Scaling Scr
Modern Enterprises

Implement Scrum and Lean-Agile techniques across complex products, portfolios, and programs in large organizations

Cecil Rupp

BIRMINGHAM—MUMBAI

Scaling Scrum Across Modern Enterprises

Commissioning Editor: Kunal Chaudhari
Acquisition Editor: Alok Dhuri
Senior Editor: Rohit Singh
Content Development Editor: Kinnari Chohan
Technical Editor: Gaurav Gala
Copy Editor: Safis Editing
Project Coordinator: Deeksha Thakkar
Proofreader: Safis Editing
Indexer: Pratik Shirodkar
Production Designer: Shankar Kalbhor

First published: October 2020

Production reference: 2051020

Published by Packt Publishing Ltd.
Livery Place
35 Livery Street
Birmingham
B3 2PB, UK.

ISBN 978-1-83921-647-3

www.packt.com

To my dear wife, Carolyn, who has stood by my side and patiently supported the countless hours I have had to commit to research and writing. Without her support, this work would not have been possible. And, to the loving memory of my parents who instilled in me the values of human decency, hard work, and carrying through a task to its completion.

– Cecil Rupp

Foreword

As an agile practitioner since 2000, I have read hundreds of books on Agile and Lean: books that talk about benefits of Agile and Lean; books that describe one or more Agile frameworks or Lean practices. What I always found to be lacking was a single book that presents the entire landscape of Agile and Lean methods. This book, *Scaling Scrum Across Modern Enterprises*, is the answer!

Cecil "Gary" Rupp is the author of two other recently released books, *SDLC Foundations* and *Tools and Templates*, which are part of his *Building Our Digital World* Series. Gary has done it again! Gary has years of experience of using Agile and Lean methods in information technology consulting, professional services, and executive management roles. *Scaling Scrum Across Modern Enterprises* does an amazing job of presenting the history of Agile methodologies, Lean development, and systems thinking.

As an Enterprise Agility Coach, I have helped customers improve their organizational agility. I have led the evolution of organizations from individuals seeking better ways to deliver products, to small cross-functional teams, to teams of teams with the same purpose in mind.

I have seen first-hand how individuals, team members, and executives struggle with understanding the various Lean frameworks. Further, leaders are looking for answers and a path toward scaling agility. This book provides a comprehensive introduction to and comparison of modern Scrum and Lean-Agile scaling strategies. It demonstrates that modern Scrum and Lean-Agile practices are not just about improving agility in software development, but also about achieving enterprise-wide business agility.

This book provides guidance on how modern scaled Scrum and Lean-Agile approaches help improve business agility across the most challenging organizational structures, product teams, portfolios, and programs. Gary articulates the most important aspects of Agile and Lean that are often overlooked by organizations. This is definitely a must-read for leaders in organizations that are serious about their commitment to scaling agility.

Manjit Singh

President and CEO

Agilious LLC

People.Powered.Agility.

Co-author of the book *The Lean Playbook: Build a Lean Organization Yourself*

Contributors

About the author

Cecil Rupp brings more than 30 years of practitioner and executive-level experience in applying the methods and tools of **information technology (IT)** for software development. His roles span IT professional services, management, business process re-engineering consulting, product management, sales, and marketing.

In addition, Mr. Rupp has directly managed more than 30 enterprise-class IT programs and projects, with the last 15 years focused almost exclusively on supporting large federal and commercial health IT programs. He is also the author of the Building our Digital World (BODW) series of books on software and systems development practices.

From the beginning, I wanted to make sure that I accurately represented the Scrum and Lean-Agile approaches described in this book, and I reached out to the experts to get their input. There are also permissions that must be sought out and granted. So many folks were kind enough to help, and I want to thank all the people who responded back to my queries, read through the sections relevant to their respective disciplines, and who were kind enough to help me with their permissions and to provide their feedback. All of their efforts helped make this a better product.

Especially, I'd like to thank the following for their contributions to reviewing and providing feedback on the content relevant to their disciplines:

Jeff Sutherland – Scrum, Scrum of Scrums, Scrum@Scale

Kurt Bittner and Patricia Kong – The Nexus Framework

Craig Larman and Bas Vodde – Large-Scale Scrum

Scott Ambler – Disciplined Agile

Michelle Stoll – Scaled Agile Framework (SAFe)®

Peter Antman and Henrik Kniberg – Minimum Viable Bureaucracy

About the reviewer

Steve Jablonski is a managing director of technology risk for a large financial services firm. He has over 25 years of technology experience in software development, database administration, project and program management, cybersecurity, governance, and risk management. Steve holds a Master's in Business Administration from the University of Colorado Denver and resides in Littleton, Colorado with his wife, Julie, their two children, and two dogs that enjoy barking and chasing squirrels.

Packt is searching for authors like you

If you're interested in becoming an author for Packt, please visit `authors.packtpub.com` and apply today. We have worked with thousands of developers and tech professionals, just like you, to help them share their insight with the global tech community. You can make a general application, apply for a specific hot topic that we are recruiting an author for, or submit your own idea.

Table of Contents

2

Scrum Beyond Basics

3

The Scrum Approach

4

Systems Thinking

5

Lean Thinking

6

Lean Practices in Software Development

Section 2: Comparative Review of Industry Scaled Agile Approaches

7

Scrum of Scrums

8

Scrum@Scale

9

The Nexus Framework

10
Large-Scale Scrum (LeSS)

11
Disciplined Agile

12
Essential Scaled Agile Framework® (SAFe®)

13
Full Scaled Agile Framework® (SAFe®)

Section 3: Implementation Strategies

14

Contrasting Scrum/Lean-Agile Scaling Approaches

Assessments

Other Books You May Enjoy

Index

Preface

Scrum is the ascendant leader in Agile practices and the primary topic of this book. But Scrum did not come about on its own, nor by accident. Nor is it the only game in town.

From the beginning, there were other Agile methodologists whose works contributed mightily to Agile-based development values and principles, as outlined in the Agile Manifesto. Many of those early Agile methodologists and practitioners developed so-called "lightweight" software development life cycle practices to overcome the deficiencies of the traditional linear-sequential and plan-driven Waterfall development model.

Scrum became the leader in this industry as a **framework** that encapsulates the customer-centric, iterative, and incremental development practices of other Agile disciplines, but also brought **empirical process control theory** (**empiricism**) to the table to help small development teams resolve *complex adaptive problems*. Such problems emerge because large and complex systems are difficult to get one's head around and fully understand how their component elements impact the system as a whole.

Scrum fosters a heuristic process that relies on its pillars of **transparency**, **inspection**, and **adaption** to visibly expose problems, experiment on ways to make improvements, and adapt the changes that most improve upon a development team's desired goals. Moreover, Scrum has proven to be a tremendously successful problem-solving framework across numerous applications, well beyond its original roots in software.

The early successes of Scrum drove organizations to implement its Agile-based approach to development at scale and in applications not addressed in the original **Scrum Guide™**. Many companies and other entities figured out how to make it work, but not without investing significant time and effort. However, the limitations in scaling guidance left the door open for other methodologists to make improvements and modifications to the basic Scrum framework. Additionally, advancements in Systems Thinking and Lean Development provided new tools to further extend the capabilities of the original Scrum framework.

This book provides evidence that Agile practices have become mainstream. However, if being Agile were only about implementing advanced software development strategies, this adoption would never have come about. Instead, modern Scrum and Lean-Agile practices go beyond supporting software development to enable business agility on an enterprise scale.

Business agility is essentially the ability of an organization to evaluate and competitively respond to changes driving both their business and their industry and do so from a customer-centric and value-added perspective. But, on the other hand, the implementation of Scrum and Lean-Agile practices on an enterprise scale involves significant structural and cultural changes that are not trivial to implement.

Ultimately, the combination of business and consumer needs and competition drive major change events across organizations. It is those drivers that are forcing the adoption of Scrum and Lean-Agile practices on an enterprise scale, spanning both product development and delivery activities. And that is what this book is about – installing the right set of Lean-Agile practices, methods, and tools, across both development and operational activities, to remain relevant in a highly disruptive, evolving, and digital world.

Purpose of the book

This book has two primary objectives. The first objective is to introduce and compare modern Scrum and Agile scaling strategies in a single reference source. The second objective is to discuss how modern Scrum and Lean-Agile practices are not just about improving agility in software development, but also about achieving enterprise-wide business agility.

Given the scope of the two objectives, the book will serve as a guide to help support the growth and management of large software and cyber-physical product development programs, and also to help organizations achieve business agility across their value creation and value delivery processes.

Who this book is for

Given Scrum's and Agile's roots in the software industry, this book will help IT practitioners, in general, learn how to work in a Lean-Agile environment. In particular, there are two critical areas in IT addressed within this book:

- Coordinating the activities of multiple Scrum Teams working in collaboration to develop a single integrated product
- Identifying the hundreds of practices that support software engineering and cross-team collaboration from both the Scrum and Lean-Agile perspectives

However, as mentioned in the previous section, the wide-scale adoption of Scrum and Lean-Agile practices supports enterprise-wide needs to operate with agility. Yes, virtually all modern businesses must operate as software businesses. The necessity of the integration of software-based product enhancements is the reality of competing in our modern digital world. Therefore, business agility requires the implementation of Lean-Agile practices on an enterprise scale, and not just within software development groups.

This book goes well beyond the scope of Agile-based software development practices to encompass agility across all value streams. A value stream is simply the set of activities within a business process that add value from a customer-centric perspective.

Several of the leading Lean-Agile practices covered in this book, provide extensive guidance in these areas. As a result, this book helps both organizational staff and executives across all domains and roles to understand modern Lean-Agile practices, and explains how to choose the options best suited for their particular contexts.

Corporations can hire consultants and send their people to various Scrum and Lean-Agile courses. But they may want to start their investigations here and have their executives and Lean-Agile team members read this book first to save a lot of time, effort, and money.

What this book covers

Chapter 1, Origins of Agile and Lightweight Methodologies, briefly touches on why Agile concepts, values, and principles evolved to address issues with the traditional plan-driven and linear-sequential software development models. We'll see how, driven by software engineers, Agile-based practices can help to eliminate the complexities, inefficiencies, and inflexibilities of the traditional software development models.

Chapter 2, Scrum Beyond Basics, introduces the fundamentals of Scrum and explains how it became the software industry leader as the preferred lightweight and Agile framework. This chapter also explains how Scrum evolved from a simple, single-team software development practice to supporting numerous industry and functional business applications to improve both operational and development efficiencies.

Chapter 3, The Scrum Approach, builds on the fundamental elements of Scrum and the factors that drove its widescale acceptance, as outlined in the previous chapter. This chapter gets into the details of how Scrum Teams operate. Specifically, you will learn the flow of activities across a Sprint as defined by its events; Scrum Team roles and responsibilities; and the artifacts that support transparency and inspection.

Chapter 4, Systems Thinking, considers how Scrum implements the concepts of empirical process control theory to help teams resolve complex adaptive problems. But we need more tools in our bag to get at the dynamics that make large and complex systems challenging to understand, let alone manage. Systems thinking provides an approach to look at complex things as a set of interconnected parts that together create a dynamic environment resulting in interactions and behaviors that are often difficult to predict.

Chapter 5, Lean Thinking, is the first of two chapters on Lean Development, and examines how these concepts and practices can help organizations maximize efficiency and value by applying Lean Development practices across all value creation and value delivery activities.

Chapter 6, Lean Practices in Software Development, is the second of two chapters on Lean Development, and focuses on how to apply these concepts and practices to the development of software and cyber-physical systems.

Chapter 7, Scrum of Scrums (SOS) Conce, teaches the principles and structures of the SoS approach. The founders of Scrum, Ken Schwaber and Jeff Sutherland, both acknowledge that the focus of the **Scrum Guide**™ is on building small, flexible, and adaptive teams to develop products, services, and other desired outcomes. Though not formalized in a guide of its own, *Scrum of Scrums* was their first documented extension to the Scrum framework, providing additional guidance on integrating the activities of multiple Scrum teams, with the potential to scale to thousands of people.

Chapter 8, Scrum@Scale (S@S), discusses how Jeff Sutherland developed this extension to Scrum and formalized it in the *Scrum@Scale Guide*®. Building on the foundations of SoS, S@S is a framework that describes a linear-scalable approach, drawing on the concepts of **scale-free architectures**, to create and coordinate multiple Scrum teams. The goal of S@S is to deliver high quality and value while simultaneously improving business agility.

Chapter 9, The Nexus™ *Framework,* examines how Ken Schwaber developed this extension to Scrum and formalized it in the *Nexus*™ *Guide*. The purpose of the Nexus Guide is to provide advanced instructions on integrating multiple Scrum teams working in collaboration on a single product. Besides learning about many useful techniques and artifacts, readers of this chapter will also learn how to install **Nexus Integration Teams (NIT)** and several new events to help manage multi-team integration, dependency, and synchronization issues.

Chapter 10, Large-Scale Scrum (LeSS), introduces the last of the relatively "pure" scaled-Scrum frameworks. LeSS provides many useful, though optional (that is, non-prescriptive) rules and guides to help Scrum teams with multi-team implementations of Scrum. Moreover, LeSS offers two frameworks, one for relatively small multi-team environments, and the other for more substantial multi-team product development activities. In this chapter, you will learn how the smaller LeSS framework functions with Scrum teams operating as Feature Teams. You will also learn how the LeSS Huge framework functions and brings the concept of Requirements Areas to manage large-scale integration and dependency issues.

Chapter 11, Disciplined Agile (DA), introduces the first of the two comprehensive Lean-Agile approaches described within this book. DA is easily differentiated by its emphasis on teams having the ability to define their **way of working** (**WoW**). DA offers six fully developed life cycles from which a team can choose. The DA toolkit provides process guidance and techniques across four levels of the **Disciplined Agile Enterprise** (**DAE**), spanning Agile, DevOps, IT, and Enterprise.

Chapter12, Essential Scaled-Agile Framework (SAFe®), is the first of two chapters on SAFe. SAFe is the second and most comprehensive of the Lean-Agile disciplines presented in this book. However, its approach is much different than that of Disciplined Agile in that it provides four configurations with detailed instructions on how to establish business agility in very large organizations while preserving the benefits of economies of scale that large organizations inherently benefit from. This chapter presents the Essential SAFe configuration, which serves as a foundation for the other configurations if they are needed.

Chapter 13, Full Scaled-Agile Framework (SAFe®), explains how to scale SAFe practices to support the development and delivery of large solutions with multiple value streams. This chapter will also help you understand how to align and manage product development, support, and enhancement investments with corporate strategies and across multiple planning horizons. Finally, we will touch on the SAFe Implementation Roadmap, which guides organizations on how to build the skills, structures, and resources necessary to support the Lean-Agile enterprise, and ultimately leverage early successes to overcome cultural and personal resistance.

Chapter 14, Contrasting Scrum/Lean-Agile Scaling Approaches, considers how, at this point, you will have learned the basics of seven unique approaches to scaling Scrum and Lean-Agile practices to enable business agility. But which approach is best for your organization? This chapter offers side-by-side comparisons for you to evaluate each framework in terms of your unique context and requirements.

To get the most out of this book

The following table lists the recommendations for a better understanding of the Scrum/Lean-Agile practices covered in this book.

Scrum/Lean-Agile practices covered in the book	Recommended requirements
The basic concepts behind Agile and the values and principles of the Agile Manifesto	Read the Agile Manifesto.
A basic understanding that Scrum is a leading Agile development approach and the need for its scaling extensions	Read the Scrum Guide, Scrum@Scale Guide, and the Nexus Guide.
A basic understanding that Systems Thinking and Lean Development practices are part of building a Lean-Agile business	NA

This book is written under the assumption that our readers will have a large range of knowledge with regard to Scrum, Scrum scaling issues, and the value of including Systems Thinking and Lean Development practices as part of their efforts to become Agile. So, the book is written for the novice, those with intermediate knowledge, and even those who have been around the block a time or two with Agile.

This book is written with all business domains and organizations in mind.

This book is useful for software developers and software development teams. But it's not limited in scope to just supporting Agile practices in the software development community. Today, Scrum and Lean-Agile practices are the necessary enablers to compete in our digitally disruptive economies. Therefore, all business domains and organizations are impacted and must embrace the concepts of *agility* to sustain organizational viability. This is the mentality you need to have when reading this book. Be it a commercial enterprise, government agency, or non-profit, this book will help your organization compete and add value in our constantly evolving digital world.

Download the color images

We also provide a PDF file that has color images of the screenshots/diagrams used in this book. You can download it here:

```
https://static.packt-cdn.com/downloads/9781839216473_
ColorImages.pdf
```

Conventions used

> **Tips or important notes**
> Appear like this.

Get in touch

Feedback from our readers is always welcome.

General feedback: If you have questions about any aspect of this book, mention the book title in the subject of your message and email us at customercare@packtpub.com.

Errata: Although we have taken every care to ensure the accuracy of our content, mistakes do happen. If you have found a mistake in this book, we would be grateful if you would report this to us. Please visit www.packtpub.com/support/errata, selecting your book, clicking on the Errata Submission Form link, and entering the details.

Piracy: If you come across any illegal copies of our works in any form on the Internet, we would be grateful if you would provide us with the location address or website name. Please contact us at copyright@packt.com with a link to the material.

If you are interested in becoming an author: If there is a topic that you have expertise in and you are interested in either writing or contributing to a book, please visit authors.packtpub.com.

Reviews

Please leave a review. Once you have read and used this book, why not leave a review on the site that you purchased it from? Potential readers can then see and use your unbiased opinion to make purchase decisions, we at Packt can understand what you think about our products, and our authors can see your feedback on their book. Thank you!

For more information about Packt, please visit packt.com.

Section 1:
Scaling Lightweight Scrum into a Heavyweight Contender

This section serves as an introduction to Scrum as a lightweight software development framework along with common approaches to scale Scrum for more complex development scenarios.

This section comprises the following chapters:

- *Chapter 1, Origins of Agile and Lightweight Methodologies*
- *Chapter 2, Scrum Beyond Basics*
- *Chapter 3, The Scrum Approach*
- *Chapter 4, Systems Thinking*
- *Chapter 5, Lean Thinking*
- *Chapter 6, Lean Practices in Software Development*

1
The Origins of Agile and Lightweight Methodologies

This chapter briefly touches on why agile concepts, values, and principles evolved to address issues with traditional plan-driven and linear sequential software development models. Driven by software engineers, the goal of agile is to eliminate the complexities, inefficiencies, and inflexibility of the traditional software development models.

This chapter explains where the traditional waterfall approach often fails due to its emphasis on detailed planning and the execution of deterministic life cycle development processes. Not everything about the traditional software development model is bad, especially with its historical emphasis on developing and applying mature business analysis and engineering practices. In this chapter, you will learn how the values and principles of agile help address the many problems associated with the traditional software development model while understanding the importance of maintaining rigor in developing your business and engineering practices.

While this is a book about scaling Scrum on an enterprise scale, we need to first understand Scrum's agile underpinnings, and why Scrum needs to be scaled.

In this chapter, we will cover the following topics:

- Lightweight software development methodologies
- Core agile implementation concepts
- The values and principles of agile
- Why engineers largely led this movement

With those objectives in mind, this chapter provides an introduction to the lightweight methodologies that preceded the development and promotion of "agile" concepts, values, and principles. Those early efforts addressed the limitations of the traditional development model and also helped refine the concepts that ultimately defined what it means to be agile. In this chapter, you will also learn why engineers largely led the initial movements to implement agile-based practices.

Understanding what's wrong with the traditional model

Since you are reading a book on mastering Scrum, I might assume you already know something about agile practices and how they evolved to address the issues of the traditional software development model, also known as the waterfall approach. Still, it's never safe to assume. So, I'm going to start this book with this section to provide a quick overview of the traditional software development model, why and how it developed, and its shortcomings.

Modern computing became a reality in the early 1940s through the 1950s with the introduction of the first general-purpose electronic computers. The introduction to modern computing is particularly relevant to our discussions on the evolution of software development practices, as the high costs, skills, and complexity of software development drove early software and **Systems Development Life Cycle (SDLC)** practices.

In the earliest days of computing, computers filled an entire room, were extremely expensive, often served only one purpose or business function, and took a team of highly skilled engineers to run and maintain. Each installation and the related software programming activities were highly unique, time-consuming, schedule-bound, complex, and expensive. In other words, early computing efforts had all the characteristics of project-based work – and development activities were managed accordingly.

It's only natural that executive decision-makers and paying customers want to manage their risks in such an environment, and the discipline of project management provided a model for managing unique and complex work in an uncertain development environment under approved constraints. Project constraints consist of the approved scope of work, budgets, schedules, resources, and quality. Specifically, project management implements detailed project planning, documentation, scheduling, and risk management techniques to guide and control complex development projects within the constraints approved by the executives or paying customers. In software development, such practices came to be known as the so-called waterfall model.

The discipline of project management is as old as the Egyptian pyramids, dating back to roughly 2500 BC, and probably older than that. Project management evolved to manage work associated with building large, complex, risky, and expensive things. If you are the person financing such endeavors, you have a strong desire to control the scope of work to deliver what you want, in the time you want it, at a cost you can afford, and with certain expectations about the quality of the deliverables. Hence the genesis behind managing work under specific and approved project constraints.

Project management looks at work from the perspective of protecting the customer's investments in risky, expensive, and complex projects. In effect, customers accept a layer of management overhead with the goal of helping to ensure on-time and on-budget deliveries.

In a modern yet classical context, projects have the following characteristics:

- An authorized scope of work – no more, no less.
- Are temporary ventures with a specific start and an end date.
- May use borrowed (for example, from functional departments) or contracted resources over the project's life cycle.
- Have specific deliverable items (for example, products, services, or expected outcomes).
- The deliverables and the type of work are relatively unique.
- The uniqueness implies that some important information is not available at the start of the project, potentially impacting the project in some way when discovered.
- The uniqueness of the product and the work also implies that there is some level of risk in achieving the objectives on time, on budget, and with the allotted resources.
- The uniqueness of the deliverables implies the customers probably don't have a complete understanding of what they want or need – as it turns out, this is especially true when it comes to building software applications and systems.

In the traditional project management paradigm, the objective is to manage work within pre-determined constraints. The constraints are the *scope* of work, *budgets*, *schedules*, *resources* allotted to the effort, *deliverables*, and *quality*. The goal of project management is to successfully deliver satisfactory products within the constraints approved by the paying customer. The philosophy behind project management is that the combination of rigorous planning, engineering, and coordinated life cycle development processes provides the best approach to managing uncertainty and risk.

The project management philosophy works well when building things that are difficult to change once construction begins. Imagine that the pharaohs decided they needed tunnels and rooms within their pyramids after construction. I suspect it would have been possible, but the effort, resources, time, and costs would have been extraordinarily higher than if they planned and designed on those requirements before starting construction. The same concept is true when building ships, high-rise buildings, energy and telecom utilities, roads, and other large, complex, and expensive physical products. The cost of change is extraordinarily higher after construction starts.

Early computer scientists and IT managers faced many of the same constraints and issues those other industries faced. In other words, the characteristics of managing software development projects mirrored those faced in other industries that build large, complex, unique, and expensive things. It, therefore, seemed logical that software development projects also required rigorous planning, architectural design, and engineering, and coordinated life cycle development processes.

All software products and IT-based systems have a life cycle. The traditional model conceptually breaks up a product's life cycle into a series of phases, with each phase encompassing a type of related work. Phase descriptions expose work through a series of decompositions, consisting of the following:

- **Processes** provide a step-by-step set of instructions describing work within the phase. Phases typically have multiple processes, each describing a different type of work or approach to work.

- **Activities** (a.k.a. summary tasks) are artificial placeholders used to aggregate information about the completion of work in the underlying tasks. In other words, activities help roll up both the original estimates and the final measures of costs, time, and resources spent on the underlying work tasks.

- **Tasks** are the lowest practical level of describing work where a deliverable outcome is definable. Project managers often use the *8-80 rule* to limit task durations to a range between 8 hours and 80 hours.

Product life cycle processes follow a common pattern of work activities. Products are conceived; requirements or needs are defined; architectures and designs are established; the products are constructed and tested. Then, they are delivered, supported, maintained, and perhaps enhanced until, one day, the decision is made to retire the products.

In the traditional plan-driven and linear-sequential software development model, the life cycle processes are laid out to show work and information flowing from one phase of work to another, as shown in the following figure:

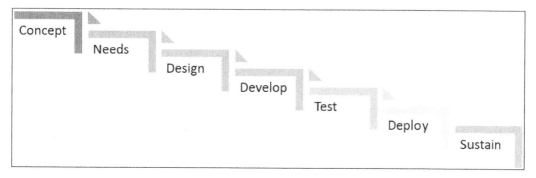

Figure 1.1 – Traditional plan-driven, linear-sequential "waterfall" software development model

The figure implies this approach to development is a straightforward process from beginning to end. Still, even in the traditional model, this is not entirely true. There tends to be some overlap of work among the phases. The traditional waterfall model is more of a conceptual framework than a mandated work structure.

But the biggest point I want to make here is that the more a team frontend-loads requirements, the more protracted the overall work becomes. The added **work in process (WIP)** adds complexity, extends the development life cycle, and limits customer input. Moreover, adding WIP delays testing that would otherwise help find and determine the cause, and quickly resolve problems at the point they arise. In short, it is that frontend-loading of work that creates all the problems in the traditional model.

There is strong evidence to support that adding size to a project under the traditional waterfall-based development model is highly correlated with project failures, while agile-based projects outperformed traditionally managed projects at every scale. For example, the Standish Group, in their 2015 Chaos Report (available at https:// standishgroup.com/sample_research_files/CHAOSReport2015-Final. pdf), which summarized data across 50,000 projects, shows agile-based projects outpaced waterfall-based projects at every category of project size – spanning small, medium, large, and combined – with the largest projects having the greatest percentage of reported failures, at 42%.

Clearly, there are other factors at work besides the frontend-loading of requirements leading to higher failures in larger projects. Let's take a moment to see how these other factors only make things worse.

It's nearly impossible to capture all the requirements for a new product concept at the start of a project. First off, customers and end-users don't yet know what they don't know. It's not unusual for a customer to get their hands on a product and quickly discover new insights into how the tool can help them in ways not previously discerned. Second, customers and end-users have other jobs and work to do, and it's difficult to get them to sit through a requirement gathering session for protracted periods. And, even if they make the time, they may initially forget about things that later turn out to be very important.

Under the traditional model, astute development teams know they can start assessing architecture and design requirements in parallel with requirement gathering. But if we accept the premise that the requirements are not likely to be completely or correctly defined all at once at the start of the project, then we also have to believe the product designers will make wrong assumptions, leading to future reworks of the architecture, designs, and code to fix errors.

Under the traditional model, the developers follow the plan. If a customer comes in with a new or revised requirement, that change request impacts the baseline plan. The scope of work can change, which in turn can change the planned schedule, resource allocations, and budgets. If the customer insists on the change but won't change the constraints of the project, the project team will likely fail to meet their obligations defined in their project's charter or contract agreements. In other words, under the traditional model, when a client proposes a new change request, something has to give in one or more of the previously defined scopes of work, budgets, schedules, requirements, and quality.

The term **scope creep** refers to an unexpected and unauthorized change to the project's planned work. Scope creep is a major cause of project failures in the traditional model, because scope creep may impact the project's authorized resources, schedule plan, and the type and amount of work approved under the project's charter or contract agreements. Changes to both functional and non-functional requirements can generate scope creep. Functional requirements are the business and user requirements, whereas the non-functional requirements deal with the quality, security, and performance of the product.

To some degree, software development and testing have always gone hand in hand. But under the traditional development model, only unit and integration testing occur in parallel with coding. System testing, end-to-end testing, acceptance testing, and performance testing tend to be put off until the completion of coding for the entire product release. By that time, the complexity and size of the code base make it much more difficult to assess the root cause of any problems and fix any bugs that crop up in the tests.

The delivery/deployment processes, within the traditional model, span most of the other life cycle development phases. The deliverables of deployment processes are not just the application code but also training aids, wikis, help functionality, sysadmin documents, support documentation, user guides, and other artifacts necessary to support and maintain the product over its operational life span. Also, the development team must coordinate with the operations group to work through hardware, network, software, backup, storage, and security provisioning needs and related procurement acquisitions. Waiting to address these issues until the later stages of the project will almost assuredly delay the scheduled release date for the product.

Collectively, these issues lead to overly complex projects, lengthy development times, cost and schedule overruns, potential scope creep, poor quality, misalignment with customer priorities, and intractable bugs. Moreover, the "soft" nature of software development made it challenging for customers to wrap their heads around the cause and effects that kept leading to so many project failures. It wasn't like they could watch a building go up and see problems as they arose. Instead, a customer's or end user's first real view into the capabilities of the software is delayed until user acceptance testing, which occurs just before the software is supposed to be delivered.

As you might imagine, the folks who most take the heat for failed deliveries under the traditional software development model are the project managers and software development engineers. An astute project manager works with the development team to identify the cause and effects of their project's failures. After all, it's the engineers who are in the best position to understand the impact of unexpected changes and other impediments that prevented delivery within the approved constraints of the project.

Starting in the 1990s, a number of software engineers came to understand that the overly prescriptive practices of the traditional plan-driven and linear-sequential development model were not well suited to software development. The traditional model implements a deterministic view that everything can be known and therefore preplanned, scheduled, and controlled over the life of a project. The reality is that there are too many random or unknowable events that make it impossible to predict client needs, market influences, priorities, risks, and the scope of work required to deliver a viable product. The real world of software development is not deterministic; it is highly stochastic.

As a result, these engineers began to experiment with lighter-weight software development methodologies that provided more flexibility to address changing requirements and information on a near real-time basis. They also developed techniques to eliminate the inefficiencies and quality issues associated with a protracted software development life cycle. In the next section, we will learn about some of the better known and successful lightweight software development methodologies.

Moving away from the traditional model

The movement away from the traditional plan-driven and linear-sequential development model was gradual and spearheaded by a relatively small group of likeminded individuals. Later in this chapter, I am going to discuss how the agile movement was led by a group of engineers, and not by management specialists. The fact that engineers led this movement has ramifications for why many agile practices did not address enterprise scalability issues from the start. But for now, I want to get into a description of some of the so-called lightweight approaches that set the stage for modern agile development concepts.

There were several lightweight methodologies available to the software development community well before the values and principles of agile were outlined in the agile Manifesto in 2001. In common across these lightweight methodologies were a reduction in governing rules and processes, more collaborative development strategies, responsiveness to customer needs and priorities, and the use of prototyping and iterative and incremental development techniques. In short, lightweight software development methodologies evolved to eliminate the complexities of the traditional software development model.

In this section, I'll briefly introduce some of the better known or impactful lightweight methodologies. These include the following:

- **Adaptive Software Development**, defined by Jim Highsmith and Sam Bayer in the early 1990s [Highsmith, J. (1999) *Adaptive Software Development: A Collaborative Approach to Managing Complex Systems*. Dorset House Publishing Company. New York, NY].

- **Crystal Clear**, evolved from the Crystal family in the 1990s, fully described by Alistair Cockburn in 2004 [Cockburn, A. (2005) *Crystal Clear: A Human-Powered Methodology for Small Teams*. Pearson Education, Inc. Upper Saddle River, NJ].

- **Extreme Programming (XP)**, by Kent Beck in 1996 [Beck, K. (1999) *eXtreme Programming eXplained. Embrace Change*. Addison-Wesley Professional. Boston, MA].

- **Feature Driven Development (FDD)** developed (1999) by Jeff De Luca and Peter Coad [Coad, P., Lefebvre, E. & De Luca, J. (1999). *Java Modelling In Color With UML: Enterprise Components and Process*. Prentice-Hall International. (ISBN 0-13-011510-X)], [Palmer, S.R., & Felsing, J.M. (2002). A Practical Guide to Feature-Driven Development. Prentice-Hall. (ISBN 0-13-067615-2).

- **ICONIX**, developed by Doug Rosenberg and Matt Stephens, was formally described in 2005 [Rosenberg, D., Stephens, M. & Collins-Cope, M. (2005). *Agile Development with ICONIX Process*. Apress. ISBN 1-59059-464-9].

- **Rapid Application Development (RAD)**, developed by James Martin, described in 1991 [Martin, J. (1991) *Rapid Application Development*. Macmillan Publishing Company, New York, NY].

- **Scrum**, initially defined as a formal process by Jeff Sutherland and Ken Schwaber in 1995 [Sutherland, Jeffrey Victor; Schwaber, Ken (1995). *Business Object Design And Implementation: OOPSLA '95 Workshop Proceedings*. The University of Michigan. p. 118. ISBN 978-3-540-76096-2]

Adaptive Software Development (ASD)

ASD starts with the premise that large information systems can be built relatively quickly, at lower costs, and with fewer failures through the adoption of prototyping and incremental development concepts. Large projects often fail due to self-inflicted wounds associated with unnecessary complexity and lengthy development cycles.

Some organizations address those problems by breaking up the pieces of a large and complex project into smaller component parts and reassigning the work to multiple teams, who work on their assignments independently and in parallel. However, that approach creates new issues in terms of providing clarity on what the components should be and do, what the final solution must be and do, and how it will all come together. In contrast, Jim Highsmith's ASD approach employed a combination of focus groups, version control, prototyping, and time-boxed development cycles to incrementally evolve new product functionality, on demand.

Highsmith was an early proponent of rapid application development. With an emphasis on speed, RAD reduced cycle times and improved quality in smaller projects with low to moderate change requirements. However, RAD was not an adaptive strategy, and it proved not to scale well in large and more complex environments that have a great deal of uncertainty associated with them.

Highsmith's approach drew from complex adaptive systems theory as a model of how small, self-organizing, and adaptive teams, with only a few rules, can find a path to construct the most complex systems. He argued that imposing order to optimize conditions in uncertain environments has an oppositional effect, making the organization less efficient and less adaptive. Plan-driven development projects continuously operate out of step and behind current organizational and market needs.

ASD implements a series of speculate, collaborate, and learn cycles to force constant learning, adaptions, and improvements. Instead of focusing on the completion of predefined work tasks, ASD has a focus on developing defined features that provide capabilities desired by customers.

The term speculate replaces the term plan in the ASD approach. The basic idea behind ASD is that a team cannot implement a plan to enforce a strategy based on a deterministic view that the world can only follow one set of rules or lead to only one perceivable and desired outcome. Instead, empirical evidence observed over the course of a project quickly reveals the underlying assumptions of the plan are flawed.

Planning is still an acknowledged requirement in an ASD-based project, but the ASD developers and project managers are aware they live in a world of uncertainty, and that plans must change. Therefore, the astute development teams know that they must be willing to experiment, learn, and adapt, and do so over short cycles so that they do not get locked up in a plan that cannot work.

The ability of a project team to be adaptive is largely contingent upon their ability to leverage the strength of their combined knowledge and collaborate on finding effective solutions to complex problems. Again, overly prescriptive plans get in the way of understanding, problem-solving, and innovations. In ASD, the focus is on delivering results, and not on completing predefined tasks.

Learning is the final part of the ASD cycle. The development team obtains input from three types of assessments: technical reviews, iterative retrospections, and customer focus groups. Learning reviews occur at the end of each iterative development cycle. Iterations are kept short to limit the potential damage from making errors that do not support the common purpose of the team and the organization it supports. Customer focus groups provide necessary and ongoing input, feedback, and validation.

Crystal Clear

Over a period of time spanning about a decade, Alistair Cockburn observed numerous development teams to determine what set of practices separated successful teams from those that were not. His study began in 1999 when an IBM consulting group asked him to write a methodology for object-oriented projects. Alistair determined that the best way forward was to interview project teams to uncover their best practices and techniques.

What he found was that success was not at all determined by the methods and tools the teams used to support object-oriented programming. Instead, the success criteria were much softer, more structural, and not so much based on the particular methods and tools used by developers to create their code.

After 10 years of continuing these interviews of successful software development teams, Alistair Cockburn wrote the book *Crystal Clear: A Human-Powered Methodology for Small Teams*. In that book, Alistair cites the following factors as being most critical to project success:

- Co-location and a collaborative, friendly working environment.
- Eliminate bureaucracy and let the team do their work.
- Encourage end-users to work directly with development team members.
- Automate regression testing.
- Produce potentially shippable products frequently.

So, in other words, it wasn't mature software development practices or tools that made the difference in building and deploying high-quality software products. Rather, it was the decluttering of bureaucratic and overly complex organizational structures that made the most difference in team effectiveness.

In a crystal-clear environment, the development team consists of anywhere from two to seven developers, and they work in a large room or adjacent offices. The team works collaboratively, often holding discussions around whiteboards and flipcharts to work through complex problems. The developers, and not specialist business analysts, work directly with end-users and customers to discern the functional requirements and capabilities needed by the product.

The team does not follow the directions of a plan or manager. Instead, they focus on the requirements they uncover during their direct communications with customers, and then they build, test, and deliver incremental slices of functionality every month or so. The most effective teams also periodically review their work to uncover better ways to build software and operate in their upcoming iterations.

Alistair believes different types of projects need different approaches and that a single methodology does not support all project requirements. Thus, he developed the Crystal family of software development methodologies to support varying project needs. For example, larger projects require more coordination and communication. Projects that are governed by legislative mandates or have life or death consequences require more stringent methodologies with repeated verification and validation testing to confirm the designs and suitability of the products for their intended environments. Smaller development teams working on non-mission-critical applications need less oversight and bureaucracy.

Alistair classified his Crystal methodologies by the number of development team members that must be coordinated on a project, and by the degree of safety required by a product. There are five Crystal colors used to define project team size. These five Crystal colors are as follows:

- *Clear* for teams of 2 to 8 people
- *Yellow* for teams of up to 20 people
- *Orange* for teams of up to 40 people
- *Red* for teams of up to 80 people
- *Maroon* for teams of up to 200 people

The *Crystal Sapphire* and *Crystal Diamond* methodologies provide additional rigor through verification and validation testing to confirm the viability of mission-critical, life-sustaining, and safety-critical applications.

The Crystal Clear methodology incorporates three properties of most effective small teams. These properties are as follows:

- Frequent delivery
- Reflective improvement
- Osmotic communication, for example, co-location of team members to improve collaboration

Alistair cites four other properties displayed by the most effective small teams. These are as follows:

- Personal safety
- Focus, for example, knowing what to work on and having the ability to do so
- Easy access to expert users
- Automated and integrated development environments

Extreme Programming

Kent Beck is another software engineer who came to realize that great software can be developed at a lower cost, with fewer defects, more productive teams, and greater returns on investment than the industry was producing under the traditional software development model. Now in its second edition, Kent Beck wrote his book titled *eXtreme Programming eXplained* to detail his approach to achieving the aforementioned goals [Beck, K., Andres, C. (2004-2005) *eXtreme Programming eXplained*. Embrace Change. Second Edition. Addison-Wesley Professional. Boston, MA].

XP places value on programming techniques and skills, clear and concise communications, and collaborative teamwork. Kent explains the methodology in terms of values, principles, and practices. Values sit at our core and form the basis of our likes and dislikes. Our values often come from life experiences. On the other hand, values also serve as a basis of the expectation we have of ourselves and others. Practices are the things we should do in support of our values. Likewise, practices performed without direction or purpose work against our stated values. Finally, principles help define our values and guide our practices in support of our values.

The values defined in XP encourage communication, simplicity, feedback, courage, respect, safety, security, predictability, and quality of life. Values are abstractions that describe what good looks like in an XP environment.

There are quite a number of principles defined in XP, and simply listing them here would not provide much enlightenment. I've summarized some of the most important principles here:

- Treat people with respect, offering a safe participatory environment that values their contributions, gives them a sense of belonging, and the ability to grow.

- The economics of software development, and the impact on our customers, is just as important as the technical considerations.

- Win-win scenarios are always preferred.

- Look for repeatable patterns that work, even though you must understand the same patterns may not apply to every similar contextual use.

- Get into the habit of designing tests demonstrating compliance before developing the code.

- Seek excellence through ongoing and honest retrospective assessments and improvements.

- Seek diversity in experiences, skills, approaches, and viewpoints when building your teams.

- Focus on sustaining weekly production flows of incremental yet high-priority slices of functionality.

- Problems or issues will arise and represent opportunities to make positive changes.

- Make use of redundancy in practices, approaches, testing, and reviews as checks and balances to improve the quality of released products.

- Don't be afraid to fail; there is something to be learned from every failure.

- Improvements in quality have a net positive impact on the overall productivity and performance of the team.

- Implement changes toward XP in small steps, as rapid change is stressful for people.

- Responsibility must come with authority.

- Team responsibility spans the entire development cycle, from the assignment of a story through analysis, design, implementation, and testing.

Principles provide the development team with a better understanding of what the practices are meant to accomplish. As with the principles, there are many practices listed in XP. Since practices are at the core of XP, we need to take a quick look at them:

- Teams work together in an open space, big enough to support the entire team.

- Ensure that teams have all the skills and resources necessary for success.

- Keep key information out in the open and visible through whiteboards, story cards, and burnup/burn down and velocity charts.

- Maintain team vitality by producing work at a sustainable and healthy rate.

- Implement paired programming where two developers work and collaborate on one computer.

- Use story formats to understand the capabilities customers and users need, and their priorities.

- Plan work 1 week ahead through the refinement of identified high-priority stories.

- Plan work ahead quarterly to evaluate ways to get better, identify areas to aggregate related work (for example, themes), and assign stories to the themes.

- Build in slack and don't overcommit.

- Install build automation capabilities and make sure product builds never take more than 10 minutes to complete.

- Implement continuous integration practices so that the developers merge their working copies of software into a source control management system throughout the day.

- Implement a test-driven development approach where tests are written before writing the code.

- Make time to incrementally improve the design every day.

As this is a book on scaling agile practices, it's interesting to note here that Kent Beck addresses the issue of scaling XP. First, add teams, but keep the basic small team model when scaling XP. Next, break down any large-scale problems into smaller elements and have the teams address each issue as simply as possible. For larger and more intractable problems, do whatever you can to stop making the situation worse, and then work to fix the underlying problems while continuing to deliver useful products.

Feature-Driven Development (FDD)

As the name implies, the feature-driven approach emphasizes the implementation of new or enhanced features at a rapid rate. Developed by Jeff DeLuca and influenced by Peter Coad, the FDD approach leverages object-oriented concepts with the **Unified Modeling Language (UML)** to define a system as a series of interacting objects. UML provides a method to describe interactions between agents and systems. An agent can be an end user or another system.

At its core, FDD is another iterative and incremental development approach that stresses customer focus and the timely delivery of useful functionality. The FDD approach integrates concepts from XP and Scrum, and, like RAD, takes advantage of modeling techniques and tools – including **Domain-Driven Design (DDD)** by Eric Evan [Evans, E. (2003) *Domain-Driven Design: Tackling Complexity in the Heart of Software. Addison-Wesley.* Hoboken, NJ], and object modeling in color by Peter Coad [Peter Coad, Eric Lefebvre, Jeff De Luca (1999). *Java Modeling In Color With UML: Enterprise Components and Process*, Prentice-Hall. Upper Saddle River, N.J.].

Peter Coad, et al., came to realize that, model after model, they built the same four general types of object classes over and over again. These four repeating object class patterns are called **archetypes**, which means a common example of a certain person or thing. The four common classes and their color classifications include the following:

- **Moment-interval** (*Pink*): Representing a specific moment, event, or interval of time

- **Roles** (*Yellow*): Defining the way some *thing* participates in an activity

- **Descriptions** (*Blue*): Methods to describe, classify, or label other *things*
- **Party, Place, or Thing** (*Green*): tangible and uniquely identifiable *things*

Many agile development approaches use stories as the structure to capture the capabilities that customers and end-users need the product to provide. The UML modeling approach describes requirements from the standpoint of client-valued interactions and functionality (a.k.a. features).

DDD has a focus on modeling domains/domain logic. Instead of working directly with customers and end-users, the DDD approach encourages collaborations between developers and domain experts to define models that accurately reflect the business domain and their problems.

The feature-driven development approach encompasses five standard processes:

- Develop a model – feature-driven, time-boxed, and collaborative.
- Build the feature list – from the models, categorized and prioritized, and time-boxed.
- Plan by feature – the assignment of features to developers.
- Design by feature – establish a design package with two weeks of work each that logically go together.
- Build by feature – keeping the development focus on developing and delivering useful features.

While FDD is considered an agile approach and often included as a lightweight methodology, the approach, by design, supports larger projects involving 50 developers or more.

ICONIX

The ICONIX approach to software development is another use-case-driven practice. However, it is a lighter-weight implementation of UML than the more widely known and practiced **Rational Unified Process** (**RUP**). Though RUP incorporates an iterative software development approach, it is a heavyweight approach that is highly prescriptive and implements a comprehensive application life cycle management approach.

Described by Doug Rosenberg, Matt Stephens, and Mark Collins-Cope, the ICONIX approach predates XP and RUP, when Rosenberg and his team at ICONIX developed an **object-oriented analysis and design (OOAD)** tool, called **ObjectModeler**. Their **ObjectModeler** tool supported the object-oriented design methods of Grady Booch, Jim Rumbaugh (OMB), and Ivar Jacobson (Objectory). The ICONIX process was formally published in 2005 in their book titled *Agile Development with ICONIX Process. People, Process, and Pragmatism* [Rosenberg, D., Stephens, M. & Collins-Cope, M. (2005). *Agile Development with ICONIX Process*. Apress. New York NY.]. The authors provided further elaboration on the ICONIX approach in their 2007 book titled *Use Case Driven Object Modeling with UML: Theory and Practice* [Rosenberg, D. & Stephens, M. (2007). Use Case Driven Object *Modeling with UML: Theory and Practice*. Apress. New York, NY]. In its modern form, the authors promote the ICONIC process as an open, free-to-use, agile, and lightweight object modeling process that is use-case-driven.

ICONIX implements a robust and relatively document-intensive process – when compared to XP – for requirements analysis and design modeling. In addition, ICONIX implements an intermediary process, called *robustness modeling*, to help developers think through the process of converting **what** is known about the requirements, into **how** to design in the desired capabilities. ICONIX implements a modeling technique called *robustness diagrams*, which depicts the object classes (for example, use case descriptions of classes and behaviors) and the flow of how the defined objects communicate with each other.

From a logical perspective, there is a different level of abstraction when modeling and analyzing requirements versus analyzing software and systems design requirements. They are two different worlds – physical versus logical. The robustness modeling approach helps designers visualize the translation of information from the physical requirements into a logical implementation.

The ICONIX approach breaks out into four delivery *milestones*, which include a requirements review, a preliminary design review, a detailed design review, and deployment.

Requirements analysis informs the requirements review milestone. The output of the business analysis includes use cases, domain models, and prototype GUIs.

A robustness analysis informs the preliminary design review milestone. The outputs of the robustness analysis include both textual and graphical descriptions of user and system interactions, both of which serve as aids to help the development team validate the requirements and designs with their customers and end-users.

A detailed design informs the detailed design review milestone. The domain model and use case text are the primary inputs to the design document.

The code and unit tests inform the deployment milestone. The term deployment is a bit confusing as this milestone serves as the completion marker for developing the code to support the requirements, and not a physical deployment of the application to the customer.

In summary, the ICONIX process is a lightweight, agile, open, and free-to-use object modeling process that employs use case modeling techniques. Its strength lies in the techniques the methodology implements to transition use case models of requirements into useful design elements.

Rapid application development (RAD)

James Martin wrote *Rapid Application Development (RAD)* to address the issue that the speed of software development activities always seems to lag behind the speed at which businesses operate. Given that computers and software were fast becoming the backbone of business operations and competitive responses, it was untenable to have 2- or 3-year development life cycles with an even larger backlog of requirements.

James Martin notes in his book that there are three critical success factors that information systems departments face:

- Speed of development – to implement new business capabilities

- Speed of application change – to respond to new needs and priorities

- Speed of cutover – to quickly replace legacy systems and operations

Martin believed the key to sustained business success was the installment of rapid application development capabilities.

Martin was an early proponent of the use of **computer-aided systems engineering (CASE)** tools, and he was the founder of **KnowledgeWare** – the company that produced the **IEW (Information Engineering Workbench)** case tools. (Later, IEW was sold to Sterling Software in 1994, which in turn was subsequently acquired by Computer Associates.) Ultimately, IEW combined personal computer-based information and data modeling tools with a code generator that expedited the process of building software applications that run on mainframe computers.

Martin's concept of RAD was to use tools and techniques to lower development costs, reduce development times, and build high-quality products. Manual processes often lead to reduced quality when attempts are made to expedite the process. However, the methods and tools implemented within CASE tools enforce technical rigor while simultaneously improving quality, consistency, and efficiencies in software development.

The modern concept of RAD lives on through **Integrated Development Environments (IDEs)**, such as Android Studio, Atom, Eclipse, Microsoft's Visual Studio, NetBeans, VIM, and many, many others.

Scrum

This book is about mastering Scrum for enterprise, and the next chapter provides much greater detail on the methodology. For now, I want to focus on introducing Scrum as an example of a lightweight software development methodology and how and why it came about.

Both the initial concepts behind Scrum and the name Scrum came from the works published by Hirotaka Takeuchi and Ikujiro Nonaka, in their 1986 Harvard Business Review article titled *The New New Product Development Game* [Takeuchi, H., Nonaka, I. (1986) *The New New Product Development Game* Harvard Business Review. Retrieved <May 21, 2020.]. This article builds on original concepts developed by Nonaka as published in a 1991 article titled *The Knowledge Creating Company.* [The Knowledge Creating Company. Oxford University Press. 1995. p. 3. ISBN 9780199762330. Retrieved March 12, 2013.] The concepts behind Scrum are built on Takeuchi and Nonaka's findings that organizational knowledge creation drives innovation.

Takeuchi and Nonaka note that the traditional linear-sequential development methods are not competitive in the *fast-paced, fiercely competitive world of commercial new product development.* Takeuchi and Nonaka cite six differentiating factors that provide the speed and flexibility necessary for competitive success: *built-in instability, self-organizing project teams, overlapping development phases, multilearning, subtle control,* and *organizational transfer of learning.*

An important insight, highlighted by the two authors, is that *knowledge creation leads to innovation, which in turn leads to competitive advantage.* Moreover, they found that learning from direct experiences, and from trial and error, are essential elements of knowledge acquisition.

Jeff Sutherland and Ken Schwaber collaborated to develop the Scrum methodology. In their book titled *Software in 30 Days*, Southerland notes that the writings of Takeuchi and Nonaka *profoundly influenced* his early works [Schwaber, K., Sutherland, J. (2012). *Software in Thirty Days. How Agile Managers Beat the Odds, Delight Their Customers, and Leave Competitors in the Dust.* John Wiley & Sons. Hoboken, N.J.]. Ken Schwaber says he was influenced by the works of Babatunde A. Ogunnaike in the areas of *industrial process control, and the applicability of complexity theory and empiricism in software development.*

Sutherland developed his views on Scrum, initially in 1993, as an alternative to the highly prescriptive and top-down project management-based methodologies typified in the traditional waterfall-based software development model. Later, in 1995, Jeff Sutherland teamed with Ken Schwaber to formalize and present the Scrum process at the **OOPSLA'95 (Object-Oriented Programming, Systems, Languages & Applications)** conference. Jeff and Ken continue to maintain the Scrum processes in the form of the *Scrum Guide.* [Schwaber, K., Sutherland, J. (2017) *The Scrum Guide*™ *The Definitive Guide to Scrum: The Rules of the Game. ScrumGuides.org.* https://www. scrumguides.org/]

In his book titled *Scrum – The Art of Doing Twice the Work in Half the Time*, Sutherland notes that detailed project plans and schedules of the traditional waterfall model gave a false sense of security and control [Sutherland, J. *Scrum The Art of Doing Twice the Work in Half the Time*. Currency (An imprint of Crown Publishing and a division of Penguin Random House). New York, N.Y.]. He also came to understand that project plans and schedules are a red herring that hinder truthful assessments of the project's real health.

Project managers know they are working with incomplete information and uncertainty when they develop their project plans. What many may not have understood is that the strung-out life cycle of the traditional model prevented discovery of most critical issues until very late into the project schedule. Moreover, by then, the issues were often numerous and cumulative, adding further complexity and challenges to identify and fix the root causes of the problems. In effect, the plans and schedules locked in requirements, deliverables, priorities, and work activities built on incomplete and dated information and wrong assumptions. Consequently, too many traditionally managed projects failed miserably.

Sutherland realized the alleged benefits of the traditional model – control and predictability through detailed planning – were at odds with reality. The traditional model attempts to force a deterministic approach to management – based on the idea that future events are predictable and controllable. In reality, the world is full of uncertainty, subject to stochastic and interlocking processes and events.

Bull riders wouldn't have a job if bulls didn't buck. However, cowboys wouldn't think that they could sit quietly on a bull's back, with a predefined plan, and not have to respond to the bull's every movement. At least, not if they have any desire to stay on the bull for the full 8 seconds. Instead, cowboys use their senses to take in real-time information about the bull's movements, and they constantly adjust their weight and position to stay in proper alignment with the bull's actions.

Bull riding may sound like an extreme analogy, but businesses are no less prone to being thrown off their game by the constant flux in their competitive surroundings. So why do we think we can ride out those fluctuations in business with a predefined strategy that is not responsive to new information and change?

Sutherland and Schwaber both came to realize that software development teams must embrace uncertainty with creativity and responsive movements. They also realized that an entirely different approach to product definition and development was necessary to resolve the self-inflicted wounds of attempting to control chaos. Resultingly, both turned to the philosophy of empiricism, which espouses a belief that real knowledge comes from information gained through sensory experiences and empirical evidence (for example, knowledge gain through observation and experimentation).

Empirical processes support knowledge acquisition through evidence-based strategies that employ the use of human senses to observe and document patterns and behaviors. Empiricism also promotes the use of trial and error practices to reveal the effectiveness of different strategies through experimentation and analysis.

Sutherland's and Schwaber's approach to empiricism is encapsulated in the three pillars of empirical process control: *transparency*, *inspection*, and *adaptation*. Transparency means process information must be fully available to those who are responsible for its execution. Frequent inspections help the team observe their progress with the desired goals. And when deviations from expectations are noted, the team responds by adjusting the process to achieve positive outcomes through adaption.

It's foolish to wait until all the requirements are fully defined, and the product is fully designed, coded, and tested, to see whether it works, and only then determine whether the product still supports the customer's needs. Instead, it makes more sense for the responsible team to frequently evaluate their progress against their goals, and their continued alignment with the customer's current needs and priorities.

Scrum is lightweight because it is not overly prescriptive. Scrum is a framework and not a methodology that might otherwise impose a lot of rules, constraints, processes, and documentation requirements. Within the Scrum framework, developers are free to use any number of tools and techniques to accomplish their work. But the Scrum framework enforces minimalism, offers an open and safe environment to try different things, and implements a frequent inspect and adapt cycle of events.

This book is largely about scaling Scrum concepts because Scrum has largely won the agile methodology wars in terms of wide-scale acceptance. Nevertheless, there are different views on how to scale the implementation of Scrum capabilities across a large enterprise or a large project. This book addresses why there is not a single method that works in all situations.

In this book, we will explore this Scrum scaling issue together in three parts. First, in the next chapter, you will learn the basics of Scrum. Then, in Part 2 of this book, you will learn about the different approaches to scaling Scrum. Finally, in Part 3, you will learn how to apply Scrum in different environments and situations.

But, before we get to the next chapter, we'll review some of the core implementation concepts implemented by the lightweight agile methodologies. Next, we need to understand how the core concepts support Agile's values and principles. Finally, I'll discuss how the agile movement was initially powered by software engineers and not by MBAs or management specialists. The development of the values and principles of agile, along with the development of lightweight software development methodologies by software engineers, had profound ramifications on adoption and scalability in both large enterprise environments and large, complex projects.

Defining Agile's core implementation concepts

You have probably already surmised that the lightweight methodologies introduced in previous sections have more in common than not. This section consolidates and elaborates on the common principles and practices that came from the lightweight software development methodologies.

I have ordered the concepts alphabetically, to avoid an inaccurate view that one concept has more or less importance than any of the others. All of these principles and practices have found wide-scale acceptance. The order of implementation within an organization is situational and usually best implemented at the team level – for reasons I'll explain in Part Two of this book.

Backlogs

In the traditional model business analysts document business and user requirements in some form of business or requirements specification, while members of the development team document functional and nonfunctional requirements and develop related technical specifications. All of that goes away on agile-based software development projects. Instead, a product owner maintains a backlog of identified requirements, typically documented in the form of epics, stories, and features. While the development team members help the product owner refine the product backlog, only the product owner has the authority to set priorities within the backlog.

Co-location

Modern electronic communication, collaboration, and source control management tools allow software development teams to work in virtual environments and across multiple locations. I've managed more than my fair share of virtual software development projects, both large and small, and I've been able to make them work.

However, an ideal situation is to locate all the development team members in a single location, working together in one room large enough to accommodate the entire team. If the organization has the resources, a common practice is to place a central table with sufficient size to sit all the team members around the table with their computers, so that they can face each other and talk comfortably while they're working. Also, the room's walls should all have whiteboards on them so that team members can conduct multiple collaborative working sessions at the boards simultaneously. The room should be dedicated to the team so they can keep the information on their whiteboards and charts out in the open at all times.

The team members also need time and space to work independently. So, again, if the organization has the resources, the ideal situation is to have individual work cubes in or adjacent to the room. The main point is that the teams can come together to work through technical implementation concerns or address problems that crop up during the project.

In Part Two of this book, you'll discover that having multiple Scrum teams associated with the development of a single product is not uncommon. Each team works as an independent group, and they may work at other facilities. However, each separate team should work together as a single unit and co-located in a single facility with a dedicated room to work and collaborate as a team.

CI/CD pipelines

The acronym **CI/CD** or **CICD** refers to the combination of continuous integration and either continuous delivery or continuous deployment practices. Continuous integration preceded the concepts of continuous delivery and continuous deployment. The term Continuous Integration was originally described by Kent Beck as part of his 12 Extreme Programming development processes. Continuous delivery is the automation of provisioning development and test environments on-demand and with proper configurations. Continuous deployment takes CI one step further to include automated provisioning and configuration in a production deployment environment. The next two subsections provide more details about these two specific areas of automation, CI and CD.

Continuous Integration

Bugs in software code are pretty much a given. The longer a development team waits to integrate and test their source, the more bugs accumulate. Also, the accumulation of both code and bugs makes the task of debugging more complex, difficult, and time-consuming. More frequent integration and testing make debugging less difficult. The causes of bugs are more easily found and more easily fixed.

Continuous Integration is the practice of frequently integrating code into a shared repository – at a minimum, several times a day. More frequent check-ins are better than less frequent check-ins. For larger sections of code, a good practice is to use stubs and API placeholders (a.k.a. skeletons) so that your code can be tested and checked into the source code repository more frequently. This allows other programmers on the team to see what you are doing and even assist with the development of the functionality delivered to the stubs and APIs.

The development team should always work from a single source code repository. Automating the build process is an important component of CI. The automation process includes compiling source code files, packaging compiled files, producing application installers, and defining the database schemas. The more repeatable, self-testing, and automated the build process, the less likely it will be that the process will introduce bugs.

Ideally, developers initiate the build process every time they check their code into the SCM system, and the build process should take less than 10 minutes, including the execution of automated tests. If the build process is manually intensive and time-consuming, developers won't do it frequently, leading to the previously mentioned bug accumulation issues.

Another good practice is to have every commit build on a dedicated integration server. Cloud-based platforms and virtualized development environments make this strategy increasingly practical. The dedicated integration system offers better visibility to available code and provides a staging environment for subsequent testing.

Continuous delivery/deployment

There are several important elements of the concepts and practices behind the implementation of continuous delivery and deployment capabilities. As a component of agility, iterative development practices generate frequent releases of potentially shippable products that can be made available to customers in a predictable cycle. The frequent availability of useful functional software impacts the organization's delivery capabilities.

Specifically, frequent releases create potential issues in the areas of provisioning. Each new release of software has the potential to impact the organization's infrastructure with new demands for computing equipment, networks, database management systems, backup and storage capabilities, security applications, and other software applications.

Continuous Delivery is the term used to define an IT organization's ability to implement changes on demand. Such changes include the introduction of new features, bug fixes, software, and system configuration changes. Provisioning concerns span the development, testing, and production environments, encompassing all software and related infrastructure requirements.

The goal of Continuous Delivery is to implement changes to the development, test, and production environments safely, rapidly, and sustainably. As an example, continuous delivery capabilities make it practical to release software at extremely short intervals, even multiple times a day.

Cloud-based **Platform as a Service (PaaS)** offerings make continuous delivery both economical and practical for many organizations. PaaS providers offer their customers a virtualized application development and hosting platform as a cost-effective alternative to building and maintaining dedicated, in-house IT infrastructures. But the same concepts and capabilities are possible within an organization's data center with the correct technologies and practices.

Continuous delivery concepts extend the automated build and integration test capabilities out into the test environments. They also generally include the ability to provision and configure necessary infrastructure resources on demand. Conceptually, continuous delivery supports the development and testing environments. After the completion of testing, the development team manually pushes the released software into the production environments. The customer's IT operations team then provisions resources and configures the hardware and software for the new release.

Continuous deployment takes the automated provisioning and configuration capabilities of continuous delivery out into the production environments. Humans are not involved, and only a failure in the automated process stops the delivery of the release. With the implementation of both continuous delivery and deployment capabilities, developers have the potential to release new product functionality within minutes of pushing their code into the test environments.

Continuous deployment capabilities create a new set of potential problems by releasing software updates to customers who don't value, or understand, or are not yet willing to adopt the changes. Also, the functionality may not apply to every type of user. Therefore, it's not unusual to set up rules that limit the deployment of automated production releases to stages or to specific communities of users.

Cross-functional

The implementation of iterative development releases by small teams is only possible if the teams have the resources and skills required to develop and test the product's features. As the teams are stood up, they must collectively have the skills to work on the product. Over time, individuals should strive to cross-train on the skills they don't have but that are necessary for the development of the product. This concept is called "multi learning" and is key to the team's self-sufficiency.

Customer-centric

The third value in the Agile Manifesto says customer collaboration is more important than contract negotiations [Kent Beck, et al. © 2001. *Manifesto for Agile Software Development.* `http://agilemanifesto.org/`. Accessed 10 November 2019]. A contract scenario creates situations where the customer defines high-level requirements and then, except for brief requirement gathering activities, disappears for the remaining duration of the project. Moreover, contract negotiations set up adversarial relationships, and not the collaborative relationships that support the iterative and evolutionary development aspects of agile.

Incremental and iterative development (**IID**) practices help simplify development by reducing the size and complexity of code, making it easier to find and debug any errors in the application. However, the IID practices also allow several very important customer alignment and collaboration opportunities.

First, the customers and end-users can look at the product frequently to ensure the implementation of features that meet their needs. Invariably, customers get new insights into how a software product can better support their needs only after they have a chance to work with a prototype or new release. The frequent releases of agile provide more opportunities for customers to get these insights.

Second, if the customer judges the software features as insufficient in some manner, the customer's priorities have changed, or their insights after viewing the software lead to new requirements, the development team can quickly adjust to meet the new requirements. In the traditional model, change requests were not desirable as they had a direct impact on the authorized constraints of the project. In other words, changes in scope cause negative impacts on project budgets, resource allocations, and schedules.

Iterative and Incremental Development (IID)

The phrase iterative and incremental development describes the agile approach practitioners take to deliver frequent releases of potentially shippable products. I have found there is often confusion about what the terms iterative and incremental mean.

The term *iterative* means development is broken up into limited time-boxed durations, typically of 4 weeks or less. In a modern DevOps environment with continuous delivery and deployment capabilities, iterations are measured in hours or minutes. Iterative development reduces complexity and work in progress, which are important elements in implementing lean software development concepts.

The term *incremental* refers to the concept that the product evolves incrementally with each development iteration. In other words, the term increment implies the release of a new slice of functionality with each iteration.

Iterative and incremental go together because the sole purpose of development, regardless of the methodology employed, is to create something that customers ultimately value. In that context, new increments of product functionality are the deliverables of the iterative development process.

Pair programming

There are several important elements associated with agile practices that allow the development team to operate rapidly, efficiently, and productively. Some of the most important elements include transparency, safety, perspective, and inspection.

An effective strategy to address all four of these elements is pair programming. In pair programming, two developers sit side by side and work together. One programmer has the role of *driver*, while the other takes on the role of an *observer*, sometimes called the *navigator*.

As the driver develops the code, they are heads-down and operating at a tactical/implementation level. The observer inspects the developer's code in real-time to help resolve any bugs and consider more efficient development approaches. The observer also evaluates the code in terms of addressing the strategic goals of the feature within the application. The developers change roles frequently to stay fresh and engaged.

Potentially shippable products

The first principle stated in the Agile Manifesto is *Our highest priority is to satisfy the customer through early and continuous delivery of valuable software* [Kent Beck, et al. © 2001. *Manifesto for Agile Software Development.* http://agilemanifesto.org/. Accessed 10 November 2019.] Agile practitioners employ IID practices in support of this principle.

However, it does not matter how frequently the development team completes new updates if the output has no functional value to the customer. Therefore, a key component of most agile practices is the concept of providing a potentially shippable product with every development iteration.

That does not mean to imply the product owner must release the product of an iteration to customers and end-users. There may be practical reasons not to do so until full business process functionality is available, or the customer is in a position to accept the product into production.

Prototyping

I noted previously that, often, customers don't know what they want until they see the product and have a chance to work with it. This is the point of having frequent customer reviews, as often as every iterative release. At the beginning of a project, there may not be much to show. Moreover, the team may want to show potential product concepts before devoting much time to developing the features.

Prototyping is an approach to quickly and cost-effectively build a mock-up of a particular product or feature. The mock-up could be as simple as a screen or user face design, or more complex with data fields, data, and algorithms that support the proposed application functionality. The prototypes are shown to customers before the implementation of the feature into a production release of the product.

An important concept of prototyping is that all prototypes are, by definition, throwaway activities. In other words, there should never be an expectation that a prototype must be deployed to a customer. Such an expectation gets in the way of the concept that *failures are not bad, or to be avoided, as they provide opportunities for learning*. If nothing else, the developers now know what not to do in the future.

Retrospectives

The twelfth and final principle of the Agile Manifesto states: *At regular intervals, the team reflects on how to become more effective, then tunes and adjusts its behavior accordingly* [Kent Beck, et al. © 2001. *Manifesto for Agile Software Development.* http:// agilemanifesto.org/. Accessed 10 November 2019]. Retrospectives support this principle.

During a retrospective, the development team looks back at the past iteration to assess what worked well, what didn't work out so well, and what they could do differently in the future, starting with the very next iteration. Retrospectives only work and have value when the development team members feel free to speak out. In other words, they must work in an environment where team members are respectful, open, and honest, with complete transparency about all customer and product information.

Safety

Pair programming, prototyping, and retrospectives all create situations for potential tension and conflict. The development team member must be open to alternative views, know that failure is not going to get them in trouble, and that they should feel free to speak out during retrospectives and other team collaboration activities. That requires the development of an environment that stresses respect and safety for its team members.

The concept of safety is 180° out from the command and control environments dictated by the traditional development methodologies. The plan-driven and linear-sequential approach to development in the traditional model created cultures where team members followed edicts driven from above. In contrast, agile encourages a bottom-up approach to planning and executing work that puts the development team and the product owner in the driver's seat for decision-making.

Self-organizing

Having team members with multiple useful skills gives the team more flexibility in the assignment of work. Development teams can expect that each iteration of work has different task requirements. If the team employs specialists and does not cross-train – both to develop missing skills and provide more flexibility in individual work assignments, they have limited ability to assign work on demand. Instead, they find themselves having to wait to take on work until the required specialist is available.

From the context of the product backlog, having teams filled with specialists causes delays in the assignment of work and bottlenecks that, in turn, creates too much work in progress. Accumulated work in progress is a form of waste and is the antithesis of lean development organizations.

Small teams

Effective software development teams must have the resources they need to deliver incremental slices of new product functionality every iteration. If a team is too small, they likely won't have the skills and resources to deliver. If the team is too large, the coordination of work grows significantly larger and more complex.

Ken Schwaber and Jeff Sutherland, in the Scrum Guide, state teams should not be smaller than three members and not greater than nine. Jeff Bezos, the CEO of Amazon.com, is famous for noting that no matter the size of the company, individual teams should never get large enough to consume more than two pizzas in a sitting. (for example, five to seven people) [Deutschman, A. (2004) *Inside the Mind of Jeff Bezos. Pizza Teams and Terabytes.* https://www.fastcompany.com/50106/inside-mind-jeff-bezos-5. Accessed November 8, 2019]. UK anthropology professor R.I.M. Dunbar, in his paper titled *Co-Evolution of Neocortex Size, Group Size, and Language in Humans*, cites the maximum useful team size is limited to no more than 10 to 12 people [Dunbar, R. I. M. (1993). *Coevolution of neocortical size, group size and language in humans. Behavioral and Brain Sciences 16* (4): 681-735], [Buys, C.J. & Larsen, K.L. (1979). *Human sympathy groups. Psychological Report.* 45: 547-553]. The **Scaled Agile Framework (SAFe™)**, another scaled Scrum approach discussed later in this book, recommends that development teams stay in the range of 5 to 11 people. [Corporate (2019) *Scaled Agile. Agile Teams.* https://www.scaledagileframework.com/agile-teams/. Accessed November 8, 2019].

Source Code Management (SCM)

Developers work on code as individuals and in groups as part of a larger team. The developers implement changes to their code incrementally, not sure if the individual changes can deliver an intended result. In such cases, they may need to retrieve the original code to start over. That is the primary purpose of an SCM tool, to serve as a repository for all source code and related artifacts, and to automate version control over each of the stored artifacts so that developers can roll back to whatever versions they require.

The SCM tool also makes it possible for developers to find and check out the latest version of the code under development. SCM is an important capability as the developers must have confidence that they are working from the most current code set. If they pick up an old code set, there are likely to be numerous changes that can negatively impact the code they are developing. SCM tools also make it easy for the members of the development team to see the completed work to date, work in the queue, and work in progress.

Stories

There are many approaches to documenting business and user requirements. Under traditional development practices, requirements documentation tends to have a focus on analyzing what a product must do to fulfill business and user needs. In other words, the focus of requirements analysis is on the product. In contrast, *story*-based formats provide a brief elaboration on what customers and end-users want to do. In other words, what are the capabilities they need to do the work of their organizations?

It's a subtle distinction but think of it this way: customers don't care as much about the list of product features as they care about what they can do with the product's features.

The basic format of a story is as follows:

As a <type of user> **I want to** <desired capability>, **so that** <expected result or benefit>.

Sustainable workflows

The eighth principle of the Agile Manifesto states *Agile processes promote sustainable development. The sponsors, developers, and users should be able to maintain a constant pace indefinitely* [Kent Beck, et al. © 2001. *Manifesto for Agile Software Development.* http:// agilemanifesto.org/. Accessed 10 November 2019]. Unfortunately, this objective is not always achieved, but it is the desired goal.

There are several keys to sustainability in iterative development environments. First, the team should never overcommit. They need the skills and resources to do the work required to support the development of the product. They need direct access to customers and users so they can fully assess the feature requirements. The team needs to develop heuristics for estimating the amount of work they can complete in a development iteration. Finally, the team must be in control of stating how much work they can accomplish in any development iteration.

Testing (test-driven and automated)

Testing is an important component of the overall software development life cycle process regardless of whether the development team is following the traditional approach or an agile-based development approach. Testing is a set of **quality assurance** (**QA**) activities that confirms the product features meet the business, user, functional, and nonfunctional requirements.

The primary difference between testing practices in the traditional model and those found in agile is the amount of work taken on before testing. As noted in previous sections, the more the development team attempts to implement new functionality before testing, the more likely there is to be an accumulation of bugs and defects that are difficult to locate and resolve. The iterative development nature of agile practices helps reduce the complexity of debugging a software product by limiting the amount of functionality implemented between testing.

Another important aspect of modern agile practices is to develop a test for each piece of code before writing the code. This practice is referred to as test-driven development.

Traditionally, the code is written first and then tested. In the traditional approach, the challenge is to develop a test, after the fact, that accurately supports the original requirement as opposed to writing a test that simply verifies the functionality of their code.

Test-driven development puts the focus on initially creating a test that fails unless the code properly implements the underlying functional requirement. It's not uncommon to have a developer run the test before they write the code to make sure it does fail, thus ensuring there is not a conflict with other code or that other code already fulfills the requirement. Next, the developer creates the code and runs the test again. If the test fails, the developer has not properly implemented the requirement. If the test passes, the developer has confidence they have properly implemented the requirements and that their code works.

Testing environments are another critical success factor in software development regardless of the software development methodology used. Sometimes, organizations take shortcuts due to costs and do not stand up dedicated test environments, forcing the development team to run their tests on their development environments or in the production environments. The problem with running tests on the development environments is that those computing systems likely do not replicate the exact conditions the software must operate in on the production environments. The problem with running tests on the production environments is that a bug could potentially bring the system down.

The only way around the problems associated with testing the production environment is to create a clone of the production environment. Again, modern **PaaS** offerings make it easier and less costly to stand up a development or test environment to make the conditions found in production environments. Likewise, virtualization makes it possible to set up independent testing environments within a set of clustered servers. Performance testing in test environments helps duplicate the demand loads expected in production environments.

Tools

The introduction of software programming tools came along almost concurrently with the introduction of electronic computing equipment. The primary focus of programming tools is to convert human-readable instructions into machine-readable instructions. The modern instantiation of software programming tools includes text editors and **IDEs**.

Text editors facilitate code development by providing syntax-aware assistance to code construction based on the type of programming code used by the developer. IDEs provide an integrated suite of tools to assist developers and code creation, software builds, and testing. The suite of tools within an IDE may include text editors, object and data modeling tools, code libraries, compilers or interpreters, debugging tools, and test platforms. IDEs help turn software development into an integrated and automated process and help reduce typing errors and bugs.

In the earliest days of agile, and also used in support of traditional software development practices, efforts were made to simplify business process and information analysis through the introduction of modeling methods and tools. Such tools fell broadly into the categories of **RAD** and **CASE**.

CASE tools attempted to reduce the complexity and speed of development by providing a suite of tools to model the physical and logical views of the customer's domain. The most sophisticated CASE tools offered integration capabilities that helped translate the information from one modeling method and tool into another.

The RAD approach, as proposed by its originator, James Martin, added methods and tools for **Joint Application Development (JAD)**. JAD is an approach to capture business requirements through a series of workshops with domain experts and knowledge workers within the customer's organization. As you can probably tell, JAD sessions supported the traditional software development model more than agile, by attempting to collect all requirements at the start of a project. On the other hand, the case tool environment had the goal of expediting development.

RAD tools still exist with an emphasis on modeling and a low-code rapid application development platform. As in the past, the primary focus of RAD tools is a modeling environment that encourages the participation of domain experts in defining and analyzing business and user requirements. However, modern RAD tools also implement capabilities to implement automated workflows and integrated forms with no or minimal amounts of software coding.

Appreciating the importance of Agile's values and principles

No book that considers agile-based practices is complete without including a discussion on the Agile Manifesto and its impact on the software development industry. If you are interested in Scrum and agile-based software development practices, and you haven't done so already, you should read through the Agile Manifesto. It's available online at `http://agilemanifesto.org/` [Kent Beck, et al. © 2001. *Manifesto for Agile Software Development*. `http://agilemanifesto.org/`. Accessed 10 November 2019]. For expediency, I refer situationally to specific values and principles throughout this book to show how a certain practice supports agile.

The main point I want to make in this section is that Agile was not and was never intended to be a methodology. The 17 signees of the Agile Manifesto represented at least 8 distinct software methodologies, by my counting, many of which are listed in the *Moving away from the traditional model* section in this chapter. Jim Highsmith, in his introduction, notes that Alistair Cockburn made the comment that he *personally didn't expect that this particular group of agilities to ever agree on anything substantive.*

The group of gathered software engineers wasn't going to agree on a specific agile methodology. But, in the end, they agreed on issues of far greater importance. As Highsmith put it, *Agile Methodologies is about the mushy stuff of values and culture.*

Agile is not about how to develop software; it is instead about implementing a culture that respects people and customers, promoting trust and collaboration, and creating organizations and cultures where people want to work. In the process, really good software is built quickly, efficiently, and with the features our customers want.

Building on a movement led by engineers

It's interesting to me that the concepts of Agile, in its earliest days, were developed and promoted primarily by software engineers. That was not by accident as software programmers were taking the brunt of the criticism for the failures created by implementations of the traditional software development model.

Being in the trenches, so to speak, many software engineers understood the root cause of the failures of the traditional model. Through experimentation, those engineers discovered new ways of working that overcame the limitations of the traditional model. In the process, they also discovered better ways to work together as a team in collaborative, safe, and respectful environments.

However, and this is not meant to be a denigrating statement, in most but not all cases they were software engineers and consultants, and not organizational executives. That very fact limited the scope of the implementations they could take on without senior management support. Their early experiments involved single products with one or a small handful of development teams.

For sure, agile-based practices showed demonstrable successes early on, bringing positive attention. Eventually, senior management caught on and began to realize that there might be something to this whole agile idea. Senior executives are ultimately pragmatic. They have a fiduciary responsibility to stockholders to implement organizational structures that are highly profitable and support the mission of the enterprise. From that perspective, there is much incentive to adopt agile-based practices.

On the other hand, there weren't many examples of large-scale agile-based implementation programs or projects. Scaled agile approaches evolved over time, but not without a lot of fits and starts. The issues with scaling agile were not so much related to the maturation of technologies or methodologies, but rather rethinking organizational designs. I'm going to table this discussion for now. But we will revisit organizational design issues in Section 2 of this book.

Summary

After reading this chapter, you should have a sound understanding of the many issues created by following the traditional plan-driven and linear-sequential development model and project management practices. Engineers, who most often bore the brunt of criticism for failed projects, began to develop so-called lightweight software development methodologies to overcome the problems associated with the traditional model.

In this chapter, you have learned that the traditional model often failed on four fronts. First, the traditional model created lengthy delivery cycles. Second, given the predefined project planning and linear-sequential processes, the traditional model is unresponsive to changes in market conditions, customer needs, or priorities. Third, the protracted development cycles made it difficult to locate and resolve bugs, and ultimately delayed deliveries and created more costs. Finally, the stochastic nature of developing highly customized software products makes it nearly impossible to predict with certainty a project plan's deterministically imposed constraints of scope, budgets, schedules, resources, and quality.

These engineers started experimenting with lightweight development methodologies that directly addressed the failings of the traditional model. This chapter introduced and contrasted a number of these methodologies, such as ASD, Crystal Clear, XP, RAD and Scrum.

Many of the lightweight development methodologies introduced in this chapter shared common concepts, many of which are retained today as techniques that facilitate agility. These practices were discussed in detail in the section titled *Defining Agile's core implementation concepts*.

Seventeen engineers involved in defining lightweight development practices met on February 13, 2001, at The Lodge at Snowbird ski resort, in the Wasatch mountains of Utah, to share their views and seek common ground. Though they practiced many of the lightweight concepts noted in this chapter, what they found they most shared in common were their philosophical views on the importance of values and culture, and not so much on specific development techniques or practices. Their collaboration resulted in the publication of the Agile Manifesto (`www.agilemanifesto.org/`) as a statement of 4 common values and 12 principles of Agile software development.

In the next chapter, you will be introduced to the basic Scrum approach, roles and responsibilities, and events defined within the Scrum Guide.

Questions

1. What makes software development unique from the development of other large, complex products, such as ships, utilities, bridges, roads, or buildings?

2. Why do plan-driven and linear-sequential development practices often fail when developing software?

3. What are some of the development practices often associated with lightweight and agile-based software development practices?

4. Why do you think the software engineers who defined the Agile Manifesto found common ground on values and principles instead of specific development practices?

5. Why is XP considered a methodology and not a framework?

6. Why is Scrum considered a framework instead of a methodology?

Further reading

- Beck, K., Andres, C. (2005) *Extreme Programming Explained, Embrace Change.* Addison-Wesley/ Pearson Education, Inc., Upper Saddle River, NJ

- Cockburn, A., (2005) *Crystal Clear, A Human-Powered Methodology for Small Teams.* Pearson Education, Inc. Upper Saddle River, NJ

- Highsmith, J. (1999) *Adaptive Software Development, A Collaborative Approach to Managing Complex Systems.* Dorset House Publishing. New York, NY.

- Highsmith, J. (2004, 2010) Agile Project Management, The Agile Software Development Suite Series. Addison-Wesley/ Pearson Education, Inc., Boston, MA

- Kerr, J., Hunter, R. (1994) Inside RAD, How to Build Fully Functional Computer Systems in 90 Days or Less. McGraw-Hill, New York, NY

- Rosenberg, D., Stephens, M., Collins-Cope, M. (2005) Agile Development with ICONIX Process, People, Process, and Pragmatism. Apress, Berkeley, CA

- Martin, J. (1991) Rapid Application Development, High Speed, High Quality, Low Cost. MACMILLILLAN Publishing Company, New York, NY

2
Scrum Beyond Basics

Scrum is, by far, the software industry leader as the preferred lightweight and agile framework to use. As a result, it is the Agile reference model of choice in this book. Due to its roots in software development, many industries and functional business areas employ Scrum to improve both their operational and development efficiencies.

The emphasis on Scrum is the instantiation of small Agile teams to develop products iteratively over short cycles. It also allows us to deliver increments of new customer-centric value much more efficiently than in the traditional plan-driven, linear-sequential development model.

Though Scrum describes the activities of small teams, many organizations use Scrum across their enterprises, which involve hundreds or even thousands of individuals, all working in small teams. Still, the Original Scrum Guide does not prescribe practices to coordinate the activities of multiple teams. Later, in module two of this book, you will learn about multiple Scrum variants that address how to scale Scrum across multiple teams.

Before we get to the subject of scaling Scrum, we need to understand how it works and why it is so successful. We'll break this topic into two parts, spanning two chapters. The primary objective of this initial chapter is to understand the nature of Scrum as a framework and the importance of its empirical process control theory foundations. In the next chapter, you'll learn how to apply Scrum.

In this chapter, we're going to cover the following main topics:

- Mastering Scrum
- Requiring executive sponsorship
- Putting the focus on products
- Forming Scrum Teams
- Identifying roles and responsibilities
- Leveraging empirical process control theories
- Defining Scrum Events
- Implementing Scrum Artifacts

In this chapter, you will learn why Scrum is based on a sports metaphor and why it's considered a framework and not a prescriptive methodology. Though Scrum is a team effort, you will learn why long-term adoption and success still depends on executives to provide leadership, as well as necessary resources and structural realignments. In this chapter, you will learn how Scrum's foundations, which were built on empirical process control theory (empiricism), help organizations resolve complex adaptive problems. Finally, you will learn about the basic elements of Scrum, including its rules, events, roles, responsibilities, and artifacts. We'll start with a discussion on what it takes to "master" Scrum.

Mastering Scrum

This book is ultimately about mastering Scrum practices and doing so at an enterprise scale. But I don't want to assume that you already know a lot about this approach to agile software development. If you believe you have a sound understanding of Scrum concepts, feel free to move on to the other chapters in this book. However, if you are relatively new to Scrum, I would recommend that you continue reading these two introductory chapters.

The content in this chapter and the next chapter align with the concepts presented in **The Scrum Guide** (`https://www.Scrumguides.org/`). Scrum employs somewhat unique terminology, and its foundations, based on empirical process control theory, may be challenging to understand as the perspective of Scrum moves from *project* to *product*, and from following *life cycle processes* to producing *increments of customer-centric value.*

Scrum evolved to implement the values and principles of Agile within software development projects. However, Scrum is a generalized approach to Agile that supports any number of business improvement applications. Though the Scrum Guide mentions its software development heritage, given its broader scope, interestingly, the Scrum Guide does not explicitly discuss how to apply Scrum in a software or systems development context.

The next three subsections introduce the basics of Scrum as a sports-based metaphor, its application in a software development context, and how it became the de-facto standard. As a person who loves all types of sports, let's start with the sports metaphor.

Applying a sports metaphor

The term **Scrum** came from a paper titled *The New New Product Development Game*, written by Hirotaka Takeuchi and Ikujiro Nonaka. Their paper introduced Scrum as a rugby-based metaphor for coordinated team play in manufacturing-related business. The basic idea behind a rugby scrum is that a team of individuals work together with a collaborative goal to take possession of the ball, across multiple iterations of play, and move it forward to score more points than their competitors.

After assessing some of the world's most successful businesses, Taguchi and Nonaka concluded that the best companies had moved away from the traditional plan-driven and linear sequential life cycle development processes. Instead, the more successful manufacturing companies employed teamwork, much like the rugby scrum teams, by employing radically different concepts, such as the following:

- Broadly defined corporate goals, as opposed to detailed product and project plans.

- Self-organizing product-oriented teams, as opposed to functional roles and responsibilities.

- Team independence, as opposed to top-down enforcement of policies and procedures.

- Continuous improvements in pursuit of excellence, as opposed to operational permanence.

- The employment of integrated and fully functioning product teams, as opposed to assignments of people across disparate functional departments.

- Concurrent phases of work, as opposed to linear sequential life cycle development processes.

- Multi-learning, as opposed to individuals having a single role and limited cross-functional skills.

- Organization-wide knowledge transference, as opposed to siloed organizations.

Scrumming in a software development context

A decade later, in the mid-1990s, Ken Schwaber and Jeff Sutherland applied Taguchi and Nonaka's principles to software development, along with their concepts of empirical process control theory – also known as *empiricism*. Sutherland and Schwaber collaborated and presented a joint paper, titled *Scrum Development Process*, at the **Business Object Design and Implementation Workshops held as part of the Object-Oriented Programming, Systems, Languages & Applications '95 (OOPSLA '95)** event in Austin, Texas. (Sutherland, Victor, Schwaber, 1995)

I was interested to know how Jeff and Ken started working together, so I reached out to Jeff Sutherland to ask him, and this is what he told me:

"In 1993, my team at Easel Corp. formalized Scrum as we know it today. We did 2 years of monthly releases with a product that Computer World said was the best they had ever seen.

In 1995, we were acquired by VMARK. I had worked with Ken on waterfall projects at a banking software company. He was CEO of a waterfall Project Management methodology company. I invited him up to VMARK to look at Scrum. I wanted to get the intellectual property out into the public domain.

I said, 'Ken, you should be selling Scrum, not waterfall, as it works and waterfall doesn't.' He spent 2 weeks embedded with the first Scrum Team and agreed that it would be better to sell Scrum. We agreed on the ground rules. It would be open-source, and we would write a paper for presentation at my annual workshop at OOPSLA '95. Ken began selling Scrum in the industry while I was implementing Scrum in multiple companies as CTO.

Ken worked with me as a consultant in all my companies, so we evolved Scrum together and showed up at the Agile Manifesto meeting in 2001. The rest is history."

Becoming the de facto standard

By and large, Scrum is the de facto standard today in agile practices. For example, according to the CollabNet | VersionOne *13th Annual State of Agile Survey*, 72% of their respondents reported they were practicing Scrum or a hybrid that includes Scrum. (CollabNet | VersionOne, 2019)

I believe long-term project managers – if they were openly honest – could quickly identify some of the deficiencies associated with developing software under the traditional plan-driven and linear sequential development model. The following are some examples:

- Customers almost always think they have given you their requirements when, in reality, they have only given you a list of high-level deliverables in their charter or negotiated agreements.

- Contract agreements too often focus on identifying expected work tasks and deliverables and ways that the contractor will prove their performance against the specified tasks and deliverables.

- Customers and end-users almost always find better or new ways to use a product only after they have seen a prototype or a working release.

- Product developers are always the best people to define and estimate project-related work.

- Software coding takes a relatively minimal amount of time across the project's duration.

- Conversely, testing and debugging often takes up the most time in a project.

- The more requirements that are added to the project plan, the longer testing and debugging will take.

As we go through this chapter, we will find out how Scrum either addresses or leverages the preceding list of facts to help achieve a more positive outcome when contrasted with the traditional development model. In the next subsection, we are going to start on this journey by understanding that the implementation of Scrum requires executive-level sponsorship.

Requiring executive sponsorship

In the previous chapter, *Origins of Agile and Lightweight Methodologies*, I mentioned that a successful enterprise implementation of Scrum requires the support of a CEO or, at a product level, a senior-level executive who can assign a Product Owner to the development effort. As we get further into this chapter, we'll explore why that's the case. I don't want to imply that it's not possible to employ Scrum concepts within a small development team as a standalone effort. However, the team members' efforts will be frustrated without the executives buying in and having a basic understanding of Scrum concepts.

The successful implementation of Scrum requires making changes to traditional software development philosophies, culture, organizational structures, and infrastructure. Any project team that attempts to leverage Scrum concepts quickly runs into a host of organizational problems related to those four areas of concern. The Scrum Team needs an executive sponsor to clear the way for them to operate successfully. Later in this chapter, we will learn that a Scrum Master clears impediments for the development team in their day-to-day activities. However, the executives must also clear impediments at the organizational level.

At a philosophical level, Scrum refutes the misconceptions of the traditional model that customers desire capabilities for a product and that the work required to produce it is known from the start. Instead, requirements must be teased out over time as customers and end-users have a chance to use prototypes and incremental releases of new functionality. Likewise, the developers have better success when they can focus on high-value and high priority tasks, and iteratively implement new product features and functions in shorter intervals and more frequent releases.

The traditional (that is, Waterfall) model follows a project-based approach to development. Project management practices break development into distinct life cycle phases that are pre-planned and highly controlled. But if a product's requirements can't be defined at the start of a project, which they seldom are, then the project team is already off to a bad start. They will build features that may not be truly valuable, and they will have too much **work in progress** (**WIP**) to build and test the product efficiently. You will learn the importance of removing all forms of waste, of which WIP is a type, in the next chapter on concepts and practices.

Organizational cultures develop over time as a set of behavioral norms influenced by corporate policies and procedures, executive expectations, social influences, and just familiarity with the way the organization conducts its business. Unfortunately, this established culture leads to complacency and resistance to change that may hinder the competitiveness of the organization.

Just as cultures are built over time, changing the culture also takes time. Change is scary for many people. Therefore, organizational change is a difficult task, even when the organization's success or the livelihood of its people depends on it.

The use of traditional waterfall-based software development practices goes back to the mid-1950s. For many organizations, those practices are ingrained not only in corporate policies and practices but in the very culture of the company. Simply put, attempts to change the project-oriented approach to development cause stress up and down the organization.

The proper implementation of Scrum requires a very different set of roles, responsibilities, and practices than those defined in a project-oriented development approach. Also, at an enterprise level, there are layers of middle management positions that are not required, nor desired, when implementing Scrum. Those folks will not be supportive of change unless senior management helps them understand the importance of the necessary transformations and proactively find new roles and responsibilities for the affected individuals. They must trust that the organization's executives have their back, or they will work to undermine the transformation efforts.

Moreover, the practices of Scrum do away with a lot of overhead in terms of inefficient development processes, review and approval cycles, and overly burdensome documentation requirements. These items, too, are ingrained within the culture of an organization. They are ingrained because of the long-term behavior and beliefs of its people, informed by those policies and practices, and the social norms that evolved to support them. In short, it's hard for people to see why these activities are no longer necessary.

Less is more is a commonly used idiom that is ascribed initially to Robert Browning, in 1855, in his poem titled Andrea del Sarto. It is also applied to the minimalist architectural views of Ludwig Mies Van Der Rohe (1886-1969). However, the term has similarly found use in describing the minimalist concepts of Scrum. In the next subsection, you will learn why Scrum stays small, no matter the scale.

Implementing small teams

Scrum implements a small team approach to development. As a general rule of thumb, the Scrum Team should not have less than three people in it, nor more than nine people. Too few people and the team may not have all the skills and resources necessary to build the product. Too many people, on the other hand, and the communication among members and integrating work become too complicated.

The formula for team communications and integration links is $x = n(n - 1) / 2$, where x is the number of potential team member connections and interactions and n is the number of team members. So, a team consisting of three members has only three potential communication interfaces between its member. However, a team consisting of nine members has 36 communication interfaces between its members. Grow the team to 50 members, and the number of networked communications connections raises to 1,225. People simply cannot manage that many potential relationships and interactions.

So, Scrum does not scale by adding team members and infrastructure. It scales through replications of small teams by following the same basic rules, roles, events, and artifacts.

As your organization moves to implement a small team structure, it's essential to provide a work environment that is conducive to supporting small teams. Setting a suitable work environment is the subject of the next subsection.

Establishing a proper work environment

Scrum has additional infrastructure-related requirements in order to support the small teams. Each team needs to be co-located in a dedicated workspace with sufficient room to hold a table where they can work together with their computers. The room should have ample space so that whiteboards that display project data can be set up. Space for break-outs into smaller work teams for collaborative work sessions must also be provided. The room should include developer laptops and provide access to all the networks, computing systems, software, and other tools the team needs to design and develop the product.

The co-located work environments allow frequent face-to-face collaborations by team members, which better supports Scrum's empirical-based development processes. The team members should be able to meet and discuss important issues and topics without scheduling delays or communications impediments. In a co-located facility, the developers can participate in pair-programming techniques. Plus, the team members are free to move about and review the data that's posted on their whiteboards and flipcharts and use those same tools to work through the requirements and related architectural and design elements.

Putting the focus on products

As noted in the earlier section *Requiring executive sponsorship*, Scrum's implementation eliminates the plan-driven approach of traditional project management practices because there are too many unknowns in terms of customer needs, priorities, risks, and potential impediments. In the next subsection, you will learn how empiricism is a better approach to managing work in a project-oriented environment that experiences random and uncontrolled events. However, before we get there, we need to understand that the focus of work must be product-specific. We also need to understand why this is the case.

A traditional organization creates hierarchical organizational structures to support business functions, such as sales, marketing, development, and so on. This decomposition continues below the functional departmental level, with teams established by their type of work or skills.

Under the traditional model, project managers follow pre-defined plans and schedules to control work that is complex, unique, and time-limited. Those programs and projects may draw resources from the functional departments on an as-needed basis, for the duration of the project or resource requirement. In this model, the projects operate as matrix organizations, and team members effectively have two managers – the project manager and their functional manager.

At first glance, the matrix organizational structures may look efficient because all skills are managed and mentored by domain-specific line managers. These domain resources are also theoretically available on an as-needed basis to any project team that needs them.

In reality, the matrix organization is very inefficient. Domain-specific training makes it more challenging to cross-train employees so that they support other skills and technology requirements. Also, the projects may find that there are organizational constraints that limit their access to resources that are deployed for other operational, production, or project needs.

Organizational needs for specific domain-oriented resources vary over time. This means there are times when there will be insufficient resources and other times when there will be too many resources available with a particular skill. Both situations negatively impact the organization. Necessary work cannot be done when the resources are the limiting factor, and, at other times, the domain-specific resources are sitting unproductively on the bench. Both situations represent costs and inefficiencies to the organization.

All this goes away under Scrum. Instead, the management focus of Scrum is always on products, not functional departments or projects. Instead of borrowing resources, the Product Owner has full access to the functional resources they require to design, develop, and deliver their products.

So, now that you understand the importance of aligning Scrum Teams around products, and not projects, let's take a closer look at how to form and operate Scrum Teams.

Forming Scrum Teams

No matter the size or complexity of a product, Scrum Teams remain small, autonomous, self-contained, cross-functional, and self-organizing. Let's go over these in a bit more detail:

- Small teams avoid the network density issues that cause inefficiencies resulting from the exponential increase in communication relationships with each added team member.

- Autonomous teams have the authority to figure out the work that's required to implement the requirements described in the product backlog.

- Self-contained teams have all the resources they require to complete their work.

- Cross-functional teams have all the knowledge and skills they require to perform their work.

- Self-organizing teams have the responsibility of assigning work tasks to team members in the most efficient manner.

Members of small Scrum Teams must collaborate to work through dependency and integration issues, they must get along, and they must be willing to jump in and help other members when meeting the commitments of the Sprint Goal are in danger.

With a product-oriented focus, Scrum Teams must have all the skills necessary to define the requirements, establish the architecture and design, construct the product, and deploy it. These software product construction skills must encompass test script development, programming, data management, component and systems integration, and testing.

Still, there are limits to what a single Scrum Team can know, such as the business drivers that justify investments in the product. Therefore, Scrum Team members must also have direct access to domain experts and other stakeholders to refine customer needs and product requirements.

Providing access to specialized skills

The Product Owner, with assistance from the Scrum manager, must make sure the developers have timely access to employees, customers, end-users, and other stakeholders who have the information they require to build the right product for their target market customers.

Ideally, Scrum Team members can reach out directly to speak to the people who have the information they require to complete their work. However, there will be times when that is not practical. The Scrum Team members may not know who has the information they need. Alternatively, the effort to locate the right resources, communicate the requirements, and get the input they need is often time-consuming.

The Product Owners and Scrum Masters must facilitate the outreach process to ensure the product's Scrum Teams have access to domain and other technical experts as needed. They also must make sure to capture all customer, market, end user, product, and Scrum Team information and ensure that the information is fully transparent – that is, that it's available to all other Scrum Teams and stakeholders.

Implementing multiple Scrum Teams

Large products may require multiple development teams to produce all the elements required by the solution. This is a fairly common reason for establishing multiple Scrum Teams. Also, organization may have multiple product lines, and each product may have one or more Scrum Teams supporting the product development efforts.

However, as a separate strategy, and often supporting a product or multiple product lines, the Scrum Team's implementations may expand to include all product promotion, order taking, delivery, and support activities, not just development activities. For example, the Scrum Teams may form by business function to include development teams, marketing teams, sales teams, order management teams, partner teams, and so on.

The formation of Scrum Teams to support business functions makes sense in that they all have information and artifacts that they develop and deliver. It also makes sense that they do so as efficiently as possible and in lock-step with the product development teams. Regardless of each Scrum Team's function, they all have the same product-oriented focus, and they all pull from the same product backlog, which is under the control of one Product Owner.

Supporting non-development activities

It's important to note that the Scrum Guide provides generalized guidance on Agile-based practices, but does not provide specific instructions regarding the types of Scrum Teams an organization may form. Scrum Teams can develop any type of product, service, or some desired outcome. Scrum supports all types of deliverable items so long as the Scrum Teams follow the basic rules mentioned at the beginning of this section; that is, small, autonomous, self-contained, cross-functional, and self-organizing.

When scaling Scrum at an enterprise-level, in support of multiple product lines, the product development teams form under the direction of the Product Owners. Scrum Teams that support business functions, such as marketing, sales, support, partner, distribution, and other functional resources, may support one or more Scrum Development teams, depending on the scope of each product. As a result, the business-oriented Scrum Teams may work with more than one Product Owner since each product should have a single, dedicated Product Owner.

For smaller products, the Scrum Teams may include members who have domain knowledge or functional skills. However, the better strategy is to have the developers work directly with these other experts when their skills are required. While it's possible to integrate those functions in a development team, there are practical limits to how much expertise the team can build across disparate domains of knowledge, and remain small.

Finally, it may make sense to combine business domain skills within a single Scrum Team to support a single product's delivery requirements. In this scenario, individuals with marketing, sales, and partnering skills may form within a single Scrum Team. This strategy works to support small products or to support product variants targeting a specific region, niche market, or type of customer.

Evolving Scrum Team formations

The construction of Scrum Teams via skills and knowledge is potentially unique across various products. But the scope of work performed by individual Scrum Teams can vary over time. Moreover, the types and the number of Scrum Teams required to support a product across its life cycle will change as market conditions and product growth change. In effect, change is the one constant you can expect across the life cycle of a product.

Each organization has to figure out what types of Scrum Teams to form based on the products they support. Moreover, those needs will evolve to support changing needs and priorities. Changing corporate strategies, customers, customer needs, customer priorities, impediments, and issues all impact the existing teams' abilities to support their product.

Now that we understand the purpose of Scrum Teams, let's take a look at the roles and responsibilities defined within the Scrum Team.

Identifying roles and responsibilities

There are only three roles in Scrum: Product Owner, Scrum Master, and developers. Adding additional roles and responsibilities does not add value in the Scrum framework and can cause more overhead, inefficiencies, and bottlenecks in the development process. Let's take a closer look at these roles.

Note that Scrum does not have the role of the project manager. However, Ken Schwaber, in his book titled *Agile Project Management with Scrum*, notes that the Scrum Master is, in effect, the project manager for Scrum-based projects. Nevertheless, the responsibilities of the Scrum Master are quite different. I'll address those differences shortly in the *Scrum Masters* subsection. But first, we will start with the first role in Scrum, which is the Product Owner.

Product Owners

It may seem counterintuitive, but the Product Owner role is a part-time position with regards to supporting the Scrum development effort. The Product Owner is effectively a product manager who is responsible for defining product development enhancements, as well as priorities that add the most value and generate the most revenue per unit of development cost.

As the product manager, their job is to assess market needs that are not satisfied and therefore represent an opportunity to the company. They spend the bulk of their time assessing the market opportunities, understanding user needs, conducting competitive assessments, and developing strategies for sales, marketing, and distribution.

In other words, the Product Owner still takes on the business, marketing, and sales support roles of the product manager, but also assumes responsibility for defining product requirements and priorities within the Product Backlog. This added responsibility might not seem like such a big deal. Still, they alone are held accountable for increasing customer desired value in the product while managing life cycle costs and ROI.

From the results of their analysis, the product managers are in the best position to develop the list of high valued ROI customer requirements. When wearing the Product Owner hat, the product managers work with the development team to establish development priorities to deliver the highest value ROI features and functions in the shortest possible time. The Product Owner is ultimately accountable for the profit and loss of their respective products and, therefore, cannot delegate the responsibilities of the Product Owner.

Business managers sometimes employ the concepts of Vilfredo Pareto's Principle of Unequal Distribution (also known as the 80/20 rule, Pareto Principle, or Pareto Analysis) to analyze which subset of people or activities have the most significant impact against a broader set of items. Vilfredo Federico Pareto's (1848–1923) academic focus was on the economics of land distribution. However, other observers found the 80/20 phenomenon (for example, 80% of consequences come from 20% of the causes) seemed to apply to many other areas of study, and in particular, business management.

What this rule implies, from the perspective of product management, is that ~80% of a product's benefit or value comes from only ~20% of the implemented features or work activities. Likewise, ~80% of the negative impact on product results from only ~20% of the issues identified. From a practical standpoint, this means that the Product Owner must prioritize work around 20% of the features that are the most useful to a customer or end user. Put another way, 80% of the identified work has little practical value and represents wasted effort.

The Product Owner is ultimately responsible for defining the right high-value set of features for their assigned products. Moreover, they must maintain the prioritized backlog of high-value product features and ensure the requirements are clearly defined and articulated to the product development team. Besides the business and user requirements, the backlog must also include the technical requirements defined by the development team, as necessary to support the architecture, design, and non-functional requirements of the product.

Finally, even if the Product Owner successfully identifyies the right 20% of the available features, a company still has to make a profit. Likewise, nonprofits and government agencies must live within their budgets. Therefore, the Product Owner is ultimately responsible for assessing the commercial viability or budget feasibility of producing a new product or feature.

Developers

There are no types or categories of developers in Scrum. Every Scrum Team member only has the title of *Developer*, and there are no senior developers or junior developers. Likewise, there are no GUI developers, testers, programmers, database developers, or any other types of developers – only *Developers*. The reason for this is simple. Effective Scrum Teams are self-organizing and cross-functional, realigning their resources on-the-fly to meet the unique needs of each Sprint. And, all developers must carry their weight. Adding titles works against this philosophy.

Developers do have different strengths and weaknesses, skills, and interests, and the team can take advantage of those differences to apply the best people to the right tasks in each Sprint. But the overarching goal is to ensure the team has an abundance of overlapping skills to maximize their flexibility and productivity as a group.

Scrum developers perform all the work that is necessary to iteratively implement increments of new functionality across the development life cycle of a product. That's a fancy way of saying they build stuff. They also test the products they create. SQA is not a role in Scrum. Instead, the development team members identify, analyze, test, and fix any bugs or defects in the products they build.

The term *iterative* refers to the frequent and repetitive nature of software development under Scrum, typically limited to individual and independent development cycles of 1 to 4 weeks. The developers work within these timeboxed constraints to deliver fully "Done" increments of new functionality. The Scrum terminology for an iteration is **Sprint**.

The term *increment* refers to the concept that each Sprint produces a new slice of useful and high valued functionality. Each increment must be fully formed and integrated with previous increments of functionality. By definition, each increment of functionality must meet the definition of done.

In other software development approaches, the closest equivalent to the definition of Done is acceptance criteria. Every increment of functionality must have a unique definition of Done, as defined by the Product Owner and Scrum Team. In other words, the term **Done** describes the acceptance criteria for each new increment of functionality.

You might be asking yourself why it is so essential to define a definition of Done for every product enhancement. There are a couple of reasons. First, code under development represents work in progress that becomes increasingly difficult to manage and more complex to debug as it accumulates. This issue is no different than a manufacturing facility that allows materials to accumulate at every piece of equipment in the factory. After a while, it's nearly impossible to track all the individual parts and concurrent workflows. Secondly, the different pieces of code under development must eventually be integrated into the product. The longer the team holds off on the integration of code, the more difficult it is to determine the cause and effects of bugs discovered after these integrations.

The better alternative is to test individual segments of code initially to make sure that each piece of code works correctly, and then integrate each segment into the baseline code for the system to ensure it doesn't break something else. If the new code does break something, at least the developers have isolated the problem and know that something about the interaction of the new code with the existing code set is causing the bug.

With these issues in mind, the ideal situation is that each Sprint results in a potentially shippable product. The Product Owner has the sole authority to release a product into production, and there may be many reasons why they choose to delay the release of a potentially shippable product to a customer. But the main objective is to ensure that the increment of functionality resulting from each Sprint is fully integrated with previous increments of functionality, and thoroughly tested to ensure there are no bugs in the product. This integration and testing strategy gives the development team confidence that they can continue to build on the completed increments in future Sprints, without worry that untested software components may cause problems in future increments.

Scrum Teams are too small to enhance their ability to function as a cohesive unit. Not including the Product Owner in the Scrum Master, Scrum limits team size to three to nine people.

It may take some time for the team to gel and require some trial and error when it comes to grouping people together. Since the team works so closely together for extended periods, they must have respect for each other and have the ability to work through difficult issues without causing conflict. The team must have diversity in terms of their skills and personalities to ensure they can attack problems with abundant knowledge and from differing perspectives. Not every approach works equally well for every type of problem.

Teams that encourage multi-learning to develop a diverse and overlapping set of skills have more ability to self-organize to address the different types of problems that arise from the Sprint. The development of cross-functional skills also makes it easier for teams to adjust when individuals are sick, on leave, or otherwise absent. There is little luxury for small teams to have individuals with specialized skills, as their skills likely cannot be fully utilized at all times. To be effective, Scrum Teams must have autonomy and freedom to self-regulate their activities so that they can apply the right set of skills and resources to the tasks identified within each Sprint. In short, waste occurs any time a team does not have the skills and resources to apply to the work at hand, or when they have specialists whose skills are not required.

The sole purpose of Scrum Teams is to develop new increments of functionality across each Sprint, typically within a single product line. The members form a cross-functional group that includes all the skills necessary to complete the work of each Sprint. They are accountable for completing each increment per the agreed definitions of done. The entire team is responsible for completing the work of the Sprint. If someone is hung up on a task, other members jump in to help out. Everyone in the team is responsible for achieving the Sprint's Goal.

Since Scrum Teams are responsible for getting the work of each Sprint done, they cannot rely on outside help. The only exception to this is when they require the skills of specialists. Even then, the role of the specialist should include training the Scrum Team members on their skills before they move on to work on other projects within the organization.

In other words, when specialists are required, they tend to rotate from Scrum Team to Scrum Team to help develop organizational skills and their areas of expertise. Once the organization builds enough organizational skills in the specialized domain of knowledge, the specialists should move on to become a member of the Scrum Team. This means the specialists must also multi-train in the disciplines required by the Scrum Teams.

As you might imagine from the preceding descriptions, effective development teams do not evolve overnight. The organization needs to give its Scrum Teams time to gel, build their skills, and learn how to work together. Given the investments required to build a capable team, it makes no sense to disband a team when a product development requirement comes to an end. Instead, the more effective strategy is for the organization to move the team onto new work, either on the existing product or different products.

Scrum Masters

Scrum Masters are the project managers of a Scrum project. But the role is different than that of the traditional project manager. First and foremost, Scrum Masters are responsible for the successful implementation of the Scrum process and the overall effectiveness of their teams. But rather than directing the activities of the Scrum Team, as the traditional project manager would do, the Scrum Master allows the team to decide how to do the work on each Sprint. The Scrum Master is ultimately responsible for the implementation of the Scrum process and spends their time supporting the team to ensure their success.

One of the primary ways that the Scrum Master role differs from the project management role is that, while they are responsible for the proper execution of the Scrum process, they are not responsible for the actual work of building a product and its delivery. The product team, as a whole, is responsible for their work and delivering increments of new functionality on every Sprint, not the Scrum Master.

Scrum Masters are facilitators whose primary work is to ensure the successful employment of Scrum rules, artifacts, and events. The Scrum Master's role is that of a servant leader. In other words, their leadership doesn't come from or through directives but rather from their knowledge and their effectiveness in supporting the team by removing impediments, mentoring and coaching, and facilitation of events.

As the team's expert in Scrum, the Scrum Master guides the Product Owner, their team members, and the organization as a whole. Guidance can take the form of one-on-one mentoring, coaching the team, and providing training to those who were not familiar with the concepts of Scrum. At all times, the Scrum Master must be careful not to impose their will on any of the team members.

As an example, a traditional project manager might view the daily Scrum meetings as an opportunity to get updates and direct work from the Sprints task list, just as they might manage work on a schedule plan. But they have missed the point when they do this. As a facilitator, their role is to get the team members to open up about the work they are doing and the challenges they are facing.

Directing work is not the same thing as facilitating work. Whenever a Scrum Master feels compelled to tell a team member what they should work on, they have missed the point of their role. The development team members have the responsibility to self-organize and assign work against the Sprint Backlog with the resources and skills available within the team.

The Scrum Master's role – for example, in daily meetings – is to ensure the team members use that opportunity to inspect their work and evaluate any variances that are impeding their work and adapt their approach accordingly. The team members may also ask the Scrum Master to help resolve any impediments so that the team members don't have to spend their limited time on such activities. Also, when the Scrum Master sees behaviors that are counterproductive to the successful implementation of Scrum, they use those opportunities to redirect the team's behaviors through coaching, training, and mentoring activities.

In support of the Product Owner, the Scrum Master's primary role is to ensure everyone has a common understanding of the issues facing the business domain, the Product Backlog priorities, and Sprint Goals and objectives. They may assist the Product Owner in finding effective ways to prioritize the Product Backlog. Again, it is not the job of the Scrum Master to make the backlog a priority, but rather to help the Product Owner develop effective techniques for managing the backlog. Besides, Product Owners may not have a sound understanding of empirical process control.

This issue becomes evident when the Product Owner attempts to pre-define every potential customer and end user requirement or assigns equal and high priorities to all of the backlog items. The Scrum Master must help the Product Owner gain confidence that they can better identify high-value requirements and priorities through the iterative and incremental development processes of Scrum, which are validated by the product being frequently inspected by customers and end-users.

The final point I want to make is that the Scrum Master must work in alignment with the organization's culture, goals, and objectives. Their primary concern is their assigned development team or teams and removing any impediments that affect their ability to meet the commitments they have made for each Sprint. And as part of their duties, they make sure all team members, the Product Owner, and the stakeholders within the organization understand the concepts and practices of Scrum. But they also must realize that, sometimes, an ideal situation can't be obtained due to corporate policies or culture.

In such cases, the Scrum Master may have no choice but to make accommodations or tweaks to the Scrum process to ensure the Scrum Team functions successfully within its corporate environment. When such situations occur, the Scrum Master must reach out to decision-makers, organizational stakeholders, the Product Owner, and affected team members to discuss the situation and potential impacts and collaborate on defining the best approach forward.

Now that you know about the unique roles and responsibilities within Scrum, we need to take a look at the meetings and activities they participate in within Scrum. Scrum calls these activities and meeting Scrum *Events*. In effect, Scrum Events establish the boundaries of Scrum meetings and help manage the flow of value-based work within the Scrum framework.

Empirical process control is the approach Scrum uses to remove impediments and resolve issues.

Leveraging empirical process control theory

Scrum's foundations lie on empiricism, as opposed to following a pre-planned process. Empiricism in the philosophy of science, which emphasizes on knowledge acquisition through hypothesis, theories, experimentation, and the validation of results. For example, the scientific method is based on empiricism.

A hypothesis is an initial – though hopefully testable – assumption, when supporting data or information is lacking, about how or why something works the way it does. In contrast, a theory is an attempt to explain the observed phenomenon based on the data and the facts that are known. Hypothesis and theories both serve as a starting point to assess our understanding of the world around us.

Next, experiments are designed that test the hypothesis or validate whether the theories work. When the evidence supports the hypothesis or theories, the scientists (developers, in the case of Scrum) gain confidence in their understanding of the phenomenon under investigation. If the evidence does not support their theories, then the experimenters at least know what will not work, and they may gain insights as to why not, as well as some alternative approaches they might explore.

The main point behind Scrum's use of empiricism is that customers and end-users, more often than not, do not know what capabilities a new product or product enhancement needs to provide to support their needs. Likewise, the developers cannot know the best approach to developing the end product until the requirements are better exposed. Even after they understand the requirements, they may need to design and conduct experiments to discover the best way to implement the desired functionality.

Scrum Teams employ trial and error techniques to expose requirements by building and showing prototypes and incremental releases of new functionality to customers and end-users. Each new increment of functionality leads to new insights into what the product can and should be.

The Bible of Scrum is *The Scrum Guide*™, co-written and maintained to this day by Ken Schwaber and Jeff Sutherland. In the Scrum Guide, Schwaber and Sutherland introduce their three pillars of empirical process control: *transparency, inspection,* and *adaptation.* These three pillars are the foundation that supports Scrum development teams in their work.

The word transparency simply means that everything is out in the open. All product and project-related information is available at all times, including stakeholders, the CEO, customers, and development team members. Such information includes the following:

- Product backlog

- Development priorities

- Work in progress

- Work completed

- Requirements in the form of Stories

- Definitions of "Done"

- Estimated delivery dates of backlog items

- Impediments

Inspection is an essential aspect of Scrum's empirical process by providing the data and information the development team needs to review and evaluate the current situation. The inspection includes any activity that serves to assess the quality of Scrum Artifacts, progress against the Sprint Goal, progress against the Sprint Backlog, impediments, team performance, and to detect any variance in the Sprint Plans. Scrum Artifacts include the Product Backlog, Sprint Backlog, and Increments, as defined in the next section of this chapter.

Adaption is the process of evolution in the empirical model. In other words, as the team continues to gather new data, they can assess both their goals and their progress to see if changes need to be made. If the customer's needs and priorities have changed, or the team is in danger of missing a Sprint Goal, adaption allows the team to make near-real-time course corrections to address these concerns.

Empiricism and the scientific process represent the technical aspects of how Scrum works, and why. But there is a softer side of Scrum that is equally important, and that is the role of the core values that make Scrum work at a human level. Core values are the subject of the next subsection.

Establishing Scrum's core values

Scrum is not limited to guiding the intellectual and physical aspects of designing and building products. However, there is a critically important softer side of Scrum that guides the development teams and other stakeholders through how they need to work together, expressed as a set of core values. The core values of Scrum include commitment, courage, focus, openness, and respect.

Commitment speaks to the team's desires and ability to evaluate the product backlog in terms of the goals established for each Sprint, scope the work, and make commitments to deliver. Making those commitments take courage. In the spirit of transparency, it also takes courage to speak out and let the truth be known with regards to all aspects of a team's work and the state of the product. The team must stay focused on delivering only the highest value items from the product backlog, and not allow themselves to get off track working on things that do not contribute to meeting the goals established for each Sprint.

Openness is another word for transparency, but not just limited to the team's performance and delivery of product increments. The concept of openness also applies to how team members work together. They must be open in their communications with other team members to work through sticky issues, without making things personal. Without respect, that degree of openness and honesty is not possible.

In Scrum, it's always about leveraging the collective skills and diversity of knowledge and experiences to make the team better as a group. Failure to respect others for their contributions is a surefire way to destroy the integrity of the team.

In summary, people are critical enablers in the implementation of Scrum. They must not only understand the core values; they must live them. Now that you've learned some of the core concepts that make Scrum what it is, we need to turn our attention to understanding some of the critical issues you will face when implementing Scrum. Let's start by discussing the pitfalls associated with partially implementing Scrum.

Partial Scrum is not Scrum

One notable comment to make about Scrum is that the original authors, Sutherland and Schwaber, are both adamant that all Scrum roles, Events, Artifacts, and rules are absolute. Though it is possible to find value in implementing only parts of Scrum, the final result is not Scrum.

I've included this issue based on real-life experience. One of my customers implemented concepts that were very similar to Scrum, including some of the terminology. However, without proper guidance, the development teams have to fill in the holes or gaps in the methodology. Not only does this cause stress throughout the organization, but it ultimately leads to project failures.

When organizations implement custom versions of Scrum, there is no definitive guide, outside the Scrum Guide, to go back to fix any problems that result. Also, human nature causes the authors of the revised Scrum methodologies to dig in and protect their approach. When things go wrong, by circumventing the Scrum processes, there is a high probability the executives and Scrum Teams won't know or won't understand the value of going back to the basics of Scrum.

Let me give you another real-life example of the impact of employing Scrum in unique or custom ways. In my situation, a program manager was used to seeing detailed requirements specifications for the products under his management. When the organization implemented an enterprise-wide but modified version of Scrum, there were no complete instructions provided on how to gather and use requirements under an iterative and incremental development process. As a result, the manager forced the contractor's development team to define all the User Stories at the beginning of the project. In effect, the program manager went back to old habits of the traditional model, such as defining all the requirements in advance of development. As you might imagine, this led to severe project schedule slippage as the customer's requirements and priorities kept changing.

Another critical issue faced by organizations that attempt to implement Scrum, without fully thinking about the consequences, is the impact that change will have on existing project teams and subcontractors working under approved project charters and legal contract agreements. We'll explore this issue in the next section.

Revising your contracts

When an organization makes a move to implement Scrum, the executives must communicate the new direction, and also appropriately modify all project charters and legal agreements that govern how employees and contractors work and deliver products. If an organization attempts to implement Scrum but fails to modify the contracts and charters, the teams have competing directives, and they will fail. The disparate directives are simply too broad to reconcile at the team level.

Project charters are directives from executive sponsors that guide the objectives of the project but also constrain the scope of work authorized for the project – usually expressed in the form of deliverable items, along with the budgets, schedules, resources, and quality constraints. A contract agreement provides similar information. However, this is a legal document with serious non-compliance consequences that cannot change without formal and written approval from the authorizing agent.

In a situation I was involved with, during a mandated mid-project implementation of Scrum-like practices, the customer's contract office never modified the contract agreements during the contract period. As a result, we had to adhere to the standard requirements for project schedules, reports, and documentation that were initially developed under the client's previous traditional software development practices. For reasons never passed down to me, the client's assigned internal program executives never changed the contracts.

Therefore, whether we wanted to or not, from a contractual perspective, we still had to develop a detailed project management plan and schedule plan. The client's program manager still insisted on providing a full definition of business and user requirements, as User Stories for the entire backlog, before starting any development work. The development team also had to provide all the documentation and ongoing reports required under the traditional SDLC model. In the end, the contracts prevented us from following the so-called mandated agile practices.

Part of the problem in this situation was that the organization attempted to deploy Scrum at an enterprise-scale without proper preparation, promotion, and training. Given the large size of the client's organization, a staged rollout, starting with some highly visible and useful pilots, would have helped the organization adjust and prepare for the changes that were coming their way.

I'll discuss the staged enterprise deployment concept in more detail in *Chapter 7, Scrum of Scrum*, which introduces the original Scrum scaling concepts. In the meantime, we need to move on and discuss the importance of providing complete visibility across all Scrum Team activities. That is the subject of the next subsection.

Making Scrum visible and transparent

Transparency means all Scrum products and project information is available to anyone who wants to see it. Teams that work in a single co-located working environment have an advantage as they can display all the product and Sprint information on whiteboards and flip charts within the room. However, when product development activities involve multiple teams, especially when those teams operate from geographically disparate locations, the organization may need to implement an electronic mechanism to distribute or otherwise make the information readily available.

Information Radiators is a common term used to describe displays of agile-based product and project information in a highly visible and available manner. Alistair Cockburn is credited for the initial description of Information Radiators in his book titled *Agile Software Development* (2001, 2007). Schwaber and Sutherland, in their book, titled *Software in Thirty Days* (2012), discuss the concept of Information Radiators as applied to Scrum.

The main point is that Product Owners and Scrum Teams do not hide what they are doing. Everything must be transparent and out in the open for inspection by anyone who believes they should have access to that information.

Information Radiators can provide access to virtually any type of product or development-related information, such as the following:

- Budgets
- Burndown and Burnup Charts
- Definitions of Done
- Impediments
- Product Backlog
- Product Increments
- Sprint Backlog
- Sprint Goals
- Sprint Velocity
- Task Boards (showing work in the queue, work in progress, and work completed)
- Testing Results

Project budgets still exist in Scrum, at least in the Scrum-based projects I've supported. By now, it should be pretty clear to you that it's impossible to define exact budgets for a large section of product development work, given the stochastic nature of the effort. In the next section, I'll present an alternative approach to budgeting that better fits the Scrum model for development.

Treating Scrum development as a fixed cost

This subject is not a part of Scrum, as outlined in The Scrum Guide, but helps further explain the economics of Scrum. Under the principles of project management, there is an expectation that funding allocations support the completion of a specific scope of work within an approved timeframe, with approved resources, and to an agreed level of quality. However, a planned budget is only reasonable if the development team can indeed specify all the work that is necessary to deliver a fully described set of product features. A project-based budget also assumes all requirements are fully defined and won't change throughout the project's duration.

Likewise, there can be no chance that the market conditions or desired features and functions will change during the duration of the budgeted effort. Finally, there can be no unexpected issues that come up to delay the project or cause more work.

Unfortunately, that's not real life. The stochastic nature of software and complex system development makes all these assumptions invalid. There are simply too many variables and unknowns to make such predictions.

Scrum turns the entire development paradigm on its head by planning and conducting work across very short intervals of time. The expectation is anything, and everything can and will change over time. So, we can only work off the information we have at the moment.

Through the three pillars of **empirical process control** – that is, **transparency, inspection,** and **adaption** – the team evaluates their progress against known requirements in the product backlog and identified impediments, and then adjusts their efforts to maximize their outcomes at the current stage of development. As long as the product's value justifies their efforts, the team can continue working against items contained within the product backlog.

For these reasons, I recommend that organizations look at Scrum-based development as a relatively fixed cost, at least in the short run. Periodically, the organization must review the level of effort being funded and adjust their budgets if something has changed in the value or delivery model. This strategy simplifies the organization's approach to justifying software and system development projects.

For example, if the value of a product justifies investments in seven development teams with an average of seven people each, and the work exists to support that level of investment, then the budget is fixed accordingly. Periodically, perhaps every quarter, and with completion of the current high-value items in the backlog, the executives and Product Owners can reassess the level of investment necessary to support continued development on emergent, high priority requirements.

Over time, a Product Owner may need a higher number or a smaller number of product teams supporting their products. A successful company will always be on the lookout for new product opportunities to grow the business, thus providing new opportunities for the developers.

Thrown objects don't stick

I will talk about enterprise-wide implementations of Scrum in the last two sections of the next chapter, but another issue I want to point out here is the tendency to throw a new IT methodology over the wall and hope it will all work out. In this case, it's the idea that Scrum will somehow stick if you just put it out there or mandate it through an edict without appropriate planning and follow-through. This strategy rarely works out.

This issue was the situation I described in the *Revising your contracts* subsection. Our client forced an enterprise-wide adoption of their version of Scrum. It came with almost no forewarning, no training, no modifications to corporate processes or contracts, and no discussion of revised roles and responsibilities across the chain of development-related responsibilities and processes. The client put out some simple training, really presentation-ware, with a proclamation that all project teams were to implement their new approach to development. The result is that they broke all their old software development practices before fully defining and implementing the new processes.

It took several years to sort some of these issues out, but in the meantime, another insidious problem began to seep in, and that was process bloat. Without proper training or proper contract guidance, some program and project managers felt compelled to mix what they knew from their experience with the traditional software development model with the new mandated agile practices. For example, project teams attempted to implement Scrum using the same project planning, detailed requirements gathering, gate reviews, documentation, and project scheduling strategies dictated by their contracts and cultural norms.

Scrum, as an agile framework, implements a lightweight set of processes and events to efficiently and quickly develop high-value products. Since the organization was not explicitly following Scrum, internal support organizations began to incorporate some of its legacy practices in the new agile paradigm. Given that Scrum is a framework and not a prescriptive methodology, that might make some sense on a situational and as-needed basis. But wholesale integration of traditional and agile concepts loses the point, and the result is not agile anymore, is it?

Now that I've discussed what can go wrong when Scrum is not applied correctly, let's discuss how to implement Scrum properly. We'll start with a discussion on the defined roles and responsibilities within Scrum, and then move on to discuss the events, artifacts, and approach to implementing Scrum at the project level.

Defining Scrum Events

Scrum implements its iterative workflow via a series of Scrum Events. These events support the three foundational underpinnings of Scrum: *transparency*, *inspection*, and *adaptation*. In other words, events provide visibility at key points of the Scrum process, offering opportunities to inspect the progress of the work and the delivery and value of the increments. If any aspect of the project places the Sprint Goals at risk, the team can adapt their work and strategies to either fix the problems or optimize the outcomes.

As an analogy, the driver of a car cannot merely set their wheels in a set direction and expect the car to stay on the road. The driver must have clear visibility to continuously inspect the trajectory of the car against the variations in the road and terrain, and then adjust their steering and acceleration to keep the car on the track. Likewise, the Scrum Team must continuously inspect and adjust its trajectory against the Product Backlog and Sprint Goals.

Let's continue for a moment with this analogy. A driver can review maps and create a detailed plan describing all the locations where they want to go, places where they want to eat, sleep, and get gas, the roads that the drivers must follow, the turns that they need to make, and speed limits along the route for an upcoming trip. Once they start the trip, reality sets in. They may encounter road construction, bad traffic, unfavorable weather conditions, unexpected points of interest, and a host of other factors that will change the outcome of their trip from the initial plan. The driver continually adjusts their plan as they encounter these unexpected conditions. They may also add or delete stopover points or pitstops based on their current personal needs.

This empirical process is precisely how software development works in Scrum. The world is full of complexity and unknown probabilities. The astute team knows that change is the norm and not something to be fought. With that in mind, let's look at how Scrum Events provide opportunities for us to observe, inspect, and adapt a Scrum Team's activities to maximize their outcome, given the conditions they face along their journey to deliver a high-value product.

Scrum Events include Sprints, Sprint Planning meetings, Daily Scrum meetings, Sprint Review meetings, and Sprint Retrospective meetings. The next five sections describe the Scrum Events under the same names.

Sprints

Scrum employs an iterative development strategy that breaks up life cycle development work into relatively small and frequent intervals. The necessary interval of Scrum is anywhere from 1 week to 30 days, with the norm following into 1-week to 2-week intervals. During the Sprint, the team works on a subset of the Product Backlog that represents the current high-value priorities, called the Sprint Backlog.

The development team self-organizes to assign work tasks to individual members, usually based on their skills and availability. For example, if someone has previously worked on a similar development task, they might be assigned the new task to reduce the time and effort to understand the problem, develop the approach, and implement the functionality. Sometimes, a task might be assigned to more than one team member if the feature is unusually large. Or, the teams may employ paired programming techniques that allow members of the team to work side by side, leveraging both their skills and knowledge to build, inspect, and adapt each segment of code in conformance with their definition of Done:

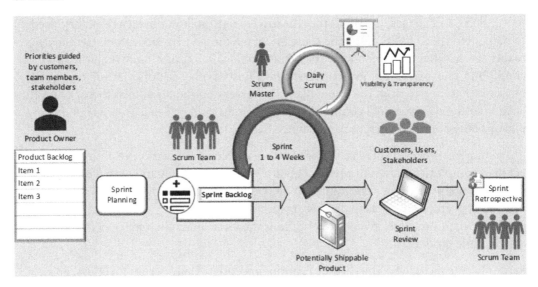

Figure 2.1 – Traditional graphical model of a single Sprint within the Scrum framework

The preceding diagram graphically depicts a single Sprint within the Scrum Framework. The graphical model starts with the Product Backlog, which is owned by the Product Owner. Before the Sprint can start, the development team must decide what the goals for the upcoming Sprint are, as well as the work they must accomplish. The Sprint Team conducts a Sprint Planning session to define the work they can accomplish from the prioritized Product Backlog, as they must also define the work tasks that are necessary to produce the Product Backlog Items. The PBIs and tasks collectively form the Sprint Backlog.

The current iteration begins, and the Scrum Team meets daily to provide visibility on their progress and to bring attention to any impediments that may cause delays. Any issues are taken offline in working sessions to address these problems. The Scrum Master may facilitate the Daily Scrums and other meetings, and they assist in resolving the impacts from identified impediments.

At the end of each Sprint, the outcome is a Potentially Shippable Product that meets its definition of Done for this Sprint. The definition of Done is a shared understanding by the Product Owner and team members of what the final state of a new incremental slice of functionality must have. In addition to achieving the customer's desired functionality, the definition of Done for each feature must also conform to the organization's standards, conventions, and guidelines.

Increments do not meet the definition of Done until the Scrum Team implements all desired capabilities, thereby meeting all acceptance criteria. Ultimately, only the Product Owners, customers, and end-users must decide whether the product meets the definition for the release and whether other items need to be added to the Product Backlog. The Sprint Reviews provide an opportunity to demo and get feedback on the product.

The last Event within a Scrum Sprint is the Sprint Retrospective. All Scrum Team members attend the Retrospectives to discuss the areas that they can improve in the next Sprint.

Now that you understand the Events associated with each Scrum Sprint, let's take a closer look at the activities involved with each Event, starting with Sprint Planning.

Sprint Planning

The development team gets together with the Product Owner at the beginning of each Sprint to inspect and adapt the Product Backlog. They do this to focus on the highest priority requirements. The Sprint Planning meeting is timeboxed limited to approximately 2 hours for every week of Sprint duration. So, if your Sprints have a 2-week duration, the Sprint Planning meeting should be limited to about 4 hours.

Though organizational stakeholders will express their preferences regarding feature priorities, the Product Owner is always the final authority on any changes to the Product Backlog; for example, additions, deletions, and changes in priorities. The reason for this is that the Product Owner is an independent and business-oriented authority who can look across all functional and non-functional requirements and accurately assess backlog priorities in terms of the highest value and return on investment.

Going back to the 80/20 rule, as discussed previously in this chapter, the highest value features form a relatively small subset of the features described within the Product Backlog. It makes no sense to work on the lower 80% of product features, which collectively require a much larger work effort when the customer only places value on the top 20% of the features contained within the Product Backlog. Yet, the traditional model forces the team to place equal value on the entire set of requirements. The Sprint Planning process helps the team avoid that type of error in thinking.

The Sprint Planning meeting has two objectives. First, the team must evaluate what they can deliver in the upcoming increment in terms of functionality. Second, the team must decide how they will build the functionality of the increment. These questions are answered in parallel during the Sprint Planning meeting, not sequentially.

To support the first objective, the Product Owner discusses their goals for the Sprint in terms of implemented functionality for the increment. An increment may include one or more features, depending on complexity. Similarly, features specified within the Product Backlog may have one or more Stories that define the requirements.

Unless the development team is just starting on a new product development effort, with few identified requirements, it's highly likely the 20% of high-value features in the Product Backlog represents more work than the team can get done during an upcoming Sprint. Working with the Product Owner, the development team evaluates the functional and non-functional requirements in terms of difficulty.

The team may use a game-based assessment strategy, such as planning poker, to assign points representing the degree of difficulty for each of the highest priority backlog items. Likewise, a mature development team will have tracked, over several Sprints, the average number of points of work they can complete within a Sprint. With these two pieces of information, the team can determine how much work they can complete in the upcoming Sprint.

An important note to make here is that only the development team can decide how much work they can accomplish within the upcoming Sprint. Executive Managers, Customers, Product Owners, and Scrum Masters have no say in the matter, as they are not responsible for completing the work. Forcing their will won't change the outcome and simultaneously undermines the team's ability to do good work. In fact, by adding work in progress beyond the team's capacity to deliver, those individuals may introduce inefficiencies that further delay the release of the desired functionality.

In support of the second objective, the development team must analyze the functional requirements to determine the best approach to build the product. The development team evaluates the functional requirements and comes up with an initial design or design enhancement. The team further analyzes the work to come up with a series of work necessary to build the features. Those work tasks form the Sprint Backlog. Once the tasks have been defined, the team self-organizes by assigning work tasks to individuals or groups within the team in the upcoming Sprint.

The deliverable of the Sprint Planning process is the Sprint Goal. Although the Product Owner is the first to specify the goals of the Sprint, it's the development team that refines the parameters of the Sprint Goal through the Sprint Planning process.

The Sprint Goal defines the increment of functionality from the Product Backlog that is the focus of the upcoming Sprint. However, rather than focusing on discrete backlog items, the objective of the Sprint Goal is to provide an abstraction that helps the individual members understand the purpose of their work as a team on this Sprint. Thorough inspection and adaption across the Sprint, the team's approach to supporting the goal may change, and not the goal itself. If the inspection activities indicate the scope of work is different than initially conceived, the team can negotiate with the Product Owner to re-specify the scope of work that's pulled from the Product Backlog.

With the completion of Sprint Planning, the team needs to make sure they keep track of their completed work, evaluate the team's progress against their goals for the Sprint, and identify and remove any impediments that are causing problems. The team discusses these three elements as a review of the Sprint's progress during their daily Scrum meetings.

Daily Scrums

The development team meets daily to plan their work for the next 24 hours. Teams hold their daily Scrums in the same location, at the same time every day, and are timeboxed limited to 15 minutes. Each member of the team always answers the following three questions:

- What tasks did they accomplish in the last 24 hours?

- What tasks do they expect to accomplish in the next 24 hours?

- What impediments are getting in the way of their work or them meeting the Sprint Goal?

The development team members must understand that they cannot just work on anything that interests them. They must stay focused on work that supports the Sprint Goals that have been agreed to by the development team. While the team members work against specific tasks from the Sprint Backlog, they must remain cognizant and focused on how they will meet the definition of Done most expediently.

The daily Scrum is a perfect example of an event that provides visibility to the work of the project in terms of the project's goals, and the ability to inspect and adapt when things appear to be going awry. Also, the information provided in meetings may indicate that additional discussion and planning is required. The affected team members will meet separately so that the other team members can get back to their work. Non-value-added meetings is another form of waste to avoid.

The Scrum Master may facilitate daily Scrum meetings, but they cannot dictate the team development priorities. Instead, the Scrum Master's primary role is to help the team stay focused on the Daily Scrum agenda. The Scrum Masters also helps ensure the team stays within the 15-minute timebox duration limit. The team must take any lengthy discussions or work on any impediments that are getting in the way of the team's ability to complete its work offline. For example, if the team needs access to a domain expert to understand the requirements of a feature, the Scrum Master would help organize and schedule that meeting or call.

In the interest of transparency, Scrum meetings are open to other attendees, such as the Product Owners, executive sponsors, customers, and other stakeholders. However, beyond listening, they cannot participate in the daily Scrum meetings, and the Scrum Master must make sure that they do not interrupt the meetings.

The team must provide complete transparency regarding the progress of their work and any impediments on an ongoing basis. These daily Scrum meetings help ensure ongoing transparency by providing snapshots of information on work progression over short time intervals during the Sprint.

However, at the end of each Sprint, the team needs to demonstrate their work and receive feedback on how well the new increments of product functionality support the identified requirements, as well as review the identified items and priorities established within the product backlog. That is the purpose of the Sprint Review meetings that occur at the end of each Sprint.

Sprint Reviews

At the end of each iterative Sprint cycle, the development team reviews their work to demonstrate completion of the new increment in conformance with their definitions of done. As a rule of thumb, the Sprint Review meeting is timeboxed limited to 1 hour per 1-week Sprint duration. In other words, a 2-hour Sprint Review meeting is appropriate for a 2-week Sprint duration.

The meeting is open to all external stakeholders, such as customers and end-users, so that they can view the implementation of the new increment of functionality within the product. The Product Owner should invite only the stakeholders who have an interest in this or are impacted by the new increment of functionality.

This meeting is another example of a Scrum event that provides opportunities for transparency, as well as inspection and adaption. For example, customers and potential users have the opportunity to see a demo of the product, inspect it in terms of their current needs and priorities, and provide feedback that's vital to the product adaption process.

One phenomenon I have seen time and again is that when customers and end-users finally have an opportunity to look at products, invariably, they will gain new insights into how they can use the products. Or, they may have realized that they forgot to tell the Product Owner about another critical feature they require.

In the traditional model, unfortunately, these insights generally came during user acceptance testing or after the product had been released. In either case, those insights come far too late to impact current development activities. Those users may have to wait another year, assuming funding becomes available for a new development project, to see the implementation of the new enhancements they've now identified as a high priority.

The Sprint Review meeting is not limited to just reviews by customers and end-users. The entire Scrum process is open to discussion. During the Sprint Review, the Product Owner will discuss new product Product Backlog requirements and priorities and work with the team to assess how they fit with existing Product Backlog priorities. The Product Owner may also discuss projected target dates for deliveries of new increments of functionality.

As a group, the attendees of the Sprint Review can address business and market considerations that impact the product's definition and development. Those discussions may lead to a new refinement of the Product Backlog, which becomes an input to the Sprint Planning meeting for the next Sprint.

After the Sprint Review, the Scrum Teams turn their attention to discussing how they can improve their team's performance. That review occurs in a separate event called the Sprint Retrospective.

Sprint Retrospectives

Just after the Sprint Review, the development team meets to reflect on how they can improve their work, starting with the very next Sprint. The timeboxed duration for this meeting is roughly 2 to 3 hours in duration. The product development team describes the work they completed during the Sprint, what went well, what didn't go so well, and what they did to address the problems.

The Sprint Retrospective needs to occur before the Sprint Planning meeting for the next Sprint. Having the Sprint Retrospectives at the end of each Sprint ensures the information is still fresh in their memories, and also allows the teams to integrate their actions for improvements in the next Sprint.

The Scrum Master should facilitate this meeting as there is potential for tension among the team members. Everyone must remember to remain respectful as they discuss the parts of the last Sprint that did not go so well. The focus needs to be on assessing better ways to do things and not blaming people. The scope of the discussions in the Sprint Retrospective should span people, relationships, processes, and tools.

The development team should not limit their conversations to just the things that did not go so well. They should also discuss the things that went well. As the facilitator, the Scrum Master can make a list of the items discussed and work with the team to prioritize their impact. Once the prioritized list is in place, the development team can create an improvement plan for the next Sprint.

The empirical process control foundations of Scrum through transparency, inspection, and adaption, and push the team to seek improvements continuously. The Sprint Retrospective implements the discipline to ensure this process doesn't stop. Without this discipline, due to competing priorities, it's simply too easy to avoid making time to assess how things are going and look for ways to improve. Over time, the work of the team will devolve and go backward in terms of productivity and performance.

Process improvement ideas do not need to be limited to merely improving work performance. It's also essential for the team to assess what they can do to make the work more enjoyable and sustainable. Scrum Teams stay together over long extended periods, usually measured in years. The teams get better due to their time and experience working together, and it's therefore vital that the team finds ways to develop a supportive and work-friendly environment.

With that, we've reviewed Scrum's roles and responsibilities and the events that guide the work across a Sprint. Before we can move on to discussing the basic workflow of Scrum, we need to understand the information available within Scrum that provides transparency about the completed and planned value of work. Scrum-related information is maintained in three forms, referred to as Scrum Artifacts. These artifacts include the Product Backlog, the Sprint Backlog, and Increments.

Implementing Scrum Artifacts

By definition, the term artifact refers to any object made by humans or something that can be observed through investigations or experimentation. In the traditional model, we are used to having an untold number of potential artifacts related to a project. Many of those artifacts take the form of physical documentation and reports of various topics. However, in a generic sense, a programmer's code and database schemas are other examples of artifacts. In the traditional model, documentation is a direct result of the detailed project planning, monitoring, and control processes.

Scrum seeks to minimize the production of artifacts, and Sutherland and Schwaber limited their list of artifacts to just three. These include the Product Backlog, Sprint Backlog, and Increments. Collectively, these artifacts portray the work and value of a project and provide the means for transparency, inspection, and adaption. The goal is to keep the team's focus strictly on the most useful information necessary to manage a Scrum project effectively.

Product Backlog

The Product Backlog provides a prioritized list of all identified requirements known to the Product Owner. No matter the size of a product, there is only one Product Backlog, and it includes the entire set of requirements that have been identified for the product under development. The Product Owner is responsible for the Product Backlog, and they alone have the authority to include what's in the list and prioritize the items on the list. Yes, the Product Owner will take input from other stakeholders and executives, but only the Product Owner is held accountable for the specification and delivery of high-value and high ROI features and the functionality built into the product.

An updated Product Backlog is necessary for as long as a product remains viable and facing competitive pressures. Using the 80/20 role and ROI assessments, the Product Owner continues to direct the development team to focus on delivering the highest in the shortest time possible. Over time, as new increments of functionality are released, with new items added to the Product Backlog, the Product Owner continues to use the same 80/20 rule and ROI assessments to determine development priorities for upcoming increments.

The 80/20 rule assessments can continue for as long as the implementation of related features has a positive ROI. This rule may seem strange because, after a while, the team will be working on features well down the list in the original 80/20 assessments. But again, as long as the development activities have value and a positive ROI, the development can, and should, continue.

A Product Backlog lists all identified features, functions, business and user requirements, identified enhancements from the Sprint Reviews, and identified bug or defect fixes. The typical Product Backlog has a tabular format with five columns, specifying **Name**, **Description**, **Priority**, **Work Estimate**, and **Value**. Higher priority items in the backlog have more details included in their descriptions than lower priority items. There is no need to define the requirements in detail unless and until their value justifies a higher ranking.

I mentioned previously that large projects only have one Product Backlog. I also mentioned that Scrum scales through the replication of the process across small teams. As a result, large products can potentially have any number of small teams working against the single Product Backlog. In such cases, it may be useful to add another column to designate the type of work performed or the team responsible for completing the items on the list.

Product refinement is the act of updating the Product Backlog, a process that never stops for as long as the product justifies new development activities. Competitive markets, business and user needs, and available technology enhancements provide reasons to update a product, thus necessitating the refinement of the Product Backlog. Also, the need for refinement naturally occurs as low priority items make their way to the top of the list.

The Product Owner and Scrum Team collaborate on the refinement of the Product Backlog. The product development team must be involved as they alone understand the details of how to build the product, as well as the impact of developing architecture and design elements to support the functional and non-functional requirements of the product. However, the team should not get carried away with this activity. The Scrum Guide suggests that a maximum of 10% of the Scrum development team's time should be devoted to this activity.

The highest-ranked items in the Backlog that are available for selection in an upcoming Sprint must have sufficient refinement that the team has confidence that they have a complete definition of Done and that the increment of work is deliverable within the Sprint. Only the development team can estimate the work effort for each deliverable increment. The Product Owner can negotiate with the development team to define or redefine the scope of work, but that is the limit of their influence on impacting the development team's estimates.

Sprint Backlog

The Sprint Backlog includes the list of Product Backlog items selected for development in the Sprint, plus the work tasks required to build the required functionality. Through the Sprint Planning process, the development team determines the type of work as tasks necessary to create this increment of new functionality. The agreed definition of Done for each backlog item, plus the Sprint Goals, informs the development team as they define the work tasks for an upcoming Sprint.

The Sprint Backlog provides transparency about both the backlog items and the scope of work agreed upon for the Sprint. Throughout the Sprint, the development team and Product Owner, as well as other interested stakeholders, can inspect and evaluate progress against the Sprint Goal and Sprint Backlogs. When there are negative variances, the development team adapts to minimize impacts. The daily Scrum is the primary Scrum Event that provides the opportunity for transparency and the inspection of progress against the backlog.

Another essential concept is that the Sprint Backlog emerges throughout the Sprint. In other words, the development team cannot know all the variables that might impact their work. As they begin to work through the Sprint Backlog items, they gain a better understanding of the work required to deliver this new, incremental functionality. The development team updates the Sprint Backlog to ensure it accurately reflects the current scope of work identified for the increment. As the team identifies new work requirements, they add them to the Sprint Backlog. Likewise, the team removes work items from the Sprint Backlog that are no longer necessary. Only the development team has the authority to make changes to the Sprint Backlog. But as with all Scrum Artifacts, the information is transparent and available to all interested stakeholders to make sure they know about both the decisions taken and the reasons the teams made them.

Increments

An increment is a term used in Scrum to specify all the Product Backlog items included in the current Sprint. Since each Sprint builds upon previous increments, the value of the current increment builds on the value of previous increments. In other words, the benefit of the current increment is not just the value of the backlog items that were added in the current release, but also the sum of the value of all previous increments.

Each increment must stand alone as a potentially releasable product. The Product Owner will decide whether they want to release the increment are not. But the development team must ensure the increment fully incorporates the requirements of the increment, meeting all definitions of done, including the potential for releasing it to a customer.

Each increment must also contribute toward the achievement of the vision established by the Product Owner for the product. If the increment does not support the vision for the product, something has gone wrong. Either the vision is wrong, or the priorities that have been established in the backlog are inconsistent with the vision. Transparency and inspection of the increment facilitate such analysis. As the development team and the Product Owner discover such inconsistencies, through *inspection*, they use the process of *adaption* to recalibrate and realign their efforts.

At this point, you know how to construct a Scrum Team, establish the appropriate Sprint events, and gather necessary information for transparency, inspection, and adaption through the use of Scrum Artifacts. We will look at how to put all these things together to manage work associated with developing, delivering, and maintaining complex products in the next chapter, which describes the Scrum approach to development.

Summary

In this chapter, you have learned the following about Scrum, as well as its relevance to agile practices in terms of development and to support operational business functions:

- The term Scrum comes from a sports metaphor related to Scrum. We also looked at why a team-oriented concept improves software and systems development and delivery.

- The importance of executive leadership and support for long-term success and enterprise-wide adoptions.

- How Scrum's empirical process control theory helps teams work through complex adaptive problems through experimentation and observation. We also looked at the importance of its three pillars: transparency, inspection, and adaption.

- Scrum has a product-oriented focus on development, not a project-oriented focus. We looked at how that helps put the focus squarely on adding customer-centric value.

- You also learned about the essential elements of Scrum so that you can include its rules, roles, responsibilities, artifacts, and events.

- Finally, you learned that Scrum is Scrum and that any attempts to modify the basic approach may have unintended and unfortunate consequences.

In the next chapter, you will learn how to apply Scrum's events to guide the Scrum Team's work across an iterative development cycle. You will get a better understanding of the responsibilities of each of the roles defined in Scrum across a Sprint. You will also learn how the artifacts of Scrum support the three pillars of empiricism: transparency, inspection, and adaption.

Questions

1. Who are the originators of the Scrum Framework?

2. The foundations of the Scrum Framework are built on what theory?

3. How many roles are there in Scrum, and what are they?

4. What are the three pillars of empirical process control?

5. Is it OK to add the role of Project Manager in Scrum? (Yes or No)

6. What are Scrum Events?

7. What are Scrum Artifacts?

8. Why is transparency so important in Scrum?

9. What is the definition of Done in Scrum?

10. What is an increment?

Further reading

Sutherland, Jeffrey Victor; Schwaber, Ken (1995). Scrum Development Process. Business object design and implementation: OOPSLA '95 workshop proceedings. The University of Michigan. ISBN 978-3-540-76096-2.

Corporate. (2019) 13th Annual State of Agile Survey. CollabNet | VersionOne. `https://www.stateofagile.com/#ufh-c-473508-state-of-agile-report`. Accessed November 24, 2019.

Schwaber, K. (2004) Agile Project Management With Scrum. Microsoft Press. Redmond, Washington.

Schwaber, K., Sutherland, J. (2017) The Scrum Guide. Scrum.org. `https://www.Scrum.org/resources/Scrum-guide` Accessed 24 November, 2019.

3
The Scrum Approach

The previous chapter introduced the fundamental elements of Scrum, including the importance of executive sponsorship, putting a focus on products, forming Scrum Teams, and identifying Scrum roles and responsibilities, events, and artifacts. This section puts these concepts into play across a Sprint development cycle.

As you read through this section, please refer to *Figure 3.1 – Scrum-based iterative and Incremental development cycle*, which provides a graphical view of the basic flow of work within the Scrum framework. As defined in *The Scrum Guide*, the Scrum events that define a Scrum workflow include **Sprint**, **Sprint Planning**, **Daily Scrum**, **Sprint Review**, and **Sprint Retrospective**. *Figure 3.1* includes additional elements not included in the Scrum Guide, but they provide useful contextual information across the Sprint cycle.

In this chapter, we're going to cover the following main topics:

- Guiding the flow of work in Scrum
- Initiating development work
- How Scrum can break down
- Identifying how Scrum can break down
- Failing implementations of Scrum

Specifically, we are going to put all of the concepts you've learned in the previous chapter together to outline the basic approach to developing a product under the Scrum framework. In this chapter, you will learn how Scrum events enforce the iterative and Incremental workflows of Scrum.

Scrum as a framework

Before we start the discussion on Scrum workflows, we need to understand the ramifications of Scrum being a framework and not an overly prescriptive methodology. In this section, you will learn how to apply the basic Scrum approach to agile as a framework and not an overly prescriptive methodology. By describing Scrum as a *framework*, the implication is that Scrum is a container that provides only minimal guidance on baseline practices, rules, artifacts, and events. The objective of the Scrum philosophy is to keep the essential framework lightweight and relatively simple to understand. Even then, Schwaber and Sutherland note, in *The Scrum Guide™*, that Scrum is still challenging to master.

Since Scrum is a framework, those who implement Scrum are free to include other business and engineering practices that support their approach to software and systems development. The framework concept is critical to understand as the intent of Scrum is to apply agile practices and empirical process control theories to resolve complex adaptive problems across any type of development or operational requirement. However, each organization and their Scrum Teams must choose the life cycle development and delivery practices that best support their needs in the moment.

For example, your development team may use different software tools than other development teams and therefore require a different set of lower-level activities and best practices surrounding the use of those technologies. Likewise, your team may choose to implement test-driven development or model-driven development concepts within the framework of Scrum. Also, your team may implement variants for testing your software, based on the complexity and scale of the code you are developing. More importantly, as your team works together over time and continues to seek constant improvements, you may develop a set of best practices within the Scrum framework that are unique to your team.

As with any development methodology, there is a flow to working within Scrum. The events and artifacts within the Scrum framework support empirical process control through transparency, inspection, and adaptation. But the events and artifacts of Scrum also provide guide rails that constrain work within the iterative and Incremental Sprints of Scrum. The remaining sections of this chapter explain the basic flow of work across each Sprint.

Guiding the flow of work in Scrum

The typical flowchart for Scrum looks quite different from traditional linear-sequential flowcharts of waterfall practices, in part due to the iterative nature of agile-based development practices (see *Figure 3.1 – Scrum-based iterative and Incremental development cycle*). Please refer to the following diagram to see the visual representation of the flow of work within each Scrum Sprint:

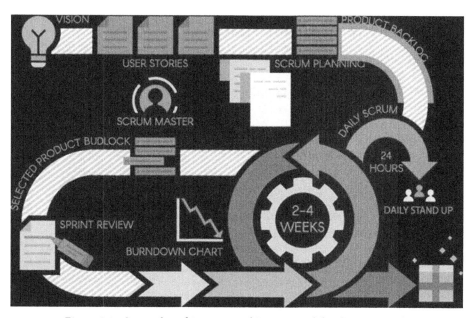

Figure 3.1 - Scrum-based iterative and Incremental development cycle

At the start of a Scrum project, the Product Owner must establish the vision for the product and create the initial product backlog of identified requirements. The vision holds until business or market conditions change sufficiently to warrant a revision. The Product Owner and Scrum Team continuously refine the product backlog to ensure the development activities stay in alignment with the highest value customer priorities.

Once the Scrum project kicks off, the basic flow of work within each Sprint iteration follows this basic pattern:

- Begin a new Sprint.
- Refine the product backlog.
- Determine the Sprint's goal.
- Plan the work.
- Develop the Sprint backlog.

- Conduct Daily Scrum meetings.

- Conduct a Sprint Review.

- Conduct a Sprint Retrospective.

In the remaining sections within this chapter, we will take a deeper dive into each of these Scrum events.

Establishing the product vision

Product development cannot begin until the vision for the product is conceived and articulated. The vision establishes the boundaries of a product. In other words, the vision specifies what's in and what's not in a product.

The vision of the product is not a statement of what it is but what it can be. The product vision refines our understanding of who our customers are and what value we will deliver to them. Moreover, the product vision represents a shared though high-level understanding of our value proposition.

A value proposition is a powerful approach to determining whether or not a new product or service is commercially viable. The information provided in a value proposition typically includes the following:

- Product name and description

- Target market customers

- Challenges or needs addressed

- Capabilities delivered

- Benefits from use

- Competitive advantages

Once the Product Owner establishes the vision for a product, the Sprint iterations can begin.

Implementing iterative and Incremental development cycles

Scrum implements an iterative and Incremental development process that starts with a product concept and vision and then Incrementally adds value through a series of iterative life cycle development workflows. Common with all agile practices, Scrum breaks the product development life cycle into a series of very short and frequent iterations. The objective of each Sprint iteration is to release a new Increment of functionality. Therefore, each Sprint in Scrum represents one iterative and Incremental development cycle.

All Scrum Teams follow the same iterative development cycles. In other words, the scheduling of Sprints across Scrum Teams should not be staggered. They are all contributing collectively to the creation of a potentially shippable product, contributing to the same Sprint Goals and all working toward the same definition of Done for the Sprint.

The Product Owner works with the Scrum Team members to prioritize and select high-value items from within the product backlog that contribute to a specific goal defined for the Sprint. This collaboration to prioritize and select items for upcoming Sprints is called product backlog refinement.

Conducting Product Backlog refinement

Through the process of product backlog refinement, the Product Owner works with the development team members to prioritize the development of features and functions with the highest value. The product backlog refinement process creates and finds the product backlog.

Product owners must determine the highest value features and functions that their product customers and users need. They must also work with the developers to determine the costs associated with developing and delivering new Increments of functionality. Also, there are technical requirements that support the implementation of user requirements. These technical considerations become part of the cost and timing factors associated with developing new product features.

As these factors come together for the highest value features, the Product Owner is in the position to prioritize the items in the product backlog. Following the concepts of the 80/20 rule, the Product Owner and Scrum development team members should not spend much time assessing the work involved to develop lower value features. Some of the lower value items may raise in relative value with the completion of higher value items or through emergent customer needs; but, until they do, the team should not spend much time assessing the work or scoping the requirements.

As part of the product backlog refinement process, the team must analyze each identified requirement to the degree that is necessary to understand the scope of work. There are many approaches to gathering, documenting, and analyzing software and systems requirements. However, within the agile community, the typical approach is to document requirements from the end user's perspective in a story format.

Creating User Stories

The Scrum Guide does not define User Stories as an artifact within Scrum. Kent Beck defined the term and this approach to requirements gathering in his book, *Extreme Programming Explained*.

Nevertheless, Stories are commonly used in Scrum as a natural language format to document customer and end user requirements. Likewise, themes and epics are not Scrum artifacts. However, Stories, themes, and epics are all commonly used within the Scrum framework to characterize and refine items within the product backlog. Collectively, these three classifications provide an efficient approach to documenting and organizing requirements as items within the product backlog.

In the context of Product Backlog refinement, User Stories provide the lowest level of abstraction necessary to define and prioritize work for an upcoming Sprint. During the refinement process, the Scrum Team collects additional information to understand the scope of work that's required. The refinement is complete when the Product Owner and Scrum Team can agree on a definition of Done for each item in the backlog.

Identifying a definition of Done

Another critical element of product backlog refinement is to ensure the team establishes a definition of *Done* for each product backlog item worked within the Sprint. Those who are more familiar with the traditional development model can think of the definition of Done as being analogous to acceptance criteria. In either case, both concepts share common characteristics, such as the following:

- Each requirement should have clear and concise descriptions of what good looks like when correctly implemented.

- The results of the requirement should be testable.

- Everyone on the team needs to understand the requirement.

- Requirements define capabilities that satisfy customer needs and objectives.

The definition of Done is situational to every product backlog item, refined by the Scrum Team members, and ultimately approved by the Product Owner. They must have a common understanding of what good looks like when a feature or function is fully installed and tested in the software or system. Also, there cannot be any bugs in the new code or the integration of the new code with the existing code.

In the last three subsections, you've learned how to refine a product backlog, develop User Stories that further refine the development team's understanding of individual requirements, and specify definitions of Done to help to ensure fulfillment of each backlog requirement. But we also need a method to decide what items within the product backlog should be considered for development within an upcoming Sprint. This process starts with the definition of a Sprint Goal.

Establishing Sprint Goals

Through the Sprint refinement and planning processes, the Product Owner and Scrum Team establish objectives for each Sprint in terms of the implementation of items from the product backlog. The Product Owner and the Scrum Team negotiate objectives and goals for the Sprint. While the Product Owner is accountable for establishing priorities, only the Scrum Team can commit to the work they can accomplish within each Sprint.

Sprint Goals are abstractions that sit above the level of User Stories and work tasks. Let's take a closer look at what I mean by this. If we are building an ATM banking application, we might have a Sprint Goal to build and test a set of features that allow bank withdrawals at an ATM. In this context, we might have two primary User Stories:

- "*As a user of the ATM banking application, I want to see my account balance when I log in so that I know whether I have sufficient funds to withdraw money for my personal needs.*"

- "*As the user of the ATM banking application, once I see my available balance, and assuming I have sufficient funds, I want to be able to withdraw as much as $250 from the ATM.*"

The Scrum Team defines the work tasks necessary to build these two features within the ATM application. Now the devil is always in the details, and there may be any number of other capabilities that might logically fit and support these two user requirements, such as having the ability to transfer funds between accounts before making a withdrawal and the ability to review pending withdrawals.

The Scrum Team negotiates with the Product Owner to determine which ancillary capabilities are of high value and critical for this release, constrained by the amount of work the Scrum Team can complete during the Sprint. Once they agree, the Scrum Team commits to deliver the negotiated and agreed features and ancillary capabilities within the Sprint.

Much of the work described so far is completed as part of the Sprint Planning event. Also, to the maximum extent possible, most Sprint Planning work is completed within a timeboxed Sprint Planning meeting, as described in the next section.

Conducting Sprint Planning meetings

At the start of the project and the start of each new Sprint, the development team analyzes the highest priority items or stories in the product backlog to identify the deliverable items within an upcoming Increment and how they will go about doing the work. This activity is referred to as Sprint Planning and is the first event scheduled within each Sprint.

The outputs of the Sprint Planning meeting and subsequent breakout sessions include a subset of product backlog items consistent with the Sprint Goals. The Scrum Team refines the agreed definition of Done and creates a list of work tasks and work assignments that are necessary to start building a new Increment of functionality. The sum of the identified work tasks forms the Sprint Backlog, which is necessary before development work can begin in the Sprint.

At the end of each Sprint Planning event, the team should be able to explain the following to both the Product Owner and Scrum Master:

- The Increment of new functionality required to support the Sprint Goal
- The scope of work the Scrum Team expects to accomplish over the Sprint
- A clear explanation of how the team intends to self-organize and allocate their work

At this point, the team is ready to begin working on developing the new Increment.

Initiating development work

All development work in Scrum must fit within timeboxed development iterations that have consistent durations, limited to a period of 1 to 4-week cycles called *Sprints*. The output of a Sprint is an Increment of functionality that meets the definition of Done, is useable without additions or modifications, and is, therefore, a potentially shippable product.

With the definition and refinement of the Sprint Backlog, the development team immediately gets to work starting to build the new Increment of functionality, consistent with the Sprint Goals. Ideally, the teams complete all identified work before the Sprint duration ends, and all completed work complies with the definition of Done.

Recall that Scrum is a framework that serves as a container for other engineering processes. Therefore, test-driven development, continuous integration, and automated testing all logically fit within the Scrum framework and help to ensure the quality of the software.

The Scrum artifacts created and refined within a Sprint include the **product backlog** and **Sprint Backlog** discussed in previous sections of this chapter and **Increments**. The term Increment represents the functionality and value of the product in its current state. An Increment represents the backlog items from the previous Sprint but built on previous Increments. Therefore, while the term Increments represents the current extended functionality of the product, it's also appropriate to think of the term as implying the sum value of the product through the implementation of product backlog items to date.

Within each Sprint are four primary Scrum events: Sprint Planning, Daily Scrum, Sprint Review, and the Sprint Retrospective. We covered the topic of Sprint Planning in the preceding section, so, now, let's take a look, in order, at the Daily Scrums, Sprint Reviews, and Sprint Retrospectives.

Conducting Daily Scrums

Every 24 hours, the Scrum Team meets, ideally at the same and same place, to discuss the progress of the team in completing the work of the Sprint. These Daily Scrum meetings should be short and to the point, usually taking 15 minutes or less. The team does not address any issues in these meetings. Instead, the affected team members and other technical or domain specialists who can help to resolve the issue, take the conversation offline in a separate meeting.

Supporting the pillars of empiricism, the Daily Scrums provide an opportunity for team members to inspect their progress and adapt their work to address any issues. The team can also agree to take on more work if it appears the team will accomplish their Sprint Goals with time to spare.

In the spirit of transparency, executives, customers, end-users, and other stakeholders can join Daily Scrum meetings. However, the Scrum Master must make sure these folks do not interrupt the meeting. The goal of the Daily Scrum is to minimize waste in the form of extended meetings that do not directly support the work of individual team members in their assigned work.

Daily Scrums continue through the duration of the Sprint. At the end of each Sprint, the team conducts a Sprint Review meeting, as discussed in the next section.

Conducting Sprint Reviews

On the last day of the Sprint, the Sprint team meets with designated stakeholders and the Product Owner to review the work of the Sprint. This meeting is called the **Sprint Review**. All work is entirely transparent to the attendees of the Sprint Review. The attendees inspect the work to see whether there are any variances from the original Sprint Goal. The development team members may provide a demo of the new product functionality to prospective users of the software.

The Sprint Review is another form of transparency that allows users and customers to inspect the product to determine whether the new functionality meets their needs. If the new Increment of functionality falls short of expectations or the users have new insights on how the product can better serve their needs, they record that information for further review in upcoming product backlog refinement and Sprint Planning meetings.

During the Sprint Reviews, the Product Owner discusses the work completed in the previous Sprint and the value it provides. They also take the time to discuss current priorities in the product backlog and their future development and release plans. The Product Owner should address performance against the project constraints of schedule, budgets, resources, and quality. Finally, the Product Owner should provide new insights on market conditions, potential business, or customer opportunities and their impact on future development priorities.

The development team reviews their work over the Sprint and explains what went well and any issues they faced and how they addressed those issues. The development team should also provide a demo of the new enhancements to the Sprint Review meeting attendees.

All attendees can participate in the discussions on current priorities, market conditions, new enhancement requests, and future releases. Though no decisions should be made in the Sprint Review, the team should update the product backlog to reflect new backlog items and priorities. The information gathered in the meeting becomes an input into the product backlog refinement discussions and Sprint Planning events.

Before the team meets to plan the next iteration of work, they need to take some time to inspect the work of the previous Sprint. The Sprint Retrospective, discussed in the next subsection, provides a scheduled opportunity for the team to discuss areas where they can adapt to improve their work and remove impediments affecting their ability to complete their work.

Conducting Sprint Retrospectives

Sprint Retrospectives offer an essential opportunity to inspect and adapt the work of the team in light of new information and issues discovered in the previous Sprints. The team's ability to act is highly dependent on the willingness and ability of the team to be transparent in uncovering and discussing their work.

Building strong bonds and trust among team members is critical, as is safety in terms of not making things personal and understanding that discussed information is not ever used to attack other team members. The team is responsible for the work they complete as a group, and they must act and work as a team.

The Sprint Retrospective meeting should occur right after the Sprint Review meeting. The goal of the Sprint Retrospective meeting is to analyze what went well in the previous Sprint and what did not go so well and to discuss ways the team can improve the quality or performance of their work in future Sprints, starting with the very next Sprint. Holding off on scheduling this meeting will make it challenging to implement any desired changes in time to affect the new Sprint positively.

The outputs of Sprint Retrospective meetings are agreements on opportunities to improve the team, and action items to make those improvements. Note that it can take several years for a Scrum Team to fully mature. In the interim, the Sprint Retrospectives help the team to grow and improve in their joint capabilities. As they reach a high level of operation, the Retrospectives help to keep the team from backsliding into old habits or unproductive routines. They also help the team to recognize new opportunities for improvement, including the development of new skills.

The Sprint Retrospective is the last scheduled event in the Sprint cycle. Assuming the Sprint Goals were achieved, with the release of a new Increment of functionality that conforms with the definitions of Done, the output of the Sprint is a potentially shippable product.

Releasing potentially shippable products

At this stage of the Scrum workflow process, the team has developed a new Increment of functionality that conforms with the agreed definition of Done and achieves the Sprint Goals. Products at this stage are potentially shippable. When a development team fails to produce a shippable product, they create an undesirable situation where each new Increment accumulates additional work in progress that the teams must eventually complete.

In other words, if a development iteration has unfinished work, and the Increment does not meet its definition of Done, the team must add the work to a future Sprint. In the meantime, the accumulation of incomplete work makes the product more difficult to work with, and it becomes increasingly more challenging to locate and fix identified bugs. This lack of discipline causes a form of accumulated technical debt that delays delivery of new functionality, slows work down, makes development work more complex, and hides bugs and defects.

So, the objective of Scrum is to have a completed Increment of functionality every Sprint, conforming to the definition of Done and thoroughly tested. The Product Owner, based solely on business reasons, will determine when to release the completed Increments into production. But in the meantime, every Sprint Increment must stand on its own, fully deployable should the Product Owner decides to do so.

That's the end of the basic Scrum workflow. The team moves on to help the Product Owner to refine the product backlog and plan the next Sprint. Now that you understand the basic Scrum workflow, we'll turn our attention to understanding the impact of systems thinking and lean development in the application of both agile and Scrum-based practices.

Identifying how Scrum can break down

Scrum is hard, much harder than it looks from a simple review of the Scrum Guide and memorization of its empirical process control foundations and product-oriented team structures, events, and artifacts. It's even more challenging to scale Scrum across a large product or as an organization-wide implementation.

In this section, you will come to understand that there are innumerable pitfalls that can lead to Scrum implementation failures, both at the product and organizational levels, and how to resolve these issues at the start. Each subsection addresses a particular issue but also provides a discussion on how the organization can avoid or at least minimize the problems.

Lacking executive sponsorship

Executive-level support is a critical success factor for any Scrum implementation. Because Scrum is ultimately about changing the values and the principles that guide the organization, a move to implement Scrum on any scale will run headfirst into impediments created by the organization's culture. Only the most senior executives have the power and authority to remove these impediments.

For example, Scrum requires a movement away from functional departments to product-oriented teams that are self-organizing, self-contained, and autonomous in their efforts to create the highest possible value at the lowest possible cost. The effect is that Scrum eliminates hierarchical organizational structures while changing employee and management positions, roles, and responsibilities. Instead, fully empowered Product Owners supported by their dedicated Scrum Teams replace the bloated bureaucracies of the traditional bureaucratic organizational structures.

Scrum also changes product life cycle development processes to release new Increments of customer valued functionality frequently, forcing the streamlining of all product life cycle development and operations-oriented processes. The streamlining requires more effective communications and collaboration between organizations that previously operated as individual silos. The efforts to streamline all development and operations activities will force the integration of business processes.

Other critical business processes eventually must follow suit. For example, marketing AD campaigns and promotions will have shorter life cycles. Sales organizations must stay current with released product capabilities, features and functions, and the specific customers targeted with each new release. Frequent releases impact product delivery and consulting partner programs, including training and support requirements. When the software is part of a more extensive system, device, or equipment, the changes affect the organization's supply chain partners and associated processes.

So, to recap, Scrum implementations at a project or product development team level have impacts across the organization and its delivery and supply chain partners. The impediments faced by the Scrum Team go beyond their scope of work and authority to address, and, for that reason, executive-level sponsorship is vital. Only a chief or **Line of Business (LOB)** executive has the authority to work through the many organizational issues that will impede the effectiveness of the Scrum Team.

The chief or LOB executive may delegate their authority situationally. But they cannot delegate their authority if they don't know what the issues and impediments are. They must stay informed and engaged in making Scrum work, no matter the scale of the Scrum implementation.

Failing to obtain buy-in

Just because the chief executive is supportive and directing the change to Scrum doesn't mean everyone else in the organization has the same commitments. The lack of organizational buy-in is likely the number one issue the enterprise Scrum implementation team will face. A corporate mandate without proper preparation, communications, early success, and ultimately lack of buy-in will virtually guarantee Scrum implementation failures and delays.

For one thing, organization-wide implementations of Scrum requires major reorganizations, away from hierarchical and functional departments, and to streamlined, product-oriented, and loosely coupled Scrum Teams. Individuals, particularly those in middle management roles, will feel threatened if they don't see a useful role for them and they believe their jobs and compensation are at risk. Yet these are the very people the business needs to buy into the change. If they don't buy in, they will resist the change.

Also, change is scary. However, the odds of achieving early successes improve when the organization stages the roll-out of Scrum through a series of pilot engagements, implemented by the organization's most enthusiastic innovators and early adopters. The odds of success increase, even more, when individuals in other functional groups see an opportunity for them in the change.

There is an adage that says success breeds success. Part of the success comes from hiring people who want to achieve great things. But another critical factor is that most people want to be part of something successful. The successes of the innovators and early adopters generate the enthusiasm required to move the early majority, late majority, and laggards to change and adopt the new Scrum paradigm eventually.

Lacking an agile mindset

Individuals across the organization must develop an agile mindset. Unfortunately, achieving an agile mindset is not all that simple. You cannot merely follow the rules of Scrum to achieve agility. The values and principles of agile must guide decisions made within the Scrum framework and not by the prescriptive rules of Scrum. The Scrum Guide implements few rules and those that exist connect Scrum's roles, events, and artifacts, guiding the relationships and interactions between them.

agile is not a prescriptive methodology with specific rules to follow. Instead, agility is a philosophy expressed as a core set of 4 values and 12 principles. Before an agile framework, such as Scrum, can be implemented, the organization must understand and embrace the core values and principles of agile. Then, and only then, can they begin to figure out how to go about achieving Agility.

agile has a widescale impact on the organization, as identified in the previous two subsections. Ultimately, the culture must change. And since organizational culture is driven by the collective views, objectives, and experiences of its people, culture can only be changed by the people who make up the organization. And that process takes time and work. If a chief executive wants to change the culture, they must generally accomplish the following tasks in roughly this order:

1. Identify the current strengths and weaknesses of the organization's existing culture in terms of values and behaviors.

2. Create and articulate a vision for the future, defining the business strategies, goals, and objectives.

3. Communicate the cultural strengths that can be leveraged but also which values and behaviors need to change and why.

4. Define and communicate the highest value of tactical priorities to meet the organization's strategic goals and objectives.

5. Establish clearly defined goals and metrics to evaluate progress against the tactical plans.

6. Implement the product-oriented teams of Scrum.

7. Establish co-location facilities with both team and individual work areas, plus install development systems and tools and networking and communications infrastructures.

8. Update employee compensation, incentive, and rewards programs to align the progression of skills and team performance with the organization's strategic and tactical goals.

9. Encourage open, honest, and respectful communications in support of Scrum's empirical process control foundations and its pillars of transparency, inspection, and adaptation.

10. Don't just mandate change; create the motivation for change by promoting successes; providing regular feedback, coaching, and mentoring opportunities to Scrum Teams; and recognizing people who demonstrate desired values and behaviors of Agile and Scrum.

Failing to invest

Another vital part of the Scrum implementation preparation is to ensure the organization has the skills, infrastructure, and resources to support the products and Scrum Teams. The implementation of Scrum involves a reinvention of organizational structures, behaviors, and work environments. More substantial investments are required to support enterprise-scale Scrum implementations.

The Product Owners, Scrum Masters, and Scrum Teams will take time to develop their skills in Scrum. I'll discuss training issues in a separate subsection. However, the organization also needs to provide access to individuals who are already trained and skilled in Scrum. Such resources may already exist within the organization. But, in most cases, the organization may need to hire outside consultants to help to guide them through the implementation process.

The organization may choose to create a **Scrum Center of Excellence (CoE)** to support, coach, and mentor the newly installed product development teams, Scrum Masters, and Product Owners. An **Executive-level enterprise Scrum Master (ESM)**, must be installed to work through organizational issues, for example, impediments that require executive-level decision-making and investment authorities. When multiple divisions are involved in the enterprise Scrum implementation, each division should have a dedicated ESM to support their efforts.

The ESMs may establish Scrum Teams solely dedicated to removing organizational-level impediments. Each ESM creates a backlog of prioritized issues that they must address. For example, the ESMs must address gaps in resources, product team alignments, compensation, and incentive plans, knowledge, experience, and infrastructure needs across the organization, both before and during the enterprise deployment of Scrum.

The Scrum Teams also need a physical place to work, ideally in a co-located facility with room to work, conduct breakout sessions, and set up their information radiators. The developers need network access, development and testing computers, and software development and testing tools. These investments advance the effectiveness of the Scrum Team.

Lacking effective communications programs

Organizations that mandate a change to Scrum without preparation are doomed to failure. People need to know why change is required. They want to know what's in it for them. They need to feel they are safe in the change situation, otherwise, they will resist it. Moreover, they need to know what they have to do to be successful in the new environment. None of this can happen overnight.

Start by building a communications plan. The organization likely has the skills in-house to do this, as both marketing staff and project managers have the skills and training to develop and execute effective communications plans. Make sure the communications plan provides a layout of the specific details of why the change is necessary, the timelines, and the expected organizational and personal benefits expected as outcomes of the change.

Make sure employees and managers know who to go to if they have questions or concerns. Provide details on training opportunities and dates. The communications strategy should include information on the staged roll-out priorities and initiation dates as that information becomes available. Also, the communications plan should emphasize early and continuing promotion of implementation successes and the specific accomplishments of individual Scrum Teams.

Failing to educate

It should be evident that organizations that wish to implement Scrum need to train their employees in advance of the implementation and then provide continuing training opportunities as the teams form and mature. But based on my experience, too many companies refuse to make the human and financial resources available to support an effective training program. Even if they do provide access to training resources, how many organizations track and provide incentives to employees who participate in training programs that are relevant to the organization's continued success?

Going back to our discussions on Shuhari, it can take years to master a new subject. The organization might start by providing access to online courses that cover the fundamentals of Scrum. But the organization should also consider bringing in experts to teach Scrum classes and directly address questions unique to the organization's implementation of Scrum. Over time, the organization will produce its experts, and these folks should be available to mentor other Scrum Teams.

Also, the training can't just be about agile and Scrum but should also encompass development practices and skills and the technologies and tools used by the development organization.

The bottom line is learning is an ongoing, never-ending requirement.

Failing implementations of Scrum

In the previous four subsections, you have learned how Scrum implementations fail from lack of executive sponsorships, foundations, agile mindsets, and communications and training programs. In the remainder of this section, you will learn how to resolve the impediments that hinder the successful enterprise or product-level deployments of Scrum.

I've touched on this subject before, but the empirical process control mechanisms of Scrum provide a practical approach to resolving Scrum implementation issues. However, the Scrum Teams cannot resolve most of the issues identified in this section as they don't have the authority to address issues outside their direct product development-related activities.

Therefore, the organization must establish an enterprise-level Scrum CoE or some other type of organizational Scrum implementation resources to resolve issues that require executive-level decisions. These decisions include issues associated with business and organizational alignment, hiring, people management, compensation plans, and investments in infrastructure, tools, training, facilities, and funding.

Adding roles that are not part of Scrum

Scrum Teams only employ three roles, ever. These are the **Product Owner**, the **Scrum Master**, and the **Developers**. The founders of Scrum were very careful not to install structures that would create an overly competitive environment that is not conducive to team building. Any organization that adds additional roles is not truly practicing Scrum. Moreover, another risk from adding roles is organizational bloat and a return to hierarchical and bureaucratic processes.

Focusing on the wrong product backlog items

Given the product-oriented nature of Scrum, there has to be someone responsible for making decisions and ultimately held accountable for the success of the product. To be held accountable, they must have the authority to make decisions on product backlog items and priorities. That is the role of the Product Manager.

There is only one Product Manager assigned to each unique product. In some of the scaled-Scrum approaches introduced in Section 2 of this book, the Product Owner may enlist the help of assistants or Teams of Product Owners working under a Chief Product Owner or Product Manager. For now, let's keep things simple. The Product Owner is the only decision-maker regarding product backlog priorities.

Not even the company's chief executive should override the decisions of the Product Owner. For sure, **Chief Executive Officers** (**CEOs**) and **LOB** executives, customers, end-users, development team members, and other stakeholders will undoubtedly have opinions and seek to influence decisions. Still, there can only be one decision-maker, and that is the person who ultimately has responsibility for the organization's **Return on Investment** (**ROI**) for the product.

Product Owners are the voice of the customer. A successful Product Owner recognizes the customer's interest must come first. If a prospective customer is not happy with a product, they will not buy it. Customers have varying needs and will value different features and functions, price points, performance, and quality uniquely. The challenge is in identifying the right set of product features and functions and priorities to make the product commercially viable.

A product with a large prospective customer base and multiple market segmentation will have a larger pool of requirements options to consider for each Increment. As mentioned in previous sections within this chapter, the Product Owner must work though a multi-dimensional problem that evaluates the size of the market for each identified requirement, the Incremental value to customers for each satisfying requirement, and the cost of producing and delivering each requirement. They must resist every attempt by outside influencers to change priorities that do not fit Scrum's value-based product backlog prioritization model.

Allowing inappropriate priorities

You may think that surely the CEO can change the priorities in the product backlog. However, unless the chief executive is the Product Owner, the answer is no; the CEO cannot change the product backlog items or priorities. The Product Owner cannot allow outside influencers to arbitrarily make decisions on product backlog items and priorities that do not fit the highest-value/lowest-cost prioritization model described previously, no matter who the influencers are.

Product Managers who are weak or ineffective will make bad decisions. For example, they may add low-value items with unsubstantiated priorities within the product backlog. Conversely, they may add items that appear to have high customer value but are not cost-justified given what the target market is willing to pay for them. Or the Product Owner may make an error by purposely choosing to prioritize the development of many low-cost items that have relatively little Incremental value, instead of focusing on the development of higher-value items.

An effective Product Owner understands the scope of knowledge and work that goes into building and sustaining a viable product backlog. When a Product Owner fails, it's likely the hiring chief executive or LOB executive who under-scoped the breadth of skills and cross-functional knowledge required to perform in the role of Product Owner successfully.

For example, the Product Owners must have credible domain knowledge to understand customer issues, capability requirements, and priorities thoroughly. To stay on top of the market trends, the Product Owner needs to spend the bulk of their time meeting with customers, industry analysts, end-users, and stakeholders. Ideally, the Product Owner should seek out opportunities to speak and present at industry forums and become a recognized thought-leader within the industry.

The Product Owner must have the business domain knowledge to assess product pricing strategies accurately, as well as costs, and value. They must have marketing skills and knowledge to understand how to identify target market customers and how best to promote their products. The Product Owner must be a competent business development specialist who can identify new market niches and product opportunities. The Product Owner must also know about sales, including the use of inside and outside sales organizations, and the use of channel partners such as **Value-Added Resellers (VARs)**, systems integrators, consultants, **Managed Service Providers (MSPs)**, **Original Equipment Manufacturers (OEMs)**, and distributors.

Do the Product Owners do all of this work alone? No, of course not. They are the ultimate decision-makers, but they must have access to functional efforts to pull the information together they need to make the right decisions. If the Scrum implementation effort is limited strictly to development activities, the Product Owner will access corporate resources in the functional departments. However, if the organization is implementing Scrum enterprise-wide, the Product Owner can establish functional Scrum Teams to provide support across sales, marketing, partnerships, and other critical product life cycle activities.

In short, the Product Owner must be a capable and knowledgeable *jack of all trades* whose responsibilities encompass the entire scope and breadth of product management. The Product Owner spends a relatively small amount of time directly supporting development-oriented Scrum events, requiring somewhere on the order of only 25% of their time. The Product Owners need time to work in parallel with functional or, more ideally, Scrum-based teams supporting marketing, sales, partnerships, distribution, and other business functions critical to the product's market success.

Directing instead of leading

A common mistake is to place a Scrum Master into a development team based on their technical skills, domain knowledge, or project management experience without making sure they are adequately trained and clearly understand their role. None of those skills are requisite justifications for hiring a Scrum Master. The potential problem is the Scrum Master with such skills may assume authoritarian control over the Scrum Team, which is in opposition to their role in Scrum.

The roles of the Scrum Masters include providing mentoring, coaching, and serving. The Scrum Master provides mentoring and coaching on Scrum practices to the Product Owner, development team members, and any other stakeholders whose views and actions can affect the product development priorities and work. In this role, the Scrum Master monitors decisions and activities, and steps in to provide guidance when the actions are taken or proposed are inconsistent with Scrum.

Moreover, in the role of a servant leader, they help the development team to resolve any impediments that would otherwise distract the team members form to complete the goals of each Sprint. In other words, the authority of the Scrum Master comes not from directives but from their knowledge, their ability to provide guidance, and their desire and ability to serve the team as opposed to leading or directing the team's activities.

Scrum Masters who approach their job as technical leaders make the mistake of trying to exert influence as the arbiter of technology, architecture, design, and development decisions. Such actions fly in the face of both agile values and Scrum practices, where the team as a whole determines the best approach to developing each new Increment of functionality. Scrum Masters who cannot resist influencing technical and development-related decisions should reconsider if they are better suited to working as a development team member.

Scrum Masters coming from a project management role need to understand they are no longer responsible for project planning, scheduling, or prioritization of work. Scrum Masters do not monitor work to control or direct the execution of work. Only the development team, operating as an independent, fully functional, and self-contained unit, can decide how much work they can take on within each Sprint.

If the Scrum Master helps to create the burndown and velocity charts, it is Done in their role to serve the team by allowing the team to stay focused on their value-added tasks. The Scrum Master never develops charts to direct the team's activities. They develop the charts so that the development team, its Product Manager, and other stakeholders can make informed decisions.

When I say the development of burndown and velocity charts are non-valued added work, I don't mean to imply the charts have no value. But the charts are measurements only and do not directly contribute to the development of a new Increment of functionality. On the other hand, the charts are part of the information radiators previously discussed that help to provide transparency and facilitate inspection and adaption processes. So, the charts have value, even though they do not directly contribute to the development of the project.

An easy way to think about value-added versus non-value-added work is to ask yourself whether the activity directly contributes to the construction of the product's Increment. If not, then the work is not value-added from the customer's perspective. The work may be necessary or useful as a vital information radiator item, but the development team cannot let such activities get in the way of developing the Increment. As a Servant Leader, the Scrum Leader steps in to help the team.

Likewise, rather than use the information from the burndown and velocity charts to micromanage and direct the team's progress, the Scrum Master provides the information freely and without judgment and as an aid to the team's decision-making process. The goal of a Servant Leader is to help the team to obtain the information so they can assess the progress of their work and their capacity as a team.

Having risks and issues are the norm and not the exception when developing large and complex software and IT-aided systems. Risk management is the reason Scrum implements the concepts of empirical process control. It's impossible to know or plan for every contingency that affects a development project. In some cases, the development team responds directly to address any issues that arise. However, the Scrum Master should work through any issues not directly related to the act of designing and building the Increment. They may schedule fact-finding meetings or need to resolve other issues that affect development team member participation.

Performing non-value-added activities

The fastest way to kill an Increment is to allow the development team to get sidetracked on non-value-added activities or work. Non-value-added work is any activity that does not directly contribute to the development of the current Increment of functionality as required to achieve the Sprint Goal. Activities that can take away the development team's focus includes the attendance of non-relevant meetings, working on development tasks or other activities not related to the current Increment, and working on issues best resolved by the Scrum Master. Over-engineering a product beyond what is required to achieve the Sprint Goal is another example.

The timeboxed events of Scrum (for example, Sprint Planning, Daily Scrum, Sprint Review, and Sprint Retrospective) provide maximum transparency while minimizing time spent in non-value-added meetings. The Scrum Master helps to ensure the teams stick to the scope of each event and within the time boundaries. When an additional discussion is required to resolve a development issue, the impacted development team members should take the meeting offline and allow the other team members and meeting participants to get back to their work.

In an ideal situation, the development team has a typical area in which they work as a team. The co-location of team members facilitates the display and use of information radiators, paired programming, and breakout sessions to discuss requirements and architecture, design, and coding issues. The developers need access to networks, computing systems, and software development tools. I also personally believe people need time and space to think without distraction and to decompress. Having cubicles or individual desks within or adjacent to the shared meeting room provides that individual space.

Scrum development teams are self-organizing. That means they must have the authority to evaluate the work necessary to fulfill a Sprint's goal and make individual assignments based on priorities, time, skills, and interests. Scrum development teams are self-contained. That means each team must have the skills necessary to complete all work. Since Scrum development teams are limited in size, the individuals must value learning new skills and developing competency in multiple skills. New product requirements and new technologies and tools will expand over time the skills needed to develop the team's assigned products. As a result, employee compensation and incentive plans must support the multi-learning objectives of Scrum.

With all of these constraints in mind, the development teams cannot afford team members who are specialists. Still, there will be times when the need for a new skill is immediate, and the team may not have the expertise needed to develop a new Increment of functionality. In those cases, the team must have access to specialists on a time-limited basis. Those specialists may come from an internal group or hire through outside contractors. However, in the longer term, assuming the new skills become an ongoing requirement, the development team should build the skills in house.

Allowing team burnout

A critical issue that comes up time and again is burnout of Scrum development team members. This issue happens when the Scrum Masters, Product Owners, chief, or LOB executives exert too much influence on individual Scrum goals and over commit the developers. Only the development team can make commitments on the scope of work they can take on during each timeboxed Increment and plan the work tasks necessary to achieve the Sprint Goal.

Executives, Product Owners, and Scrum Masters who do not recognize the development team must have the final say on Sprint Goals and work tasks make two mistakes:

- They have not understood that value trumps functionality.
- They have not understood the importance of transparency.

In the first case, Product Owners who focus on making value a priority understand that releasing something customers want and will pay for is more important than waiting to implement a product with the most features and functions. The 80/20 rule is a prime consideration, as we've learned previously that ~20% of a product's features provide approximately 80% of the product's value. The other 80% of the identified prospective backlog items are expensive and time consuming to deliver and offer little value in return to the customer.

In the second case, transparency is critical as it provides timely and accurate information for accurate decision making. Transparency enables trust, which is why Scrum's three pillars of empirical process control, *transparency*, *inspection*, and *adaptation*, are so important. The organization's executives and Product Owners may question whether the development team is putting their full effort toward meeting their target release dates. Such concerns are reasonable and open for discussion. However, interference with a team's decisions is not. Only the Scrum Team can adequately access the scope of work they can take on within an Increment. But the Scrum Team also has a responsibility to provide sufficient and accurate information to have informed conversations.

For example, if the Product Owner or executives have concerns about the team's *velocity*, they can have a conversation to see whether there are external impediments that are limiting the scope of work completed within each Increment. It also might make sense to evaluate the economic feasibility of adding additional Scrum Teams to help to work through the product backlog.

Failing to provide full transparency

Scrum development teams, when properly implemented, can determine the amount of work they can complete withing an upcoming Sprint. They must have the authority to make decisions on workloads. But they must also show accountability through the visibility of their velocity charts and by meeting their commitments.

Besides the Scrum events, velocity and burndown charts and other useful metrics provide evidence of the team's ability to both judge and complete the work they have committed to complete within each Sprint and planned for future releases. Over time, the development team builds a profile of their capabilities by estimating the work they can complete in each Sprint, often expressed as story points, and then tracking their performance against their estimates. The team charts this data across each completed Sprint. The measure of their performance, expressed as story points per Sprint, is called velocity, and the charts showing velocity over time are called velocity charts.

Burndown and velocity charts are not the only items that provide transparency on the team's activities and capabilities. The team can employ any number of handwritten, drawn, printed, or electronic displays of their work and their decisions. For example, they may have the User Stories written on 3" by 5" index cards and posted on a Scrum Board to show those that are in a queue, work in progress, tested, and Done. They may have architecture and design drawings displayed on whiteboards or flip charts. They may also draw out the screen displays, application reports, and screen navigation features. Test scripts and test results should be displayed.

There is no limit to what can be displayed so long as the information is useful and relevant. Such information, when publicly displayed for all to see, is referred to as an *information radiator*.

Continuing development beyond economic value

We can think about this issue in another way; how many features in a mature word processing application do you use, let alone across the entire suite of products? As an author, there may be certain features I use more than you might in a word processor. There may be other features you use that I do not. Other users will have different feature sets they prefer. The question is how many features have the team implemented that do not have sufficient economic value to justify the effort?

Figure 3.2 – Word processor application needs

One of the primary roles of the Product Owner is to look at the intersection of our needs and other market opportunities, to determine the sweet spot for maximizing value at the lowest production delivery costs. See *Figure 3.2* on *'Word Processor Application Needs'* as an example. The **Sweet Spot** identified in the graphic offers the maximal economic return to the organization's investments in the product as it includes the subset of features desired by all types of customers.

That's not to say the sales opportunities within the author, market, or your collection of needs might not economically justify further investments. The Product Owner needs to gauge whether features should all go into a generalized product or whether it might be better to offer niche variants of the product. A generalized product costs less to promote, sustain, and sell. However, niche products may avoid turning off customers who believe the full-featured product has become too complicated. Niche products may also support a higher price and a higher ROI.

The Scrum Teams stay together for as long as the addition of the new features and functions continue to add value sufficient to justify continued investments. Of course, the product's accumulated costs continue to increase with added development activities. But that does not matter so long as the revenues from new product sales and from existing customers for maintenance, support, and upgrades offset the ongoing costs of continued product development activities.

Failing to support market segment opportunities

Some products have a large and diverse customer base. The Product Owner, working with the product's marketing staff, segments their market opportunities based on groupings of common characteristics, such as customer demographics, interests, needs, and locations. The Product Owners follow the same rules of prioritizing identified backlog items with the highest-value and lowest-cost.

Take a quick look at the graphical example of *Figure 3.3* – Market Segmentation Priorities – Intersecting, which is a generalized view of the graphic presented in *Figure 3.2*. You can see there is an area of overlap where the customers' *needs* span all three market segments, for example, the **Sweet Spot!** From Increment to Increment—this is the area where the Product Owner knows they can maximize sales opportunities:

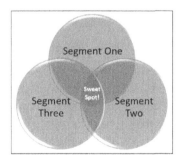

Figure 3.3 – Market Segmentation Priorities – Intersecting

At some point in time, the developers may complete the implementation of all features within the intersecting needs of the three marketing segments. Now the market segments must carry their weight to justify further development investments.

The reason for pointing this out is that markets are seldom this easy to segment. For example, *Figure 3.4* displays a situation where target market segment two does not intersect the customer needs of either target market segments one and two. There is a sweet spot among the needs of the first two market segments, and that may be a logical place to start development.

However, what do you do if the customers in segment three will pay more for a product than the customers in market segments one and two? Be careful here. The easy answer is to assume we'll build the product for segment three customers. However, the needs may be so unique and challenging that the development costs outstrip the additional revenues.

In the meantime, perhaps segment two customers will pay more for additional features, beyond the sweet spot, that are relatively simple and inexpensive to implement. Now the Product Owner should consider making those segment two features a higher priority, along with those identified in the sweet spot:

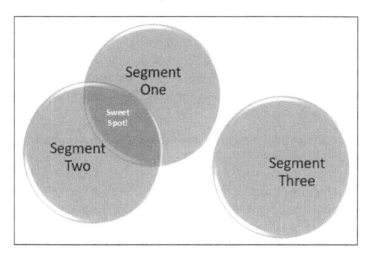

Figure 3.4 - Market Segmentation Priorities – Non-Intersecting

The bottom line is that, across Increments, the product backlog may include items that address the needs of one or more market segments. There still is only one product backlog. Also, the Product Owner still makes the priorities based on the highest-value/lowest-cost prioritization model.

Regardless of the situation, when producing a new release for a product with multiple market segments and niches, your marketing and sales campaigns must be in sync for each new release. Otherwise, your company may not achieve the sales goals that justified the investments. In other words, the Product Owner cannot solely focus on development priorities; they must also make sure the rest of the product marketing, sales, delivery, and support functions are operating in sync.

Pushing deliveries beyond capacities

Companies exist because there is a profit incentive to create things that customers want. The same paradigm holds for government agencies and non-profits. Rather than profit, legislative mandates and goodwill drive government agencies and non-profits to create products and services their customers want. Motivation is useful in that it drives our economies and citizen support systems.

But unbridled motivation can also destroy a company by releasing products and services that are not ready for delivery. When we are not honest, disaster follows—usually in missed delivery dates, cost overruns, and reduced profitability.

Here, again, the answer is transparency. Product Owners need to determine and communicate the identified product backlog items with the highest customer-centric value. The Scrum teams need to make visible their capacities to deliver. Executives need to communicate to investors and their customers the organization's capacities and plans to deliver.

Putting undue pressure on the development teams will not fix the problems of misinformed expectations. Moreover, putting more pressure on the development organization is likely to backfire, creating stress and long hours that hinder the team's performance. The developers need to work at a sustainable pace or they will burn out and mentally and emotionally check out.

The development team's primary focus must continuously remain on only providing the highest value product features with the lowest cost, across each development iteration. But that statement also assumes you have a legitimate market opportunity and capacity to deliver within a competitive timeline. If your competitors beat you to the market and your organization does not have a compelling and unique value proposition, then, most likely, your company shouldn't be making this product or service anyway.

Failing to work as a team

This subsection discusses a catch-all area of behaviors that can hinder the success of a Scrum Team. For example, a dominant team member may seek to lead instead of jointly collaborating on critical decisions. The Scrum Master needs to get involved and mentor the team member on more effective ways to work with their team members.

Some team members may not pull their weight at work. For example, a team member may be late to Scrum events or may not adequately participate and engage in the development work. They may also have a limited skill set and may not learn new skills that would otherwise help the team to more efficiently self-organize, be self-sufficient, and evenly allocate work across each Increment.

The team can positively address these concerns with the individual during their Sprint Retrospective meetings, though the discussions need to remain respectful to retain the integrity of the team. If the member is defensive or non-responsive, the Scrum Master needs to get involved, listen to everyone's concerns, and see whether there is a resolution that works for the individual and the team.

Failing to evolve the product Incrementally

Sometimes, a new product concept is enormous in scope and complexity, making it difficult to immediately assess the features, functions, priorities, and architecture and design requirements. And, in some cases, it may be difficult to refine the vision without some experimentation. But how is the team supposed to proceed in those cases?

After all, without a solid vision and specific product goals and objectives, the development team can't know how to get started. If they start on development, they can't know what they need to deliver. Finally, without a complete vision, the team won't know whether they are off track working on items that have little or no value.

Still, we have to start on something. Though it may be tempting, it's not a great idea to put a new product out to market too quickly. It's much better to build a series of prototypes until the functionality reaches a stage that the product has enough value to attract customers and end-users.

I'll admit, this approach is not textbook Scrum. But as digital remove systems continue to merge into increasingly complex products, we need to manage our risks. It takes time to figure out what our customers want, and releasing a product before it's ready will do more harm than good. It's better to set expectations correctly upfront with customers, stakeholders, and investors.

Keeping the development focus on continually delivering only the highest-value Increments allows the product to mature gracefully. It also provides that fastest path to deliver a viable release.

The value-cost development priority model does not change. The Product Owner still defines a prioritized list of requirements within the product backlog. The development team works through the product backlog as expeditiously as possible, but not to the point of exhaustion and burn out. It's the CEO's job to manage shareholder or customer expectations. As mentioned in the Scrum Team burnout section, productivity will go down if the work pace is not sustainable, and your best people will leave.

By definition, prototypes are potentially disposable products. The reason for this is the developers, the Product Owner, and the paying customer or executive sponsor must be able to walk away from an early architecture or design that cannot meet the business goals that justified the investments. Modern evolutionary architecture concepts help to address these risks by allowing the architecture to emerge in lock-step with the product.

Prototypes also allow the customer to provide early guidance from customers and end-users. The team should find out early on what the customers and end-users do not like or want in the product so that they can cut their losses and remain focused on developing the features and functions the customers do want. The development team works through multiple development iterations until the baseline product can justify a release of the product to customers. The Product Owner decides with input from targeted customers when the product is ready for release.

Summary

At the beginning of this chapter, you learned some of the history and basic concepts behind Scrum. Later, you were introduced to the roles and responsibilities, events, and artifacts associated with Scrum. We learned that modified Scrum is no longer Scrum and why. We also learned that enterprise Scrum is hard to implement as it requires a change in the culture of the organization. Moreover, the changes will remove layers of middle management, and those people must have new opportunities within the organizational deployment of Scrum, or they will resist all efforts to make the deployment successful.

This chapter presented the basic workflow associated with the iterative and Incremental development cycles of Scrum, which are called Sprints. In this section, you learned the use and purpose of Scrum roles, events, and artifacts across each Sprint.

In the next chapter, you are going to learn about *systems thinking*. Systems thinking is not a software development methodology. Instead, it is a way of thinking about complex systems to understand how the collective parts work as a whole to accomplish some purpose or function. However, it's important that you understand the fundamentals of systems thinking as many of the scaled Scrum and Lean-agile practices you'll learn about in *Section 2* of this book employ these concepts.

Questions

1. Why is Scrum described as a framework?

2. How does the traditional development model most differ from the Scrum model?

3. Who has the final say on the scope of work that a Scrum Team can complete within a Sprint?

4. Why does the Product Owner have the final say on the items and priorities established within the product backlog?

5. What is the purpose of the Daily Scrums?

6. What is the purpose of the Sprint Reviews?

7. What is the purpose of the Sprint Retrospectives?

8. What are some of the issues that can cause a Scrum Team to fail?

9. What is the potential problem with hiring a Scrum Master based solely on their technical skills, domain knowledge, or project management experience?

10. What is the primary issue with continuing to develop a product beyond its economic value?

4
Systems Thinking

The whole is greater than the sum of its parts.

Paraphrasing Aristotle, Metaphysics, Book 8

Scrum has been an amazingly successful Agile methodology and has largely won the Agile wars as an industry standard. Scrum's strength comes from the following critical success factors:

- Its foundations in empirical process control theory help teams to solve complex adaptive problems.

- Relatively simple to learn.

- Minimizes prescriptive practices.

- Teams and organizations can implement their preferred business and user requirements analysis and engineering practices within the framework.

By now, you should have a strong understanding of how the basic Scrum framework supports Agile-based values and principles.

In this chapter, we'll turn our attention to systems thinking, which is an important branch of management, social, and engineering sciences. Most succinctly, systems thinking is an approach to looking at complex things as a set of interconnected parts that together create a dynamic environment, resulting in interactions and behaviors that are often difficult to predict. For example, biological organisms, plate tectonics, weather, business and manufacturing processes, and management and social organizations all represent types of complex systems. Relevant to this book, IT-based products, product life cycle development and support processes, and organizational structures are all examples of complex systems in software and systems development.

Systems thinking has become an increasingly important issue as organizations attempt to scale Agile and Scrum practices, both at the product and organizational levels. In later sections in this book, you will learn how systems thinking is an important concept within the **Large-Scale Scrum (LeSS)** and **Scaled-Agile Framework (SAFe)** methodologies.

In this chapter, you will learn the basic concepts behind systems thinking. Next, you will learn how to apply systems thinking to address the complexities of large products and software development processes. Lastly, you will learn how systems thinking is critical to assessing the complexities associated with implementing Agile and Scrum practices across the entire organization.

In this chapter, we will cover the following topics:

- Real-life application of systems thinking
- Learning to think holistically, and seeing how the sum of the parts is greater than the whole
- Basic terminology and concepts of systems thinking
- Applying systems thinking to Agile development practices
- Applying systems thinking to manage large and complex product-development efforts
- Applying systems thinking to manage enterprise-scale Scrum transformations

Applying systems thinking

I can't help it: I was trained to apply critical thinking when faced with complex problems. But I also enjoy figuring out how complex things work and how to make them work better. I'll start this chapter with a real-life story of how I used systems thinking to discover and help resolve a series of design problems affecting an advanced manufacturing facility. But bear with me for a moment while I first describe the educational, business, and technical training that allowed me to look at the situation differently than the engineers who were designing and developing the manufacturing plant, its equipment, and its processes.

Benefitting from interdisciplinary studies

The charter of the U.S. Naval Academy is to prepare young Navy and Marine Corps officers for leadership roles in military combat, spanning a diverse set of highly technical disciplines. As a result, every midshipman receives a multidisciplinary education that includes subjects from science, mathematics, engineering, economics, and the humanities.

I was commissioned as a United States Marine Corps officer and later graduated as a flight officer from the Navy's flight school in Pensacola, Florida. I went on to obtain additional training and flew over 2,000 hours in the Phantom F-4 aircraft, both reconnaissance and fighter/attack models, over eight years.

The F4 was an extremely complex aircraft with tens of thousands of separate parts making up the airframe and its electrical and electronic, pneumatic, hydraulic, jet propulsion, fuel, and weapon systems. Everything in the plane was designed to support its combat or reconnaissance missions. Because of the aircraft's complexity, any number of individual component failures could negatively impact the aircraft's mission and safety. Systems design and redundancy helped minimize those issues.

I also obtained an MBA while I was in the Marine Corps, with an emphasis on finance, statistics, and management principles. This was my educational and technical background when I took my first civilian job to work in a high-tech manufacturing firm. Specifically, my assignment was to serve as the project manager overseeing the development of an advanced manufacturing facility to build then state-of-the-art printed circuit boards for a Department of Defense client. As it turned out, the diversity of my education and work with complex systems, such as the F4, became instrumental in my ability to assess the critical issues facing this start-up manufacturing facility.

Understanding integrated circuit board manufacturing

Printed circuit boards provide the electrical connections between power sources, other circuit boards and system components, and the electronic components, such as integrated circuits, capacitors, and resistors, that are mounted on the circuit boards. Each circuit board contains layers of fiberglass and epoxy resins that have copper foil bonded on to one or both sides. Electrical circuits are printed and chemically etched into the copper foil.

The fiberglass layers are stacked and compressed together under heat to form the hardened circuit board. Then, holes are strategically drilled through the circuit board in specific places, a conductive metal is then plated through these holes to form the electrical connections between layers. Referred to as through-hole technology, the drilled and plated holes are mapped to hit metal pads, printed on each layer, that serve as the electrical connection points between layers.

One of the issues with through-hole technology is that the holes that are drilled through the circuit board take up a lot of space in the interior layers of the boards, and also constrain the location of connections points. For example, if layers one and five in an eight-layer board need a connect point, then the through-hole forming the electronic connection takes up space on the top and bottom of the board—limiting the number of electronic components that can be mounted on a circuit board, and through the other layers—which limits the space available to etch the circuitry.

In contrast, our circuit boards were designed to support a large number of surface-mounted components that had to fit in relatively small physical spaces on both the top and bottom of the circuit boards. In a manufacturing process called **surface-mount technology** (**SMT**), the surface-mounted components are attached to copper pads that are etched on the board surfaces, as opposed to being connected through wire leads that are inserted into plated holes drilled through the boards. With SMT, our shop could fit many more electronic components on each board than was feasible with the through-hole process.

To eliminate the through-holes, our engineers defined processes to build circuit boards, layer by layer, more analogous to the fabrication approach to building integrated circuits. This approach allowed the drilling and plating of holes between each discreet layer, and not through the board. Our engineers also used lasers to design and etch much smaller circuit patterns on each layer—enabling more complex circuitry—and to discretely drill much smaller holes between each new layer added to a circuit board. This strategy provided more space on the surface of each board to attach surface-mounted components.

Adding layers increased defects

The downside of this approach was a huge increase in the number of manufacturing steps. The manufacturing process for each layer of the board included all the steps of a through-hole board, with a few additional steps, but these steps were also multiplied by the number of layers. So each discrete-hole board had more than eight times the manufacturing processes as the through-hole boards. In addition, the increased number of steps per board also increased the number of potential defects and failures per board.

For example, let's suppose a through-hole board has a theoretical failure rate of, say, 1 defect per 1,000 manufacturing steps—to keep the math simple—and that each board has 100 manufacturing steps. In this scenario, we should expect an average of 1 failure for every 10 boards produced; however, if our discrete-hole boards have the same number of manufacturing steps per layer, times 8 layers, then our average defect rate is now 1.25 boards per defect.

Evaluating the manufacturing facility and processes as a system

I joined the team when the participating organizations were six months into the pilot development phase. The engineering team had obtained equipment that they took over from another prototype printed-circuit development team. Space was extremely limited, and the equipment was shoe-horned into the old development shop with no logical design to support the flow of work through the manufacturing processes. In addition, the engineers had to borrow equipment from other shops in the facility as they designed some of their new manufacturing processes. All of the new equipment was custom built and required months to build and deliver.

I spent my first two months working in the shop with the fabricators, across all shifts, helping to build the circuit boards. I wanted to understand the processes intrinsically. Within the first month, I began to get a very unsettled feeling that we would not be able to deliver the volume of boards required under our contract, nor within the approved budget constraints. It was clear to me that the engineers were optimizing their workflow around their processes, but were not looking at the operations of the manufacturing system as a whole. They were all very bright individuals, but their primary direction was to focus on developing the individual equipment and processes within their area of expertise.

I completed some simple queuing theory and defect-per-unit calculations, and the results were not good. We were not going to make our product numbers, and we would be late in delivery and be over budget. I would like to say that my concerns were immediately addressed, but I was the new kid on the block, and nobody wanted to hear this news from me.

Fixing a broken system

As you might imagine, when we went into the initial production phase, the truth was exposed, and we found ourselves the bottleneck in a $1-million-per-day systems development project. Now that is not a fun place to be, and all of a sudden, we had more senior management attention than anyone wants. The company brought in an expert on **Failure Mode and Effects Analysis (FMEA)**, and he and I were assigned to figure out how to fix the design problems of our complex manufacturing system. FMEA is an approach to evaluating components, assemblies, and subsystems to identify potential failure modes in a system, along with their causes and effects.

I also started looking at the manufacturing systems from the perspective of **Six Sigma** and the **theory of constraints**. In the end, it was not our engineering processes, defect rates, or our state-of-the-art manufacturing equipment that were the drivers behind our failures to meet our delivery and cost obligations. We could address all our failures and meet our performance cost objectives through the simple realignment of the equipment and matching product flow rates across the manufacturing processes. Plus, we had to strategically add equipment capacity to some stages of the development flow.

Netting out the problems

I have spent a number of paragraphs explaining the complexities that we dealt with in that prototype circuit board manufacturing facility. But now, let's set out what the real problem was. Can you precisely state in one sentence what the real issue was?

Quite succinctly, the engineers developing the equipment and processes were practicing **local optimization**.

Local optimization simply means that each engineer was evaluating the needs of their equipment and processes in isolation, as if they had no effect on the other elements that made up the manufacturing system as a whole. And it's a complex problem to solve. For example, my first attempt was to use relatively simple queuing theories to evaluate the flow across the development activities. Those models gave me an approximation of the issues we would face when the plant went live, but they were only approximations, and I knew the situations would, in fact, be much worse—and they were.

The mathematical models in queuing theory could not adequately reflect the queues that would form over hundreds of mixed/matched batch processes and cycle times, extensive setup requirements, and multicyclical flows. For that kind of modeling, we needed to use simulation modeling, which we ultimately did. And our simulation models were amazingly accurate, all things considered.

However, this was also about the time that Eliyahu Goldratt wrote his famous book, *The Goal: A Process of Ongoing Improvements* (Goldratt, 1984). This book introduced the **theory of constraints** to the world's manufacturing communities. With the theory of constraints, we learned how important it is to match production flows in even the most complex manufacturing systems. Now we had a practical theory as to how to go about solving our complexity issues. Bear with me through one more section as I explain how we resolved our systems-oriented complexity issues.

Addressing causes and effects

The primary causes and effects of our issues were the mismatched capacities and processing rates of the manufacturing equipment, and how long a board could stay in-queue between certain processes before the integrity of the board was compromised, resulting in higher defect rates. For example, if a board came out of the plating process and had to wait for the plasma etcher to free up, and the moisture content built up in the boards while it was waiting, parts of the boards would explode inside the plasma etchers—or, to phrase it more technically, there would be violent delamination or separation between layers of the board.

The problem was that the plating line could simultaneously plate many more boards than the plasma etchers could handle on delivery. Plus, the plasma etching process took longer than the plating and was often bottlenecked by other downstream processes. The initial fix was as simple as installing an oven between the two processes to keep the boards dry while sitting in-queue. We also had to add additional capacity in the plasma etchers to better match flow rates across the combined manufacturing processes.

There were other process bottlenecks that occurred as boards in the process cycled back though the same equipment that was busy working on other boards in production. The cyclical nature of the discrete-hole development process, building each circuit board one layer at a time, meant that the boards recycled continuously back through the same equipment.

The required changes were much more challenging to implement in production than it would have been had we addressed the plant design issues as a whole before we designed, purchased, and installed all the capital equipment. For example, we had to offload some of the work in our low-volume, high-tech facility to the company's high-volume shop to make room to move all our existing equipment plus new equipment to support a better flow and capacity. We had to purchase additional equipment to align capacities across the fabrication process, causing further delays in production. We had to move the equipment. We had to redesign equipment and tooling to support the flow of work further. We also had to redesign the product's substrate to use a less dangerous and less costly material.

In the end, our budget ballooned to more than three times the original planned costs to build the advanced interconnected facility. On the other hand, the efficiencies gained provided significantly more capacity than was needed to support our original client's demand, and our per-board costs were less than half of our original budgeted cost estimates.

As a result of our team's efforts, the new circuit boards had the speed and low-cost economics to support the emerging **very high-speed integrated circuit** (**VHSIC**) chips, which expanded the company's market opportunities for the advanced circuit boards. Moreover, the commercial VHSIC option might never have been considered under the economics that justified the development of the advanced circuit board shop for our government client.

This real-life story, though somewhat lengthy, demonstrates how systems complexity issues are challenging to resolve. Hopefully, you got the point that local optimizations were killing the productivity of the entire plant. If we had continued to optimize individual processes and not looked at the manufacturing system as a whole, it's likely the whole program would have been shut down. This type of analysis is a prime example of how systems thinking was key to fixing problems that had nothing to do with the viability of the underlying development tasks and processes.

Thinking holistically

Definition of holistic

Relating to or concerned with wholes or with complete systems rather than with the analysis of, treatment of, or dissection into parts (© 2020 Merriam-Webster, Incorporated)

Systems thinking provides a way to untangle the complexity caused by the stochastic impacts of interrelated elements within a system. *Stochastic* is a mathematical term that simply means the elements that are measured—in this case, the components of our product development and organizational systems are subject to the whims of seemingly random variables. The term *elements* includes anything that can impact the system or be impacted by other elements within the system. In other words, elements are the parts that make up a system.

System complexity increases exponentially with the number of elements involved in the system. The mathematical expression for such growth is $n(n-1)/2$. *Figure 4.1* is a graph that shows the exponential growth in system connections with linear growth, from 2 through to 100, in the number of participating elements:

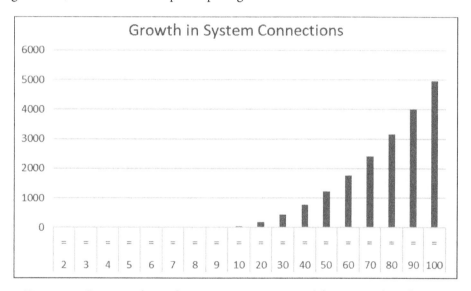

Figure 4.1 – Exponential growth in system connections with linear growth in elements

As components are added to the system, the number of potential connections increases beyond our ability to rationalize all of the potential impacts and their causes and effects. Because of the exponential rise in the number of potential interrelationships, the complexity of the system as a whole is indeed greater than the sum of its parts.

For example, *Figure 4.1* shows that there is only 1 potential relationship between 2 elements in a system, and this grows to nearly 5,000 with 100 elements. Using software developers as an example, if we have 2 people in a paired-programming team, then they will have only that 1 relationship between them while programming. If we have 10 developers within our team, then the number of potential relationships grows to 45. Increase the number of developers to 100, and the number of potential interfaces between them exponentially increases to 4,950.

In other words, the number of potential interrelationships and types of interactions in a multinode system makes it increasingly difficult to predict the total impact of any changes to the system. Instead, we have to break out and assess the elements participating in the system, by modeling their relationships and interactions between individual elements and across the system. You'll learn how this is done later in this chapter.

Visualizing causes and effects

The type of modeling used in systems thinking is called *causal modeling*, which evaluates the causes and effects of behaviors between elements that participate in a system. Elements include events, tangible or intangible things, processes, or states within the system. Causal modeling diagramming technics, such as the **causal loop diagram (CLD)**, visually depicts the causal relationships between the elements identified within a system. The basics of causal diagramming include the following:

- System variables are displayed as nodes.

- Arrows indicate causal influence between two or more nodes.

- Arrowheads indicate the direction of causality.

- Causal influences can have balancing or reinforcing impacts.

- Causal influence arrows can indicate the impact of a trend in the same direction or indicate an opposing impact.

- Causal arrows can form paths between two or more nodes.

We'll use causal loop diagrams in subsequent sections to model systems related to IT. We'll start with a straightforward CLD of a single-element system and then add much more detail and complexity as we go along. But before we get to those examples, we need to make sure that we have a common vocabulary and understanding of the terms used in systems thinking and causal modeling.

Understanding the concepts and vocabulary of systems thinking

The concepts and vocabulary that describe systems thinking are surprisingly simple. All systems have elements and interconnections, and collectively they serve a purpose or function. All systems have stocks that change dynamically because of the flow of the stocks between elements within and across the system. The queuing of stocks within the system causes delays in flows with both positive and negative consequences. Finally, feedback loops provide information that can modify flows to bring a system into balance or to reinforce a positive or negative trend.

Before we get into the application of systems theory to Scrum and Agile practices, let's first explore the basic terms and concepts of systems theory in a bit more detail. We'll start by looking at the definitions of the more common terms:

- **Systems**: These are complex structures of tangible and intangible things, principles, procedures, and social and political environments that collectively act together to serve some purpose or function.

- **Elements**: This term refers to the collection of parts that make up a system. These could be tangible and intangible things, principles, procedures, or social and political environments that participate in and guide the behaviors of the system.

- **Interconnections**: The relationships—including physical, informational, formal, or informal linkages—that bind elements together within the system.

- **Function**: The purpose, goal, or objective of a nonhuman system.

- **Purpose**: The purpose, goal, or objective of a human-based system.

- **Stocks**: These are tangible, quantifiable, and measurable variables within a system that are subject to dynamic changes over time through the actions of a flow. Where the term *element* implies a type of thing at any given time, the term *stock* implies attributes of the elements that have observable values at specific points in time.

- **Flows**: These are actions that dynamically change the directions of stocks within a system as inflows and outflows.

- **Inflows**: These indicate a direction of flow that serves to increase the measurable amount of stock. Inflows are shown in causal loop diagrams as arrows that point to the elements accumulating stock.

- **Outflows**: These indicate a direction of flow that serves to decrease the measurable amount of stock. They are shown in diagrams as arrows that point to the elements accumulating stock. Outflows are shown in causal loop diagrams as arrows that point away from the elements losing stock.

- **Delays**: These are formed when inflows are greater than outflows, resulting in an accumulation of stock. Delays are typically indicated by writing the work *delay* on the arrow connecting elements or with a double hashmark on the connecting arrow.

- **Feedback loops**: These are mechanisms that adjust flows to either stabilize a system or reinforce a certain trend within the system.

- **Balancing feedback loops**: These provide information or resources that bring a system or elements within a system into equilibrium and maintain them within a desired range.

- **Reinforcing feedback loops**: These provide information or resources that support a trend within a system or elements within a system. The trend can be either positive or negative.

- **Positive causal link**: This means that the cause-and-effect impact of two linked nodes are changing the observed attributes in the same (positive) direction, increasing the value of the monitored attributes.

- **Negative causal link**: This means that the cause-and-effect impact of two linked nodes are changing the observed attributes in the opposite (negative) direction.

- **Open systems**: These are characterized by having inflows and outflows external to the system—that is, things that can enter or leave the system.

- **Closed systems**: These are characterized by having no flows in or out of the system—that is, the system is fully self-contained.

- **Labels**: Use labels on everything displayed within your causal diagrams so that reviewers know what the elements and links represent within your system model.

So now, let's run through a few exercises to see how the terms depicted in the preceding list help describe the workings of a system. We'll start with the most basic of systems, comprised of a single element that has both an inflow and an outflow.

Causal modeling of a single-element system

As depicted in *Figure 4.2*, the most basic system includes a single element acting as a stock, with some sort of incoming and outgoing flow:

Figure 4.2 – Single-element system

The system might represent a manufacturing process with the incoming flow of raw materials, a queuing of materials as stocks, and the outgoing flows of a finished product. Or the system could represent an information-oriented transaction, such as the data for a customer order moving to a queue formed in a fulfillment specialist's inbox who then reviews and approves the shipment of the product, which is the outflow.

Causal modeling of a basic Scrum Team system

The preceding system model could depict a Scrum Team working from an external set of requirements from the Product Backlog. In that scenario, the inflows are stories from the Product Backlog, the team's stocks are the work in progress, consisting of tasks and code, and their output is a product feature that meets the definition of *done*.

Now, let's step up the complexity a little bit by adding the two additional elements within our Scrum system model—the **Product Backlog** and **Product Features**. Note that *Figure 4.3* is essentially the same display as *Figure 4.2*, but with additional information added to show the most basic elements of a Scrum Team as a system. The revised labels also provide more information about the types of stocks, inflows, and outflows within our Scrum system model:

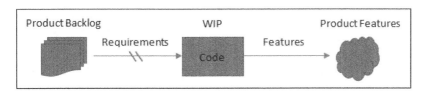

Figure 4.3 – Sample Scrum Team system

From a workflow perspective, requirements flow in from the Product Backlog, forming a queue as a delay at the Sprint Backlog, from which code is developed, and the result is an outflow of new or enhanced product features. As requirements are pulled into the sprint, they temporarily sit in a queue with the development team. The delay is indicated by the double hashmarks on the **Requirements** arrow. If requirements come in at a faster rate than developers can create the features, then the requirements will stay in the queue, and the work in progress will build from sprint to sprint when no actions are taken to reduce the inflow or improve the outflow.

Implementing feedback loops

This model of a Scrum Team as a system is still too elementary, and in this section, we'll continue to add typical types of complexity to the system to demonstrate how system thinking is applied. So now that we have described the basic inputs and outputs of the Scrum Team system, let's put in some feedback loops.

A very common feedback loop in Scrum is the Sprint Planning event. The product owner, Scrum Master, and development team meet to assess Product Backlog priorities, determine the sprint goal, and determine the stories that support the sprint goal. The development team must also assess how much work they can complete within the sprint's duration:

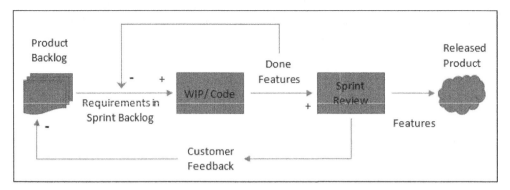

Figure 4.4 – Scrum Team system with feedback loops

Figure 4.4 adds the sprint review meeting with a customer feedback link looping back to the Product Backlog. Note the - sign, which indicates the link from the sprint review's oppositional effect on the Product Backlog. In other words, the values of the two linked nodes are changing in the opposite direction. If the customers are satisfied with the features, then the effect is to remove the requirements from the Product Backlog. If the reviewers are dissatisfied with the new features, or discover the need for new capabilities, then the effect is to add those new requirements back into the Product Backlog.

Note that there is also a negative causal effect, such as the one between **Done Features** and **Requirements**. This link tells us that as the requirements are coded, meeting the definition of *done*, the number of requirements in the **Sprint Backlog** queue are reduced. If the implemented code does not meet the definition of *done*, then the requirements stay in the **Sprint Backlog**.

One final point to be made on this model is that the arrows from the **Product Backlog** to the **WIP/Code**, **Sprint Review**, and **Released Product** nodes represent the flow of requirements and features as a positive linear sequence. So, where the **Done Features** and **Customer Feedback** links are informational, the remaining arrows show the flow of tangible items in the form of requirements and features.

This is a very high-level model of a single sprint, and we can get a lot more granular in the model to further break down other parts of the sprint events. So let's do that and apply these concepts, using **CLDs** to show how systems thinking is applied to analyze Agile practices applied to the **Sprint Planning event**.

Supporting Agile working through systems thinking

In this section, you will learn how to apply systems thinking to work through the entities and relationships involved in analyzing the Sprint Planning event within Scrum. Sounds like a relatively small and simple task, right? Let's find out.

Diagramming causal linkages in Sprint Planning

We do not need to continue adding to our original Scrum Team system models when we are trying to focus in on one particular area within the system. Moreover, the causal diagramming loop modeling approach is better suited to modeling larger and more complex systems. In this section, we will introduce the causal loop diagram, modeling the elements and linkages within Sprint Planning. Look at *Figure 4.5*:

- Customer/end user Requirements
- Flow of Items from Sprint Review
- Flow of Items from External Sources
- # of items in Product Backlog
- Refined items in product backlog
- Prioritized items in Product Backlog
- Defined Sprint Goal in context with product backlog priorities
- Define Design requirements
- Scope the work effort
- Define initial tasks

- Type of work in Sprint Backlog
- Determine team capacity
- Obtain item clarifications from PO and other sources
- Determine tradeoffs
- # of items in Sprint Backlog
- Negotiate items included in Sprint
- Sprint

Figure 4.5 – Elements identified governing the Sprint Planning event

In this model, I have identified the elements related to Sprint Planning, as depicted in the previous figure.

Modeling the requirements flow

Now we need to explore the individual links between these elements. We'll start with a model of the relationships between customer and end user requirements and the flow of items from sprint reviews and external sources.

In *Figure 4.5*, customer and end user requirements flow to the Sprint Planning process from the previous sprint review and from other external sources that the product owner has collected. This is our first example of a causal loop diagram, with many more to follow in this chapter.

The arrows show that there is a positive causal relationship between the requirements and their flow into the sprint review and product owner. There is also a positive causal relationship between the flows and the Product Backlog. In other words, and in all cases, the values of all the linked nodes are changing in the same direction:

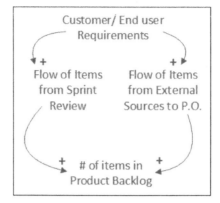

Figure 4.6 – CLD model of analyzing Product Backlog priorities

Now that we have modeled the elements and relationships involved in creating the Product Backlog, let's look at the elements and relationships involved in refining the Product Backlog.

Modeling Product Backlog refinement

If we had a large whiteboard or an electronic equivalent, we could continue to build our Sprint Planning event model from the Product Backlog model shown in *Figure 4.6*. To keep each part of the Sprint Planning model manageable for a book format, I'm going to break each aspect of Sprint Planning into a separate CLD model:

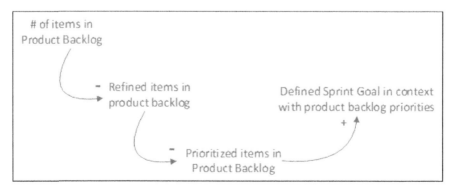

Figure 4.7 – Open CLD model of Product Backlog refinement activities

Figure 4.7 shows the flow of information during the Product Backlog refinement process. This section does not form a loop, and that's OK, since we are only looking at a subset of the larger Sprint Planning event model. This component of the system is closed by other segments that we'll look at later in this section.

This segment starts with the *number of items in the Product Backlog* node and flows to the refined items and prioritized items nodes, before ending with the sprint goal definition node. Note that the first three nodes have a negative causal link. The Product Backlog holds the entire subset of identified requirements, but only a smaller set of the items makes it through the refinement and prioritization activities. On the other hand, the flow of Product Backlog items from the refinement and prioritization activities has a positive causal link, as the selected items add information to the sprint goal definition activity.

Modeling design and task clarifications

The next set of activities related to Sprint Planning have to do with determining the design and scope of work necessary to finalize the sprint goal. This segment includes the previously identified *Defined Sprint Goal in context with Product Backlog priorities* node.

Figure 4.8 includes two loops. The bottom loop shows how the sprint goal impacts both the product design and work-scoping efforts, and how both have a positive causal relationship. The upper loop includes a couple of important causal relationships. First, the product design activities impact the scope of work required to complete the development effort. In addition, both the design and scoping efforts are impacted by clarifications from the product owner, customers, users, and other stakeholders:

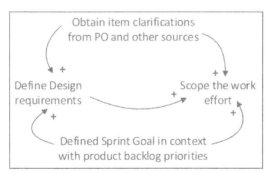

Figure 4.8 – CLD model of design and work clarifications

Typically, the development team directly seeks out those experts for clarification of requirements, and those interactions could be included in our CLD model; however, I would also argue that the impact of those interactions is outside the Sprint Planning system, unless the impact of the interactions serves to delay the clarification process. If that situation occurs, then I would add them to our CLD model.

At this point, we have a couple of paths to follow: we can follow the path that describes the negotiation and tradeoff activities with the product owner or we can look at the path the development team takes to determine the work that is required and their capacity to complete it in the upcoming sprint. Let's start with a model of the onward path.

Modeling sprint capacity assessments

The CLD shown in *Figure 4.9* provides a visual model of the entities and relationships identified that were identified to compare the anticipated work to the team's capacity. The assessment begins with the **Define Design requirements** node, which has a direct and positive impact on the work-scoping effort. In other words, the **Scope of the work effort** node changes in the same direction as changes to the design:

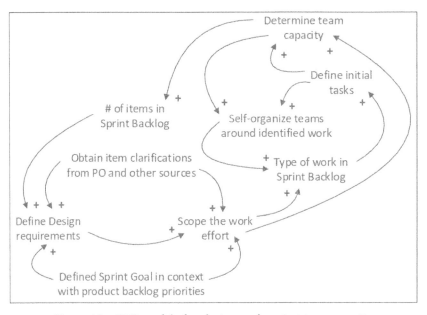

Figure 4.9 – CLD model of analyzing work against team capacity

The model retains the *Obtain item clarifications from P.O. and other sources* node, as the input is necessary to fully assess the design requirements and the scope of work required to develop the desired features and functionality. The scoping effort has a direct and positive causal relationship with the *Type of work in Sprint Backlog* node. In other words, as the scope of work is identified, the type of work required to support the development effort moves in the same direction.

The type of work that is identified has a direct and positive impact on the *Define initial tasks* node, as the identified tasks are dependent upon the identification of the scope of work and type of work proposed for the Sprint Backlog. Similarly, as the initial tasks are identified, the team can begin to self-organize, allocating work to those who are best suited to complete each task, as depicted in the direct and positive link to the *Self-organize teams around identified work* node. At the same time, the development team must decide how much work they can take on, which is identified in a direct and positive link to the *Determine team capacity* node.

The *Determine team capacity* node has direct and positive impact on the team's ability to self-organize, and on the number of items selected for the Sprint Backlog. Both of those relationships are direct and positive, indicating the impacts' trend in the same direction. For example, when the team's capacity allows the inclusion of additional work, the number of items in the Sprint Backlog increases and the team is better able to self-organize in support of the work. Likewise, the items in the Sprint Backlog and the team's ability to self-organize are limited when the team's capacity is limited.

As complex as this visual model already is, this section of the Sprint Planning process can be enhanced. For example, the development team may consider adding elements and linkages to indicate the skills within the development team, as that relationship has an impact on the team's capacity and ability to effectively self-organize to accomplish the proposed work.

We're almost done with the construction of our CLD diagram for Sprint Planning. What remains is modeling the elements and relationships that define the sprint negotiations and tradeoff activities.

Modeling sprint negotiations and tradeoffs

Figure 4.10 displays a CLD diagram that models the negotiation and tradeoff activities that the development teams conduct with the product owner to bring the scope of work in alignment with their capacity to deliver within the sprint. This visual diagram starts with the *Define Design requirements* node and loops to the left to indicate a direct and positive relationship with the *Determine tradeoffs* node.

In other words, as the design complexity changes, which also involves feedback from the work-scoping and clarifications loop, the tradeoff options change in the same direction. If the design and work is more than the team can take on, or there is insufficient information to start the development work, then the development team must meet with the product owner to evaluate potential tradeoffs and to possibly renegotiate the scope of work anticipated for the sprint:

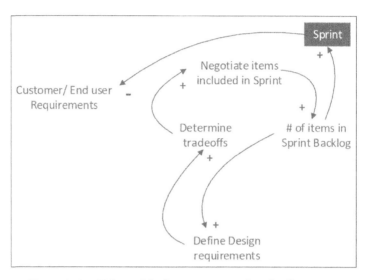

Figure 4.10 – CLD model of negotiations and tradeoff activities

The link between the *Determine tradeoffs* node and the *Negotiate items included in Sprint* node is direct and positive as changes in the tradeoffs require similar changes in the negotiations. In other words, a request for a tradeoff requires a similar agreement in the negotiations, and vice-versa. One the negotiations are complete, the number of items included in the Sprint Backlog change in the same direction, as indicated by the direct and positive causal arrow between the *Negotiate items included in Sprint* node and the *number of items in Sprint Backlog* node.

We have now modeled all the primary elements and relationships involved in the Sprint Planning event. So far, the individual CLD diagrams have modeled individual loops to make it simper to discuss and display important activities, participants, and relationships within the Sprint Planning event. In actual practice, the participants in the modeling effort would collaborate on the entire Sprint Planning event and build the CLD model incrementally as they identify participating entities and relationships. We'll see what this looks like in the next section.

Putting it all together

When a team is working collaboratively at a large white board, they may choose to brainstorm the Sprint Planning event to define the entities and relationships incrementally, and in an ad hoc manner. In other words, they may come up with a lesser or greater number of entities and relationships, and these may not be defined in the order presented in the previous sections. They may also have a different set of entities and relationships, depending on how they conduct Sprint Planning. Over time, they will expose the entire model, and it can be quite large and complex, as shown in *Figure 4.11*. This CLD diagram shows all the elements and relationships for Sprint Planning previously described in this chapter:

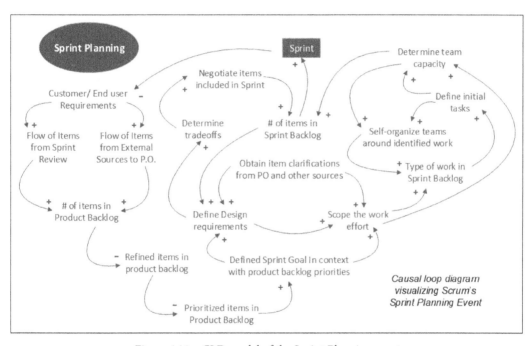

Figure 4.11 – CLD model of the Sprint Planning event

The Sprit Planning event is but one component of the Scrum framework. Other Scrum events and roles have equal levels of complexity that should be modeled by the participants most affected. Every product-development effort is unique, and the Scrum Teams should model their identified entities and relationships to understand the complexity of their product-development systems.

In addition, modern systems often involve the simultaneous development of multiple and integrated components and products. Coordinating events across development teams that are working across portfolios and programs adds to the complexity. Systems thinking is necessary to deal with such complexities. We'll explore how systems thinking is an important analysis tool for developing large and complex products in the next section.

Applying systems thinking to large, complex, and integrated products

I've noted in previous sections that the original developers of Scrum, Jeff Sutherland and Ken Schwaber, both intended it to scale beyond the small product or single project. Interestingly, both Sutherland and Schwaber have extended the basic Scrum concepts to include new guidance on methods to scale Scrum across large products and at an enterprise level.

For example, Jeff Sutherland founded his new company Scrum@Scale for this purpose, and Ken Schwaber introduced his Nexus framework at Scrum.org for scaling Scrum.

We'll discuss both of these Scrum scaling approaches, along with several others, in Section Two of this book. But before we get to those chapters, we need to understand how systems thinking aids in the analysis required to deal with the increasing complexity of scaling Scrum, Lean, and Agile practices on an enterprise scale.

Putting the focus on products, not projects

In this section, you'll learn how to use systems thinking to analyze the complexities of deploying and maintaining multiple teams working on developing a single, large, and complex product. Before we begin, let's start by taking a quick look at how large projects were managed under the traditional project-based development model. This comparison helps set the as-is baseline that most organizations start from before we move on to Scrum.

Traditionally, using program-management concepts, the oversight of large and complex product-development efforts fell to the program manager and their **program-management office** (**PMO**). Under the traditional **systems-development life cycle** (**SDLC**) model, the program manager and PMO staff break up the overall work effort across multiple project teams, and the integration of work is managed via **an integrated master schedule** (**IMS**).

There is no fast rule on how to divide development work activities. The work assigned to each project team may be broken down by systems, applications, modules, types of related functionality, skills, or other criteria. Each project team defines the activities and tasks necessary to produce and deliver their assigned deliverables and then sends their planned schedules and updates back to the PMO for inclusion within the IMS. In other words, the IMS includes all identified deliverables and related activities and tasks supporting the authorized scope of work and spanning all participating project teams.

By definition, all programs and projects have constraints on budgets, time, scope of work, deliverables, resources, and quality. These constraints form the boundaries for what's in and what's out of a project.

Moreover, project-management philosophies hinge on the principles that all project-based work is unique and, therefore, at least some of the details are identified or fine-tuned throughout the project. The project's constraints help the executives monitor progress against the budgets and schedules that justified the investments, and help prevent unapproved scope creep from setting in.

The traditional project-management model does not look at the long-term life cycle requirements of developing, maintaining, and enhancing a product. New programs and projects must be approved, typically on an annual budget cycle, to address new product requirements or enhancements that were not identified in the previous program or project specifications. Consequently, project-based development philosophies are not inherently responsive enough to address evolving market opportunities or changes in customer or end user needs.

Scrum eliminates project-oriented practices and instead puts the focus on products. Moreover, continued development and support activities are sustained across the life of the product. Ideally, each new budget cycle simply determines the amount of funding required to sustain the development and support team activities for each product over the next fiscal planning period, until the product reaches its end of life.

Let's move on and look at some of the elements and relationships involved in transforming the development activities from a program or project-oriented development activity to a product-oriented development activity. As with the Sprint Planning CLD modeling activity, we'll start by identifying the elements and relationships involved in this transformation.

Modeling project-to-product team transformations

The previous section, with its focus on Sprint Planning, looked at a relatively small part of the Scrum framework. This section provides a model of the rest of the Scrum events and the added complexity of supporting the development of a large and complex solution involving multiple Scrum Teams.

The scope of this model is fairly large, so for this exercise, we will stay at a fairly high level in our analysis. In practice, the Product Owners and other planning participants will further decompose many of the elements to analyze their unique circumstances.

Similar to the strategy employed with our analysis of the Sprint Planning event, *Figure 4.12* provides a list of identified elements. The model is based on several assumptions: the product already exists, and the organization's executives are looking for a better approach to aligning further development in support of customer's needs, while also benefitting from improvements in productivity:

Elements impacted by project-to-product team transformation	
• A burning platform situation • Executives read this and other books on Scrum • Executives feel pressure to make changes to product development approach • Enterprise Scrum team established • Number of missed requirements • Product release delays • Product Quality Issues • Development of Scrum teams • Determine Product-oriented team needs • Alignment of development resources • Optimized Scrum teams • Number of Scrum Teams • Scrum training • Promote Initial successes	• Decision to scale Scrum to improve large and complex product development activities • Remove impediments to deploying Scrum and Scrum teams • Product owner establishes product backlog based on priorities and value • Focus on high priority backlog items • Focus on high value product backlog items • Sprint goals established on backlog priorities • Required Scrum team skills and experience • Roll-out of pilot teams • Staged roll-out of additional Scrum teams

Figure 4.12 – Elements involved in implementing Scrum on large and complex products

Bear in mind that there is no single approach to laying out a CLD diagram, and organizations have unique issues that they have to deal with. This model is but one potential set of elements and issues facing an organization that wishes to implement Scrum to support the development of a large and complex product or service.

Modeling a burning platform situation

Figure 4.13 is a visual model of the response that an organization might take to address a **burning platform** situation involving the long-term development and sustainment of a large and complex product offering. The term *burning platform* is a business analogy involving a situation where the company is facing a critical problem that is putting the firm at risk of going under.

The analogy comes from the story of a fellow who was on a burning oil platform at sea and was faced with a decision to jump into freezing waters, and perhaps perish, or face the certainty of dying if he stayed on the burning oil platform. He jumped and lived. The point of the story is that it's often better to take an action that might cause failure than staying where you are and facing certain failure:

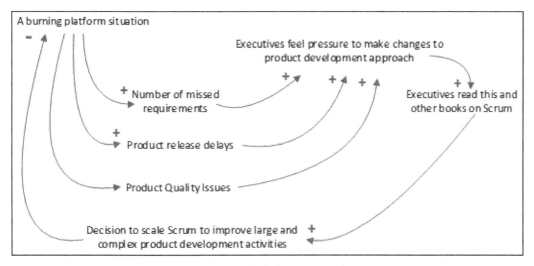

Figure 4.13 – CLD model of a burning platform situation

In our model, the executives have observed that they are missing important customer requirements, missing release dates, and having product quality issues. All these effects are direct and positive indicator of the burning platform situation facing the company. Faced with these situations, the executives do some research, read mine and other books on scaling Scrum, and decide it's time to jump into the Scrum waters. That decision had a direct but negative (oppositional) effect on the burning platform.

Modeling Scrum scaling activities

Figure 4.14 is a visual model of the elements that are identified for the system to scale in an Agile manner in support of the development of a large and complex product. Remember from the previous subsection that the executives decided to jump off their burning platform and into the unknown waters of implementing Scrum on a large scale. That decision is where this diagram starts.

As the first order of business, the organization has implemented an enterprise Scrum Team to oversee the implementation of Scrum. The enterprise Scrum Team both evaluates the needs for the implementation and removes any impediments that arise during and after the implementation. This team operates at the enterprise level, not at the product level.

Some of the issues they must address include determining the needs to implement product-oriented teams, understand the skills and experiences needed on each team, and deciding how many teams are required and the makeup of each team in terms of skills. These are all direct and positive (in the same direction) effects of the establishment of the enterprise Scrum Team.

Those same elements directly impact the organization's ability to define optimized Scrum Teams for their product. Again, the relationships are direct and positive. The removal of impediments impacts the organization's ability to optimize the teams and ensure the teams receive adequate skills, through training, coaching, and mentoring resources. These relationships are negative, or oppositional, in effect. In other words, with the removal of impediments, more Scrum training is provided, and more optimized teams are created:

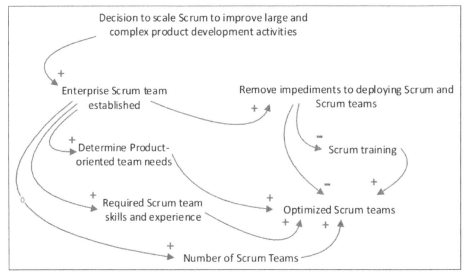

Figure 4.14 – CLD model of Scrum scaling activities

At this point, we can start to look at the elements involved in developing and refining the Product Backlog, and the assignment of Scrum Teams to develop the desired product capabilities.

Modeling the development of the Product Backlog and rolling out Scrum Teams

Figure 4.15 looks at the issue of missing requirements and how the organization can develop Product Backlogs and ultimately establish Scrum development teams to build the highest-value and highest-priority features. Both product value and priority assessments have direct and positive outflows from the identification of missing requirements relationship.

For simplicity, the model does not get into the elements involved in finding and developing a product owner to support the development and refinement of the Product Backlog. But certainly, those are important factors that the enterprise Scrum team must address.

With the assessment and identification of high-priority and high-value items, the product owner builds the Product Backlog. Items with higher priorities and value flow into the backlog with direct and positive relationships.

The development of the Product Backlog allows the subsequent development of sprint goals and backlogs. Before we do this, we need the development and assignment of Scrum Teams. In the previous section, we modeled the elements in our system that remove the impediments to providing Scrum training and the definition of optimized Scrum Teams. Those elements allow the organization to assign the Scrum Teams. The relationship between removing impediments and the assignment of Scrum Teams is negative, as they move in opposite directions—that is, having fewer impediments leads to the capacity to have more team assignments. The definition of optimized Scrum Teams has a direct and positive relationship with the assignment of Scrum Teams.

The assignment of Scrum Teams has a direct and positive relationship with the rollout of pilot Scrum Teams and with the rollout of additional Scrum Teams over time. The assignment of Scrum Teams also has a direct and positive relationship with the establishment of sprint goals. In other words, the teams are available to develop the sprint goals and Sprint Backlog:

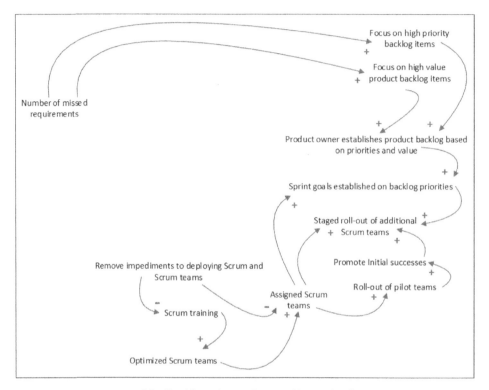

Figure 4.15 – CLD model of building the Product Backlog and rolling out Scrum Teams

We could go on and model the elements and relationships involved in running the development sprints. I've stopped the model here as this is the scope of the effort that is most involved in realigning the organization's development resources into product-oriented teams. Now let's look at what these models look like when combined.

Modeling the rollout of Scrum in a large product environment

Figure 4.16 puts all the previous models from this section into a single model. The visual model shows the burning platform situation that helped us understand the issues that put the company at risk. That assessment led to the organization's executive conducting research and discovering how scaled Scrum concepts could help resolve those issues.

Two causal loops evolve from the burning platform situation and assessment. One loop, shown in the lower left-hand side of the diagram, shows the elements and relationships that lead to the assignment of Scrum Teams. The other loop, shown on the right side of the model, depicts the identified elements and relationships that lead to the discovery of the highest-priority and highest-value requirements, which become the baseline items making up the Product Backlog. As the Product Backlog is defined, the Scrum Teams are assigned to develop the desired features, starting with pilot teams and rolling out additional Scrum Teams over time.

Note that an additional line was shown to form a linkage between the *Staged roll-out of additional Scrum Teams* node to the initial *Burning platform situation* node. This relationship completes the causal loop. The relationship is negative to indicate the oppositional effect the implementation of Scrum Teams has on the burning platform— that is, adding more Scrum Teams should reduce the effect of the burning platform situation:

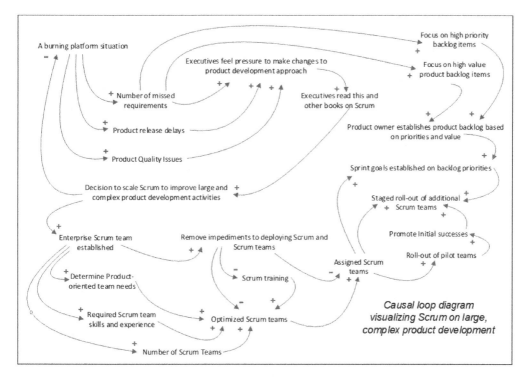

Figure 4.16 – CLD model of a large product rollout of Scrum

In the next and final section of this chapter, you will learn how to apply systems thinking to enterprise implementations of Scrum.

Applying systems thinking to enterprise implementations of Scrum

The organizational structures, roles, and responsibilities in Scrum are very different than those employed in the traditional hierarchical organization that employs program and project-management concepts to deliver products. Scrum eliminates the need for functional departments and flattens the organization by providing only three roles: product owner, Scrum Master, and developers. Scrum also eliminates the need for detailed project planning and scheduling, and instead employs empirical process control concepts to iteratively deliver new increments of functionality as market, customer, and end user priorities dictate:

Elements impacted by enterprise Scrum transformation	
• Chief/ LOB Executives make business decision for transformation	• Assign Resources to work Transformation impediments
• Burning Platform	• Number of development teams
• Competitive Advantage	• Remove scrum deployment impediments
• Identify Resources to work transformation impediments	• Selection of Product Owner
• Size and Complexity of Organization	• Selection of Scrum Master
• Scrum Team needs assessment	• Selection of Development Team members
• Reassignment of department level resources	• Assignment of Scrum teams to support product promotions and marketing
• Reassignment of Program Manager	• Assignment of Scrum teams to support product-oriented partnerships
• Reassignment of PMO resources	• Assignment of Scrum teams to support product support
• Reassignment of Project Managers	
• Reassignment of Project Team Members	• Assignment of Scrum teams to support delivery
• Determine	• Assignment of Scrum teams to support product supply chain
• Elimination of detailed project plans	• Self-organizing teams
• Elimination of Product Specifications	• Self-contained teams
• Elimination of project schedules	• Implementation of product backlog
• Establish roll-out plan	• Implementation of sprint planning events
• Establish coaching and mentoring resources	

Figure 4.17 – Identified elements involved in an enterprise Scrum implementation

In the previous section, you learned how to begin to assess the elements that could potentially impact a project-to-product development team transformation. In this section, you will learn how to apply systems thinking to an enterprise-scale deployment of Scrum. This section is not meant to provide an all-inclusive systems-oriented assessment of the project-to-product team transformation. But it will serve as a starting point for you and your teams to think about your unique transformation situations.

As with the previous two sections, the Scrum implementation analysts use the same CLD diagramming techniques to assess the causal relationships between elements in the enterprise Scrum transformation program. *Figure 4.17* provides the list of elements identified for the enterprise-scale Scrum transformation activity.

Modeling the business drivers affecting business transformation decisions

Similar to the large product Scrum implementation, this model starts with a set of issues that can drive executive management to look to some type of major organizational transformation initiative. The business drivers identified include a burning platform, seeking a competitive advantage, the pursuit of market opportunities, more responsiveness, and the reforming of bloated, bureaucratic, and unwieldy organizational structures:

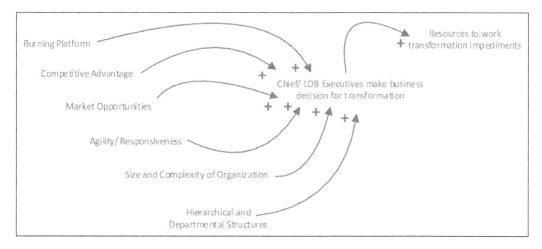

Figure 4.18 – CLD model of business drivers affecting business transformation decisions

All of these elements provide direct and positive impacts on the organization's executive in providing some sort of business transformation, such as the implementation of Scrum on an enterprise scale. Once that decision is made, resources are required to eliminate any impediments to the transformation.

Modeling the impact of resources to remove organizational impediments

Figure 4.19 shows the resources identified to carry out the enterprise transformation to Scrum. The resources identified follow Scrum's basic guidelines on limiting roles to those of a product owner, scrum master, and Scrum team members. The primary difference in this model is that these roles operate at an enterprise level, and the product they support is enterprise Scrum:

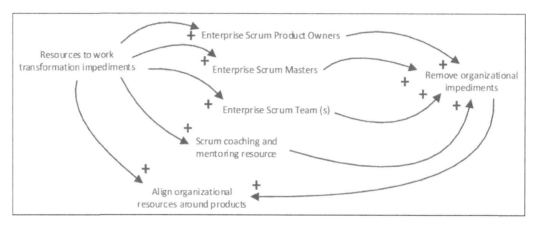

Figure 4.19 – CLD model of resources to remove enterprise-level impediments

Additional resources for Scrum training, coaching, and mentoring are also identified as necessary elements to eliminate impediments to the enterprise deployment of Scrum. All relationships identified in this CLD model of the resources required to remove enterprise-level impediments are positive. As resource requirements increase, the resources should respond in the same direction. Likewise, as enterprise Scrum resources become available, the organization's ability to remove impediments increases.

Modeling the impact of Scrum Team needs assessments

Figure 4.20 is a larger and more complex CLD model that depicts how a decision to implement Scrum on an enterprise-scale affects the development of Scrum Teams, not only at the product-development level, but also across product-support functions. The identified product-support teams in this model include development, marketing, partnerships, product support, delivery support, and supply chain.

There is no single or correct way to align organizational resources in support of its products. Not every organization requires all of the product-support functions listed, while other products may have additional support requirements. This model stays purposely at a very high level. Ideally, the enterprise Scrum product owner will identify functional teams to model each of the product-support functions and ultimately determine the best structures for their enterprise Scrum implementations.

To simplify this model, I have bounded the Type Scrum Teams and Scrum Teams within rectangular boxes. Each of the types of Scrum Teams require a deeper dive to understand the elements and relationships that impact the organization's ability to provide adequate support services for each of their products. Each type of team requires further assessment on the number of teams required, the number of people needed to support each effort, and the necessary skills and experiences of those team members.

Figure 4.20 is not a closed loop. The loop is closed when other elements are included in later sections. Instead, this section of the larger CLD diagram shows how the need to align organizational resources around products impacts decisions on product definitions, Scrum Team needs assessments, the functional activities of identified Scrum Teams, and training, coaching, and mentoring requirements. All relationships are positive, meaning that the impacts trend in the same direction between elements:

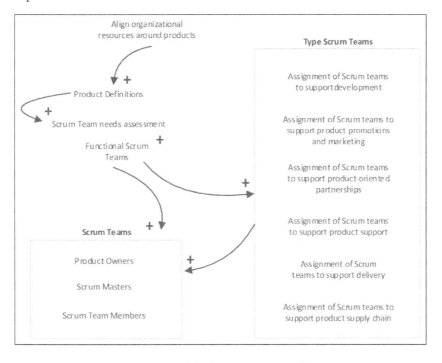

Figure 4.20 – CLD model of Scrum Team needs assessments

For example, the impact of deciding to align organizational resources around products leads to an increase in the need to define products. With an increase of defined products, there is an increase in the need to assess Scrum Team requirements. An increase in the Scrum Team needs assessments leads to an increase in defining the functions of identified Scrum Teams. The identification of Scrum Team functions leads to further definition of the types of Scrum Teams required, which also has a positive impact on the definition of Scrum Team Member requirements.

Modeling the elements supporting Scrum events and Scrum Team deployments

At this point in the model, we have analyzed the business drivers that impact the executive decisions to seek business transformations and identify the need to install a team to work through the impediments of the change initiative. Next, we explored the types of resources needed to manage the enterprise-scale transition to Scrum and its impact on the organization's ability to addresses impediments that hinder the transition. Finally, in the last section, we looked at the elements involved in defining the organization's products, determining the supporting functional requirements and types of Scrum Teams and resources needed to support those efforts.

Now, in *Figure 4.21*, we will look at the parts of the enterprise Scrum implementation system that both impact and support the organization's ability to roll out the Scrum Teams on an enterprise scale. The assessment starts with the same Scrum Team requirements box identified in the previous *Figure 4.20*:

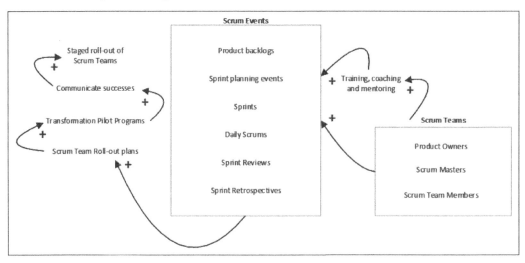

Figure 4.21 – CLD model of the rollout of Scrum Teams and events

In the CLD model, the identification of the need for Scrum Team Members has a positive impact on the need to provide training, coaching, and mentoring to ensure each team's success. In turn, the training, coaching and mentoring allows the identified Scrum Teams to support the Scrum events as they deploy.

The ability of the teams to support Scrum events, as each are stood up, has a positive impact on the organization's ability to plan the rollout of the Scrum Teams, initially as pilot engagements. The success of the pilot engagements, or lack thereof, has a direct and positive impact on the organization's ability to proceed with a staged rollout of additional Scrum Teams. Now we can look at how the staged rollout impacts the business drivers that caused the enterprise Scrum transformation.

Modeling the elements that close the loop to address business drivers

We left off with the staged rollout of Scrum Teams in the last section. *Figure 4.22* shows that the staged rollout of each new team has different impacts on each of the business drivers that justified the organizational transformation to enterprise-wide Scrum:

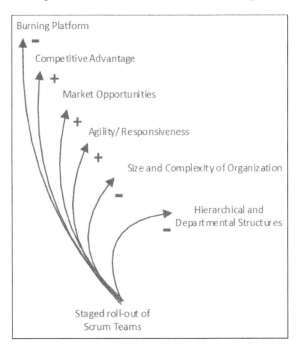

Figure 4.22 – CLD model of Scrum Teams' impact on business drivers

Again, remember that the positive sign indicates that the changes between the elements trend in the same direction, while a negative sign indicates that the trend between elements is oppositional. So this section of the model indicates that each successful deployment of a Scrum Team reduces the impact of the burning platform situation, reduces the size and complexity of the organization, and decreases the organization's reliance on or need for hierarchical and departmental structures.

On the other hand, each successful Scrum Team deployment improves the organization's competitive advantage, allows the organization to pursue attractive market opportunities, and be more Agile (that is, more adaptive) and responsive to their customers' and end user needs.

Modeling the entire enterprise Scrum transformation

Now, as shown in *Figure 4.23*, we can put the entire enterprise Scrum transformation model together. This is a highly simplified model; in a real-world situation, this model would only serve as an initial baseline for the transformation. Many of the elements would require much deeper analysis, with increasingly complex CLD diagrams, to explore all the potential elements involved, and their *cause-and-effect* relationships:

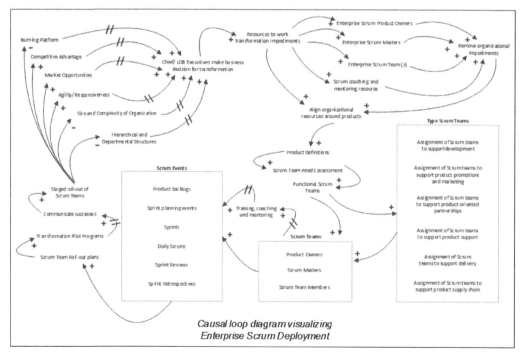

Figure 4.23 – CLD model of enterprise Scrum transformation

If you have a keen eye, you may have noticed the hashed lines added to the preceding CLD model. These represent delays in the effects of the relationships between nodes. We'll take some time in the next section to better understand the potential cause of the delays.

Modeling delays between enterprise Scrum transformation elements

To keep things simple, I haven't yet addressed the subject of delays since the initial model of the sprint cycle in *Figure 4.1*. Now that the baseline model is complete, let's take a look at some of the more obvious relationships that may experience delays between causes and effects.

As noted in the previous section, the CLD displayed in *Figure 4.23* includes double hashmarks (//) on several of the arrows. These hashmarks indicate delays between causes and effects among the connected elements. Depending on each organization's unique circumstances, there may be causes for delays at virtually all of the elemental connections. But to keep things relatively simple, let's focus on these.

Note that all of the business drivers connected to the chief/L.O.B. executives which delay the business decisions for transformation elements. The delay occurs because it takes time for the chief executives to diagnose the issues, and to set a course of action.

Another potential source of delays is in the provisioning of training, coaching, and mentoring services to newly formed Scrum Teams. Likewise, their ability to effectively implement Scrum events is dependent upon the time it takes for the individuals and team as a collective to master the elements of Scrum.

Finally, there is a delay between the deployment of the pilot Scrum Teams and the communications of their efforts. Until product features are released and available for demonstration, there is not much to report, and there will not be a commercial success to indicate a success until the product is released.

Review of CLD patterns

This chapter has introduced a number of causal loop diagrams to describe the complexity of various Scrum and Agile event patterns. *Figure 4.24* provides a listing of all the CLDs presented in this book:

Figure 3.2 - Single element system	Figure 3.3 - Sample Scrum Team System	Figure 3.4 - Scrum Team System with Feedback Loops	Figure 3.5 - Elements identified governing the sprint planning event
Figure 3.6 - CLD model of Analyzing Product Backlog Priorities	Figure 3.7 - Open CLD model of Product Backlog Refinement Activities	Figure 3.8 - CLD model of design and work clarifications	Figure 3.9 - CLD model of Analyzing Work against Team Capacity
Figure 3.10 - CLD model of Negotiations and Tradeoff Activities	Figure 3.11 - CLD model of Sprint Planning Event	Figure 3.13 - CLD model of burning platform situation	Figure 3.14 - CLD model of Scrum Scaling Activities
Figure 3.15 - CLD model of building the product backlog and rolling out Scrum teams	Figure 3.16 - CLD model of a large product roll-out of Scrum	Figure 3.18 - CLD model of business drivers affecting business transformation decisions	Figure 3.19 - CLD model of resources to remove enterprise-level impediments
Figure 3.20 - CLD model of Scrum team needs assessments	Figure 3.21 - CLD model of roll out of Scrum Teams and events	Figure 3.22 - CLD model of Scrum teams' impact on business drivers	Figure 3.23 - CLD model of Enterprise Scrum transformation

Figure 4.24 – Index of Scrum/Agile CLD patterns

This concludes the content on systems thinking. Before we go, let's take a moment to summarize what you have learned.

Summary

In this chapter, you have learned that systems thinking provides a way to analyze the complexity caused by the stochastic impacts of interrelating elements within a system. Complexity in a system goes up with each increase in the number of participating elements and relationships.

You have learned that a system is more than the sum of its parts. This complexity arises because of the exponential growth in potential cause-and-effect relationships as the number of elements increases.

 We also went through the concepts and vocabulary of systems thinking and learned how to apply those concepts to issues related to the implementation of Agile capabilities. In addition, you also saw how to apply systems thinking to analyze the elements and relationships within a Sprint Planning event when employing Scrum to support a large and complex product-development activity, and as part of an enterprise Scrum transformation.

In the next chapter, we will learn how to apply lean–agile concepts in similar scenarios.

Questions

1. Provide examples of complex things that act as a system related to information technology.

2. Explain why complexity increases with the number of participating elements and relationships within a system.

3. Use the mathematical model of $n(n-1)/2$ to demonstrate how system complexity increases.

4. What is an element or node within a system?

5. Explain the difference between negative and positive causal links.

6. What are the primary differences between open and closed systems?

7. What are stocks within a system?

8. Explain the concept of flows within a system, including inflows and outflows.

9. What types of feedback loop exist within a system, and what are their differences?

10. What is the purpose of causal modeling?

Further reading

- Capra, F., Luisi, P.L. (2014) *The Systems View of Life. A Unifying Vision*. Cambridge University Press. Cambridge, UK.

- Kuppler, T., Garnett, T. Morehead, T. (2013) Build the Culture Advantage. *The Culture Advantage*, LLC. Washington Township, MI.

- Meadows, H., Wright, D. (2008) *Thinking in Systems*. Chelsea Green Publishing. White River Junction, VT.

- Rutherford, A. (2018) *The Systems Thinker. Essential Thinking Skills for Solving Problems, Managing Chaos, and Creating Lasting Solutions in a Complex World*. Kindle Direct Publishing. San Bernardino, CA.

- Rutherford, A. (2019) *The Elements of Thinking in Systems. Use System Archetypes to Understand, Manage, and Fix Complex Problems and Make Smarter Decisions*. Kindle Direct Publishing. San Bernardino, CA.

- Stroh, D.P. (2015) *Systems Thinking for Social Change. A Practical Guide to Solving Complex Problems, Avoiding Unintended Consequences, and Achieving Lasting Results*. Chelsea Green Publishing. White River Junction, VT.

5
Lean Thinking

This chapter discusses how to improve organizational efficiencies and value by applying Lean development practices across all value creation and value delivery activities.

Scrum is a well-defined and optimized framework at the small project team level. However, the addition of multiple development teams, products, and customers quickly introduces complex dynamics that the original Scrum Guide does not address. In effect, the life cycle of the product development function becomes a very complex system at larger scales.

The application of Lean development principles focuses organizational resources on improving customer value, eliminating waste, improving the flow of work, building only what is wanted as its needed, and seeking perfection. These principles help address the complexities of software and systems development when scaling Scrum or any other set of Agile practices.

In this chapter, you will learn the basics of Lean concepts and the application of Lean concepts as applied to Agile software development practices. It's important to make this connection as Lean-Agile practices are at the heart of modern scaled Agile practices, such as the **Scaled Agile Framework (SAFe®)**. After learning the basic concepts, we're going to dive deeper into the application of Lean-Agile practices to software and systems development.

Lean practices originated to enhance manufacturing capabilities within Toyota, a Japanese automaker. The practice of *Lean production* in manufacturing employs the basic concept of doing more with less by eliminating all forms of *waste*. The simplest way to define waste is any activity in the development and delivery of a product or service that the customer doesn't value and therefore doesn't want to pay for.

The application of Lean concepts to software development is a more recent development. But, before we get to that discussion, we need to understand the basic concepts of *Lean Thinking* as they originated in manufacturing. That is the subject of the first section of the chapter.

Before we move on to this discussion, let me address a question you might already have: *why do we care about how Lean was developed to support manufacturing practices?* There are two parts to the answer. First, though initially developed to address efficiency issues within manufacturing companies, the principles apply equally well to service-oriented industries, such as the software industry. The second issue is that scaled Agile and scaled Scrum implementations often involve the management of very large and complex products with parallel development activities. In addition, modern **cyber-physical systems** involve the integration of manufactured products and associated software and control system components, creating more development complexities. Therefore, the management philosophies of Lean development and Agile-based software development practices need to be likewise aligned and integrated.

The discussions on Lean thinking strategies span the remaining two chapters of this module. This chapter introduces the basics of **Lean development**, while the following chapter discusses how Lean development practices apply in the domains of software and systems development.

We'll start our introduction to Lean development by covering the following topics:

- Introduction to the basics of Lean Thinking
- Eliminating all forms of waste
- Creating customer-centric value
- Improving value stream efficiencies
- Moving from Push to Pull production scheduling approaches
- Seeking perfection is always the goal

OK, let's get started on understanding the basics of Lean Thinking.

Understanding the basics of Lean Thinking

In their book *Lean Thinking*, James Womack and Daniel Jones summarized the five principles of Lean Thinking as follows:

> *Precisely specify value by specific product, identify the value stream for each product, make value flow without interruptions, let the customer pull value from the producer, and pursue perfection.*

These five principles – value, value stream, flow, pull, and perfection – form the foundations of Lean Thinking. In this section, we will explore each of these five Lean principles in some detail. Before we get into the details, however, let's start with the basics.

The original concepts of the Lean movement were born in the Toyota Motor Company and are maintained by Toyota to this day in what is now referred to as the **Toyota Production System (TPS)**. Toyota continues to promote the guiding principles of Lean and its managerial approach and production as a philosophy called The Toyota Way.

The founder of Toyota, Sakichi Toyoda, his son Kiichiro Toyoda, and industrial engineer Taiichi Ohno are credited with creating the initial Lean manufacturing concepts, which were then referred to as **Just-in-Time (JIT)** production or JIT manufacturing.

Classifying types of waste

At its most basic level, Lean Thinking employs methodologies to dramatically improve the efficiencies and throughput of business and production processes through the elimination of all forms of waste. The Japanese word *Muda* means waste and is often used in that context when discussing Lean production concepts.

For of this book, we'll use the English word *waste* going forward. In the context of Lean Thinking, waste is any form of human activity that employs organizational resources but creates no value in the eyes of the customer.

Taiichi Ohno identified the most common forms of waste as follows:

- **Waiting** – delays in processing, including any time products spend waiting or in a queue with no value being added
- **Overproduction** – producing more of something than you need, or than your customer's currently want
- **Extra-processing** – over-processing or conducting any non-value-added activity
- **Transportation** – wasted time, resources, and costs moving products and materials from one location to another

- **Motion** – unnecessary movement, motion, or activities by people

- **Inventory** – carrying and storing any materials and products not undergoing a value-added activity

- **Defects** – in the product or services produced

Lean thinking embodies these same categories of waste to this day. Although, an eighth category was later added to refer to the waste of **unused human talent and intellect**. The elimination of waste is the defining characteristic of Lean Thinking.

As mentioned at the start of this chapter, the five primary elements of Lean Thinking are value, value streams, flow, pull, and perfection. Before we look at these principles in detail, in later parts of this chapter, let's start with a quick introduction to each term.

Introducing the foundational principles behind Lean Thinking

Value is defined as what our customers want – usually expressed as goods or services. Value is not simply what we can deliver or what our markets or competitors are delivering, because those items may not be the things that customers really want. Value is an assessment of the whole product and the definition of value is subject to continuous refinement as customer needs and competitive factors change over time.

The term **solution** is a more accurate representation of what value is as opposed to the terms products, goods, and services. The term solution implies a product or service that specifically addresses identified end-users and customer needs, and not simply filling a niche.

Finally, the concept of value in Lean looks at costs from the perspective of what the lowest total price can be if all waste is eliminated. A more traditional approach to pricing is to assess what customers are willing to pay, reduce that number by the desired profit margin, and then work backward to estimate the highest costs the organization can tolerate However, organizations that simply focus their process improvement activities on meeting current customer and market pricing expectations will find themselves at risk from competitors who strive to do better.

Value streams include all the seller's activities or tasks from the start of value creation until the delivery of value in the form of products or services to end-user customers. Every product or service has multiple value streams defining how the products and services are conceived and designed, how they are produced, how they are sold and ordered, and how they are delivered to customers. Moreover, large and complex solutions may involve value streams extended across their external suppliers and solution delivery partners.

The goal of every Lean effort is to make each value stream as small and efficient as possible. In other words, value streams should have the least possible number of steps, use the least amount of resources, and take the least amount of time possible. Value stream analysis requires the identification of all activities from the final delivery of a product or service backward through all delivery, production, order taking, and design processes. Large and complex products with multiple components may have multiple value streams that span delivery, production, order taking, and design processes for each component.

Value streams consist of two types, **value creation** and **value delivery**. Value creation includes the activities to design, engineer, test, and produce a product or service that people want. Value delivery includes all the activities necessary to satisfy the customer and improve their experience in acquiring and using the product or service. For example, order processing, inventory management, supply chain and partner management, fulfillment, distribution, warehousing, transportation/delivery, product support, and product maintenance are all forms of value delivery activities.

As you go through this chapter, you will find that many of these activities include huge amounts of waste that need to be aggressively eliminated. The lean organization constantly challenges whether each activity is necessary and, if it is, whether it can be simplified and streamlined.

Flow is an expression of efficiency spanning value creation and value delivery activities. Flow includes the movement of materials, components, and finished goods, resources, and information. Batch processes, mismatched production rates, queuing, and delays for any reason are all a nemesis of efficient flows across value streams. Improving the effectiveness of flow is what makes it possible for small and efficient value streams. Improvements to flow reduce both development and operational costs and time to deliver, while simultaneously improving quality.

Flow is improved in a stepwise fashion, as follows:

1. Identify value stream activities.

2. Identify the objects (that is, raw materials, components, information, and so on) that flow through the value streams.

3. Work to eliminate any impediments to efficient flow and activities that do not add value, while ignoring all organizational, cultural, supply chain, and other barriers that would otherwise hinder the effort.

4. Eliminate work practices, mismatched equipment capacities, batch processes, lengthy setup and tool changes, or other resource limitations that cause delays, defects, reworks, scrap, or the backflow of objects across value stream activities and equipment. Backflows are caused by reworks or redundant activities performed across the same production equipment or other resources.

5. Identify and eliminate any other impediments that prevent synchronized and continuous flows.

Pull is a value stream scheduling approach that reduces **Work In Process (WIP)** by enforcing a simple rule that downstream activities take in new work only when they are ready. Materials and components are never pushed from one value stream activity to another. Instead, a value stream activity can only pull new work into their area when there is a customer requirement and they have the capacity to immediately start the work.

From a practicable standpoint, this means downstream activities can take in work only after a customer has submitted an order and the preceding upstream activities have completed their work and signaled that new work is available to the downstream activities. When those conditions are met, the downstream value creation/value delivery activities are allowed to *pull* the existing orders in for processing.

Relatively speaking, in the context of Lean, upstream activities are those that are closest to the provisioning of raw materials and the start of value stream production processes. In contrast, downstream activities are those that are, relatively speaking, closer to delivering the product or service to customers. So, if we specify an activity in the middle of a value stream, as shown in *Figure 5.1*, upstream activities precede it, while downstream activities follow:

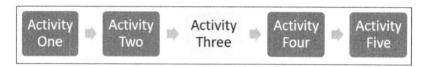

Figure 5.1 – Upstream versus downstream activities

This pull-oriented approach is in contrast to a traditional approach where orders are pushed into production immediately upon order entry or to fulfill expected demand, whether there is the capacity to start the work or not. Pushing work into a value stream process will only cause queues and delays that mask defects that ultimately increase non-value-added reworks and scrap, add carrying costs, and introduce excessive process complexities and inefficiencies.

Perfection is always sought but never quite achieved, but is still a tangible goal to obtain. In previous chapters, we spoke about using retrospectives as an approach to continuously look for ways to improve our software development activities continuously. Similarly, early Lean practitioners discovered early on that no matter how much they improved their value stream activities, they always found new areas for improvement.

The drive for continuous improvements makes sense when you recall the *80/20 rule* (a.k.a. the **Pareto Principle**) discussed in previous chapters. When we look at the cause and effects of any activity or set of activities, we find that roughly 80% of the effects impacting our systems come from ~20% of the identified causes. If we fix the most impactful 20% of influences across our value stream and run a Pareto analysis, the same 80/20 rule applies to the new set of identified causes and effects. Continued retrospectives will always lead to the discovery of new impacts and causes to address, with the team incrementally improving performance over the duration of their charter.

But another important aspect of seeking perfection is that the failure to pay constant attention to identifying new areas for improvement leads to complacency. Such complacency will always lead organizations and teams to backslide to inefficient and error-prone practices.

Lean practices are substantially different than the traditional business practices that largely facilitated the United States' growth and dominance in manufacturing industries until the 1970s. However, a competitive global economy – led initially by Japan, but later by other nations that adopted Lean practices – forced U.S. manufacturers to respond in kind. Now we can find Lean practices applied across industries in the United States and across the World.

Now that you understand the basic principles behind Lean practices, we need to take a quick look at the benefits of Lean. This is the subject of the next section.

Profiting from Lean practices

As discussed in the previous sections of this chapter, Lean Thinking is a business enhancement approach that seeks to eliminate all forms of waste while also ensuring the organization stays focused on providing enhanced customer value. At their most basic level, Lean practices evaluate value-creating actions to dramatically minimize the size, non-value-added activities, and complexity of identified value streams.

The benefits of Lean include the following:

- Eliminates interruptions and delays in value stream processes.
- Aligns and adjusts value stream activities to support continuous and streamlined flows.

- Implements continuous efforts to drive out all waste so that value stream activities are performed most efficiently.

- Creates more value, as perceived by the customer, with less human effort, less equipment, less time, and less space than traditional business approaches.

- Customers are more likely to purchase products and services when the focus of the business is squarely centered on adding customer-centric value.

- Lean practices do not have the goal of eliminating jobs, as was typical under business process reengineering practices. Instead, the focus is to improve employee satisfaction through the expansion of their roles to identify and eliminate waste and to identify opportunities to add value to the products and services they produce.

- Lean practices create new ways of working that are ultimately more efficient and add more value, and thereby more profitable for the producer.

- You now understand the basics of Lean Thinking and the benefits derived. So, let's move on to explore the practical implementation aspects of the five aforementioned Lean principles. In the next few sections, you will gain a deeper understanding of how Lean practices improve both business efficiencies and value. We'll start our discussions with an understanding of how to determine value.

Determining value

Placing a focus on value is the first and most critical step in Lean Thinking. Value is not just about product features and functions. It requires the organization to look beyond producing what they or their competitors already produce and instead constantly look for ways that positively change the customer experience throughout their value creation and value delivery activities. Adding value is hard work and takes imagination because virtually everything in an organization's value chain contributes to value.

Value is defined in terms of specific products and services, useful product variants that fulfill niche market needs, specific capabilities provided by each variant, prices as evaluated by the customer, and the satisfaction of the customer experience from product awareness, through order entry, delivery, and support. Because value has such a broad scope, the surest way to fail is to build a product based on our ability to leverage existing facilities, processes, equipment and tooling, and resources. Simply put, the focus is on the wrong thing.

The focus always has to stay on the customer, and what they want. Then we must evolve our facilities, processes, equipment, and resources to deliver what they want. The evolution may not occur overnight, but every incremental change we make along the way improves our value, and subsequently our competitive average.

Organizations that choose to improve value can start by identifying the following elements of their value streams:

- Describe the complete set of activities from product conceptualization and design to the launch of production capabilities.

- Describe the flow of information from initial customer interest to order entry and on to delivery.

- Describe the complete product development process from the procurement and staging of raw materials on through the production and delivery processes.

In other words, the organization must completely understand the process of product conceptualization and design, demand creation and order handling, and product development and delivery. These three areas encompass the central value streams of Lean.

Later, in the section on *Flows*, we will see that it may make sense to subdivide these value streams into smaller increments. But for now, to establish a foundational understanding of adding value, it's easier to focus on describing these three higher-level value streams.

Designing to value

A useful concept to understand and implement Lean practices is *design to value*. Design to value includes the specification of requirements and designs that maximize value as defined by the customer.

In a traditional sense, design to value is a marketing function that involves market research, competitive intelligence, product differentiation, branding, defining the customer experience, and often the inclusion of focus groups and prototyping to test out various product concepts. However, under Lean practices, design to value goes beyond the definition of product requirements and designs and includes the full spectrum of value creation and value delivery activities that ultimately define the complete customer experience.

In other words, the organization designs to value all value stream processes. Any weakness in any value stream can negatively impact the customer's perception of value.

Just think about this logically. We can build a product that meets every customer need. But if they don't know it exists or don't know how to buy it, what good is it? We can build the best marketing campaigns to promote our new product, but if it fails to deliver value as perceived by the customer, they won't buy it. And, if we build a good product and promote it well, we could still mess things up by failing to price it correctly or failing to deliver it promptly.

Therefore, value is an all-encompassing concept that looks across value streams to ensure we are delivering the right product, at the right time, to the right customers, at the right price, with the right delivery and support services. If we do these things well, we will establish a competitive advantage that cannot easily be surmounted by our competitors – unless we stop looking for ways to constantly improve upon value.

In conclusion, the achievement of value is not an instant process. It's not even an end goal. Rather, the achievement of value is a constant journey and an evolutionary process.

Now that we have a deeper understanding of what value is, we can move on to understand how value streams affect our ability to deliver value. That is the subject of the next section.

Understanding the value stream

The analysis of our value streams is the second step in Lean Thinking. A value stream is the set of all specific actions required to bring a product or service to the customer. In the previous sections, we spoke of three critical value chains an organization must identify and analyze. Let's take a look at those three areas in a slightly different manner.

- **Value Identification Tasks** – include all activities to create the right product, from the initial product concept to design, engineering, and building out production capabilities.

- **Information Tasks** – include all activities to identify customers, generate demand, address customer questions, take and fulfil orders, and support the product after delivery.

- **Physical Transformation Tasks** – activities from the procurement and receipt of raw materials and the transformation to finished products ready for delivery to customers.

Identifying the states of value

As with the identification of value, analysis is required to truly understand the dynamics and scope of work involved in each value stream. The organization must identify the value streams for every product and every product family with the goal of exposing and eliminating all forms of waste. During this analysis, the organization can expect to find three states of value across each of the activities they identify and analyze. These three states are as follows:

- Unambiguous value

- Unavoidable waste

- No value

The best-case scenario for an activity is of course that it adds unambiguous value, which is the first possible state. In other words, the activity clearly and provenly provides capabilities that a customer is willing to pay for. In this situation, there is no need to change anything.

In some cases, technology limitations or investments in existing capital may add waste to an activity, but realistically the organization does not have a viable approach to address the issue in the short term. This is the second state of value where there is non-value-added waste. In the Toyota production system, this type of waste is referred to as *Type I Muda*. While this type of waste is non-value-adding, the activity is required – at least in the short run – to support our customer's needs. Over time, as technologies and economics permit, the organization may be able to eliminate some or all of their Type I Muda.

The third possible state is that an activity provides no value to the targeted customer. In the Toyota production system, this type of waste is referred to as *Type II Muda*. This type of waste must be eliminated as soon as possible. The elimination of Type II Muda provides the quickest opportunity to improve the value of a product or service.

As you conduct value stream analysis, don't forget to look across all third parties that participate in your value stream, including suppliers and partners. This should be a collaborative and voluntary effort to remove all waste in the value stream. If your value-stream partners do not see the value in eliminating waste or helping your organization improve your value stream, then start looking for new partners.

Providing transparency across your value streams

A Lean enterprise is an entity that seeks to eliminate any activity that does not directly contribute and add value to the products and services it develops and delivers. Lean development places the focus on value creation and the elimination of waste and unnecessary activities. While some entities may practice Lean development in an ad hoc manner, the Lean enterprise installs the principles of Lean development as the foundation of its culture.

The hallmark of a Lean enterprise is complete transparency and efficiency across the value stream, including the activities supported by external partners and suppliers. If your suppliers are unwilling to participate in a value stream analysis activity, then perhaps they're not the partners you should be working with. Also, if you're partners and suppliers are not open to being completely transparent in their activities that support your value stream, they too are probably not the right set of suppliers and partners you should have going forward.

Now that we understand the basics of analyzing value streams, we need to expand our understanding of how the flow of objects across value streams impacts our assessments and our value. This is the subject of the next section.

Identifying and improving flows

The third step in Lean Thinking is to identify flows across the value streams. Flows are identified in terms of objects that participate in the activities across each value stream. The objects can be information, raw materials, resources, components, and finished goods.

In traditional business models, organizations often aligned resources around functions and departments. The thought behind these practices is that functional and hierarchical organizational structures lead to better management and more efficiencies by logically grouping resources and skills around specific business or technology processes. In actual fact, the opposite is true. The movement of work through functional departments and hierarchical organizational structures creates a number of problems. These problems include the following:

- Large batch sizes that make it difficult to match production to demand.
- Inefficient changeovers between product variants.
- Queuing and delays across business and production processes.
- Inefficient flow across value-creating steps and activities.

When organizations align their resources by functional departments, there is a tendency to seek economies of scale through the procurement of high-capacity equipment and large-scale production processes. This is the antithesis of Lean Thinking, where the ideal goal is to build each product one at a time, just in time, and in the most efficient and rapid process possible. Instead, large-scale production processes and equipment become behemoths that need constant feeding and attention, and thereby become barriers to efficient production flows.

Feeding the monster

Since the organization may have a number of functional departments, each individually optimized around the tools and technologies they employ, it's virtually impossible to match their production flow rates. As a result, products that move into the functional departments often sit in a queue until an economically efficient volume of work is ready for processing and the equipment is set up for the new batch run. Anytime we have queues and delays, we can expect to see higher levels of defects, the result of which is increased reworks and scrap, and extended production cycle times.

For example, materials that accumulate in queues before processing may hide any number of defects. The defects cannot be found and fixed until they move on to downstream processes. When they do move, a shop may find they have a batch load of defective products.

Also, large-scale and batch production processes base their efficiencies on the volume of products that can be handled simultaneously. Intuitively, it may seem that a batch production process is more efficient than a process that can only work on one product at a time. However, products accumulating in queues, simply because they are waiting on enough products to economically run the batch process, adds to the overall time it takes to get the final products finished and ready for delivery.

There is also a tendency to want to feed these monolithic systems, whether there is customer demand or not. After all, the organization has invested heavily in these large-scale systems and the executives and managers will feel a great deal of pressure to keep them constantly busy and running at their most efficient capacities. But busywork is not necessarily – in fact, probably is not – value-added work.

As a result, an organization so aligned may not see value in expending time and resources to simplify tooling and reduce setup and changeover times as they represent a relatively small amount of the total time involved in the overall batch production process.

In contrast, Lean Thinking seeks to eliminate batch production and concentrate on developing efficient flows and developing products on a JIT basis to meet current customer demands. This means that the objective of Lean processing is to eliminate batch processes while simultaneously reducing setup and changeover times.

It is difficult for a manufacturer to walk away from investments they have made in expensive large-scale manufacturing processes and equipment, and so they may instead be inclined to keep their existing equipment and run it with smaller batch sizes. However, there are two problems with that strategy. First, the batch equipment is not likely economical to run with lower batch sizes. Second, if the manufacturer produces multiple product lines and product variants, the changeover and setup times become significant factors in terms of lengthening the overall production cycle times associated with the smaller batch sizes.

The bottom line is that corporate investments in large-scale production assets add to the resistance to change over to Lean practices. Moreover, the executives and managers of those facilities may not fully understand the production inefficiencies caused by their functional organizational structures and investments in large-scale batch processes.

Waiting, always waiting

Delays in production processing are a huge problem in the traditional model. There are several factors that contribute to delays, such as mismatched cycle times across activities, inconsistent batch sizes across disparate activities, significant setup and changeover times, and the impact of introducing multiple product variants across the same production lines. As a result, it's not uncommon, under the traditional model, for materials and finished goods to spend way more time sitting in queues than they spend undergoing the value-added production-oriented processes.

In addition, manufacturers need a place to store all this, accumulating inventories. As a result, the built-in delays from mismatched flows force the organization to spend money on the expansion of facilities to hold the increased materials. Compounding the problem, there are increased inventory carrying costs associated with procuring the additional raw materials that end up waiting in multiple queues along the length of the value stream. Finally, the queuing of materials and delays in work in progress hide product defects and errors, which leads to additional reworks and scrap, also contributing to increased costs.

Mapping the value stream

The concept of mapping value streams also originated in the **Toyota Motor Corporation**, though the concept was originally referred to as *material and information flows*. I prefer the latter term as every business manages the flow of both information and materials. The flow of information and materials is what we manage across a value stream. A value stream map provides a way to visually display and analyze the flow of information and materials across the organization, and their contributions, or lack thereof, to adding value.

In their book *Lean Thinking* (Womack and Jones, 2003), the authors describe value streams as *a set of all specific actions required to bring a specific product (whether a good or service, or, increasingly, a combination of the two) through the three critical management tasks*. They list these three management tasks as follows:

Problem-solving tasks – includes activities spanning product conceptualization through design and engineering to production launch

Information management tasks – includes all information handling activities required to take and process an order, and then schedule and deliver the product or service

Physical transformation tasks – includes all activities to transform raw materials into a finished product delivered to the customer

Value stream mapping is a useful tool to show the flows across each identified value stream across the three management tasks. An organization often creates separate maps to show the current state and the desired future state for each value stream. The objective of the contrasting value stream maps is to identify all forms of waste in the current state and show how they are eliminated when achieving the targeted future state.

For those readers who have further interest in this subject, there are a number of vendors who provide tools and templates as aids in value-stream mapping. There is not an overarching standard, particularly when it comes to value stream mapping symbols. So, my recommendation is to work with your organization to establish a governance body to determine standard tools, templates, and symbols.

In the next section, you will see a very simple map of a value stream and learn how the information is used to analyze and improve the flow within the value stream.

Identifying and fixing value stream flows

Figure 5.2 shows a basic sequential flow across a value stream consisting of five activities, from Activity A to E. The arrows represent the direction of flow. For this example, we'll assume no effort has yet been made to reduce batch sizes or match the rate of flow across each participating activity.

Looking at the data in the columns below each activity, we can see that **Activity A** can process two parts in 5 minutes for an average of 2.5 minutes per part. Following this logic across the remaining activities, we see **Activity B** has a flow rate of 3 minutes per part, **Activity C** has a flow rate of 2.5 minutes per part, **Activity D** has a flow rate of 1.33 minutes per part, and **Activity E** has a flow rate of 2 minutes per part:

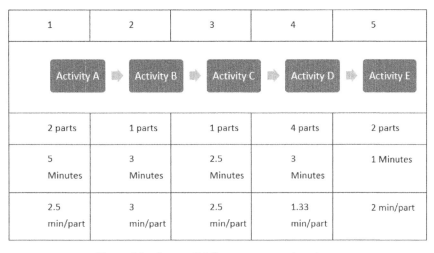

1	2	3	4	5
Activity A	Activity B	Activity C	Activity D	Activity E
2 parts	1 parts	1 parts	4 parts	2 parts
5 Minutes	3 Minutes	2.5 Minutes	3 Minutes	1 Minutes
2.5 min/part	3 min/part	2.5 min/part	1.33 min/part	2 min/part

Figure 5.2 – Sequential flows across a value stream

Based on this data, it should be apparent that the primary bottleneck in our system occurs at **activity B**, as its flow rate of 3 minutes per part is the slowest across the five activities. However, if parts are released into the value stream rate of 3 minutes per part or slower, we should not see queues of parts building at **activity B** or any of the other activities. This strategy ensures that the rate of entry of parts into the system does not exceed the ability of the system to handle the flow of incoming parts.

However, if parts come in at a quicker rate than 3 minutes per part, the parts will begin to queue at the slowest activities. For example, if the parts come in at 2.5 minutes per part, we should expect to see the parts begin to queue at **activity B**. If there are no limits placed on the work in progress, those incoming parts will continue to queue at **activity B** for as long as the organization allows assuming there is space to store the parts.

If we increase the incoming flow rate to 2 minutes between parts, our queuing problems become worse. Now activities A, B, and C cannot handle the load and parts will queue at all three activities. The best-case scenario, at least in the short run, is to limit either the incoming flow of parts to a rate of 1 part every 3 minutes to prevent the buildup of parts at any of the activities. At this rate of flow, the production through our value stream system is a constant 20 parts per hour.

In the long run, if the higher customer demand rate of two parts per minute is sustained, the organization must improve the efficiency of their value stream if they want to address the full demands of the market. That's the subject of the next several subsections.

Fulfilling increased customer demands

So, you may be wondering what you should do if customer demand is greater than the slowest rate of production? The short answer is you cannot fulfill market demands until you improve your production capacities and flows. Pushing in all the additional orders when you do not have sufficient capacity will make matters worse, that is, increased carrying costs for raw materials, increased production complexities and inefficiencies, the hiding of defects, and therefore increased scrap and rework.

If you are the only provider of the product, under the economic concepts of supply and demand, you may be able to raise prices and obtain a higher profit, even though you cannot fulfill all the orders. But that assumes you have an inelastic market. In other words, customer demand will not change markedly with increased prices.

In this case, you can safely produce up to your full production rates and use the excess profits to improve value stream efficiencies. These improved efficiencies will further lower your costs and you can thereby sell even more products at higher margins – until the competition steps in with a viable product at a lower price.

If you have an elastic market, where customer demand is highly correlated with changes in pricing, your only choice to capture the remaining market is to improve your capacity and production efficiencies. In other words, your customers won't pay a higher price, and the only way you can capture the larger market is to increase capacity while lowering your product costs. As we'll see in the next subsection, that may not be easy to do in the short run.

Matching demand and production rates

Going back to our example in *Figure 5.2*, let's assume customer demand supports a production rate of 60 parts per hour, that is, a flow rate of one part per minute. If we push parts into our value stream system at that rate, the parts will only queue at all the activities since none of the activities have the capacity to match that rate of flow.

The best long-term solution is to add capacity at each activity by streamlining and improving the efficiency of work at each activity to handle the flow rate of one part per minute. That will take some time and effort to achieve. In the shorter run, the organization may be able to add capacity in the form of new equipment and additional resources to achieve the desired flow rate of 1 minute per part. That approach comes at a higher cost.

Building in takt time

It should be clear that, regardless of the circumstances, the organization needs to limit the intake of new customer orders to match the production capacity of its slowest value creation activities. We accomplish this by measuring the **takt time** between the intake of customer orders matched to the total time available for production.

The term takt time was initially derived from the German word *Taktzeit*, which translates in English to *cycle time* or *pulse time*. The *pulse time* aspect of this term describes a precise interval of time, such as the rhythmic timing of music, while the *cycle time* aspect of the term came from the German aircraft industry in the 1930s as a production management technique to gauge the interval of time an aircraft spent between assembly stations. Toyota implemented the concept of takt time back in the 1950s and continues to employ the concept to this day.

From a mathematical perspective, takt time is calculated as the total time available for production divided by customer demand in terms of individual products or services. The equation looks like this:

$$T = \frac{Ta}{D}$$

Here, T = takt time; Ta = total time available to work; and D = customer demand in terms of units per time period.

In a single product situation with no product variants, the calculation is quite simple. Using the example cited in *Figure 5.2*, customer demand is 60 parts per hour, which is its takt time. But let's see how we got to that figure.

If we assume two 8-hour shifts per day, with a total of 18 full days and 4 half days, and no downtime, the total hours available for production are calculated as follows:

$$\left(\frac{2\,shifts}{workday} * \frac{8\,hours}{shift} * 18\,workdays\right) + \left(\frac{1\,shift}{workday} * \frac{8\,hours}{shift} * 4\,workdays\right)$$

$$= 320\,hours$$

Ideally, the estimates for customer demand come directly from customer orders. For this exercise, let's assume the order backlog for the upcoming month is 19,200 widgets. We now have enough information to calculate the takt time:

$$320\,hours/month/\,19{,}200\,widgets/month) = 60\,widgets/hour$$

OK, I cheated a bit in that I had already defined the takt time as 60 widgets per hour in the previous subsection. But you should now be able to see how I got there.

Changing over between product variants

Note that in this example we have not even discussed setup or tooling requirements associated with changing over equipment to build variants of a product. Those activities add time to each step of the value stream that requires a changeover. Moreover, the amount of time and resources devoted to the changeover accumulates with each product variant introduced into the production schedule, as measured over a specific period of time. Changeover and setup activities are a form of Type I Muda, unavoidable in the short term, but an area of improvement that we should address as soon as it's practical to do so.

To the greatest extent possible, the organization should set up individual value stream processes to accommodate unique activity flows to reduce, if not eliminate, setup and changeover activities. Also, we know that the organization should aggressively work to build capacity at each activity to match expected demand rates either by improving the efficiencies of each process or by adding capacity in the form of new equipment and resources to match the demand for each product variant.

One of the first books to demonstrate why a system cannot exceed its slowest activity in the production system was *The Goal* by Eliyahu Goldratt, first published in 1984 (Goldratt, 2014 – 30th-year edition). The book was written as a fictional novel, which made it an interesting and entertaining read. Here are two story-form but fictional books related to I.T. that discuss similar concepts: *The Phoenix Project* (Kim et al. 2016) and *The Unicorn Project* (Kim, 2019).

Managing the transformation to Lean Thinking flows

Many, if not most, markets are highly segmented with multiple niches having customers that prefer products with different features and options. In large-scale operations with batch processes, the introduction of new product variants can dramatically increase the amount of queuing and delays across value stream activities. The organization has to continue feeding its production monsters and production managers will resist slowing down production to support the setup and changeover required to work on new product variants. As a result, the tendency is to accumulate enough customer demands for each product variant until the volume justifies changing over the equipment.

In contrast, Lean Thinking seeks to implement the continuous flow of individual products across the value streams, at a constant rate, with virtually no setup or changeover requirements. Rather than implementing large-scale batch processing systems, Lean Thinking practitioners prefer lot sizes of one, with matched activity processing speeds, no delays, no cues, no non-value-added activities, and no requirement to move or transport parts or people between value stream activities. The infrastructure within an existing business may be a long way off achieving these goals. In truth, there is no short-term solution to address the business transformation problem to implement Lean Thinking concepts.

The most ideal situation is to implement Lean Thinking before the organization makes significant investments in capital equipment and value stream processes. Nevertheless, that's not the reality for most existing organizations. Depending on the business situation, the organization may choose to implement Lean Thinking concepts in support of developing and introducing new product lines. But if the organization is facing competitive pressures and financial troubles, they may have to move aggressively away from their existing processes and systems.

Moreover, when an organization is facing a crisis, they must look at their previous investments as *sunk costs*. In other words, their previous investments cannot be refunded or recovered, and the organization must be willing to walk away from equipment and processes that prevent them from being competitive. It may be possible to reduce setup and changeover times and improve operational efficiencies sufficiently to extend the life of some of their production equipment. But the longer-term solution is to invest in developing flexible value creation and value delivery systems that are efficient and Lean.

Likewise, the organization must move away from suboptimal organizational structures built around functional departments and instead align their assets and resources around the creation of value. The existing organization must work diligently to connect and aggregate activities and resources to optimize the flow of information and materials across value streams to improve their value creation and value delivery capabilities.

Furthermore, the organization cannot stop its efforts to implement Lean practices at the boundaries of the organization. Instead, the organization must assess value stream activities across the entire value chain, to include third-party suppliers and partners. In other words, the components, subassemblies, services, and information provided by external parties that contribute to the development and delivery of the final solution are all included in the whole product concept of Lean Thinking. Therefore, value stream analysis has to reach across the activities of those third-party contributors.

Obtaining buy-in across the enterprise

Organizations that choose to implement Lean Thinking principles must avoid disruption in business functions and reduced morale among employees during the transformation. Organizational resistance is a real phenomenon that must be addressed. Much of what an organization does is embedded in its culture, and people working in that environment often perceive their value, roles, and opportunities through the prism of the cultures they work in.

A practical approach to building buy-in among employees and other stakeholders is to help them reimagine their work as contributing to value creation and value delivery activities, as opposed to denigrating past practices or their previous contributions to the organization. They must see themselves in the Lean enterprise as valued and empowered employees who can make a difference and have a positive impact. It is, after all, to their benefit to support the development of a viable and profitable organization. Employees will feel more inclined to support a change to Lean practices when they know they have a direct and important role in the organization's future.

The successful Lean enterprise rethinks existing conventions, organizational structures, business functions, and career progressions around product line value. When the employees, contractors, and suppliers believe they are important to the long-term success of the business and will be valued for their efforts, they will support the transformations to create and deliver value-based products and services. Alternatively, if they feel their jobs are at risk, they will resist or leave.

It's important to note that the installment of Lean development practices across an enterprise doesn't happen overnight, and neither does overcoming organizational resistance. Largely, people want to be part of successful activities and organizations. And therefore, people will adapt and adopt over time as the new Lean development strategies prove successful.

While it is possible to adopt a Lean development practice across a single product line, it's not likely to stick if that's as far as the organization is willing to go. Executives and managers will view the effort as out of line with their mainstream practices. It's better to have executive sponsorship and make any initial changes part of a longer-term adoption strategy.

Smaller organizations can look across their product development streams and begin to align and synchronize their process flows, and reduce activity cycle times, to quickly obtain better efficiencies while simultaneously ensuring they are building the products their customers want. Those successes will help drive similar improvements in the value delivery streams.

Larger organizations may start out with reorganizing production facilities along high-value product lines and then begin to work on the synchronization and coordination of flows and reducing cycle times to eliminate bottlenecks. Over time, other product lines and value delivery streams can begin to work on improving their activities.

But no matter the size of the organization, continuous improvements are the norm in Lean development, not the exception. Cultural change must ultimately occur to help make Lean stick within the organization.

Moving from Push to Pull oriented deliveries

In our initial discussions around the example described in *Figure 5.1*, we assumed a push scenario where the organization allowed customer demands to set the rate of flow through the value stream. That is not an ideal scenario and is made worse as additional product variants are introduced into the value stream, each having different flows, setup and changeover requirements, and activity processing speeds.

Pushing parts into a value stream based upon customer demand causes issues when capacity is not sufficient to meet demand. Even if capacity exceeds demand, it's still a bad practice to fill a shop with work simply to prevent the idling of equipment and people within the facility. You may end up building products customers never want. In the meantime, you are spending money on things that you can't sell. It's better to limit the introduction of new work into the facility based on capacity, as set by the slowest activity in the value stream, up to the limits of proven customer demand.

The best approach to limit work into a facility is by implementing a pull-based order entry strategy, which is the subject of the next section.

Changing from Push to Pull

The fourth step in Lean Thinking is to move from Push to Pull oriented systems. Pull processing supports three important Lean objectives:

- Forces the organization to convert from functional departments and batch processing to product and value-oriented value streams and flows

- Minimizes the time to take a new product or service from concept to launch, through order-taking, and to delivery

- Minimizes the time, delays, and carrying costs associated with converting raw materials into finished goods

A Lean enterprise eliminates the traditional paradigm of pushing products to market based on estimates of customer needs or to reduce inventories of products made due to excess capacity. Instead, the Lean enterprise pulls work into production when capacity is available and limited to actual customer orders or proven demand levels. A push-based production system exists solely to maximize the economies of scale across functionally aligned and large-scale batch processes. But, as noted in the previous section, feeding these production monsters does not come without inducing serious and unintended consequences.

Managing production rates

The problem with push-oriented systems is that it's very unlikely input flows will match production capacities, or that production capacities will be matched across the value streams. Also, push-based production systems evolved to *feed the monsters* so as to achieve maximum economies of scale across large batch processes. Tending to those monsters are teams of highly skilled specialists, which makes it more challenging to align resources around value.

This concern should be pretty apparent from the *Figure 5.1* example in the previous section. And that example is actually relatively simple. Imagine working in a machine shop that must produce any number of parts and product variants, each of which has a different setup and changeover requirements, different production rates, and also different flows through the shop. Pushing parts into such an environment quickly introduces production complexities and queuing that are impossible to predict and address.

The previous discussions on flow demonstrate that one part of the solution is to define value streams with predictable flows across similar product variants and set up the production processes and equipment accordingly, and to minimize setup and changeover requirements. That's only half of the solution. The other half is that we must limit demand to the minimum capacity of the value stream activities. The best way to achieve that goal is the implementation of pull production concepts.

Recall from the *Figure 5.1* example that the slowest production process was Activity B at a flow rate of 3 minutes per part. That is the maximum rate that value stream can support. Any attempts to introduce new objects into the stream at a faster rate will only result in the formation of queues and subsequent production delays.

Early **Manufacture Resource Planning (MRP)** systems attempted to address the scheduling problem by maintaining accurate records of orders, inventories, and production sequencing information. But they were push-based systems that only exacerbated the queuing and delays associated with batch processing. Instead, the manufacturing facilities needed an approach to pull work into their operations only when capacity becomes available with materials and order information made available JIT to sustain an efficient flow.

Processing work just in time

The fix to these sorts of problems came with the implementation of **JIT** concepts, first introduced by Taiichi Ohno at Toyota. First and foremost, JIT addresses the issue of flow with a concentrated effort to align value stream activities with the goal of implementing efficient flows and minimizing setup and changeover requirements between product variants. The next step is to implement *level scheduling* concepts, which simply ensures information or objects are not introduced into the value stream any quicker than the slowest activity that can accept them.

But if we have multiple product variants flowing through a value stream, each with different activities, flows, and flow rates, how can we determine the optimal flow rate for the system at any given time? To manage flow rates in such an environment, we need an effective way to visualize and control work in process. This flow-rate sequencing strategy is what pull-based production systems accomplish.

Pulling work on a first-in, first-out basis

Pull-based production systems implement a **first-in, first-out (FIFO)** production scheduling philosophy. In a product manufacturing context, this means orders come into the value stream for processing as they are received. The scheduling typically occurs at the beginning of a new shift, and the schedule consists of a list of each product requirement for each product variant, in FIFO order, plus the number of products required for each variant. The manufacturing facility then pulls those orders into the shop as production capacity becomes available in the downstream processes.

So, using our example from back in *Figure 5.1*, the operators at *Activity A* would see the new order list at the beginning of the shift and they would pull the highest-ordered item from the list to work on. When *Activity A* is completed, a visual aid – usually in the form of a Kanban card – indicates to the operators at *Activity B* that there is work that they can pull from *Activity A*.

Each Kanban card is a visual representation of a requested work item. The purpose of a Kanban card is to inform people in subsequent downstream activities to move, procure, or develop more of a component for delivery against a customer order. The Kanban card simply lists the information about the order and the product variant associated with it.

The data provided on Kanban cards can vary significantly, based on the unique requirements of each production environment. Basic information on a Kanban card often includes the part number, part description, quantity, lead time, the name of the supplier, the name of the scheduler/planner, bin location, order date, and due date.

In a traditional manufacturing environment, Kanban cards physically move with their associated work items. In modern Lean practices, a Kanban card may be information written on sticky notes placed in lanes on a whiteboard, with each lane representing a sequence or state of processing through the value stream. You'll see how the sticky notes work in Lean software development practices in later sections of this chapter. But before we move on to discussing the application of Lean practices to software and systems development, let's finish this section with an expansion on the Lean concept of continuously seeking perfection.

Seeking perfection

Seeking perfection is the fifth and final step in Lean Thinking. Conceptually, in Lean Thinking, perfection is the elimination of all waste while providing maximum customer value. At this point in time, the organization has implemented the first four elements of Lean: defining and delivering value, value stream identification, balancing flows, and pulling work in lockstep with customer demands. Now we need to make sure we keep improving.

At a more granular level of understanding, the organization has developed systems and processes to fully understand what customers value; the organization has identified their value streams that support value creation and value delivery activities they have structurally reorganized their functional departments and batch processing systems to support continuous flow along the value streams; and the organizations have established pull-based scheduling mechanisms to match demand to its production flows and capacity.

But there is always more that can be done to improve value and value stream performance. And that comes with improvements through the continued discovery and elimination of waste. That is, recall that waste is defined as any activity that consumes resources but creates no value for the customer.

Producing something that customers don't want is a form of waste. You've also learned that other common forms of waste include waiting, overproduction, extra-processing, transportation, motion, inventory, and defects. The continued discovery and removal of waste in all these areas is how we travel the road to perfection.

Finding perfection is a journey, not a destination

With all the work that has been done to understand value in the eyes of the customer, identify our value streams, improve the flows across our values streams, and pull work in at a rate equal to customer demand, it's tempting to sit on our laurels and think we are done. But we can still do better. This is the underlying concept behind the Lean principle of continuous improvement – the reality is we are never done!

For example, it's a certainty that customer preferences and needs will continue to evolve over time, which will change our customers' definitions of value. Also, following the principles of Pareto analysis, we can continue to look at the leading causes of bottlenecks, failures, and defects in our systems to make those activities more efficient, thus improving our production flow rates and efficiencies across a value stream.

Continuous improvement takes time, energy, and resources, but it's critical to the long-term success of the organization. In practical terms, the more we continue to improve, the less likely it is that a competitor will be able to find a way to leapfrog our production capabilities or offer more value.

Finding waste through transparency

Another critical enabler to seeking perfection is the concept of *transparency*. This concept was discussed in *Chapter 3, The Scrum Approach*, albeit in a slightly different context. In Scrum, the concept of transparency is that all information should be made freely available to all team members, executives, and other stakeholders. The goal is not to hide issues but rather bring them to light so that everyone can get involved to eliminate the impediments that are preventing the team from achieving its goals.

In Lean Thinking, transparency gives the organization access to the information it requires to accurately assess customer value and value stream efficiencies. So, the concept of transparency has similarities in Scrum and Lean Thinking, though the point of reference is somewhat different, that is, eliminating impediments versus improving value and flow.

The concept of transparency in Scrum has a focus on providing visibility of information that is necessary to support the inspect and adapt elements of empiricism, that is, using empirical evidence through sensory experiences and experimentation to make sound decisions. In contrast, transparency in Lean is providing access to information that allows the organization to analyze all value stream activities in terms of enhancing customer value, that is, transparency helps identify waste. Nevertheless, in both cases, the act of transparency is what allows the organization to continuously improve.

There's another aspect of the Lean principle of continuous improvement that we need to understand if we truly want to seek perfection, and that is defining metrics that accurately define our current state and desired future state. In the next subsection, you'll learn some of the metrics that aid the Lean Thinking team toward their goal of constantly seeking perfection.

Defining the metrics of perfection

Truly, perfection is the goal from the very start of any Lean Thinking approach to improving value creation and value delivery activities. Many of the metrics that we use to assess value stream performance and measuring value do not change over time. In other words, many metrics remain useful for as long as the organization exists to create value for its customers.

We can assess progress from the very beginning of a Lean change initiative, as we begin to analyze existing capabilities when the organization is still functionally aligned around large-scale batch processing systems. We continue to measure performance as we work to align value stream flows and implement JIT capabilities with pull-based scheduling techniques. And, when we have achieved high value and value stream efficiencies, we continue to use those same metrics to assess the current state against potential future state improvements.

The following list shows some of the metrics that every Lean-thinking organization should track and seek to improve over time:

- Labor productivity as measured against product throughput and costs
- Type I and Type II Muda in value streams
- Production throughput times
- Inventories and inventory carrying costs
- Space and facility utilization
- Error and defect rates
- The cost of scrap and rework
- Setup and changeover times between product variants
- Transport distance and time for resources and materials moving between value stream activities
- Matching demand rates against value stream flows and capacity

You should not view the items noted in the preceding list as the only metrics your organization will need. Every organization has unique business situations and needs and should always assess their activities in terms of value and efficiencies. During those assessments, other factors come up that need to be improved, and therefore measured and monitored.

When seeking perfection, the focus is not on the competition. That's a moving target, and you can likely improve upon whatever the competition is doing, anyway. Instead, compete against imperfections by improving value and identifying and eliminating all forms of waste.

Summary

In this chapter, you have learned the basics behind Lean Thinking and its emphasis on adding value by eliminating waste. You now know that there are eight common forms of waste: waiting, overproduction, extra-processing, transportation, motion, inventory, defects, and unused human talent and intellect. And you have learned the five foundational principles behind Lean Thinking, including value, value streams, flow, pull, and perfection.

You should understand why value is always defined by the customer. With that understanding, you also know that the concept of design to value includes the specification of requirements and designs that maximize value as defined by the customer.

You've learned that a value stream is the set of all specific actions required to bring a product or service to the customer and that there are three critical value chains the organization must identify and analyze. These include value identification tasks, information-oriented tasks, and physical transformation tasks.

Next, you learned that Lean Thinking requires an organization to look at the efficiency of their flows across value streams. Flows include the efficiencies of movements and transactions of materials and information that participate in the activities spanning each value stream. Improvements to flow come from the elimination of batch processes, reductions in setup and changeover times, and matching capacities and throughput across each activity within the value stream.

Improving the efficiencies of flows is not the whole story. You now know that pushing information or materials into a value stream at a rate greater than the capacity of the slowest activity will break the value stream as a system. You've learned how to calculate production rates in the form of takt time.

Pushing orders into value creation and delivery activities causes queues to form, which delays throughput and hides defects that increase reworks and scrap. In addition, pushing in work just to fill large-scale batch processes increases costs and the probability that you will spend time and effort making things customers don't want. Instead, each value stream should pull items in at a rate that does not exceed customer demand, and never faster than the slowest activity in the value stream.

Finally, you've learned that seeking perfection is a desired goal that can never be obtained, but is always necessary. There are always things that can be improved, and sitting on one's laurels is a sure-fire way to slip back into bad habits and mediocrity.

We've spent enough time understanding the basic concepts of Lean Thinking. Since this is a book on scaling Scrum-Agile processes, let's see how Lean concepts help improve value and efficiency in software and systems development practices. That is the subject of the remainder of this section (in the next chapter).

Questions

1. Why is the concept of value important in Lean Thinking?

2. What are the five foundational principles of Lean Thinking?

3. What are the eight common forms of waste?

4. What are the three primary types of value streams?

5. What is the purpose of takt time, and how is it calculated?

6. Explain why large-scale batch processes are not efficient.

7. What is the purpose of changing production scheduling from a push-oriented system to a pull-oriented system?

8. True or false: A principle of JIT is to procure and store raw materials so that they are available when customers send in their orders?

9. How does the concept of transparency support the goal of perfection?

10. What are the three states of value and can you define them?

Further reading

- Dalio, R. (2017) Principles. Simon & Schuster, New York, NY.

- Goldratt, E.M. (2014) The Goal: A Process of Ongoing Improvement. 30th Anniversary Edition. The North River Press Publishing Corporation. Great Barrington.

- Highsmith, J.A. (1998) Adaptive Software Development: A Collaborative Approach to Managing Complex Systems. Dorset House Publishing Co. New York, NY.

- Haunts, S. (2018) A Gentle Introduction to Agile & Lean Software Development. Published by Stephen Haunts, Ltd. UK.

- Kim, G.; Behr, K.; Spafford, G. (2014) The Phoenix Project: A Novel About IT, DevOps, and Helping Your Business Win. Second Edition. IT Revolution. Portland, OR.

- Kim, G. (2019) The Unicorn Project: A Novel About Developers, Digital Disruptions, and Thriving in the Age of Data. IT Revolution. Portland, OR.

- Liker, J. K. (2004) The Toyota Way: 14 Management Principles from the World's Greatest Manufacturer. McGraw-Hill. New York, NY.

- Metcalf, G. (2019) Lean Software Development: Avoiding Project Mishaps. Ingram/Lightning Sources. Milton Keynes, UK.

- Reinertsen, D.G.; Smith, P.G. (1997) Developing Products in Half the Time: New Rules, New Tools, 2nd Edition. John Wiley & Sons, Inc. Hoboken, NJ.

- Poppendieck, M.; Poppendieck, T. (2007) Implementing Lean Software Development: From Concept to Cash. Addison-Wesley. Upper Saddle River, NJ.

- Poppendieck, M.; Poppendieck, T. (2010) Leading Software Development: The Results Are Not The Point. Addison-Wesley. Upper Saddle River, NJ.

- Poppendieck, M.; Poppendieck, T. (2003) Lean Software Development: An Agile Toolkit. Addison-Wesley. Upper Saddle River, NJ.

- Poppendieck, M.; Poppendieck, T.; Kniberg, H. (2014) The Lean Mindset: Ask the Right Questions. Pearson Education Inc. Upper Saddle River, NJ.

- Womack, J.P.; Jones, T. (2003) Lean Thinking: Banish Waste and Create Wealth in Your Corporation. Free Press. New York, NY.

- Womack, J.P.; Jones, D. T.; Roos, D. (2007) Machines that changed the World. The Story of Lean Production-- Toyota's Secret Weapon in the Global Car Wars That Is Now Revolutionizing World Industry. Free Press. New York, NY.

6
Lean Practices in Software Development

Creating efficiencies and value by applying Lean development practices
to software and systems development

The use of Lean development practices has expanded beyond its origins in manufacturing to include services and information-oriented businesses of all types. Regardless of the industry, Lean practices help the organization compete in their markets and ideally attain a sustainable competitive advantage. Lean practices also help government agencies and non-profits deliver services that citizens and other beneficiaries want in the most efficient way.

Today, Lean Thinking is the backbone of several Scrum-based Agile frameworks, such as the **Large-Scale Scrum (LeSS)** Framework and the **Scaled-Agile Framework (SAFe®)**. Both frameworks will be discussed in later chapters. But before we can get to those chapters, it's important that you first understand the basic concepts of how Lean Thinking is leveraged in software and systems development practices.

Specifically, in this chapter, you will learn how Lean principles and practices improve value and efficiencies in software and systems development. Building on the foundational concepts of Lean Thinking, as outlined in the previous chapter, you will learn how to apply common Lean practices across software and systems development life cycle activities.

This chapter covers the following topics:

- Applying Lean principles to software development
- Practicing Lean in software and systems development
- Achieving continuous improvements (Kaizen)
- Building in quality
- Delaying decision-making and commitments
- Detecting defects through automation (Jidoka)
- Eliminating mistakes (Poka-Yoke)
- Eliminating waste
- Ending multitasking/task switching
- Practicing Gemba
- Optimizing the whole
- Producing **just-in-time (JIT)**
- Rejecting unfinished work
- Respecting people

Let's get started!

Applying Lean principles to software development

The subject of Lean Thinking applied to software and systems development is quite broad in scope. Most importantly, Lean practices have become the centerpieces to several modern Agile approaches, such as Disciplined Agile and the Scaled Agile framework® (SAFe®), we must cover the concepts behind Lean Thinking and Lean Development practices before we get to those chapters. Because of the scope of this subject, this book includes two chapters devoted to introducing Lean Development. This chapter introduces the historical roots of Lean and its generalized concepts and practices. In contrast, *Chapter 7, Scrum of Scrums* applies Lean Development concepts and practices to software and systems development.

Leaning on principles

As noted in the preceding section, the concepts and principles behind Lean practices apply equally well across both manufacturing and services-oriented industries, the latter of which includes the software industry. However, looking across the information that is available from software industry professionals, you will find that the naming, definition, and number of principles applied to Lean Thinking varies significantly among the experts.

For example, Womack and Jones, in their book Lean Thinking (Womack and Jones, 2003), initially described the five Lean Principles of Value, Value Stream, Flow, Pull, and Perfection. However, Mary and Tom Poppendieck in their book Lean Software Development: An Agile Toolkit (Poppendiecc hk & Poppendieck, 2003) introduced seven principles governing Lean software development.

Other analysts have identified many other principles and practices that apply to Lean concepts, both in manufacturing and service-related industries. For example, Professor Jeffrey Liker, at the University of Michigan at Ann Arbor, studied Toyota extensively and outlined 14 management principles that he associates as the guiding principles behind **The Toyota Way** as a culture and philosophy that is manifested in the **Toyota Production System** (**TPS**). When you look closer at Professor Liker's 14 Lean principles, you'll find that many of the individual principles describe multiple practices associated with Lean Thinking.

As I thought through what I would write for this section, it occurred to me that virtually all the Lean principles and practices applied to the manufacturing industry (and later to service industries as a whole) also apply to software and systems development. While the application and practice of Lean principles in software development require some tweaking, the overall goals remain the same: focus on adding value and eliminating waste.

Practicing Lean in software and systems development

Rather than trying to stay at a higher level of abstraction by defining only Lean principles, this book will dive deeper to describe the application of lower-level Lean practices in the field of software development. Accordingly, the following list contains 18 Lean practices commonly applied to software development, at least from my point of view:

- Value

- Achieving continuous improvements (Kaizen)

- Applying visual controls to manage intake and flows

- Building in quality

- Improving knowledge

- Delaying decisions and commitments

- Detecting defects through automation (Jidoka)

- Eliminating mistakes (Poka-Yoke)

- Eliminating waste

- Ending multitasking/task switching

- Practicing Gemba (that is, go to the source)

- Implementing single-piece flows

- Improving knowledge

- Leveling workloads (Heijunka)

- Optimizing the whole

- Producing **JIT**

- Rejecting unfinished work

- Respecting people

Note that I have left out discussions on the principles of *Flow*, *Pull*, and *visual controls* (for example, Kanban boards) as those concepts, as they apply to software development, were previously discussed in *Applying Flow and Pull concepts to Scrum* section. We'll review each of the listed Lean principles in the order shown here, starting with the Lean principle of building in quality.

Adding value

The concept of adding value in the software industry is no different than the concept of value applied to manufacturing firms or other types of service-oriented industries. Value is always defined by the customer. It doesn't matter how much experience we have or how bright we are; any idea we come up with is, at best, a risk until properly validated by the target customers.

Value is anything and everything your customer is willing to pay for. That concept is common sense when building commercial software applications, as customers won't buy what you make otherwise, and you won't be in business for long if you get it wrong. But the conceptual model of value in Lean also applies to software development projects that support government agencies and non-profits.

For example, government agencies provide services, and we taxpayers pay for those services. Similarly, non-profits raise money to help or advocate other people or organizations, such as a religious or school affiliation, or to improve art and culture, or to help the environment and other charitable purposes. In either case, the benefactors want those agencies and organizations to use their resources most efficiently and provide value.

So, the concept of adding value has two parts. First, the term value includes the capabilities, features, and functions that customers want. Second, value includes the price customers can pay. You might argue that functionality and pricing are subjective. But your customers will quickly let you know if your product is lacking in either category. They simply won't purchase the product, or they will return it, and they will give your product bad reviews if they do happen to procure it.

At the end of the day, adding value is all about maximizing customer satisfaction. In the previous chapter, you learned that customer satisfaction is highly dependent upon two types of value streams: *value creation* and *value delivery*. The Lean concepts of value streams, including adding customer-centric value and eliminating waste across both development- and business-oriented activities, is every bit as necessary in the software industry. In software development, value creation and value delivery activities can be broken down as follows:

- Activities to learn what customers want
- Activities to design the right solution
- Activities to validate that customers agree it is the right solution
- Activities to identify resources and establish efficient production processes necessary to build the right product

- Activities to identify resources and establish efficient demand-creation processes necessary to generate awareness and calls to action to procure products and services

- Activities to identify resources and establish efficient order taking and fulfillment processes necessary to receive payments and deliver the right product or service at the right time

- Activities to build and test products in accordance with customer requirements, acceptance criteria, and product demands

- Activities to identify resources and establish efficient operational processes necessary to support the product, once delivered

The preceding list includes the primary value streams that help add value and improve customer satisfaction. Your organization may choose to implement value streams differently. There is no problem with identifying value streams differently as long as the activities are efficient (that is, through the constant elimination of waste) and contribute to customer satisfaction.

Before we leave this subject, there is one other aspect of value that must be addressed, and that is product completeness. An incomplete product, in the eyes of the customer, is not value-added. Put another way, the product has unrealized value in terms of customer expectations. We've all experienced this situation when we've purchased a product that requires batteries, but the vendor doesn't supply them.

Customers want a whole product that fits the purpose and function it was purchased to provide. If your organization provides gaming consoles, but doesn't provide the hand controllers or the games, that's an incomplete product, and you will have unhappy customers. If your organization markets specific capabilities for your software products, but customers later find out they are only available as a pricy upgrade, they will be unhappy.

Bait and switch tactics are never a good option. Delivering a product without all the necessary components or software will only lead to unhappy customers. Releasing a product before it is fully tested, only to find it's full of bugs and missing features, is not a whole product. I could go on, but I think you get the idea.

Achieving continuous improvements (Kaizen)

This topic is conceptually tricky to implement, and I believe some analysts oversimplify what it takes to continuously improve performances and capabilities within an organization. The primary point to be made in this section is that Scrum and Lean-Agile teams build upon "good practices" to implement better practices over time, or at least to improve upon good practices in terms of supporting current business, development, and operational needs.

The term "best practices" has fallen out of favor in the software industry because of the implication that there is only one right way to do things, and that those so-called "best practices" cannot be improved upon. As noted previously in the sections on *Seeking perfection*, perfection is never actually achieved, even though it's always the desired goal. But building a foundation on good practices is not only possible – it's desirable.

Developing good practices

While there might not be such a thing as best practices, there certainly are good practices. On the other hand, I believe there is such a thing as **good engineering practices** comprised of suitably appropriate methods, procedures, and techniques. Building a library of good engineering practices helps improve quality and outcomes while reducing costs.

The basic idea is to not reinvent the World every time you come across a new problem. Instead, start with a basic approach, and then improve upon it. This concept supports two Lean principles outlined by Professor Linker, as part of The Toyota Way. The first is that standardized tasks are the foundations for continuous improvement. The second principle is that we should use reliable, thoroughly tested technologies that we can trust to support our people and processes.

The software industry has produced hundreds, if not thousands, of methods and tools. Most methods and tools fall out of favor over time, and many methods are specific to a particular technology or vendor's offering. Still, based on the standards approved for use by your development organization, some good practices already exist, so start from there. Alternatively, you can define your own good practices; but again, why start from scratch?. You need a baseline to start with in order to know if your team is improving or not.

Leveraging the 80/20 rule

You learned about the 80/20 rule in the section on *Perfection* in the previous chapter. Following Pareto's Principle (that is, the 80/20 rule), once we successfully address the first 20% of the most impactful activities – the ones that cause ~80% of our current problems – a subsequent review of the remaining most impactful activities results in the same pattern of 20% of the causes, thus creating ~80% of the most impacts. The refinement events in Scrum use these principles to improve performance over time.

However, the same 80/20 rule concepts apply to customer requirements in terms of identifying high-value opportunities within the Product Backlog. At any given time, only a relatively small number of identified features and functions have real value to the targeted customers.

In Product Backlog refinement, across every iteration, we need to re-evaluate two pieces of the value puzzle. First, what do customers now want from the product in terms of capabilities implemented as features and functions? Second, which of the highest value items in the backlog have the lowest development and delivery costs?

Value stream analysis in the software industry leverages the principles behind the 80/20 rule to continuously improve performance and add value. This repeating pattern of assessing the currently highest customer-centric value priorities, while eliminating all forms of waste, allows the organization to achieve tremendous improvements over time, usually well beyond the organization's initial expectations.

Avoiding radical change

Teams that attempt to continuously change out their practices, tools, and technologies will reduce their productivity as they master the new methods and tools. These will also have higher costs. So, those types of radical changes need to be considered carefully before you investment and implement something that's going to cost time, money, and effort before you see a viable return on investment.

Radical improvement concepts were initially associated with **business process reengineering** (**BPR**). BPR initiatives seek to redesign an end-to-end process and achieve radical improvements all at once. The goal of a BPR project is to improve business performance by streamlining activities, cutting costs, improving customer satisfaction, and achieving a significant and rapid competitive advantage.

At that level of detail, BPR sounds a lot like Lean. But BPR encourages rapid and radical changes, while Lean is more of a continuous process improvement effort. Radical changes are very disruptive to the organization, and it's difficult to obtain buy-in from those affected by the change. Those are the very people your organization needs in order to implement the changes. Moreover, it tends to be difficult to find practical approaches to both radically and quickly improve a business process.

There are times when radical improvements are both available and potentially viable. Sometimes, new technology is a potential driver for a radical change initiative. Or, there may be a new market opportunity driving the decision. However, more often than not, a BPR initiative is driven by a competitive market situation where the organization can no longer survive without radical change.

In the latter situations, the organization is already under extreme duress. As mentioned previously, the downside is that radical improvements usually entail extremely disruptive and rapid changes that can lead to massive resistance by all employees and stakeholders who are impacted. In contrast, Lean is a continuous improvement-oriented activity that seeks to implement incremental improvements over time. Incremental improvements tend to be less stressful on the organization and its people, particularly when the employees and other stakeholders participate in the improvement activities, and their jobs are not threatened by the improvement activities.

That's not to say that Lean practices cannot lead to rapid or breakthrough improvements. But, if done correctly, continuous improvements, through the implementation of Lean development philosophies, tend to be less disruptive to the employees and stakeholders the organization must count on to discover and implement the changes required to add value and eliminate waste.

Documenting good practices

A major tenant of Agile is that the focus of the development team is on creating working products, and not producing "comprehensive" documentation. This is true, but this doesn't mean there is no documentation. It's pretty hard to improve a process or practice, add value, eliminate waste, or know that you have achieved those goals if you haven't first documented your standard practices.

No, you don't need to write a book, but you do need an outline of *what good looks like*. In other words, we need the right amount of documentation to help us understand the minimal steps and acceptance criteria to perform an activity in a high-quality manner. Those procedural outlines serve as a baseline that lets us analyze broken processes and inefficiencies, and ultimately assess proposed changes that can have the most significant impact with the smallest level of effort or investment.

Don't worry if your initial attempts to build good practices fail. The whole point is to create a baseline and continuously improve from there. This continuous improvement process is another reason why it makes no sense to write detailed documentation. You probably aren't going to figure everything out at first and get it right the first time. Instead, go with the best information you have and improve your practices and value stream activities through trial and error thereafter.

Finally, we do not ever want to write documentation for documentation's sake. No value is added from the perspective of the customer. However, all documentation must be created, because it somehow helps the customer obtain the benefits of the product.

Starting with a focus on achieving stability and predictability

When a Lean software development team starts out, their primary focus is on achieving a degree of stability and predictability. It will be impossible for a team to accurately estimate their production capabilities until they achieve some level of stability with the skills, processes, and tools available to the team. In effect, during the initial startup, the team's continuous improvement activities focus on developing skills while implementing good practices around the technologies they employ. Then, through continuous refinement, the team improves their practices so that their collective performance improves with each iteration and release.

Measuring improvements

No matter how good our intentions are, it's easy to aim high and miss the mark because we never first figured out what *good* might look like. In other words, if we reduce the cycles times on 10 activities, but one of the 10 has twice the cycle as the others, we will have bottlenecks. So, one of our metrics might be to keep all cycle times within a specific range.

Let's take a quick look at some of the metrics our Lean software development organization should focus on:

- **Blockers**: Anything that causes a work item to sit in a queue is called a blocker. Very often, blocks in throughput occur because the next activity in line is missing some critical piece of information, materials, or components necessary to complete the activity. We need measures to not only see the areas of blocking, but also their causes, so that we can fix them.

- **Cycle time**: This metric operates at two levels. The first is the cycle time of each activity in a value stream, while the second is the cycle time for the combined activities across a value stream. This information is important to balance loads to prevent queuing and to improve throughput across the value stream.

- **Issue closure rates**: Neither Lean nor Agile practices can eliminate risks and issues. If it takes us a month to know there is a problem, then that's a problem.

- **Leadtime**: This metric is a variant of throughput and provides an indicator of how long it takes a new requirement to go from concept to delivery.

- **Mean time between failures** (**MTBF**): Customers need their applications and other solutions to be available. MTBF provides a measure of how often customers can expect to lose access to or use of the product.

- **Mean time to repair** (**MTTR**): Equally important as the preceding MTBF metric is MTTR, which is a measure of how long it takes to discover the failure, repair the problem, and then bring the solution back online.

- **Team velocity/Throughput**: Velocity (also known as throughput) is a measure of how much work a team can accomplish, usually measured in terms of story points. Teams estimate how much effort is involved with each new Product Backlog item and assign it an estimated degree of difficulty. The teams measure how many story points of work they accomplish across each Sprint and use these metrics to help rationalize how much work they can complete in future iterations. The metrics can also help the team gauge how many Sprints are required to complete a specific release of functionality.

- **Virus infection rates**: We might have the most functional software on the market, but it's of little value if the software is susceptible to viruses or other forms of malicious malware, such as adware, spyware, browser hijacking software, and fake security software. We want to measure those events and strive to move them all to zero.

- **Work in Progress/Progress** (**WIP**): Excess WIP contributes to lengthier cycle times and higher likelihood of bugs and defects. We want to measure, reduce, and then sustain an acceptable level of WIP, which is usually one item per task in the pipeline.

- **Queue size**: Queues are highly linked to excessive WIP, in that they are the location where work and materials accumulates. As noted previously, an ideal WIP measure is one item per task. Therefore, it should be apparent that, beyond the initial orders, as defined in the Product and Sprint Backlogs, we don't want any queues.

- **Queue waits**: When we have queues, the problems are exasperated when work items sit in the queue for lengthy periods of time. Lengthy waits in the queue add to the product delivery cycle time, and they often hide defects and bugs that become increasingly difficult to resolve.

Continuing to improve through refinement

The team must also evaluate flow and how much work they have in progress on every iteration, as discussed in the upcoming section, titled *Applying visual controls to manage intake and Flows*. Visual aids, such as a Kanban board, help the team not only see the flow, but also work stoppages. Work stoppages are impediments to the team's flow. As they are identified, the team comes together to eliminate the impediments in the current Sprint. However, they should also use the refinement event to further analyze how they can prevent the impediments from occurring in the future, or at least reduce their impacts in the future.

The whole point of having relatively short iterations is to reduce the amount of work in progress so that impediments and bugs are quickly discovered and resolved. This strategy conforms with the Lean principle of continuous improvements. In contrast, under the traditional plan-driven and linear-sequential software development model, there is little or no opportunity, during the life of the project, to observe and fix problems since testing activities where problems and bugs can be uncovered are held off to the very end of the project.

Applying visual controls to manage intake and flows

In the previous chapter, you learned about visual aids in the form of Kanban cards and Kanban boards to support pull-based intake strategies that match customer orders to production capacities. The same principles on the implementation of Flow and Pull concepts apply to managing work within a Scrum-based Sprint.

Instead of a product order list, we have a Sprint Backlog, which serves the same purpose of identifying the order list of work. We also have standardized activities in a Scrum, such as design, development, and testing.

However, since Scrum Teams, by design, are self-contained and self-organizing, every team member or subset of team members should be able to pull and work on any story or task off the Sprint Backlog. As a result, the Scrum Kanban board tends to be a bit of a simpler process than a Kanban card used in manufacturing.

An example of a Scrum Kanban board is shown in the following diagram. The Scrum Kanban board is very often a simple whiteboard hung in the common work area supporting the Scrum Team. Lines are drawn on the whiteboard to segment different stages of work completion across the Sprint. Information describing the identified Stories and Tasks are written by hand onto individual sticky notes. These sticky notes are placed on, and later moved across, segments on the whiteboard to indicate the current status of each defined Story and Task.

Scrum Teams can choose to segment their whiteboards into whatever numbers and types of segments that they believe best supports the visualization of their development and testing activities. The following diagram provides a simple segmentation consisting of stories identified in the Sprint Backlog (that is, **Story**); the set of stories and tasks that are refined and available to start working on (that is, **To Do**); a segment showing the work that is currently in process (that is, **In Progress**); another segment that indicates the completed work undergoing verification (that is, **To Verify**); and a segment that shows the stories and tasks that are complete, meeting the **definition of Done** (that is, **Done**):

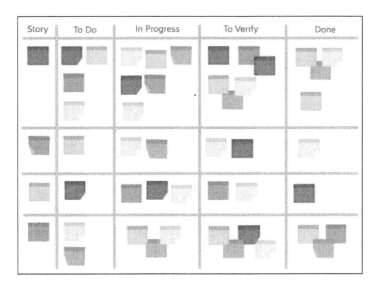

Figure 6.1 – Scrum Kanban board with sticky notes listing tasks for teamwork and visual management

I mentioned that the Scrum Team could choose the number and types of segments they prefer on their Scrum Kanban boards. As an example, they may prefer to modify and split the segment titled To Verify to show work progressing through **Testing** and **Peer Review** activities, if those terms are more indictive of the team's verification process. Likewise, some Scrum Teams may prefer to use the term **Backlog** or to further segment the Backlog section into separate **Product Backlog** and **Sprint Backlog** sections.

By using the Pull production concepts defined earlier in this section, upcoming work is initially displayed as a queue in the Story or Backlog segments. As individuals within the team have the capacity, they pull stories from the Backlog queues to refine their understanding of the work. But they should never pull more than one task at a time.

In an ideal situation, those who have refined the Stories should be able to complete the work, and they will pull the refined stories as work into their WIP queue. The whiteboard is updated by moving the sticky note describing the work from the To Do segment to the WIP segment. However, there is nothing that prevents another developer or paired programming team from pulling the refined stories and tasks from the To-Do segment. In those cases, the sticky notes need to be updated with an annotation to indicate the refinement process is completed. Alternatively, the Scrum Team members can simply talk to each other to get an update on the status of work in each segment on the whiteboard.

In the previous chapter, you discovered that retrospectives are key events within a Scrum Sprint that allow the Scrum Team to assess their performance and uncover better ways of working. This concept is also a critical component of Lean Thinking. In Lean Thinking, continuous improvements are part of the Lean concept of seeking perfection.

Building in quality

In the traditional software development model, quality is a lengthy and arduous process that spans the requirements, design, development, and testing phases. Identified functional and nonfunctional requirements translate into system components and features through the architecture and design activities. The developers create test scenarios and test scripts and identify acceptance criteria that their code must eventually pass. Once the code has been developed, the developers or testers run the tests to see if the code passes. If not, the code is sent back to the developers to debug and fix. Since testing is the last phase of overall development activity before deployment, it's very difficult to find the source of bugs and defects, leading to delays and extra costs. By that time, the software code is too big and too complex to efficiently debug.

Testing incrementally

Under Scrum and Agile processes, the requirements, analysis, design, coding, and testing process is expedited by only building a small increment of new functionality over relatively brief development iterations. Bugs are found more quickly and dealt with immediately. Simply put, it's easier to find the underlying problems causing defects when coding and testing are frequently iterated, as well as when integrated tasks are performed throughout the development life cycle of a product.

Instead of tracking bugs and defects, the goal is to avoid them in the first place. Allowing defects to accumulate in the team's software code is a form of partially done work, which you'll learn about in the *Rejecting incomplete work* section.

Test-driven development (**TDD**) and **CI** (**CI**) help the developers identify bugs early on. TDD implements a discipline used to write test scripts that meet predefined acceptance criteria prior to writing the source code. The tests are also run before the code is written to make sure they fail. This ensures the new code will not implement functionality that interferes with other existing routines.

Once the code has been developed, the TDD scripts are run again as part of unit and integration testing to ensure the new code functions as intended. If the test fails, then the developer knows they need to fix their code before moving on to writing any new code.

Development teams using CI practices to merge their code into a central repository multiple times a day. As part of the merge process, an automated build process integrates and tests the new code with the existing code to see if errors crop up. If there are errors, the developers analyze the cause of the defect so that they can resolve the issue before proceeding with new work.

It should be pretty clear that building in quality means writing less software at a time and implementing incremental testing to find and resolve any errors before the code becomes so complex that the source of the error is masked. Also, the developers should not be afraid to fail. A trial and error approach to development is not a bad thing. Rather, it turns out to be an effective and efficient approach to quickly developing and testing code, and also provides an overall reduction in the amount of time spent on debugging software.

Refactoring software code

It's rare that a new piece of software code or newly integrated software is written in its most efficient form. The goal of refactoring is to improve the internal structures of software code so that it runs more efficiently, without changing its external behaviors, which would introduce new bugs into the previously working product. In short, refactoring makes software perform its purpose more efficiently, especially when new components are added and integrated. So, developers should refactor their software often as part of their efforts to build quality into their products.

Delaying decisions and commitments

The Lean concept behind this principle is that decision-making should never be rushed. In fact, you should wait until that last practical moment to make most decisions. This strategy is the exact opposite of what occurs in the traditional waterfall-based software development model. The waterfall model forces project teams to make detailed project plans based on highly uncertain and speculative information. Then, the development team was expected to follow those plans as if they were gospel.

In contrast, Agile-based software development methodologies, such as Scrum, recognize that markets change and that customer needs to evolve over time. Given those facts, if we make decisions early, it's very likely they will be wrong. The more uncertain the market or the more dynamic the customer environment is, the more likely this statement is true.

Delaying decisions on priorities, the architecture, and system designs until we have better facts on what customers perceive is value helps keep us from making the wrong decisions. Making wrong decisions leads to lost productivity and may also involve having to make significant changes to existing software code to get things right. Instead, it's better to leave all the options open until we have better information to make final decisions.

In the long run, delaying decisions until we have reliable information to work with saves time, lost productivity, and money building products that customers want and value. In effect, delaying decisions is a valuable risk mitigation strategy.

Detecting defects through automation (Jidoka)

The manufacturing concept of **Jidoka** is the implementation of human intelligence-like capabilities used to constantly monitor production equipment and processes to identify defects. The goal of Jidoka is to quickly identify and isolate any errors or equipment shutdowns to minimize harm so that the issues can be addressed immediately. Jidoka-based systems may also have capabilities to resolve specific issues without human intervention.

The software development equivalent includes CI and testing capabilities. You have already learned about several techniques that improve software testing as part of Agile development practices, so they do not need to be repeated here. However, I will add that Jidoka concepts also apply to network and system performance and security monitoring in an IT operations environment. When networks or systems shut down, their performance is reduced, or their security is compromised, automated systems can discover and react much more quickly than humans can to address the problems, assuming the right protocols are in place.

The main point is that CI software testing, plus network and system performance and security monitoring capabilities, help make the IT organization Lean in two ways: first, to quickly find and resolve any problems that negatively impact value creation and value delivery activities, and second, to streamline flows to improve efficiencies across IT value stream creation and delivery activities.

Eliminating mistakes (Poka-Yoke)

Any time there is a mistake, no matter the cause, the software development team can expect an impact in the form of delaying product or feature deliveries or wasted time spent debugging and fixing a faulty software product. Mistakes do not just show up as bugs in the software code. Mistakes also show up as defects when requirements are not accurately defined to begin with.

Implementing effective software testing strategies, such as TDD, CI, and continuous delivery capabilities, all help prevent mistakes from accumulating to the point that the team's productivity is hindered due to extended software debugging and break-fix activities. In addition, development strategies such as paired programming and peer reviews also help eliminate buggy or inefficient software. Refactoring software is another strategy used to enhance the performance of existing software code.

While it may not be possible to eliminate mistakes, it is certainly possible to find them early and reduce their impact on the quality of the software. Accumulating defects and bugs also hurts the team's ability to deliver incremental value on a timely basis. Having effective and proven software development methods and tools helps eliminate errors and mistakes, particularly as the team's proficiency improves over time.

Many modern software development tools and **Integrated Development Environments (IDEs)** have integrated text and source code editors that help the developer write correct code for the language they are using. Most have integrated debugging tools that find and indicate errors in the code in real time as the developers incrementally develop their code. Another capability that supports the concept of Poke-Yoke is the use of pre-tested code libraries, which eliminates the need for developers to rewrite similar code over and over again.

Eliminating waste

Taiichi Ohno identified the most common forms of waste as waiting, overproduction, extra processing, transportation, motion, inventory, and defects. Let's look at how those concepts of waste apply to software and systems development.

Waiting

Waiting is a problem because that means we are not getting something done that the customers want, or it is impacting the productivity of the team. For example, if the team is waiting on requirements, or information necessary to refine the requirements, they can't build the features that the customers want. If they are waiting on items from the Product Backlog to be prioritized, they cannot deliver the features and functionality that the customers value the most.

Items identified within a Product or Sprint Backlog are, by definition, waiting to be worked on. However, as you will see in the next subsection on overproduction, this is not a bad thing as long as they are not the highest priority items. In other words, priority always goes to the highest value, lowest cost items. From the perspective of the 80/20 rule, the highest 20% of the high priority-low cost items may provide as much as 80% of the value.

When systems and networks go down, the developers do not have access to the tools they need to develop, test, and deploy their software. Customers are similarly impacted when they do not have access to the applications they need, which can be a huge issue in the era of **Software as a Service (SaaS)**.

Overproducing

Overproduction occurs when a development team continues to build software products and features simply because they have the capacity or the skills to do so, not because the items have the highest priorities in the Product Backlog. A typical scenario is when a team has capacity but not the skills or resources to work on the highest value items in the Product Backlog. This is an issue that most often crops up in multi-team development environments, especially when teams are specialized. If a team does not have the skills to work on the highest priority items in the Product Backlog, there will be pressure to have them work on something, even if that means working on lower priority items.

The problem with having a team work on lower priority items is the same problem functionally aligned manufacturing organizations have when they produce items. While they may have additional capacity, their capacities are not matched and working in lockstep with the other functional units. When the higher capacity workstations continue processing work, the inevitable result is queuing at other stations. If the products cannot be immediately utilized because they rely upon other components still under development, the net result is a wasted effort with no real-time value added. Even if the lower value products can be released, they will not have the value and profit contributions available if the team could have instead worked on delivering the higher-value items in the backlog.

For this reason, all development teams need to be fully self-contained with all the skills necessary to support the product's development requirements. The more an organization relies upon specialists, the more often they will be faced with situations, and feel pressure, to have those specialists building components and features that do not have high or immediate value. This strategy of reaching is a waste of time and resources. The solution to this problem is to encourage cross-training within the development teams, and to encourage continuous learning activities.

Extra or non-value-added processing

Similar to overproducing, extra processing occurs when features, enhancements, or higher levels of quality are added to a product that are not valued by the customer. However, in this case, the features are added by the Product Owner or developers based on their views of what adds value to a product; they are not validated by their target market customers. Worse, the decision makers may not have a complete understanding of the potential markets for their products and services.

This situation occurs most frequently when a highly technical CEO or group of highly technical individuals build products that they know would help them address the technical issues they face or faced as developers. In other words, they have viewed the potential market and requirements through the narrow lens of their direct experiences.

Yes, their perception of needs may have an initial market value that's enough to start a business. However, their vision for the market, as a whole, is often incomplete and not sufficient to sustain the business in the long run. And, if the ego of the CEO or Product Owner is involved, they may not have the discipline to overcome their perceptions to find out who their larger prospective base of customers might include, or what their expanded needs are.

I've seen this situation occur multiple times over my career, spanning a diverse amount of technical solutions, such as developing **computer-aided systems engineering (CASE)** tools, workflow tools, **IDEs**, portals, and middleware products. While there was an initial market for identified technical enhancements, the decision makers often missed the larger market opportunities by not directly addressing the needs of the business and domain users who mostly benefit from applications created by those software development tools.

For example, I believe an early failure of **CASE** tool vendors is not pushing harder on their code generation and testing capabilities. CASE tools evolved to include business domain experts and business analysts in modeling business functions, processes, data and information requirements, and the definition of objects in support of object-oriented modeling. But I believe the CASE tool vendors missed an opportunity to entrench those products in the much larger business community by going the next step to automate code generation and testing.

Interestingly, the software industry is seeing a resurgence of this concept through *No-code development platforms*. No-code software development platforms provide GUI-based drag-and-drop tools that allow businesses domain experts to develop software applications quickly and without coding.

I've similarly experienced first-hand vendors of **middleware** integration products that made similar mistakes. They did not quickly implement GUI-based modeling capabilities that would otherwise encourage involvement of domain experts and business analysts in modeling and analyzing business processes that span multiple business systems. GUI-based modeling capabilities help domain experts link disparate, geographically dispersed, and even cross-organizational applications to set up the integration and data transformation rules across applications in support of cross-functional/cross-organizational business processes.

Some middleware vendors were so focused on developing products for other technical specialists or solving complex technical problems that they did not see their competitors were expanding the overall middleware customer base. Instead of selling directly to IT shops, other competitors expanded the middleware markets by selling more compelling products, with GUI-based modeling and integration capabilities, directly to business executives, process owners, business analysts, and business process consultants.

Here's an interesting point to think about. In my opinion, it didn't really matter whether non-technical domain experts directly used the modeling tools. More importantly, the GUI-based modeling tools made metadata mapping, data integrations, and data transformations visible to the domain experts, as opposed to a black-box approach where the customers had to trust the accuracy of the developers' middleware integrations.

Another example of extra processing occurred in the early portal software industry. As the name **portal** implies, portal software provides a gateway to other corporate and external applications and information resources. In other words, portal software development tools allow organizations to create an internet or intranet-based website that serves as a highly graphical interface and launch point for users to discover and interact with any number of back-end applications and information resources.

Again, some of the early Portal products were built by engineers to solve particular technical problems, including application and data integration, business intelligence, executive dashboards, web services, and GUI-based intranet and internet-based information and marketing hubs. And all that's before we speak about business domain portal applications, such as Human Resource Portals.

A modern portal software development environment includes all those capabilities with product variants that address specific domain user needs. Those vendors who stayed focused on developing point solutions did not remain relevant as the industry matured.

The main takeaway from this section is that Product Owners and developers must look past their biases to develop features, enhancements, and levels of quality that are validated by customers in the targeted markets. Otherwise, there is a high probability that the intended customers will not value them. The bottom line is that extra processing is a form of wasted effort, which causes lost productivity and developer time that cannot be gotten back. So, avoid extra processing at all costs.

Transportation

The waste of transportation occurs when value stream activities are delayed waiting on components or functionality produced by entities not located with the development team that requires them. This type of queuing problem is an issue in modern globalization where development teams are geographically dispersed off-site, across the country, and often across the world. When the negative consequences of working across disparate time zones is added in, the resulting lost productivity can be quite significant.

Realistically, we are not going to get away from leveraging human resources residing in different locations and working in virtual environments. But there are some things that can be done to mitigate the risks. For example, it may make sense to organize product lines so that development occurs in locations with similar time zones. Alternatively, it may make sense to organize work into subsystems or large components that require minimal interactions between development teams to resolve data exchange and integration issues.

Motion

The issues related to wasted motion are similar to those of transportation, except the scale is limited to motion within the development team's work environment. An example of waste in motion occurs when development team members are not co-located and must move away from their desks to find and work with another team member. Another example of wasted motion occurs when information is not available to team members and they must leave their work environment to find it. Likewise, if developers do not have access to their desktop computers to the development tools, networks, or applications they require, they will have to move to another location to obtain the necessary access to the tools they need.

The solution to wasted motion is to provide co-located work facilities for your development teams. Ideally, a co-located facility has a central meeting area, individual workspaces, open walls, and whiteboards for Big visible charts. The developers also must have network access, computing equipment, and the software tools they need to do their jobs.

One area of motion that may be necessary is to visit with customers or users to discuss and refine their understanding of requirements. In other words, there will be times where it makes sense for the developers to leave their work environments to visit the customers or other stakeholders who have the information they need. But, whenever possible, it's a better practice to bring those individuals to the work location of the developers.

Inventory

In the traditional concepts of Lean manufacturing, the waste of inventory involves carrying costs for raw materials sitting in queue or in storage waiting on processing. Not only are the delays potentially hiding defects that will require rework or generate scrap, but there is additional cost associated with procuring and storing the materials. Maintaining an inventory of excessive hardware components or building software components that do not have the highest current value are examples of building inventories in software and systems development. Both forms of inventories are examples of non-valued-added waste.

We've previously discussed how the traditional Waterfall-based software development model forced development teams to identify and build all features within a single product development and test cycle. And we also discussed how that approach to software development hides bugs and defects that become very difficult to debug and fix. So, in an Agile paradigm, we use iterative and incremental development practices to reduce the number of identified requirements in development at any given moment.

We've also discussed the use of Kanban boards to visualize and limit the amount of work in process within the development team. Ideally, development team members pull individual tasks, one at a time, from the Sprint backlog when they become open and thereby have the capacity to take on new work. This approach mimics the single-piece development principle of Lean, helps maintain a constant flow, and implements the Lean principle of Pull.

Defects

Wasting defects occurs when software products or related services deviate from what the customer requires. Note that not all defects result from lousy coding. A defect can arise simply because the requirements were not properly identified or understood in the first place.

In the traditional Waterfall-based development model, the business analysts and developers interview customers and end users to document their needs and then write detailed specifications that outline the identified business, user, and nonfunctional requirements. All development work is based upon what's written in those specifications. The problem is that there is a high chance that what's written in the specifications is wrong. Worse, those errors won't be discovered until nearly the end of the project, during user acceptance testing.

In the Agile development paradigm, the Product Owner identifies requirements and writes them down, typically in the form of epics and user stories. These epics and user stories are managed within the Product Backlog. Working with input from the development team, the Product Owner assigns priorities to each epic and user story based upon their values and costs to deliver. That is, those items with the highest value and lowest costs to develop will have the highest development priorities.

Next, the development team determines which items they will work on within an incoming Sprint based on alignment with the goals of the Sprint and the amount of work that is achievable within the duration of the Sprint. Certainly, before the Sprint, but even during the Sprint, developers will seek information from the Product Owners, customers, end users, and other stakeholders to better refine their understanding of the requirements. Then, at the end of the Sprint, the developers conduct a Sprint review where customers and end users can view a demo of the product. This constant review of the product while it's under development helps ensure the customers agree that the product conforms to their requirements and has value.

Wasting defects also occur when the development team does not employ proper and continuous testing procedures during development. This subject was discussed extensively in the *Continuous improvements* and *Detecting defects automation* sections.

Ending multitasking/task switching

In case you haven't already figured this out for yourself, multitasking is a bad habit. Almost everyone thinks they are good at it, but no one really is. It turns out we humans are sequential thinkers. The best you might be able to say is that you are quick at *context switching*, which means you are comfortable with quickly changing your train of thought from one subject to another. Nevertheless, there are delays associated with changing subjects or moving from one task to another.

Scientists who have analyzed the process of multitasking have come to realize what we are really doing is task switching. In other words, we're not very good at doing more than one thing at a time. Instead, we compensate by repeatedly moving from one task to another, and then back again. Worse, multitasking hurts decision-making, makes us less efficient, increases our stress, and makes us less friendly (*6 Reasons You're Actually Not Good at Multitasking*: `https://www.goodtherapy.org/blog/6-reasons-youre-actually-not-good-at-multitasking-0831167`).

Lean analysts, such as Mary and Tom Poppendieck (Poppendieck, 2003) concluded that task switching in software development is a bad practice. Every time a person switches tasks, they require time to change their train of thought and redirect their activities to the new task. When developers are assigned to multiple teams, the constant interruptions of task switching reduce their productivity and contributions.

Another form of task switching occurs when a development team takes on too much work and tries to work on those tasks in parallel. Instead of having an efficient flow and pulling work to each team member as they have capacity, the team members find themselves constantly switching back and forth between tasks. The result is that every time they switch tasks, they lose time coming back up to speed with the requirements of the revisited task.

In short, task switching is a waste of human talent and intellect that needs to be avoided at all costs.

Practicing Gemba

Gemba is a Japanese business management term that roughly translates to *the place where things happen* or *the real place*. In the context of Lean, Gemba is the place where value is created. Therefore, in the context of software development, Gemba is the place where developers create value.

Toyota implemented the practice of *Gemba Walks*, where managers literally walk the floors of their manufacturing facilities to view the processes and talk with the people performing the work. The in-person visits and discussions allowed the managers to see first-hand what actually takes place on the production floors. This time on the production floors allowed the managers to promote a collaborative environment, build trust with their employees, and make more informed decisions.

Though I didn't know the term at the time, this is exactly what I was doing when I started working in the printed circuit board shop. Intuitively, I understood I would not get a true understanding of how circuit boards were built, let alone understand any of the issues the fabricators and engineers faced, unless I went down and worked on the floor with them. No spreadsheet or computer printout was going to tell me what I needed to know.

In Agile-based software development, especially in Scrum-based practices, the concept of Gemba plays out in the concepts of transparency, inspect, and adapt. To improve transparency, many Agile disciplines recommend the employment of *Big visible charts* in work locations, or adjacent to work locations, so that anyone who walks by can quickly see and understand relevant project data. If they have questions, they can ask the developers right then and there.

The practice of Gemba does not just include executives and business managers going out to get first-hand knowledge from the developers. Product managers, Product Owners, and marketing staff also need first-hand knowledge of development impediments that would delay or prevent the implementation of a new marketing strategy.

Product managers, Product Owners, and marketing staff need to understand the issues and not get ahead of what's possible. The danger is that they will push for a product enhancement that is not commercially viable or promote a product or services in advance of the development team's ability to provide the value customers want. No matter how big the opportunity, value-based priority assessments must always include the time, effort, development costs, and lost opportunity costs necessary to raise the priority within the Product Backlog of a new product, a new feature, or a new functionality.

Implementing single-piece flows

Single-piece flows is a discipline where each activity across a value stream can only process one item at a time. Optimized layouts and flows, the elimination of batch processes, reduced setup times, and limited waste due to transportation, queuing, or unnecessary motions makes single-piece flows possible.

Working on one component at a time dramatically improves efficiency, improves quality, and ultimately moves items through a value stream at the most practical pace that won't cause queuing and resulting delays. The ideal goal in Lean is to implement single-piece flows across all value stream processes.

The implementation of Kanban boards, with a restriction of developers pulling only one item at a time from the WIP queue or Sprint Backlog, effectively implements single-piece production in a software development environment. All the traditional benefits of single-piece flow, as listed in the preceding paragraph, apply to the implementation by a software development organization.

Improving knowledge

Virtually, all Agile approaches to software development, including the Scrum framework, relies on relatively small and autonomous teams. Each of the small teams has all the skills and resources they need to self-organize and get a new increment of prioritized work completed, fulfilling each increment's definition of Done, within relatively short iterations of time.

> **Note**
>
> The **Definition of Done** is a common term and concept that's employed across Agile-based practices, including those cited in part two of this book.

Over time, the team can expect new needs to emerge that they may not have previously addressed. A basic philosophy in Scrum is not to rely on the concept of using specialists to perform work that is new to the team, except in a short-term and emergency situation. Even then, if the specialist's need is a long-term requirement, the team is expected to have one or more members learn and acquire the skills.

Given this philosophy, the team must be willing to constantly improve their knowledge. In fact, rather than promoting individuals based on their time in their company or years of experience, a better practice is to base salaries and promotions on the relevant training and professional certifications they receive.

With that goal in mind, the organization's human resources staff and executives must constantly evaluate organizational training needs and ensure sufficient resources are made available to train and certify their Scrum Team members across the skills and disciplines required by the organization. Moreover, the organization's executive staff must ensure their compensation and incentive programs are in alignment with this philosophy of continuous learning.

Finally, another form of waste is having to relearn something. When constructing new or infrequently created logical routines or software components, take a few moments to document the process and maintain the code in a code library for reuse when it's needed at a later date.

Leveling production (Heijunka)

The Lean lexicon defines **Heijunka** as *Leveling the type and quantity of production over a fixed period of time.* (`https://www.Lean.org/search/?sc=Heijunka`) The concept of leveling production in Lean simply means the production rates need to match customer demand rates. Production leveling is the most efficient way to meet customer demands by eliminating batch processes and simultaneously reducing work in progress. Those improvements, in turn, reduce delays and complexity in production while improving flows.

It's very likely that the Product Owner, in collaboration with a multitude of stakeholders and customers, has identified a share a common understanding that systems fail through of potential features and functions that will take multiple Sprints and releases to implement. Those items need to be pulled by the development team only when they have the near-term capacity to work on them. And then they need to try and not work on everything in their queue (that is, the Sprint Backlog) at once. Individual team members pull individual items from the Sprint backlog and work on them until they meet the definition of Done. This is how product leveling occurs in an Agile-based development system. The primary tool that aids in leveling production in a software development environment is the Kanban board.

Optimizing the whole

The traditional software development model employs a project-based development paradigm. Each project has a specific objective that is pre-planned, budgeted, scheduled, and approved. This strategy is suboptimal over the life of a product as funding for new enhancements is never assured, and each project is constrained to complete a scope of work approved by the customer or executive sponsor. Such a development strategy is suboptimal on a number of levels.

Failing through suboptimization

Systems and Lean Thinking share a common understanding that systems fail through suboptimization. Recall from *Chapter 4, Systems Thinking* that we need to look at the whole of a system and not its individual parts if we are going to improve the performance of a system. Similarly, in the initial sections of this chapter on Lean Thinking, we found that the performance of an integrated system is bound by its slowest activity within the value stream. Both concepts are related.

Suboptimization occurs when a process or system, as a whole, fails to meet expectations because there is a lack of integration or coordination between the activities that make up a process or the elements that make up the system. In other words, the process or system is said to be suboptimal.

You can argue that the expected outcome of a process or system is relatively subjective. The expected outcomes of a business process or system are typically based on business or organizational goals that live apart from the realities of what's currently possible. So, for example, the business might have targeted goals to produce 100 widgets per month at a cost of $1,000 per widget. Whether that goal is possible or not is another matter.

Such was the situation when I worked in the printed circuit board shop cited at the beginning of the previous chapter. Our government contract specified we deliver a certain number of surface mount circuit boards at a specific price within a fixed time frame. The primary reason our shop got into problems is that the engineers designed their processes in isolation of the other manufacturing processes. As a result, the engineers did not have a complete understanding of how their processes impacted other manufacturing processes as a collective system. Using our Systems Thinking vernacular, the engineers were practicing local optimizations.

Fixing just one element within the system is not likely going to help the organization achieve its overall business goals. Instead, we must look at the entire value stream to make sure all activities are synchronized and coordinated. This will help us produce a constant flow of products within the target costs that are in line with customer delivery requests.

The software industry was not quick to understand that the same principles apply to their development processes. I say this from personal experience, not necessarily because some other consultant or industry expert says it's true. The traditional Waterfall-based software development model implements a suboptimal batch process.

Pushing software products through development

The waterfall approach to software development is a pure push-oriented approach to product development. Think about how the Waterfall process work. Software products start out as loosely defined requirements, pushed through development, and then sent on directly to customers or into a production environment where the customers will hopefully find value.

Let's take a closer look at Waterfall software development practices from this perspective:

1. First, a contract or charter is released that specifies high-level requirements and authorized constraints governing budgets, schedules, resources, and quality expectations for a new software application or system. The project team initially preplans all the work by defining a typical set of activities required to produce an application using standard development practices and metrics attained on previous software development projects. Once the initial project plans are completed and approved by management, they are pushed to the development team, and the team must abide by them.

2. Next, the business analysts and senior developers analyze and refine the business and user requirements, and then describes them in detailed requirements specifications. The requirements outlined in the specifications are pushed to the software architects and software designers, who then create detailed architecture and design documents outlining the components of the application, their interactions, and how the software team is to build out the products.

3. Next, the architecture and design documents serve as input to the developers who begin to code the applications. Now, there are a lot of bright software engineers who know they should conduct unit and integration tests concurrently with coding, and most do. However, it's a common practice under Waterfall to push out additional systems testing, user acceptance testing, regression testing, and performance testing activities until after the developers have finished all their coding activities. At that late stage, the testing activities will uncover a number of defects and bugs that are entrenched so deeply in the software code that debugging becomes a lengthy and tedious task. This late testing approach results in more delays.

4. Eventually, the product is ready to be released into deployment, which may involve any number of other activities to produce documentation for system administration, installation, configuration, and product support, plus user help guides and training aids. Finally, the software product is pushed to the customer or to a production environment where the IT operations team takes over to maintain and support the product across its life cycle.

In short, the plan-driven and linear-sequential waterfall process implements a push-oriented development system end-to-end with no expectations of allowing major changes to the initial requirements, which might work to change the predefined set of processes. To do so would negatively impact the plans, approved by customers and senior managers, that support the approved budgets, schedules, resources, and quality constraints.

It turned out that the Waterfall approach is suboptimal in terms of producing the products customers want, with the features they want, when they want them, and with the quality they really want at a price they are willing to pay. Let's find out why.

Waterfalling is suboptimizing

The length of each of the software development activities described in the previous subsection are different, which means the flow of work across this value stream is suboptimal. Moreover, the combined requirements, design, development, testing, and release processes should never have been viewed as a single, sequential, end-to-end operation. From a Lean perspective, requirements analysis and design are a separate value stream, while the set of development and test activities are another value stream. Finally, the production release and support activities are a third value stream.

The mistake was viewing the process of software development as a fixed set of activities bound by predefined project constraints. It was the wrong paradigm for several reasons:

- **The software industry is highly dynamic in terms of technology changes, customer applications, and the competitive landscape**: Plans based on previous practices and metrics are suboptimal to meet current needs.

- **Customers often don't know what they want until they see it**: Products built solely from high-level requirements are suboptimal in the implementation of user-centric features and functionality.

- **Customer priorities and needs change quickly**: Products built from a plan are suboptimal because they cannot evolve in line with the customers' needs.

- **Competitive markets rapidly change business requirements**: Products built from a plan are suboptimal because they cannot evolve in time to address competitive issues or support the company's emergent market opportunities and strategies.

Changing from project to product-oriented development

The solution to suboptimization is to get away from the project-oriented development paradigm and move to a product-oriented development strategy. Where projects have a fixed duration and scope of work, product-oriented development strategies look across the entire life cycle of the product as a continuum. In a product orientation, the organization continues to make investments in the product or service for as long as the product has value and we can make a profit from continuing development and sustainment efforts.

Product-oriented development involves different organizational structures and financial strategies. Since development and sustainment activities are ongoing across the life of the product or service, it's more efficient to maintain the development and support teams over a set duration. Project-oriented development forces the organization to essentially start over every fiscal year, build a new team, and find new funding. Moreover, project management is predicated on the concept that progress is measured against detailed plans and schedules. Therefore, project-oriented development work is antithetical to the notions of allowing responsive change to address new requirements, strategies, and priorities.

In a product-oriented strategy, funding must be sustained over the life of the product. Funding may change based on the opportunity to develop new value-added enhancements, or perhaps get reduced if the product has maximal value but requires ongoing sustainment and support services.

Producing just-in-time (JIT)

Taiichi Ohno conceived JIT at Toyota as a strategy to reduce the time between when a customer placed an order until the company collected payment. To achieve this goal, the objective was, and still is, to match production rates to customer demand and eliminate all waste in activities that do not add value across the production processes.

The elimination of waste goes beyond the identification of non-value activities, to also include the elimination of raw material inventories and work in progress. Matching production capacity to demand involves pulling orders into the production operation only at the rate the facility can handle, which is effectively the rate of its slowest process.

We don't need to elaborate much further on this subject as we already discussed the application of these principles in software and systems development across many of the previous sections in this chapter, including the sections on *Leveling production* and *Applying visual controls*. The main takeaway is that the principles of JIT are manifested in the software development organization that implements a pull system that limits work in progress to the capacity of individual team members performing the work. In such cases, a Kanban board helps implement this pull strategy while also providing visualization of work in progress. The Kanban board also supports the FIFO ordering of work based on product and Sprint Backlog priorities.

Rejecting unfinished work

Unfinished work is any work in progress that's not meeting the **definition of Done**. Unfinished work is not a bad thing as long as the product is flowing through the development system with proper cadence, one feature at a time, and with minimal waste. But when work is delayed for any reason, we have a problem.

A common cause of delays occurs when developers move on to develop new code before completing the work they had started. They may have run into a bug that's proven difficult to resolve. Or, they may not have the knowledge or skills to implement a particular feature. Hopefully, by now, you know that the solution is to reach out to other team members, even as an all-hands effort, to fully address the problem before moving on. Otherwise, the team, as a whole, risks missing the objectives of their Sprint goals.

Another common form of unfinished work in software development occurs when a developer moves on to write new code before completing their unit and integration tests. By now, you know that every committed segment of software code must meet its definition of done before moving on. Otherwise, the developer runs the risk of creating buggy or defective code that becomes increasingly difficult to resolve the longer they delay testing.

Finally, we've previously discussed that humans cannot multitask. So, it's a misnomer to think developers can work on multiple tasks simultaneously. Instead, they will either work through their selection of tasks sequentially – the best-case scenario – or they will attempt to work on them in parallel – the worst-case scenario. Neither scenario is ideal as work declared in process by the developer is really delayed. But the issues of context switching, as the developers moves back and forth between tasks, adds to the complexities and time required to finish the work; that is, the features not being worked on are both unfinished and delayed.

Respecting people

The concept of respecting people is a part of Lean principles that date back to Taiichi Ohno's work at Toyota. But the principles also found their way into the Agile Manifesto and virtually all Agile-based approaches to software development, including Scrum.

Respect doesn't imply that employees and team members get to slack off or accept low-quality work. There is accountability. But we always treat people the way we want to be treated. In other words, we follow the Golden Rule. Let's see how this principle applies to software development team members:

- Work normal hours, eliminate overtime, and maintain a sustainable pace.

- Help team members understand the value they provide to customers.

- Build compensation and incentives plans around continuous learning and skills.

- Challenge team members without belittling them.

- Hold teams, not individuals, accountable to their commitments.

- Implement safe working environments so that team members are not punished for seeking help when problems arise.

- Involve team members in analyzing problems, their cause and effects, and coming up with methods to resolve the issues at hand.

- Remove impediments to minimize frustration.

- While seeking stability, also provide variety to prevent boredom.

- Protect the organizational knowledge base by developing stable personnel, promotions based on demonstrable development of relevant knowledge and skills, and very careful succession plans.

This concludes this chapter on applying Lean practices to software and systems development. In the concluding *Summary* section, you'll have a chance to review the primary concepts and knowledge you should retain from this chapter.

Summary

In this chapter, you learned how to take the basic principles of Lean, as introduced in the previous chapter, and apply them to software and systems development projects. Though many of the practices are tweaked a bit, the basic principles of Lean still apply across the board. And the basic goals of Lean, which are to increase value and eliminate waste, are just as important to being competitive in the software industry as they are in manufacturing or other service industries.

Altogether, you have reviewed the practical implementation of 18 Lean practices to enhance value and eliminate waste in software development activities. You've also seen how the values and principles of Agile inherently implement many Lean concepts.

This chapter also completes *Module One* of this book. You now have the foundational knowledge necessary to understand how to apply modern Scrum practices at scale. In the next module, you will learn about the current thought leaders and methodologist who are developing scaled-Agile concepts. These include Scrum@Scale, Nexus, **Large-Scale Scrum (LeSS)**, Disciplined Agile, and the **Scaled-Agile Framework (SAFe®)**.

Chapter 14, Contrasting Scrum/ Lean-Agile Scaling Approaches includes a comparative analysis of all scaled Scrum and Lean-Agile practices introduced in this book. Every approach mentioned in this book has something to offer and different sets of strengths in terms of capabilities and applications. In this chapter, you have learned the capabilities and benefits of this approach. *Chapter 14, Contrasting Scrum/ Lean-Agile Scaling Approaches* offers more context with the contrasts against other Scrum/ Lean-Agile approaches.

Questions

1. What two aspects of Lean Thinking are applicable across industries, government agencies, and non-profit organizations?

2. Identify common value streams that apply to the software industry.

3. Is designing a product a value creation or value delivery value stream?

4. Is developing a software product a value creation or value delivery value stream?

5. Is order taking a value creation or value delivery value stream?

6. Identify Lean practices that support building in quality.

7. Explain how traditional waterfall-based practices differ from Lean-Agile practices in terms of handling feature development flows.

8. What are the three primary purposes of a Kanban board in software development?

9. Explain the differences between overproducing and extra or non-value-added processing.

10. Explain the type of waste associated with multitasking and context switching.

Further reading

1. Dalio, R. (2017) Principles. Simon & Schuster, New York, NY.

2. Goldratt, E.M. (2014) *The Goal: A Process of Ongoing Improvement. 30th Anniversary Edition.* The North River Press Publishing Corporation. Great Barrington.

3. Highsmith, J.A. (1998) *Adaptive Software Development: A Collaborative Approach to Managing Complex Systems.* Dorset House Publishing Co. New York, NY.

4. Haunts, S. (2018) *A Gentle Introduction to Agile & Lean Software Development.* Published by Stephen Haunts, Ltd. UK.

5. Kim, G.; Behr, K.; Spafford, G. (2014) *The Phoenix Project: A Novel About IT, DevOps, and Helping Your Business Win.* Second Edition. IT Revolution. Portland, OR.

6. Kim, G. (2019) *The Unicorn Project: A Novel About Developers, Digital Disruptions, and Thriving in the Age of Data.* IT Revolution. Portland, OR.

7. Liker, J. K. (2004) *The Toyota Way: 14 Management Principles from the World's Greatest Manufacturer.* McGraw-Hill. New York, NY.

8. Metcalf, G. (2019) *Lean Software Development: Avoiding Project Mishaps.* Ingram/ Lightning Sources. Milton Keynes, UK.

9. Reinertsen, D.G.; Smith, P.G. (1997) *Developing Products in Half the Time: New Rules, New Tools, 2nd Edition.* John Wiley & Sons, Inc. Hoboken, NJ.

10. Poppendieck, M.; Poppendieck, T. (2007) *Implementing Lean Software Development: From Concept to Cash.* Addison-Wesley. Upper Saddle River, NJ.

11. Poppendieck, M.; Poppendieck, T. (2010) *Leading Software Development: The Results Are Not The Point.* Addison-Wesley. Upper Saddle River, NJ.

12. Poppendieck, M.; Poppendieck, T. (2003) *Lean Software Development: An Agile Toolkit.* Addison-Wesley. Upper Saddle River, NJ.

13. Poppendieck, M.; Poppendieck, T.; Kniberg, H. (2014) *The Lean Mindset: Ask the Right Questions.* Pearson Education Inc. Upper Saddle River, NJ.

14. Womack, J.P.; Jones, T. (2003) *Lean Thinking: Banish Waste and Create Wealth in Your Corporation.* Free Press. New York, NY.

15. Womack, J.P.; Jones, D. T.; Roos, D. (2007) *Machines that changed the World. The Story of Lean Production – Toyota's Secret Weapon in the Global Car Wars That Is Now Revolutionizing World Industry.* Free Press. New York, NY.

Section 2: Comparative Review of Industry Scaled Agile Approaches

This section serves as an introduction to commercialized approaches created specifically to implement Agile development concepts, values, and principles on larger and more complex development portfolios, programs, and projects.

This section comprises the following chapters:

7
Scrum of Scrums

Very often, Scrum finds its way into an organization at the project level as a single team experiment. Such experiments occur when the potential benefits are so high that the organization is willing to assume the risk of adopting a new software development methodology. However, the originators of Scrum, Ken Schwaber and Jeff Sutherland, always intended that Scrum could scale across an enterprise.

This chapter discusses the original concepts of scaling Scrum as defined by its founders, including the concepts of the **SoS**. In this chapter, you will learn three approaches to scaling Scrum across an organization. These three approaches include the following:

- Bottom-up approach
- **Center of Excellence (CoE)**
- Top-down approach

Both Schwaber and Sutherland continue to refine Scrum scaling concepts in their respective companies: Scrum@scale.com (Jeff Sutherland) and Scrum.org (Ken Schwaber). You will learn about those two approaches in the next two chapters. For this chapter, we will start our understanding of Agile scaling concepts with an introduction to the original ideas for scaling Scrum.

The topics in this chapter include the following:

- Original Scrum scaling concepts

- **SoS**

- The bottom-up approach

- The top-down approach

- CoE

Original Scrum scaling concepts

During all four years of participating in the **U.S. Naval Academy** (**USNA**) Indoor and Outdoor Varsity Track programs, I don't recall a single day when I didn't hear my field coach, Al Cantello, a former American Olympian Javelin thrower, tell us to avoid thinking we could find instant success. Of course, his point was clear; no one achieves great things overnight. It takes hard work, diligence, and time. The same principles apply to the organizations that have sponsors who want to implement Scrum practices across an enterprise. It will not happen overnight, and there is a lot of sweat equity required in the interim and beyond. If our goal is to seek excellence and be competitive, we have to work like an Olympian, or more precisely, as an Olympian team.

The founders of Scrum, Ken Schwaber and Jeff Sutherland, always intended that Scrum should scale across the enterprise. Many of their books, listed in the *Suggested reading* section, offer extensive examples of large-scale Scrum implementations.

This chapter introduces two conventional approaches to scaling the basic concepts of Scrum. One method employs a *bottom-up approach* to scaling that is driven by early adopter teams, and the other is a *top-down approach* directed by the chief executives. The primary difference between the two methods is the level of sponsorship:

- The bottom-up approach occurs when an engineering team decides to implement Scrum on a project, and the success of the project drives interest and enthusiasm for further deployment throughout the organization.

- The top-down approach occurs when a chief executive drives the initiative to improve organizational efficiencies and competitiveness.

There is also a third approach, described at the end of this chapter, that takes a middle of the road approach, by implementing an infrastructure to support one or more simultaneous Scrum projects on an as-required basis. The Scrum infrastructure includes the development of a **CoE** that product teams can employ on demand, as resources become available and priorities merit it. The business drivers for using the CoE might include existing and costly project failures or identified risks on upcoming projects, or if timely entry into new product markets justify an agile approach to development. This chapter discusses all three methods in detail.

Before we get into the three implementation approaches, we need to spend a little time learning about the initial scaling Scrum concepts, usually referred to as the **SoS**.

Scaling with the SoS

To understand SoS, you must first understand this is not a new way of doing Scrum nor is it a new formalized Scrum framework. Rather, the purpose of SoS is to minimally extend the basic Scrum framework to manage large product dependency, coordination, and integration issues across multiple teams, with negligible overhead and complexity.

Some people refer to SoS as a **Team of Teams**, while others sometimes refer to SoS as a type of **MetaScrum**. That's not a good practice, as different people tend to have varying opinions on what these terms really mean. For example, a Team of Teams is not defined in any Scrum framework, and MetaScrum is a defined pattern in Sutherland's more recent *Scrum@Scale Guide*. Sutherland also expands on the concept of MetaScrum as *a pattern* in his book, *A Scrum Book: The Spirit of the Game*.

Jeff Sutherland describes the "*first scaled Scrum*" implementation as occurring at IDX Systems (now G.E. Healthcare). The first implementations at IDX started in 1996 and quickly expanded to include *hundreds of teams* (Sutherland, 2015).

With this understanding, let's get into the basics of what a Scrum of Scrums is.

Understanding the basics

An SoS is a scaled Scrum technique to integrate the work of five to nine Scrum teams (see *Figure 7.1*). Each SoS operates independently on the development and delivery of a large product. In effect, a Scrum of Scrums serves as a new event in the Scrum framework to address cross-team coordination, integration, and dependency issues.

Figure 7.1 shows a Scrum of Scrums configuration of five Scrum teams. Conceptually, the SoS operates more like an event than an organizational structure. In other words, the teams operate independently from their respective locations and send Ambassadors to attend periodic meetings to coordinate their work:

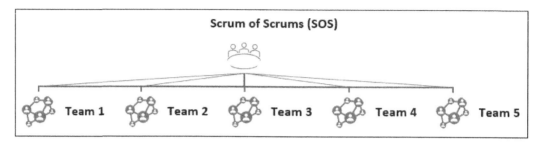

Figure 7.1 – Scrum of Scrums

Some commentators view implementations of SoS as a unique Scrum organizational structure. That's really not true. The Scrum of Scrums retains the original small team structures as identified in the Scrum Guide. SoS merely provides guidance on how multiple teams working on a single product collaborate and coordinate their work.

Be careful not to fall into the trap of thinking Scrum needs to be extensively modified to scale. For example, I have seen consultants recommend breaking up the role of the Product Owner into multiple positions. This concept is not consistent with the practices outlined in *The Scrum Guide*. For example, there is only one product—ever—one Product Backlog, and one Product Owner within a Scrum of Scrums. A single Scrum Master may serve up to three Scrum teams that are collaborating on the development of a single product. However, the assignment of one Scrum Master per development team is preferred.

I acknowledge the SoS concept can get confusing as the founders of Scrum have expressed views that seem in conflict. For example, Sutherland talks about the organizational restructuring at IDX where directors ran SoS, and VPs became leaders at sites with multiple SoS, coordinating the activities of 600 developers across eight business units (Sutherland, 2015). In contrast, Schwaber describes SoS as short, daily Scrum meetings of an engineer from each team working on an integrated product (Schwaber, 2007).

In the chapters on **Scrum@Scale** and **Nexus**, Sutherland and Schwaber, respectively, identify additional roles in their newest concepts on scaling Scrum. We'll not address that here as the initial Scrum of Scrum concepts do not employ any roles other than **Ambassadors**.

As you learned in *Chapter 4, Systems Thinking*, a crucial concern when scaling any organization is controlling the exponential growth of communications and relationship connections between its members. The Scrum of Scrums concept deals with this concern by limiting the number of people who can interact across teams and by limiting the number of teams within SoS. The team representatives are the *Ambassadors*.

Designating Ambassadors

Each of the teams designates "Ambassadors" to interact with the other Scrum teams within SoS and who represent the interests and concerns of their respective teams. The role of Ambassador is not a permanent position. Rather, teams rotate members from time to time.

Caution is advised here again. I have seen Scrum of Scrum advocates promote the idea that team members can form vertical communications slices with their counterparts in other teams within the Scrum of Scrum. That's problematic for a couple of reasons:

- Development teams are supposed to be fully self-contained and cross-functional so that they can take on any high-priority work within the Product Backlogs. Working on low-priority items is not value-added and is a form of waste. But that's exactly what happens when a team must go down the list of priorities to find work they can do.

- The vertical slice strategy immediately opens the teams up to the **network density** issues defined in *Chapter 4, Systems Thinking*.

Let's take a moment to revisit the subject of network density but in the context of managing multi-team communications via a Scrum of Scrums.

Eliminating network density

In a traditional hierarchical organization, inter-organizational connections are managed along functional lines with layers of bureaucracy between those who are doing the work and those who can make decisions. Moreover, the organization must implement cross-functional business processes to facilitate communication, decision making, and flow. The problem, of course, is the standard cross-functional business processes then constrain organizational flexibility, improvements, and innovations.

In SoS model, each team assigns Ambassadors who attend recurrent Scrum of Scrums meetings to discuss and resolve dependency and integration issues. Limiting the number of Ambassadors who meet keeps the communications networks to a minimum.

For example, a full complement of nine development teams will have nine Ambassadors. Following the network density equation introduced in *Chapter 4, Systems Thinking*, *N(N-1)/2*, the number of potential connections is *9*(8-1)/2 = 36* connections. In other words, these Ambassadors have potentially 36 lines of communication between them.

However, let's assume that the organization decides each team member is free to talk to everyone else across the teams. In that case, we have 45 people directly collaborating. Using the network density equation, *45*(45-44)/2 =* **990 potential lines of communication**. Is it any wonder we can't get anything done?

Moreover, this problem happens on a larger scale with our unconstrained email and IM network communications. These are all time wasters. Strive to keep things simple.

In a Scrum of Scrums, the independent Scrum teams minimize the number of their interconnections by keeping their teams small and by limiting the number of their members who meet directly with the other teams.

Beyond that, a Scrum of Scrums is still basically Scrum with a couple of caveats. Let's see what they are.

Building on Scrum

Scrum of Scrums teams follow the Scrum Guide in terms of employing the same basic roles, events, artifacts, and rules at the team level. However, there are some additions. For example, you have already learned that SoS itself is a new type of multi-team event that serves as a coordinating mechanism supporting five to nine Scrum teams. Also, you've learned that a Scrum of Scrums implements a new role in the form of Ambassadors.

The Ambassadors meet periodically to address development dependencies and integration concerns. For example, multiple teams may touch the same components, and one team's coding activities may affect or drive the development of capabilities needed by another team.

The ultimate objective of SoS is to ensure the teams work in collaboration to deliver a single, integrated, and potentially shippable product at the end of every Sprint. Teams can assign different Ambassadors and even different numbers of Ambassadors to each SoS event. However, the combined number of Ambassadors attending the meetings should always be limited. As with any team event, smaller is better than larger, with an optimal range falling between seven (plus or minus two) people (Miller, 1956 and Sutton, 2014).

Now that you know that SoS is more of an event as opposed to a structure, let's review the purpose of Scrum of Scrums meetings.

Supporting Scrum of Scrums meetings

SoS meetings are not status meetings for management consumption. Rather, they enable cross-team synchronization to address emergent concerns on dependencies and integration issues. Scrum of Scrums meetings are attended by the technical experts from each Scrum team who are best situated to discuss and resolve the issues.

SoS meetings are typically scheduled once or twice a week and are timeboxed limited to 15 minutes. Some organizations have daily Scrum of Scrum meetings. There is no right or wrong answer as to how many SoS meetings need to occur. But keeping them short and to the point is crucial as the goal is to get the right people together to communicate the issues, and then take the resolution activities offline in separate working meetings.

As a basic principle, Scrum does not advocate having meetings just for the sake of it. Nevertheless, there is nothing that prevents the Scrum of Scrums meetings from being scheduled as often as the situation warrants. Dependency, coordination, and integration issues will drive such decisions.

As with any Scrum event, Scrum of Scrums meetings are timeboxed so that people can focus their time and efforts on value-added work. When issues are identified in Scrum of Scrum meetings, the Ambassadors take the issues back to their respective teams to resolve locally. If warranted, the Ambassadors can help to organize an offline meeting with the appropriate cross-team representatives to resolve dependency and integration issues. In the Scrum of Scrum scaling approach, the Scrum of Scrum meetings typically start at the end of the Daily Scrums.

The Scrum Masters of the affected teams may also help to coordinate and facilitate offline meetings. But it's the responsible team members, potentially involving external stakeholders and domain experts, who must collaborate to resolve the identified cross-team dependency and integration issues.

Coordinating and integrating work

In the traditional Scrum team model, the developers still have a requirement to integrate, test, and commit their code with the existing code base. However, the developers working in an SoS pull from a single Product Backlog and the same code base has additional issues related to scaling. For example, how will the developers communicate across the teams within the SoS? How will they integrate and test their software to form a cohesive solution?

The SoS has the same scaling issues with network communications and linkages discussed in *Chapter 4, Systems Thinking* (review *Figure 4.1– Exponential growth in system connections with linear growth in elements*). When multiple teams work in collaboration to develop large and complex solutions, they are dependent on each other and must address the communications and linkage issues between them.

SoS Ambassadors must also address three types of dependency and integration issues that create cross-team dependencies when scaling Scrum:

- Overlapping requirements and scope of work

- Distribution of business and technical domain knowledge across teams

- Processes and tools to turn requirements into working software and test artifacts

An organization can minimize cross-team impacts in development when it installs and develops fully functional and self-contained Scrum teams that address these three areas of concern. The goal is to optimize productivity by eliminating cross-team dependencies.

Establishing useful metrics

Scrum of Scrums meetings are not ad hoc events. They serve a purpose—to help teams to coordinate their related work and identify dependencies and integration concerns. Moreover, they help the teams to put the right actions into play to resolve these issues. In the parlance of Scrum, Scrum of Scrums meetings provide the transparency that enables the teams to inspect and adapt their coordinated activities.

If we agree with these principles, then the next obvious question should be: "how do we know whether we are getting this right?". To answer that question, we need to identify specific questions, metrics, and goals for the Scrum of Scrum. Also, we need to make this information available across SoS as part of our information radiators. The following list provides some ideas on how to get started:

- *How do we know the teams are resolving dependency and integration impediments?*

  Visually display identified dependency and integration impediments.

  Track delays caused by cross-team impediments.

- *How many* **Product Backlog Items (PBIs)** *have dependencies?*

  Identify dependencies in Product Backlog during refinement.

  Ensure cross-team dependencies are addressed in the Sprint Planning.

  Visually display cross-team dependencies.

- *How many stories have dependencies?*

  Identify dependencies in Sprint Planning.

  Ensure related tasks are identified in Sprint Backlogs.

  Install visual aids to show cross-team task dependencies.

- *How do we know whether the dependency and integration issues were properly addressed?*

  Deliver a fully tested and potentially shippable integrated increment at the end of each Sprint.

  Obtain customer, stakeholder, and user feedback on the implementation of integrated increments during Sprint Reviews.

Note that some consultants recommend building a separate Scrum of Scrum backlog. In this context, the backlog is more like a Sprint Backlog of dependency- and integration-related work tasks and not a new type of Product Backlog. Remember, there is only one Product Backlog, ever.

Answering contextually useful questions

Given the timebox nature of the Scrum of Scrum meetings, it should be no surprise that the Ambassadors should come prepared to report both the progress of their teams and identified dependency- and integration-related impediments. To keep the meeting within its 15-minute timebox, each of the Ambassadors should limit their interactions to addressing the following questions for their respective teams:

- What has the team accomplished since the Ambassadors last met?

- What problems (impediments) has the team faced since the Ambassadors last met?

- What does the team plan to accomplish before the Ambassadors meet again?

- What cross-team dependency or integration issues has the team identified or still need to resolve?

These conversations will inevitably lead to more discussion. But resist the temptation to try to resolve issues in the Scrum of Scrum meetings. The Ambassadors must take detailed discussions and the offline work to separate working meetings.

Scaling SoS

There are development organizations that claim to have more than one product and more than one Product Owner in their Scrum of Scrums. Such a practice is not consistent with the basic principles of Scrum, that is, that multiple teams pull from the same Product Backlog and only one Product Owner can be responsible for the items included and their priorities.

As a basic rule, when you have multiple large products requiring multiple Scrum teams, create multiple Scrum of Scrums—with one SoS for each product. Each SoS has one Product Owner, one Product Backlog, and up to nine development teams. Still, large organizations often have products that are so large that a single Scrum of Scrums is not adequate to handle the organization's development objectives. Recall that an SoS is limited to no more than nine Scrum teams, each having no more than nine members. Ergo, a Scrum of Scrums can have no more than 81 people involved in development. So, what's the organization supposed to do when they need to employ more than 81 people?

Unfortunately, the Scrum Guide does not provide any direction, and the initial SoS concepts that came from papers written by Sutherland and Schwaber provided few details. If you have the time, you can read all the books in my *Suggested reading* lists, where more guidance and examples can be found.

But a quicker approach is to continue reading the remaining chapters in this *Section* to discover some of the more common formalized approaches for implementing Scrum on a very large scale. Then, you can dive into the books on the approaches you have specific interest in and may consider adopting.

Now that you have learned the foundations of scaling through Scrum of Scrum practices, let's discuss the three approaches to scaling Scrum across an organization. We'll start with an introduction to method one, which is the bottom-up approach.

Method one – building on a foundation of success

Method one of scaling Scum is the bottom-up approach. Schwaber and Sutherland note in their book, *Software in 30 Days*, that historically, Scrum implementations across an enterprise have been driven by the bottom-up approach (Schwaber, K. and Sutherland, J., 2012). In a typical scenario, a development team implements Scrum for a project and its success generates further interest throughout the organization, which other development teams and programs want to emulate.

Recall that software engineers and consultants developed the original concepts behind agile and lightweight software development methodologies as a response to the negative outcomes produced under the traditional waterfall software development model. These engineers recognized the plan-driven and linear sequential nature of the traditional approach created a host of problems.

Let's review in detail some of the issues these software engineers faced:

- The plan-driven nature of the traditional approach forces developers to attempt to gather all business and end-user requirements at the start of the project. At the same time, the development team begins to specify the software architecture and designs. This level of detailed planning takes time and delays the start of development.

- Customers do not always understand the need for detailed requirements analysis, and they have limited time to apply to the effort. They may also think it is the developers' job to define the requirements for them. Therefore, more often than not, customers place little value in supporting the requirements analysis effort.

- The plan-driven approach implements a deterministic view to development, imposing the idea that all elements of a project can be predefined and implemented within the specified budget, resource, and cost constraints of the project. This immediately sets up a situation where customers and project managers are reluctant to implement major changes over the course of the project. Moreover, it's a no-win situation for developers. If they agree to make the changes, the project schedules and budgets are negatively impacted. If they don't agree to make the changes, their customers and end-users are unhappy.

- With an expectation that all requirements are fully defined, the developers generate the code for the entire application while limiting initial testing to unit testing and perhaps integration testing. The developers hold off on other types of testing, such as system testing, end-to-end testing, regression testing, and non-functional testing, until after the code is fully developed. The problem with this strategy is that the increased complexity and size of the code in the completed code base makes it extremely difficult to find and fix the source of any bugs or defects, further adding time and cost to the project. Customers don't want to pay the developers to fix products that they believe should be finished and ready for deployment.

- Under the traditional model, the end-users do not get to evaluate the software until user acceptance testing, which is scheduled after the developers complete their coding and testing activities. At this stage of the project, the project team expects the application is virtually complete and ready for deployment, save the final finding and fixing of errors by end-users. However, invariably, the customers find defects in the product in the form of features they want but are not included in the release. The customers and end-users may have forgotten to mention certain requirements during initial requirements gathering activities. But often, these users have simply got new insights into how the product can be enhanced to support their needs.

All of the preceding issues drove many project teams to try alternative approaches to development, usually driven by the software engineers who wrongfully took a lot of the blame for past failures caused by strict adherence to the traditional model. Still, it takes an enlightened customer who is willing to accept new risks by trying a new approach. Likewise, the project manager must be willing to work within a new project management framework.

There is an old saying that success breeds success. This is a true statement but with caveats. The only way the engineering-led and bottom-up approach of method one works is when the early agile projects are so successful that they represent a paradigm shift of such enhanced productivity that the rest of the organization takes notice. Change represents risks, and organizations are reluctant to take on new risks unless there is strong evidence that a different approach is warranted. In addition, the cost benefit of any proposed change must substantially override the potential downside of staying with the status quo.

The early successes of Scrum provided a model that other teams within the organization could follow. In some cases, those early successes were enough to overcome resistance to large-scale change across the enterprise. Nevertheless, the more typical scenario is that the resistance to change is so great that only active participation by the organization's chief executives can drive the organizational changes necessary to implement Scrum across an enterprise.

> **Note**
>
> Schwaber and Sutherland observed that Scrum implementations in the early days usually followed a bottom-up deployment that aligns with my personal experience. For example, the agile-based projects I managed from the mid to late 1990s through to 2015 occurred only on projects where the engineers controlled the development approach. All other projects I managed in that timeframe followed traditional waterfall practices as mandated by corporate policy.

Agile practices have become the norm for many organizations. For example, the CollabNet VersionOne Thirteenth Annual State of Agile Report (`https://www.stateofagile.com/#ufh-c-473508-state-of-agile-report`) and HP's online survey of 601 software developers and I.T. professionals report enterprise adoption rates of between 48% and 54% (`https://techbeacon.com/app-dev-testing/survey-agile-new-norm`). As shown in *Figure 7.2*, these statistics place Agile in the early to late majority on the innovation adoption curve (Moore, 2005):

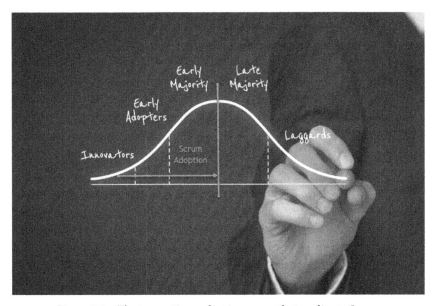

Figure 7.2 – The innovations adoption curve that applies to Scrum

As more and more companies realize the benefits of Agile and Scrum, I see no reason why this innovation adoption trend won't continue.

> **Note:**
>
> Geoffrey A. Moore adapted the **technology adoption life cycle**, originally developed by agricultural researchers Beal and Bohlen in 1957, to define five high-tech market segments: *innovators, early adopters, early majority, late majority*, and *laggards*. Moore argues that each target market, in order, is sufficiently different than the preceding types of users, with different needs and degrees of comfort in taking on new technology. Therefore, each market must be addressed independently, starting with the early adopters, and then build on the early successes to market the benefits to the next group in line. Note also that Moore's concepts only apply to disruptive technologies, as mainstream products have already achieved widescale acceptance.

As noted previously, the historical tendency was to deploy Scrum within an organization from the bottom up. However, Schwaber and Sutherland both discussed tactics to scale Scrum across an enterprise. The next subsection introduces their original concepts to scale Scrum from the top down.

Method two – starting with big things in mind

The second approach to scaling Scrum is an enterprise approach driven by executive management. However, implementing Scrum at an enterprise level is a non-trivial effort. Patience and commitment are necessary to see the transition through from front to end.

The organization's executives can expect to spend the first three to six months, or longer, training personnel and running several concurrent initial Scrum pilot engagements. As the pilot projects begin to rapidly deliver new increments of functionality, the executives must communicate the early successes to build enthusiasm throughout the organization. The executives can further expect the transition to enterprise-scale, across all product lines, to take at least one to three years, depending on the size of the organization.

With the successful deployment of Scrum across all product lines, you might think the organization is over the hump. Not quite! Expect to spend the next three to five years helping these teams to master the concepts so that their approach to work within the framework of Scrum becomes second nature. Continuous improvement concepts are built into Scrum, so the organization continues to see gains in both productivity and quality throughout the learning and maturation process.

The notion of continuous improvements is both part of and yet separate from mastering a subject. Mastery comes with learning and applying principles to different situations. Individuals and teams must be willing to experiment to improve and becomes masters in their disciplines. Let's take a look at this from the Japanese discipline of *shuhari*.

Mastering Scrum through Shuhari

It takes time for individuals to master new skills and get to the point where the execution of the new skill becomes instinctual and applied creatively. Many Agile practitioners promote the concepts of *shuhari*, a Japanese martial arts description of the three stages individuals go through to master a new discipline. The term *shuhari* roughly translates as *first learn, then detach, and finally transcend*.

The three stages of *shuhari* break down as follows:

- *Shu*: Learn and strictly follow the rules and learn from the experts.

- *Ha*: Perfect the skills, learn from other masters, and occasionally try new things.

- *Ri*: Master the acquired knowledge and skills and apply them in innovative and evolutionary ways to fit your situation.

Today, there are many other I.T. experts who discuss the applications of *shuhari* to Agile adoptions, including Martin Fowler in his blog; Jeff Sutherland and Ken Schwaber in their book, *Scrum, The Art of Doing Twice the Work in Half the Time*; and Craig Larman and Bas Vodde in their **Large-Scale Scrum (LeSS)** certification courses.

Building the foundations for Scrum

The executives who wish to implement Scrum must recognize that Scrum changes the way that businesses operate foundationally. Likewise, roles and responsibilities throughout the organization must change to support the new approach to business. Affected individuals need to master the skills of Scrum. As with any enterprise change initiative, change is scary and will be resisted. Count on it.

With that in mind, start small, promote your successes, and build from there. Most people ultimately want to be part of something that is successful. Many who might have otherwise resisted will come around to the new way of thinking and working because they want to be part of the success. Some folks will leave, but you may be better off without them. Let me explain through a real-life story, though not a Scrum-based example, of how people can be motivated to outperform their expectations, and why it's essential to stick with the people who want to be part of something bigger than themselves.

Setting expectations

I enlisted in the Navy and attended the U.S. **Naval Academy Preparatory School (NAPS)** prior to receiving an appointment to the **United States Naval Academy (USNA)** as a midshipman. Later, as a midshipman, I had the opportunity to go back to serve as a platoon leader for an incoming NAPS class. At the start of the bootcamp, I had to take my midshipmen candidates on a somewhat lengthy double-time march; I had the platoon stop so that I could address them. I asked the members of my platoon a simple question: *"How many of you have never run a mile in your life?"* About a third of the troop claimed they had not. It turns out they were incorrect, as we had just completed a mile.

The whole point of the exercise was to demonstrate that their life from here forward was going to be about accomplishing things they may have previously thought were impossible. This new lifestyle was a scary proposition for some, and a challenge for others. As a result, a couple of the Napsters left within 24 hours of our conversation, but the rest went on to graduate from both NAPS and the Naval Academy. Our team also became stronger in the process and won the top platoon award for the bootcamp. Moreover, I was running right beside them, which is where a leader needs to be.

Leading through example

Please, do not think that you need to be a drill sergeant to lead a Scrum team. The military is a different environment where a lack of order and discipline has life and death consequences. Nor do I mean to imply that those who left were somehow better or worse as human beings—they just wanted a different life. But to find success, a team must be cohesive, dedicated, and trained, with leaders who stand beside their teammates.

In your enterprise, the pursuit of excellence is not wrong. But to maintain the long-term support of your team while in the constant pursuit of excellence, it's far more important to be a leader who sets a positive example while communicating a vision, providing clear directions for the team—coaching and mentoring along the way and removing any obstacles that hinder your team's success.

Organizing around products

Let's get back to the subject of implementing Scrum on an enterprise scale through executive mandates (for example, the top-down approach). In Scrum, it all starts with organizing work around products supported by Product Owners and Scrum teams.

A Product Owner gathers the requirements and prioritizes the work around the development of high-value capabilities, usually expressed as features and functions. Larger product development efforts may require multiple teams.

Keeping Scrum teams small

No matter the size of the organizational implementation, individual Scrum teams are always kept small, product-oriented, self-organizing, empowered, and self-contained. There are always only two roles in every Scrum team, developers and the Scrum Master. The developers perform the work necessary to create the products. Since Scrum teams are self-organizing and self-contained, the developers should each bring multiple skills and experiences to the table with sufficient diversity as a group to complete the full scope of assigned work. Scrum Masters provide day-to-day guidance and may support only one Scrum team or potentially several Scrum teams.

A typical metric for sizing a Scrum team is seven plus/minus two members. Therefore, at an enterprise level, there are many independent Scrum teams, all operating under the same set of rules. For example, for every 100 people involved in developing software or software-based systems, you should expect to have between 11 and 20 Scrum teams, around an average of 14 teams. Scale the organization to 1,000 people involved in development, and you now have somewhere between 110 and 200 Scrum teams.

Maintaining one Product Backlog

Scrum is a product-centric approach to development. Each Scrum team is assigned to work on a single product, under the control of a single Product Owner. For larger and more complex products, there can be any number of Scrum teams assigned to support the development effort, and they all pull items to work on from the same Product Backlog. In addition, all assigned Scrum teams must pull work from the highest priority backlog items. In a couple of paragraphs, I'll discuss why it's important to never pull lower prioritized items from the Product Backlog. For now, it's important to understand that at the beginning of each Sprint, during the Sprint Planning meetings, the Scrum teams must collaborate to decide how to allocate work from the highest priority items in the upcoming Sprint.

The Product Owner is ultimately responsible for decision making with regards to selecting and prioritizing items contained in the Product Backlog, as it's their job to understand market considerations, user needs, and the value of desired features within the Product Backlog. The Product Owner must always evaluate the value of each product feature in contrast with the cost of production and delivery.

Prioritizing development on value

Higher value features with the lowest costs should have the highest backlog priorities. Going back to the 80/20 rule, if approximately 20% of the desired features have roughly 80% of the value, why would the team expend any time working on 80% of features that collectively only have 20% of the value? This aphorism is why all Scrum teams supporting a product must always pull from the highest priority (for example, the highest value and lowest cost) items within the Product Backlog.

Each Scrum team supports the Product Owner by assessing the scope of work in the Product Backlog and providing input on architecture and design considerations and development efficiencies. Though the Scrum team is not in a decision-making role, they must inform the Product Owner of architectural and design considerations that impact timelines, costs, and their ability to implement key features while supporting the specified nonfunctional requirements.

In theory, agile-based projects can operate continuously, running on from year to year without stopping. In reality, every organization needs to constantly re-evaluate the appropriateness and effectiveness of their investments. All organizations have constraints, typically defined under the categories of scope, budgets, resources, time, and quality. In addition, market conditions change, and corporate strategies must evolve to ensure the organization remains relevant and viable.

Changing your paradigm

Many, if not most, companies and agencies fund and approve bespoke (for example, custom or non-standard) work as programs and projects across annualized and quarterly budget cycles. Programs and projects are not part of Scrum, per se, but are still useful to management and customers alike as the means to allocate budgets and monitor work. Likewise, Portfolio Management, which is an approach to analyze product, program, and project investment decisions in light of corporate strategies, is not part of Scrum.

When corporate executives elect to implement Scrum enterprise-wide, they need to make sure their predilections to practice portfolio, program, and project management concepts do not degrade their efforts to practice agility. For example, detailed project plans and schedules are not part of Scrum, and their implementation will quickly undermine a Scrum team's efforts to remain aligned with current product priorities.

When practicing Enterprise Scrum, and if implemented at all, portfolios, programs, and projects simply become higher-level abstractions to align work and resources around corporate strategies, goals, and objectives. But ultimately, under Scrum, the focus is always on products.

Focusing on the highest value work

Since Scrum has a product-oriented perspective, the focus of each Scrum team is limited in scope to work on implementing the currently highest value features that fit within the larger vision for their product assignments. Again, all of the Scrum teams assigned to a product pull from the same Product Backlog. As you might imagine, the coordination of efforts between multiple Scrum teams assigned to a product and its backlog becomes the critical aspect of scaling their efforts.

Some organizations implement Scrum of Scrums meetings to coordinate cross-team work. Under SoS, each team assigns an *Ambassador* to attend periodic meetings with the Ambassadors from other Scrum teams. How the Scrum teams organize their work is situational but tends to take advantage of individual team skills, experiences, and preferences. For example, if a team has experience with another application or strengths in middleware, they may take on integration work between the integrated products.

Individual Scrum teams may have specific technical or domain knowledge that gives them advantages in working on selected aspects of a large application. However, the Product Owner and Scrum Masters need to be careful to ensure that the Scrum teams are not so specialized that they cannot work on the highest priority items in the backlog.

Turning on a dime – not likely

Beyond these basic scaling extensions, the execution of work in Enterprise Scrum and product development activities spanning multiple Scrum teams follow the same basic principles outlined in the early part of this chapter. But now that I've defined the desired end state for enterprise-scale Scrum, the question still remains about how the organization builds Scrum competencies and capabilities on an enterprise scale. Having been involved with one large organization that simply mandated implementation of Scrum-like practices, virtually overnight—so it seemed to us in the field—I can assure you that approach is doomed to failure, at least in the short run.

I like to compare the situation to steering an aircraft carrier. It takes time and distance from the first command issued by the skipper to initiate a turn until the commands are executed, the rudder is applied, and the ship reacts. Not seeing an immediate response, the skipper might bring the whole ship to a stop. The same concepts apply to implementing enterprise change in a large organization. Not seeing immediate results, the executives may kill the enterprise Scrum initiative.

Having been involved in another large organization that simply made Agile available as an option to product teams, my experience suggests that approach will not achieve the benefits of a directed and planned approach. Moreover, the organization may not even track the metrics to know whether their agile implementations were successful, so what's the real point beyond appeasement to a few maverick development teams? While the organization might have a few successes, what is their strategy for building on those successes?

Leveraging Scrum to implement organizational agility

So, let's talk about a third and more practical approach to the enterprise-wide deployment of Scrum, one that involves executive directives and ongoing communications, but through a staged rollout that builds on early successes. This approach also addresses the issue that every organization is different and has unique issues to deal with. It will take time for the organization to work through those issues. There is not a one-solution fits all deployment strategy for Scrum—or any other Agile-based methodology for that matter.

The first thing to consider is using Scrum to roll out Scrum. In other words, Scrum is the product of the Enterprise Scrum development effort. In this scenario, the **Chief Executive Officer (CEO)** must provide leadership for the enterprise effort to implement Scrum practices and must continually demonstrate their commitment to the effort. In effect, the CEO serves as the Product Owner over the organization's Scrum product. And they are ultimately responsible for deciding the organizational Scrum implementation priorities.

As with any Scrum-based development project, the enterprise implementation of Scrum requires one or more Scrum Masters to support the Scrum product teams. We will call this person an **Enterprise Scrum Master (ESM)**. The CEO needs to appoint an executive sponsor for this role. Very large organizations with more than one operating division may have a dedicated ESM appointed to every division.

The first order of business is to reform the business around product lines, with each product having a dedicated Product Owner. In most cases, an existing product manager can step up into this role, so long as they see the value of moving their products into the Scrum development and organizational model. They must also be willing to accept the new responsibilities and accountability for gathering requirements and defining product development priorities around the highest value features and functions.

Though my career is in I.T., I have been fortunate to have roles as a practitioner, as well as in business process reengineering and process improvement consulting, management consulting, and as a professional services executive, as well as senior leadership roles in marketing, business development, and sales. The reason I bring this up is that I see no reason why Scrum can't scale across these functions. In other words, instead of creating functional departments to support sales, marketing, partnerships, consulting, and distribution, each Product Owner can establish cross-functional Scrum teams to support these activities for their products.

Staging Scrum team deployments

I mentioned the need for implementing organizational Scrum as a staged roll-out. Here, communications and some high-level training must start at the frontend. The point is to prepare the organization for the desired future state and make sure all employees understand the business drivers and potential benefits of the roll-out. The organization also needs to set and communicate expectations on the roll-out of Scrum.

The initial deployment of Scrum in a top-down driven implementation begins with pilot engagements. A top-down-driven implementation means executives and managers provide the vision for the organizational deployment of Scrum and help to remove organizational-level impediments, but otherwise, they step out of the way to let the teams do their work.

The organization's executives must communicate their intentions early and often. After the initial communications and executive-level training is complete, the assigned ESM(s) will work with the product level Product Owners to identify pilot engagements that have high value and potentially have a big impact in terms of meeting the organization's strategic priorities. The initial teams must be carefully selected to ensure they have the right mix of skills and experiences and that assigned team members are committed to learning and using the Scrum process.

Upon successful launch and deliveries by the initial pilot projects, which can occur as early as three months into the transition, the organization must prepare to stand up new Scrum teams. Depending on the size of the organization and the product lines they maintain, the new teams may support products that had initial pilot engagements or other products that are just starting out with Scrum.

With each new transition to Scrum, the primary role of the Product Owners is to decide what needs to be built and in what order. In their role as Servant Leaders, Scrum Masters work with their development teams to ensure the team figures out how to deliver on the vision within the Scrum framework. The Scrum Masters also help to remove impediments that hinder their team's ability to complete their tasks and deliver their increments. The development teams make commitments and incrementally deliver new features that support the vision for the product.

Preparing the organization

In the meantime, other project and functional managers who are waiting in queue need to continue their work while being aware of the organization's longer-term objectives and progress to implement Scrum. The groups who are waiting can prepare through training and studying the work of the Scrum teams that preceded their entry into the organizational Scrum deployment. The division's assigned ESM works with the Product Owner and the functional managers to assess the qualifications and alignment of employees and contractors necessary to stand up the product's Scrum teams.

During the transition period, the organization's employees need to understand that they must make the effort to learn and transition into the new Scrum-based organization. The employees must also understand that their job descriptions, roles, and responsibilities will change as their products move over to Scrum-based practices. They will have to learn and master new skills.

On the other hand, this commitment and loyalty cannot be a one-way street. If the executives don't offer safety, new opportunities, organizational support, and training, the resistance will mount, and the Scrum implementation efforts will be sabotaged.

Some folks will not want to change. As a result, there will be some attrition, but that's OK. Implemented correctly, the organization should achieve sufficient productivity gains that the organization may not need to immediately rehire replacements, if at all.

The organization must resist the desire to roll out Scrum all at once, no matter how successful their initial pilots. Each new product and the new teams will face unique impediments that must be removed. This type of deployment strategy takes time and focus, with proper attention from executive-level management. With each new rollout, the assigned Product Owners, Scrum Masters, and developers must all be trained, and their work must be monitored and supported. New teams must be nurtured through executive-level attention and with sufficient oversight to quickly address uncovered impediments.

The bottom line is the organization's sponsoring executives must rationalize how fast they can drive the required organizational changes with the time, energy, and mental capacity required to deal with each new Scrum deployment scenario. At some point, they will reach bandwidth limitations that impact their ability to adequately monitor and support the concurrent addition of new teams.

On the other hand, the limitations in bandwidth cannot be the justification to slow-roll the deployment of Scrum. The ESM must work with the Product Owners and Scrum Masters to develop their skills and capabilities. In turn, those individuals will go on to train, coach, and mentor the members of new teams. Just as a snowball gathers momentum and grows while rolling downhill, the top-down organizational Scrum deployment should gather momentum and grow.

Redeploying organizational assets

Another issue that the organization will face is the need to reorganize all functional departments into the self-organizing and cross-functional teams. This activity has to be rationalized and planned around the product lines. The anticipated changes must be communicated and explained. Again, the roll-out of the new teams has to be managed within the bandwidth of the organization's executive sponsors to handle the impediments that are sure to follow each deployment of Scrum to a new part of the organization.

As the organization is reformed, the division-level ESMs meet periodically with their product line Product Owners and Scrum Masters to discuss the impediments they face in the organization's transition to Scrum. This list of impediments represents not only problems that need to be solved but also the list of items in the organizational-level Scrum product Backlog. Working with the product teams, the ESM prioritizes the organizational Scrum requirements to form the Organizational Scrum product Backlog.

Organizational-level Scrum teams work the items contained in the Organizational Scrum product Backlog. These teams follow the same cross-functional and self-organizing patterns of the product-level Scrum teams. They also follow the same Scrum rules of performing work in time-boxed increments (for example, Sprints) with Scrum events and artifacts.

Under Scrum, the tiers of middle management go away. What remains are executives, Product Owners, Scrum Masters, and development team members. The focus is always on supporting the teams and helping them be successful as a whole. Under the traditional model, too often selected individuals, in particular executives and managers, get the credit for meeting performance objectives. That contradicts the Scrum philosophy. Simply put, effective teams outperform the collective output of independent individuals.

The culture has to evolve to take advantage of team-based performance efficiencies. This is one of the reasons Scrum limits the definition of roles to Product Owners, Scrum Masters, and developers. Giving titles too often serves as a means to elevate an individual over their peers and to allow an individual to specialize. Scrum expects all team members to contribute to the cross-functional mix of skills. Therefore, employee compensation scales need to benefit those who acquire the most skills, as evidenced by their education and professional training and certifications.

Likewise, to promote the understanding that team performance counts above individual performance, the organization should implement team-based performance merit incentives and bonuses. While individuals can improve their compensation through the acquisition of additional useful skills and knowledge, the team-based incentives help them to understand their bonuses come from helping to make the team operate and perform better.

At this point, you should have a good understanding of the two most common approaches to implementing Scrum on an enterprise scale, bottom-up (team-led) and top-down (executive-led). We'll now turn our attention to a third strategy, which installs a Scrum CoE to assist with enterprise-wide implementations. The CoE strategy is really an extension of the top-down/executive-led approach as the commitment of time and resources plus the authority to operate require executive-level sponsorship.

Method three – Scrum CoE

Scrum and Agile *CoEs* provide teams of subject matter experts who can provide thought leadership, education, guidance, coaching, and mentoring services throughout the organization both during and after a transformation to establish enterprise-scale agility. CoEs can have a wide berth of knowledge and skills or provide a smaller slice of expertise and guidance around narrow domains of knowledge. A CoE might not even be called a CoE, but it's considered a CoE if it's providing skills and expertise as a centralized support group to a wider community during a transition phase or beyond to help to sustain and mature organizational practices.

Companies often establish Scrum and Agile CoEs to support a larger Scrum transformation effort. In this context, a Scrum-based CoE provides the following support services:

- Define and promote an organization-wide Scrum methodology.

- Tailors Scrum implementation to meet organizational needs.

- Expand knowledge of Scrum practices across the enterprise.

- Answer questions from Scrum team members.

- Implement organization standards for methods, tools, and templates.

- Establish product-oriented Scrum teams.

- Remove organizational impediments to establishing enterprise Scrum capabilities.

- Identify gaps in Scrum team deployments and areas for improvements.

The concept of implementing CoEs is a fairly established practice in the software and systems development community, though different organizations may use different terms for the same concept. For example, the project and program management community promote the use of **Project Management Offices (PMOs)** as a centralized source of domain knowledge, good organizational PM practices, and resources.

Mike Cohn, a co-founder of both **Agile Alliance** and **Scrum Alliance** and the founder of **Mountain Goat Software**, suggests that **PMOs** can support a transition to Scrum. Since PMOs support the implementation of corporate I.T. practices, they can help or hinder an organization's move to implement Agile-based program management practices.

A move to implement Agile requires the organization to replace program and project management and project team roles with the Product Owner, Scrums Master, and development team roles of Scrum. In addition, the traditional project planning and scheduling activities are replaced with a Product Backlog, Product Backlog refinement, and Sprint Planning. The linear-sequential product development life cycle gets replaced with Scrum's Sprint iterations with incremental deliveries of the highest priority Product Backlog items, as viewed from the eyes of the customer.

It should be obvious there is a lot of work to do to support a successful transition to implement Scrum across a large, multi-team product or on an enterprise scale. An Agile PMO can support the transition to Scrum with the following activities:

- Develop a training program.
- Provide coaching.
- Select and train coaches.
- Challenge existing behaviors.

Over time, some traditional project-oriented responsibilities go away though some will remain, including the following:

- Assist with reporting.
- Assist with compliance needs.
- Manage the inflow of new projects.

The need for corporate I.T. processes does not go away with the implementation of Scrum practices, though the nature of the processes will change to align with the values and principles of Agile and the empiricism of Scrum. The revised corporate I.T. processes should include the following:

- Assist in establishing and collecting metrics.
- Reduce waste.
- Help to establish and support communities of practice.
- Create an appropriate amount of consistency across teams.
- Provide and maintain tools.
- Coordinate teams.
- Model the use of Scrum.
- Work with other groups.

Cohn further notes the PMOs, over time, may change their name to something that is more descriptive of their role in leading Scrum transformation and sustainment activities. Perhaps they become the core group to implement a Scrum Center of Excellence.

This section has only briefly touched on Mike Cohn's thoughts on these areas. Additional details are maintained on Mike's Mountain Goat Software website on this web page: `https://www.mountaingoatsoftware.com/articles/the-roles-of-the-project-management-office-in-scrum`.

Disciplined Agile (now a part of PMI), discusses the use of a CoE, or **Center for Excellence (C4E)** as

> *"a group of people with specialized skills and expertise whose job is to provide leadership and purposely disseminate that knowledge within your organization"*

(`https://www.pmi.org/disciplined-agile/people/centers-of-excellence`).

As a final example, Ken Schwaber's **Scrum.org** has implemented Nexus as its Scrum scaling strategy. The **Nexus integration team** is an implementation support team that provides the skills and resources to build the infrastructure for large-scale development, such as build, integration, and application life cycle management tools. Though it provides CoE expertise on tooling to other Scrum teams, it operates as an autonomous Scrum team (`https://techbeacon.com/app-dev-testing/enter-nexus-ken-schwaber-scaling-scrum-future-agile`).

As you can see from the preceding examples, CoEs can have different names or a different domain of focus and provide varying types of support services. In our context, a Scrum CoE provides expertise and guidance in the practices of Scrum. The need for Scrum-based CoEs became apparent as organizations began to scale Scrum in support of large product development efforts and to improve overall organizational agility.

Growing a foundation of excellence

The Scrum Guide claims Scrum is *simple to understand*, yet *difficult to master*. Individuals, Scrum teams, and the organization as a whole need time to learn and internalize the new disciplines of Agile. As a result, it is not unusual for a Scrum team to take several months to achieve full productivity. Part of the equation is related to mastering new skills. The other part of the equation is the team must learn how to effectively work together.

Some Agile and Scrum experts, such as Martin Fowler, Alistair Cockburn, and Craig Larman, point to the Japanese martial art concept of *Shuhari* (learn the tradition, detach/innovate, and transcend) as a model that describes the stages of learning to mastery. Simply put, it takes time and deliberate practice for individuals to become experts at something.

In addition, the Scrum team must learn to work together. Organizational experts often cite *Tuckman's stages of group development* (forming–storming–norming–performing-adjourning) as an idealized model for group development. The bottom line here is that teams can go through as many as four stages before they function at a high level. The fifth stage is related to the team disbanding and needing to say their goodbyes and adjust to a new situation.

Though we have digressed a bit from the subject of CoEs, it is important to understand Scrum CoEs help individuals and their Scrum teams to build their knowledge, skills, and effectiveness through these transitional periods. Let's take a look at some of the drivers for expanding Scrum implementation and support services.

Expanding organizational Scrum capabilities

The initial successes of Scrum within an organization often come from small, passionate teams that willed their way to success. Sometimes, those teams may have taken advantage of an opportunity to operate independently. This happens most often on small development projects unhindered by excessive oversight and bureaucracy. However, sometimes development teams are forced into a situation to save a failing project or where a project is of such importance that the organization is willing to grant the team more flexibility in how they operate.

A third possible scenario occurs when the organization's executives have decided to move forward with implementing agile-based practices on an enterprise scale. There is a risk in making and going forward with such a decision. The best way to manage those risks is to start with the implementation of small, independent Scrum teams operating as prototypes for guiding future expansion.

However, an additional risk management strategy is to develop a Scrum or Agile-based CoE in parallel with installing the initial Scrum teams. The CoE can serve as a mentor and coach to the new teams. The CoE is set up as a Scrum team and its product is the implementation of Scrum on an enterprise scale. The Scrum CoE is not a large team, at least not at first. The CoE might only have a single CoE Product Owner, a single CoE Scrum Master, and maybe a handful of expert Scrum practitioners or consultants.

The CoE Product Owner works with the Scrum team Product Owners to help them to develop an integrated Product Backlog and understand the refinement, integration, and coordination processes. The CoE Scrum Master works with the Scrum Team Scrum Masters to help to remove organizational impediments and support mentoring and coaching needs within the new Scrum teams. Collectively, the CoE captures and distributes lessons learned to the Scrum teams throughout the transformation.

Regardless of the initial drivers for installing Scrum, the importance of a CoE expands considerably once the organization's executives decide to implement Scrum practices on an enterprise scale. Furthermore, it is not possible to obtain sponsorship and funding to establish a CoE before the organization's executives buy into the potential benefits of implementing wide-scale agility.

Identifying Scrum CoE benefits

Once the executives make the decision to implement Scrum and other Agile practices on an enterprise scale, they should explore the benefits of creating a CoE to assist with the efforts. Let's take a look at some of the areas where a CoE can be of benefit.

Establishing a Scrum scaling framework for agility

No two enterprise Scrum implementations are alike. The CoE defines and builds the Scrum scaling framework that fits the political and business dynamics within the organization. In addition, the CoE assesses Scrum team needs and capabilities across the organization, constantly evaluates the gaps, and works to fill the gaps with functional Scrum teams. On an enterprise scale, Scrum teams fulfill other functional roles besides product development. For example, some Scrum teams may support operational needs, such as marketing, order entry, supply chain management, channels, transportation, and distribution.

Building organizational skills and expertise

As the organization's subject matter experts, the Scrum CoEs provide coaching, training, and mentoring to the Scrum teams. They also train the Scrum Masters to become mentors and coaches to their respective Scrum teams. Having a cascading training, coaching, and mentoring framework is a force-multiplier in developing enterprise-scale Scrum.

Eliminating waste while adding value

Since you are reading this book, you will, of course, guide your team to implement *Lean development* and *systems thinking* concepts with the implementation of enterprise-scale Scrum. In that context, the CoE helps the Scrum teams to identify and eliminate waste in all its forms, as outlined in *Chapter 5, Lean Thinking*, which improves delivery of value.

The Scrum CoE is the organization's pool of Scrum experts. But, ideally, they also have expertise in systems and Lean thinking, and Agile practices in general. The CoE's domain experts provide training, coaching, and mentoring to the Scrum teams in those areas.

Lowering procurement and sustainability costs

The CoE assesses the methods and tools in use by the organization and establishes a common technical reference guide and governance policies that establish organizational standards. The standards and governance policies help the organization to manage procurement and sustainment costs and supportability issues that would otherwise explode if every internal Scrum Team chose to go their own way.

Some Scrum practitioners may bristle at this thought. User and team preferences for methods and tools are often an emotional issue for folks. After all, who wants to learn something new if you are doing well with what you already know? Nevertheless, organizational costs and sustainability issues are important factors the CoE must consider.

Developing useful information radiators

The CoE provides guidance to the Scrum teams on useful **information radiators**. The emphasis is not on the traditional project-based constraints data of managing the pre-planned scope, schedules, costs, and quality metrics. Instead, the focus is on providing information that demonstrates how well the teams are performing in terms of delivering the highest customer-centric value.

Fulfilling compliance requirements

A Scrum CoE can help to ensure the organization's Scrum teams meet federal compliance requirements, such as the **Gramm–Leach–Bliley Act (GLBA)** and the Sarbanes-Oxley Act, and other industry- and government-related compliance requirements. In a general sense, **I.T. compliance** is about implementing I.T. controls, goals, objectives and defining outcomes. From a practical perspective, we would care to implement a compliance program to ensure business and I.T. goals are aligned, measured, and monitored. In particular, controls are critical elements to manage organizational and I.T. risks.

I.T. compliance has another important role. The control mechanisms help to ensure the organization's information and data are protected, secure, and available. With an increasing number of autonomous Scrum teams, compliance assurance can become a bigger issue. The Scrum CoE for compliance can provide the guidance and oversight necessary to ensure compliance requirements are met across the organization.

Closely related to I.T. compliance is I.T. governance. We will look at that next.

Providing I.T. Governance

As a general concept, governance defines the "rules of the road" for an entity in terms of specifying corporate policies and standards. The objective of governance is to specify desired business outcomes that drive revenue and protect the organization.

I.T. Governance is another type of framework that contains the processes necessary to ensure I.T. investments meet desired business outcomes. In that context, it should be no surprise that I.T. governance is a subset of the overall corporate governance process.

In most organizations, corporate and I.T. governance is an executive-level function. For example, the organization may employ a **Chief Compliance Officer (CCO)** or give the role over to the **Chief Information Officer (CIO)** or **Chief Technology Officer (CTO)**.

However, in Enterprise Scrum, there is no such role as COO, CIO, or CTO. Yes, an organization may choose to keep those roles, but the Scrum Police will tell you it is not Scrum. However, there is nothing that prevents the organization from placing the executive-level roles and responsibilities within a Scrum CoE.

I.T. Governance executives are responsible for decision making regarding technologies, strategies, standards, procedures, and processes across the organization's I.T. function. All such decisions must consider the needs of customers, stakeholders, partners, and employees. In a modern context, I.T. Governance supports organizational needs to focus value creation efforts on alignment with the entity's mission and corporate strategies.

Also tied to I.T. compliance and governance is risk management. In fact, the three capabilities are so closely linked, they are often identified by the acronym GRC (Governance, Risk, and Compliance). As an example, see *GRC360: A framework to help organizations drive principled performance* at `https://link.springer.com/article/10.1057/palgrave.jdg.2050066`.

By now, if you are guessing that a Scrum CoE has a role to play in risk management, you would be right. Let's see why.

Identifying and mitigating risks

Risk management is an important part of project management practices. The Scrum Guide mentions risks but indicates risks are limited in scope due to the iterative development nature of Scrum. But what happens when you have multiple teams working in an integrated fashion? Obviously, with multiple Scrum teams building parts of an integrated solution, the opportunity for risk increases for each Sprint. Therefore, as the organization moves to implement Enterprise Scrum, the risk management function implemented in the traditional project management model needs to be replaced.

Risk management involves four key components: risk identification, risk mitigation, contingency planning, and risk monitoring. For those who may not be familiar with the discipline of risk management, risks represent potential threats in the form of danger, harm, or loss. In contrast, issues represent risks that are realized. Risk identification and mitigation strategies work to discover risks before they become issues and to develop strategies to prevent or live with them. Contingency plans are a form of predefined action plan on what to do should a risk become an issue. Monitoring helps us to identify the points at which risks are becoming issues that we must address.

Risks can be measured in terms of both likelihood and potential impact. We identify potential risks early, try to avoid or eliminate the negative impacts, and then monitor the situation to see whether they come about. Sometimes, we even agree to accept the impact of a risk, should it come about. Ideally, particularly for those risks that have significant negative consequences, we develop contingency plans at the risk stage. That way, we have the plans in place should the risks become issues, and we have to execute them.

Rather than having a Scrum of Scrums team responsible for these activities, it may be better to assign the function to a Scrum CoE—especially on larger and more complex products. It's not that SoS teams cannot perform risk management duties. The concern is how much focus they can give it, particularly when identified risks and issues may play out over multiple teams and across multiple sprints.

CoEs also have a role to play in strategic planning and portfolio management. That's the subject of the next subsection.

Determining portfolio investment strategies

In previous subsections, you learned that I.T. Governance and I.T. compliance play a role in aligning I.T. strategies with corporate mission and strategies. You can think of those activities as having a focus on foundational technologies, procedures, and processes. There is another level of alignment that must be considered, and that is the alignment of I.T. and other corporate investments in terms of supporting the products and services delivered by the enterprise.

In other words, there is an executive-level function that must determine what set of potential investments in new products and services, or enhancements to existing products and services, maximizes the goals and objectives of the business and are in alignment with its mission.

Again, since Scrum eliminates hierarchical structures and much of the existing executive structures, something has to take over the roles and responsibilities that guide organizational strategies. That does not happen at the Scrum team level—at least, not at the development Scrum team level. Here, again, is a role a Scrum CoE can support.

So far, the CoE examples provided have a focus on providing some form of specialized skills or services and doing so within a formalized organizational structure. But the CoE does not have to be the only organizational structure that provides training, coaching, and mentoring. The CoE can help to form **Communities of Practice (CoPs)** that augment the capabilities of the CoEs.

Establishing CoPs

The CoE may help the organization to establish CoP across the enterprise. The CoPs play a different role than the CoEs by proving an opportunity for interested domain practitioners to collaborate, share their ideas and practices, and develop functional skills organization wide. This is a low-cost yet high-impact way for an organization to build domain skills and capacity across the enterprise.

CoPs are organized groups of professionals who share common interests within specific domains of knowledge. They may form to resolve issues, improve their skills, and learn from each other. One obvious area for a CoP is Scrum. The Scrum CoP can help the CoEs with coaching and mentoring Scrum team members, both during and after the transformation to Enterprise Scrum.

Over time, the Scrum CoEs identify domains where a CoP can help the organization through its Scrum transformations and support the development of the CoPs until they are self-supportive or no longer needed. Given the empirical process control mechanisms of Scrum, the CoEs encourage the team to try out new ideas, share practices, and participate in retrospectives.

Avoiding CoE failures

Despite all of the positive things CoEs can bring to the organization, they can also bring a lot of problems with them. In this section, you will learn what pitfalls need to be avoided when establishing Scrum CoEs and how to avoid them.

Agile practices, in general, seek to eliminate hierarchical and bureaucratic structures. The goals and objectives map back to the Product Backlog, which is the prioritized list of items that add the highest value to a product or service under development. The Product Owner collaborates with the development team to refine the backlog and establish Sprint Goals. The Scrum Master facilitates events and removes impediments. The CoEs must support those efforts.

In this context, let's take a quick look at bad CoE practices and how to avoid them:

- If the CoE implements a bureaucratic formality or seeks to centralize authorities, the entire Scrum framework comes apart. Scrum implements self-contained and autonomous teams that act in a coordinated way to achieve specific goals and objectives, and the CoE simply brings skills and experience on an as-needed basis.

- If the CoE dictates I.T. governance policies and standards, they run the risk of stopping flexibility and innovations at the Scrum team level. I.T. standards and policies must be decided in collaboration with the Scrum teams to ensure maximal flexibility with minimal technical debt.

- If the CoE enforces centralized planning the effect is to impose on the Scrum teams the same plan-driven limitations of the waterfall approach to development. Leverage the empirical process control theories upon which Scrum is based to provide transparency, inspection, and adaption, via Scrum events and artifacts, to create the highest value at the lowest possible cost.

- If the CoE resources have more loyalty to supporting bureaucratic interests or following traditional practices, the product development organization will quickly devolve to working on non-value-added activities. The CoE members need to view their role as augmenting change to: through fully participating resources of the Scrum teams they support, abiding by the same rules, and they must not impede the empirical processes of Scrum.

- If the CoE team members, as the experts in their domains of knowledge, dictate practices, they will not create learning opportunities to enable the teams to grow and become self-contained and fully autonomous. Rather, employ a Socratic teaching approach to convey new knowledge while also teaching critical thinking skills.

By the very title of the function, the people within a CoE are deemed experts. As the organization's experts, there is a strong tendency for them to tell people what to do or how they should think. The experts better serve the Scrum teams they support when they use Socratic teaching principles that have a focus on asking questions and not so much on providing answers. This approach allows the team members to actively participate in the learning experience and gain a deeper understanding of the concepts under discussion.

Now that you understand the potential dangers of implementing Scrum CoEs, let's take a look at how we can avoid some of those pitfalls.

Building effective CoEs

You might want to start by not calling them centers of excellence. Find a more innocuous name, such as Scrum Advocates, Scrum Implementation Champions, or Scrum Working Groups. That avoids the notion that these folks are the experts who are somehow superior to the Scrum team members. While the CoE staff may have greater knowledge and experiences, they are still learning human beings. If your organization decides to retain the Scrum CoE verbiage, then focus on the word "excellence" as indicating their role to help the organization continuously improve and achieve excellence.

Avoid any notion that the CoEs are somehow in charge of the day-to-day operations of the Scrum teams. While they may have some governance responsibilities, they cannot over-govern. Mostly, they are a body of experienced resources available to the Scrum teams as collaborative and participative partners. Some CoEs have executive powers, but those powers are used to help to remove organizational impediments that prevent business transformations to an agile enterprise.

In the next chapter, you will learn about the Scrum@Scale concept of a *network* of autonomous teams. This is a better mental model than the traditional hierarchical or bureaucratic structures of the past.

Continuous innovations and change with the goal to improve value creation and value delivery are the hallmarks of agility. The CoE exists solely to improve agility and help the organization to avoid locking into existing ways of doing things. In their roles as organizational experts and leaders, the CoE staff must learn as must as they teach. As the CoE staff work with the Scrum teams, they have a responsibility to make sure that recently discovered good practices, methods, and tools are shared across the organization.

If the CoE staff are sitting in an ivory corporate tower, they are not learning and they are not teaching. What they know has a shelf life in an agile world. Therefore, they need to constantly get their hands dirty performing real-life activities and dealing with real-life impediments, working side by side with the Scrum teams to deliver value.

Scrum CoEs need legitimacy. In other words, they must have a purpose to justify the cost of implementing the team, just as the organization's executives must justify the investment costs in any type of Scrum team. The best way to ensure legitimacy is to have the organization's executives listen to the Scrum teams to learn what organizational impediments are getting in their way and what they need to solve those problems.

When appropriate, the executives should establish CoEs to address the organizational impediments, plus define metrics and measurements to indicate how well the CoEs are performing against the identified impediments and contributing to business value. Each CoE should have a stated mission and purpose and have a cross-organizational function. The CoE team incentives and rewards must be directly linked to the success of the Scrum transformation and the Scrum teams they support.

The CoE provides leadership and vision to the Scrum teams. Rather than enforcement of standards and controls, an effective CoE provides recommendations and alternatives for the Scrum teams' consideration. The CoE should provide guidance on techniques, useful templates, and tooling relevant to their area of focus. Above all, the Scrum CoEs must view the Scrum teams as their customers. As with any Scrum team, the CoE's existence is justified by providing value to its customers.

Finally, the CoE staff cannot become another form of bureaucratic layer that obstructs the business from being agile and innovative. Like it or not, bureaucracy is just another form of waste in a Lean-Agile organization.

Evaluating best fits

The Scrum of Scrums is largely an incomplete strategy, though it set the stage for what was to follow in modern formalized scaled Scrum strategies, such as *Scrum@Scale*, *Nexus*, and *Large-Scale Scrum*. Organizations that are run by pure Scrum advocates appreciate the SoS approach does not provide complex rules or bureaucratic structures and excessive overhead when scaling. The SoS is a generic Scrum approach that is easily adopted across organizations spanning commercial enterprises, federal agencies, and non-profits. However, beyond implementing the initial SoS structures, it's on the organizations' executives to figure out how to synchronize the activities of multiple SoS teams.

Given this context, unless the chief executive insists on going it alone when scaling Scrum beyond a single SoS team, this scaled Scrum approach is best limited to organizations that do not require more than nine Scrum teams and 81 people working in collaboration on a single product. Also, large organizations with multiple products may consider implementing individual SoS teams for each product, again constrained by having no more than nine Scrum teams and 81 people within each product group.

An SoS, like Scrum, does not provide specific guidance on how to handle regulatory and compliance issues. Both Scrum and SoS predate the concept of **Development Operations (DevOps)**. And though **Continuous Integration (CI)** concepts were well established when Sutherland and Schwaber first introduced Scrum, modern continuous delivery and test automation capabilities were not yet available. Systems thinking and Lean development practices were well understood but not yet applied to software development in a formalized approach. Finally, neither SoS nor Scrum provide detailed guidance on integrating operational value stream activities.

Given these limitations, organizations adopting the SoS approach should seek out additional consultative support to develop customized strategies in these other areas of concern. The alternative is to move on to adopt one or more of the modern scaled Scrum approaches identified in the upcoming chapters on *Scrum@Scale*, *Nexus*, *LeSS*, the **Scaled-Agile Framework (SAFe)**, or **Disciplined Agile (DA)**.

Summary

This chapter introduced the original SoS concepts to scale Scrum beyond one or two teams. An SoS scales Scrum to support large products and for implementations spanning an enterprise as the organizational standard for development. In addition, you learned three methods to scale Scrum: bottom-up, top-down, and CoE-led. Regardless of approach, the goal is to remain true to Scrum's empirical process control theories established by Schwaber and Sutherland in the Scrum Guide.

As described for method one, you learned that the historical deployment of Scrum occurred at the product or project team level. In such cases, an engineering or technical lead is able to drive the implementation of Scrum to fix the inefficiencies associated with a failing traditional plan-driven and linear-sequential development approach (that is, waterfall). A bottom-up approach to Scrum deployment indicates members of the product development team are driving the adoption of Scrum on a larger scale.

In this chapter, you learned that both Ken Schwaber and Jeff Sutherland always intended that Scrum should scale across both large products and as an enterprise development framework across all products. On the other hand, that objective requires buy-in from executive management. As described in method two, the top-down approach to scaling Scrum is driven by corporate executives or business owners, usually as a mandate.

Scrum's *network-oriented* team structures are radically different than the traditional functional and hierarchical organizational structures. On the positive side, Scrum offers a customer-centric approach to development that offers significant competitive advantages. Still, all too often, it takes a "burning platform" situation for chief executives and business owners to justify such radical change on an enterprise scale.

Finally, method three describes a *best of both worlds* approach as it has executive support but implements Scrum from the bottom-up. In this approach, a Scrum CoE with skilled resources is stood up to support the construction of Scrum teams in support of high-value and high-risk projects. Over time, the CoE helps the organization to scale Scrum across the organization as part of a corporate-sponsored and staged rollout.

Both the CoE and the top-down scaled Scrum implementation strategies require executive support and mandates. But the CoE strategy provides the resources to help to make the transition successful and with the foundations to stick and establish a cultural norm.

In the next chapter, we will explore how Jeff Sutherland's **Scrum@ Scale** extends the original Scrum scaling concepts as a formalized framework. *Chapter 14, Contrasting Scrum/ Lean-Agile Scaling Approaches* includes a comparative analysis of all scaled Scrum and Lean-Agile practices introduced in this book. Every approach mentioned in this book has something to offer and different sets of strengths in terms of capabilities and applications. In this chapter, you have learned the capabilities and benefits of this approach. *Chapter 14, Contrasting Scrum/ Lean-Agile Scaling Approaches* offers more context with the contrasts against other Scrum/ Lean-Agile approaches.

Questions

1. What is the purpose of SoS?

2. What are the two typical approaches taken to scaling Scrum in the original Scrum model?

3. In the context of an innovation's adoption curve applied to Scrum, what stage is Agile adoption within the software industry?

4. Why did software engineers and consultants largely lead the movement to promote agile practices?

5. What does it mean to prioritize Product Backlog items in terms of the highest value?

6. Instead of hierarchical organizations, which business structures better fit the scaled Scrum model?

7.   What are the two elements necessary to build a foundation of excellence?

8.   What are the five stages of team development?

9.   Since Scrum does not advocate the use of the traditional hierarchical management structures, where is it most logical to place executive-level functions, roles, and responsibilities? And what is their primary function?

10. Scrum has two seemingly conflicting objectives in I.T. governance. What are they?

Suggested reading

- Coach Bio (2019) *NAVY. Men's Cross Country. Al Cantello. Men's Cross Country Head Coach / Track & Field.* Retrieved from `https://navysports.com/sports/mens-cross-country/roster/coaches/al-cantello/150.` Accessed 26 November 2019

- Corporate. (2019) *13th Annual State of Agile Survey. CollabNet | VersionOne.* `https://www.stateofagile.com/#ufh-c-473508-state-of-agile-report.` Accessed November 24, 2019

- Fowler, M. (2014, August) *ShuHaRi.* Retrieved from `https://martinfowler.com/bliki/ShuHaRi.html`

- Jeremiah, J. (2019) *Survey Says... Survey: Is agile the new norm?* `https://techbeacon.com/app-dev-testing/survey-agile-new-norm.` Accessed 29 November 2019.

- Kuppler, T., Garnett, T., Morehead, T. (2014) *Build the Culture Advantage, Deliver Sustainable Performance with Clarity and Speed.* Sterling Heights, MI. The Culture Advantage, LLC.

- Moore, G. A. (2005, 2008) *Dealing with Darwin: How Great Companies Innovate at Every Phase of Their Evolution.* New York, NY. The Penguin Group (USA)

- Schwaber, K., Beedle, M. (2002) *Agile Software Development with Scrum.* Upper Saddle, NJ. Prentice-Hall, Inc.

- Schwaber, K. (2004) *Agile Project Management with Scrum. Best practices.* Richmond, WA. Microsoft Press.

- Schwaber, K. (2007) *The Enterprise and Scrum. Developer Best Practices.* Richmond, WA. Microsoft Press.

- Schwaber, K., Sutherland, J. (2012) *Software in 30 Days: How Agile Managers Beat the Odds, Delight Their Customers, and Leave Competitors in the Dust.* p.162. Hoboken, New Jersey. John Wiley & Sons, Inc.

- Sutherland, J. (2001, November) *Agile Can Scale: Inventing and Reinventing SCRUM in Five Companies*. Retrieved from `https://www.cutter.com/article/agile-can-scale-inventing-and-reinventing-scrum-five-companies-408271`.

- Sutherland, J. Sutherland, J.J. (2014) Scrum. *The Art of Doing Twice the Work in Half the Time*. New York, NY. Currency, an imprint of Penguin Random House, LLC.

- Sutherland, J. (2015, June) *IDX Case Study - The First Scaled Scrum*. Retrieved from: `http://www.scruminc.com/wp-content/uploads/2015/06/IDX-Case-Study-The-First-Scaled-Scrum.pdf`

- Sutherland, J., Coplein, J.O., et al. (2019) *A Scrum Book. The Spirit of the Game*. Raleigh, NC. The Pragmatic Bookshelf, LLC.

- Sutherland, J.J. (2019) *The Scrum Fieldbook. A Master Class on Accelerating Performance, Getting Results, and Defining the Future*. New York, NY. Currency, an imprint of Penguin Random House, LLC.

- Sutton, B. (2014, March) *Why Big Teams Suck*. Retrieved from `https://www.linkedin.com/pulse/20140303152358-15893932-why-big-teams-suck/`

- Tuckman, Bruce W (1965). *"Developmental sequence in small groups"*. Psychological Bulletin. 63 (6): 384–399. doi:10.1037/h0022100. PMID 14314073

- Tuckman, B.W., Jensen, M. A. C. *Group & Organization Studies*, Volume: 2 issue: 4, page(s): 419-427. Issue published: December 1, 1977. `https://doi.org/10.1177/105960117700200404`

8
Scrum@Scale

This chapter introduces the **Scrum@Scale (S@S)** approach to scaling Scrum, which is the latest thinking from Jeff Sutherland, one of the two developers of Scrum. In this chapter, you will learn how Scrum@Scale extends the original Scrum framework to support the development of large and complex products, processes, services, and systems. You will learn how Scrum@Scale offers a linear scalable approach to installing and coordinating multiple Scrum Teams with the goal to deliver high quality and value, while simultaneously improving business agility.

This chapter outlines the basics of this scaled Scrum approach, consistent with Sutherland's *Scrum@Scale Guide* (`https://www.scrumatscale.com/`). You will learn how the *Scrum@Scale Guide* builds upon the concepts outlined in the original Scrum Guide and on the values and principles outlined in the **Agile Manifesto**. But where the original Scrum Guide operates at the single team/single product level, the Scrum@Scale Guide has a broader focus to ensure the business remains adaptive at an enterprise scale as Scrum Teams and products are added.

In this chapter, you will learn how scale-free architectures enable scaling and coordination of Scum teams with "minimum viable bureaucracy." You will also learn about the new roles and organizational structures that help the teams resolve dependency, redundancy, and integration issues.

Over the course of this chapter, we're going to cover the following main topics, in order:

- Coordinating multiple Scrum Teams
- Defining the S@S use case
- Implementing scale-free Scrum architectures
- Scaling Scrum with S@S
- Facilitating S@S events
- Installing executive leadership
- Intersecting the PO and SM cycles
- Building healthy organizations
- Evaluating best fits

With this preliminary introduction, let's now dive into the details. We'll start with a discussion on the issues that crop up when organizations need to have multiple Scrum Teams working together in a collaborative way.

Coordinating multiple Scrum Teams

Jeff Sutherland notes that the original Scrum Guide worked very well at defining how a single Scrum Team works collaboratively to achieve optimal outcomes, capabilities, and sustainability. Over time, the success of Scrum led organizations to scale Scrum to increasingly larger product development efforts that required the expansion and coordination of multiple Scrum Teams. Scrum proved scalable in these larger product development efforts. Nevertheless, Jeff also concedes that new extensions to Scrum were necessary to overcome two major issues that arose when scaling Scrum across multiple teams:

- Declining Scrum Team efficiencies
- Unclear management structures at scale

The Scrum Team inefficiencies came from the same network density and non-value-added waste issues you learned about in the previous chapters on *Chapter 4, Systems Thinking,* and *Chapter 5, Lean Thinking.* The most critical issues associated with scaling Scrum are the exponentially increasing lines of communications produced by the geometric rise in team members. As multiple Scrum Teams are formed, there needs to be a coordinating structure to simplify communications and to guide priorities as a collective to responsively support evolving business strategies, customer needs, and competitive market conditions.

This principle acknowledges the facts, borne out time and again, that adding human resources only causes more delays. There are two reasons for this:

- It takes time to bring added software developers up to speed on the work.
- The increased communication overhead creates more inefficiencies.

The goal of S@S is to focus multiple Scrum Teams, in a coordinated manner, around the strategies, goals, and objectives of the business. At a more granular level, Scrum@Scale implements structures to integrate, coordinate, and synchronize the work of multiple teams around value creation.

Defining the S@S use case

S@S stays true to Scrum's origins of defining a framework to resolve complex adaptive problems through installing empirical process control theory (empiricism) within an iterative and incremental development framework. S@S preserves many of the roles and events of the original Scrum Framework.

However, as the organization continues to scale beyond the level at which a single Product Owner can manage, S@S implements new roles, organizational structures, and events that help support the coordination and integration of the underlying teams. You will see that S@S extends the original Scrum Framework by repeating small team patterns, thus creating fractal-like organizational structures.

But before we can define those new roles, events, and structures, you need to know something about the underlying theories upon which S@S is built. These theories are the topics that will be covered in the remainder of this section.

Overcoming Brooks's Law

Fred Brooks is famous for making the following observation: *adding manpower to a late software project makes it later* (Brooks, F. 1995). Brooks succinctly put into words the impacts of network density problems, where geometric additions of human resources create an exponential rise in potential participant integration and communications links.

The S@S framework bypasses the impacts of Brooks's Law, and network density issues in general, by limiting the size of individual team structures and the number of team members who can communicate with other teams. S@S also installs the team concept at scale as nodes to further limit the type and number of interactions across teams. Let's look at how this works.

Repeating structural patterns

Scrum@Scale is all about scaling Scrum through repeating structural patterns. Within the S@S Framework, small teams collaborate in fractal-like patterns, with information-hiding capabilities mimicking object-oriented designs.

Fractal patterns exhibit similar structural designs, no matter the scale at which you view the components that make up the larger and more complex system. In other words, no matter the scale of view, the component elements all look virtually the same. Moreover, the larger elements are built from the smaller elements.

The term *information hiding* means the teams are fully self-contained and only share the information they need to complete and integrate their work. The teams also limit communications with other participating teams through a small number of individuals (for example, the *Ambassadors* defined in the Scrum of Scrums (SoS) model). In the context of object-oriented designs, those individuals who communicate with other teams serve as the *interfaces* for their respective teams.

These fractal-like designs, with information hiding and a constrained number of interfaces, radically reduce the number of communication paths. Put another way, multiple Scrum teams working within the S@S framework operate as a network of loosely coupled teams, with well-defined interfaces that limit network density issues through preferential connections, or nodes. More about that later. First, we need to talk about how S@S limits organizational bureaucracy.

Minimizing bureaucracy

One of the biggest problems with the traditional hierarchical management structures is the amount of bureaucracy that becomes necessary to coordinate functionally aligned resources around product-oriented development and delivery activities. Each organizational structure has differing goals and objectives. However, align the organization's resources around its products and the bureaucracy-related issues will largely go away.

The Scrum@Scale structure enables large networks of teams to interoperate under a **minimum viable bureaucracy (MVB)** via **scale-free architectures** and **networked teams**. These strategies overcome Brooks's Law to achieve linear scalability. The objective of linear scaling is that there should be no decrease in performance per team when adding Scrum Teams in a collaborative environment.

In this chapter, you will learn how these concepts work together to maintain autonomy with the empirical process control mechanisms of Scrum's small team structures at scale. But first, let's take a deeper dive into understanding how scale-free architectures, team networks, fractal geometries, and object-oriented metaphors describe the interoperability of multiple Scrum Teams operating at scale, starting with an introduction to networking concepts.

The original concept of **MVB** is largely credited as a description of the internal implementation of Agile practices at **Spotify**. Henrik Kniberg, a developer, Agile/Lean coach, and blogger at Crisp AB, initially used the term in the Spotify Cultural video part 2, originally released in 2014 (`https://labs.spotify.com/2014/09/20/spotify-engineering-culture-part-2/`). Later, Peter Antman, who was then working as an Agile consultant at Spotify, and is now a Spotify employee, popularized and defined the term as having a *"small enough structure to help but not be in the way"* (Peter Antman. 2016, *Growing up with Agile – Minimum Viable Bureaucracy at Spotify*: `https://blog.crisp.se/2016/04/29/peterantman/growing-up-with-Agile-minimum-viable-bureaucracy-at-Spotify`).

Scrum@Scale implements these concepts and expands its definition as *"having the least amount of governing bodies and processes needed to carry out the function(s) of an organization without impeding the delivery of customer value."* (Sutherland, Scrum@Scale Guide, 2020)

MVB helps an organization achieve business agility by reducing the amount of time and effort it takes to get a decision. Instead of working through multiple layers of bureaucracy, Scrum Teams have direct access to the individuals who have the power and authority to remove organizational impediments and to make business decisions.

The challenge all businesses face is that it's difficult to scale organizational structures and retain any level of efficiencies. The issue is one of latency, as everything takes more time and effort to move through organizational processes, and bureaucracy in a multi-level, hierarchical organizational structure. As it turns out, *nothing scales*, and a new type of organizational architecture is required to effectively deploy and coordinate the activities of multiple Agile teams across an enterprise.

Networking concepts and metaphors

Scram@Scale preserves the basic Scrum Teams and empirical process control and complex adaptive systems theories articulated in the original Scrum Guide. However, the philosophy of Scrum@Scale is that these teams operate as a network of independent but highly collaborative entities. The effectiveness of the collaboration comes through communication hubs that allow large-scale connectivity with a minimal number of paths and transmissions.

Anyone who has worked in middleware understands the inefficiencies of point-to-point interconnections. It's the same network density problem (that is, $n(n\text{-}1)/2$ connections) we identified in *Chapter 4, Systems Thinking*. The middleware industry largely solved this problem by going to hub-and-spoke and messaging-based integration architectures.

Architectures that rely on random connections quickly fail as there is no information or structure to simplify routing communications. The way to overcome the inefficiencies of random connectiveness is to establish *very connected* hubs that constrain the types and routes of communications and interoperability:

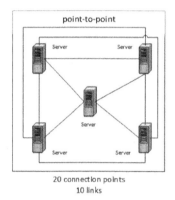 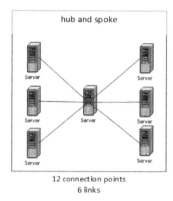 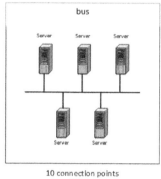

Figure 8.1 – Network communications/integration strategies

Before we leave the topic of networking, the preceding diagram shows how communications links and connection nodes can vary significantly based on the networking strategies being used. This example uses server-based applications as an example, but you can switch out servers with teams or people to show how they are similarly affected.

Building scale-free architectures

There are different strategies that use hubs to support preferential interconnections at scale, but they are largely lumped together under the concept of **scale-free networks**. Structural designs that employ node-based interoperability preferences are called **scale-free architectures**. Power grids operate as scale-free architectures, as does the internet.

Scale-free networks provide a useful example for us to understand how a large collection of loosely connected objects can interoperate in organized and constructive ways. In such an architecture, each object is self-contained and relatively autonomous. But each object also knows what hubs it can communicate with, and what information it must exchange to support its functionality.

Object-oriented programs work in a similar manner. Each defined object is fully self-contained in terms of data, methods, and instructions to guide their purpose or function. The methods in **object-oriented programming** (**OOP**) have specific procedures that guide their work, as well as associated messages that describe how to invoke an object's services.

The following diagram graphically portrays how multiple Scrum Teams scale linearly and minimize the network density issues of exponential growth by marshalling communications through a limited number of preferentially interconnected nodes. These preferential interconnections are the hallmarks of scale-free architectures:

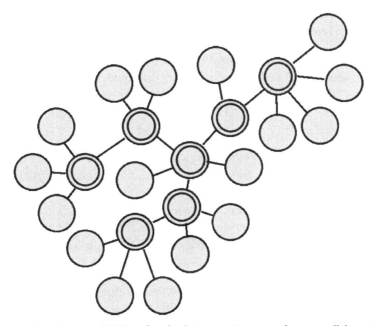

Figure 8.2 – Linear scalability of multiple Scrum Teams working in collaboration

Human beings, of course, are not objects; but there is merit behind the idea of applying the concept of object-oriented designs and scale-free architectures to organize and sync multiple Scrum Teams. Scaled as network-based systems, Scrum Teams are the objects.

Sutherland also introduces the notion that **linear scalability** is what enables scaling without the loss of productivity per Scrum Team. Following guidance from research that concludes that five communication nodes are optimal, Scrum Teams can scale in a **fractal**-like pattern. Fractals are structures that display similar patterns that reoccur at progressively larger or smaller scales and emerge from seemingly random or chaotic processes.

The preceding diagram also provides an example of how Scrum Teams within the S@S framework take on a fractal-like display pattern. Note that the circles with the double lines serve as hubs to connect other objects within the network, similar to the hub and spoke example shown in the middle diagram in *Figure 8.1*. These nodes are examples of very connected hubs, as defined in the context of scale-free architectures.

In this chapter, you will come to understand why Sutherland applies the concepts of networks of teams, scale-free architectures, and fractals to describe the Scrum@Scale approach to scaling Scrum. However, before we get started, let's first look at how Scrum@Scale defines a **Minimum Viable Bureaucracy (MVB)**, and why it's important.

Nothing scales

Jeff Sutherland credits the **Intel Corporation**, where they implemented Scrum at an enterprise scale involving 25,000 engineers, as the originators of the notion that *nothing scales* and that we need scale-free architecture to solve the problem. (Sutherland, 2017. *Give Thanks for Scrum 2017. Scrum@Scale.* – `https://www.Scruminc.com/give-thanks-Scrum-scale-free-architecture/`)

Well now, that's an odd statement. If nothing scales, how do we scale Scrum? The key is the concept of *scale-free architectures*, which implies the connective properties of the Scrum Teams remain consistent and capable, regardless of scale. Scale-free architectures are abound in the world around us. For example, they support connectivity and expansion in power grids, stock market transactions, the growth of cancer cells, and the transmission of viruses. OO programs are another example of scale-free architectures.

Scale-free architectures allow the efficient interoperability of many *very connected* components with hubs that facilitate linkage and communications between the disparate nodes. This is a critical concept behind the theories of Scrum@Scale in terms of how large numbers of autonomous Scrums teams collaborate and work collectively toward a common purpose and set of goals. While the foundation of Scrum@Scale is still the basic Scrum Team, scaling starts with the implementation of an SoS.

Implementing scale-free Scrum architectures

In both the original *Scrum Guide* and the *Scrum@Scale Guide*, the Scrum Team is the idealized development unit. The Scrum Team has all the skills to take a concept and run with it until it is ready for deployment. Scrum@Scale keeps the fundamentals associated with the basic Scrum Team and builds scale by simply adding new Scrum Teams as needs arise.

More importantly, Scrum@Scale implements a scale-free architecture through networked structures and scaled roles. Building on the basic Scrum Team, interconnections form in relatively small **SoS** Teams, ideally consisting of five people per Scrum Team and five Scrum Teams per SoS. Likewise, SoS Teams combine, as needed, to form **Scrum of Scrum of Scrum (SoSoS)** Teams. Situationally, the numbers can vary somewhat, but the ideal is five members for each type of team structure:

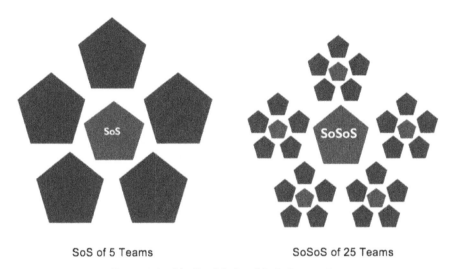

SoS of 5 Teams   SoSoS of 25 Teams

Figure 8.3 – Idealized SoS and SoSoS team sizes

The preceding diagram graphically portrays the idealized SoS team size of five Scrum Teams, each having five team members, and a SoSoS Team having five SOS teams for a total of 25 Scrum Teams. As a metaphor, think of the *Russian Matryoshka Nesting dolls*. Lower-level Scrum Teams nest within upper level SoS and SoSoS Teams, but they all look and act similarly.

Again, these figures are representations of ideal team size goals and are not meant to be absolutes. Product and team resource needs always surmount to idealism, but within boundaries. For example, ±2 is a good limit to place on the idealized team size of 5. We will revisit the SoS and SoSoS pentagonal structures later in this chapter.

The SOS and SoSoS Teams collaborate to produce a fully integrated set of potentially shippable increments of new product value at the end of every Sprint, with contributions from all participating teams. Both the SoS and SoSoS operate as scaled Scrum Teams and have scaled versions of the original Scrum roles, events, and artifacts.

Scaling Scrum with S@S

Scrum@Scale helps organizations scale Scrum by essentially repeating the common small Scrum team pattern but minimizing the team members who participate in cross-team communications and work sessions. This strategy helps teams avoid the network density issues we described in *Chapter 4, Systems Thinking*. In this context, S@S looks a bit like its predecessor, SoS, where Scrum Teams assign ambassadors to represent their interests in SoS meetings. The SoS team concepts still apply to developing a single product, just as Scrum teams only support the development of one product. The SoS operating as a team of Scrum Teams has the responsibility to develop and deliver
a potentially shippable product at the end of each development iteration. And at this level of scale, SoS and S@S are essentially equivalent Scrum scaling strategies.

However, at some point of scale, the Product Owner has more work than they can handle. At that point, S@S installs multiple Product Owners working in collaboration under the direction of a Chief Product Owner, and together they form a Product Owner Team. Each SoS has a dedicated Product Owner Team. The Chief Product Owner Team establishes the vision by prioritizing the Product Backlog items within a single Product Backlog. Collectively, the Product Owner team works through SoS team level integration, dependency, and synchronization issues.

Similarly, as the number of Scrum Teams grows, a **Scrum Master (SM)** of the Scrum of Scrums is appointed, called the **Scrum of Scrums Master (SoSM)**. The SoSM is accountable for delivering new increments of value produced by the Scrum Teams that make up the SoS. The SoSM is responsible for providing visibility and dealing with impediments at the SoS level that cannot be resolved at the Scrum Team level.

Installing SoS artifacts, roles, and events

Recall that Scrum implements three artifacts: *Product Backlog*, *Sprint Backlog*, and *Increments*. Scrum@Scale has the same artifacts but scaled at the SoS, SoSoS, and enterprise levels. The underlying Scrum Teams still maintain their artifacts. However, depending on the size and needs of the organization, the SoS, SoSoS, and enterprise levels have artifacts that drive the underlying team-level artifacts.

Unlike Scrum, SoS implements the role of a **Product Owner Team (POT)**. Members of the POT collaborate to establish priorities within a single enterprise backlog. Each SoS and SoSoS Team has a Product Owner who is responsible for selecting items and establishing priorities within a Team Backlog. The Team Backlog may include a collection of items pulled from a shared SoS backlog, or independently established for the team.

The POT includes a person fulfilling a SM role and another person who has a **Chief Product Owner (CPO)** role within the team. Those roles support the POT, but otherwise operate identically to their counterparts at the Scrum Team level. The CPO must also coordinate the generation of a single SOS Backlog and prioritization of its items.

Each SOS has a Scrum Master, called the **Scrum of Scrums Master (SoSM)**. The SoSM makes progress visible, helps remove impediments at the SoS level, including resolution of cross-team dependencies and the distribution of SoS Backlog items. The SoS Teams work in collaboration to develop independent yet integrated increments of potentially shippable products. The CPO, in collaboration with the Product Owner Team, determines when to release the fully integrated and tested products. The SOSM coordinates their teams' incremental deliveries in support of the Product Owner's release plans.

In the previous chapter, you learned that the SoS concept implemented a Scrum of Scrums Meeting as the event used to resolve cross-team dependency, coordination, and integration issues. In the Scrum@Scale framework, these events are called a **Scaled Daily Scrum (SDS)** event. As the name implies, this is a scheduled daily event, and there is no formalized title for the attendee. (that is, there is not a defined ambassador role). Otherwise, the two events are essentially identical in terms of purpose and function.

Scaling Scrum is not just about coordinating multiple Scrum Teams. There must be a business to justify the resources, time, expenditures, and organizational disruptions caused by realignment. In fact, scaled Scrum changes the entire corporate operating system.

Applying an Agile operating system

Both the *Scrum@Scale Guide* and *Scaled-Agile, Inc.* refer to the term **operating systems** as a business management construct; however, if you have not studied business, you may wonder what this term really means. In a general context, a corporate operating system is the standard collection of business processes employed by an entity, be it a government agency, commercial company, or a non-profit.

A traditional corporate operating system supports functional-hierarchical organizational structures through the implementation of corporate policies and cross-functional business processes. In contrast, an Agile operating system seeks to minimize complexities to improve value streams efficiencies by eliminating all waste. Moreover, an Agile operating system seeks to build only the things customers want, when they want them.

The Scrum@Scale Guide promotes the basic Scrum Team as a prototypical structure upon which to create an Agile operating system that enables scale-free organizational architectures. Later, you will learn about Scrum@Scale's **Executive Action Team (EAT)** as the organization responsible for developing and executing a transformational strategy. In effect, the EAT establishes an Agile operating system as a **reference model** that includes corporate operational rules, procedures, and guidelines for business agility.

Leveraging Scrum's team process

Scrum, SoS, and SoSoS Teams follow the basics of Scrum, as originally outlined in the Scrum Guide, which the Scrum@Scale Guide refers to as the **team process**. In other words, the team process is Scrum practiced at a team level. The primary difference in Scrum@Scale is the concept of what constitutes a Scrum Team. The goals of the team process are to maximize flow, increase team performance, provide a healthy and sustainable environment for its team members, and fast-track customer feedback via Sprint reviews.

It's important to note that Scrum Teams are not just for software development. While the basic small-team structure and roles of Scrum do not change – comprising developers, a **Product Owner (PO)** and a **Scrum Master (SM)** – each new team is built to support a specific business, development, or operational requirement. Therefore, different Scrum Teams have different sets of knowledge, skills, experiences, methods, and tools necessary to support their particular business function.

Optimizing Scrum and SoS Teams around sets of fives

The Scrum@Scale Guide cites Harvard research conducted by J. Richard Hackman, Edgar Pierce Professor of Social and Organizational Psychology, (Hackman, J. R. 2002). It found the ideal team size is more limited than they originally thought. Recall that the original Scrum Guide specified the ideal Scrum Team size as 3 to 9 people. Instead, Professor Hackman concluded that an ideal team size is 4.6 people (on average):

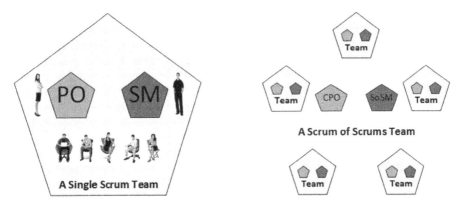

Figure 8.4 – Scrum Team versus an SoS Team

The preceding diagram displays both a Scrum Team and a SoS as a team organizational structure that includes five Scrum Teams. Sutherland's Scrum@Scale approach builds on this average team size of ~5 people to create a repeating pattern of pentagons to build and then coordinate the activities of multiple Scrum Teams. Of course, there is nothing that prevents individual Scum teams from having fewer or more people; five is simply an idealized objective.

Consistent with what you learned in *Chapter 6, Lean Practices in Software Development*, the SoS operates as a large Scrum Team, following the same team processes, with similar roles, events, and artifacts, but scaled to support the underlying Scrum Teams. The SoS, operating as an autonomous unit, has a set of **potentially shippable products (PSP)** as its incremental delivery of value across each development iteration.

Just like with the Scrum Team, a SoS needs leaders to define what gets built and how things get built. The SoS has a **Chief Product Owner (CPO)** who works with the Scrum Team-level POs to define and prioritize the build-related work. Similarly, the SoS has a **SoSM** who works with the Scrum Masters within the SoS to coordinate the activities necessary to build the deliverables. The pentagonal structure limits the number of CPO/PO and SoSM/SM networking connections to five peers within the SoS.

The SoS brings a Scrum-based structure to organize and direct the work of up to five Scrum Teams and 25 developers, involving any number of disciplines and business functions. However, many organizations and product teams have many times that number of people working on business operations and product development-related activities. The Scrum@Scale Guide provides guidance on how to continue this pentagonal scaling structure to whatever level of scale is necessary.

Leveraging pentagonal structures, ad infinitum

If necessary, the pattern of pentagonal scaling continues in S@S by adding the **SoSoS** structure to support linear scalability for up to 25 Scrum Teams, as shown in the following diagram. And there can be more than one SoSoS, if needed:

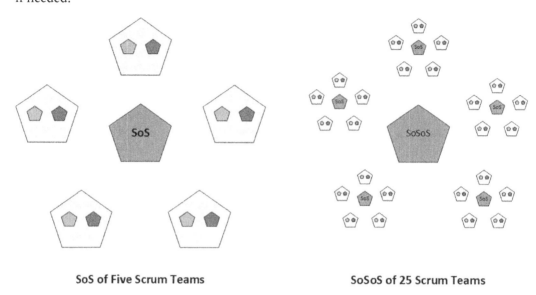

SoS of Five Scrum Teams   **SoSoS of 25 Scrum Teams**

Figure 8.5 – SoSoS teams

Again, it is an idealized state to have five SoS teams within a SoSoS, with each Scrum Team having exactly five people. An organization can have fewer than five SoS Scrum Teams within an SoSoS, but ideally no more than five. Likewise, Scrum Teams may have more or less than five people each – depending on resource needs, with five being an idealized state.

Just like with the Scrum Team, a SoSoS needs leaders to define what gets built and how things get built. The SoSoS has a **CPO** who works with the Scrum Team-level POs to define and prioritize the build-related work. Similarly, the SoSoS has a **SoSM** who works with the Scrum Masters within the SoS to coordinate the activities necessary to build the deliverables.

The scaling of Scrum Teams does not need to stop at 25 teams, but the pattern of up to 25 teams within individual SoSoS structures repeats as often as necessary to support the organization's product, process, and service development and operational needs. This is shown in the following diagram:

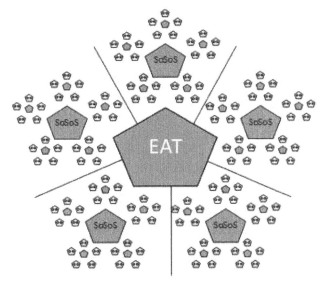

Figure 8.6 – Executive Action Team (EAT) used to coordinate multiple SoSoSes

The fractal structures continue to scale in S@S, following the same basic optimal of 5 ± 2 team members, as shown in the preceding diagram for the **EAT**. An EAT serves as an executive-level SM for the scaled Agile organization. However, before getting into that topic, we need to look at the events and cycles implemented by S@S.

Facilitating SoS events

As the organization builds to a level requiring the implementation of an SoS organizational structure, the SoSM and CPOs form into leadership groups. These groups support the scaled versions of SM and PO cycles and their corresponding events.

The Scrum@Scale events correspond to the same types of events outlined in the Scrum Guide. For example, the SoSM facilitates a **Scaled Daily Scrum (SDS)** meeting, attended by at least one representative from each Scrum Team. As with the Daily Scrum, the SDS is a 15-minute timeboxed event where members discuss team and cross-team impediments and dependencies. Also, recall from the basics of Scrum that impediments and dependencies are directly tied to accomplishing the **Sprint Goal**.

In the Scrum of Scrum Retrospectives, the Scrum Masters within the SoS get together and discuss and create a plan for improvements for the upcoming Sprint. Different than the Scrum Guide, the Scrum@Scale Guide discusses the act of *inspection* as planning and conducting **experiments** to drive continuous improvement results.

There is only one Product Backlog in a scaled Scrum organization. All Scrum Teams pull items from this prioritized backlog of highest-value requirements. The construction and refinement of the backlog is a joint responsibility of the **POT**, under the guidance of the CPO, who has final authority over vision, goals, and priorities. The Product Backlog remains a value-based representation
of customer needs.

The CPO ensures the PO teams conduct SoS-level Sprint Planning events and that the CPO facilitates the SoS-level Sprint Review to ensure the customers agree that the deliverables meet their requirements and fulfill the definition of Done. The SoS-level POT conducts a scaled version of Sprint Planning with assistance from the SoSM team.

Coordinating the what and the how

The original Scum Guide is a framework that implements a bare-bones Agile process bounded within a single but repeatable iterative and incremental development cycle. The Scrum Team, SM, and PO all interoperate and collaborate within each of those iterative cycles.

In contrast, Scrum@Scale integrates two SoS-level iterative and incremental cycles that operate in concurrence with the original Scrum development cycle. The SoS-level cycles include an **SM cycle** and a **PO cycle**.

The PO cycle has components that guide *what* gets developed, while the SM cycle has a set of components that guide *how* the development work gets done. The Scrum@ Scale concept also employs a **Component** concept, which allows organizations to customize their Agile transformation and implementations strategies. While many of the components are unique to one cycle or the other, two components serve as connection points while another is shared. Let's take a closer look at both the SM and PO cycles and their components.

Intersecting the PO and SM cycles

Scrum@Scale is billed as an Agile framework to address complex adaptive problems and deliver high-value products. The framework includes a minimum set of components that support two integrated cycles: the *Product Owner cycle* and the *Scrum Master cycle*. The Product Owner cycle implements a strategy to guide decisions on *what* is to be built (the product) in terms of highest-value development priorities. Adjacent yet overlapping the PO cycle is a SM cycle that informs *how* the product is to be built (the process):

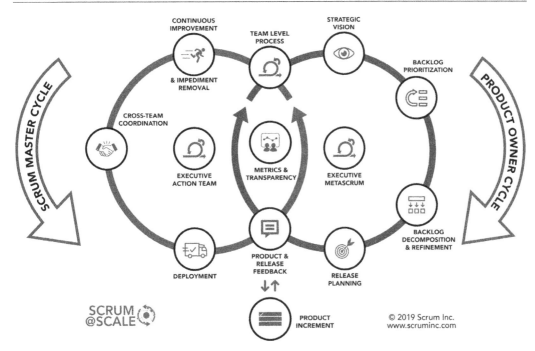

Figure 8.7 – Scrum@Scale Framework components

As shown in the preceding diagram, the SM cycle includes six components, while the PO cycle includes seven. Both the SM and PO cycles have three of the components in common, two of which are intersection points – **Team Level Process** and **Product & Release Feedback** – while the other is shared – **Metrics and Transparency**. The **Team Level Process** is the original Scrum guidance operating at the team level. The **Product & Release Feedback** component coordinates and consolidates feedback on the collective, potentially shippable, products for release. The **Metrics and Transparency** component ensures an SoS wide view to team metrics through Scrum Team and SoS team information radiators.

The SoSM is responsible for facilitating the SM cycle. Collectively, the SoS Scrum Master team, as a group, is accountable for the joint SoS releases of potentially shippable products. In that role, they are responsible for continuously improving throughput, lowering costs, and delivering higher quality. They ensure transparency across the SoS through appropriate and widescale use of information radiators. In short, they coordinate how work is accomplished and improved across the SoS.

The CPO is responsible for facilitating the PO cycle. Collectively, the POT, as a group, is accountable for guiding team-level processes toward delivering the highest-value items within the Product Backlog, articulating the strategic vision, backlog prioritization, decomposition, and refinement and release planning. They have a common touchpoint with the SoSMs to verify product alignment with customer needs through the Sprint Reviews. They are equally involved in reviewing and analyzing metrics and ensuring transparency across the SoS through highly visible and up-to-date information radiators.

Note that the **Product Increment** component stands alone. Potentially shippable products are released with each iterative development cycle based on their meeting the definition of Done for each incremental delivery of value. However, those incremental deliverables may not form a complete product in the eyes of the customer. Therefore, deployment to customers as a fully developed product increment is outside the boundaries of the SM and PO cycles.

The intersections of the PO and SM cycles is intentional. For much of their cycles, each team works on their respective functions. The SoSM teams define processes and facilitate effort to building the right products. POTs define what those deliverable products need to be and to ensure the development priorities are established around value.

The intersection at the Team Process helps ensure the Scrum Teams are focused on the right things with aligned guidance from the SoSMs and POs. The intersection at Product and Release Feedback serves as frequent intervals for verification and validation that the customers approve of the capabilities and direction of the product. If not, it is better to find out early when there are problems. Having metrics in place is what allows for verification and validation. Without metrics, no one would know for sure what the goals and objectives are, nor would we know how well we are meeting them.

With that, you now understand the boundaries and scope of activities surrounding the PO and SM cycles. Now, we need to take a look at what keeps these two cycles aligned with their respective functions of *what* gets built and *how* things get built.

Installing executive leadership

Recall from its previous introduction in the preceding diagram that the S@S Framework components show two cycles that create flow around their related components. One of the flows is the Scrum Master cycle, while the other flow is the Product Owner cycle. The **EAT** sits at the center of the SM cycle, while the **Executive MetaScrum Team (EMT)** sits at the center of the Product Owner cycle.

The executive level teams sit above the SoS or SoSoS – or whatever level of scale is reached by the S@S organization – to support the teams at an executive management level of authority. The primary thing to remember is that S@S implements one set of executive leaders to support the Scrum teams, and another set to support the Product Owners.

The EAT, sitting at the center of the SM cycle, focuses on the implementation and development of knowledge, resources, skills, and processes to develop and deliver high-value products. The EMT also works to eliminate impediments that must be dealt with at an executive level of authority.

In contrast, the EMT fulfills the Product Owner role for the entire Agile enterprise. In that capacity, the EMT brings together the CPO, key executives, and critical stakeholders to discuss and negotiate priorities with the POTs, adjust budgets if need be, and realign teams around the delivery of value, as prioritized within the Product Backlog. The EMT establishes product visions and aligns product investments with corporate strategies.

You now have a high-level understanding of the roles that the EMT and EAT play. Now, let's take a deeper dive to better understand their responsibilities. We'll start again with the EAT and its role at the center of the SM cycle.

Executive Action Team

The **EAT** has the same function as the Scrum Master role but serves an entire Agile organization. The EAT is a leadership team, not a single individual. Moreover, all Scrum Masters report to the EAT. The EAT structure provides resources to ensure sufficient planning and the completion of items identified and managed within the Organizational Transformation Backlog.

Teams operating under the EAT live in the Scrum-Agile world. However, there may be parts of the organization that are not operating in a similar manner, and it is the responsibility of the EAT to integrate with any part of the organization that is not operating in the same Agile umbrella. The EAT ensures the Agile organization implements Scrum values, roles, events, and artifacts with the necessary support systems.

Recall that the preceding diagram provides a representative display of an EAT that is coordinating five groupings of 25 teams. Again, there is no need to have exactly five groups of teams with five teams each. The number of teams in each SoS, and teams of teams operating within the EAT, is situational, and based on the needs of the organization. The number five is simply an optimal number of connected nodes in a network to minimize network density concerns.

Removing impediments

Identified impediments move up from the Scrum Teams to the SoS, and ultimately to the EAT when they cannot be resolved at the lower levels. Usually, impediments that make their way to the EAT operate at an executive level of authority. The EAT has executive-level authority, and members of the EAT are empowered, politically and financially, to resolve whatever impediments come their way, similar to the executive authorities within a traditional hierarchical organization.

The EAT operates as a high-level Scrum Team, and its members include a single Product Owner, a Scrum Master, and necessary team members to carry out the executive-level authorities. The Product Owner maintains a single though transparent Product Backlog for the EAT, which includes the items that create transformational value across it.

Transforming with the EAT

The EAT is responsible for the implementation of Scrum across the enterprise as a whole. In this context, the EAT's role is to help accomplish the transformation to a large-scale Scrum organization. The EAT's Product Owner is responsible for the Organizational Transformation Backlog, which is a prioritized list of identified items deemed as necessary to support the transformation, growth, and sustainment of a scaled Scrum organization. The items can take the form of work activities to implement structural changes, provide training, and even help identify needs and assist the Scrum Teams with selecting and procuring environments to support continuous integration, testing automation, and DevOps toolchains.

As with all Scrum-based teams, the EAT has a Product Owner. The EAT's Product Owner is responsible for maintaining the Organizational Transformation Backlog, including item identification and prioritization. As with an SoS or SoSoS, the EAT Product Owner is responsible for creating and funding a Product Owner Team and for making sure that their collective concerns are represented within the EAT.

The EAT's responsibilities include, but are not limited to, the following:

- Creating an Agile operating system
- Including corporate operational rules, procedures, and guidelines to enable agility

- Measuring and improving the quality of Scrum across the organization
- Building capability within the organization to support business agility
- Establishing a center for continuous learning for Scrum professionals
- Exploring new, more effective ways of working

Executive MetaScrum Team

Whereas the EAT fulfilled an organization-wide Scrum Master (like) Role as a team, the **EMT** fills a Product Owner (like) role as a team for the entire scaled Scrum organization. The EMT is a leadership team that defines the organizational vision, establishes strategic priorities, and ensures the teams are operating in alignment with the organization's goals.

Owning the products

Though the EAT's Product Owner is responsible for creating and funding the Product Owner organization, the Product Owner Team operates under the direction of the EMS. This linear-network design ensures an Agile organization is infinitely scalable with any number of associated Scrum of Scrums.

Recall that each SOS has a Chief Product Owner who may also have a Product Owner Team. Likewise, each SOSOS has a Product Owner Team that consists of the SOS-level Products Owners. Coordinating the activities of the SoSoS Product Owner Team is an SoSoS-level Chief Product Owner.

So, Scrum@Scale recognizes that naming these roles the same thing for each level is confusing. Their guidance is to have organizations come up with customized names that best describe the scope of work or responsibilities spanning each SoS and SoSoS level. The Scrum Master, Product Owner, and Chief Product Owner titles merely indicate the type of work these folks perform.

With this understanding, the following diagram portrays five SoSoS Teams, each of which have a Chief Product Owner who works as part of a Chief Product Owner Team under the direction of an EMT). The Chief Product Owner Team meets with essential stakeholders from the EMT:

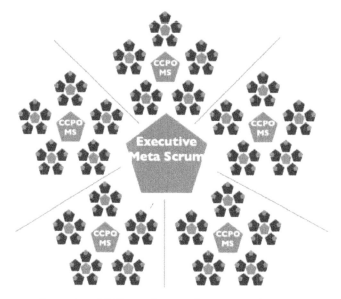

Figure 8.8 – EMT coordinating five groups of 25 teams

In the preceding diagram, the very smallest orange pentagonal figures are depicted as being individual Scrum teams with five members each, and that each Scrum Team has a Product Owner.

1. Those Scrum team-level Product Owners, in turn, participate as members of the Product Owner Teams at an SoS level – as shown in each of the larger dark grey pentagonal shapes – and each SOS will have a **CPO** Let's look deeper:

2. Next, five SOS teams (dark grey pentagonal shapes) collaborate as a SOSOS (larger orange pentagonal shapes), and I presume they have someone who is filling a Chief Product Owner role at the SOSOS level.

3. Next, the five SOSOS Teams collaborate as a larger group with a designated **Chief Product Owner Meta Scrum** (**CPOMS**) role. In effect, the CPOMS role participates as a member of a Chief Product Owner Team at the **EMT** level.

The EMT facilitates a **MetaScrum Event** at least once per Sprint. The MetaScrum events serve as a stakeholder alignment meeting to provide transparency on the operations of the Agile organization as a whole. This transparency supports inspecting the teams' activities and focuses on supporting the organization's business objectives and facilitating adaption where necessary. The scope of the MetaScrum Event includes the following:

- Organizational decision-making: Strategic planning impacts on funding, new products, product releases, and resource allocations; Product **End of Life** (**EOL**) plans; Organizational backlog priorities

- Seeking EMT approvals on funding, personnel, and customer commitments

- EMT and CPO agreeing on Product Backlog items and prioritizations

As a minimum, the Scrum@Scale Guide suggests metrics around the following business performance criteria:

- **Productivity**: The number of working products delivered per Sprint

- **Value delivery**: The business value per unit of team effort

- **Quality**: The defect rate or service downtime

- **Sustainability**: The team's ability and willingness to continue

We have now covered the basic elements that make up the Scrum@Scale approach. Now, let's talk about how these elements work together to make a healthy organization.

Building healthy organizations

Though neither Scrum nor Scrum@Scale subscribe directly to Lean development practices, they all place a premium on adding value, as defined in the eyes of the customer, which is the primary reason for their existence. Customers pay our bills and give the organization purpose.

The iterative and incremental approach to Scrum-based development provides frequent opportunities to build new capabilities, obtain client feedback, and use their inputs to refine the product going forward. At its core, the empirical process control mechanisms of Scrum provide an experimental or *trial and error* approach that helps guide the organization to build the right products, for the right customers, at the right time.

Scrum@Scale retains the original Scrum values of openness, courage, focus, respect, and commitment. Empiricism, established on the three pillars of transparency, inspection, and adaptation, is not possible without adherence to these values. Information must be fully available (transparency), for all to see (inspection), and the organization must be willing and able to respond appropriately (adaption). If people are fearful to tell the truth, or not able to bring up issues and opportunities for discussion, then the organization, as a whole, cannot operate efficiently, appropriately, nor adaptively.

This approach will work for those organizations that want to employ the basic concepts of Scrum in a scaled manner, and who want some guidance on scaling organizational structures, but do not want a lot of management overhead. In the next section, we'll take a closer look at where the Scrum@Scale approach best fits from an organizational perspective.

Evaluating best fits

Scrum@Scale is one of the four relatively *pure* Scrum scaling strategies presented in this book, which also includes *Scrum of Scrums*, *Nexus*, and **Large-Scale Scrum** (**LeSS**). However, of these four scaled Scrum approaches, only *Scrum@Scale* and *LeSS* present an approach to expanding beyond a total of nine Scrum teams. While the other approaches have demonstrated such capabilities, there is limited written guidance on how to organize or manage very large expansions of Scrum.

Scrum@Scale introduces a linear network approach to scaling Scrum at an enterprise scale that leverages concepts embodied in scale-free architectures, OO design, and fractal geometries. These concepts are not difficult to master and are more informational than something the participants need to understand to implement the structures and disciplines of Scrum@Scale. At the end of the day, it's still Scrum.

There is some additional overhead that comes with Scrum@Scale, in terms of implementing new team structures on top of the basic SoS teams, plus associated leadership roles. Again, these are relatively minor adjustments and the overall approach still adheres to Scrum's basic philosophy of leveraging small, autonomous teams using empirical process control and complex adaptive systems theories to develop, deliver, and sustain complex products. In addition, the scaled structures of SoSoS, along with the EAT and EMT leadership teams, offer agility while addressing network density concerns.

With these extensions, the Scrum@Scale approach broadens the potential applications for implementing LeSS. For example, this approach provides direct guidance on how to expand beyond nine teams and 81 developers, as outlined in the original Scrum of Scrums scaling approach. The Scrum@Scale Guide also provides some, though limited, instructions on implementing executive authorities, and dealing with political and financial issues associated with scaling Scrum across an enterprise.

The Scrum@Scale Guide specifically states that the approach *"can be applied across multiple domains in all types of organizations in industry, government, or academia"* (The Scrum@Scale Guide, 2019). As with any scaled Scrum approach, such organizations must integrate the employment of domain experts in support of its scaled Scrum practices.

Jeff Sutherland's career includes extensive experience as a **Chief Technology Officer (CTO)** and business entrepreneur in the healthcare, software, and high-tech industries. Though he is a co-founder of Scrum, his Scrum@Scale approach is more oriented to installing appropriate organizational structures and roles for scaling across multiple products and a large enterprise. This is in direct contrast to the Nexus and LeSS Frameworks, where the focus is much more on integration and coordination issues in a multi-team development environment.

The differences in scaling approaches is not a good or a bad thing, just different. All three approaches build on the foundations of Scrum. However, executives who want specific guidance on how to scale and manage Scrum across multiple products and across a large enterprise, regardless of the type or mix of products under development, may gravitate to the Scrum@Scale approach.

On the other hand, executives who are more concerned with integration, dependency, and coordination issues associated with developing large software products may find more value in the Nexus and LeSS approaches to scaling Scrum. You will learn about the Nexus and Less Frameworks in the next two chapters, respectively.

Summary

In this chapter, you learned how Scrum@Scale employs the concepts of scale-free architectures, built around the basic Team Processes of Scrum, to grow an Agile organization without adding hierarchical and overly bureaucratic organizational structures. Instead, multiple Scrum Teams can operate semi-autonomously with minimal oversight by simply adding tiers of Scrum Master and Product Owner guidance around pentagonal structures.

The first structure is the original Scrum Team, which is limited to an average of five people per team. The Scrum Teams include the developers, Scrum Master, and Product Owner, and all they work within the original Scrum framework's empirical process control theory.

The next level is the **SoS**, which can expand to five Scrum Teams while adding an additional SoS-level Scrum Master and CPO. The SoSM and CPOs have similar roles and responsibilities as their counterparts at the Scrum Team level, and they have similar events. The primary difference is they create a larger team of teams to provide guidance and assistance to the teams contained within the SoS.

The final level of Scrum@Scale involves the **SoSoS**, which expands the basic Scrum Team structures and Team Process to more than 25 Scrum Teams. At this level, the organization implements the **EAT**, as a central hub guiding the SM cycle, to provide SM type support for the entire Agile organization. Similarly, the **EMS** event is a hub within the PO cycle that serves as a forum for key executives and critical stakeholders to discuss and negotiate product development priorities, change budgets, and realign Scrum Teams with high-value priorities.

Finally, you learned about the components of the SO and PO cycles, their intersection points, and shared components. The SM cycle components collectively work to help define and install the Agile processes necessary to build the right set of products and other deliverable items. The components of the PO cycle ensure the organization stays focused on defining the right (that is, the highest value) set of products and services for the right customers at the right time.

This completes our work on the Scrum@Scale approach to scaling Agile, developed by Jeff Sutherland, one of the two co-founders of Scrum. In the next chapter, we are going to learn about the Nexus Framework, the scaled Scrum approach developed by the other co-founder of Scrum, Ken Schwaber. *Chapter 14, Contrasting Scrum/ Lean-Agile Scaling Approaches* includes a comparative analysis of all scaled Scrum and Lean-Agile practices introduced in this book. Every approach mentioned in this book has something to offer and different sets of strengths in terms of capabilities and applications. In this chapter, you have learned the capabilities and benefits of this approach. *Chapter 14, Contrasting Scrum/ Lean-Agile Scaling Approaches* offers more context with the contrasts against other Scrum/ Lean-Agile approaches.

Questions

1. True or false: The purpose of Scrum@Scale is to extend the original Scrum framework to support the development of large and complex products, processes, services, and systems.

2. How many Scrum Teams did the original Scrum Guide anticipate as working in its framework at optimal capacity while maintaining a sustainable pace?

3. What are the two goals of the Scrum@Scale framework?

4. The Scrum@Scale framework is described as a network of teams operating consistently with the Scrum Guide to address complex adaptive problems, while creatively delivering products of the highest possible value. What type of architecture is this an example of?

5. What is a business operating system?

6. What are the two cycles within Scrum@Scale?

7. What is meant by the term "Team Process?"

8. A **Scrum of Scrums (SoS)**, in an idealized structure, looks like what?

9. A **Scrum of Scrum of Scrums (SoSos)**, in an idealized structure, looks like what?

10. What are the roles of the **Executive Action Team (EAT)** and the **Executive MetaScrum (EMS)**?

Further reading

- Sutherland, J. (2006-2020) *THE SCRUM@SCALE GUIDE, Version 2.0. The Definitive Guide to the Scrum@Scale Framework*. Scrum Inc., Released under Creative Commons 4.0 Attribution-Sharealike License. All Rights Reserved© Scrum Inc. `https://www.Scrumatscale.com/wp-content/uploads/ScrumatScaleGuide-Published3.15.20.DrJeffSutherland.pdf`. Accessed 20 April 2020.

- Brooks, F. Jr. (1995) *The Mythical Man-Month*: *The Essays on Software Engineering, Anniversary Edition*. Boston, MA. Addison-Wesley.

- Hackman, J. R. (2002). *Leading teams*: *Setting the stage for great performances*. Boston, MA.Harvard Business Press.

- Sutherland, 2017. *Give Thanks for Scrum 2017*. Scrum@Scale. `https://www.Scruminc.com/give-thanks-Scrum-scale-free-architecture/` Accessed 21 April, 2020.

- Peter Antman. 2016, *Growing up with Agile – Minimum Viable Bureaucracy at Spotify*. Crisp's Blog. `https://blog.crisp.se/2016/04/29/peterantman/growing-up-with-Agile-minimum-viable-bureaucracy-at-spotify`. Crisp AB. Stockholm, Sweden. Accessed on 21 April, 2020.

9
The Nexus Framework

The Nexus Framework is the latest update to Scrum from Ken Schwaber and his company Scrum.org. He has published a **Nexus™ Guide** (*The Definitive Guide to Scaling Scrum with Nexus: The Rules of the Game, published January 2018.* `https://www.Scrum.org/resources/nexus-guide`) as a complement to the original Scrum Guide that he and Jeff Sutherland wrote and still maintain. The objective of the Nexus Framework is to provide additional information on how to develop and sustain scaled product and software delivery initiatives.

In this chapter, we're going to cover the following main topics:

- Building on Scrum
- Reviewing the Nexus Framework
- Learning the basics of Nexus
- Conducting a Nexus Sprint
- Getting into the details
- Establishing value

- Extending Scrum to form a Nexus
- Evaluating best fits

Let's get started.

Building on Scrum

Like Sutherland, Schwaber recognizes that the original *Scrum Guide* had a focus on creating an Agile-based development framework that installed empiricism as a means to improve the effectiveness of small Agile teams. Scrum does not specifically address the unique issues associated with scaling work across multiple teams, though Scrum has been employed effectively in large products and even enterprise-wide implementations. Ken Schwaber refers to Nexus as *"acting as an "exoskeleton resting" on many Scrum teams."* (Bittner et al., 2018)

The issue of using solely the Scrum Guide to scale these concepts is that there is no guidance on how to do so. As a result, organizations have had to figure out how to do this for themselves. Ken and Scrum.org addressed this issue with the introduction of the Nexus Framework, which implements roles, organizational structures, events, and artifacts to scale the original Scrum concepts. Most importantly, *the Nexus Framework provides guidance on connecting teams as a vital element to resolve integration and dependency issues.*

Connecting multiple Scrum Teams

The choice to use the term **Nexus** as a descriptor for this approach to scaling Scrum was not by accident. A general definition of a Nexus is *a connection or series of connections linking two or more people or things*. In this context, a Nexus within Scrum connects the work of the collective Scrum Teams across each Sprint. The purpose of the Nexus is to help improve teamwork by anticipating and managing dependencies that would otherwise cause impediments when building a larger, integrated, and fully tested product.

The Nexus Framework leverages the original Scrum concepts, as outlined in the Scrum Guide, as a building block for a Nexus. In this chapter, you will learn the basics of how to employ the Nexus Framework as a scaling extension to Scrum. As you review this chapter, it's important that you remember that you must have Scrum Teams that are working well and producing Done increments before taking on the efforts to form a Nexus of Scrum teams.

As a personal note, Kurt Bittner elaborated and made the point that an organization *"needs more than people who (think they) have mastered the concepts of Scrum."* The organization needs at least a few teams to be installed who have learned how to self-organize, removed impediments, and successfully delivered potentially shippable increments. Without this foundation of working Scrum Teams to build on, the organization will struggle to help the Scrum Teams learn how to work successfully in collaboration as a Nexus.

Scaling Scrum Teams within a Nexus

Nexus builds off the Scrum Framework. If you have development teams that are already familiar with Scrum, then adding Nexus roles, artifacts, and events should feel familiar. Moreover, the existing Scrum Teams should already be comfortable with refining items from a single Product backlog and working in collaboration with a single Product Owner.

Like Scrum, Nexus is a framework consisting of roles, events, artifacts, and the rules to implement Agile-based development around the empirical process control theory. The Nexus Framework specifically defines how work is accomplished across three to nine Scrum Teams. You will learn how Schwaber came to specify this range of numbers later in this chapter. For now, it's important to understand that the Scrum Teams within a Nexus work in collaboration to deliver the highest customer value against a single Product backlog of identified and prioritized items. The objective of the Nexus is to build integrated increments of value that meet specific goals established for each Sprint.

As Scrum Teams are added to work within the Nexus framework, the primary difference is building the **NIT (NIT)** and implementing the additional Nexus events and artifacts. Scrum practitioners already understand the concept that Scrum Teams add integrated increments of value across each Sprint. What makes scaled Scum more challenging is the need to discover and eliminate cross-team dependencies, coordination, and integration concerns. This is a strength of the Nexus approach to scaling Scrum.

Establishing the Nexus foundation

An integrated Increment in Nexus simply means that multiple Scrum Teams deliver value across each Sprint, and that those individual increments of value must be integrated to form a complete solution. This doesn't mean that each team delivers value separately, though there will be times when teams independently deliver an independently valuable feature. Still, most teams collectively contribute to delivering a single Increment of value. In such cases, the Nexus of Scrum Teams produces numerous artifacts, and their activities must be coordinated to create a "Done" Increment.

As you will discover in this chapter, work is divided across the Scrum Teams during the Nexus Sprint planning events. This work must be decomposed to minimize and, ideally, eliminate cross-team dependencies and sequence work to coordinate the integration and testing of individual team deliverables. Sometimes, these dependencies can't be completely eliminated. If they could, refinement might be sufficient to eliminate these dependencies, and teams would not need any other techniques.

At the Scrum team level, developers continue to use their Scrum practices to develop increments of useful product functionality across each Sprint. The primary difference is that their individual outputs must be merged, integrated, and tested throughout the Sprint with the artifacts, especially code, that are produced by the other teams in the Nexus.

Reviewing the Nexus Framework

Scrum.org refers to Nexus as a process framework that allows multiple Scrum Teams to work in collaboration to build integrated increments. The practices within Nexus are consistent with the original Scrum practices, but more attention is paid to eliminating dependencies and facilitating interoperation between the Scrum Teams.

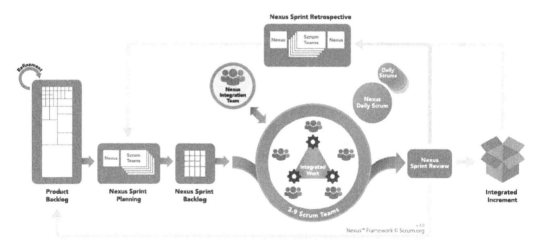

Figure 9.1 – Nexus™ Framework for scaling Scrum

The preceding diagram shows the events and artifacts associated with the Nexus Framework. By now, you should be able to quickly see that the Nexus Framework is conceptually similar to the original Scrum Framework. This is intentional as the goal of Nexus is to extend Scrum practices, not replace them.

The Nexus Framework provides new roles, artifacts, and events. However, for the most part, Nexus roles, events, and artifacts inherit the purpose and attributes of their corresponding Scrum roles, events, and artifacts, as documented in *The Scrum Guide*.

Defining Nexus roles

Nexus maintains the original Scrum roles at the Scrum Team level, which are the Product Owner, Scrum Master, and Developers. Nothing changes in Nexus with regards to the roles at the Scrum team level.

However, Nexus implements a new team role to guide the efforts to eliminate cross-team dependencies and to establish common integration, test, and commit strategies. This new role is the **Nexus Integration Team** (**NIT**), which is really a new type of Scrum team as much as it is a new role. The members of the NIT coach the Scrum Teams on how to apply the concepts and use the methods and tools to deliver integrated increments across the Nexus. They may or may not be members of the Scrum Teams. If they are, their primary commitments are first to the NIT, and then to their assigned Scrum Teams. On occasion, they may help the Scrum Teams in their efforts to resolve cross-team dependency and integration issues.

However, the operative word in the previous sentence is *help*, as members of the NIT are not tasked to do the work. The NIT doesn't coordinate or supervise work unless they are operating in an *emergency mode*. Under normal circumstances, the members of the NIT serve a role that is similar to that of a Scrum Master. Where Scrum Masters help ensure the teams perform Scrum well, the NIT helps ensure that the Scrum Teams are integrating well. Just like a Scrum Master, the NIT doesn't coordinate, manage, or supervise. It consists of mentors, coaches, and servant leaders.

The NIT members include the Product Owner, a Scrum Master, and the NIT members.

Creating Nexus artifacts

Like roles, Nexus maintains all the original Scrum artifacts. These artifacts include the *Product backlog*, *Sprint Backlogs*, and *Increments*. Nothing changes at the Scrum team level in terms of building and maintaining these three artifacts. All teams work from the same single Product backlog. All Scrum Teams create a Sprint Backlog as a subset of the Product backlog items they are developing within the Sprint. The Increment is the sum of the Product backlog items that are completed during the Sprint, plus the value of the increments of all the previous Sprints. Finally, the Scrum Team artifacts are made transparent, as discussed in the original Scrum Guide.

Nexus implements a new **Nexus Sprint Backlog** artifact to provide transparency on all **Product Backlog Items (PBIs)** under development within the Sprint. While the Scrum Teams continue to maintain their individual Sprint Backlogs, the Nexus Sprint Backlog provides a holistic view of work across the Nexus. The Nexus Sprint Backlog also provides transparency on which Scrum Teams will do the work on each of the PBIs within the Sprint.

Implementing Nexus events

The original Scrum events include the *Sprint, Sprint Planning, Daily Scrum, Sprint Review,* and the *Sprint Retrospective*. Events is one area where Nexus makes significant changes to support scaling dependency management requirements within the original Scrum Framework.

Nexus implements six new events, which are **Refinement, Nexus, Nexus Sprint Goal, Nexus Daily Scrum, Nexus Sprint Review**, and the **Nexus Sprint Retrospective**. The Nexus events augment, surround, or replace their Scrum event counterparts.

Understanding the Nexus process flow

The process flow for Nexus was depicted in *Figure 9.1*. The Nexus process flow enables multiple cross-functional Scrum Teams to work together and deliver an Integrated Increment of potentially releasable value across every Sprint. The individual Scrum Teams evaluate the cross-team dependencies, self-organize as necessary to take on the work associated with the selected PBIs, define the work tasks, and then identify the most appropriate members to complete the work.

The activities associated with the Nexus process flow are as follows:

- Refine the Product Backlog
- Nexus Sprint planning
- Development work
- Nexus Daily Scrum
- Nexus Sprint review
- Nexus Sprint retrospective

The primary purpose of the product refinement activity is to analyze the scope of work associated with each high-value PBI, and to assess which PBIs support the current Sprint Goal while maximizing value. Nexus adds the additional complexity of needing to work through cross-team dependency issues.

Sprint planning activities help define and assign work tasks associated with selected items within the Sprint Backlog, around an agreed Sprint goal. Nexus Sprint planning extends Sprint planning activities to address cross-team dependency issues. Just as the Scrum Teams have individual Sprint goals and Sprint Backlogs, the Nexus has a Nexus goal and Nexus Backlog. But now. the individual Scrum Team Sprint goals must be in alignment with the overarching Nexus goal.

The Nexus Sprint Backlog contains the PBIs that have cross-team dependencies or impacts. In other words, the purpose of the Nexus Sprint Backlog is to provide cross-team transparency on the subset of items that have dependency concerns. Cross-team dependencies would otherwise be difficult to see and track across all the items listed in the team-oriented Sprint Backlogs.

Development work across Scrum Teams operating within a Nexus must be integrated, tested, and committed to form a potentially shippable product. In a software development environment, those builds need to occur frequently on a common automated build or continuous integration environment.

During the Nexus Daily Scrum, the members of the NIT and representatives from the Scrum Teams discuss cross-team dependencies, impediments, and integration issues. These issues are taken back to the Scrum Teams in time for their Daily Scrums so that they can build a plan to work on the problems.

The Nexus Sprint reviews replace the traditional Sprint reviews as an opportunity for the Nexus to obtain input on the Integrated product Increment, delivered as a potentially shippable product. This is the most efficient use of the reviewers' time. Reviewers can still assess the contributions of the individual teams. Therefore, all Scrum Team members should attend the Nexus Sprint reviews.

The Scrum Teams still conduct individual Sprint retrospectives in Nexus. However, the NIT holds two Nexus Sprint retrospective events that bracket the individual team retrospectives. Representatives from each Scrum team attend the initial Nexus retrospectives to discuss issues that challenged the ability of the Nexus to deliver an Integrated Increment. Those issues are taken back to the Scrum Teams so that those who are closest to the problems can use their first-hand knowledge of the situations (also known as **bottom-up intelligence**) to define practical solutions. These proposals are then taken back to the NIT in a second Nexus Sprint retrospective to discuss any cross-team actions that are necessary.

You will learn more specifics about these activities later in this chapter. But for now, let's review some of the fundamental instructions outlined in the Nexus Guide.

Learning the basics of Nexus

In this section, you will learn how the Nexus Framework extends the original Scrum Framework to support multiple Scrum Teams that are working in collaboration to build large, complex, and integrated products. Will start with an introduction to the NIT.

Defining a Nexus

A Nexus consists of a **Nexus Integration Team (NIT)** and approximately three to nine Scrum Teams. If Nexus is needed, then there is one product and one product Increment. Each individual team within a Nexus does not produce their own product Increment. Since the Nexus is a collaborative development effort, the individual increments must be integrated and tested as a whole to ensure accomplishment of the Nexus goal.

The NIT is responsible for completing an Integrated Increment that meets the definition of "Done" within each Sprint. In that role, the NIT must help the team assess and eliminate impediments and cross-team dependencies that would complicate their work and reduce their effectiveness. The outcome of a Sprint in Nexus is a potentially shippable product that aggregates PBIs from multiple Scrum Teams as an integrated and working solution.

Only the Product Owner has the authority to release a potentially shippable product to customers or end users. For business reasons, they may hold off on a product release until sufficient business value justifies the efforts involved, and the product is sufficiently complete to meet the needs of its intended users.

Establishing a NIT

The primary role of the NIT is to provide mentoring and coaching services to help resolve non-technical integration and dependency issues. The NIT is also responsible for ensuring a new Integrated Increment is delivered with every Sprint. NIT team members may be the "experts" in some business domains or technical discipline, but their primary focus is helping the teams achieve greater self-organization and autonomy. NIT members are not functional area leads nor team leads, as those roles are inconsistent with Scrum.

The NIT helps determine the appropriate methods and tools for integration and may help with installing the common SCM, integration, and test infrastructure. The NIT members do not perform the software integration work. That is the responsibility of the Scrum Teams. Instead, the NIT ensures the Scrum Teams are capable of delivering the integrated increments that meet the definition of Done.

Rather that resolving problems directly, the NIT leverages the strength of individual Scrum Team members, through bottom-up intelligence, to achieve optimal resolutions to identified problems. If the Development Teams lack technical integration skills, the NIT may help find external experts. In emergency situations, assuming they have the relevant skills and experience, members of the NIT may jump in to help the teams resolve difficult issues.

The focus of the NIT can change over time. They may start with coaching the Scrum Teams on refinement practices to eliminate dependencies. As the Scrum Teams grow in numbers, the NIT may take on some work to support the development and maturity of the common build and test automation framework. Over time, the NIT members will devote much of their time to helping the Scrum Teams work through cross-team dependencies and integration issues.

Some NIT members may be experts in the use of development and testing tools, software engineering practices, and systems engineering in general. When standards are adopted by an organization, NIT members are accountable for making sure that they are followed. In some cases, the NIT members may be responsible for defining standards in development, testing, networks, infrastructure, security, and architectural standards. More often than not, the standards may be defined in a corporate compliance or IT governance organization.

The NIT is often, if not usually, a member of one of the Scrum Teams within the Nexus. However, their first priority is supporting the work of the NIT. In other words, resolution of cross-team integration and dependency issues must always take precedence over their team-level development responsibilities.

If a NIT member does not have the bandwidth to support their NIT and Scrum team activities, their NIT responsibilities take precedence. In addition, the NIT's composition may change over time, depending on current integration needs and priorities.

The NIT addresses both technical and non-technical issues and constraints affecting cross-team integration capabilities. The NIT may help assess needs and install an **integrated development environment** (**IDE**) or DevOps toolchain to resolve these technical integration issues. However, the best outcome is when the Development Teams in the Nexus collectively do these things; the NIT's role is to ensure that it gets done.

Now that you understand what an NIT is and does, let's take a closer look at the individual roles within the NIT.

Organizing and resourcing a NIT

The Nexus Integration Team, like a Scrum Team, only has three roles: the Product Owner, Scrum Master, and the NIT members. As noted previously, there is only one Product Owner who is in charge of the products developed by the Nexus.

Product Owner

As with Scrum, only one Product Owner is assigned to support the product under development within the Nexus. This single Product Owner assignment is consistent with the Scrum philosophy that only one person can be held accountable for defining and releasing value to customers. While the PO retains the role they have in Scrum, their work is much more challenging due to the increased number of Scrum Teams they have to work with.

The **Product Owner** is a member of the NIT, just as they are a participating member of the individual Scrum Teams. The Product Owner has the final say on the inclusion of PBIs and priorities within the Product backlog. As with Scrum, they are accountable for maximizing product value within the Integrated Increments of new functionality built by the Nexus.

Scrum Master

The NIT includes a Scrum Master, and their role is similar to those of a Scrum Master at the Scrum team level. In fact, the NIT's **Scrum Master (SM)** may be a Scrum Master of a Scrum Team within the Nexus. The primary responsibility of the NIT's Scrum Master is to provide mentoring and coaching for elements of the Nexus framework to the Scrum Teams within the Nexus.

The NIT SM must monitor the Scrum Teams to ensure the Nexus events, artifacts, and roles are implemented correctly, and make suggestions for improvements. Ultimately, the NIT SM is responsible for ensuring all Scrum Teams understand and work effectively within the Nexus Framework and are focused on delivering maximum value.

Nexus Integration Team members

The members of the NIT are ultimately responsible for ensuring the Scrum Teams collectively develop high-quality integrated increments. In this role, the NIT members' primary job is to help the teams identify and work through cross-team dependency and integration issues.

Ideally, the NIT is composed of a balance of skills, ensuring that the NIT is cross-functional. If roles are siloed in the Nexus, then the NIT members may have different skill profiles to augment the skills and resources of the collective teams.

The NIT members are usually members of the Scrum teams, though they may be borrowed specialists that have been brought in from other functional support groups within the organization. Examples of specialized skills that an NIT might need include operations staff, domain experts, security experts, enterprise- or system-level architects, or other experts in **Source Control Management (SCM)**, **Continuous Integration (CI)**, and automated provisioning.

For example, the NIT may include systems engineers who are skilled in the methods and tools employed within the Nexus for software development, integration, and testing. In that role, they work with members of the Scrum Teams to ensure they resolve software development dependencies, as well as follow modern practices to frequently integrate and test their code and components under development via an integration server.

When NIT members also support other Scrum teams, their NIT work must always take precedence over their Scrum team's work. These are usually the most skilled and experienced individuals within the Nexus, and they may have specialized skills that can be leveraged across the Nexus of Scrum Teams.

In contrast, the specialists that are brought in from external functional organizations may provide temporary support until the Scrum Teams within the Nexus develop these skills. NIT members form external support functions provide specialized skills that are not available within the Scrum Teams and that do not require a full time resource. Otherwise, it makes more sense for the specialist to become a permanent member of the NIT.

Making work and value transparent

Nexus artifacts are deployed to facilitate transparency to both work and value, which enables opportunities for inspection and adaptation. The Nexus artifacts include the Product backlog, the Nexus Sprint Backlog, and the Integrated Increment.

Product Backlog

Having multiple teams does not change the basic model of working from a single Product backlog. When the Scrum Teams are working to develop an integrated product, then they must only work from a **single** Product backlog. Trying to figure out ways to break down the Product backlog for a single product only adds unnecessary complexities – so, don't do it.

This does not imply that there are no other types of backlogs within the Nexus. For example, Scrum already implements a Sprint Backlog that allows Scrum Teams to identify and track PBIs and work associated with achieving their Sprint Goals. You will learn about Nexus Sprint Backlogs in the next subsection.

As with Scrum, the Product Owner maintains accountability for the items specified within the Product backlog. They must make the Product backlog available to the Nexus and Scrum Teams. The Product Owner also establishes the prioritized ordering of items in the Product backlog to maximize customer value, lower development costs, and increase ROI.

The development team works with the Product Owner to refine the PBIs at a level of granularity (also known as **"thinly sliced" functionality**) that enables detecting and eliminating cross-team dependencies. PBIs are ready for Nexus Sprint planning when the Scrum Teams believe they have eliminated or at least sufficiently reduced the potential impacts of cross-team dependencies.

Nexus Sprint Backlog

The Nexus Sprint Backlog provides an aggregated view of all the items in the Sprint Backlogs that were selected by the Scrum Teams for inclusion in the Sprint. The purpose of the Nexus Sprint Backlog is to highlight cross-team dependencies and the flow of work during the Sprint. The Nexus Sprint backlog is updated daily, if not more often.

Integrated Increment

An Integrated Increment is a term in Nexus that defines the current aggregation of all integrated work completed by the Nexus. This includes work completed both before and during the current Sprint. Each Sprint produces a usable and potentially shippable product that meets the definition of "Done" for the Integrated Increment. Each instantiation of an Integrated Increment is inspected within the Nexus Sprint reviews.

Now, let's take a closer look at the importance of establishing and maintaining Nexus artifacts to improve transparency.

Creating transparency with Nexus artifacts

When scaling Scrum to build larger and more complex products, there is no escaping the fact that work must be integrated across multiple Scrum Teams. As with most Agile practices, Scrum-based development is built around small teams. As the work scales, the Scrum Teams have no choice but to break up the product development effort into smaller bits, and then later combine their deliverables into an integrated whole.

The NIT works with the Scrum Teams to ensure the Scrum and Nexus artifacts are fully transparent. The word transparent simply means no one should attempt to hold back information, and that all information should be readily available to anyone who needs it to do their jobs. This is especially critical since there are so many development and integration dependencies that must be managed across each Sprint. Lack of transparency leads to inefficiencies in flow and use of resources, as well as delays.

Scrum and Nexus are both based on the idea that all information must be fully transparent to minimize risks and to maximize value. Otherwise, lacking sufficient details, bad decisions will be made, though the impacts are potentially much more consequential in the scaled environment of a Nexus.

In the case of the Nexus, a major concern is exposing dependencies that can negatively impact the output and effectiveness of Scrum Teams. Dependencies must be identified and resolved to avoid the accumulation of technical debt. The NIT works in collaboration with the Scrum Teams to ensure complete transparency of all artifacts and that they are depicted in a way that interested or effected stakeholders can understand them.

Nexus artifacts are used to record the results of work that's been performed. In effect, the Nexus artifacts provide visible transparency of findings from ongoing inspection and adaption activities. These Nexus artifacts include Product backlog, Nexus goal, Nexus Sprint Backlog, and Integrated Increment. Discussions on artifact transparency and the definition of Done further round off our understanding of the important role transparency plays within the Nexus. Let's take a look at these Nexus artifacts a little bit more closely.

Product Backlog

As with Scrum, there is only one Product backlog for the entire Nexus, from which all the underlying Scrum Teams pull work. Since there is only one only Product backlog, there is only one Product Owner who is ultimately accountable for the value identified in and produced from the Product backlog.

Just because an item is listed within the Product backlog doesn't mean it's ready for development. The NIT works with the Scrum Teams to decompose the high-level requirements into PBIs that have minimal cross-team dependencies. When prioritizing the Product backlog items, the Product Owner must consider each item's customer-centric value and the cost of delivery. While customers may value a certain capability, they may not want to pay or afford the price to have it.

In this context, the Product backlog provides transparency on the highest priority items in terms of achieving the highest customer value with the lowest development and delivery costs. Moreover, the Product backlog provides the transparency the Scrum Teams need to select items to work on in an upcoming Sprint.

Nexus goal

Just like Scrum Teams work to achieve Sprint Goals, the Nexus, as a whole, works to achieve a common goal, called the Nexus goal. During the Nexus Sprint planning meeting event, the Product Owner introduces their objectives for the Sprint. Since there are multiple Scrum Teams involved in a Nexus, the Nexus goal provides a summation of all the work and Sprint goals spanning the Scrum Teams within the Nexus. In other words, the Nexus goal provides transparency on the sum of the features, capabilities, and functions that must be demonstrated in the Nexus Sprint Review.

Nexus Sprint Backlog

The Nexus Sprint Backlog contains the subset of **Product backlog Items** (**PBIs**) that have dependencies spanning two or more Scrum teams. The Nexus Sprint Backlog is updated daily, usually during the Nexus Daily Scrum event.

The Nexus Sprint Backlog is broken out from the Product backlog to provide transparency of the PBIs that have dependency, integration, and workflow issues. These must be addressed during the Sprint. The individual Scrum Teams within the Nexus still maintain their Sprint Backlog to provide transparency on the subset of Product backlog items each team expects to deliver during a Sprint in support of their Sprint Goals.

Integrated Increment

The Integrated Increment is the summation of all work across all Scrum Teams that must be accomplished during the upcoming Sprint. As with Scrum, the output of the Sprint is a fully integrated and potentially shippable product that meets the definition of "Done," as defined by the Development team. The Product Owner is ultimately accountable for what's included within the Integrated Increment, and they define the acceptable quality and acceptance criteria for the Increment of new functionality.

In this context, the Integrated Increment provides transparency regarding the expected outcome of all Scrum Teams working in collaboration to build a new Increment of value.

You should now have a solid understanding of the roles, events, and artifacts that form the foundations of the Nexus Framework. In the next section, you will learn how to conduct a Sprint in Nexus.

Conducting a Nexus Sprint

A Sprint within Nexus is very similar to the traditional Scrum Sprint. There is one additional event: the Daily Nexus Scrum. Also, modifications are made to the Sprint review and Sprint retrospective events. For example, there is only one Sprint review for the Nexus. The reason for this is that the product must be viewed as a whole solution, and not individual parts.

Sprint retrospectives are a bit more complex in that there are Nexus retrospectives scheduled both before and after each Scrum Team conducts their retrospectives. The reason for this is that the NIT and select members from the Scrum Teams meet initially to review dependency and integration issues that have impacted or more of the Scrum Teams. These assessments go back to the effected Scrum Teams for their consideration during their Sprint retrospectives. The Scrum team retrospectives will likely result in cross-team actions that must be taken back to the Nexus to consider and implement.

The outcome of the Nexus Sprint is an integrated Increment that is the sum total of the deliveries developed by the Scrum Teams. This is integrated to work as a fully functional and potentially shippable product. Whether or not the integrated Increment has sufficient value to justify a release to customers is the sole decision of the Product Owner.

With this brief introduction, let's dive into the details of conducting a Nexus Sprint for maintaining flow through a series of Nexus events.

Maintaining flow with Nexus events

Nexus events define the flow of work across a Nexus Sprint and are superimposed over the original Scrum events. If your organization has not yet implemented Scrum, Nexus advocates would discourage you starting a Nexus before building an initial foundation of effective Scrum Teams who are skilled in the use of the original Scrum practices. Nexus is additive, and not a replacement for Scrum. Another way to think of this is that Nexus is overlaid as an extension of an existing Scrum development organization.

All Nexus events are time-boxed in the same manner as their corresponding events outlined in the original Scrum Guide. We'll work our way through them in sequence, starting with refinement.

Refinement

Unlike Scrum, where refinement is a recommended but not mandatory event, this is a necessary event in Nexus. The reason for this is that the Scrum Teams must work together to evaluate both the scope and dependencies of individual items and related development tasks.

The Product Owner and the Development teams collaborate on Nexus refinement. The Nexus refinement event serves two primary purposes:

- Decompose PBIs that are too large to complete in a single Sprint
- Break down PBIs to minimize cross-team dependencies

To the greatest extent possible, Nexus refinement should be coordinated across the Scrum Teams as an all-hands event. The teams collaborate on refining their collective understanding of backlog items. The goal is to provide enough granularity that items can be pulled by the Scrum Teams from the Product backlog with minimal cross-team dependencies. Each Scrum Team has input on which PBIs they prefer to work on.

The output of refinement is an ordered list of Product backlog items and Scrum Team assignments. The goal is to deliver the highest possible value with minimal risks and complexities. There is no timebox for refinement – it's an ongoing process.

Refinement is performed periodically during the Sprint, whenever the Scrum Team feels that they need to invest time in improving the quality of PBIs. Refinement on each PBI continues until enough information is available to plan and execute their development activities, without causing dependency or scope assignment conflicts across the teams.

Customer input on desired product capabilities tend to be vague and unactionable from the perspective of a development team. Typically, high-level requirements must be decomposed into more granular assessments of user needs, acceptance criteria, and implementation features and functions. The modern trend is to decompose high-lever user or customer capability requirements into epics and user stories.

Having said this, although PBIs may be clear from a requirements perspective, they simply represent too much work to complete in a Sprint. In those cases, the goal is to break the work up into smaller deliverable items that fit within a Sprint. The teams must become proficient at estimating so that the Nexus only takes on work that produces a Done product Increment within a single Sprint. Knowing their capacity, the Development teams in the Nexus can forecast how much work they can undertake in each Sprint.

Additionally, refinement activities might involve refactoring or technical debt reduction. Refinement would work on improving these items too, as well as working on making improvements to ways of working that have come out of Sprint retrospectives.

In Case You Forgot

Refactoring involves restructuring and improving application or component code to improve its performance and readability without altering its base functionality. In other words, after refactoring, the software should still be able to do what it originally did, only better.

Technical debt (also known as design debt or code debt) is the accumulation of deferred work that happens when a developer or team delivers software that is inefficient, incomplete, not properly integrated, or has known defects and bugs. While releasing such incomplete code may be expedient and useful somehow in the short run, eventually, those issues need to be addressed. The biggest concern is that the accumulated technical debt makes the code increasingly complex and difficult to fix with each new Increment of functionality.

The number of participants and frequency of Product backlog refinements is driven by the uncertainty of the scope of work within the Product backlog. The decomposition process may take several iterations before the work is fully exposed as a number of actionable backlog items.

The optimal goal of refinement is to specify PBIs at a level of granularity that allows a single Scrum Team to complete the work within a single Sprint. However, this may not be possible if different teams have different skills or areas of competency. Over time, the Scrum Teams should work to become more cross-functional to make the goal obtainable.

Since the refinement event is ongoing, refinement activities for each defined high-level requirement can proceed through multiple Sprints and involve multiple Scrum teams. This helps ensure each item is ready for selection within a future Nexus Sprint planning event. We will learn about this further in this section.

Nexus Sprint goal

The Nexus Sprint goal is the joint objective for the Sprint and encompasses the sum of all the work that's been performed by the Scrum Team in terms of their individual Sprint goals. The definition of Done for all work PBIs must support the Nexus goal, and the Scrum Teams must be able to demonstrate completeness in the Nexus Sprint reviews to stakeholders.

The Nexus Sprint goal is an important input for Nexus Sprint planning. However, the Nexus Sprint goal is not locked in. It can be refined during Nexus Sprint planning.

Nexus Sprint planning

The refinement process should have already identified and removed dependencies for selected PBIs. The purpose of Nexus Sprint planning is to coordinate the activities of all Scrum Teams within the Nexus across the duration of a single Sprint. The NIT members look to the Product Owner for domain knowledge and PBI selection and priority decisions.

The highest priority PBIs and initial Sprint goal are the inputs to Sprint planning. The Product Owner discusses the Nexus Sprint goal to explain the purpose of the Sprint and how selected PBIs support the Nexus goal.

The outcome of Nexus Sprint planning is a jointly planned and agreed upon list of PBIs that minimize cross-team dependency and integration issues. The goal is to create a balanced workload across the Scrum Teams that is actionable within the timebox of the Sprint and achieves the Sprint goal.

There are three parts to Sprint planning:

- Validation of the Product backlog by the Scrum Teams to ensure the work is properly decomposed into chunks that the individual teams can support within a Sprint.

- Determine the collective Sprint goal as an integrated Increment of value.

- Conduct Sprint planning sessions to define Sprint backlogs and expose and minimize the dependencies across teams.

During Nexus Sprint planning, all Scrum Team members collaborate to validate and adjust the ordering of work. Where dependencies exist, the Scrum Teams need to synchronize their activities to avoid unnecessary queuing of work and resulting work delays over the course of the Sprint. PBIs may need to be split up to enable syncing of component builds, testing, and integration across multiple Scrum Teams. Ideally, the Scrum Teams select and volunteer for the work they believe they can take on and complete.

Once the overall work for the Nexus is understood, Nexus Sprint planning continues with each Scrum Team performing their own separate Sprint planning events. If new dependencies crop up during Sprint planning, the teams share this information and work through the issues in a collaborative manner.

During the Sprint planning process, the work associated with developing the PBIs is decomposed into individual work tasks. It's important to understand that cross-team dependencies may impact the sequence of work and are accounted for in the planning process. The Nexus planning event is complete when all Scrum Team planning is complete, and any identified dependencies have been removed or resolved.

All PBIs identified for the Sprint (but not team-level tasks) and all dependencies are made transparent within the Nexus Product backlog. Team-level tasks are not included in the Nexus Product backlog as that would add unnecessary detail and complexity. The lists of team-level tasks are maintained in each team's Sprint Backlog.

Nexus Daily Scrum

Representatives from individual Development teams meet daily with the NIT members to inspect the current state of the Integrated Increment in terms of progress against the Nexus goal. The event also provides the opportunity for a daily sync in order to evaluate the impact of current integration activities and dependencies.

The Nexus Daily Scrum provides transparency on how well integration is working across the Scrum Teams. Integration issues that arise can be addressed immediately by the affected Scrum Teams before they have an opportunity to create technical debt. For this reason, the Nexus Daily Scrum is always held before the Scrum Teams conduct their Daily Scrums.

Note that scheduling Nexus Daily Scrums before the teams conduct their Daily Scrums is opposite to the approach that's taken in Scrums of Scrums. In Scrum of Scrums, the teams drive the need to conduct integration discussions. In Nexus, the NITs help the teams identify their integration and dependency issues and the need for team-level actions.

In the long run, information from the Nexus Daily Scrum helps the NIT assess integration and process failures, and to evaluate potential longer-term solutions. This might involve building out a common infrastructure to enable Continuous Integration and testing.

During the Nexus Daily Scrums, the participants discuss identified integration issues or newly discovered cross-team dependencies and their impacts. An effective way to uncover potential integration and dependency issues is to have the NIT members ask the participating Scrum Team members the following questions:

- Was the previous day's integration work completed? If not, why not?
- What new dependencies or impacts have been identified?
- What information needs to be shared across Scrum Teams?

When I asked Kurt Bittner to review this chapter, he noted that, *"as with Daily Scrums, asking these three questions can be good at first. But at some point, asking the same questions over and over again will become stale, and people will start to disengage. The Nexus must find ways to make sure these meetings remain relevant and engaging."*

On a daily basis, information made available by the Scrum Team participants is used to adjust the Nexus backlog to provide up-to-date transparency on the status of work completed by the Scrum Teams, and the progress of work in the context of the Nexus goal.

The output of information from Nexus Daily Scrum serves as input to the Scrum Team's Daily Scrum events. The Scrum Teams use this information to plan and adjust their work as necessary to minimize impact from the identified dependencies and integration issues. The Daily Scrums continue through the duration of each Sprint.

At the end of each Sprint, all planned work and PBIs should be completed in conformance with the corresponding definitions of Done. At that point, the Scrum Teams make their deliverables fully transparent during the Nexus Sprint reviews.

Nexus Sprint review

The Nexus Sprint review is held at the end of the Sprint to solicit feedback from customers, end users, and other interested stakeholders on the Integrated Increment that the Nexus has built over the Sprint. In other words, the Nexus Sprint review enables inspection of the Sprint deliverables as an Integrated Increment. The output of the Nexus Sprint review serves as input to help the Nexus adapt the Product backlog, as needed.

The Nexus Sprint review replaces the Scrum Sprint review to provide an integrated view of the Sprint deliverables accomplished by the Nexus. The objective is to obtain feedback from customers and other stakeholders on the value of the integrated increment, areas for improvements, and an understanding of new priorities or concerns.

The Nexus Sprint review replaces individual Scrum Team Sprint reviews because the focus in a Nexus is on providing transparency to inspect and adapt the entire Integrated Increment. It would be both inefficient and impractical to perform individual Scrum Team Sprint reviews and assess the functionality of the Integrated Increment. It doesn't make sense to conduct individual Sprint reviews. If the teams can review separate subsets of the Increment, they're probably not collaborating and building an Integrated Increment.

Finally, since there is only so much time our customers will give us to participate in Sprint reviews, we need to make sure that we maximize the value of their time when they are available. The reviewers are not likely to want to sit through multiple Scrum Team reviews on a bi-weekly basis.

> **Note**
>
> In the *Organizing Nexus Sprint reviews* section, you will learn about several techniques you can use to improve customer and stakeholder participation and contributions in the Nexus Sprint reviews.

As in the original Scrum Framework, Sprint reviews for the Nexus occur at the end of each Sprint. Now that the Scrum Teams have conducted their Sprint reviews, they should have sufficient information to begin their retrospectives.

Nexus Sprint retrospective

The Nexus Sprint retrospective enforces a continuous improvement strategy by scheduling time at the end of each Sprint to inspect and adapt both the functionality of the NIT and the Scrum Teams. The output of the Nexus Sprint retrospective is an action plan for the next Sprint to improve identified cross-team dependency and integration issues. Therefore, the Nexus Sprint retrospective must be completed prior to the next Nexus Sprint planning event.

Each Nexus Sprint retrospective includes three separate events:

1. The NIT members and representatives from each of the Scrum Teams meet to discuss integration and dependency issues impacting more than one Scrum Team.

2. The Scrum Teams hold their own Sprint retrospectives while taking in the information coming from the Nexus Sprint retrospective as input. The output of the Scrum Team Sprint retrospective is proposed action items to take back to the NIT.

3. The NIT members and Scrum Team participants meet again to discuss and agree on how to visualize and track identified action items in the upcoming Sprint.

It's important that each Scrum Team provides a representative to attend the initial and final NIT retrospective events. The Nexus Sprint retrospective facilitates the inspection and adaption elements of the empirical process control theory to discover and eliminate cross-team impediments. Issues that address more than one Scrum Team are taken back to the Scrum Team retrospectives for discussion, along with any other issues that were identified by the individual Scrum Teams.

The goal of the individual Scrum Team retrospectives is to both address impediments that affected their team and to address cross-team integration impediments. Once the Scrum Teams have completed their retrospectives, the members of the Nexus Sprint retrospective meet again to discuss how they will make the actions identified by the Scrum Teams transparent, including the measures and visual aids that demonstrate improvements.

The types of integration challenges that the Nexus will face when scaling Scrum are fairly common. As a result, there are common questions the teams can ask in each Nexus Sprint retrospective, such as the following:

- Was any of the planned work not completed?

- Is there technical debt that needs to be addressed?

- Were the teams able to frequently integrate their code and product artifacts?

- Were the teams able to avoid the accumulation of unresolved dependencies?

Is any of these issues are identified, the teams should answer the following set of questions:

- Why did this issue happen?

- How can we eliminate the technical debt?

- How can we prevent this issue from happening again?

The Nexus retrospectives must address cross-team scaling issues, such as planned work left undone; the frequency and success of Scrum team integrations; and whether the software components were built, tested, and deployed frequently enough to prevent the accumulation of unresolved dependencies. For each question, the participants in the Nexus Sprint retrospective discuss why the issues occurred, how the Nexus can reduce technical dept, and how the recurrence of these issues can be prevented.

This completes the discussion on Nexus events. We are going to revisit this topic in the *Improving through Sprint retrospectives* section. However, before we do, we need to go back and discuss the techniques we can use to obtain useful customer input during the Sprint reviews.

Organizing Nexus Sprint reviews

It's usually impractical to have each of the Scrum Teams within a Nexus have independent Sprint reviews. There is only so much time customers, users, and other stakeholders will devote to the reviews, especially given the iterative updates across each Sprint. Therefore, it makes more sense to schedule a single Nexus Sprint review that consolidates the product updates in one integrated demo.

Nexus promotes two approaches to conducting Nexus Sprint reviews. One is to use an exposition (expo) format, while the other is to employ an offline review. In the expo format, each Scrum Team has a display table set up in an open hall where interested stakeholders can come in and rotate through each of the updates they are interested in viewing. The offline reviews are recoded demos or videos of each Scrum Team's updates that can be viewed online at the leisure of interested stakeholders. The offline review format works best when the location, time, and availability of stakeholders are factors in obtaining stakeholder feedback.

Bittner also discusses the potential use of World Café and Open Space workshop techniques and technologies to create a dialogue with customers, users, and stakeholders. The idea is to change things up across Sprints so that the stakeholders don't get bored and remain engaged in participating in the assessments.

It's also important to remain aware of the purpose of product reviews. They are not just for entertainment purposes. The goal is to collect valuable feedback from those most impacted by the product, on both the new capabilities implemented in the current Scrum, and guidance on how the product can be improved.

Improving through Sprint retrospectives

One of the common elements across all Lean and Agile practices is the notion that the development organizations must always seek ways to improve. Once the organization becomes complacent, you can expect performance to begin to decline and competitors will quickly have the opportunity to catch up and displace the market leaders. As with *The Scrum Guide*, the Nexus guide implements Sprint retrospectives as a mechanism for implementing continuous improvements across each Sprint.

The Nexus Sprint retrospective is more complex than the original Sprint retrospectives. This is because the Scrum Teams must look across their independent efforts to evaluate areas where dependency and integration issues have negatively impacted their performance as an interoperating Nexus. Nexus implements a three-step Nexus retrospective process, as shown in the following diagram.

In step one, the NIT members meet with representatives from each Scrum Team to discuss any dependency and integration issues the teams faced during the previous Sprint. The representatives from the effected teams take this feedback to their respective Scrum Teams for review and analysis. In step two, all the Scrum Teams have their normal print retrospectives. The primary difference in Nexus is that the Scrum Teams will also discuss, analyze, and assess potential resolutions to the dependency and integration issues. In the third step, the Scrum Team representatives take their respective team's ideas back to the NIT in a follow-up Nexus retrospective. The NIT members consolidate the results, look for common themes, and determine how they should proceed across the Nexus:

Figure 9.2 – Nexus Sprint retrospective process

During the initial Nexus retrospective, it's useful to ask the following questions:

- Was the Nexus goal achieved?
- Was all the planned work competed? If not, why not?
- Did the Nexus generate any technical debt?
- Were all the artifacts, especially code, continuously and successfully integrated?
- Were all software builds (integration, tests, and commits) successful and sufficiently frequent to avoid the accumulation of cross-team dependencies?

For every question listed here, if an answer is a negative response, then the NIT and participating Scum Team representatives need to discuss why they believe they had these issues, how can they fix these issues, and how they we keep this from happening again. But, ultimately, it's up to the Scrum Teams to finish the analysis and propose working solutions, as they are closest to the issues.

As a quick reminder, technical debt is the implementation of working but not optimal code or other solution components. Technical debt occurs when a team implements an expedient solution that addresses the immediate business or user needs but does not adequately address the efficiencies or sustainability of the software design, code, security, or integration elements. Over time, technical debt accumulates, causing performance, scalability, and security issues that must be addressed.

Bittner (Bittner et al. 2018) suggested implementing two tools to facilitate the Nexus retrospective process. These are the *Simple Sprint Retrospective Board* and the *Plan-Do-Check-Adapt Sprint Retrospective Board*.

The Simple Sprint Retrospective Board, shown in the following diagram, provides a tool that can be used to capture and organize team assessments that had been discussed during the Nexus Sprint retrospectives:

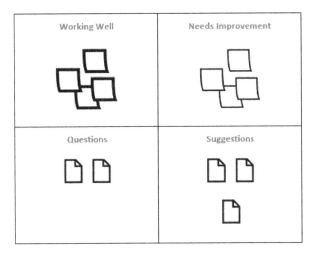

Figure 9.3 – Sample Simple Sprint Retrospective Board

As the name suggests, the tool provides a simple four quadrant block that's used to track items that worked well, items that need improvement, questions the team has, and suggestions for improvements.

You have probably already gathered that the Plan-Do-Check-Adapt Sprint Retrospective Board, shown in the following diagram, is a take-off on Deming's PDCA Wheel (that is, plan–do–check–act or plan–do–check–adjust):

Plan	Do	Check/ study	Adapt	Done
Improvement ideas	Agreed items to review	Items ready to evaluate	Items that need to be adapted before adoption	Ideas that are adapted and adopted

Figure 9.4 – Sample Plan-Do-Check-Adapt Sprint Retrospective Board

This tool offers a robust way to guide the work across the dependency or other items that must be addressed to improve Nexus and Scrum Team performance.

Defining "Done" in a Nexus

The NIT is responsible for defining what **Done** means, as applied to an Integrated Increment, and all Scrum Teams complete their work according to that same definition. An Integrated Increment is only "Done" when the output of the Nexus is integrated and usable.

At this point, you have learned the basic of Nexus, as defined in *The Nexus*™ *Guide*. In the remaining sections of this chapter, you'll dive into more details on the implementation of a Nexus and the common methods and tools used across the Nexus Framework.

Getting into the details

The Nexus Guide is a quick introduction to the basics of the Nexus Framework. Ken Schwaber and the folks at Scrum.org make the point that, like Scrum, Nexus is simple to understand, yet difficult to master. The remainder of this chapter provides an overview of the implementation details that must be mastered.

Building products, not running projects

As with most Agile-based approaches to development, Scrum and Nexus place the focus on building products, not running projects. There are multiple reasons for this, but the primary issue is one of staying focused on doing the things that add value.

Projects are relatively short-lived development efforts, having a set duration with a defined beginning and an end, and living within the constraints of scope, budgets, schedule, resources, and quality. The outcome of a project is a product, service, or outcome. Once the project ends, all activity stops unless a new project is chartered and initiated.

In contrast, **products** represent the value an organization brings to its customers. Most organizations don't simply produce one product and then go away. Rather, development entities set up organizational structures, processes, methods, and tools that enable continuous delivery of the products for as long as they have paying customers and it's economically feasible to develop and deliver the products.

Similar to project teams, product development organizations plan and work under the constraints of budgets and resources. However, where projects have costs, products are viewed as a revenue stream providing business value. That's a very different mindset that ultimately makes products more apparently valuable to an organization than its projects.

Product-oriented work is ongoing across fiscal years, and the organization does not differentiate the importance of development activities devoted to building, sustaining, or enhancing products, as they are all value-added activities. A product-oriented focus is always about creating and enhancing customer value.

Establishing value

Scrum was designed as a system to help development organizations overcome complex adaptive problems to deliver products with the highest value possible. Nexus is no different, with the exception that it also addresses the complexities of dependencies and communications across multiple Scrums working in collaboration to achieve a common goal.

Nexus exists because many, if not most, products are too complex to deliver with a single product development team. Integrating work at scale is difficult due to added complexities of dependencies at scale. This is the same issue we discussed in *Chapter 4, Systems Thinking*. But now, we must deal with managing the complex adaptive problems associated with managing two large systems – the product under development and the multiple Scrum Teams working in collaboration to build and deliver the product.

Keeping things simple

Complexity is the enemy of scaling. Scum is simple and Scrum.org takes the view that scaling Scrum should be simple too. Nexus solves the complex adaptive problems related to scaling Scrum by minimizing its extensions to Scrum. Nexus scaling in support of large products is still fundamentally Scrum. Put another way, scaled Scrum is still Scrum.

Staying small

Nexus is a framework that supports multiple (three to nine) Scrum Teams collaborating on development from a single Product backlog to deliver at least one "Done" integrated increment every Sprint. The limit of nine Scrum Teams follows the same restrictions placed on Scrum Team size.

The optimal size of a Scrum Team, as defined by The Scrum Guide, is based on the works of George Miller, a cognitive psychologist and Harvard University professor who concluded, based on his research, that most humans can only hold 7 ± 2 items in short-term memory. This constraint affects how much information one person can effectively manage at any given time.

The human limitations of information management are compounded by the network communications issues we discussed in *Chapter 4, Systems Thinking*. Recall that system complexity increases exponentially with the number of elements involved in the system. The mathematical expression for such growth is $n(n-1)/2$, as shown in *Figure 3.1*. Just as it's difficult to predict the interactions of numerous disparate parts in a system, it's also difficult to predict the actions and consequences of multiple teams working as a system.

So, keeping things simple and keeping things small are the two key elements of Nexus that are used to manage the complexities associated with scaling Scrum.

Extending Scrum to form a Nexus

You've learned how Nexus keeps things small and simple in the *Reviewing the Nexus Framework* section of this chapter. Let's do a quick review, but in the context of keeping things small and simple:

- Nexus modifies one artifact to eliminate dependencies: Product backlog

- Nexus adds two Nexus artifacts: Nexus Sprint Backlog, Integrated Increment

- Nexus adds five additional Nexus events that resemble the five original Scrum events: Refinement, Nexus Sprint planning, Nexus Daily Scrum, Nexus Sprint review, and Nexus Sprint retrospective

- Nexus adds one new Nexus role **Nexus Integration Team (NIT)**

At first glance, Nexus does appear to be a relatively simple extension to Scrum. Now, let's get into the details that allow for its mastery, starting with a more in-depth discussion of how a Nexus is formed.

Creating a Nexus

Since a Nexus is a scaled Scrum strategy, it makes sense to take some time to think through the types and focus of each of the Scrum Teams within the Nexus. The developers of Nexus have concluded that it's not generally a good idea to align teams around the development of software components. The primary issue is that software components represent small slices of functionality, and many components may not have a development requirement within the current Sprint.

In addition, component-based Scrum Teams tend to become highly specialized in the business and technical aspects associated with their respective components. As a result, it's very hard to keep all the component-based Scrum Teams actively engaged on value-added work from Sprint to Sprint.

Aligning Scrum Teams around personas and value

Similar in concept to the practices you learned in the chapters on Lean development, Nexus suggest that Scrum Teams form around increments of business value. Value is defined through the eyes of the customer. In some cases, we may have a very strong understanding of the unique types of customers and their specific needs. In other situations, we may view our customers in a more generalized sense. With this in mind, the authors of *The Nexus Framework for Scaling Scrum* (Bittner et al., 2018) suggest two work partitioning strategies:

- Persona-outcomes-oriented Scrum Teams
- Value areas-oriented Scrum Teams

Persona-outcomes-based Scrum Teams implement functionality in support of unique types of users and the outcomes those prospective customers expect from using the product once it's been released. Scrum Teams can support more than one persona. If a certain persona has more outcomes than a single Scrum Team can accomplish, then the identified outcomes can be split among multiple Scrum Teams.

The choice of using the word "persona" to describe that this type of Scrum Team building strategy is not by accident. In this development strategy, the teams define typical types of users and give them a unique name for ease of identifying with their potential customers. These personas are not real customers, but they represent a large swathe of a particular type of customer that uses their product. Each defined persona includes specific details about their fictional person so that the developers gain empathy for the needs of their customers, as well as how the users will use the products they are building.

Scrum Teams built around value areas take a more generalized approach to development. Though conceptually similar to the persona-outcome-based teams, Scrum Teams that support value areas map more closely to Lean development practices. In other words, value area teams support the organization's defined operational and development value streams.

Regardless of which Scrum Team construction strategy is implemented, the organization must ensure that each Scrum Team develops both deep and broad skills related to the business domains they work in regarding the methods and tools they employ. The idea is that all work associated with each Nexus goal can be equally divided among the Scrum Teams.

Establishing good team development practices

When a Nexus is working well, it is always building an Integrated Increment of value across each Sprint. This strategy means the code base must be completely transparent, can be shared, and be readily accessible to the members of all Scrum Teams. Bittner et al (2018). suggests five development practices to allow the teams to work effectively together when building Integrated Increments. These strategies are as follows:

- Trunk-based development
- Continuous Integration
- Automated API-based testing
- Versioned API management
- Code review

Any development team that is properly using a configuration management or source control management tool understands the importance of implementing trunk-based development. The objective is to have one code base that all developers work from. All the branches on the development tree are temporary and any code that's developed on the branches is integrated with the main trunk continuously. This is so that other developers who pull code from the trunk base know they are working from the most current and tested code set.

Continuous Integration is the second part of the trunk-based development requirement. As developers build their code, they frequently commit their changes to the source code repository. With each commit, the code is put through a series of tests to ensure the new code doesn't break anything in the existing code. Code commits can occur every few minutes, but never less than once a day.

An **Application Programming Interface** (**API**) is simply a defined method for disparate software components and systems to communicate and interoperate. The term API integration refers to the use of APIs to interconnect software components, modules, or systems to participate in a joint process. The APIs enable synchronous or asynchronous data exchange and data transformations that allow the disparate systems to communicate and work with each other.

With automated API testing, all software components, modules, and systems have published APIs that all Scrum developers use. The APIs need to be tested to ensure they aren't broken as new functionality is added. In fact, APIs should never be extended as any components that rely on them could fail due to these changes. The better strategy is to replace the APIs when new functionality is required, and then allow the original APIs to persist until the developers are confident that none of their software components still use the original APIs. All original and modified APIs need to be placed under version management so that the developers can track which versions of the APIs their components are using.

The developers within the Scrum Teams must consistently build high-quality code. Though the Scrum Teams work aggressively to build deep and broad skills, different developers will have different strengths and weaknesses. In addition, humans make mistakes. A common practice in Agile is to employ paired programming techniques to improve the quality of the software produced by each team, and Nexus recommends this practice.

In paired programming, the developers take turns writing code. While one is writing, the other is observing and reviewing the other's code. This puts two sets of eyes on every line of code to detect errors and omissions, while also providing a real-time forum where the two developers can share their ideas on the best way to implement the desired functionality.

Evolving the Nexus

Rather than building all the Scrum Teams at once and hoping for the best, the better strategy is to start small and build the teams as it becomes apparent more resources are required. This gives each Scrum Team, and the Nexus as a whole, time to build their skills, learn how to work together, and build their culture.

As more Scrum Teams are required, the team may spin off members of existing Scrum Teams to form the new team. Nexus goes further by following the Agile principles of self-forming teams. This suggests the members should have a say on which team they wish to join. As needs evolve, members may rotate from one team to another.

The ideal situation is to use experimentation (that is, use empirical process control theories) to put the right teams and team members together, and then let them settle down and mature the practices of their team. It might take 6 months to form a fully capable and efficient Scrum team, and that team should stay together for as long as it makes sense. Over time, some additional rotations will occur to prevent stagnation and to provide more opportunities for the developers.

In addition, new team members joining from outside the organization or Nexus may rotate through one or more teams before finding a permanent home with one of the existing Scrum teams. In effect, the newly hired developers work as interns while they learn the necessary domain knowledge and skills, understand the culture of the enterprise, and build relationships across the Nexus. They also gain an intimate understanding of how the Nexus works to build and deliver Integrated Increments of high value.

Planning a Nexus Sprint

The initial planning events in the Nexus are obviously going to require more work than simpler and smaller scale Sprint planning events. This is because the Product backlog must be refined not only in terms of understanding high-value development priorities, but also understanding how the work should be divided to minimize dependencies across the participating Scrum Teams. After the initial Sprint, Nexus planning still involves refining the work to eliminate dependencies, but the effort is more along the lines of a traditional Sprint planning session.

The book The Nexus Framework for Scaling Scrum highlighted a number of Nexus planning techniques in their book *The Nexus Framework for Scaling Scrum*, (Bittner et al., 2018). This book will only provide a quick overview of each technique, so I highly recommend that you read Bittner et al.'s book to gain a more solid grounding on each of the Nexus planning techniques. The suggested Nexus planning tools include the following:

- Impact maps
- Cross-team Product backlog refinement board
- Story mapping
- Cross-team visual dependency refinement board
- Relative sizing board
- Outcome and measures planning board
- Nexus Sprint Backlog board (that is, Nexus Kanban board)

Impact maps

As originally conceived, an **impact map** visually displays connections between **Goals**, **Actors**, **Impacts**, and **Deliverables**, as shown in the following table:

Goals	Actors	Impacts	Deliverables
Process Performance Support Reduce Order Entry Time			

Figure 9.5 – Impact map

The **Goals** are statements defining why specific work items are prioritized for the upcoming Sprint. The **Actors** represent individuals who either impact or are impacted by the product under development. In other words, the product under development must support the needs of these actors. The **Impacts** are statements or outcomes that are expected by the linked actors. Impact statements describe what the product needs to do for the actors, or the capabilities desired by the actors, to support their individual needs. Finally, the **Deliverables** are statements of what the Nexus or Scrum Team needs to do to deliver the linked impacts. Deliverables can take the form of activities, features, and functions that the final solution must provide to our customers.

Kurt Bittner has improved upon the basic impact map format by adding a *Personal Outcome* field and improving the **user experience** (**UX**) modeling terminology Nexus uses to describe users and customers and the outcomes they are looking to achieve. In the revised format, *Customer Outcomes* has been added as a new column, the term *Personal* replaces the term *Actor*, the term *Deliverables* has been changed to *PBIs* (Product backlog Items), and *Impacts* has been changed to *Business Impacts* (see the following table).

Bittner's paper on his revised impact map is located on the Scrum.org website at `https://www.scrum.org/resources/blog/extending-impact-mapping-gain-better-product-insights`. Now, let's take a look at the following table to see how the Nexus-based impact map works.

Goals	Personas	Customer Outcome	Business Impact	PBIs
Goal 1				
Goal 2				

Figure 9.6 – Revised Nexus-based impact map

For the purpose of this example, let's assume that the application is an online game. In this map, we have three goals:

- Bring in high-paying customers

- Extend our customer base at the lowest possible cost

- Find new high-value niche market opportunities

There are three personas – Jay, Mary, and Joe – one each to represent our three goals. Jay wants high-end performance, Mary is on a budget, and Joe has a relatively unique, or niche, requirement.

Let's also assume that Jay's requirements will take some time and are expensive to implement. On the other hand, Jay's persona is the primary target customer and represents the largest potential revenue stream.

Mary's persona represents a sizable target market among those that value entertainment over competition. Mary's needs are fulfilled more quickly and at less cost than those of Jay's persona. However, these customers don't want to pay as much for a gaming product.

Finally, Joe represents a segment of the market that values gaming from the perspective of social networking. Though Joe values some of the same capabilities that Mary and Jay want, he's actually easier to satisfy as long as he has the opportunity to make new friends.

Ok; this was a little bit of a simple and slapstick example. But hopefully, you got the point of the exercise and the tool. Now, we are going to move on and look at a method and a tool that can help refine PBIs impacting multiple Scrum Teams.

Cross-team Product Backlog Refinement Board

After creating the impact map, the development teams will quickly realize that the high-level deliverables require further refinement to expose the **Product backlog items (PBIs)** as potential product features or functionality. However, since the PBI development work must be broken out among the Scrum Teams, the teams also need to minimize the dependencies across the work. The cross-team Product backlog Refinement activity provides both a method and a tool to visualize dependencies during the Product backlog refinement process. The method is to list identified PBIs in context with the Scrum Teams that must deliver the functionality and those impacted by the implementation of the PBIs. This visualization is facilitated in the cross-team Product backlog Refinement Board shown here:

Product Backlog Item	Persona 1 Scrum Team	Persona 2 Scrum team	Value Area Scum Team
1. Application Installation Feature			
1.1. Install from Internet			✓
1.2. Install from Compact Disk			✓
2. Product Search Feature			
2.1. Search by product type	✓		
2.2. Search by order number		✓	

Figure 9.7 – Cross-team Product backlog Refinement Board

Now that the Scrum Teams within the Nexus can visualize their dependencies, they continue their refinement work to break up these features into specific development tasks. The work items must be refined with sufficient granularity to eliminate the dependencies between the Scrum Teams.

The Scrum Teams do not need a new technique or tool to do this work. They are simply decomposing the PBIs we identified in *Figure 9.4* into more granular activities while taking care to minimize cross-team dependencies. The end result is the same cross-team Product backlog Refinement Board with many more development tasks identified and no cross-team dependencies.

As the Scrum Teams refine the Product backlog, they must be careful to consider the dependencies that can impact their work. For example, there are people dependencies based on skills and knowledge sets. Business domain experience may be required to properly support critical business processes affected by the product. Integrated systems that leverage both hardware and software components may require that the teams carrying out certain work items have technical expertise in the specific components affected by the identified work. There may be organizational authority dependencies that must be considered, such as changing code that impacts the security of the overall solution, or when components of the system are subject to compliance or security regulations. Some work items may affect the existing architecture or reusable components that must be considered. Finally, there can be external dependencies associated with supply chain, development, and delivery partners.

Story mapping

As the Product backlog grows, it's important to ensure the Nexus and its associated Scrum Teams stay focused on delivering work that is customer-centric and has the highest value. Story mapping is a technique and a tool that helps keep the Nexus focused. The story map lists the most critical capabilities (that is, goals) in context with the actors that need those capabilities. These relationships may be shown on the horizontal axis. On the vertical axis, phases or releases show the features in context with the goals and actors they support. See the following diagram for an example of this.

Cross-team Visual Dependency Refinement Board

The story maps do a great job of displaying development tasks in terms of goals and the spread of phases or releases. But the Scrum Teams also need to determine how they will allocate their work over the Sprints and the dependencies that impact their work. Yes, the previous Nexus refinement process has eliminated dependencies associated with performing each work task, but not the time-dependent sequencing of work for integrating their respective deliverables:

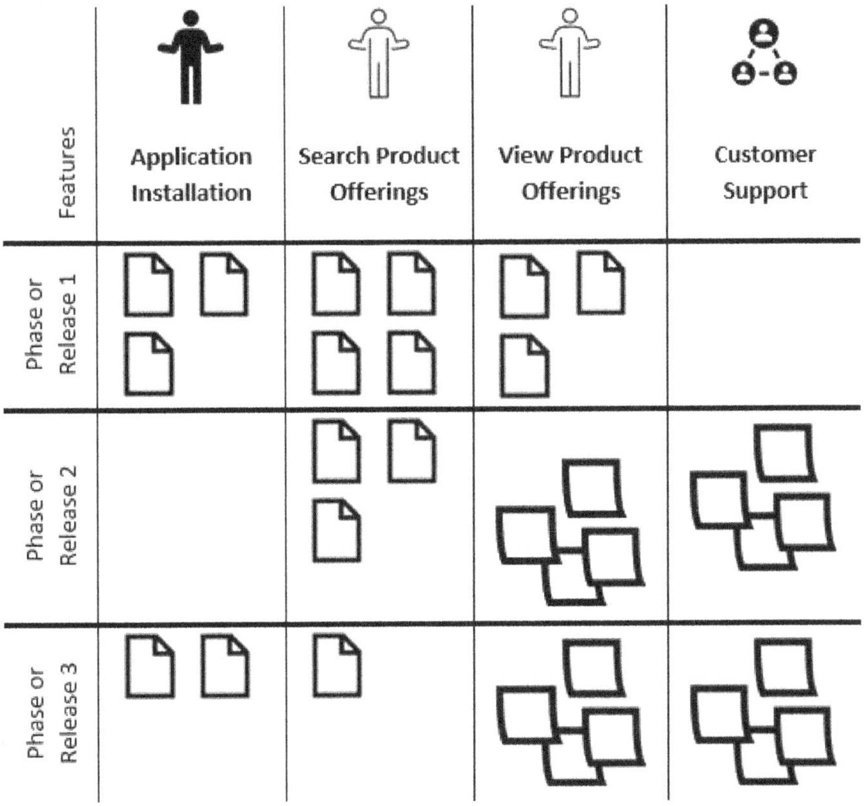

Figure 9.8 – Story map

For example, Scrum Team one may be working on developing the user interface for a new feature, while Scrum Team two is building the backend processes that implement the feature. Though Scrum Team two can develop and test their logic independent of the application, at some point, those capabilities must be integrated with the user interface on the client-side of the application. There is a dependency in that relationship. Both Scrum Teams one and two can both perform some of their tasks independently, but the final integrated tasks cannot occur until the user interface is competed. The cross-team visual dependency refinement board shows these types of relations by team and across the planned Sprints.

The arrows depicted in the cross-team visual dependency board shown in the following diagram have different colors to make it easier to visualize the types of dependencies; in this case, the hardware, software, and third-party dependencies. You can have whatever dependencies and colors make sense for your product development clarification needs:

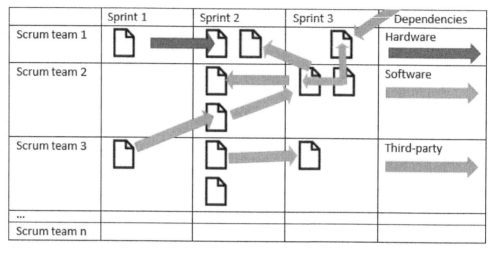

Figure 9.9 – Cross-team visual dependency refinement board

Note that the direction of the arrows also conveys important information:

- Horizontal arrows: Dependencies between PBIs within the same team

- Vertical arrows: Dependencies between individual items across teams within the same Sprint

- Arrows point to the left: Indicates a successor task has a dependency on a predecessor task

- Arrows pointing to the right: Indicates a predecessor task has a dependency on a successor task, which is a risk that must be resolved

- Angled arrows: Dependencies between separate teams but across Sprints

This is a very quick overview of the cross-team visual dependency refinement board technique. More detailed information is available on page 45 of Bittner and Kong's book titled *The Nexus™ Framework for Scaling Scrum – Continuously Delivering an Integrated Product with Multiple Scrum Teams*.

Relative sizing board

With the aforementioned techniques, the Nexus is now ready to move from Backlog refinement to Sprint planning. Because the Scrum Teams must work through their dependencies, Sprint planning is an iterative process. The outcomes of the Sprint planning sessions are Sprint goals for each Scrum Team that support both their team objectives and the Nexus goal.

During Sprint planning, the Scrum Teams continue to refine the Product backlog, and they develop both the Nexus Sprint Backlog and individual Sprint Backlogs for each Scrum Team. The Scrum Teams within the Nexus must decide how to divvy up the work among their teams. As part of that exercise, they must understand the relative size of each PBI selected for the Sprint. Nexus suggests the use of a Fibonacci-based estimating technique to make relative size estimations.

For example, the teams might use the numbers 1, 2, 3, 5, 8, 13, and 21 for estimating the degree of difficulty for each PBI, with each number representing a multiple of the first estimate in the series. In other words, an estimate of 5 for a selected PBI means the teams judge the development work is five times greater than the work associated with an estimate of 1. Also, PBIs with estimates of 5 or greater likely need more refinement to break up the work into small increments that a team feels confident can be completed within a single Sprint.

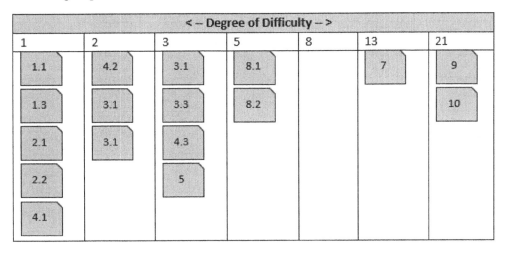

Figure 9.10 – Relative sizing board

The objective of Nexus and Sprint planning is to ensure each team, individually, and the Nexus, as a whole, can accomplish the work taken on within the Sprint. For planning purposes, the Scrum Teams place cards listing the selected PBIs on a relative sizing board (see the following diagram). The Scrum Teams and NIT members are the experts in development, so to prevent second guessing by management and other stakeholders, the planning estimates are not shared outside the Nexus. Visibility to stakeholders is made available through the Nexus and Sprint goals, the Nexus Sprint Backlog Board, and velocity charts.

Outcome and measures planning board

So far, we have not addressed how the identified work items support the value streams that justified the investments, nor how the work items relate to specific business outcomes and what "good looks like" when the business achieves these outcomes. This is a critical issue that must be addressed during Nexus and Sprint Backlog refinement and planning activities.

The most expedient way to map PBI work items to business outcomes and desired outcomes is to extend the relative sizing board as a matrix with columns and rows to map related work items by the outcomes and their key measurements. The following diagram shows an example of this:

1	2	3	5	8	13	21	Outcome	Measure
1.1	4.2	3.1	8.1		7	9	O 1	M1.1
1.3	3.1	3.3	8.2			10	O 2	M2.1
2.1	3.1	4.3					O 3	M3.1
							O 4	M4.1
2.2		5					O 5	M5.1
4.1							O 6	M6.1

Figure 9.11 – Outcome and measures planning board

Note that, here, outcome 4 has no work items assigned to the effort. Now, the Nexus knows they have some additional work to do to flesh out this requirement.

Nexus Sprint Backlog Board (Nexus Kanban board)

The final technique listed for Nexus planning is the Nexus Sprint Backlog, which, for all intents and purposes, is a Kanban Board used to visualize work in progress during the upcoming Sprint. This planning board is updated throughput the Sprint to indicate the current status of each work task. This can be seen in *Figure 9.12*.

Notice that the card for work item 2.1 overlaps the bottom-left corner of the card for work item 2.2. This indicates that work item 2.1 must proceed with work item 2.3. Similarly, the card for work item 6 overlaps the bottom right-hand corner of the card for work item 5. This indicates that another task is dependent on work item 6:

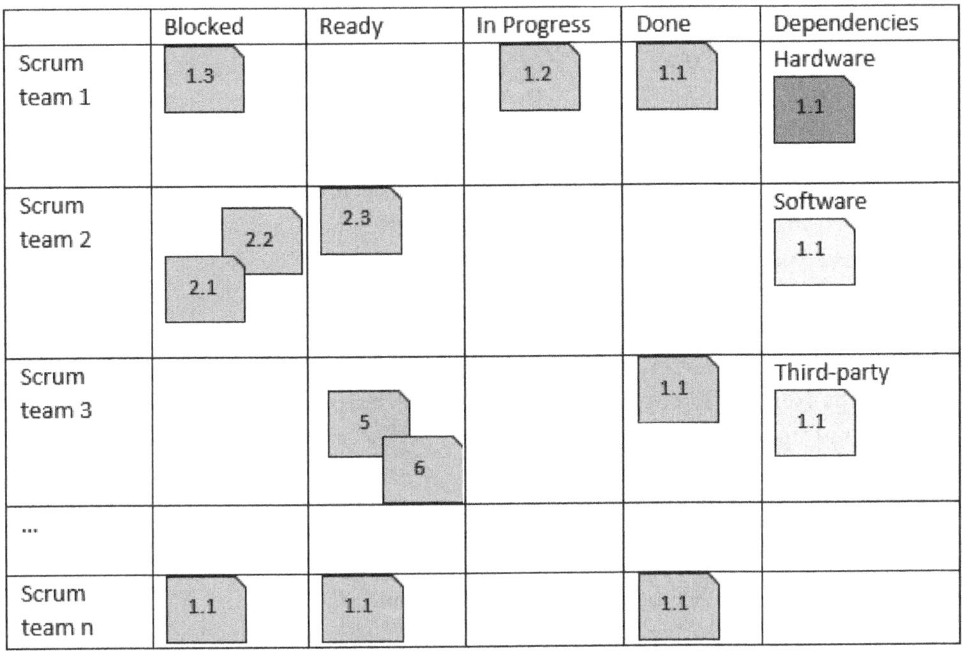

	Blocked	Ready	In Progress	Done	Dependencies
Scrum team 1	1.3		1.2	1.1	Hardware 1.1
Scrum team 2	2.2 2.1	2.3			Software 1.1
Scrum team 3		5 6		1.1	Third-party 1.1
...					
Scrum team n	1.1	1.1		1.1	

Figure 9.12 – Nexus Sprint Backlog Board (Nexus Kanban board)

This completes this section on Nexus and Sprint planning. While the initial Nexus planning may take additional time to complete, future Nexus planning events should follow the same timebox pattern as the traditional Scrum planning events. A good rule of thumb metric is 2 hours of Nexus/Sprint planning for every week of development within the timeboxed Sprint.

Now that you have covered the Nexus/Sprint planning event, let's move on and review the activities and tools associated with conducting Sprints.

Building products incrementally

The baseline code (also known as the trunk, mainline code, and master) is managed in a **source control management (SCM)** repository. Modern practice is to automate the build and test processes so that only a single command is required to execute the build and test processes. Once the new code successfully passes the tests, the developers should commit their code to the mainline code. This allows other developers know that the code they are going to be working on represents the most current working code. Developers should commit their code daily, if not more frequently.

Conceptually, SCM repositories use a "tree" metaphor to describe the build and test process. SCM allows the developers to collaborate in developing a single set of code, called the trunk, that is, at all times, fully tested, integrated, and working. Developers check out the code to build and test their extensions. SCM tracks the checked-out code as "branches" on the trunk. Once committed, the newly developed, integrated, and tested code becomes part of the trunk.

Besides minimizing the opportunities for bugs and defects to accumulate throughout the software, which makes debugging an increasingly difficult and resource-intensive task, the CI process has another direct benefit in Nexus. Nexus places a prime emphasis on addressing integration and dependency issues as early as possible. By forcing Continuous Integration and testing, issues are quickly discovered and resolved. If a developer has an issue and believes it's a problem with the existing code, they can take the problem to the NIT during the Nexus Daily Scrum. If the problem is particularly challenging, the NIT members can jump in to help work the problems to resolution.

Building a Product Backlog tree map

In the previous section, you learned how Nexus implements the Nexus Sprint Backlog Board as a type of Nexus Kanban board to visualize and manage work in progress. The cross-team Product backlog refinement board also offers a visual display of PBIs by Scrum Team assignments. Another useful visualization tool is the Product backlog tree map, which is a different approach to displaying work items under development in the Sprint, their status, and their relative size, which combines elements of both the Nexus Kanban board and the cross-team Product backlog refinement board:

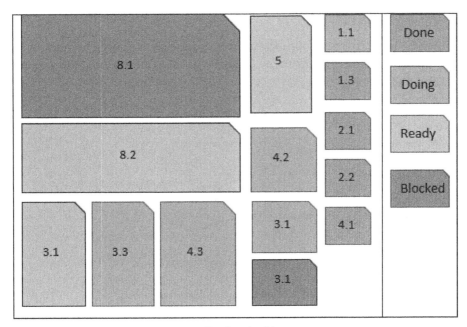

Figure 9.13 – Product backlog tree map

This section provided a very brief introduction to the Product backlog tree map. If you want to learn more about this technique, please go to page 63 in Bittner and Kong's book titled *The Nexus™ Framework for Scaling Scrum – Continuously Delivering an Integrated Product with Multiple Scrum Teams*.

Now, we can view the relative size and status of our identified work items. In the last section, you learned that Nexus uses a Fibonacci approach to estimating. Next, we'll take a look at how Nexus uses velocity charts to display progress against the Product backlog.

Measuring and judging velocity

Product backlog burndown, burnup, and velocity charts are fairly common across most Agile methodologies. The Scrum Teams estimate work item effort in terms of points, such as those ascribed in the Fibonacci sequence of numbers.

Constructing a velocity chart

A velocity chart shows the total number of story points that have been completed in each Sprint. These story points come from the estimates derived from Sprint planning, where members use numbers from the Fibonacci sequence as measures of estimated difficulty:

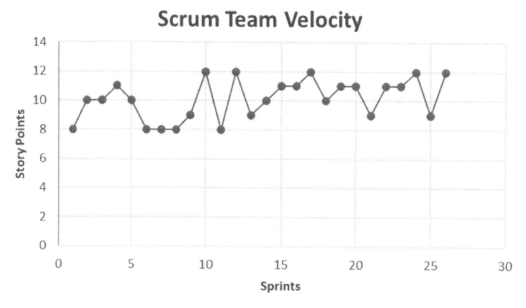

Figure 9.14 – Sample velocity chart

The velocity chart, as shown in the preceding diagram, is particularly useful at the start of a development effort or for a new team to help them determine how well they are estimating work, how they are improving over time, and to help them determine what their average velocity is over time.

Constructing a burndown chart

The burndown chart displays the number of points remaining in the Product backlog across each completed Sprint. The graph typically starts in the top left-hand quadrant with a measure of total estimated points in the backlog, and is then reduced by the number of points completed in each Sprint, with the line trending downward and to the right:

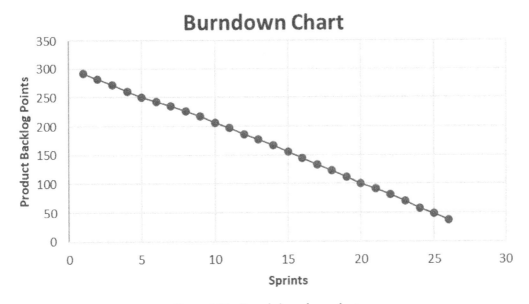

Figure 9.15 – Sample burndown chart

A burndown chart may also show a projection of points per Sprint into the future, until it reaches zero remaining points (items) in the backlog (see figure 9.15).

Constructing a burnup chart

In direct contrast, a burnup chart shows the number of points accumulated across each completed Sprint. The graph displaying the Sprints starts off in the lower left-hand quadrant and grows progressively with each Sprint with the accumulation of completed points:

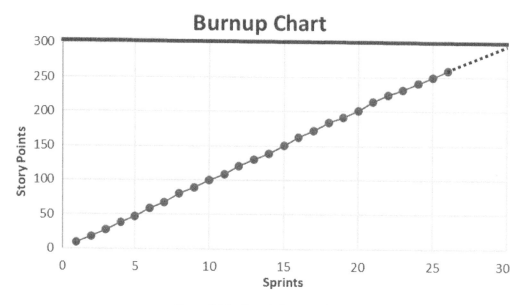

Figure 9.16 – Sample burnup chart

Usually, the burnup chart also displays a horizontal line that indicates the total estimated number of points in the backlog. As with the burndown chart, the burnup chart can show a projection into the future based on the estimated velocity per Sprint.

Earning continued support

Nexus has a basic philosophy that visibility into Sprint planning needs to be just enough to gain and sustain the trust of customers, executives, and other critical stakeholders. Estimating is an art form more than a science, and the primary benefit is to aid the team in assessing how much work they can realistically accomplish within an upcoming Sprint. Still, there is value in displaying the burnup, burndown, and velocity charts to demonstrate ongoing progress in completing the PBIs.

I've made this point before, but it's worth repeating: those who are funding a development project must feel comfortable that their investments are paying off. Otherwise, they will pull the plug. These charts, along with the Nexus Sprint reviews, are the tools the development teams have to demonstrate progress and alignment with the customers' and users' objectives.

Evaluating best fits

The Nexus Framework is another relative pure extension to the original Scrum Framework, as defined by Ken Schwaber, one of the two co-founders of Scrum, and his associates at Scrum.org. Therefore, organizational leaders who are comfortable with adopting the network-oriented organizational structures of Scrum on a large scale will find this approach attractive.

Nexus does not provide prescriptive guidance on how to implement scaled Scrums across organizational value streams. Nor does Nexus provide direct guidance on how to implement scaled Scrum in regulated industries, federal agencies, or non-profits. Nexus was defined by developers for developers. That's not to say Nexus cannot be expanded across all business functions, but the organization is on its own to figure out how.

A Nexus works from one Product backlog, with one responsible Product Owner, and with *multiple* Scrum Teams working in collaboration to develop a single integrated Increment that meets its definition of Done across every Sprint. As mentioned in the description of a Nexus, the term *multiple* typically includes three to nine Scrum Teams. As with the Scrum of Scrums approach, this limits each Nexus to a practical maximum of ~81 developers.

Bittner and Kong point out that the recommended limit of nine teams is not absolute, and that there may be situations where it's possible to include more teams. (Bittner & Kong, 2018) Still, it's up to the organization to figure out what those situations might be, and how they will limit the potential network density issues. In addition, Nexus does not provide guidance on how to implement multiple Nexus Teams in support of a single product.

Given these factors, the best situations for Nexus implementations involve up to nine Scrum Teams and 81 people who collaborate to develop a single product. Another practical implementation is in a large enterprise with multiple Nexus product teams that are aligned to support individual products. In other words, there's one Nexus per product. The organization must be careful when defining their products to prevent overlapping requirements that would necessitate cross-Nexus collaborations.

As with most scaled Scrum approaches, organizations should consider investing in external consulting resources to assist with implementation in a very large product or large enterprise deployment.

Summary

In this chapter, you learned how Ken Schwaber, through his company, Scrum.org, implement Scrum scaling practices via their Nexus Framework. The Nexus Framework does not replace the Scrum Framework; rather, it extends Scrum to organize and coordinate the work of three to nine Scrum Teams in order to deliver Integrated Increments of value across each planned Sprint.

You have learned that Nexus modifies one artifact, adds two additional artifacts, adds five new events, and adds one new role. Artifacts provide transparency to help avoid bad decision-making from having bad information. Events guide the flow of work across each Sprint. The roles define the responsibilities of the Nexus integration and Scrum Teams.

As with Scrum, there is only one Product backlog for the entire Nexus, from which all the underlying Scrum Teams pull work. Since there is only one only Product backlog, there is one Product Owner who is ultimately accountable for the value that's identified in and produced from the Product backlog.

Within Nexus, a **Nexus Integration Team** (**NIT**) works with the Scrum Teams as a coach, mentor, and facilitator to remove cross-team dependencies and address product integration issues. In that role, they may help implement the infrastructure to enable continuous integration and testing capabilities.

Nexus retains the role of Scrum Masters, who are the servant leaders for both the Scrum Teams and the NIT. The Scrum Master for the NIT provides mentoring and coaching on elements of the Nexus Framework to the Scrum Teams. They also monitor the Scrum Teams to ensure the Nexus events, artifacts, and roles are implemented correctly. They also offer suggestions for improvements.

The Nexus events guide the flow of work across multiple Scrum Teams collaborating to achieve a common Nexus goal. Within the Nexus planning events, the Scrum Teams may implement a number of useful techniques to plan the work spanning multiple Scrum Teams. Other techniques were introduced to provide visibility of the progress of the work being done during the Sprint.

This completes this chapter on the Nexus Framework. In the next chapter, you will learn how the folks at Large-Scale Scrum implement their flavor of Scrum scaling practices. As a quick hint, they are advocates of Ken Schwaber's scaled Scrum concepts, but with their own unique twists. *Chapter 14, Contrasting Scrum/ Lean-Agile Scaling Approaches* includes a comparative analysis of all scaled Scrum and Lean-Agile practices introduced in this book. Every approach mentioned in this book has something to offer and different sets of strengths in terms of capabilities and applications. In this chapter, you have learned the capabilities and benefits of this approach. *Chapter 14, Contrasting Scrum/ Lean-Agile Scaling Approaches* offers more context with the contrasts against other Scrum/ Lean-Agile approaches.

Questions

1. What is the definition of a Nexus?

2. What is the primary objective of Nexus Sprint planning?

3. What are the five Nexus events?

4. What are two common Scrum Team work partitioning strategies?

5. What are the five strategies listed for large-scale development efforts?

6. What were the Nexus planning visual aids that were mentioned in this book?

7. Why are Nexus Daily Scrum meetings held in advance of the Daily Scrum Team meetings?

8. What are the three methods and tools identified for measuring and judging Sprint velocities?

9. What is the primary reason Nexus implements a single Nexus Sprint review in lieu of holding multiple Scrum Team product reviews?

10. What are the steps in the Nexus Sprint retrospective process?

Further reading

- Schwaber, K. (2018) *The Nexus™ Guide.* The Definitive Guide to scaling Scrum with Nexus: The Rules of the Game. Scrum.org. Retrieved from `https://www.Scrum.org/resources/nexus-guide`

- Miller, George A., (1956) *The Magical Number Seven, Plus or Minus Two: Some Limits on our Capacity for Processing Information* (Harvard University) Psychological Review, 63, 81-97. `http://psychclassics.yorku.ca/Miller/` Accessed 5 May 2020.

- Bittner, Kurt, Kong, P., West, D. (2018) *The Nexus™ Framework for Scaling Scrum – Continuously Delivering an Integrated Product with Multiple Scrum Teams.* The Professional Scrum Series. Scrum.org. Boston, MA. Prentice Hall.

10

Large-Scale Scrum (LeSS)

This chapter introduces the **Large-Scale Scrum** (**LeSS**) approach to scaling Scrum. The LeSS approach applies to situations where many teams work together on a single product. But that definition is also incomplete. Craig Larmon, the co-founder of LeSS, describes LeSS in this manner:

LeSS scales product dev by descaling the org.

In other words, with LeSS, many teams can work collaboratively on one product with more success by simplifying the organization.

In this chapter, you will learn how LeSS implements two frameworks, depending on scale. As the name implies, the LeSS approach is considered another extension to the basic Scrum framework. Consistent with the original intentions of Scrum, LeSS is still considered a minimalist framework, providing just enough guidance to support team and business agility.

LeSS extends Scrum with a few basic rules that practitioners apply to scale Scrum practices across multiple teams participating as a collaborative effort to develop large products. LeSS also provides a number of optional guides that practitioners can adapt to meet their situational needs, when and if it makes sense to do so.

The benefits of the LeSS approach are its conformance to the fundamentals of Scrum's empirical process control theories and minimalist framework. However, LeSS provides a robust set of frameworks and extensions to scale Scrum across multiple teams that are working together on the development of a single software-based product.

In this chapter, you will learn how LeSS extends the basic Scrum framework to support multiple teams at two levels of scale—fewer than 8 teams and more than 8 teams. The number 8 is not a definitive rule meant to form a specific demarcation line between the two frameworks. Instead, organizations make the move to the larger LeSS framework when they begin to see a pattern evolve in which the workload on a single Product Owner becomes too extensive for them to maintain a whole-product vision.

You will also learn the LeSS extensions to Scrum in terms of rules, guides, roles, responsibilities, events, and artifacts. Finally, you will be able to define the basic LeSS workflow in terms of the LeSS events in the two LeSS frameworks.

To accomplish the aforementioned learning objectives, we're going to cover the following main topics in this chapter:

- Introducing LeSS

- Focusing on systems thinking and organizational design

- Building on Scrum

- Leveraging LeSS principles, roles, guides, and experimentation

- Implementing LeSS and LeSS Huge frameworks

- Adopting the LeSS frameworks

- Evaluating best fits

Introducing Large-Scale Scrum (LeSS)

Created by Craig Larman and Bas Vodde, the LeSS framework is all about implementing Agile and Scrum practices at scale. The core concept behind LeSS is that scaled Scrum is still Scrum. In this context, Larman and Vodde describe LeSS as "*Scrum applied to many teams working together on one product*" (*Large-Scale Scrum: More with LeSS*, Larman and Vodde, 2017).

LeSS can help organizations to deal with development complexities at scale while still maintaining the simplicity of Scrum with minimal changes to the original framework. On the other hand, within the LeSS frameworks, LeSS encourages organizations and teams to adapt practices and structures to support their unique needs.

You will find, later in this chapter, that LeSS employs systems thinking practices as a collaborative process to determine appropriate adaption strategies that address product and organization complexities. In other words, if the teams can do systems analysis in collaboration, they can grasp for themselves whether certain organizational design elements are consistent or inconsistent with adaptiveness as the global system optimization goal. Since it's a team-driven effort, this approach to adaptive change minimizes organizational resistance.

The framework was developed to extend Scrum to handle large and complex development activities while retaining the small self-managed teams and empirical process control theory embodied in Scrum. The LeSS approach has proven successful in scaling development activities across international operations and technically complex environments.

Like Scrum, LeSS is a nearly sufficient framework that is deliberately incomplete and allows for situational learning through observation and experimentation, as opposed to enforcing prescriptive rules and formulas. Continuous attention to achieving technical excellence along with continuous experimentation are the hallmarks of this approach.

The whole point of any organization's efforts to scale Scrum is to eliminate complexity, bureaucracy, and overhead, with the goal to achieve agility on a larger scale. LeSS asks the question *how can we simplify the organization to be Agile?* It should be no surprise then that LeSS shuns excessive extensions to Scrum in the way of added roles, artifacts, and rules.

When I attended the LeSS Practitioners course, Craig Larman made the comment multiple times that "*companies have too much money.*" What he meant by this is too many companies lack sufficient motivation to change their organizational structures and processes to become truly efficient and value-added. But Larman also makes clear that the true goal of LeSS is not simply to help to make companies more efficient. Rather, LeSS has an expanded objective to enable global system optimization for adaptiveness. In other words, all organizations must have the ability to change direction in unanticipated ways and do so cheaply and easily.

In *Chapter 4, Systems Thinking*, you learned that the term *burning platform* is a business analogy used to describe a situation where the company is facing a critical problem that is putting it at risk of going under. While most companies can significantly improve their business operations and simplify their organizational structures and bureaucracies, most simply lack the motivation to do so.

So, in this context, there is an interesting paradox addressed by advocates of LeSS: perhaps larger development activities appear complex because the organizational designs implemented by management have created the illusion of complexity. Instead of asking the question of whether we need to get bigger, perhaps we should first ask ourselves whether we can better achieve our goals by getting smaller and simpler? With this line of thinking, the initial focus of implementing LeSS is on descaling and simplifying.

To be more precise, LeSS helps companies and other entities to create an organizational design that is globally optimized for adaptiveness. So, the question to ask is whether an existing structure is consistent with global adaptiveness that requires a less complicated organization. Moreover, changes contemplated by a team or larger organization must be consistent with some defined system goal.

Of all of the Scrum and Agile training courses I have attended, Craig Larman's LeSS Practitioners course was the only course that dove deeply into the use of systems thinking to analyze an organization's design as a complex system. This was not a simple minutes-long discussion but was a hands-on activity carried on throughout the entire three-day class. So, let's start this chapter with a discussion on simplifying organizational design through systems thinking.

Focusing on systems thinking and organizational design

In *Chapter 4, Systems Thinking*, you were introduced to the concepts around systems thinking and how to apply causal modeling and **Causal Loop Diagrams (CLDs)** to visually depict the causal relationships between the elements identified within a system. This is the same approach used by practitioners of LeSS to visually assess system dynamics as a collective effort among affected stakeholders.

Causal modeling is used in LeSS as an approach to generate conversation about the organization's development systems and to reach a collective understanding of the systems as a whole. The purpose of the exercise is to avoid local optimizations that are endemic in traditional organizational design practices. Local optimization is directly tied to wastes as defined in the lean development chapters of this book—*Chapter 5, Lean Thinking*, and *Chapter 6, Lean Practices in Software Development*. Examples of Lean waste include the following:

- Production of non-value-added increments
- Excessive work in progress
- Non-value-added processes

- Inefficient flows, delays, and queuing of work items

- Task switching

- Fixing bugs and defects

- Waiting on resources and skills

- Hierarchical and bureaucratic lines of communications

Since we've covered the subject in detail in the systems thinking and lean development chapters, we don't need to elaborate further here. The main takeaway is that both systems thinking and lean development practices help the organization to avoid undue complexity and local optimizations when Agile-based development needs to support large products or must scale across an enterprise.

Less is Scrum applied to larger product groups and provides more structure to the original Scrum framework. The goal is to scale what works well at the team level on a much wider basis with a few additional rules and guides. The simpler structures of Scrum replace the need for organizational complexities.

In this chapter, you will learn how LeSS extends the Scrum framework and the application of some of the LeSS rules and guides enable scaling Scrum across multiple teams working together on one product. As always, we will start with the basics.

Building on Scrum

The success of Scrum as the dominant Agile framework is largely due to its simplicity and extensibility. It addresses the values and principles outlined in the Agile Manifesto without imposing excessive prescriptive guidance. Users only need to learn a few simple roles, artifacts, and events to get started. While gaining mastery may take some time, the team can get started using Scrum with minimal effort or learning.

Let's employ the same small *feature* teams as Scrum, with three to nine people, cross-functional skills, fully self-contained to independently deliver complete end-to-end solutions to external customers, and operating in an autonomous fashion. While **The Scrum Guide** focused on describing Agile practices across a single team, Larman and Vodde describe LeSS as a *barely sufficient methodology* for two or more teams working together on a single product.

The notion of having a barely sufficient methodology is an important concept. Agile practitioners have long realized that traditional software development practices forced the use of prescriptive processes that got in the way of innovation and staying focused on adding customer value. Scrum and LeSS are frameworks that contain the minimal roles, events, and artifacts necessary to implement iterative development practices to frequently produce increments of potentially shippable products with customer-centric value.

Within those frameworks, developers are free to use any number of practices, methods, and tools that are situationally useful. No two teams should expect to have the same needs, and the needs of the development teams change over time. So, there is no such thing as a best practice in Lean, Agile, Scrum, or LeSS. Developers need to use those practices that make the most sense given their needs of the moment.

Rather than focusing on prescriptive practices, LeSS builds on Scrum through the application of experiments, guides, rules, and principles. Before we get into the specifics of implementing LeSS, let's look at these four concepts in a bit more detail.

Leveraging LeSS principles, roles, guides, and experimentation

Detailed in their book, *Large-Scale Scrum: More with Less*, Larman and Vodde describe the LeSS framework as consisting of numerous LeSS rules and LeSS guides. This book will not cover all of them. Instead, you will obtain an understanding of how LeSS works in a generalized sense. For more information, please refer to Larman and Vodde's books and website. In their books and their website (https://less.works/), Larman and Vodde provide a wealth of knowledge on the use of LeSS rules and LeSS guides. *Figure 10.1* shows the relationships between LeSS principles, frameworks, guides, and experiments:

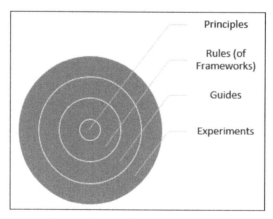

Figure 10.1 – LeSS complete picture

The LeSS principles establish the core upon which LeSS is built. The Less and LeSS Huge frameworks are next, establishing the rules and foundations for empiricism and whole-product focus with Scrum on a large scale. The guides potentially extend the rules of the frameworks on a situational basis. And experimentation is ultimately how LeSS teams determine the value of specific LeSS Guides and other practices in support of their unique product development needs. Let's take a closer look at each of these four elements.

Applying LeSS principles

LeSS principles guide decision making on the use of LeSS rules. As a general definition, principles outline the underlying or guiding theories and beliefs behind a certain way of life. In the context of this book, principles outline a belief system that defines how we conduct product development work. With this understanding, LeSS principles include the following:

- **Large-Scale Scrum is Scrum**: Learn how to apply the principles, roles, elements, and purpose of Scrum in a large-scale context.

- **Transparency**: Provide visibility in context with the definition of Done and the artifacts and events of Scrum.

- **More with Less**: We don't need more roles, artifacts, or processes; instead, LeSS funnels personal responsibilities and ownership to the lowest possible levels.

- **Whole-product focus**: No matter how many Scrum teams there are, there is only one Product Backlog, one Product Owner, one shippable product, and one Sprint.

- **Customer-centric**: Evaluate value from the eyes of the paying customer and eliminate everything else as forms of non-value-added waste.

- **Continuous improvement toward perfection**: While perfection is never truly achievable, it's always the goal, that is, frequent deliveries of potentially shippable products, with lowest costs, no defects, adding only customer value, and no external impacts.

- **Lean thinking**: This is as defined in *Chapter 5, Lean Thinking*, and *Chapter 6, Lean Practices in Software Development.*

- **Systems thinking**: This is as defined in *Chapter 3, The Scrum Approach.*

- **Empirical process control**: As noted in *The Scrum Guide*, use observation and experimentation to constantly learn and improve and allow complete transparency with inspection and adaption to improve the product.

- **Queuing theory**: Consistent with the concepts you learned in *Chapter 4, Systems Thinking*, on Lean development, LeSS applies queuing theory to the R&D domain.

LeSS principles provide the necessary context to appropriately apply LeSS rules and LeSS guides. In the next subsection, you are going to learn about LeSS rules.

Implementing LeSS rules

LeSS implements a set of 42 rules that form the foundation of the LeSS framework. The rules must be in place to support the empirical process control and whole-product focus of the LeSS framework.

LeSS framework rules are mapped to the elements of structure, products, and Sprints within the two LeSS frameworks, LeSS and LeSS Huge. The following list provides some examples of mapping LeSS rules to the LeSS and LeSS Huge frameworks:

- The LeSS framework applies to products with two to eight teams.

- LeSS Huge applies to larger products where one Product Owner cannot maintain complete visibility over its entire scope. Avoid applying LeSS Huge to smaller product groups as it will result in more overhead and local optimizations.

- All LeSS rules apply to LeSS Huge unless otherwise stated. Each requirement area acts like the basic LeSS framework.

These are only three of the 42 defined LeSS framework rules. The entire list of rules is maintained at the leSS.works website, on the rules web page: `https://less.works/less/rules/index`.

Employing LeSS guides

LeSS guides are less strict than LeSS rules in that they offer recommendations based on years of experience of implementing and using the LeSS framework across numerous entities and industries. Readers can learn more about successful LeSS adoptions at the leSS.works website, on the case-studies webpage: `https://less.Works/case-studies/index`.

As noted previously, Larman and Vodde make it clear that development processes cannot be strictly enforced and that any development methods must be applied situationally in context to be useful. Also, some experimentation is necessary to figure out the best way to apply predefined methods to inspect and adapt them to the team's current needs.

While the guides have proven useful elsewhere, each organization must apply them appropriately as an experiment to see whether and how they would work in their unique development environments and situations.

LeSS guides span elements of Adoption, Customer Value, Management, Scrum Masters, Product, Product Owner, Product Backlog, definition of Done, Product Backlog Refinement, Sprint Planning, Coordination and Integration, and Review and Retrospective. As of this writing, Larman and Vodde offer 103 LeSS guides.

Understanding experimentation

We've already discussed the importance of experimentation in the preceding guides section. The main point to be made is that experimentation is very situational and that some experiments may not be worth trying. In other words, one or more of the development teams may have used a specific development technique or procedure successfully in previous Sprints, but that does not at all guarantee they will be useful in future Sprints.

Similarly, some of the LeSS guides may be useful in certain situations while others may find a useful application across the entire development lifecycle of a product. Both Ken Schwaber and Jeff Sutherland make the point in their *Scrum Guide* that learning Scrum is easy but mastering Scrum is very hard. Larman and Vodde make the same statement about LeSS. So, let's revisit how mastery is achieved.

Revisiting Shu-Ha-Ri

As noted in previous chapters, many Agile advocates ascribe to the Japanese martial arts principles of Shu-Ha-Ri. Alistair Cockburn is credited by Martin Fowler as being the first to apply this learning and mastering analogy to software development. Larman and Vodde similarly promote this model of learning and define the Japanese expression of Shu-Ha-Ri to mean the following:

- Shu: Follow the rules to learn the basics.

- Ha: Break the rules to understand the context.

- Ri: Master and find your own way.

So, in other words, you first learn, then experiment, and finally, with practice, evolve to a higher level of understanding in your use of the underlying principles. Mastery only comes with time and practice. With this understanding, let's get into the details of how to go about implementing LeSS.

Implementing the LeSS and LeSS Huge Frameworks

In this section, you are going to learn about the two LeSS frameworks and their purposes. The two LeSS frameworks are as follows:

- LeSS framework (applies to two to eight teams as a typical pattern.)
- LeSS Huge framework (applies to eight or more teams, also as a typical pattern but not a hard and fast rule)

Larman and Vodde make the point that there is no magic behind the number eight as the demarcation between the two LeSS frameworks. Leveraging the concepts of empiricism, they have come to the opinion, through experimentation, that eight teams seem to be the number where it begins to make sense to implement the larger scaling techniques of LeSS Huge. They also make the point that, under certain circumstances, such as situations involving very complex goals with multisite and inexperienced foreign language teams, it may make sense to employ LeSS Huge techniques with fewer than eight teams.

The compelling events that drive a Less Huge implementation include the following:

- A product becomes too large and complex for a single Product Owner to grasp.
- The Product Owner work balance is pulled between competing external and internal factors.
- The Product Backlog is too large for one Product Owner to manage.

There are three common elements within both the LeSS framework and LeSS Huge framework, which are as follows:

- One Product Owner and one Product Backlog
- One common Sprint across all teams
- One shippable product increment

Now, let's take a closer look at how these two frameworks differ. We will start with an overview of the smaller LeSS framework.

Implementing the LeSS Framework

The LeSS framework applies to relatively smaller multi-team development efforts. At this level, the extensions to the original Scrum framework are minimal. The primary objective is to ensure the teams implement rules and structures to facilitate cross-team interactions:

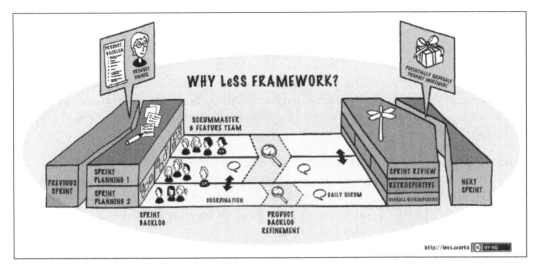

Figure 10.2 – The LeSS Framework

Figure 10.2 shows the general flow of *items* (that is, *features*) across a Sprint as defined by LeSS events. The term *features* in LeSS is simply another word for describing the customer-centric items defined within the Product Backlog. However, it's important to understand that LeSS installs the concept of "Feature Teams" at this level. In this model, Feature Teams retain Scrum's concept of employing fully capable (that is, self-managing and cross-functional) product development teams but segmenting the work across the teams around major product features.

LeSS also describes a flow of teams through the events within a Sprint. The objective of looking at Less as a flow of teams is not to emphasize the importance of attending meetings. Most of the time, people are working on their tasks. But it is useful to understand how multiple teams interact throughout a Sprint, over the course of the events and other types of collaborations, such as the multi-team **Product Backlog Refinement (PBR) workshops** and **multi-team design workshops**.

LeSS builds on the same elements implemented in Scrum to include roles, artifacts, and events. As noted in the previous section, LeSS also implements specific rules and useful guides to help LeSS teams with decision-making in large product development situations. Since the roles and guides of LeSS have already been discussed, let's take a moment to dive deeper into understanding LeSS roles, artifacts, and events.

Understanding LeSS roles

LeSS employs the same roles as described in the original *Scrum Guide*, though implemented at scale. For example, there is still only one product owner, anywhere from two to eight Scrum *Feature* Teams, and one Scrum Master for every one to three teams.

Product Owner

The Product Owner in LeSS, particularly in commercial environments, typically has a dual role. Besides the Product Owner role and responsibilities, they also fulfill the product management or product marketing functions. Product management and product marketing business functions focus on defining the product vision and direction, performing competitive analysis, identifying potential value-add innovations, and evaluating market niche opportunities.

When large product teams build products for internal consumption, the product management function is assigned to a lead internal user who has deep domain skills in the application of the product. This *superuser* may be a corporate executive or mid-level manager, as they provide product direction in terms of meeting the needs of affected business operations and delivery functions.

I would also argue that within nonprofit and government agencies, there should be a similar product management role, even if it's not called that. For example, someone or some group must define the target market for their services and their customer requirements and priorities within cost and budget limitations.

In all three scenarios (that is, commercial, non-profit, and government) that have legislative and other industry-based mandates and compliance requirements, the Product Owner must address these with the development teams as prioritized items within the Product Backlog.

Scrum Masters

The role of Scrum Master in LeSS is very similar to the role as described in *The Scrum Guide*. They are the teachers of Scrum and LeSS principles, and they provide coaching and mentoring both during the initial adoption and across the ongoing Sprints over the lifecycle of the product's development and sustainment activities. They provide guidance to team members on how they can best support the product's value creation and value delivery activities using Scrum and LeSS principles.

The primary role of the Scrum Master in Scrum is to help their teams to succeed. Besides providing mentoring and coaching services to team members, Scrum Masters help their teams by coordinating and facilitating events, improving communications, eliminating impediments, and taking on non-development related tasks that would otherwise consume the developers' time.

Scrum Masters must be totally committed to Scrum and should be experts in the use of the Scrum and LeSS approaches to development. The danger is assigning someone from another function within the organization into the Scrum Master role and have them bring their old ways of working and thinking to the position.

Scrum Masters, for example, are not project managers. They don't encourage long-term planning and scheduling of activities. They don't assign work nor dictate the activities of team members. Instead, they encourage the developers to use empiricism, operating within the frameworks of Scrum and LeSS, to frequently deliver new increments of customer-centric value.

Another danger is having an organization define their own versions of Scrum and LeSS, implementing unique rules, roles, responsibilities, events, and artifacts. The elements of Scrum and LeSS are well tested. So, while experimentation is greatly encouraged to continuously improve development and delivery capabilities, the organizations should not stray from the basic elements of the Scrum and LeSS frameworks. In this context, there is no need or benefit in defining new titles, roles, and responsibilities for the Scrum Master.

LeSS views the role of Scrum Master as one of two meta-feedback loops that indicate the degree to which Scrum is working within the organization. The other is the Retrospective. In this context, the Scrum Masters support their teams, and the LeSS product development organization as a whole, reflect and improve in their efforts to continuously seek perfection.

The role of Scrum Master retains the name originally defined in *The Scrum Guide*. There is no such thing as a LeSS Master. But, in LeSS, the Scrum Masters must help to ensure the teams apply systems thinking and whole-product focus, retain the simplicity of Scrum, and ensure complete transparency across all participating teams. The Scrum Master is a full-time job, though they can support up to three teams.

There's one final comment on Scrum Masters in LeSS. Larman and Vodde point to the *The Scrum Master Checklist* by Michael James as an excellent Scrum Master tool. The Scrum Master Checklist provides a series of questions divided into four parts:

- How is my Product Owner doing?
- How is my team doing?
- How are our engineering practices doing?
- How is the organization doing?

The current version of the Scrum Master Checklist also provides a series of *Organizational Impediment Forms*. Michael James makes the point that he would be surprised if a Scrum Master could check off most of these items and still believe they have any extra time left in their day to work on other things.

The Scrum Master Checklist is offered by Michael James under a *Creative Commons Attribution 3.0 Unported License* at the following URL: `https://scrummasterchecklist.org/`.

Feature Teams

Note that LeSS uses the term **Feature Teams** as opposed to Scrum teams or LeSS teams. LeSS makes this distinction to make it clear that each team has cross-functional skills and is able to work across all application and system components to implement whatever features that they sign-on to build.

In the parlance of software developers, they are *full-stack teams*, capable of working across the entire computer system or application under development. That includes having the skills to define the architecture, develop or enhance the frontend user interface, utilize the backend server-based technologies such as middleware, databases, and security components, plus develop the software code that implements the application logic and connects the disparate components of the system.

Teams that do not have full-stack capabilities tend to become single-specialists in specific components of the application or system. That type of specialist focus becomes a limitation in terms of individual teams being able to take on work from the higher priority items listed within the Product Backlog. When development teams must reach further down the Product Backlog to find something they are capable of working on, that is a form of waste in terms of conducting non-value-added work.

> **Note**
>
> It's quite acceptable to have team members who have specialists' skills in several areas. Multi-area specialists provide greater flexibility to a team. For example, a developer who operates as a programmer may have additional "specialist" skills in architecture, requirements analysis, security, or data management.

LeSS provides very specific guidance on structuring Feature Teams as contained in the list that follows:

- Team members are dedicated to one and only one Feature Team.
- Feature Teams are stable with infrequent changes to its members.
- Feature Teams are long-lived, spanning multiple years.
- Feature Teams are cross-functional, cross-component, and fully self-contained.
- Feature Teams are co-located in one facility and one common room.

This completes our introduction to Feature Teams. Now, let's take a look at the artifacts associated with the LeSS extensions to Scrum.

Understanding LeSS artifacts

Recall from *The Scrum Guide* that Scrum implements three artifacts, to include the Product Backlog, Sprint Backlogs, and Increments. Similarly, there are three corresponding artifacts in LeSS:

- One potentially shippable product increment
- One Product Backlog
- Separate Sprint Backlogs for each team

In other words, the Feature Teams as a collective build one potentially shippable product as a new increment of value every Sprint. All of the Feature Teams pull from the same Product Backlog. During Sprint planning, each of the Feature Teams follows the basic Scrum practices of defining Sprint Backlogs in support of their Sprint Goals.

Understanding LeSS events

LeSS maintains the Scum Events of the *Sprint, Sprint Planning, Daily Scrum, Sprint Review*, and *Sprint Retrospective*. LeSS events guide the flow of items through a Sprint, providing opportunities for team members and other stakeholders to meet at planned intervals throughout each Sprint cycle.

It's important to note that, the majority of the time, members of the Feature Teams work on their planned task assignments and do not attend meetings. The primary purpose of Scrum and LeSS events is to provide touchpoints for enabling transparency, planning, coordination, and problem-solving. As with Scrum, transparency enables inspection and adaption based on observation and experimentation. All events are timeboxed to minimize the likelihood of meetings becoming overly long and non-value-added.

Part one of LeSS Sprint planning

Sprint planning is broken out into two parts to collaboratively decide what is to be built and how. The first Sprint Planning session is attended by the Product Owner and the teams or representatives from the teams. The purpose of the first Sprint Planning session is to make a first pass at determining which items in the Product Backlog will be worked on and by which team. Similar to the Nexus approach, the teams look for opportunities to work together while also ensuring they minimize any cross-team dependencies.

Product Backlog Refinement (PBR) workshops

PBR in LeSS is an activity that is familiar to all Scrum variants but now performed on a scale that involves multiple development teams. LeSS implements PBR as a workshop where participants clarify their understanding of the items with users and other stakeholders. Larger items are split and (re)estimated.

Product Backlog Items (**PBIs**) assignments come after the refinement process so that all teams participate in the learning process and gain a broader perspective of how the PBIs fit within the whole-product concept. Having all of the teams acquainted with the PBIs strengthens each team's ability to engage where needed, which improves overall agility. Moreover, having the teams work together during the PBR workshops helps them to identify and resolve coordination and integration issues at the earliest stages of Sprint Planning.

LeSS identifies four types of PBR workshops to include an **Overall PBR**, a **Multi-team PBR**, a **Single-team PBR**, and an **Initial PBR**. Of the four, the most important is the Multi-team PBR, as it provides an opportunity for the members of two or more teams to collaborate on the refinement of specific PBIs before making team assignments. The teams take on PBI assignments, often by volunteering, based on best fits and interests.

During the first Sprint Planning session, the participants conduct an overall **PBR** workshop to clarify the requirements. Multiple Feature Teams may collaborate on the assessments of certain items during the PBR. The team should decide as late as possible which team will do which work. This ensures the teams as a collective retain maximum agility and responsiveness to customer priorities until the product group is ready to finalize their Sprint Goals and Sprint Backlogs.

During Sprint Planning, it's important that the representatives take care to spread the work out so that no single team has all of the high priority items. Balancing high priority items across teams spreads the risk and reduces the possibility that one team could negatively impact the ability of the product group to deliver a potentially shippable increment.

Volunteering preferred

In LeSS, the Feature Teams are encouraged to volunteer in the selection of items from the Product Backlog that they would prefer to work on. They may choose items because they have specific interests or skills that make them well-suited to develop the item. Having said that, it's important that the items selected from the Product Backlog are among the highest priority items viewed by the Product Owner and team representatives as contributing to the Sprint Goal. It's important that the teams do not simply choose the easiest items to avoid the more difficult but higher priority items.

Feature Teams may identify opportunities where it makes sense to work together because their tasks are related during the upcoming Sprint. This is conceptually similar to the concepts in Nexus where teams collaborate to address dependency and integration issues. The primary difference is that LeSS does not implement a formalized role that is similar to the **Nexus Integration Team** (**NIT**). Dependency and continuous integration requirements are worked out directly amongst the team representatives.

As you'll see in later sections, the LeSS frameworks rely much more heavily on Continuous Integration and Automated Build processes, plus communications by code strategies, to facilitate cross-team integrations and dependencies at scale. Where NEXUS allows for specialist operating within the NIT, LeSS prefers the teams build these skills organically.

Part two of LeSS Sprint Planning

The second Sprint Planning sessions are conducted at the team level where they will decide how they will do the work associated with building their selected items. The output of the Sprint Planning Two sessions is the definition of work required to construct a single, integrated, and potentially shippable increment that meets a common definition of Done.

In LeSS, the Feature Teams may choose to go it alone from the start, or they may choose to participate in a multi-team Sprint Planning meeting to review how they will go about implementing closely related items. In other words, the multi-team Sprint Planning Two sessions allow the teams to conduct a deeper dive into resolving dependency and integration issues.

Conducting multi-team planning sessions

The multi-team Sprint Planning Two sessions are timeboxed. The session starts with a brief 10-minute introductory session to discuss shared work and design issues. This brief meeting helps to ensure the teams have a common understanding of the details they need to work out. In the next stage, the teams spend 30 minutes at a whiteboard to talk through the issues and visualize potential solutions.

After 30 minutes, the teams break out into separate areas within the room to conduct their team-focused Sprint Planning Two sessions. The teams work through the design issues and work tasks related to constructing their items within their individual Sprint Planning Sessions Two events. As with Sprint Planning in Scrum, the output of Sprint Planning Two sessions is the individual team Sprint Backlogs.

LeSS includes three multi-team PBR guides to improve cross-team understanding and diversity of views during the planning sessions. These three multi-team PBR guides are as follows:

- **Team mixing**: This creates temporary groups with members spanning all participating Feature Teams to increase diversity of views, experience, skills, and interactions.

- **Rotation refinement**: Rotate the mixed teams on 30-minute increments to different locations and whiteboards, to take over the previous group's refinement activities. One or two members of the original group, who are usually the domain experts, stay behind to explain the previous group's work.

- **Diverge-merge cycles**: After working separately, the teams merge into one large group to share their insights, ask questions, and assess areas for coordination.

LeSS employs two types of workshops to support Sprint Planning, one for multi-team level planning and the other to support team-level Product Backlog Refinement. These workshops are the subjects of the next two subsections.

Conducting multi-team design workshops

As the individual teams work through their design issues, it may become apparent that the teams need to get together to build a joint and consistent design for their related work items. The multi-team design workshops allow the affected teams to work through their design, dependency, and integration issues as a collaborative effort. This is a 1-hour timeboxed event at a whiteboard that allows the teams to visualize their joint approach and bring attention to common technical tasks.

Taking a bite

LeSS teams are usually working on very large, integrated, and complex business and systems related problems. During the refinement process, there will be times when the Feature Teams do not have sufficient information to decompose a backlog item into lower-level stories and tasks. However, if the item is a high priority, they may not be able to hold off on getting started. In such cases, the teams take a slice of the larger problem to fully understand and implement it. This is called **taking a bite** in LeSS.

The initial bite may not solve the overall business problem or requirement. However, the act of clarification and development leads to a greater understanding of the larger problem. Through ongoing development and feedback, taking one bite at a time, the teams can incrementally expose and build out the component details of the larger requirement.

This completes the introduction to LeSS Sprint Planning Events. Now let's move on to looking at the events associated with LeSS Sprints.

LeSS Sprints

As with all Scaled-Scrum approaches, all Feature Teams participate in a single Sprint event and all working in parallel to deliver a new increment of value. In other words, the Feature Teams cannot schedule and conduct their Sprints asynchronously, nor can the teams pull items from the Product Backlog that are inconsistent with the priorities established for the Sprint.

The work of each Sprint is to develop and test code to produce desired features, each conforming to their definitions of done and producing an integrated and potentially shippable product. Since the increment involves collaborative work spanning multiple development teams, it's important that the teams work from a common integration environment and that they integrate and test their code continuously and frequently.

Developing code

Larman and Vodde encourage development techniques that originated in **Extreme Programming (XP)** and especially **Test-Driven Development (TDD)**, unit testing, and mob programming.

TDD is a style of programming that combines three activities as a single integrated process: design, coding, and testing. But, as the name implies, the critical aspect of this technique is to first write a test in which a successful pass indicates the code's compliance with requirements and acceptance criteria.

In other words, programmers write a test, then develop the associated code, and run the test to ensure the code passes. Also, developers should run the test against the mainline code before writing their new code. The initial test against the mainline code helps to ensure the new code will not replace or interfere with other code that's already written.

Developers should always strive to write just enough code, as simply as possible, to pass the test and no more. If the code does not pass, then the developer knows they missed something. Whether the code passes the test or not, the developers should look for ways to refactor the code into even simpler constructs that meet the compliance criteria. Refactoring helps to make the code more readable, less complex, sustainable, and—if later needed—extensible.

Unit testing is also an important part of TDD. Unit tests are much more granular scripts that specify a set of conditions and inputs and the expected outputs that should result from the execution of a small *unit* of code. A *unit* of code is the smallest subset of code that can standalone. Here, again, developers write unit tests before they develop as it forces the programmers to think through their code design and implementation.

Mob programming is a technique where the whole team works together on solving a particular coding problem. One programmer does the coding (also known as the driver), and their code is displayed on a screen or projector large enough for the other team members to observe. To keep things fresh for all members, the team will rotate the members through the driver position across agreed intervals of time.

Mob programming is useful across the entire devilment cycle, including the refinement of user stories, producing a working design, coding, testing, and deploying software. The team may invite customers and business and domain experts to provide information.

Resolving issues

Issues and questions will arise during each Sprint that must be addressed in a timely manner. Any process or organizational structure that impedes quick resolution is inconsistent with the value and principles of Agile. A rule within LeSS is to decentralize decision making to the lowest levels and allow information coordination and communications. This rule is further outlined in the LeSS guide of *Just Talk*.

Communication among developers does not always have to be in written or verbal form. When a product group implements a continuous integration environment, all developers have visibility to all of the other developers' code. Since code is built using common programming languages, the developers can, in effect, communicate via their code.

Communicating in code

As described previously in the sessions on Nexus and XP, the LeSS approach identifies the need to develop a common **continuous integration** environment. However, Larman and Vodde describe continuous integration as an opportunity to communicate in code. A key aspect of communicating in code is the idea of developers *breaking the build*. When a team works from the same mainline truck, as managed in a source control repository, new builds are bound to break. Having a build break is not a bad thing to happen, as it serves as a prompt that the teams need to get together to communicate and coordinate their activities.

In short, communicating in code simply means the developers can see who else is changing the code they are working on and, therefore, know when they need to reach out to other developers to coordinate their activities. In effect, the code offers a way to inform and support their coordination activities.

Automating tests

Similarly, Larman and Vodde promote **TDD** to write test automation scripts before starting the right code. This strategy ensures the continuous integration of the developers' code and their associated test automation scripts. The objective of having a continuous integration and test environment is to discover and fix any bugs immediately with each code integration. The accumulation of bugs is a form of technical debt that makes it increasingly difficult to resolve and ultimately increases waste in the form of non-value-added bug-fix work.

Running the test automation scripts with the integrated code quickly identifies any bugs that have cropped up as a result of implementing the new code. While unit testing helps to fix bugs in each developer's new code, integration testing ensures their new code functions with the existing mainline code that is maintained in the shared repository.

However, the developers need to determine whether the integration problem is with the implementation of their code or their understanding of the implementation of the other developers' code. In short, code integration failures indicate it's time for the developers to get together and talk. The goal is to make sure the mainline code is always maintained in a shippable state.

Maintaining a potentially shippable state

Having many teams working in collaboration sets up the same issues faced by developers in the traditional Waterfall model, in that the large code base developed across each Sprint is likely to contain numerous bugs that need to be discovered, located, and fixed. Building tests scripts in advance of writing code and then integrating both the code and tests frequently with the mainline code prevents a mad rush at the end of each Sprint to get all of the teams' code integrated and tested. In short, TDD along with CI practices ensures the product is always maintained in a potentially shippable state.

So, in summary, during the Sprint, the development team continuously integrates and tests their code, uses automated testing to streamline the dev-test process, and stops and fixes any problems when and as they arise. They do not let problems accumulate as errors in the code. Such a strategy ensures the code is always potentially ready for release into production. CI also eliminates the need to install separate integration and testing teams that only add costs, delays, and unwanted complexity to the development value stream.

LeSS Daily Scrum

The smaller LeSS framework implements the Daily Scrum events as originally described in *The Scrum Guide*. Each team has its own Daily Scrum. And the members within each team discuss their accomplishments, upcoming tasks, and any impediments that they need help resolving. There is not a formal joint-team Scrum meeting such as with Scrum of Scrums or the Nexus Daily Scrum implementations.

> **This is a specific rule within LeSS:**
>
> Cross-team coordination is decided by the teams. Decentralized and informal coordination is preferred over centralized coordination. Each team has its own Daily Scrum.

Rather than incorporating a new role and event for managing cross-team dependencies and integration requirements, LeSS encourages the use of informal *Scouts* to observe Daily Scrum events and coordinate cross-team activities. The Scouts are simply individual team members who volunteer to participate in another team's Daily Scrums when they have related tasks to synchronize.

Scrum Masters also help to coordinate cross-team and stakeholder communications when required to resolve the issues. However, the team members should never wait on a formal or informal process to communicate. When collaboration is needed, the members should get together and *just talk*—which is one of the LeSS guides associated with coordination and integration issues. There should be no impediments that prevent team members from talking to other members and stakeholders to resolve problems or collaborate in decision making.

LeSS Sprint Review

The LeSS framework implements only one common Sprint Review and all team members from all Feature Teams participate. Members from external organizations or departments, interested stakeholders, users, trainers, and customers are also invited to participate. External participants are drawn from the community of organizations and people who are most impacted by or benefit from the delivery of the new increment.

The Sprint Review starts off with a one-hour timeboxed event to showcase the increment. These events are typically conducted as a **Bazaar** or **Science Fair** type format. With multiple Feature Teams contributing to the increment, the product group sets up multiple tables with computing equipment and other devices to allow participants to visit the displays with the features they are most interested in.

Some Feature Team members will stay with their team's display throughout the Bazaar, while others will migrate through the other displays to review the new features. As those members visit each display, they listen in to comments and participate in conversations to gain a broader perspective on how the increment is perceived as a whole by the participants.

At the end of the hour, the participants and team members come together in a joint session to answer any questions and provide further commentary and feedback. The Product Owner also uses this time to discuss market and competitor factors and to provide guidance on where they believe the product needs to go to remain competitive and value-added.

LeSS Sprint Retrospective

Each team conducts a separate Sprint Retrospective after the Sprint Review meetings. There is no discernable difference in LeSS-based team-oriented Sprint Retrospectives than those identified in *The Scrum Guide*. The outcome of the team Sprint Retrospectives is experiments to run in the upcoming Sprints, plus a list of cross-team and systems related issues that need to be brought to the larger product group for improvements.

LeSS also implements an **Overall Retrospective** to give the teams an opportunity to discuss cross-team dependency, integration, and system-wide issues. Rather than force yet another event on the last day of the previous Sprint (that is, Sprint Reviews and team Retrospectives) or try to cram it in with the Sprint Planning sessions, the Overall Retrospective is pushed out to at least the second day of the new Sprint.

The outcomes of the Overall Retrospective are improvement experiments to conduct in the current Sprint. Product Owners, Scrum Masters, and team representatives attend the Overall Retrospectives. Business executives and managers (if they exist) may also attend.

LeSS rules and guides

You have already learned the concepts behind LeSS rules and guides. The important takeaway in terms of this section on the smaller LeSS framework is that certain LeSS rules apply only to the LeSS framework, while the LeSS guides apply to both the LeSS and LeSS Huge frameworks.

Now that you have a fundamental understanding of the LeSS framework, let's move on to discuss the LeSS Huge framework.

Implementing the LeSS Huge Framework

As with the smaller LeSS framework, the LeSS Huge framework comes with a series of LeSS rules and LeSS guides to assist with the implementation and sustainment of Scrum practices applied across multiple teams working on a single product. The larger LeSS Huge framework typically applies to eight or more teams working in collaboration on a single product. The issue with applying LeSS Huge to a smaller number of collaborating teams is the unnecessary amount of overhead and local optimizations induced by the larger organizational structure. The LeSS Huge framework is shown in *Figure 10.3*:

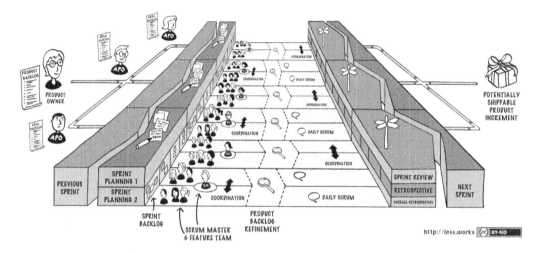

Figure 10.3 – The LeSS Huge Framework

Notice that it follows the same basic pattern as the smaller LeSS framework, depicted in *Figure 10.2*. But also note the repeating pattern in the LeSS Huge graphic, depicted in *Figure 9.3*. You may be wondering what it is that is repeating. In the next subsection, you will find these are teams assigned to unique Requirements Areas.

LeSS Huge product development efforts may involve hundreds to thousands of people trying to work in a coordinated fashion to build a large and complex product. There is literally no other option but to split the work out among the participating teams. But the question is how? To answer this question, we need to take a look at the extended roles, artifacts, and events of the LeSS Huge framework that enable scaling and then discuss the concepts behind coordinating the activities of eight or more feature teams.

Defining artifacts, roles, and events

LeSS Huge installs some variations on the traditional Scrum roles, artifacts, and events. Let's review these elements before moving on to discuss the organizational structures that allow scaling beyond eight Feature Teams.

LeSS Huge artifacts

The artifacts of LeSS Huge include the artifacts of the smaller LeSS framework to include the one potentially shippable product increment, one Product Backlog, and a separate Sprint Backlog for each Area Feature Team. In addition, LeSS Huge implements the **Requirements Area** artifact.

Requirements Areas are compositions of the larger product along the lines of its unique features. Requirement Areas include multiple Feature Teams but with additional structure to help to align the teams around specific categorizations of the requirements. We can think of product categorizations as different views into the Product Backlog.

The overarching Product Owner slots each PBI into one and only one requirement category (that is, Requirements Area). The area Product Owners have the responsibility to guide the development of the PBIs assigned to their assigned product categories, guiding the efforts of the Feature Teams within their associated Requirements Area. The groups of PBIs within a product category are supported by its Requirements Areas, which are effectively scaled up Feature Teams:

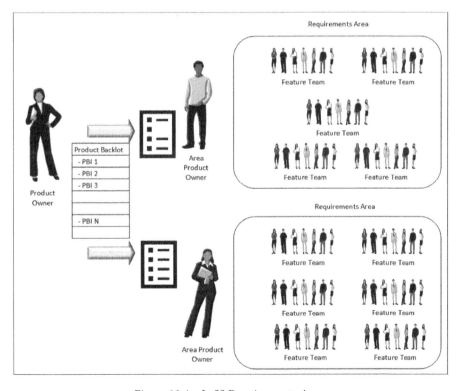

Figure 10.4 – LeSS Requirements Areas

Requirement Areas support customer-centric requirements, and their Feature Teams speak in the vernacular of the customer. The assigned Feature Teams have collective ownership of the subsystem code that they support. Requirement Areas are temporary organizational structures, and they will change and evolve over the life of the product. However, change should not occur with every development iteration.

Finally, a Requirement Area is a large cohesive group of related customer requirements that may span the entire code base of a product. Hence, the Feature Teams must have the domain and technical skills to support the entire product. Now, let's move on to discuss the roles of LeSS Huge.

LeSS Huge roles

LeSS Huge includes two additional roles, the **Area Product Owner** and **Area Feature Teams**. With increased scale, it becomes progressively more difficult for a single Product Owner to grasp all the details when managing the entire Product Backlog. While the Product Owner is still responsible for optimizing the value of the larger product, the Area Product Owners take on the responsibility of managing the details of feature level prioritization and capabilities. Collectively, the Product Owner and the Area Product Owners make up the Product Owner Team.

LeSS Huge manages the complexity of coordinating a large number of Feature Teams by dividing the work into unique Requirements Areas. The Feature Teams assigned to a Requirements Area take on the role of Area Feature Teams. Area Feature Teams have deep domain knowledge that is relevant to their assigned Requirements Areas.

LeSS Huge events

As with the smaller LeSS framework, LeSS Huge maintains one common Sprint for all Requirements Areas and their Area Feature Teams. The outcome of the Sprint is one common potentially shippable product increment.

Now that we understand the artifacts, roles, and events of LeSS Huge, we can move on to understand how to coordinate the activities of eight or more Feature Teams.

Scaling with LeSS Huge

The traditional functional-based organizational decompositions don't work for all the reasons described in *Chapters 5, Lean Thinking,* and *Chapter 6, Lean Practices in Software Development on Lean Development*. Functional decompositions lead to non-value-added waste in the form of carrying too much work in process and batching delays, which leads to an accumulation of excessive bugs and defects that are difficult to locate and fix.

Functional organizations increase the time to achieve an ROI, install unnecessary operational complexity and inefficient bureaucracies, and put the focus on managing cross-functional business processes instead of adding value.

The goal of the LeSS, as with all Lean-Agile development approaches, is to always retain a customer-centric focus. Internal politics, excessive organizational structures, and bureaucracies are not customer-centric. They do not add value. Instead, they add complexities, inefficiencies, and costs, which are all forms of waste.

The LeSS framework avoids these issues by scaling the small team concept of Scrum to break the work out along *features*. However, at roughly eight teams and beyond, the management and coordination of all of the small teams become increasingly complex and challenging tasks. To avoid these issues of scale, LeSS Huge organizes the Feature Teams around common areas of work called **Requirement Areas**.

Establishing Requirements Areas

Requirement Areas are defined by strongly related features from the perspective of our customers. In other words, the Feature Teams within a Requirement Area all work to develop items that collectively deliver customer value across a slice of the larger whole-product. Feature teams instantiated within LeSS Huge are assigned to a Requirement Area and become specialists in that area for as long as their expertise is needed, at which point they may move into another Requirement Area.

Requirements Areas are features based and contain between four and eight Feature Teams. In effect, each Requirement Area is an instantiation of the smaller LeSS framework around a slice of the larger product requirement.

Requirement Areas are dynamic and not static organizational structures that persist over time. In fact, a Requirement Area can grow and shrink over its existence, based on current development needs. Individual Feature Teams may join together or split apart (that is, merge and diverge) and move from one Requirement Area to another.

Since the Requirements Areas work as a collective, let's take a closer look at how they operate.

Area Product Owners

LeSS Huge retains the requirement to have one and only one overall Product Owner who maintains responsibility for item prioritization and team assignments to Requirement Areas. However, each Requirement Area has assigned one Area Product Owner who works with the Overall Product Owner to provide further clarification on their features and requirements. This minimizes the burden placed on the overall Product Owner to address questions across the numerous Feature Teams.

Organizations with large product groups often have multiple product managers who as a collective are responsible for developing the overall business and marketing strategies behind the product, specifying its functional requirements, and deciding on the priorities and timing on the release of features. Such product managers are typically good candidates to take on the additional responsibilities of the Area Product Owners roles.

However, this strategy may not be possible for much larger products where the product management works too large to take on additional responsibilities. Regardless of where they come from, the Area Product Owner is a specialist in their Requirement Area, and they have direct responsibility for achieving their Area Product Backlog assignments.

Area Feature Teams

Teams assigned to work within a Requirement Area are called an Area Feature Team. Area Feature Teams only work in one Requirement Area and they work directly with the assigned Area Product Owner during Sprint Refinement and Sprint Planning Events. Conceptually, each Area Requirement Area functions in a coordinated fashion that is similar to how Feature Teams operate in the smaller LeSS frameworks. It's critical that each Area Feature Team becomes, if they are not already, experts in the domain of the Requirement Area.

An added benefit of implementing domain-specific Area Feature Teams is that they tend to work with a limited subset of the code base that is directly related to their work. This strategy limits how much of the code they must master to become proficient.

As with the smaller LeSS framework, the number of Feature Teams within each Requirement Area is limited to eight. However, a Requirement Area should never have fewer than four Area Feature Teams. The objective is to not create overly broad Requirement Areas that have minimal value-added benefit. For example, the addition of smaller Requirement Areas leads to the following problems:

- Lowers Feature Team visibility into product-level priorities

- Tends to increase local optimizations

- Increases the number of teams increases coordination complexity

- Adds overhead with increased numbers of Area Product Owners and Scrum Masters

- Feature teams become too narrow and specialized, the opposite of being Agile

- The Area Product Owner position becomes more of a business analyst role—meaning they spend more of their time acting as a middleman running requirements between the domain experts and the Feature Teams

The one exception to having a limit of four teams assigned to a Requirement Area is during the startup of an area and when rebalancing teams during product transition periods.

Area Product Backlog

You learned previously that LeSS has one and only one Product Backlog. Feature Teams then take a slice of the Product Backlog, during Sprint Planning, to define a Sprint Backlog that encompasses the work they expect to achieve in the upcoming Sprint. But their Sprint Backlogs are still a slice or a view of the larger Product Backlog.

Similarly, each Requirements Area establishes a view of the Product Backlog that represents the slice of work their Feature Teams have agreed to take on. The Area Product Backlog is not a separate artifact. Rather, each item in the Product Backlog has a field or annotation to indicate its assigned Requirement Area.

Running a LeSS Huge Sprint

Events within a LeSS Huge Sprint are similar to other Scrum approaches, such as Backlog Refinement, Sprint Planning, Daily Scrums, Sprint Reviews, and Sprint Retrospectives. But it's the mechanics within LeSS Huge that make the difference in scaling Scrum across eight or more teams. In this section, you will learn how LeSS Huge implements Scrum events at scale.

Product Owner team meetings

So long as they pull high-priority items from their respective Area Product Backlogs, Area Product Owners operate autonomously in decision making. Other than for reasons of clarity, there is no need for the Area Product Owners to seek verification of themes, item priorities and alignment from the overall Product Owner. Nevertheless, there is the risk that the Area Product Owners can lose context in terms of themes, item priorities, and alignment of their respective Areas relative to the whole product. The resolution is to schedule Product Owner team meetings prior to the start of Sprint Planning Events.

The objective of Product Owner team meetings is to align and coordinate the activities between Area Product Owners and their respective Requirements Areas. The Product Owner outlines the objectives for the upcoming Sprint and provides guidance on current product priorities and direction. This meeting also provides an opportunity for the Area Product Owners to share their current situations and upcoming goals and objectives.

Area Product Backlog Refinement

In LeSS Huge, PBR occurs at the level of the Requirements Area, with each Requirements Area acting in the same manner as a LeSS framework PBR. The items selected by the Requirements Area for refinement come from their respective Area Product Backlogs.

As with all variances of Scrum, there is only one Product Backlog. Area Product Owners do not spin off a subset of the items in the Product Backlog into a separate Area Product Backlog. Rather, LeSS Huge extends the Product Backlog to include information fields to annotate which Requirements Area each defined item is assigned, providing visibility on all item assignments. This approach helps to retain the whole-product focus that is necessary to keep the disparate development efforts aligned with the objectives and priorities established by the overall Product Owner.

Figure 10.4 shows how the annotations might look within a Product Backlog, using the applications of an **Electronic Health Records (EHR)** system as a sample set of the Requirements Areas:

EHR System Product Backlog	
PBI Item	**Requirement Area**
AB	Administration
AA	Billing
AF	Patient Information
AG	Medical Histories
AD	Diagnostics (ICD-10 Codes)
AH	Pharmaceuticals
AF	Immunizations
AE	Radiology Imaging
AG	Laboratory Testing & Results
AC	Progress Notes

Figure 10.5 – EHR System: Product Backlog item assignments by Requirements Area

Note that the identified Product Backlog items, as annotated in *Figure 10.3*, are uniquely assigned to just one Requirement Area. These are just two of the information fields provided in the Product Backlog. The other fields within the Product Backlog are those found in traditional Scrum practices, such as PBI ID, PBI Name, PBI Story/Description (Optional), Epic (Optional), Theme (Optional), Estimate, and Priority.

EHR System Product Backlog	
PBI ID	**Requirement Area**
AA	Billing
AI	Billing
AN	Billing
AZ	Billing
BA	Billing
BC	Billing

Figure 10.6 – EHR System: Billing Requirements Area Item Assignments

Figure 10.5 is a subset of the Product Backlog sorted by the items assigned to the Billing Requirement Area. This slice of the overall Product Backlog represents the Area Product Backlog for the Billing Requirements Area.

Figures 10.5 and *10.6* provide fairly simple examples of Product Backlog Refinement. Sometimes the identified Product Backlog items are too large to complete within a single Sprint or by a single Area Feature Team. In those cases, we need to split the PBIs into two or more smaller and more granular stories.

Splitting PBIs

So far, the PBR process as expressed is fairly simple. But once the Area Teams begin to drill down into the requirements of each PBI, some will turn out to be too large to be defined as a single story. In such cases, they must be split into two or more smaller stories. However, PBI splitting causes another set of issues in the Product Backlog that must be addressed.

For example, splitting PBIs creates additional clutter and granularity issues that make it difficult for the overall Product Owner to absorb. Also, the split stories may have different priorities than the original PBI before it was split.

There are two strategies offered by LeSS Huge to address these issues. One strategy is to define a new field in the Product Backlog and call it *Annotations* to indicate the stories split off from the original PBI. The split items are clones of the original PBI but with their own item numbers to establish their individual priorities. The annotations field data indicates the original PBI from which the new story was split. Product Backlog reviewers can use filters to expose the desired level of detail. *Figure 10.6* shows a product backlog that includes split PBI IDs in the PBI column plus an Ancestors column to show their associated higher-level PBIs:

EHR System Product Backlog		
PBI	Requirement Area	Ancestor
AB	Administration	
AA-1	Billing	AA
AF	Patient Information	
AA-2	Billing	AA

Figure 10.7 – PBI Story splits prioritized within the Product Backlog

Care must be taken when a PBI decomposes into a number of Stories that have a wide range of priorities. There must be a balance between how information is exposed at the Product Owner's level of detail and the need to provide granularity on stories and items at the development level. An Area Product Owner may choose to create a separate artifact to manage all of their splits, but that strategy takes away visibility that allows the overall Product Owner and other Requirements Areas and Feature Teams to see the whole-product picture and dependencies. On the other hand, keeping everything in the Product Backlog with filters to limit displays increases complexity and opens up each Story to micromanagement by the overall Product Owner.

There's one final note on splitting in LeSS Huge. It's possible that split stories also end up being too large to work with. Consequentially, the Area Product Owner and Requirements Area teams may be inclined to split yet again some of their original PIS splits. This is simple to accomplish with appropriate identifiers in the Annotations field. However, LeSS Huge discourages splitting PBIs into more than three levels. The issue is the splitting becomes more of a convenience than an exercise to define a unique and separate customer-centric objective to justify the split.

The PBI Refinement process is an ongoing activity. A refined and prioritized Product Backlog allows the LeSS Huge teams to conduct their Sprint Planning events. As with the smaller LeSS framework, there are two Sprint Planning sessions in the LeSS Huge framework: Sprint Planning One and Sprint Planning Two sessions. Sprint Planning One is a multi-team event at the Requirement Area level, while Sprint Planning Two sessions can include a combination of multi-team and single-team events at the Feature Team level.

Part one of Area Sprint Planning

Sprint Planning in LeSS Huge occurs at the Requirement Area level. Conceptually, each Requirement Area operates identically as the smaller LeSS framework Sprint Planning sessions. The difference in LeSS Huge is the Requirement Areas pull from the list of PBIs annotated in the Product Backlog as belonging to their Area Product backlogs. There are no other special rules for Sprint Planning in LeSS Huge.

Area Product Owners participate in the Sprint Planning One sessions and provide guidance to the teams on the objectives and focus of the desired product increments over the next few Sprint iterations. Working with the Product Owners and domain experts, the feature teams evaluate the items assigned to their Requirements Areas (that is, Area Product Backlogs) to assess the estimates and work tasks associated with each item. They also assess architectural and design impacts associated with the new item priorities.

Domain experts who have relevant experience in terms of the current Sprint Goals are encouraged to attend both the Sprint Planning meetings and PBR workshops. This ensures their knowledge helps to inform the decisions being made by the teams during planning.

Teams are encouraged to take a bite out of the larger high-priority tasks that are as yet unrefined. This allows the teams to get started and use experimentation with feedback to further decompose the requirements, which, in turn, drive future development activities.

Product development priorities change over time. During Sprint Planning, based on input from the Product Owner and Area Product Owners, the Requirement Areas prepare for the addition and reduction of Area Teams to ensure they stay aligned with current and upcoming priorities.

Multi-team planning

In LeSS Huge, each Requirement Area holds an initial Sprint Planning One meeting. Since this is a LeSS Huge Sprint Planning event, there are, at a minimum, eight teams involved. Organizing the teams along Requirements Areas minimizes the number of teams involved in the initial multi-team Sprint Planning Event. Still, each Requirements Area has anywhere from four to eight teams to organize and coordinate. This is why LeSS Huge implements the multi-team PBR.

Multi-site Sprint Planning

Another challenge often associated with organizations engaged in large product development is the need to coordinate and integrate work across teams that are geographically dispersed. The teams may have been obtained through an acquisition or established by the company to take advantage of available labor, skills, and lower costs not available at their corporate and other development sites.

LeSS discourages the use of multi-site teams whenever practicable. The issues associated with timely communications and WIP delays associated with managing work across multiple time zones greatly reduces the operational efficiencies of the LeSS Huge Requirement Areas. Language barriers also present a problem when there is not a common language shared among the team members. In short, the organization must weigh the economic benefits and impacts of efficiencies when considering the employment of teams operating across geographic and international boundaries.

Nevertheless, many if not most large product organizations will have multiple development sites, and there are many cases where the costs and access to labor and skills make economic sense. The factors to consider include the following:

- Labor and skills are not locally available.

- Labor and operational costs are considerably reduced at other geographic locations.

- Dispersed teams have in-depth product and domain knowledge.

- Each independent team is self-managing, cross-functional, co-located, and long-lived.

- Scrum Masters are co-located with their respective teams.

- There is a minimum number of time zones between the site locations.

- The teams speak a common language, even if it's a second language to some members.

- All teams are willing and able to participate in the joint LeSS Huge events.

- A travel budget that provides some opportunities for face-to-face meetings with the Area Product Managers, domain experts, and team members.

To facilitate the multi-team and multi-site LeSS Huge events, each site must provide a large room with remote network connections, laptops, overhead projectors, audio-video conferencing software, online collaboration and document sharing tools, adequate wall space for breakout sessions, whiteboards, and access to backend computing services.

Part two of Area Sprint Planning

With the completion of the multi-team/multi-site Sprint Planning sessions, the individual teams break out to conduct their Sprint Planning Two sessions. The simplest approach is to have the individual Feature teams within each Requirement Area meet separately. Though the Feature Teams meet separately, they are encouraged to meet at approximately the same time. The goal of the Sprint Planning Two sessions is to review design requirements and create their Sprint Backlogs of PBIs and associated tasks.

Larman and Vodde also promote the use of multi-team Sprint Planning Two sessions for both LeSS and LeSS Huge. This is a particularly relevant strategy when two or more teams previously collaborated during a PBR workshop, and now need to coordinate and integrate their activities during the Sprint Planning Two meetings. Multi-team Planning Two sessions are multi-stage and typically include the following sessions:

- Whole-group question and answer session

- Whole-group design and related work session

- Single-team design and planning sessions

- Merge, if required, to discuss emergent issues from the single-team sessions

Multi-team Sprint Planning sessions help teams that are strongly related—across requirements and designs—to work through design, coordination, and integration issues across shared work.

Identifying new Requirement Areas

Over the course of the life of a product, there can be numerous drivers that create the need for standing up new Requirements Areas. For example, there can be legislated compliance requirements, such as the **Sarbanes-Oxley (SOX)** Act of 2002 and the Dodd-Frank Wall Street Reform and Consumer Protection Act of 2010. In addition, the product management group might identify new niche market opportunities that drive the need to install new product features or applications not previously anticipated.

When these opportunities present themselves, the Product Owner must identify an Area Product manager who has the domain knowledge and experience to support the development initiative. Similarly, a Scrum Master and Feature Teams must be identified or constructed to support the development activities. Ideally, these folks will come from other Feature Teams whose activities are winding down. Additional teams can be developed from scratch over time as conditions warrant.

Once the Area Product Owners and initial teams are identified, the Area Product Owner conducts an initial PBR to begin the refinement process for the list of items identified for the new Requirement Area. Given that this is a new initiative, it's likely that the requirements are not yet well defined. This is the perfect opportunity to use the *Take a Bite* guidance to get the initial development activities started. Once started, through experimentation, reviews and feedback, the Area Product Backlog grows and matures in definition.

One common Sprint

Just as the Feature Teams in the LeSS framework cannot operate independently of the other Feature teams, Requirement Areas have the same discipline. There is only one Sprint at a time, and all Requirement Areas and their Feature Teams operate in the single Sprint event.

LeSS Huge implements the single Sprint requirement as a rule.

> **In LeSS Huge, integrate continuously in one common sprint**
>
> There is one product-level Sprint, not a different Sprint for each Requirement Area. It ends in one integrated whole product, and all of the teams across all Requirement Areas are striving to integrate continuously across the entire increment.

From this LeSS Huge rule, it should be apparent that all of the rules of continuous integration apply, as described in the previous LeSS framework section. It's also important to note that the large item requirements, dependencies, and integration issues require time and effort to resolve. The Feature Teams should fully expect to spend between 10% to 15% of their time on learning and clarification activities.

Multi-area reviews and retrospectives

Less Huge does not implement special rules for multi-area Reviews and Retrospectives. Instead, all Sprint LeSS rules apply to each Requirement Area.

Although not required, LeSS allows via its guidance the opportunity for multiple teams, including up to all teams participating in the full Product Group, to provide a whole-product Review. There are logistics issues associated with coordinating a whole-product review, and oftentimes, users and other stakeholders have a specific focus in one or maybe a handful of the Requirement Area increments.

Given the logistical complications and interest levels, it usually doesn't make sense to facilitate a whole-product review in every Sprint. Instead, it's better that users and stakeholders can focus on the Requirements Areas Review they are most interested in and have the ability to contribute to the most.

For similar reasons, LeSS Huge does not have a rule that requires whole-product Retrospectives. However, there are times when a whole-product Retrospective is needed. Whole-product Retrospectives are helpful when the teams spanning the Requirements Areas are not working well together or when they are facing similar issues. Whole-product issues tend to span cross-team integration, dependency, and coordination issues.

One final comment on Sprint Planning and Retrospectives in Less Huge: it's not unusual to have multiple Feature Teams that span multiple Requirements Areas working in collaboration on common capabilities or integrated work. In such cases, it's best to have the teams working from the same site location to facilitate communications, joint learning, and relationship building. Everything gets harder with multi-site locations.

This ends the section on LeSS Huge, and you should now have a fundamental understanding of the LeSS framework and LeSS Huge framework. Before we move on to the next chapter, let's take a little time to understand how to implement and improve the adoption of LeSS.

Adopting the LeSS Frameworks

In this section, you will learn the LeSS rules and guides associated with LeSS adoptions. These rules and guides make it easier to get started and minimize the opportunities for things to go wrong.

LeSS adoption rules

Many if not most people are afraid of change, particularly when they feel they or their jobs are threatened or if they fear marginalization of their roles and authorities. LeSS adoption rules offer instruction on how to overcome organizational resistance. Specifically, LeSS implements two general rules for LeSS adoption:

- For a product group, establish the complete LeSS Structure *at the start*; this is vital for a LeSS adoption.

- For the larger organization beyond the product group, adopt LeSS evolutionary *Go and See* to create an organization where experimentation and improvement is the norm.

Based on these LeSS rules, a few things should be quite clear. First, don't attempt to short-change the LeSS adoption. LeSS is rules and guides have been tried, tested, and improved over time and build on the even more tested foundations of Scrum. Moreover, in the smaller conditions that warrant a LeSS framework adoption, go ahead and implement the entire LeSS framework all at once—that means all of the teams, roles, artifacts, and events necessary to implement LeSS across the large product development effort.

Second, the discipline of LeSS is a product development strategy. Larman and Vodde do not attempt to describe a LeSS adoption in other areas of the business beyond encouraging the adoption of *empirical process control theories*, as described in *The Scrum Guide*. Empirical process control, or *empiricism*, asserts that knowledge comes from experience, observation, and experimentation. Having the concepts of empiricism installed, over time and organization-wide, so that it becomes an accepted cultural norm, will make it easier for the LeSS teams to operate.

The second rule of LeSS adoption also emphasizes the use of a LeSS guide titled *Go See*. **Go See** is another term for the **Gemba** practices described in *Chapter 5, Lean Thinking* applied to software development.

LeSS adoption guides

LeSS guides are not meant to be prescriptive rules. Instead, they provide information on strategies that have proven useful in certain situations. However, it's up to the LeSS team members to decide on their usefulness in their particular situations. LeSS implements a number of guides for adoption, as outlined here:

- **Three Adoption Principles**: These are as follows:

  a. **Go deep and narrow over broad and shallow**: Choose one area for LeSS adoption, and do it well before attempting to install additional Feature Teams and Requirements Areas.

  b. **Top-down and bottom-up**: People at the top support the adoption, while people at the bottom bring the enthusiasm and energy to make the adoption a success; both ends benefit.

  c. **Use volunteering**: As opposed to dictating the initial adoptions. The teams should decide which products initially move to LeSS and the Feature Teams and people should have input on the teams they want to join.

- **Getting started**: This is done by educating everyone, defining the scope of the product, defining the definition of Done, creating approximately correct teams, having only one Product Owner, and not installing project managers to run the teams.

- **Culture follows structure**: The organization cannot force cultural change; the change in culture comes from successful adoptions where people see the results and buy-in to the new way of working.

- **Job safety but not role safety**: People need to know their employment is secure in the LeSS adoption, even if their former roles are eliminated.

- **Organizational perfection vision**: This is with a focus on global systems improvements over local optimizations, and encouraging experimentation, agility, and innovations.

- **Continuous improvement**: This means implementing retrospectives, with everyone involved, to achieve true improvements in terms of quantifiable customer-centric value.

- **Growing your adoption**: This can be done across products, with better definitions of done, with new teams, and through expanded product definitions, shared learning, and better support and by leveraging the energy and enthusiasm of the preceding teams.

The preceding LeSS adoption principles and guides help the teams to overcome the natural resistance to the changes associated with the adoption of the LeSS frameworks and their development strategies. Now that you understand the usefulness of LeSS rules and guides on adoptions of the smaller LeSS framework, let's look at how the LeSS rules and guides that apply to the LeSS Huge framework.

LeSS Huge adoption rules

Existing large product groups, those that ultimately require numerous Requirement Areas and more than eight feature teams, will find much more resistance to the LeSS adoption. Some of the resistance comes from the need to fulfill customer commitments and the fear the transitions will get in the way. A scaled Scrum adoption always brings political challenges when executives and managers fear losing the positions of authority they have within the traditional hierarchical and bureaucratic organizational structures. And it's hard to provide qualified coaches, mentors, and trainers at scale.

With these issues in mind, LeSS implements two general rules for LeSS Huge adoption:

- LeSS Huge adoptions, including the structural changes, are done with an evolutionary incremental approach.

- Remember each day: LeSS Huge adoptions take many months or years, infinite patience, and a sense of humor.

From these rules, it should be clear that the adoption can't be forced. Instead, the organization must take an incremental approach to implement the complete LeSS Huge structure over a period of time, often months or even years in duration.

What will help to get the organization through the LeSS adoption process is the continuing improvements along the way and the patience to see it through. And since we know perfection is always sought, but never fully achieved, we know there's always more we can do to further improve the adoptions.

LeSS Huge adoption guides

Just as you learned in the section on LeSS framework adoptions, LeSS guides for LeSS Huge adoptions provide ideas that have proven useful in larger multi-team LeSS adoptions. The following list introduces LeSS Huge guides for adoption:

- **Evolutionary Incremental Adoption**: This means a gradual and incremental adoption across the whole product group, with a focus on deep LeSS implements at the start before trying to implement LeSS more broadly.

- **One Requirement Area at a Time**: Where benefits are high and risks are relatively low, build on successes from there.

- **Parallel Organization**: During the adoption, keep the new LeSS requirements separate from the existing development operations using coordination and integration techniques where synchronization is necessary.

The initial teams adopting LeSS cannot operate as a Pilot. They are responsible for building, testing, and delivering a potentially shippable increment at the end of each Sprint. They must follow LeSS rules and guides to be successful and to demonstrate the strengths of the LeSS approach.

Assuming the organization is using a single source control management system and integration servers, which we know they should, the new Requirement Area teams must refrain from branching their code base. In other words, they must not maintain a separate code base for the product as it's extremely difficult to merge their code into the mainline. The teams need to operate in parallel, working from the same product and central codebase, and creating feature branches directly off the mainline code.

One final point on LeSS Huge adoptions. Unlike the smaller LeSS adoptions, where LeSS is installed immediately across the product group, LeSS Huge is implemented incrementally over time. Developers working in the existing development organization must understand the LeSS adoptions are the way of the future. Executive management must make it clear in their communications that everyone will eventually move into a LeSS Requirement Area and related Feature Team.

The communications need to be consistent and continuous to avoid creating a situation where the old and new development organizations establish a competitive rivalry. Competition is not the point of installing LeSS Team. Creating potentially shippable increments of customer-centric value at the lowest possible cost is the point of LeSS.

This ends the content related to understanding the LeSS. In the next section, you will learn the best use cases for LeSS adoptions.

Evaluating best fits

The two LeSS frameworks are all about scaling the theories and practices of Scrum beyond the implementation of two teams. In this context, LeSS fits well where the empirical process control theories and principles of Scrum are preferred. However, the organization has begun to experience growing pains with its initial Scrum team implementations, and the executives know something has to change. In other words, the organization needs to expand the number of Scrum teams but also needs to understand how to operate successfully in a large product development environment.

A start-up organization can adopt LeSS from its beginning if they already know they will need to expand in size to justify three or more Scrum teams immediately. However, a more likely scenario is the start-up company has already grown such that the original Scrum framework needs modifications to support its continued growth.

Another scenario occurs when an existing large product operates within a traditional organizational structure (that is, hierarchical, bureaucratic, or project-oriented). Eventually, the organization's executives will find they are unable to meet customer demands or compete in their markets or are losing money and their skilled people. In such cases, senior management must be willing to make the commitments necessary to reorganize their development operations around value.

The previous section on LeSS adoptions includes the *LeSS Guide* on the *Three Adoption Principles*, which states that implementations require a combination of top-down and bottom-up endeavors. That is undoubtedly true. No matter how strongly the existing Scrum practitioners may feel about the need to scale their Scrum structures and practices, it won't happen without executive management support and their commitments to see it through.

Commitment means the senior executives and managers must be willing to let go of their previous titles and authorities. They must embrace the fact that change is necessary for the good of the organization and their employment or monetary considerations. Most people don't want to be on a *burning platform*. But therein also lies the problem: lots of people don't recognize when they are on a burning platform. Or they try the same old approaches that got them into trouble in the first place—as Albert Einstein said:

> *Insanity is doing the same thing over and over and expecting*
> *a different result*

The reality is that it's hard to jump off a burning platform into a sea of change. But that's precisely what it takes for a traditionally managed organization to adopt LeSS successfully. If their current situation is not sufficiently harsh enough to force them off their platforms, the chief executives and business owners should still consider taking preemptive actions. They need to be able to visualize the future benefits of building efficient business and development operations that have an organic ability to compete in all market conditions.

If the company is a public company, they have a more significant hurdle to cross. Now the Chief Executive Officer must convince their board, shareholders, and market analysts that this change is in the best interests of the company and its shareholders. Such a move will be considered risky, and the CEOs must establish a clear vision, timeline, and expected results.

So, in conclusion, chief executives and business owners have to make two decisions before adopting LeSS. First, they must subscribe to the benefits of implementing Scrum's empirical process control theories and organizational structures. Second, they must be willing to communicate and stand behind their vision of a changed organization and oversee its execution from start to finish.

Summary

In this chapter, you have learned how the LeSS approach implements Scrum at scale in the development of Large Products. The LeSS framework provides the structure to manage between three and eight Scrum teams, while LeSS Huge provides the structure necessary to manage eight or more teams.

Beyond the addition of Requirements Areas in LeSS Huge, LeSS does not try to change the basic roles, artifacts, and events of Scrum. Rather the goal is to maintain the simplicity of Scrum at scale. Adding complexity through new roles, artifacts, and events or maintaining hierarchical and bureaucratic organizational structures are antithetical to the values and principles of Agile, and not in alignment with the goal to create an innovative organization.

You have learned that LeSS implements a series of LeSS rules and LeSS guides. LeSS rules are minimal though prescriptive to ensure the organization stays true to the LeSS philosophies of scaling Scrum with minimal changes to the original Scrum framework. LeSS guides are based on past heuristics (that is, trial and error) of practices that sometimes work in certain contextual situations. Product Groups, Product Owners, Requirements Areas, and Feature Teams use observation, experience, and experimentation to evaluate potential options to achieve desired outcomes and for improvements. LeSS does not believe in the use of so-called *best practices*—as they seldom are.

LeSS is differentiated from the other pure Scrum scaling concepts, such as Scrum of Scrums, Scrum@Scale, and Nexus, through the inclusion of systems thinking and Lean development concepts. In this regard, LeSS has an advantage for those organizations that understand and wish to employ systems thinking and Lean development concepts in their scaled Scrum adoptions. LeSS also offers additional guidance in the form of LeSS rules and LeSS guides that users may or may not decide to implement in support of their specific situations. For those who want to learn more, LeSS offers a number of case studies to review on their website (`https://less.works/case-studies/index`).

This concludes this chapter on the **Large-Scale Scrum (LeSS)** frameworks. In the following chapter, *Chapter 11, Disciplined Agile* you will learn how **Disciplined Agile (DA)** extends the basic Scrum framework with Lean-Agile and DevOps practices. Moreover, DA provides hundreds of optional techniques to explore in context with process goals and decision points. *Chapter 14, Contrasting Scrum/ Lean-Agile Scaling Approaches* includes a comparative analysis of all scaled Scrum and Lean-Agile practices introduced in this book. Every approach mentioned in this book has something to offer and different sets of strengths in terms of capabilities and applications. In this chapter, you have learned the capabilities and benefits of this approach. *Chapter 14, Contrasting Scrum/ Lean-Agile Scaling Approaches* offers more context with the contrasts against other Scrum/ Lean-Agile approaches.

Questions

1. True or False: LeSS is a nearly sufficient framework that is deliberately incomplete and allows for situational learning through observation and experimentation, as opposed to enforcing prescriptive rules and formulas.

2. Why does an organization use LeSS to scale Scrum?

3. Production of non-value-added increments, excessive work in progress, and non-value-added processes are all examples of what?

4. What is Shu-Ha-Ri?

5. What are the three common elements in LeSS and LeSS Huge?

6. What is the dual role of the Product Owner in the LeSS framework?

7. What is the outcome of a Sprint in LeSS?

8. What is the unique artifact associated with LeSS Huge, and what is its purpose?

9. What is the major difference in rules between LeSS and LeSS Huge adoptions?

10. Why do the initial LeSS Huge teams operate in parallel but in distinctly different reporting structures during LeSS adoptions?

Further reading

- Larman, C. and Vodde, B., *Scaling Lean & Agile Development Thinking and Organizational Tools for Large-Scale Scrum*, Pearson Education, Boston, MA: Inc. (2009)

- Larman, C. and Vodde, B. *Practices for Scaling Lean & Agile Development: Large, Multisite, and Offshore Product Development with Large-Scale Scrum*, MA: Pearson Education, Inc., Boston, (2010)

- Larman, C. and Vodde, B., *Large-Scale Scrum: More with Less (Addison-Wesley Signature Series (Cohn))*, Pearson Education, Inc., Boston, MA (2017)

11
Disciplined Agile

So far, you have learned how Scrum evolved to support Agile practices at the team level, as well as the importance of systems thinking and Lean development practices to reduce complexity and improve efficiencies. You have also learned a good bit about the leading Scrum-based practices that provide extensions to scale Scrum across multiple teams, if not on an enterprise scale. Now we are going to turn our attention to the first of three approaches that extend the original Scrum framework with systems thinking, DevOps, Lean–Agile, and portfolio-management practices. This approach is called **Disciplined Agile (DA)**.

As implemented by DA, systems thinking helps organizations to look at complex products and organizational structures as an integrated whole, and not the sum of their parts. Systems thinking prevents local optimizations that work against system-level functionality and performance. DA's implementation of Lean–Agile practices integrates value-creation and value-delivery processes to support business agility on an enterprise scale.

In this chapter, you will learn about six different Tooling your W approaches that support Lean–Agile development and delivery. The choice of which life cycles to use is left to the participating DA teams. You will learn how to apply the four layers of the DA toolkit that support different scales of implementation and serve as the foundations for business agility. You will also learn how DA provides guidance on hundreds of potentially useful techniques in context with Process Goals and Decision Points. The key differentiator in DA is its emphasis on having choice as opposed to following prescriptive guidance.

The following list describes the main topics we will cover in this chapter.

- Determining your way of working

- Finding context

- Tooling your way of working

- Choosing your level of agility

- Putting it all together

- Lean governance and milestones

- Best fits

The Project Management Institute Inc. (PMI), has recently acquired the rights to Disciplined Agile. As a result, all graphics and information cited in this book, related to Disciplined Agile, are now copyrighted under PMI. Copyrighted materials include Project Management Institute Inc., Disciplined Agile Website, 2020. Copyright and all rights reserved. With this introduction, let's begin your learning journey with DA. We'll start with an introduction to DA's concept of defining your '*way of working*'.

Determining your way of working

Disciplined Agile is unique among scaled-Agile Scrum and Agile concepts. Its ethos is that teams should have flexibility in choosing their **way of working** (**WOW**). We are going to use the WOW acronym a lot in this chapter, and if you decide to continue your studies in DA, you will see the WOW acronym used frequently. If you get stuck trying to understand why DA uses the WOW acronym in a sentence, just remember to interpret the term *WOW* as *way of working* and know that DA presents an alternative way of working that team members can evaluate for their use.

Scrum and all of its scaling variants claim not to be formalistic or prescriptive. They are considered **frameworks**, which means that they serve as a container to enforce the disciplines of empiricism within an iterative and incremental development paradigm. Beyond that, development teams can use whatever practices, methods, and tools they believe will best suit their needs.

The primary caveat to the use of preferred practices, methods, and tools within Scrum is that they should not interfere with its empirical model, and Scrum teams should never become complacent in their efforts to improve upon their practices. In this context, all Scrum variants lay claim to the notion that they are not prescriptive, and when compared to the traditional plan-driven, linear, sequential development model, that statement is true.

DA claims that other Scrum variants are, in fact, prescriptive in that they force teams to adopt a particular Scrum practice across the entire organization. Without getting into methodology wars, that statement is somewhat true. If the executives of an organization choose and mandate a specific scaled Scrum strategy, the executives expect all teams to follow suit.

In this chapter, you will learn that DA implements *six product life cycle* approaches that each team within an organization can choose from, regardless of the life cycles selected for use by other groups across the organization. Moreover, DA identifies **Process Goals**, with common **Decision Points** that in turn provide instruction on the hundreds of potential, yet optional, approaches to address issues that the teams may face.

This decision making is what DA means when it advises you to *choose your WOW!* Each team faces unique situations and issues, and therefore each team should be free to try out different sets of options to see what works best for them. Their selected approaches become their WOW until their needs and situations evolve, necessitating new ways of working.

Those who are familiar with Scrum are probably rolling their eyes and saying something like, *Agile practitioners are free to use whatever practices, methods, and tools they prefer in Scrum; what's so unique about DA's view?* The answer is a bit complicated, but the bottom line is that each Scrum variant brings a relevant, though situational, strength.

We'll look at this difference between Scrum-based Agile methodologies more closely in *Chapter 14, Contrasting Scrum/Lean-Agile Approaches*. For now, the essential thing to know about DA is that it is unique in its view that each team is free to choose a scaled-Agile approach that best suits their specific needs. Moreover, DA provides context-sensitive information on hundreds of potentially useful but optional techniques supporting common desired process outcomes.

With this understanding, we can now move on to discuss how context drives your WOW.

Finding context

DA allows disparate teams within the same enterprise to choose their WOW based on situational needs and context-specific choices. This statement means that each team must evaluate their needs and select the techniques that best apply to their situation. Still, if the team members are not aware of the potential solutions to their problems, they'll have to spend time and effort on research to uncover proven and applicable approaches. Moreover, if the team is under pressure to make a decision and move on, they may employ a suboptimal strategy.

The better approach is to have a library or knowledge base of identified practices, placed in context with the types of problems that the development team is likely to face. This context-based knowledge base of potential techniques is the approach that DA takes to help guide team decision making.

In this sense, DA is a toolkit of hundreds of optional methods and tools with decisions and tradeoffs for the team to consider before choosing an approach to address their problem. While DA takes a lot of the guesswork out of decision making, teams must make the appropriate context-specific choices based on their intentions and activities for any given option.

Under DA, teams make context-specific choices through the lens of four perspectives: *Mindset*, *People*, *Flow*, and *Practices*. This chapter will provide an overview of each of these four perspectives. Let's start with a quick look at the DA mindset

Mindset

As a means to achieve business agility, DA encourages the development of a Lean–Agile mindset on an enterprise scale. Instead of enforcing, the adoption of a specific set of practices to cover all needs, DA encourages team members to learn how to evaluate and apply Lean and Agile practices based on desired goals and objectives. In this sense, DA extends the foundations of Agile and Lean while establishing a mindset grounded on specific **Principles**, **Promises**, and **guidelines**.

Principles

Organizations that employ DA improve their business agility by eliminating waste and improving customer value on an ongoing basis by implementing Lean development and optimized flow concepts. But the DA organization must also establish a set of guiding principles that help the team in decision making. The following *Figure 11.1* includes a display of DA's principles in the left-hand panel.

Promises

People do business with people, as my mentor and friend, Jim O'Malley, used to tell me when I worked as a consultant helping our customers use our CASE-based modeling software to work through their production and business efficiency issues. If you believe this adage to be accurate, then you must also understand that there is an unspoken but vital WOW that creates a trusted business relationship. DA practitioners make promises to establish trust, as shown in the middle frame of *Figure 11.1*.

Guidelines

So far, we have learned that DA helps organizations establish a Lean–Agile mindset to achieve business agility, provides principles to guide our behaviors, and offers a set of mutual promises that allows DA teams and stakeholders to work cohesively and collaboratively. The final view of decision making is to follow a set of guidelines that help us improve and be more successful in our way of working. *Figure 11.1* displays the DA guidelines in its right-hand frame:

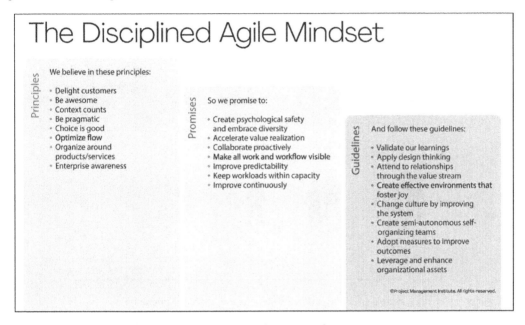

Figure 11.1 – The DA mindset

This section concludes the discussion on mindset as a perspective to evaluate team intents and activities and make appropriate context-specific choices from listed DA options. Now let's learn how **people**, in the form of roles, responsibilities, and team structures, assist in this process.

People

DA implements roles that appear similar to those of other Scrum-based practices, though some of its terminologies are a bit different. The founders of DA, Scott Ambler and Mark Lines, prefer terminology that has explicit semantic meaning as opposed to an esoteric or domain-specific language that is difficult for laypeople to understand. Also, DA implements roles that map well to traditional software-development team structures, Agile or otherwise. So, let's get started by looking at the roles at the **DA delivery (DAD)** at team level.

Staffing small DAD teams

DAD teams have pretty much the same types of roles as described in the Scrum Guide, with a couple of modifications to the names and responsibilities; however, the most notable change is the inclusion of a new **Architecture Owner** role. While this role is new to Scrum, it comes from Agile modeling practice-based methodology, conceived around the 2004–2005 time frame. *Figure 11.2* shows the most common model for configuring a small DA team. (For more information on Agile modeling, go to http://www.Agilemodeling.com/essays/architectureOwner.htm):

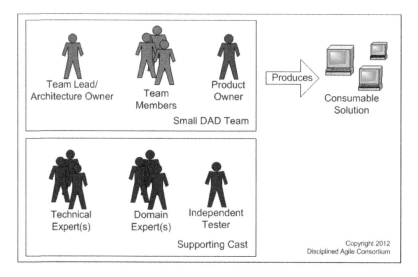

Figure 11.2: Organization structure of a small Agile team

The following subsections describe the DA roles and responsibilities at the DA-team level.

Stakeholder

The **stakeholder** is a role that includes customers, end users, managers, executives, operations team members, and anyone else whose needs are supported by the solution under development. stakeholders are listed first to remember who we work for and why.

Product Owner

As with Scrum, the **Product Owner** represents the collective interests of all stakeholders and presents a single voice to clarify their needs and priorities. In DA, the Product Owner is responsible for tracking down the answers to questions about specific needs or clarifications so that the team members can stay focused on their work tasks. The Product Owner is the team's direct point of contact for stakeholders, and the Product Owner sets up demos and provides product status updates to stakeholders.

Team Lead

The Team Lead role is similar to the Scrum Master role in terms of responsibilities, providing leadership to the team as a guide, mentor, and coach to help the team discover and improve their WOW and to continuously deliver incremental value. They may also serve as a team member in DA or be assigned to serve two to three teams on larger projects.

When DA teams do not have a Project Manager, the Team Lead may pick up some of their duties, such as providing team members' assessments, managing the team's budgets, obtaining resources, and facilitating meetings. Smaller DAD teams may have Team Leads who are also team members. Or, if they have the skills and time, the Team Lead may also have the Architecture Owner role.

Scott Ambler, one of the founders of DA, adds this additional guidance on the Team Lead role:

> *"Team Lead is really a meta role, or more accurately a superclass role in OO terms. Different teams need different types of Team Leads. A Scrum team needs a Scrum Master, or Senior Scrum Master. A project team needs a project manager or project leader. A functional service team needs a functional manager such as a Chief Architect, CFO, or Chief Procurement Officer. So, we introduce the role of Team Lead to reflect this idea – have a fit for purpose leader of a team, and that's not always a Scrum Master. It's also an agnosticism issue."*

It should be clear from Scott's statement that DA's WOW concepts apply to leadership and management roles and structures. Where traditional Scrum-based practices attempt to force organizations to adapt their structures and verbiage, DA doesn't attempt to fight battles that the DA team members and proponents cannot win. In other words, oftentimes we have to live within the organizational structures installed by the entities' executive leaders and the business domains and value streams the organization must support.

Architecture Owner

The Architecture Owner role is unique in DA's agile-based teams, but will not be unfamiliar to many project-oriented development teams. DA implements the Architecture Owner role to ensure that the team has someone with the appropriate skills to guide the architecture and design decisions for the solution under development.

The traditional project-oriented development model initiates and completes product-requirements analysis and architecture and design-related activities before starting development. DA's agile lifecycle supports iterative development practices to build, test, and deliver new increments of value frequently as customer needs and priorities evolve. Architecture and design requirements under Agile methods need to develop in lockstep to support new and changing customer requirements and preferences. As a result, the Architecture Owner must be skilled in the discipline of building and supporting evolutionary architectures (*Building Evolutionary Architectures, Ford, Kua, Parsons. 2017*).

Team members

Team members collaborate to produce a solution (product, service, or result) for stakeholders. Members perform activities in iterative cycles that support the development and delivery of a product. The iterative activities include requirements analysis, planning and estimating, architecture and design, programming/development, testing, provisioning, and deployment.

DA includes three leadership roles within a DAD team:

- **Product Owner**: The **Product Owner** has the responsibility to make sure that the teams build the right product.

- **Architect Owner**: The **Architecture Owner** has the responsibility to ensure that the teams build the product correctly.

- **Team Leader**: The **Team Leader** is responsible for making the product fast—that is, in the Leanest, most efficient manner possible.

> Note
> There are no senior members among these three leadership roles.

They work in collaboration to build the right product, correctly, and in the quickest time possible. If one of the coleaders assumes more power over the others, the result is an imbalance that affects the desired outcome against the other leaders' responsibilities.

The roles defined in this section are organic to the DA-based development teams. But sometimes we need specialists, which is the topic of the next section.

Supporting DAD team roles

DA takes a pragmatic attitude to the adoption of Lean–Agile practices and roles, at least initially, by understanding that the DAD teams may require access to supporting skills that are not available within their teams. In both the short and long run, it may make sense for the organization to maintain roving professionals. These professionals should have specialist skills as independent testing, domain and technology expertise, and system integration. Likewise, nondevelopment teams, such as those supporting business domains or delivery value streams, may require access to specialists and consultants in their fields. Additionally, DA does not confine roles as strictly as the Scrum-based practices. Instead, DA describes a number of roles, each with unique skills, operating on different levels of the DA toolkit. This is the topic of the next section.

Supporting organizational roles at scale

So far, this section on DA roles has had an IT-based orientation; however, to support business agility strategically across the organization, it's important to recognize that non-IT roles need to evolve too. This issue is one of the reasons why there are so many roles in DA—to ensure support for both value creation and value-delivery activities across value streams and product lines.

DA Process Blades introduce additional roles and responsibilities. For example, the Portfolio Management blade introduces the role of Portfolio Manager/Coordinator and the Operations blade introduces the roles of Operations Manager and Operations Engineer. At the time of writing, DA includes descriptions of 39 roles spread across the original DA layers, as depicted in *Figure 11.3*:

DAD Scaling Roles	Disciplined DevOps	Disciplined Agile IT	Disciplined Enterprise Roles
• 8 Roles	• 10 Roles	• 9 Roles	• 12 Roles

Figure 11.3: DA roles and the layers of DA

> **A word of caution.**
>
> Roles define a type of skill and related responsibilities. The organization's executives must resist the temptation to make the additional roles formalized positions. Roles are temporary, and individuals may assume more than one role at any given moment and over time. The whole point of being Agile is to have the flexibility to do what's right for the moment. Formalized positions tend to move the organization back to hierarchical and functional organizational structures.

For more information on the topic of organizational roles in DA, visit the webpage at `https://www.pmi.org/disciplined-Agile/agility-at-scale/disciplined-Agile-roles-at-scale`. In addition, DA is in the process of updating this section to reflect its new layering strategy. The designated DA roles should remain, but will be moved around into the new layers.

Managing larger Agile teams

DA recognizes the research that suggests a preferred Agile team size of between 5 and 9 members is best; however, from a pragmatic perspective, the organization may have limited resources to build separate locations as a DAD team grows beyond the desired small team size. It may also be challenging to divide work constructively among a relatively small development organization that still has more than 11 people.

Regardless of the size of a product-development organization, a DAD team structure forms the nucleus of all DA development efforts—that is, Product Owner, Team Lead, Architecture Owner, and team members supporting and interacting with external stakeholders. As the team grows beyond the small team size, the Team Lead and Architecture Owner roles are broken down into separate positions, as shown in *Figure 11.4*. Also, the teams usually include one or more specialists, who augment the core DAD team's capabilities.

In such cases, DA organizations have implemented Agile teams with as many as 25 people and still manage network-density issues. For example, having the teams stand around whiteboards during the daily coordination meetings is one way to facilitate team communications while simultaneously keeping the meeting length under control.

Establishing the team-of-teams

As an Agile team grows to 25 to 50 people, DA promotes splitting the group into a **team-of-teams** structure. The teams can be broken down by components, features, functions, or as an open source collaboration, as discussed in the next subsection.

In a team of team structure, each subteam conducts daily coordination meetings (also known as daily standup meetings and daily Scrum events). Within DA, cross-team integration, dependency, and coordination activities are resolved in a traditional **Scrum-of-Scrums (SOS)** meeting, as defined in *Chapter 8, Scrum@Scale* on SOS concepts. A typical medium-sized DA team-of-teams organizational structure is shown in *Figure 11.4*:

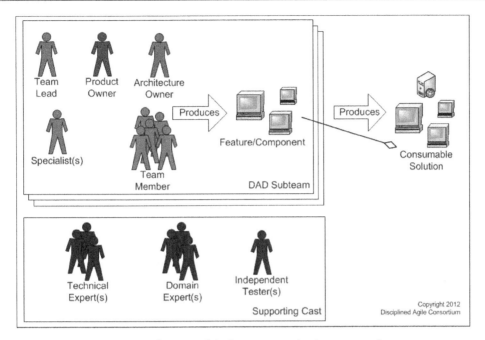

Figure 11.4: Medium-sized Agile team organized as a team of teams

Now that you understand how DA scales from small- and medium-size DAD teams to DAD team of teams, let's revisit the subject of how the subteams may be organized.

Organizing subteams

As noted in the previous subsection, DA recommends four approaches to splitting large Agile teams into team-of-teams structures. Each approach has pros and cons associated with it, and each team's unique circumstances will guide their preferred WOW.

In a component team structure, each subteam develops one or more subsystems or modules. While this is a logical breakdown, recall the issues identified with this strategy in *Chapter 9, The Nexus Framework*—that is, *software components represent small slices of functionality, and many components may not have a development requirement within the current sprint*. This strategy means that the component teams may have to reach down into their product backlog to find work, and those items may not have the current highest priorities. Also, the instantiation of features and functions often involves changing multiple software components, making it more challenging to coordinate dependency issues.

The feature team structures are ideal if each of the subteams has the depth and breadth of skills to work across the technical scope of identified work within a vertical slice of functionality. For example, large enterprise solutions may have applications or large software modules devoted to supporting one vertical slice of a business, such as order entry, payroll, procurement, or financing. On the other hand, this structure is suboptimal if a feature does not justify full-time development by at least one DAD team.

A functional team structure breaks out subteams based on life cycle aspects of the solution under development, such as an architecture team, a development team, a testing team, an integration team, and a deployment team. This structure is inconsistent with the fully self-contained and autonomous team ideals of Agile and Scrum. But if the volume of work is large enough, it may work well in a Lean development structure. The biggest concerns, though, will be in managing task-switching, sequencing, and **Work in Process (WIP)** issues associated with product handoffs between functional teams. Product-oriented Kanban boards with a pull-oriented development philosophy can help address those issues.

Scott Ambler adds this additional guidance regarding functional team structures:

> *"This really isn't a recommendation that we make, although it can happen. What we do recommend is that large programs adopt an approach where the Architecture Owner get together to become part of an AO team to negotiate evolution of the architecture over time, the Product Owners get together to manage the evolving requirements, and the Team Leads get together to coordinate management issues that fall outside what the AOs and POs take on."*

In other words, since we are dealing with multiple teams working in collaboration, rather than break down their skills along functional lines, it's much better to employ cross-functional teams and leverage the Team Leaders to discuss, negotiate, and agree on how to proceed at the points of overlapping concerns and dependencies.

Figure 11.5 shows the preferred organization structure of a large team:

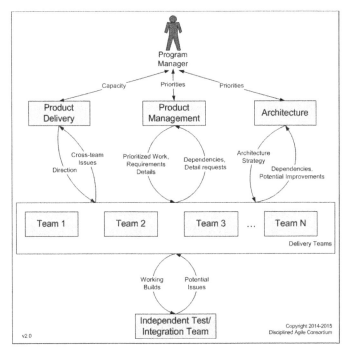

Figure 11.5: High-level organization structure of a large DA team

The internal open source teams' strategy mimics the public-oriented open source development practices. In other words, developers from multiple teams can work on any of the components to evolve them over time as needs, priorities, and team availabilities dictate. Rather than assign one component or one feature to a team, any team or developer can improve on a component or feature of the solution at any time. The critical issue here is to ensure that each team has the necessary technical and domain skills to span the scope of work across the solution.

Supporting large teams and programs

The founders of DA have observed that the SOS-based coordination begins to fail at the scope of 4 to 5 subteams. Once a DAD team grows to 35 or more people, the organization expands the team-of-teams concept to include as many teams as necessary to support the larger products or multiple products under development, but with new leadership and integration structures.

Similar to the concepts presented in *Chapter 8*, *Scrum@Scale* approach, the organization installs leadership teams to support communications and collaborations across the subteams while minimizing network-density issues through the hub and spoke concept. These leadership teams form around product coordination, product ownership, and architecture ownership.

In other words, the members of the Product Coordination Leadership Team include the team leads supporting the DA subteams. In contrast, the Product Management Leadership Team (also known as Product Owner Leadership Team) includes the Product Owners, and the Architecture Owner Leadership Team includes the Architecture Owners. Also, an Independent Test and Integration Team may be required to help the teams with their large-scale integration and testing concerns.

Let's take a closer look at how these leadership teams operate.

Product Management Team

DA does not mandate the concept of a single Product Owner identifying and prioritizing work as items from a single product backlog. Instead, as you might imagine, DA offers alternative approaches for managing and prioritizing work items. For example, DA allows the use of **Work Item Pools**, **Task Boards**, **Work Item Lists**, and **Requirements (Product) Backlog** to track and prioritize requirements, or the teams may not maintain a prioritized work item list at all. Once again, the teams choose their preferred WOW.

However, most important to our discussion on building a Product Management Team is the notion that all subteams have a Product Owner. The Product Owner role in DA is the person who represents the interests of all product stakeholders. In this context, each Product Owner serves as an intermediary and liaison between the DAD team and the product's stakeholders, facilitating two-way communications and collaborations. Not only are the Product Owners expected to be domain experts, but they are also experts in the product and may demonstrate the product during stakeholder reviews.

As a participant in the Product Management Team, they take their direction from a Portfolio, Program or Product Manager, or Chief Product Owner, as assigned by the organization under its development strategies and the scope of the work undertaken by the DAD teams. Again, the type of lead established for the Product Management Team supports the organization's WOW.

For example, organizations may implement Portfolio Management structures to align product-development budgets and priorities with corporate strategies. Other organizations may prefer to implement program-level structures, usually below the Portfolio Management function, to manage and coordinate organizational resources and budgets more effectively. On the other hand, an organization that seeks to remain consistent with Scrum practices may prefer to have a Chief Product Owner who coordinates the requirements and priorities of the Product Owner Team against a single product backlog.

As a group, the Product Management Team manages requirements, technical issues, and management concerns. The assigned Portfolio, Program, or Product Manager guides the Product Management Team. Whichever role is assigned, that person ensures that the three leadership teams (that is, the Product, Architecture, and Coordination Team Leads) are working well together and are coordinating their activities. Note that, in DA, the subteams and leadership teams are free to operate on different schedules and cadences, or they can operate on the same schedules and cadences, as DA provides options, not prescriptions.

Product Coordination Leadership Team

The **Product Coordination Leadership Team** consists of the Team Leads, and they are collectively responsible for matters relating to onboarding, offboarding, budgeting, reporting, scheduling, and people management, including coaching, mentoring, and knowledge/skills development across the teams. In other words, the Product Coordination Team effectively combines the servant–leader activities of the Scrum Master with the financial and team management responsibilities of the traditional Project Manager.

Depending on the preference of the organization, the Product Coordination Team may be called a *Team Lead Team*, or a *Program/Project/Portfolio Management Office* or *Program/Project/Portfolio Management Office Team*, or more simply a *Management Team*. The overarching Portfolio, Program, or Product Manager or CPO provides direction to the Team Leads who collectively make up the Product Coordination Team.

Architecture Owner Team

The Architecture Owner Team (also known as the Architecture Team, Agile Architecture Team, or Enterprise Architecture Team) develops an architectural strategy at either the enterprise or large-product level. Consistent with the Agile-based concepts of evolutionary architectures, the Architecture Teams continuously evaluates the architectural and design changes necessary to support the currently planned extensions to the products under development. They must communicate the architecture strategies to both the DAD teams and business stakeholders.

As architectural and design issues arise, the Architecture Teams has the responsibility to resolve the issues and communicate necessary changes. For example, the user interface may evolve to support new user needs, and integration concerns may affect the implementation of web services and integration brokers. And, as product services expand, the Architecture Team may need to evolve its **service-oriented architecture (SOA)** or microservices implementation strategies. Their goal is to address architecture and design issues associated with, changes to functional, enterprise, application, and infrastructure services.

Independent Test and Integration Team

Regardless of the size of the DA environment, the local DA subteams retain all responsibilities to create the test scripts and perform local testing. These tests can include, integration testing, acceptance testing, and regression testing; however, as the DA environment grows, or because of regulatory compliance, it may become necessary to install a separate team or multiple teams to manage large-scale testing and conformance verification and validation requirements.

In large product-development requirements, the organization may form an Independent Test/Integration Team to facilitate end-to-end integration testing, performance testing, load, and stress testing, or other system-wide and expensive forms of testing. For example, many of the system-wide performance tests require production-equivalent environments, including hardware, software, and network components. Advanced and expensive software is required to run performance, load, and stress testing that mimics anticipated production volumes, usage, and cross-application/cross-system transactions.

Also, quality-control requirements, particularly in heavily regulated industries and federal agencies, may dictate the use of independent testers to validate conformance with governance policies, safety considerations, and legislated mandates.

CoPs and other Teams

Lean–Agile practices move the organization away from establishing functional departments and hierarchical structures to build, manage, and deploy skills throughout the organization. Such functional structures do not provide sufficient agility to support iterative and incremental delivery of value. Functional organizational structures also do not support the instantiation of integrated and efficient value creation and value-delivery teams working in collaboration. Still, the organization needs some way to build and develop their people's skills and knowledge. In DA, skill and knowledge development is accomplished through the support of **Communities of Practice (CoPs)**, **Centers of Excellence (CoEs)**, and Work Teams.

CoPs are typically informal social learning groups, while **CoE**s are formal learning and skill-development organizations. In contrast, Work Teams support a specific functional requirement, such as Enterprise Architecture and Portfolio or Program Management. The Continuous Improvement Process Group and related Decision Points guide all three types of team in their implementation and improvement activities.

Deciding life cycle flows

This section introduces DA's six **full delivery life cycles** that provide options that DA teams select from based on preferences, situations, and the maturity of each team. As with all things DA, teams get to decide their WOW concerning the selection of their preferred life cycle development approaches. DA's optional life cycle delivery strategies include the following:

- **Exploratory Life cycle**: A Lean startup life cycle

- **Agile Life cycle**: A Scrum-based project life cycle

- **Continuous Delivery**: Agile: Evolved Agile-based life cycle

- **Lean Life cycle**: A Kanban-based project life cycle

- **Continuous Delivery**: Lean-Evolved Lean-based life cycle

- **Program Life cycle**: For a team of teams

The following graphic, *Figure 11.6*, provides a display of DA's high-level system life cycle. This graphic is an abstraction representing the fundamental phases of a products life. The upper part of the DA system life cycle model, depicted through the arrows, shows the initial activities required to develop the product's concept, followed by iterative development cycles. Each new iteration provides an increment of new value that must be transitioned, supported, and eventually retired. The middle bar displays DA's life cycle phases. More about that later. At the bottom section of the figure the double-headed arrows indicate the span in which delivery and DevOps activities take place:

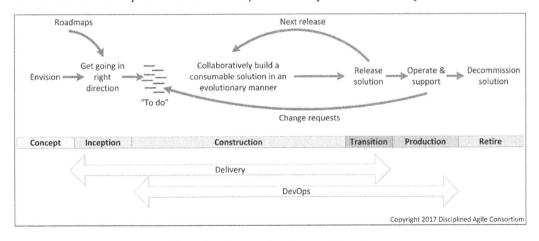

Figure 11.6: A high-level system life cycle

Since there are six life cycles to choose from, DA does not offer a single defined life cycle diagram or product workflow. Instead, each DA life cycle has a unique flow to support its implementation. Before we discuss each of the six life cycles, it's essential to understand the figure's high-level system life cycle view of DA.

At first glance, it may seem that the high-level view mimics the **phases** of the traditional waterfall type **Systems Development Life Cycle (SDLC)**. While there is a commonality in using defined phases to portray significant events in a product's life cycle, the implementation is much different. As the saying goes, *the devil's in the details.*

Rather than get hung up on the word phases, it's more important that we understand the context of their use, as there was nothing inaccurate in these original product life cycle concepts. The only issue with the life cycle phases is that we need to eliminate the plan-driven and linear–sequential processes of the traditional waterfall model.

With this understanding, let's take a quick look at the system life cycle phases:

- **Concept**: The initial phase of a product where the idea is developed and a business case substantiates the market opportunity that justifies the investments.

- **Inception**: Even in Agile practices, time is needed to explore the customer and end-user requirements and define an initial architecture and design (that is, sprint 0 which is when the project is initiated).

- **Construction**: This phase contains the development iterations that deliver incremental value across the life of the product (note the *Next Release* return arrow).

- **Transition**: This phase contains the activities that set up a successful product deployment, such as systems setup, configuration, and support information and training aids.

- **Production**: This phase contains the activities that support a deployed product, such as product release, administration, operations, and support functions.

- **Retire**: This section contains the end-of-life activities necessary to properly migrate data and destroy and dispose of software, data, and hardware assets.

Within the high-level system life cycle sits the six DA full delivery life cycles. We'll review each of the DA life cycles over the next six subsections in the order presented in the open section.

Exploratory Life cycle

The Exploratory Life cycle, as shown in *Figure 11.7*, is used in start-up or research situations for the development of a new product concept where the customer and end-user requirements are ill defined:

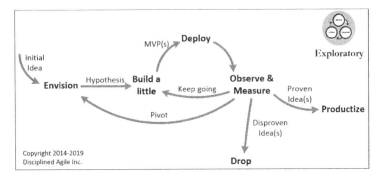

Figure 11.7: DAD's Exploratory Life cycle

In other words, this life cycle can either replace or support both the Concept and Inception phases of a product's life cycle. As the initial requirements are defined and validated by customers, the DA team will move into either an Agile or Lean Development Life cycle. Also, an Exploratory Life cycle may be employed during the life cycle of a mature product when a major overhaul is required to address competitive factors or to explore ways to address niche market opportunities.

After defining the product concept, the DA team may move to implement one of the other DA life cycles, such as the Agile Life cycle introduced in the next subsection.

Agile Life cycle

The **Agile Life cycle** (*Figure 11.8*) is DA's implementation of Scrum and XP practices and supports the Delivery Phase of a product's life cycle. The Agile Life cycle best supports DA teams that are new to Agile or whose teams have not worked together long enough to develop more advanced **Continuous Delivery** (**CD**) skills and capabilities. This life cycle is often adopted by teams taking a project-based approach to delivery:

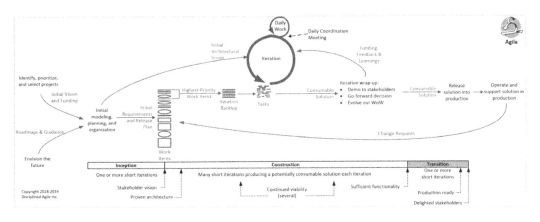

Figure 11.8: DAD's Agile (Scrum-based) project life cycle

The Agile Life cycle incorporates timeboxed iterations to deliver new increments of value with each iteration. DA purposely does not use Scrum-based terminology, opting to apply commonly understood and agnostic terms, such as the word *iterations* instead of *sprints*. Still, DA teams are free to use Scrum's terminology. Again, DA teams are encouraged to use their preferred WOW.

DA teams using the Agile Life cycle have a work item list as their source input for tasks, an extension of Scrum's product backlog. The idea here is to enforce the notion that each DA team must look across all activities that require their time, not just a list of customer requirements. So, for example, a worklist will include tasks to reduce technical debt, fix bugs, take training, or anything else that can require time from its team members. The goal is to make sure that everything is accounted for when planning the work of an iteration.

Note that there are lightweight, risk-based milestones associated with the three phases (listed within its timeline) to support Lean governance.

Continuous Delivery Agile Life Cycle

With maturity and continuing improvements, the DA teams that have implemented Agile practices may evolve to implement continuous-delivery capabilities within the Scrum–Agile framework. Now, instead of two-week or lengthier development cycles, the teams may go to one-week or quicker releases of new capabilities. Some of the critical enablers for continuous delivery are the implementation of test-driven development, continuous integration, test automation, and automated-provisioning capabilities.

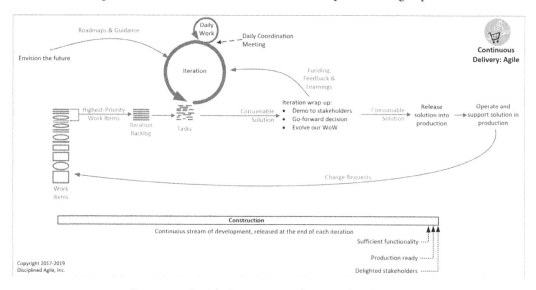

Figure 11.9: DAD's Continuous Delivery Agile Life cycle

This life cycle is typically adopted by teams in organizations with an effective DevOps strategy in place. The preceding *Figure 11.9* provides a graphical display of the Continuous Delivery Agile Life cycle.

Lean Development Life cycle

The DA Lean Development Life cycle implements the concepts outlined in *Chapter 5, Lean Thinking*. DA's Lean Development Life cycle has a focus on minimizing WIP, improving flow, supporting a continuous stream of work (as opposed to timeboxed iterations), and pulling items as capacity allows. *Figure 11.10* depicts the typical DA Lean Life cycle with its Kanban-oriented structure:

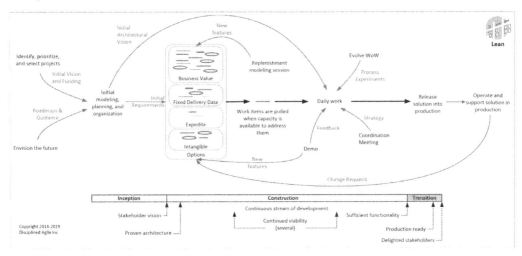

Figure 11.10: DA's Lean Life cycle: a Kanban-based project life cycle

DA's Lean Development Life cycle uses a *Kanban board* to provide visibility on work in progress and to manage the flow. Given the pull-oriented nature of Lean, cadence is set by the slowest activity in the flow (that is, requirement refinement, test script development, programming, integration, testing, and system provisioning). As a result, the DA team practicing this approach should continuously seek ways to refine their processes to streamline the flow by minimizing the setup and cycle times for each activity within the flow.

Interestingly, DA promotes this life cycle as potentially useful on project-based work. The idea is that, by their very nature, projects have detailed plans and schedules that allow work to be pulled from an identified queue of tasks.

The continuous-development nature of Lean also means that there is no reason to implement the formalized ceremonies of Scrum, such as Sprint Planning, Daily Scrums, Sprint Reviews, and Sprint Retrospectives. These activities create interruptions to the flow, and therefore represent forms of non-value-added activities, or waste, in Lean. Instead, teams only meet when they identify a need that justifies stopping the work of the team or its members.

The ceremonies of Scrum implement a discipline that helps keep the team focused on what they need to do across each sprint. Lacking such formalized structures, Lean Development requires the teams to continuously assess and improve constraints within the system that are inefficient.

Moreover, Lean Development practices eschew all forms of batch processing. This strategy is the opposite philosophy of Scrum, where the development team pulls a batch of product backlog items to work on as part of a Sprint Backlog. Instead, Lean Development views all work tasks as individual *orders* that the development team can take on in whatever priority is agreed by the Product Owner and Development Team. But those items are pulled one-at-a-time from a **work item pool**.

The *Lean Development* approach does not require much if any automation to implement. Still, it is exceedingly efficient, so long as the team works aggressively to streamline their activities to eliminate potential bottlenecks.

Continuous Delivery: Lean Life cycle

The **Continuous Delivery: Lean Life cycle** implements the most advanced forms of modern DevOps and life cycle automation processes. These processes include the same test-driven development, continuous integration, test automation, and automated-provisioning capabilities noted in the Continuous Delivery: Agile concepts, along with the implementation of automated-deployment capabilities.

Together, these automation capabilities allow Lean development teams to take on very narrow slices of work, then refine, build, test, and deploy the new capabilities multiple times a day, and in some very advanced environments, every few minutes.

Note that there is nothing wrong with holding back the release of new product functionality to less frequent iterations. This delayed-release strategy supports the deployment of applications that support a critical business process, where frequent releases would be disruptive to the organization, or where the features developed in an iteration depend on other features that are not yet built. On the other hand, in large retail applications, having frequent releases in support of new product offerings can form a distinct competitive advantage.

Figure 11.11 portrays the workflow supporting the Continuous Delivery: Lean DAD
Life cycle:

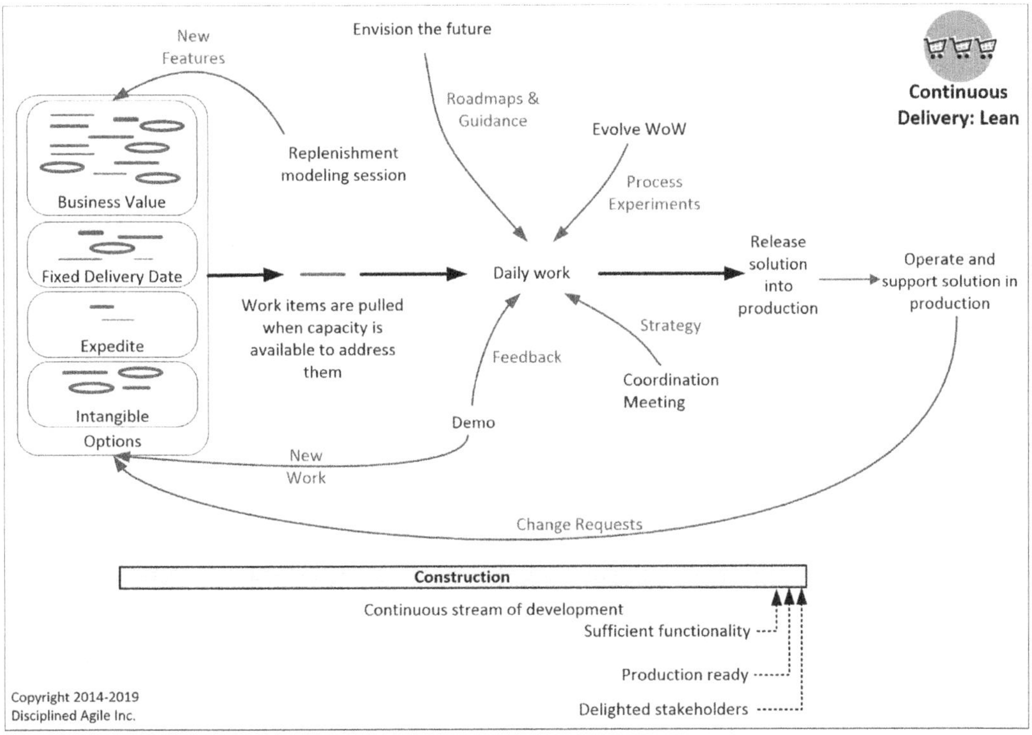

Figure 11.11: Continuous Delivery Lean DAD Life cycle

DA's Continuous Delivery Lean Life cycle provides the most efficient and Agile approach
to supporting business agility. But it also requires some investment to implement the
automation capabilities that enable continuous integration, automated testing, and
continuous provisioning and delivery.

Program Life cycle for a team of teams

The DA Program Life cycle supports the team of teams' requirements when an initial
Agile-based development project has grown too large to manage as a single Agile team.
Before we get into this life cycle, it's important to note that DA's underlying philosophy
is that the need to employ team-of-team requirements is rare. DA's view is that most
organizational teams should be free to adopt an Agile strategy that best works for their
team, irrespective of what the other teams across an organization might be doing.

The deployment of independent teams works so long as each development team is supporting a uniquely differentiated product, and the scale is such that a single Agile team can handle all the work. Still, the need for team-of-team management capabilities exists when developing large and complex products where cross-team communication, dependency, and integration issues substantially impact the work.

Figure 11.12 provides a display of the Program Life cycle as a team-of-teams structure:

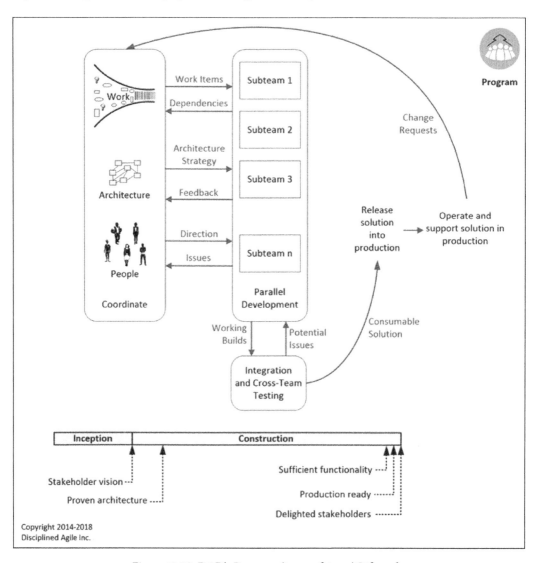

Figure 11.12: DAD's Program (team-of-team) Life cycle

Many new products have information technology components integrated as part of the solution. In many cases, the IT components provide the capabilities that uniquely differentiate or enable the solution. As a product category, the term **cyber-physical system** (**CPS**) refers to such IT-enabled products, and there are few if any industries that have not been impacted by this trend.

Large robotic systems, industrial control systems, autonomous vehicles, large ships, and fly-by-wire aircraft are all examples of large and complex systems that exhibit CPS capabilities. Yet the companies that make these products also strive to be Lean and Agile. Moreover, the disparate groups that build the components of these solutions must ultimately link up and deliver a fully integrated, tested, and functional solution. These are all examples of where team of teams or similar large-scale Agile concepts become necessary.

In a team of team's life cycle scenario, the Inception Phase is much more critical. Depending on the size and complexity of the cyber-physical system under development, there can be significantly more work involved in defining development needs, onboarding, and setting up the development infrastructures.

Under DA, each of the subteams (also known as **squads**) can still choose their WOW. Unlike SAFe, each squad can also choose its cadence. A big caveat, however, is that the teams must still figure out a way to manage their cross-team dependencies and integration issues, and decide how they will link up for testing, product demonstrations, and delivery purposes. DA, of course, provides options to do these very things.

As you can see from *Figure 11.12*, DA coordinates work at the team level: **Work** (*what we need to build*), **Architecture** (*how we will build it*), and **People** (*who is going to do what*). And, as described in the People section within this chapter, the Product Owners, the Architecture Owners, and the team leads coordinate work across their respective areas.

DA recommends a separate team perform overall system integration and cross-team testing. Continuous-integration and automated-testing environments help reduce the workload while also integrating and testing new components immediately after development. For logistical reasons, because of the need to involve external stakeholders, DA recommends that the integration team conduct whole-product usability and **user-acceptance testing** (**UAT**) as a separate set of processes.

DA suggests that the squads can work as feature teams or component teams. A feature team works on a vertical slice of a solution to implement a specific product capability. A component team works on delivering a system-level functionality, such as security, transaction processing, device controls, or data management. These types of teams were described earlier in the *People* section.

For software-related solutions only, DA recommends a continuous delivery approach to deployment; however, there are many situations where the Product Owner may choose to hold back deployment until the product archives a sufficient level of capability to justify the release. Moreover, the release of a sizeable cyber-physical system makes it impractical to have incremental releases. Imagine receiving incremental deliveries on a ship or an aircraft. However, conducting iterative reviews make a lot of sense, even on these large systems.

PMI maintains complete descriptions and life cycle diagrams for each of the preceding DA life cycles at `https://www.pmi.org/disciplined-Agile/life cycle#Agile`. The same information is also available in a book titled *Choosing Your WOW!* (*Introduction to Disciplined Agile Delivery*, *Scott Ambler* and *Mark Lines*, 2020).

Providing industry-proven practices

One of the unique differentiators and useful constructs of Disciplined Agile is the installment of hundreds of useful techniques supporting software and systems development. Rather than come up with an entirely new set of practices, DA recommends practices that have already proven useful across the software and systems development industry. *Figure 11.13* lists many of the industry sources that DA claims has influenced its practices:

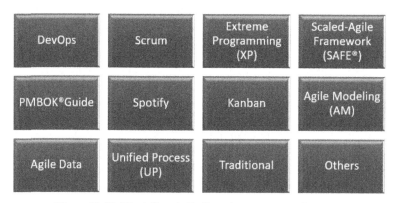

Figure 11.13: Discipline Agile Practices—source adoptions

There are too many many techniques listed to do any justice in terms of describing the available content. However, what is worth spending some time on is understanding the DA processes that are supported, and that DA implements **Process Goals** and **Decision Points** to help teams find the potential options available to improve their WOW.

Improving incrementally

Consistent with the concepts of Lean Development, the DA **Guided Continuous Improvement (GCI)** method is a *Kaizen* approach to incremental improvement. A Japanese term, Kaizen means *change for the better* or *continuous improvement.*

The initial step to DA's Kaizen approach is to identify an area for improvement. DA teams use the Process Goals relevant to a situation they currently face and select one or more of the optional techniques as a potential approach to try out as an experiment. After conducting their experiment, the team assesses the degree of improvement, if any. If the experiment proves successful, the team should adopt the new technique as part of their WOW. If not, the team should move on. Regardless of the result, the team should share their learning with other teams across their organization.

Achieving Process Goals

DA is a goal-driven approach to improving team and organizational agility. DA expresses goals in the form of *21 Process Goals* that help the organization implement new capabilities across the four product life cycle phases: Inception, Construction, Transition, and Ongoing. *Figure 11.14* shows the 21 Process Goals spanning the DA life cycle phases:

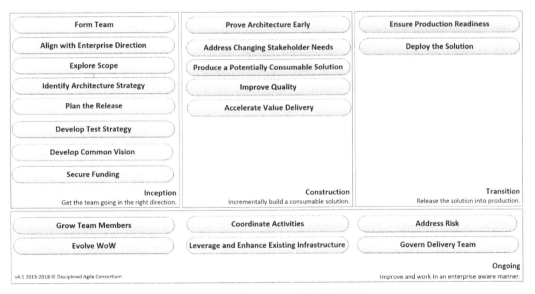

Figure 11.14: The Process Goals of DAD

This completes the section on finding context. We now know how mindset, people, flow, and life cycle practices create the contexts for decision making in DA. Now, we will turn our attention to understanding how to find the techniques DA has to offer and decide which are most appropriate in the context of our team's current situation.

Tooling your WOW

In the previous sections, you were reminded that Scrum and its scaled variants are frameworks, and that DA is considered a toolkit. So you might be wondering what the difference is. DA certainly shares the elements of a framework in that it serves as a container for implementing various Lean–Agile practices. But DA is also a toolkit as it contains listings of useful techniques across common desired process outcomes in the context of product development.

In this sense, the DA toolkit is also a knowledge base of useful techniques. But no matter how many techniques are available, they are only useful if we know when and how to apply them. That is the subject of the next section on the use of **Process Goal Diagrams**.

Using Process Goal Diagrams

DA teams do not need to memorize all the hundreds of techniques maintained in the DA knowledge base. Instead, they only need to understand how to use the Process Goal Diagrams, as shown in *Figure 11.15*, to find useful techniques that are associated with the problems they are facing or capabilities they wish to install:

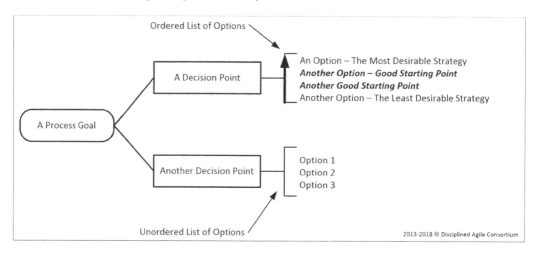

Figure 11.15: Goal diagram notation overview

The team enters the diagram using the Process Goal most similar to the area they need to improve. For example, if a team isn't sure how to go about scoping the work involved in the development of a new product or solution, the team will know to look at the Inception Phase Process Goals and select the **Explore Scope** Process Scope as a potential option. If they aren't sure which Process Goal is appropriate, they can quickly look through each goal to see which is most appropriate to their specific needs. See *Figure 11.16* of the Explore Scope Process Goal diagram:

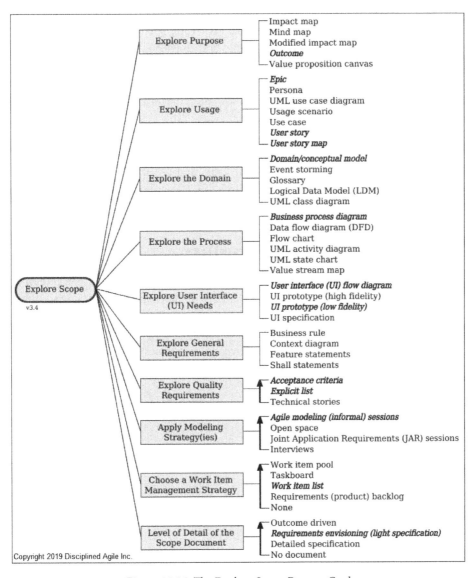

Figure 11.16: The Explore Scope Process Goal

Once the team enters the Process Goal, they will find a decision tree with multiple Decision Points, each with multiple associated techniques listed as potential options to select. A Decision Point represents an area of potential interest or intention within the selected Process Goal. So, for example, in our Explore Scope Process Goal, we may want to evaluate techniques to improve our team's ability to explore our clients' UI or usage needs, or better methods to uncover process or domain-related information.

Once we decide which Decision Point or Points offer a potential solution to our problems, we can select from the available options. Note that the example provided in *Figures 11.15* and *11.16* shows two types of options lists. The top list is an ordered list. The arrow indicates the rank order, from the least desirable option (bottom of the list) to the most desirable option. The proposed techniques that are in **bold** indicate good or practical starting points. For example, the higher-ordered techniques may require investment in skills and tooling that make them impractical for some organizations to adopt immediately.

The bottom list of techniques is unordered. Disciplined Agile has judged them all equally acceptable, and DA teams are free to experiment freely with any or all of them.

This section concludes the introduction to the tools that DA provides to support your WOW. Now let's move on to understanding how DA allows you to choose your level of agility.

Choosing your level of agility

Disciplined Agile does not expect an enterprise to implement the full complement of capabilities in one fell swoop. Instead, the enterprise can start small, starting with only one team, and then build on initial successes to implement increasingly advanced concepts such as DevOps, value stream management, and enterprise-wide agility. *Figure 11.17* shows the scope of the DA toolkit, which includes four layers of processes to scale business agility:

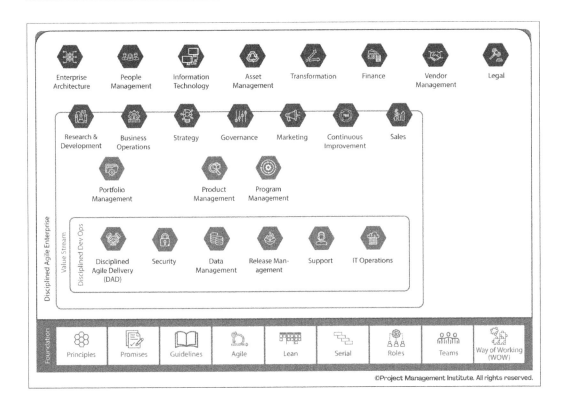

Figure 11.17: The DA toolkit

The bottom-most layer is the **Foundation**, followed by **Disciplined DevOps**, then by **Value Stream**, and finally, the **Disciplined Agile Enterprise** layers.

The process layers of the DA toolkit build on each other, adding Lean and Agile practice capabilities from the bottom up. In other words, DA enterprise processes build upon the processes of the Value Stream layer, which builds upon the capabilities installed at the Disciplined DevOps layer, which in turn builds on the capabilities established in the Foundations layer.

Disciplined Agile implements the concept of **Process Blades** that aggregate Process Groups with their Decision Points and optional techniques for each affected area of business across the scope of the DA toolkit. Each Process Blade is described in terms of mindset, people, flow, and practices, as described earlier, applying a level of consistency across the toolkit that is fractal in nature. The icons displayed in *Figure 11.17* indicate the Process Blades supported by each DA layer. The DA toolkit, in effect, provides a knowledge base of proven yet optional practices that allow each team to establish a WOW that best supports their current situation.

Scaling Disciplined Agile

The Disciplined Agile toolkit is key to scaling agility across the organization, both at a tactical and strategic level (that is, agility at scale). DA defines **tactical agility at scale** as the application of Lean–Agile strategies at the individual team level. In contrast, DA defines **strategic agility at scale** as the application of Lean–Agile strategies broadly across the entire enterprise. In other words, strategic agility goes beyond the software-development teams to address all value creation and value delivery streams.

Now that you understand the basic concepts behind the scope of the DA toolkit and its scaling concepts, let's quickly review the type of work encompassed within each of the four DA layers, starting with the innermost layer—DAD.

Building on a solid foundation

The Foundation Process layer implements the core components of the Disciplined Agile Toolkit, which includes its principles, promises, and guidelines, as described at the beginning of this chapter. The Foundation layer also includes the Process Blades that inform decisions on Agile, Lean, and traditional serial-development processes. Finally, guidance on DA roles and team structures are found in this layer, along with information on how and why teams must experiment and implement a WOW that best fits their situation.

The DA toolkit is deployed as an open strategy that implements nonproprietary processes and terminology. The hybrid nature of the DA life cycles allows each team to choose their WOW, while the predefined roles define appropriate Agile-based responsibilities. Moreover, DA implements nonprescriptive techniques and goal-driven process guides that give teams a head start in evaluating potential experiments to improve their WOW. In DA, having a choice is a good thing.

DA's foundational layer offers guidance on processes to scale Lean and Agile practices. Still, this is only the start, as we'll see in the next subsections spanning the remaining DA toolkit process layers. The next layer up is Disciplined DevOps, which provides the process guides and techniques necessary to improve communications, collaborations, and efficiencies across the organization's development and operations groups.

Installing Disciplined DevOps

DA defines DevOps as "the streamlining of the activities surrounding IT solution development (Dev) and IT operations (Ops)" (`https://www.pmi.org/disciplined-agile/process/disciplined-devops`). Remember our previous discussions that DevOps started as a communications and collaborations strategy to break down the silos that often exist between development teams and operations groups; this is still a primary objective. However, it quickly became apparent that the increased collaborations also necessarily tied the work of the groups together. And, as with any business-process reengineering effort, it became logical that those activities could be integrated, streamlined, and automated. This integration and automation strategy is the modern vision for DevOps.

DA takes a system thinking view when describing the affected elements and complex relationships surrounding DevOps implementations, as shown in *Figure 11.18*:

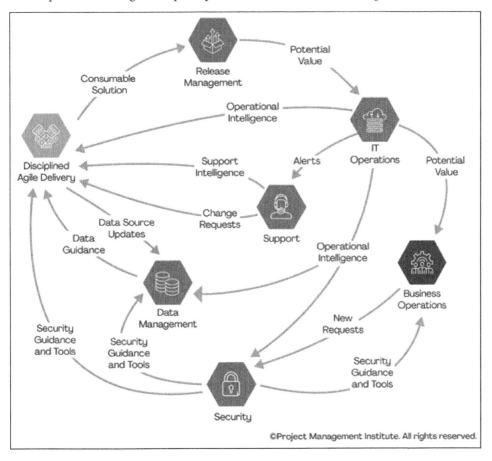

Figure 11.18: Disciplined DevOps, a systems view

Based on your training in *Chapter 4, Systems Thinking*, you should be able to work your way through the displayed relationships. DA's DevOps diagram presents a very high-level view, and each organization and its affected teams and stakeholders will need to refine the model to fit their specific needs and situations. But the model provides a start to your discussions.

Figure 11.19 displays the traditional DevOps diagram shown as an infinite-process loop. Those readers who are already familiar with the conventional *infinity-loop* display often associated with DevOps may wonder why DA has taken a systems-oriented view to DevOps. After all, the infinity-loop model does an excellent job of portraying the usual activities of development and operations as a recurring pattern. Moreover, the infinite-loop model of DevOps effectively communicates the notion of continuous development and delivery into operations with continuous monitoring and feedback as a closed-loop system.

One interesting thing to note about DA's version of the infinity loop (*Figure 11.19*) is that they place *test* before *code* to promote a test-first strategy. In other words, DA's DevOps infinity loop includes the concept of employing test-driven development:

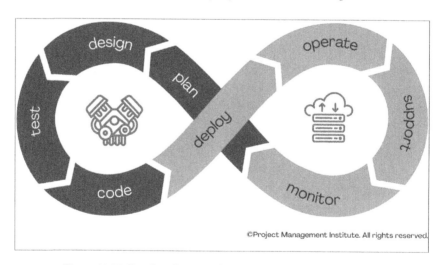

Figure 11.19: DevOps diagram shown as an infinite-process loop

Still, the infinite-loop model oversimplifies both the activities and influences that affect such cross-team coordination, hence the need for a more complex systems-level view and analysis of DevOps, as shown in *Figure 11.19*.

DevOps is still a new way of thinking, and often more of an idealized goal than immediately practical. That's not to say that there aren't organizations that have demonstrated great success with their DevOps implementations. For example, an article by *TechBeacon*, written by *Chris Kanaracus* and titled *How they did it: 6 companies that scaled DevOps*, identified five companies that have successfully implemented DevOps enterprise-wide: *PayPal*, *Kaiser Permanente*, *Starbucks*, *Yahoo*, and *Capital One*. See `https://techbeacon.com/devops/how-they-did-it-6-companies-scaled-devops` for more information.

Organizations that choose to implement mature DevOps practices must deal with the following issues, many of which are also true when evolving Lean–Agile practices in general:

- Team members cannot be specialists and must understand a broader scope of work and professional IT disciplines.

- DevOps toolchains are still evolving and are typically cobbled together.

- Toolchain product integration concerns are primarily borne by the deploying IT group unless they choose to go with solutions from DevOps-as-a-service providers. Still in those cases, you must adopt the solution providers' preferred tools and cloud-based services, which may be difficult to change at a later date.

- Development systems are more mature, integrated, and streamlined than operations-oriented methods, practices, and tools.

- DevOps requires an investment by executive management, and they may not understand the scope of the effort in terms of training, tools, time, and costs.

- There are multiple views of what DevOps means, such as BizDevOps, DevSecOps, DevDataOps, plus the inclusion of Release Management, Support, and IT Operations functions.

The systems view of Disciplined DevOps, shown previously in *Figure 11.18*, takes the preceding issues into account so that the organization can, you guessed it, determine their best WOW.

The DevOps layer implements six Process Blades to guide improvements in this area. These Process Blades include DAD, Security, Data Management, Release Management, Support, and IT Operations. Each of these Process Blades has unique Process Goals, Decision Points, and optional techniques for improvement experiments. Collectively, the Disciplined DevOps Process Blades allow the IT organization to address their concerns spanning BizDevOps, DevSecOps, DevDataOps, release management, support, and IT operations requirements.

DevOps may seem like the be-all and end-all in IT improvements because of its comprehensive approach to integrating and streamlining disparate IT functions and processes and automating wherever possible. However, DA also implements a Process Blade for information technology at the Disciplined Agile enterprise level that is substantially more comprehensive. For example, the IT blade has ~60 DA Process Goals that provide additional guidance on IT-improvement strategies.

With the first two DA toolkit layers, the organization has addressed its foundational Lean–Agile and DevOps implementation concerns, along with related role, team, and WOW considerations. At this point, the organization needs to look beyond development to explore the broader issues associated with value-stream management, spanning both Value Creation and value delivery activities. This end-to-end business agility strategy is the focus of the DA toolkit Value Stream layer, and the topic of the next subsection.

Adding value streams

IT development teams do not have the responsibility to define value streams across the whole product. The organization or product management function must also address the business-operations aspect of delivering customer-centric value. Business-oriented value-stream management is the scope of the Value Stream layer. In the context of Lean Development, DA's Value Stream layer encompasses value-delivery activities.

Recall from *Chapter 5, Lean Thinking*, that value streams include all the seller's activities or tasks—from the start of value creation until delivery of value—in the form of products or services to the end-user customers. In other words, if we genuinely want to be a Lean enterprise, we cannot merely focus on just the development tasks. Such an imbalance would never address issues of organizational waste or inefficiencies beyond the control of the development teams. The imbalance would also not align business, operations, and development strategies to deliver whole-product value.

Also recall from *Chapter 5, Lean Thinking*, that value streams consist of two types of activities, *value creation* and *value delivery*. Value creation includes the activities to design, engineer, test, and produce a product or service that people want. Value delivery includes the activities to support customers, including things like product management, portfolio management, order entry, order processing, inventory and supply chain management, product delivery or fulfillment, product maintenance, and customer support. Though not meant to be an all-inclusive list, these are the types of activities supported in DA's Foundation and Disciplined DevOps layers.

Flexing your value streams

Disciplined Agile's Value Stream layer is modeled after the concepts developed by Al Shalloway and others that is called **DA FLEX (FLow for Enterprise Transformation)**, which was acquired in September 2019 by the **Project Management Institute (PMI)**. Details on FLEX are currently maintained at `https://portal.netobjectives.com/`. This approach has been fully integrated with the DA toolkit and will soon be maintained at PMI's main website.

Somewhat similar to the philosophies outlined in Disciplined Agile, the DA FLEX approach to business agility is to provide a set of patterns and potential solutions that can be adapted by an organization. The focus of DA FLEX is on improving the sequence of work that takes place to create value. FLEX scales to fit all sizes of small and large enterprise needs and complexities. Moreover, as with the DA toolkit, those who choose to implement the concepts of DA FLEX can start small but high-impact localized improvements, and then build and refine their integrated value streams over time.

Figure 11.20 depicts the DA FLEX workflow for improving value streams:

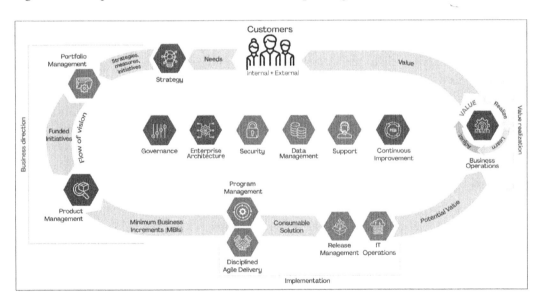

Figure 11.20: The DA FLEX workflow

Note that the workflow structure encompasses the Process Blades associated with the DA toolkit's Disciplined DevOps layer. The way to think about this is that the value-delivery aspects of DA's Value Stream layer support and extend the value-creation components of DA's Lean–Agile development foundations. From a practical implementation perspective, however, the value-creation activities must be synched, integrated, and streamlined to provide efficient flow across both value streams.

DA FLEX implements a six-step approach to achieve business agility:

1. Determine the to-be state for organizational structures and workflow as a Lean–Agile development environment.

2. Evaluate the gaps between the current and desired states and the challenges the organization faces to make the transition.

3. Identify strategies to help make the necessary transitions.

4. Apply systems and Lean thinking to determine the most value-added approach to prioritize transition activities keeping in mind the influences of people and culture.

5. Implement the proposed transition activities as experiments, and measure and monitor performance improvements against the baseline methods and metrics.

6. Use the PDSA cycle to plan, do, study, and act on the results to improve your value streams over time.

The Value Stream layer of DA FLEX implements Lean Development concepts within the DA Toolkit. But there is also a systems thinking orientation to this layer to assess value delivery activities as parts of a complex system. That is the topic of the next subsection.

Delivering whole-product value

Value delivery includes all the activities necessary to satisfy the customer and improve their experience in acquiring and using the product or service. DA's Value Stream layer primarily, though not exclusively, addresses the issues of improving value delivery.

At the time of writing, there are 10 Process Blades associated with the Value Stream layer within the DA toolkit. The Research and Development Process Blade helps improve product conceptualization and proving efforts. The Business Operations Process Bade ensures that activities that tangentially impact the customer, such as order taking, order processing, and order delivery, are in alignment with customer needs and are efficient from a whole-product delivery perspective.

The Strategy, Portfolio Management, and governance Process Blades help ensure that the products support the corporate strategies and mission of the business, are appropriately evaluated and managed from a portfolio investment perspective, and that they meet all compliance requirements. The Market and Sales Process Blades ensure that the organization is aligning its promotional and target market sales activities, while also improving their operational efficiencies.

The Product Management Process Blade helps tie all the value-creation and value-delivery activities together to ensure delivery of the whole product. This set of activities goes beyond the responsibilities of a Product Owner, as the Product Manager typically has full **profit and loss (P and L)** responsibilities for a product. Having P and L responsibilities, the Product Manager guides all decisions and activities spanning the life cycle of the product, including the following:

- Business case analysis and planning
- Customer and market validations
- Revenue forecasting
- Developing pricing models
- Deciding product launch and release dates
- Marketing promotions and communications
- End-of-life decisions

The Program Management Process Blades ensure the efficient use of resources, plus they support ongoing training, mentoring, and coaching needs. They also have traditional Program and Project Management functions, such as managing budgets, reporting, compliance, and other oversight activities that the customers and executives may direct.

Finally, the Continuous Improvement Process Blade provides improvement guidance on how to improve across all value streams continuously. Value-stream efficiencies require alignment across all teams that participate in the value-delivery and value-creation activities. For example, the activities of the teams must be synched, integrated, and improved in a coordinated fashion to avoid creating bottlenecks or delays across value-stream activities.

Promoting and selling value

A quick side note here. I've managed both IT solutions delivery and IT product sales and marketing organizations. The IT products I supported include software-development, business-intelligence, e-commerce, portal, and middleware tools. There is nothing worse than having to sell products and services that customers don't want or value. But it happens, and I've seen this disconnect happen in three general ways.

Sometimes an organization is run by a technical or domain expert who has a strong vision and directs the build of a product that has value. Still, the marketing and sales staff may not truly understand who the target market customers are or what their needs are, and they end up trying to sell the wrong thing to the wrong people.

Sometimes, the product vision looks good on paper but is not entirely validated. And, it may take significant investments in time and resources to deliver a whole product or a competitive product. In those cases, there is a great deal of pressure to sell a product that is not market ready.

I've also seen situations where the development organization, mainly when led by a particularly strong-willed technical leader, has a vision, but has no idea if there is a real market opportunity or who the paying customers are. For example, a technical team may build tools and technology that improve IT functions, but then fail to address the business concerns that would justify investments by the executives who make such purchase decisions.

All three scenarios are bad situations. It's no fun trying to sell or deliver something that customers don't understand, don't value, and don't want. Most people want to promote, sell, and deliver things that have real value, as perceived by the paying customer. Nobody enjoys being on the receiving end of an unsatisfied customer. I can't stress enough how important it is to align value-stream activities to build, promote, sell, and deliver the right products for the right customers.

So, now you've learned how to go about building a Lean–Agile foundation. You've learned about the collaboration, integration, and automation capabilities of DevOps, and you've learned how to link value-delivery and value-creation activities to quickly build the right products for the right customers most efficiently, and at the lowest possible costs. But there's still more work to do at the enterprise level, which is the topic of the next subsection.

Leveraging economies of scale

The first three layers of the DA toolkit already provide all the roles, organizational structures, methods, and tools to deliver value at an organizational level. So why do we need an Enterprise layer?

The answer is because there are functional areas that support the Lean–Agile enterprise that don't go away, and in fact, can improve an organization's ability to compete. Simply put, larger companies have significant competitive advantages with their access to corporate and financial resources, and in leveraging their large-volume production efficiencies. But the larger organizations must operate as Lean–Agile enterprises to successfully maintain their competitive advantage against smaller and nimbler upstart competitors.

Disciplined Agile Enterprise (**DAE**) helps the organization implement Lean and Agile strategies on an enterprise scale. Since IT and software development touches almost everything across an organization, it should be reasonably apparent that the integration points across all business functions must also operate in a streamlined and efficient manner.

This whole-company strategy is the essence of enabling business agility by establishing enterprise-wide flexibility, responsiveness, operational and development efficiencies, and providing customer-centric value for competitive advantage. With this in mind, the DAE layer is an acknowledgment of three basic facts:

- Virtually every modern business is driven by software.
- Modern digital technologies are disrupting traditional business practices.
- Business agility is critical to staying competitive and viable.

At the enterprise level, we start to evaluate improvements in functional areas that support all value-stream operations. DAE currently implements eight Process Blades to help the organization experiment and improve the following functional operations:

- Enterprise Architecture
- People Management
- Information Technology
- Asset Management
- Transformation
- Finance
- Vendor Management
- Legal

Realistically, your organization will often have different names for these functions. For example, People Management is most often referred to as Human Resources Management. Vendor Management can encompass several different types of relationship, such as supplier, product or service-delivery partner, or contractor.

The Enterprise Architecture and Information Technology functions help encourage reuse and quality standards, both of which can reduce costs and improve customer satisfaction. Asset Management, Finance, and Legal are all business functions that must exist to protect the company and to ensure that it has the financial resources and discipline to stay in business. Finally, the Transformation function not only supports the enterprise-wide implementation of Lean–Agile practices across the four layers of the DA toolkit, but it also serves as a crucial continuous improvement function on an enterprise scale.

Putting it all together

The Process Blades, Goals, Decision Points, and techniques of the Disciplined Agile toolkit are too numerous to cover in a single chapter. As a result, in this section, we will have a quick and summary overview of how the DA toolkit supports the transformation of teams and organizations through increasing levels of maturity. The remaining sections follow the same pattern of organizing DA Process Blades in the context of DA's associated *Inception, Construction, Transition Phases*, and *Ongoing Processes*.

We'll start our discussion on DA Transitions by initiating team-level improvement opportunities, as identified in DA's toolkit as potential Process Goals.

Initiating your DA teams

Building a DA team is a set of activities that occurs in the **Inception Phase** of Disciplined Agile. The objectives are to find and hire the right people, determine the scope of work, create an initial architectural strategy, and plan for the first release. Research by DA indicates that the typical *Inception Phase* of work spans 11 workdays. *Figure 11.21* lists the Process Blades and the number of related Decision Points spanning the Initiating Your Team Process Blade:

Initiating Your Team		
	Form Team	12 Decision Points
	Align with enterprise Direction	5 Decision Points
	Explore Scope	10 Decison Points
	Identify Architecture Strategy	9 Decison Points
	Plan the Release	8 Decison Points
	Develop Test Strategy	16 Decison Points
	Develop Common Vision	6 Decison Points
	Secure Funding	3 Decison Points

Figure 11.21: Initiating Team Process Blade | Process Goals | Number of potential Decision Points

As you can see from the figure, DA teams have 8 process objectives to choose as opportunities for experimentation and improvement, with a total of 69 potential Decision Points. Remember that each defined Decision Point has a list of techniques provided as potential options for the organization to experiment with and ultimately improve their WOW.

Now that the team has formed, they should logically start to assess how they are going to add value from a customer-centric point of view and construct the appropriate solutions. This scope of work is the topic of the next section.

Creating business value

The previous *Inception Phase* of DA includes the activities to form the DA teams. Next in line is the *Construction Phase*, where the team begins to explore how they will go about creating a **Minimum Business Increment** (**MBI**).

The MBI is a **consumable solution** that is potentially releasable to its markets. DA purposely uses the term consumable to differentiate from the Scrum-based **Potentially Shippable Product** (**PSP**) concepts. In other words, a product cannot be merely functional; it must include the elements of **working** (that is, functional), **useable** (that is, works well and is easy to use), and **desirable** (that is, it must delight, not merely satisfy, the customers). Furthermore, it is referred to as a solution, not just software. A solution is potentially comprised of software, hardware, supporting documentation, business-process changes, and organizational changes:

Producing Business Value	Prove Architecture Early	2 Decison Points
	Address Changing Stakeholder Needs	7 Decison Points
	Produce a Potentially Consumable Solution	6 Decison Points
	Improve Quality	4 Decison Points
	Accelerate Value Delivery	9 Decison Points

Figure 11.22: Producing Business Value | Process Goals | Number of Decision Points

Figure 11.22 shows the 5 desirable process outcomes of this Process Blade with a total of 28 Decision Points. Each defined decision point includes a listing of potential techniques to experiment with to improve your WOW in this area. Now that your team is working to produce value-added products, they need to understand what must be done to release those products into production successfully.

Going into production

The Process Blades of the **Transition Phase** guide the DA teams in improving the activities associated with releasing consumable products as solutions into the target markets or internal production environments. In a Scrum-based development framework, product teams typically build new increments of value on a set timeboxed schedule of 1 to 4 weeks. During the timebox, the team members spend a substantial portion of their time on activities that help ensure that the product is ready for release; however, in a fully realized continuous and automated integration, testing, and delivery environment, the entirety of the transition-related activities might only require a few minutes.

Note that DA often uses the term *solutions* as an alternative to the word *products*. The implication here is that customers value things that address some needs or issues they have. For example, I was taught years ago to think of customers as having three overarching concerns when they evaluate alternative product purchasing options:

- Does the product offer better performance?

- Does the product offer a better price or better value for the money?

- Does the product somehow improve their image in front of their peers, superiors, and subordinates?

People haven't changed, and this adage still holds. People want solutions to their needs and problems, not products, features, and functions. Without context, the latter terms have little meaning to users and customers.

Figure 11.23 lists the two desired process outcomes (goals) associated with releasing a product into production with a total of 6 optional Decision Points, each having a list of potential techniques to try out as improvement options:

Releasing Into Production	Ensure Production Readiness	2 Decision Points
	Deploy the Solution	4 Decision Points

Figure 11.23: Releasing into production | Process Goals | Number of Decision Points

So, now we have learned how DA goes about helping us build our DA team(s) and defining our scope of work. We have learned how to construct a minable marketable release, and we have learned how to improve our abilities to transition our consumable solutions into our markets or deploy them into a production environment. But other *ongoing* activities do not fit so neatly into these three categories. These ongoing activities are the topic of the next subsection.

Sustaining and evolving your teams

The ongoing group of Process Goals is not so much in support of a life cycle phase in development as they are a collection of ad hoc activities that go on throughout the life of each DA team. In other words, these Process Goals have a focus on helping to sustain and improve your team's development and delivery capabilities over time.

There are five desirable Process Goals associated with this group. The overarching objective of the ongoing Process Goals is to help sustain and improve the outcomes of your DA teams. For example, there are Process Goals to develop their skills and knowledge, to coordinate activities within and across DA teams, and to manage risks.

Another ongoing Process Goal is to ensure that the organization improves its performance and efficiency through the reuse of application functionality, data, security components, integration environments, and other infrastructure elements. Finally, two of the most critical ongoing Process Goals are to ensure that the teams continuously work to improve their way of working and that they have sufficient but Lean governance to implement the appropriate policies, standards, and practices to improve performance and manage risks.

Figure 11.24 shows the 5 desirable Process Goals that support ongoing efforts to sustain and improve DA teams with a total of 42 alternative Decision Points:

Sustaining and Enhancing Your Team	Grow Team Members	3 Decision Points
	Coodinate Activities	8 Decision Points
	Evolve WOW	12 Decision Points
	Address Risk	7 Decision Points
	Leverage and enhance Existing Infrastructure	5 Decision Points
	Govern Delivery Team	7 Decision Points

Figure 11.24: Sustaining and enhancing your team | Process Goals | Number of Decision Points

As always, each Decision Point has a list of optional techniques presented to experiment with and evaluate as potential ways to improve your team's WOW. You now have a broad, though not deep, understanding of how the DA toolkit helps organizations develop Lean–Agile practices on an enterprise scale while also exposing hundreds of potentially useful techniques to improve the individual-, team-, and organization-level performance or outcomes.

We have one remaining topic to cover before ending this chapter, and that is the subject of Lean governance and milestones.

Lean Governance and Milestones

In the last set of ongoing Process Groups, you will see governance listed as one of the identified desired process outcomes. Some Agile practitioners view governance as antithetical to the notion that Agile teams should be autonomous and free to make choices regarding standards and practices, and simply use transparency to expose their work.

In contrast, DA takes the view that Lean governance practices, along with associated Milestones, are essential regardless of the type of development practices that are employed (that is, Agile, Lean, or traditional). Lean governance helps to ensure that the teams build in quality, increase their knowledge, deliver quickly, eliminate waste, optimize the whole system with systems thinking, and respect people. Specifically, DA cites the following reasons for establishing Lean governance capabilities and Milestones:

- To ensure that teams stay focused on adding business value and positive ROI
- To facilitate the adoption of Lean–Agile processes and organizational structures
- To ensure compliance with legislative mandates and legal and safety concerns
- To ensure sufficiency in transparency to identify and minimize risks and issues
- To guide effective work practices across teams, team members, and stakeholders
- To sustain and extend tactical and strategic strategies and business objectives

A key component of DA's governance strategy is to use risk-based Milestones and both formal and lightweight milestone reviews as necessary to confirm the completion of a desired goal or task. Formal milestone reviews are less desirable, but sometimes necessary to ensure compliance with regulatory or other legal and safety requirements.

Lightweight milestone reviews are preferred and support Lean governance strategies, with less formality and less documentation. Where formal Milestones often set up a combative mindset, informal Milestone Reviews support a collaborative decision-making environment. In other words, the focus is on enabling the teams, and not using inspections to find fault.

Think about it this way: Lean governance supports continuous monitoring, as opposed to periodic phase gate or milestone reviews, where identified issues would be more challenging to resolve. Our goal should always be to identify and resolve issues when and as they arise. Failure to do so leads to technical debt, and the accumulation of technical debt makes the issues increasingly tricky, expensive, and time-consuming to resolve. In other words, the accumulation of technical debt is the modern IT equivalent of 'kicking the can down the road,' instead of, metaphorically, picking up our messes. In addition, failure to address issues as and when they arise can lead to cybersecurity and refresh concerns, both of which have negative direct and indirect cost implications.

Finally, lightweight milestone reviews support the goals and objectives of open transparency, and not just following a formal management-reporting requirement. DA guides the types of Milestones and Reviews that the DA teams might consider. For example, each of the six DA life cycle diagrams—presented in *Figures 11.3* through *11.8*—include timelines underneath each diagram to indicate the affected life cycle phases along with their associated Milestones. Each milestone has arrows that indicate where on the timelines to consider reviewing the identified goals and objectives.

This section concludes your introduction to the Disciplined Agile approach to implementing Lean–Agile WOW to deliver consumable, whole-product solutions. Now, let's look at the best fits for DA implementations.

Best fits

Disciplined Agile is in the same category as the **Scaled-Agile Framework (SAFe)** in terms of its comprehensive scope and broader inclusion of Lean–Agile concepts. These Lean-Agile strategies are much more comprehensive in scope than the pure Scrum-based frameworks of **Scrum of Scrums (SOS)**, Scrum@Scale, Nexus, and **large-scale Scrum (LeSS)**. In some ways, with its expansive lists of Decision Points and techniques, DA is a broader and more comprehensive approach to implementing Lean–Agile practices than SAFe. Still, on the other hand, their emphasis is different.

Both DA and SAFe extend the empiricism of Scrum with the application of systems thinking, Lean development, and business agility on an enterprise scale, not just limited to software and systems development. As a result, both methodologies encompass the Lead Development concepts of integrating value-creation and value-delivery functions to enable business agility. Moreover, both approaches address the issues associated with aligning value to business strategies and the management of corporate investments through portfolio management.

Where they primarily differ is in SAFe's emphasis on large-team organization, alignment, integration, and coordination strategies versus DA's emphasis on providing a detailed knowledge base of useful Process Goals, Decision Points, and optional techniques to improve your team's and organization's WOW.

PMI comparatively recently acquired Disciplined Agile as the backbone of its strategy to transform its traditional portfolio, program, and project-management disciplines to align with modern Lean–Agile practices. For all the reasons outlined throughout this book, competitive pressures will force all companies to compete in the Lean–Agile paradigm, or face going out of business. In this context, PMI's decision to acquire both DA and FLEX were wise decisions.

With nearly one million certified practitioners, 500,000 global members, and more than 300 local chapters internationally, PMI provides a broad base of skilled resources to help organizations adopt and apply Lean–Agile practices at both tactical and strategic levels. PMI's certified practitioners will require a bit of a transition period to come up to speed with Disciplined Agile. On the other hand, the adoption of Disciplined Agile is the clearest path forward for these practitioners to adopt and learn how to apply Lean–Agile practices.

Organizations that have already employed PMI's practices and certified **Project Management Professionals (PMPs)**® will find a clear transition strategy and available resources to move forward in their adoption of Lean–Agile practices. There will be some training costs involved, plus the time required to make the transformations. But that statement would also be valid for the adoption of all Scrum and Lean–Agile approaches.

Disciplined Agile is more applicable than SAFe for smaller organizations that may be in a start-up phase or have simply not evolved in size to worry about coordinating product or solution teams involving 50 or more people. If the small organization does grow in size, then DA is still a viable approach to help evolve Lean–Agile practices across the expanding enterprise.

Finally, many organizations will see value in having access to DA's hundreds of optional techniques in context with common Process Goals and decision criteria. Other Scrum and Lean–Agile practices assume that their teams understand where to find and evaluate potential methods and tools available to improve their development and operational capabilities. Moreover, DA preserves the Scrum concept of leveraging empirical evidence (that is, observation of effectiveness through experimentation) to determine which techniques improve a team's or organization's WOW.

Summary

This section concludes the chapter on the DA approach to implementing Lean–Agile practices on a team and organizational level. In this chapter, you have learned that DA is uniquely different in its view that each team within an enterprise should decide their preferred WOW. There are no executive mandates or edicts that should ever override a team's decision as to their preferred choices.

You should have a sound fundamental understanding of how and when to employ DA's six product-development life cycles, and how to access the hundreds of DA techniques in concert with the desired Process Goals and Decision Points. Moreover, you should now have the skills to employ the layers of the DA toolkit to implement the various levels of business agility.

The primary benefit of the DA approach is its flexibility and less dogmatic instructions that might otherwise hinder the acceptance of scaling Lean–Agile practices across the organization.

In the next chapter, you will begin your exploration of the SAFe. SAFe is the second Lean–Agile approach presented in this book. But where DA takes an approach of flexibility and choice, SAFe provides much more direction as to organizational structures, cross-team coordination, planning, roles, and responsibilities. The goal of SAFe is to leverage existing economies of scale and organizational resources to retain a competitive advantage in an increasingly disruptive digital world.

Questions

1. What does WOW mean in DA, and why is it important?

2. What are the components of establishing a Lean and Agile mindset in DA?

3. What are the essential DA team-level Roles?

4. Within a DA team of teams, cross-team integration, dependency, and coordination activities mimic what type of organizational structure?

5. What types of leadership teams support large team and program-level DA implementations?

6. What are the six types of product life cycles promoted by DA?

7. How do Continuous Delivery: Agile and Lean product life cycles differ from their Lean and Agile counterparts?

8. What are the components of a Process Goal Diagram?

9. What are the four layers of the DA toolkit?

10. How are the Process Blades, Goals, Decision Points, and techniques of the DA toolkit organized?

Further reading

- Ambler, S. (2012) *Agile Modeling: Effective Practices for Extreme Programming and the Unified Process.* New York, NY. John Wiley and Sons, Inc.

- Ambler, S., Lines, Mark. (2012) *Disciplined Agile Delivery: A Practitioner's Guide to Agile Software Delivery in the Enterprise.* Boston, MA. Pearson Education, Inc.

- Ambler, S., Lines, Mark. (2017*) An Executive Guide to Disciplined Agile: Winning the Race to Release Agility.* Disciplined Agile Consortium.

- Ambler, S., Lines, Mark. (2020) *Choose Your Wow! A Disciplined Agile Delivery Handbook for Optimizing Your Way of Working.* Newtown Square, PA The Project Management Institute, Inc.

- Ford, N., Kua, P., Parsons, R. (2017) *Building Evolutionary Architectures: Support Constant Change.* Sebastopol, CA. O'Reilly Media, Inc.

12
Essential Scaled Agile Framework® (SAFe®)

The **Scaled Agile Framework**™ (**SAFe**®) is a Lean-Agile approach to developing large-scale products and solutions that integrate computing and physical products or components (also known as **cyber-physical systems**). The business drivers for implementing SAFe are the need to compete in our digital age with compelling, value-added solutions, minimal waste, and optimized value stream efficiencies.

Consistent with the philosophies of Lean development, SAFe implements Lean practices on an enterprise scale spanning both *value creation* and *value delivery* activities—that is, the set of development and operational processes and activities. Collectively, these value streams provide an end-to-end view of how the organization creates customer-centric value.

SAFe is also an amalgamation of Scrum, Lean, Extreme Programming, Kanban, and other Agile practices to improve small team development and delivery performance. While SAFe preserves the small team concepts of Agile, it also provides organizational structures to coordinate and integrate the efforts of multiple Agile teams, working in collaboration across value streams to produce and deliver large, integrated solutions.

Moreover, SAFe includes specific guidance to align product portfolio investment priorities with the mission and strategies of the business, and across multiple planning horizons. SAFe implements a Lean Portfolio Management competency to apply Lean and systems thinking approaches to product investment funding, Agile portfolio operations, and governance.

SAFe is a comprehensive approach that requires two chapters to cover, one devoted to the essential elements of SAFe, and the other devoted to the SAFe Large Solution and Portfolio Management concepts. In this chapter, we're going to cover the following main topics related to the Essential SAFe configuration:

- Becoming SAFe

- Improving business agility on an enterprise scale

- Taking the train

- Configuring SAFe

- Building on Essential SAFe

- Developing core competencies

- Defining roles and responsibilities

- Installing Lean-Agile practices

- Maintaining flow

- Establishing a solution context

- Breaking down silos with DevOps

- Building in quality

- Remaining Essential SAFe artifacts

- Evaluating best fits

By the end of this chapter, you will understand how the Essential SAFe configuration provides the enabling infrastructure to establish Lean-Agile practices in development activities involving 50 or more people. The skills addressed in this chapter include building small Agile teams, coordinating and synchronizing their work through Program Increments (PIs), developing continuous flows across the product development life cycle, breaking down organizational silos, and how to take a solutions-oriented view to product development.

Becoming SAFe

In this section, you will learn the basic concepts that are the foundations behind SAFe. Scaled Agile, Inc. develops and promotes SAFe as a comprehensive Lean-Agile methodology to achieve business agility. The target market for SAFe includes "*the world's largest and most sophisticated software applications, networks, and cyber-physical systems.*" – https://www.scaledAgileframework.com/enterprise-solution-delivery/.

The previous chapter on **Disciplined Agile** (**DA**) also presented a Lean-Agile approach to development. However, the focus of DA is on providing structured guidance on potentially useful, but optional, techniques in context with various process goals. In contrast, SAFe's Lean-Agile approach places more focus on how to implement organizational structures and processes to integrate and coordinate teams on a massive scale. For example, where DA implementations start at the single, small team level, SAFe integrates multiple Agile teams into **Agile Release Trains** (**ARTs**) of *50 to 125* people and scales upward from there.

SAFe is a large and complex methodology to implement Lean-Agile practices on an enterprise scale. SAFe was never about merely making software development teams more productive; instead, SAFe has the objective of making an entire organization Lean and Agile around its product lines, integrating both development concepts.

Integrating Lean and Agile development concepts

Agile practices have evolved to optimize activities at the development team level to primarily develop software products through iterative and frequent development cycles, allowing rapid responsiveness to change and incremental deliveries of customer-centric value. Thus, as initially conceived, Agile was primarily a team optimization concept.

In contrast, Lean development has always been about the optimization of the entire set of value creation and delivery stream activities across the life cycle of the organization's products. Lean developers look across value streams to optimize all flows as an integrated system. Lean practitioners typically use value stream mapping to visually display the current and future states of all activities necessary to deliver a product or service to the market.

> **Note**
> Recall that the goal of value stream mapping is to analyze and optimize the entire set of value stream processes as an integrated system. Therefore, the objective of SAFe's Lean-Agile practices is to leverage the team-level improvement capabilities of Agile with the comprehensive and organization-wide value-stream improvement capabilities of Lean.

The values and principles of Agile, as outlined in the Agile Manifesto (`https://agilemanifesto.org/`), had a massive impact on improving the performance of the software development industry. But before the Agile Manifesto became a thing, Lean development practices had already become a dominant strategy for improving manufacturing efficiencies from a customer-centric and value-added perspective. The integration of computer and interconnected systems with physical products made it inevitable, in my mind, that impacted industries would integrate Lean and Agile practices.

Scaled Agile, Inc., the developers of SAFe, also understand the political and social disruptions caused by attempts to affect organizational change on an enterprise scale. In this chapter, you will learn how SAFe supports a *dual business operating system* that takes advantage of the large organization's economies of scale, with minimal disruptions, while implementing Lean-Agile practices at the product level. Over time, as the organization sees the benefits, the new Lean-Agile operating system becomes the norm and the culture follows.

For further information on SAFe's dual operating system vision, please refer to this article: `https://www.scaledagileframework.com/whats-new-in-safe-5-0/`

Leveraging economies of scale

The previous paragraph made it clear that SAFe has a unique and beneficial value proposition for existing companies that have significant economies of scale, which usually prevents competitors from entering their markets. However, the competition has changed, and many existing companies face disruption within their industries from smaller, more Agile entities that leverage advanced digital technologies to gain a competitive advantage.

These disruptions occur in established physical and software products companies as well as brick and mortar retail companies. Manufacturers of physical products now find their competitors employing computing technology and internet-based connections to provide enhanced capabilities. Large brick and mortar retail firms must establish online marketing and sales capabilities to compete against online retailers such as Amazon.com. And large software development companies must learn how to employ Lean and Agile practices across their value creation and value delivery activities on an enterprise scale.

Building cyber-physical systems

Of all the methodologies presented in this book, SAFe is unique in its application to supporting the construction of large cyber-physical systems. In other words, SAFe provides an approach to implement both Lean and Agile practices on large, complex products that involve an intermixture of digital and physical components.

The number of products that fit this criterion is large and growing. For example, self-driving automobiles, trains, aircraft, ships, manufacturing control systems, robotics, and even large buildings with **Building Information Management** (**BIM**) systems fit into this category. Additionally, the large-scale production of **Internet of Things** (**IoT**) products also qualifies as large cyber-physical production systems and would similarly benefit from using SAFe's Lean-Agile practices and organizational structures.

Building large software products with SAFe

Large software companies are not immune from disruptors in their industry, given the dynamic and rapid pace of technology change in the information technology industry. Plus, the move by retail companies from brick and mortar infrastructures to online sales platforms makes them large software companies. The software industry as a whole, and regardless of product offerings, must adopt Lean-Agile practices to retain the benefits of their established customer base and economies of scale.

Many enterprise-class systems and large software product companies have challenging scaling issues that would benefit from the employment of SAFe's Lean-Agile practices and organizational structures. Though not dealing in physical products *per se*, these companies produce multiple products that have unique value propositions, customers, and users.

In effect, each of the software modules or software-based services has both value creation and value delivery activities that must be synchronized and integrated, with work pulled on demand. Examples of representative large software product companies include developers of **enterprise resource planning** (**ERP**) systems, **health information management** (**HIM**) systems, insurance claims management software, and online retail software applications.

Limiting factors when scaling Scrum

In previous chapters, you learned that other Scrum-based practices mostly take a *wash, rinse, and repeat* approach to scaling agility across an enterprise or large product development requirement. In other words, there is very little modification to the basic Scrum framework as the organization scales Agile capabilities across the enterprise.

Instead of making Scrum Teams bigger, or adding more organizational layers or roles and responsibilities, the traditional Scrum-based model duplicates the basic small Scrum Team structure. Each small team has the same roles, events, and artifacts, and rules are ideally fully self-contained and operate autonomously within a single product line.

As you learned in *Chapter 6, Lean Practices in Software Development* through *Chapter 9, The NEXUS Framework* new extensions to the basic Scrum framework evolved to support coordination, synchronization, and integration issues when multiple Scrum Teams work on a single product (that is, Scrum of Scrums, Scrum@Scale, Nexus, and LeSS). However, those methodologies do not guide the scaling of Scrum on an enterprise-scale in the context of supporting and integrating operational value streams. Their primary focus is on coordinating development value streams.

That type of limited focus doesn't work for every company. While the theories of empiricism and the complex adaptive systems approach of Scrum are useful and extendable across business functions, organizations are left on their own to figure out how to employ them.

Most of the Scrum methods provide little guidance on how to improve value stream flows, as the very notion of product backlogs and Sprints implies a push-oriented development strategy. Recall from the chapters on Lean development that the best value streams operate as pull-based systems with streamlined and coordinated flows of activities. Such activities flow as a sequence in lock-step, with minimal cycle times and cycle time variances across activities. Additionally, Lean development processes eliminate all batch processes and queuing with pull-based order entry and processing.

The pure Scrum methodologies do not discuss the alignment of product investments with business strategies, or managing costs within **return on investment** (**ROI**) constraints. The basic principles behind Agile and Scrum do not address how an organization goes about the work of defining and evaluating product or solution investment opportunities and priorities, nor how to align organizational resources to the mission and strategies of the business.

There are other issues to consider when implementing Agile practices at an enterprise level. For example, in highly regulated industries or government organizations, more structure and oversight may be required to address compliance requirements. In other cases, the resistance to change when it comes to implementing network-oriented organizational structures of small teams on a large scale may be impossible to overcome, at least in the short run.

None of these limitations are indictments against Scrum. But these issues must be addressed by any organization that attempts to implement Scrum on an enterprise scale. In contrast, SAFe is a comprehensive and enterprise-class Lean-Agile methodology that guides all of these areas, and more.

Expanding agility on an enterprise scale

SAFe employs the empirical process control theories of Scrum while adding the analytical capabilities and benefits of systems and Lean thinking. SAFe leverages existing organizational resources to achieve improved economies of scale. It implements sound Portfolio Management practices to define, prioritize, and align investment opportunities with corporate strategies over multiple planning horizons. In short, SAFe is a framework to implement business agility on an enterprise scale.

Compared to Scrum and all its variants, SAFe is by far the most prescriptive approach to scaling Agile practices. It incorporates numerous Agile techniques within its framework, such as Lean development, systems thinking, Kanban, Scrum, **Extreme Programming (XP)**, and DevOps. Moreover, SAFe provides detailed guidance on how to integrate these capabilities on an enterprise scale:

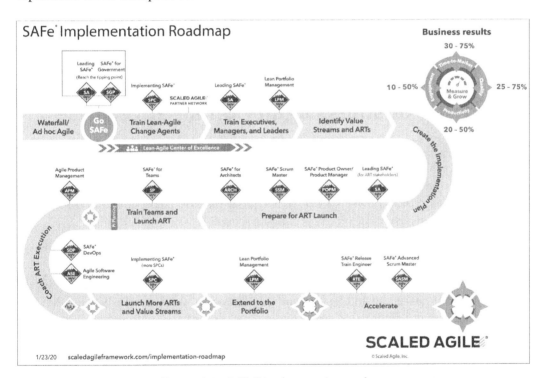

Figure 12.1 – SAFe™ implementation roadmap

Given the scope of its knowledge base of useful and integrated practices, SAFe is a more comprehensive development framework than the Scrum framework is alone. As a result, Scaled Agile, Inc. provides a comprehensive implementation roadmap to guide the implementation effort, as shown in *Figure 12.1*. The company also provides detailed guides, instructions, and certification programs to help the organization implement its team structures, roles, responsibilities, events, and artifacts.

These are the areas where SAFe shines. However, it comes at a bit of a cost in terms of education, time and cost to implement, disciplined efforts on the part of the executive leadership to drive adoption, plus some additional overhead and structure. It would be a mistake to think other Scrum and Agile scaling approaches wouldn't have similar issues. Scaled Scrum does not minimize the efforts to create an Agile enterprise.

The SAFe methodology implements some relatively unique concepts and terminology. This chapter introduces you to the basics of how SAFe works, and how it is implemented and why. But there is much more to learn. The *Scaled Agile, Inc.* web page provides a SAFe graphic where you can click on any of the terms and concepts that you want to explore further at `https://www.scaledAgileframework.com`.

Improving business agility on an enterprise scale

We live in an era that is defined by the **digital economy**. The term *Digital Economy* is most often ascribed to Don Tapscott's 1995 best-seller *The Digital Economy: Promise and Peril in the Age of Networked Intelligence*. In his book, Tapscott talks about a new economy where *the age of networked intelligence is a digital economy*.

We often think of the digital economy as conducting e-commerce via the internet and the World Wide Web. However, it's bigger than that. For example, the average automobile has more computer power than the systems NASA used to guide and sustain living conditions within the Apollo spacecraft and Space Shuttles. Think how much more advanced the AI-based autonomous vehicles currently under development are. In other words, our digital economy is also driven by the computing power and systems employed directly within our modern products.

We also have the concept of the **IoT**, whereby networking capabilities via the internet enable two-way communication of information between products and suppliers or their third-party support organizations. The IoT infrastructure is enormous. For example, *"Gartner, Inc. forecasts that the enterprise and automotive Internet of Things (IoT) market* will grow to 5.8 billion endpoints in 2020, a 21% increase from 2019."* (`https://www.gartner.com/en/newsroom/press-releases/2019-08-29-gartner-says-5-8-billion-enterprise-and-automotive-io`). IoT connects the products of our digital economy, driving rapid and continuous feedback on product performance and customer demands, while also enabling instantaneous upgrades to deployed smart products.

Driven by a combination of global markets, instantaneous information, and digital disruptions, business entities must be Agile to remain competitive in their markets. Likewise, government agencies and non-profits do not operate in a vacuum and must practice agility to remain useful and relevant.

SAFe implements many Lean-Agile practices and configurations at scale, all of which work together to help the organization compete in diverse market conditions. SAFe's conceptual model is that organizations can leverage the capabilities of SAFe to achieve business agility in the digital age in which we live.

Before we get into those discussions, it's important to note that the developers of SAFe understand how difficult it is to effect change on an enterprise scale. People who feel threatened or just uncomfortable with change will dig their heels in and resist. A more effective strategy is to start small, demonstrate success, and then build on those successes until the new business methods become the norm, and the culture adjusts on its own. To use an analogy that is consistent with SAFe's approach to scaling Lean-Agile practices, *everyone jumps on the train!*

However, it's premature to jump into introducing the concept of *trains* in SAFe. Before we get there, we need to understand the business drivers that created a need to have Lean-Agile Enterprises, plus we'll dive into the core values and principles that guide the implementation of SAFe. We'll start with a discussion on the business drivers that led to SAFe's implementation of a **dual operating system** for business agility.

For more information on this topic, please refer to the *New Business Agility* section at `https://www.scaledagileframework.com/whats-new-in-safe-5-0/`.

Implementing a dual operating system for business agility

It's important to understand that SAFe is not intended for start-up entities unless they somehow have the resources to start with at least 50 to 125 people. The more common situation occurs when an existing large entity has realized they are no longer sufficiently competitive or nimble to service their customers adequately. To reduce the organizational disruptions and resistance, SAFe implements a dual business operating system that facilitates innovations while preserving the foundational strengths of the organization.

One operating system retains the functional and hierarchical operations that allowed the large companies to compete in their traditional markets, leveraging their economies of scale to protect against intrusions from new entrants into their markets. The second operating system is an overlay of networked-oriented small teams and trains that support operational and development value streams around the organization's large products and solutions.

In our modern digital economy, many existing large enterprises have faced off against small competitors who have used disruptive digital technologies to change the dynamics of their markets. Think, for example, how robotics has made manufacturing in the United States competitive again. Likewise, online companies such as Amazon.com have made many "brick and mortar" retailers largely uncompetitive in local markets.

Existing organizations that want to survive through the disruptions caused by the emergent digital economy must adapt, which requires a high degree of agility. Companies that do not adapt will lose their competitive edge and may not survive. If they do survive, they will not enjoy the market shares, revenues, or market-dominating positions they previously enjoyed.

Fortunately, existing companies can compete, leveraging the same people, resources, and economies of scale that made them secure in the first place. But they need to rediscover the innovative networks and culture that initially helped build the organization.

SAFe addresses the issues of reinstalling innovations and business agility through the implementation of a dual operating system. In other words, the organization can implement network-oriented structures of small teams alongside the hierarchical structures. Where the hierarchical structures continue to provide efficiencies, stability, and economies of scale, the smaller, network-oriented teams foster entrepreneurial activities and innovations.

Over time, the network-based teams may replace the hierarchical structures in the form of product and solution-oriented value streams. But that's a decision that can wait, usually after the advantages become apparent to the organization as a whole. In the meantime, people do not need to fear that the transition to SAFe will cause them to lose their jobs or their positions. They will have time to adjust to their new roles and the new way of doing business.

Establishing a Lean-Agile mindset

Organizations that install SAFe promote a **Lean-Agile mindset** that embodies the concepts of Lean development with the values and principles outlined in the Agile manifesto. As a matter of choice, or *mindset*, individuals and organizations can choose to remain fixed in their views, or they can choose to seek opportunities to grow. In other words, we choose whether we prefer having a **fixed mindset** to keep things the same or a **growth mindset** that allows us to expand both our knowledge and our abilities.

The implementation of Lean-Agile practices is a significant change for most organizations, and the leaders and its people must be willing to adopt a growth mindset to achieve success. As a simplified model of Lean-Agile practices, SAFe conceptualizes these practices as living in the **SAFe House of Lean**.

For more details on the SAFe House of Lean, refer to the related section within
`https://www.scaledagileframework.com/whats-new-in-safe-5-0/`.

For information on SAFe's views regarding Lean-Agile mindsets, review the article at
`https://www.scaledagileframework.com/lean-agile-mindset/`.

Later in this chapter, you will learn about the four SAFe configurations that define the entrepreneurial and innovation-based teams of SAFe. These configurations include *Essential SAFe*, *Large Solution SAFe*, *Portfolio SAFe*, and *Full SAFe*. But, before we get to the introductions to those four configurations, we need to review the core values and principles that guide all SAFe teams.

Building on the four core values of SAFe

SAFe embodies three bodies of knowledge previously described in this book. These three bodies of knowledge include *Agile*, *Lean Product Development*, and *Systems Thinking*. We don't need to go through those subjects again, suffice to say that those three disciplines bring a wealth of capabilities that allow SAFe to scale deep and wide across the organization. Chief among the capabilities are *alignment, built-in quality, transparency,* and *program execution,* as shown in *Figure 12.2.* Together, these four capabilities form the core values that drive SAFe practices:

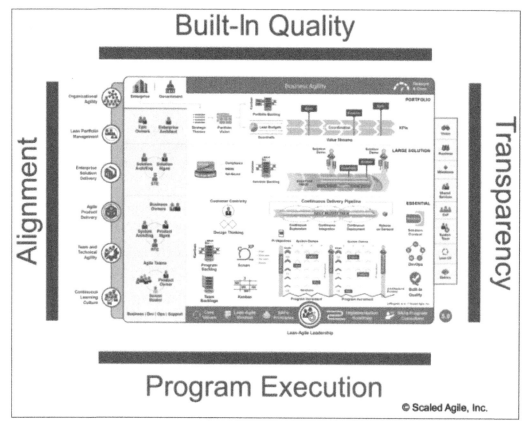

Figure 12.2 – The four core values of SAFe (https://www.scaledagileframework.com/safe-for-lean-enterprises/)

The following list outlines the scope of capabilities embodied in each of the core values:

- **Alignment**: With the corporate mission, strategies, and attendant investment priorities

- **Built-in quality**: From the start in relation to five specific areas—Value Stream Flow, Architecture and Design Quality, Code Quality, System Quality, and Release Quality

- **Transparency**: Providing accurate and timely information to make informed decisions, and with safety in mind, to those who deliver the message

- **Program execution**: Across portfolios, teams, trains, and value streams

Values and principles go hand-in-hand. Where values form an underlying belief system for the individual or an organization, principles define the rules or standards of conduct that guide the individual or organization's behavior. SAFe implements 10 principles, which we'll review in the next subsection.

The 10 principles of SAFe

The 10 principles of SAFe help guide the organization to implement the disciplines of Lean-Agile practices, systems thinking, and value-based flows. The 10 principles do not take the place of the wealth of knowledge available on these topics. Instead, they blend the disparate concepts into a workable structure of useful and implementable practices, as described in the following list and at `https://www.scaledagileframework.com/safe-lean-agile-principles/`.

The 10 principles of SAFe are as follows:

- **Take an economic view**: Look at customer value from the perspective of providing only those things that customers want, and to eliminate all forms of waste that a customer would refuse to purchase.

- **Apply systems thinking**: SAFe evaluates complex systems across three critical elements – products, the enterprise, and value streams. Organizations must resist local optimizations and instead concentrate on synching activities, identifying system boundaries and environmental interactions, and improving interfaces and dependencies to maximize the flow of value.

- **Assume variability; preserve options**: Delay making any decisions until the last possible moment.

- **Build incrementally with fast, integrated learning cycles**: Provide more frequent opportunities to test assumptions with customers, provide new increments of functionality more frequently to customers and end users, reduce the opportunity for defects and bugs to propagate to the point that they are difficult to isolate and resolve, and review past efforts to discover better ways of working to deliver value.

- **Base milestones on an objective evaluation of working systems**: Define acceptance criteria and conduct product demos to obtain objective evaluations of new increments of value in terms of usefulness and economic benefit.

- **Visualize and limit WIP, reduce batch sizes, and manage queue lengths**: Following the practices of Lean development, use Kanban Boards to visually display work in progress and establish pull-based rules to take on new work only when team capacities become available.

- **Apply cadence, synchronize with cross-domain planning**: All activities across all value streams need to work in a coordinated and integrated fashion and at the same pace.

- **Unlock the intrinsic motivation of the knowledge workers**: Provide incentives around team accomplishments and the development of useful skills, respect for others, safety to be open and honest, and provide team-level autonomy within constraints that support the mission, strategies, identified value streams, and budgets of the business

- **Decentralize decision making**: Eliminate artificial boundaries, friction, and delays that prevent the rapid resolution of issues identified at an operational level.

- **Organize around value**: No functional, hierarchical, and bureaucratic organizational structures that only delay decision making and inefficient processes.

Now that you understand what the core values and principles of SAFe are, let's explore the seven core competencies necessary to implement SAFe within and across an enterprise.

Developing the seven core competencies

As the term *competencies* implies, the seven core competencies of SAFe are the skills and capabilities the organization must build and maintain in order to properly execute the operating systems to achieve business agility and thrive in the digital age. Put more succinctly, the seven core competencies of SAFe are what allow the organization to be agile, and to practice agility. For more details on SAFe's Measure and Grow Self-Assessment tool, please refer to the section entitled *Measuring business agility* at `https://www.scaledagileframework.com/whats-new-in-safe-5-0/`.

Across the 7 core competencies are 21 dimensions that enable business agility. SAFe implements a business agility self-assessment tool, as part of SAFe's *Measure and Grow* capability, that helps portfolios assess and improve their state of business agility across these 7 core competencies.

The 7 core competencies and 21 dimensions of SAFe include the following:

Team and Technical Agility	Agile Product Delivery
• High-performing cross-functional, Agile teams • Business and technical teams build business solutions • Quality business solutions delight customers	• The customer is the center of your product strategy • Develop on cadence, release on demand • Continuously explore, integrate, deploy, and innovate
Enterprise Solution Delivery	**Continuous Learning Culture**
• Apply Lean systems engineering • Coordinate and align the value chain • Continually evolve live systems	• Everyone learns and grows together • Exploration and creativity are part of the organization's DNA • Everyone is responsible for continuously improving solutions, services, and processes
Lean Portfolio Management	**Organizational Agility**
• Align strategy, funding, and execution • Optimize operations around the portfolio • Lightweight governance empowers decentralized decision making	• Create an enterprise-wide, Lean-Agile mindset • Lean out business operations • Respond quickly to opportunities and threats
Lean-Agile Leadership	
• Inspire others by modeling behaviors • Align mindset, words, and action to Lean-Agile values and principles • Actively lead the change and guide others to the new way of working	

Figure 12.3 – List of SAFe's 7 core competencies and the 21 dimensions of business agility

As shown in *Figure 12.3*, SAFe implements 7 core competencies that support the development of a Lean enterprise, plus 21 dimensions that enable business agility. These core competencies and dimensions are shown in the proper context in *Figure 12.4*. The graphic may be hard to read, so feel free to review it on the Scaled-Agile, Inc. website at `https://www.scaledAgileframework.com/safe-for-lean-enterprises/`:

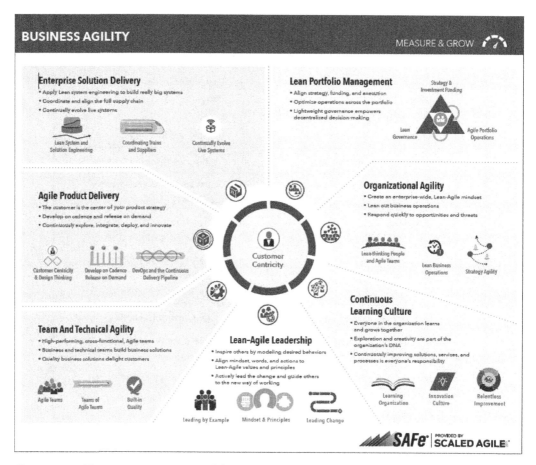

Figure 12.4 – The 7 core competencies of the Lean Enterprise and the 21 dimensions of business agility (`https://www.scaledagileframework.com/safe-for-lean-enterprises/`)

The core competencies list in the frame on the left-hand side of the graphic provide a focus on the execution of SAFe practices. At the same time, those on the right focus on supporting business strategy and organizational development. Lean-Agile leadership is the foundation of SAFe, since implementation is futile without their active support and encouragement. By the way, that statement is true of any enterprise-scale implementation of Agile and Scrum practices.

Customers have center stage in the graphic to remind SAFe practitioners as to the purpose of the organization, to add value as seen in the eyes of the customer. The **Measure and Grow** icon in the top-right is both a reminder and a link to a self-assessment tool to track the organization's progress in implementing the SAFe principles and practices that enable business agility. For more information on SAFe's Measure and Grow, please review the article at `https://www.scaledagileframework.com/whats-new-in-safe-5-0/`.

Now that we've covered SAFe's dual operating systems, Agile-mindset, core values, principles, and core competencies that enable business agility, we can get started on our SAFe journey. We'll start by taking the train.

Taking the train

SAFe implements Scrum within its framework and shares some of its attributes, such as iterative development practices, incremental deliveries of new value, small teams, and customer centricity. But SAFe also implements modern concepts that are often associated with **development operations** (**DevOps**), which ties together development and support functions through closer communication and collaboration, plus automation and integration of product life cycle processes. Together, these capabilities make continuous development and delivery practices possible.

Rather than view the release of new product enhancements as discrete offerings, each with their beginnings and ends, SAFe conceptualizes the ongoing release of new products and enhancements as a part of a **continuous delivery pipeline** around value streams. SAFe defines value streams as *the series of steps that an organization uses to implement Solutions that provide a continuous flow of value to a customer.*

The concept of a continuous delivery pipeline is also consistent with the principle in the Agile Manifesto that states "*Agile processes promote sustainable development. The sponsors, developers, and users should be able to maintain a constant pace indefinitely.*" (Beck *et al.*, 2001)

To provide continuous delivery, you must implement an organizational structure that provides continuity across its products and solutions. SAFe implements **ARTs** and **solution trains** in support of this objective. SAFe defines an ART as "*a long-lived team of Agile teams, which, along with other stakeholders, incrementally develops, delivers, and, where applicable, operates one or more solutions in a value stream.*"

A solution train is an organizational structure within SAFe that supports the development of large and complex solutions that require coordination of the activities of multiple ARTs and the suppliers that support the organization. Solution trains align the integrated ARTs to a mission and strategies of the business around a shared solution vision, backlog, and roadmap. Each of the ARTs and solution trains operate on the same iterative cadence, which SAFe refers to as a **Program Increment (PI)** – `https://www.scaledagileframework.com/program-increment/`.

For more information on SAFe's continuous delivery pipeline, visit `https://www.scaledagileframework.com/continuous-delivery-pipeline/`.

For more information on SAFe's Agile release trains, visit `https://www.scaledagileframework.com/agile-release-train/`.

For more information on SAFe's continuous delivery pipeline, visit `https://www.scaledagileframework.com/solution-train/`.

Building on cadence, releasing on demand

A **PI** is a timebox duration in which the ARTs and solution trains, when implemented, deliver incremental value in the form of working, tested software, systems, and large-scale solutions. The iterative cadence of a PI is typically *8 to 12 weeks* long. The most common pattern for a PI is four development iterations, followed by one **Innovation and Planning (IP)** iteration. IP iterations provide a cushion to complete PI objectives that are not completed in the development iterations, plus they provide time for working on innovative ideas, continuing education, PI planning, and **Inspect and Adapt (I&A)** events.

A key concept in SAFe is that ARTs and the solution train iteratively define, build, test, and deliver products at a common cadence, but they *release on demand*. This practice is an important concept when building large-scale and complex solutions that take many iterations to deliver a complete product or solution. In SAFe, the cadence of the PI ensures the creation and delivery of incremental value throughout the entire development cycle. Each PI ensures solution-level testing and customer validations across each iteration. However, the product is not releasable until it fully meets its definition of done, and the product owner approves the release.

The amount of time specified for the PI's timebox duration is a subjective decision made by the organization, but, once decided upon, should remain the same for the life of the product. The PI duration has no tie to the amount of work accomplished within each iteration. To believe otherwise is to fall into the same trap as the Waterfall model, which forced a set scope of work within an arbitrary set duration. Instead, with SAFe, the organization accumulates deliveries of incremental value across each PI, until the product is at a level of maturity for release to the external customer.

You've already learned that SAFe implements teams in the form of ARTs and solution trains, and you learn how these trains operate in this chapter. But living within each train are smaller-sized Agile teams that do the work and produce the deliverables of the value streams. Like the ARTs and solution trains, they are long-lived to support the product or product line across its development life cycle and often its operational life. Agile teams also work to a cadence, but on a smaller timescale, as discussed in the next subsection.

Scaling small Agile teams

As noted in the previous subsection, ARTs are a collection of "*long-lived Agile teams*." SAFe Agile teams are fundamentally Scrum teams, implementing the same roles, events, artifacts, and rules. However, Agile teams may also include the disciplines of Kanban and XP. Safe recommends a hybrid of the **ScrumXP** approach for teams, explicitly working on software development activities. Scrum installs empirical process control and complex adaptive systems capabilities across small teams. At the same time, XP implements 12 useful software development techniques, such as user stories, paired programming, continuous integration, and **test-driven development** (**TDD**).

The small Agile team profile eliminates the complexities and inefficiencies that negatively affect the performance of large teams. The smaller duration iterations, usually timebox-limited to 2 weeks, enable flexible responses to link up with other Agile teams and the ARTs and solution trains, and ultimately deliver more customer-oriented value more frequently.

As you will discover later in this chapter, the research behind both the ART and Agile team sizes provides the best of all worlds. That is, small team agility to frequently provide customer-centric value, with more significant team integrations and synchronicity to develop large-scale solutions. Agile teams and trains within SAFe scale to enable the development of increasingly more substantial and more complex products and solutions via four SAFe configurations. The scaling starts with SAFe's roles and responsibilities.

For more information on SAFe's Agile teams, review this article at `https://www.scaledagileframework.com/scrumxp/`.

For more information on SAFe's Agile teams, review this article at `https://www.scaledagileframework.com/test-driven-development-2/`.

Scaling roles and responsibilities

Keen observers of the SAFe configuration graphics have probably noted that SAFe implements a repeating pattern of three primary roles across each level of product and solution development. You will learn about SAFe's roles and their responsibilities in the sections on SAFe configurations. For now, you can think of SAFe as implementing three generic responsibilities to three specialized roles at subsequent levels of scale, as follows:

- **What gets built**: **Product Owners (POs)** | product management | solution management

- **How it gets built**: Agile teams | system architect/engineering | solution architect/engineering

- **Servant leadership, coaching, and mentoring**: Scrum Master | **Release Train Engineer (RTE)** | **Solution Train Engineer (STE)**

This cascading structure of roles and responsibilities is what allows SAFe to scale Lean-Agile practices with increasing size and complexity of products and solutions.

Now that you understand the essential elements of SAFe, let's get into the details of the SAFe configurations.

Configuring SAFe®

SAFe is a comprehensive Lean-Agile approach to providing the organizational structures, roles, events, and artifacts to achieve business agility on a large scale. Not every organization needs every element of SAFe, and those that do will take some time and effort to get there. Rather than trying to eat the whole elephant at once, so to speak, SAFe implements four configurations, as shown in the following list:

- **Essential SAFe**: `https://www.scaledagileframework.com/essential-safe/`

- **Large Solution SAFe**: `https://www.scaledagileframework.com/large-solution-safe/`

- **Portfolio SAFe**: `https://www.scaledagileframework.com/portfolio-safe/`

- **Full SAFe**: `https://www.scaledagileframework.com/`

Essential SAFe and **Large Solution SAFe** are the basic building blocks for organizing large teams to develop large and complex products and solutions. Of the scaled Agile approaches presented in this book, **Portfolio SAFe** is the only approach to address Portfolio Management in the context of an Agile enterprise. **Full SAFe** brings everything together, as many organizations will have more than one instance of the three other SAFe configurations.

The four configurations are too broad to cover in one chapter. So, we will cover the initial Essential SAFe configuration of SAFe in the remainder of this chapter, and then cover the remaining configurations in the next chapter. This type of separation is logical as, collectively, the remaining configurations build to the Full SAFe configuration.

Building on Essential SAFe

At the very beginning of this chapter, you learned that SAFe is a Lean-Agile approach for developing large-scale products and solutions. That is a true statement beginning out of the gate with the first level of configuration, Essential SAFe.

SAFe implements four configurations that guide different levels of implementation. These four configurations are *Essential SAFe*, *Large Solution SAFe*, *Portfolio SAFe*, and *Full SAFe*. We'll start with the introduction to Essential SAFe, as shown pictorially in *Figure 12.5*.

Essential SAFe is the most basic configuration of SAFe and includes a minimal set of roles, events, and artifacts required to deliver value at scale. As with other Scrum-based practices, SAFe incorporates the use of small Agile teams to reduce the issues of complexity that arise with increasing numbers of active participants.

However, since SAFe is an approach to implement Agile practices at scale, the Essential SAFe configuration introduces a higher-level organizational structure known as **ART** to plan, organize, and manage work at scale:

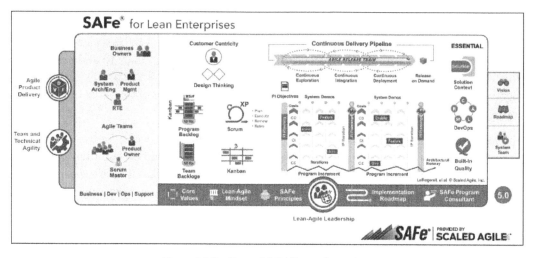

Figure 12.5 – Essential SAFe configuration
(https://www.scaledagileframework.com/safe-for-lean-enterprises/)

Purpose of Essential SAFe

Essential SAFe is the fundamental configuration of SAFe in that it is a fully self-contained framework to support large and complex product development efforts. In other words, Essential SAFe provides the minimum elements necessary to implement Lean-Agile practices in support of developing large and complex products. Essential SAFe also provides the foundations that are necessary to implement *Large Solution SAFe*, *Portfolio Safe*, and *Full SAFe* configurations, should the organization require those capabilities.

In the following subsections of this chapter, you will learn the essential roles, events, and artifacts that make up Essential SAFe, plus the specific SAFe core competencies that support this configuration of SAFe.

Elements of Essential SAFe

SAFe coordinates the activities of multiple small Agile teams to plan, integrate, and synchronize their work to build large and complex products. As noted in the previous sections of this chapter, SAFe implements a Lean-Agile approach to product development that has a focus on creating customer value while making value streams as efficient as they can be. These activities start with Essential SAFe.

Essential SAFe incorporates a number of Agile practices within its framework. These include the use of Kanbans, backlogs, Scrum, **XP**, iterative development, incremental additions to value, and continuous delivery. You've already learned about most of these concepts in previous chapters. In the remaining sections within this chapter, you will learn how SAFe implements these practices in a coordinated manner to build and deliver large and complex products effectively.

As you will see, there are numerous elements that make up the Essential SAFe configuration, and some conceptual organization as groups or related knowledge helps facilitate the learning process. These groupings are not part of SAFe, but make sense from a taxonomic (in other words, knowledge classification) perspective. With this strategy in mind, the remainder of this chapter breaks down the elements of Essential SAFe into the following groupings:

- Developing core competencies
- Defining roles and responsibilities
- Installing Lean-Agile practices
- Maintaining flow
- Understanding the solution context
- Breaking down silos with DevOps
- Building in quality
- Evaluating best fits

We'll goes through these groupings in the same order, starting with the core competencies associated with Essential SAFe.

Developing core competencies

In the introductory section of this chapter, you learned that SAFe implements 7 core competencies supporting the Lean Enterprise and their 21 dimensions that enable business agility. The SAFe core competencies associated with Essential SAFe include **Agile Product Delivery** and **Team and Technical Agility**.

The competency of Agile Product Delivery helps ensure that the organization takes a customer-centric approach to define, build, and release products and services as a continuous flow. The dimensions of Agile Product Delivery include customer centricity, design thinking, developing on cadence while releasing on demand, DevOps, and the continuous delivery pipeline.

The Team and Technical Agility competency implements the skills and Lean-Agile principles and practices that create high-performing Agile teams and Agile release teams that can deliver high-value and high-quality products and solutions for their customers. The dimensions of Team and Technical Agility include the installment of multiple small Agile teams, coordinating, synchronizing, and integrating the work of multiple Agile teams as teams of Agile teams, and building in quality.

For more information on Agile Product Delivery competencies, please visit `https://www.scaledagileframework.com/agile-product-delivery/`.

For more information on Team and Technical Agility competencies, please visit `https://www.scaledagileframework.com/team-and-technical-agility/`.

Defining roles and responsibilities

SAFe installs three sets of roles and responsibilities across the various SAFe configurations. The Essential SAFe configuration is unique in that there are two sets of identified roles and responsibilities. One groups operations at the small Agile team level, while the other operates at the product level.

Essential SAFe introduces the minimum number of roles and responsibilities required to implement SAFe within an organization. These roles include Agile teams, PO, Scrum Master, RTE, system architects/engineering, product management, and business owners. You will learn the roles and responsibilities in the next subsection.

The Essential SAFe configuration implements its seven roles conceptually across three levels. Three roles span the Agile team level, three other roles support the ART level, and Business Owner informs the other groups regarding the scope and priorities of the product or solution under development.

Conceptualizing essential team responsibilities

Agile teams have the traditional Scrum team members, consisting of a Scrum Master, PO, and developers. With a couple of exceptions, the Agile teams operate as any Scrum team operates. One exception is that SAFe recommends the employment of XP techniques for software development teams. Another exception is the role of the PO, which is limited to defining stories and prioritizing the team backlog items consisting of features and components.

The ARTs have a **Release Train Engineer** (**RTE**), a systems architecture or systems engineering function, and a product management function. Recall that an ART encompasses multiple Agile teams and has anywhere from 50 to 125 people. Therefore, roles at the ART level have directional and oversight responsibilities to help the Agile teams coordinate and integrate their work in conformance with product and solution backlog priorities.

The RTE serves in a Scrum Master type role for the entire ART. The product management function has a broader responsibility than the PO in that it identifies and defines customer needs, understands the solution context, and develops the program vision, roadmap, and features required for the whole product or solution under development. The system architect/engineering function defines and communicates a shared technical and architectural vision for the ART to help ensure that the product or solution under development fulfills its intended purpose.

At the product level, ARTs support the value streams and operate as a team of Agile teams. Therefore, another level of leadership is required to coordinate, integrate, and synchronize the activities of the underlying Agile teams.

Now that you have a conceptual model to work from, let's take a deeper dive into each of these roles and responsibilities within this section, starting with the most basic function—Agile teams.

Agile teams

Consistent with Scrum practices, SAFe implements small, cross-functional, self-organizing, and autonomous Agile teams, typically containing 5 to 11 individuals each, at the lowest levels of its configurations. Like Scrum, SAFe Agile teams, as a collective, provide a broad and diverse set of skills necessary to support the business needs of the organization. SAFe Agile teams can support any number of value streams – spanning both business and development requirements, and therefore, different Agile teams can have a varying mix of skills. Also similar to Scrum, SAFe Agile teams define, build, test, and deliver an increment of value in short time-boxed iterations.

Agile teams support the ARTs and solution trains. Whereas the ARTs and solution trains operate on the PI intervals, the Agile teams operate on more frequent iterations. Each development iteration is a standard, fixed-length timebox interval, where the teams deliver incremental value in the form of working, tested software and systems. The recommended duration of the timebox is 2 weeks. However, 1 to 4 weeks is acceptable, depending on the business context.

For more information on SAFe's Agile teams, please review this article: `https://www.scaledagileframework.com/agile-teams/`

Scrum Masters

As with Scrum, the primary role of the Scrum Master is to act as a servant leader and coach for the Agile teams. The knowledge level of a SAFe Scrum Master is broader than is required in Scrum, as the SAFe Scrum Master must have a solid understanding of the application of Scrum, XP, Kanban, and Lean development practices. Moreover, they need to understand how to integrate these practices into a cohesive whole.

The SAFe Scrum Master must, of course, understand the concepts, principles, and practices of SAFe, and coach their teams in SAFe practices. They also work with other Scrum Masters, including RTEs and STEs, to improve and sustain the implementation of SAFe practices across the enterprise.

For more information on the Scrum Master role, please review this article: `https://www.scaledagileframework.com/scrum-master/`

Product Owners

Each Agile team has a **PO** who is responsible for managing the priorities within the team backlog. At a cursory level, the SAFe PO has many of the same duties as the traditional Scrum PO; as follows:

- Defining the Product Backlog

- Refining and prioritizing the work in the backlog

- Creating or assisting in the creation of user stories for the development teams

- Reviewing and accepting completed user stories in terms of acceptance criteria

Unlike Scrum, the PO in SAFe has a more limited role in that they do not have product management responsibilities. Product management is a separate function in SAFe. On the other hand, SAFe POs have a much closer relationship with their assigned teams and interact daily. As a result, a SAFe PO is typically assigned to one or two teams, but never more than two teams.

For more information on the PO role, please review this article: `https://www.scaledagileframework.com/product-owner/`.

RTE

If you look closely at the Essential SAFe graphic, you will notice that the ARTs implement a similar three-pronged organizational structure to the Agile teams. This pattern applies at the large solution train level as well. We'll get to that section later.

The RTE has a similar role to the Scrum Master at the Agile team level. They are the servant leader and coaches for the ARTs. The RTEs facilitate the ART events and processes, assist the teams in delivering value, communicate with stakeholders, and help remove impediments at the ART level. Consistent with SAFe's focus on implementing Lean-Agile practices, the RTEs drive the ARTs to be relentless in their efforts to improve across each PI.

The RTEs facilitate PI planning events to both plan activities and coordinate Agile Teams and value stream activities. With its emphasis on Lean-Agile practices, and employing tools such as program and solution Kanbans, the RTEs help their teams manage and optimize the flow of value. The RTEs also leverage their time with the Agile Team members during the PI planning event to identify and mitigate potential risks. You will learn more about how SAFe implements risk management strategies in the section on planning PIs.

For more information on the RTE role, please review this article: `https://www.scaledagileframework.com/release-train-engineer-and-solution-train-engineer/`

System architect/engineering

As with any software, system, or product development effort, someone or some team must first define the architecture and designs for the products. This activity occurs both before and during development. In SAFe, this role may belong to a single individual or a team. Regardless, they provide architectural or engineering support and technical leadership within the ART and across its Agile teams.

The system architect/engineer's primary role is to assess functional and non-functional requirements and, ultimately, to define the solution context and solution intent for the product. They define the technical vision for the product and create the architecture that specifies the components that make up the product or system. They also define the interfaces between the product or system components.

The architecture and engineering function is a collaborative effort with other team members, partners, and stakeholders to define the solution and validate assumptions, look at alternatives, and feed the continuous delivery pipeline. Collectively, they work to define the technology infrastructure, solution or system components, and subsystems, and to define and manage component interfaces and APIs.

Finally, since SAFe involves multiple teams and trains, the individuals having the system architect/engineering role must work across Agile teams, ARTs, and solution trains to ensure there is alignment in the technical vision and also the implementation of the technical vision.

For more information on the system architect/engineering role, please review this article: `https://www.scaledagileframework.com/system-and-solution-architect-engineering/`

Product management

In SAFe, program backlogs are the responsibility of an assigned product manager, while POs maintain team-level backlogs. Product managers are external facing and have the responsibility to evaluate product vision and strategies based on their research of customer needs and market opportunities:

Product Management Responsibilities	
Collecting market information and analyzing trends	Establishing consumer and reseller financing capabilities, if required
Conducting market research and planning	Overseeing product designs and development to achieve objectives
Facilitating focus group meetings with customers and potential users	Performing sales channels assessments (in other words, direct sales, inside sales, online sales, partner and reseller sales channels)
Determining a product's value proposition	Determining packaging and labeling requirements to provide unique visibility and product protection
Creating marketing plans	Branding a product to establish a unique identity
Establishing product pricing consistent with its value proposition and market objectives	Establishing and overseeing advertisements and promotions programs
Assessing distribution, transportation, and warehousing concerns	

Figure 12.6 – Product management responsibilities

Figure 10.6 depicts the product management responsibilities. Unlike Scrum, SAFe breaks out product managers as a role separate from those of the POs. Product managers of large and complex products, or products with emergent market opportunities, already have a full-time job before adding in the responsibilities of the POs. For large products and solutions, the workload is too large to put on the shoulders of one individual.

Still, the SAFe product managers and POs must work together in close collaboration to be effective in communicating value creation and value delivery objectives and priorities to the ARTs and Agile teams.

For more information on the product management role, please review this article: `https://www.scaledagileframework.com/product-and-solution-management/`

Business owners

The business owner is another role that is unique to SAFe. There is not usually a single business owner, but rather a small group of stakeholders who have relevant business or technical knowledge for the product under development by an ART. Business owners are responsible for governance, compliance, and return on investment. They are ultimately responsible for the business outcome of the products.

You now have a detailed understanding of the roles and responsibilities related to Essential SAFe. In the next section, you will learn how Essential SAFe integrates Lean and Agile at both the Agile team and ART levels.

For more information on the business owner role, please review this article: `https://www.scaledagileframework.com/business-owners/`

Installing Lean-Agile practices

Conceptually, this segment of the Essential SAFe configuration implements structures and practices to install Agile, Lean development, and design thinking practices to develop customer-centric products and services at scale. Specifically, in the subsections that follow, you will learn how SAFe integrates the concepts and practices of customer-centricity, design thinking, Kanban, XP, and program backlogs as the underpinnings to value-centric development.

For more information on the Agile practices, please review this article: `https://www.scaledagileframework.com/agile-product-delivery/`

For more information on the Lean-Agile principles, please review this article: `https://www.scaledagileframework.com/safe-lean-agile-principles/`

Building value with customer centricity

Consistent with what you learned in the Lean chapters, the Lean-Agile practices of SAFe place a premium on delivering value in terms of supporting customer needs by delivering the highest value capabilities – from the perspective of the customers and economics, and by doing so in the most efficient manner. Anything else is waste.

Waste is harmful to an organization for two reasons:

- Waste does not support our customers' priorities.
- We open our organization to competitive threats.

SAFe practitioners view customer centricity as a mindset. SAFe organizations focus on their customers, evaluating their needs, putting themselves in the customer's shoes – so to speak, evaluating whole product needs, and looking at customers as a lifetime relationship, and not a short-term or transactional sale.

For more information on SAFe's concepts of customer centricity, please visit `https://www.scaledagileframework.com/customer-centricity/`.

Thinking about design

Design thinking supports customer-centric development with the goal to create high-value products while ensuring profitability and sustainability over the life cycle of the product. Companies that focus on putting out "unique" or "me too" features and functions miss the point. Customers buy things because the products fulfill a purpose in terms of the capabilities provided that enhance their performance, their budgets, and their image.

The focus of design must be on identifying customers and user needs and putting the focus there. Products that miss the mark are those that implement the wrong features, implement the right features incorrectly, or fail to implement desired features altogether.

The objectives of the design thinking process are to evaluate success across four broad measures:

- Desirable – Is this what our customers and users want?
- Feasible – Can we build and deliver the right solution?
- Viable – Is the solution we provide profitable or within budget?
- Sustainable – Can we maintain and support the product over its product-market life cycle?

The design thinking process activities flow as follows:

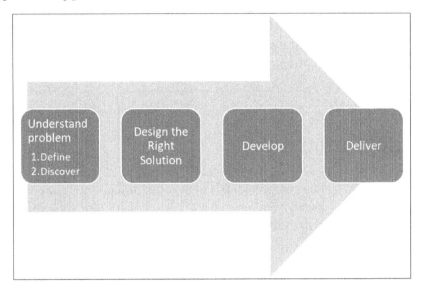

Figure 12.7 – Design thinking process

The design thinking process is not a one-time activity. Rather, the organization continuously evaluates these criteria across each PI.

For more information on the design thinking practices, please review this article: https://www.scaledagileframework.com/design-thinking/

Managing via Kanbans

Those who have a keen eye may have noticed that the word Kanban shows up twice under the Essential SAFe graphic. One instance is to indicate the need for program- and solution-level Kanbans, and another level to support the Agile teams. In all cases, Kanban Boards help the organization to visualize workflow, establishing **Work in Process** (**WIP**) limits, measuring throughput, and continuously improving their processes.

Kanbans are such important tools within SAFe's Lean-Agile practices that they are implemented at multiple levels, including *teams*, *portfolios*, *programs*, *solutions*, and *value streams*. Kanbans provide visibility to priority backlog items, work in progress, and work completed. Kanbans provide visibility on blockages that are impacting flows.

Most importantly, Kanban-oriented visibility makes it easier to identify the blocks, their impacts, and the reasons for the blocks. Having visibility on flows makes it easier for the ARTs and teams to discover and fix their immediate problems and ultimately address the root causes for longer term improvements.

For more information on the SAFe Kanbans, please review the following articles:

- Team: `https://www.scaledagileframework.com/team-kanban/`

- Program and solution: `https://www.scaledagileframework.com/program-and-solution-kanbans/`

- Portfolio: `https://www.scaledagileframework.com/portfolio-kanban/`

Integrating Scrum with XP

SAFe merges these best elements of Scrum and XP development practices. The concept behind this merger is that Scrum represents a time-tested and proven framework to implement iterative, incremental, and small team-based organizational agility. At the same time, XP provides a comprehensive and proven set of technical practices for software development.

Establishing backlogs

Essential SAFe implements two levels of backlogs: one backlog supports the program-level work, while the other backlog supports the Agile teams' work. Both backlogs are required to manage the deliverables across PIs and the underlying Agile team increments.

For more information on SAFe's program backlogs, please refer to the article at `https://www.scaledagileframework.com/program-and-solution-backlogs/`.

For information on SAFE's team backlogs, go to `https://www.scaledagileframework.com/team-backlog/`.

You now understand how SAFe integrates Lean-Agile practices across the life cycle of a product. Now we are going to look at how flow is managed in SAFe.

Maintaining flow

From what you have read in *Chapter 4, Systems Thinking* and *Chapter 5, Lean Thinking*, you know that Lean is all about keeping the focus on adding value. You also know that means customers do not want to pay for "extras" in the way of non-value added activities, features, and functions. Assuming we have the customer centricity and design thinking parts right, we must also ensure that the flows across our value streams are efficient. Plus, we must implement Lean flows in an agile way. This integration is not as awkward as it might seem.

Agile practices inherently employ iterative development practices to frequently develop Increment of new or enhanced and customer-centric value. Lean development seeks to deliver customer-centric value continuously and efficiently. A Lean-Agile enterprise seeks to integrate these two concepts. In other words, there are Agile-based activities that must be synchronized, coordinated, and integrated to deliver new functionality on a predictable and standard cadence. On the other hand, there are elements of Lean to ensure that the organization is operating in an efficient manner with synchronized flow that eliminates bottlenecks and excessive work in progress.

SAFe implements iterative development cycles via PIs and Agile development cycles. The Kanbans, noted in the previous subsection, help ensure efficient flow through pull-oriented work intake processes. Since we've already looked at the employment of Kanbans within SAFe, let's now turn our focus to how SAFe implements cadence at both the Agile Team and ART levels.

Maintaining cadence via PI

SAFe differs from traditional Scrum approaches by having, in effect, two concurrent iteration cycles. The primary iteration is the PI, which is a timeboxed duration at which the ARTs and solution trains operate. Organizations tend to bound PI intervals in 8 to 12 weeks in duration.

Within each PI is any number of Agile teams that operate in a traditional Scrum fashion (in other words, 1- to 4-week timeboxed iterations). Team-level Increment are also timeboxed, but much more frequent in occurrence, depending on business needs. For example, Agile teams typically operate on two-week iterations. However, 1- to 4-week iterations are acceptable, with each iteration delivering an Increment of value toward the broader goals of the PI. As with Scrum, each Increment includes time to plan work, assess their progress through daily team meetings, conduct reviews and demos, and look for opportunities to improve. Moreover, the Agile team iterations provide more frequent opportunities to synch up and coordinate their efforts with other Agile teams.

For more information on PIs, please refer to the article at `https://www.scaledagileframework.com/program-increment/`.

For more information on iteration execution within SAFe, please review this article: `https://www.scaledagileframework.com/iteration-execution/`

Planning PIs

Each PI has a unique set of business and technical goals collectively referred to as **PI objectives**. Agile teams and ARTs accomplish the PI objectives across many iterative development cycles within an upcoming PI. As with PIs, the Agile team and ART development iterations have a constant cadence, but of a shorter time duration – usually, a timebox limited to 2 weeks. Anything between 1 and 4 weeks is acceptable. For more information on PI objectives, please refer to the article at `https://www.scaledagileframework.com/pi-objectives/`.

Each team iteration delivers value incrementally by completing PI objectives associated with the PI. The ARTs establish their goals for the PI during the **PI planning** event. The PI planning events are face-to-face meetings that allow all ART members and stakeholders to plan the PI objectives, down to the Agile team level, and in support of the product's solution context and vision. For more information on PI planning, please refer to the article at `https://www.scaledagileframework.com/pi-planning/`.

PI planning events are two-day events conducted during **the IP iteration**. The IP iterations have the same duration as other Agile team iterations within each PI. Still, they serve as a buffer to complete unfulfilled PI objectives and to perform innovative work, work on continuing research and education, the PI planning activities, and inspect and adapt events. For more information on innovation and planning iterations, please refer to the article at `https://www.scaledagileframework.com/innovation-and-planning-iteration/`.

The face-to-face meetings provide the opportunity to build social networks and relationships that allow the teams to collaborate and coordinate their work. The organization needs to find or create facilities to hold large gatherings, with abundant space for whiteboards, tables with chairs, and break-out areas for cross-team meetings.

Organizations that have teams operating across disparate locations and geographic regions must find or create facilities that allow their teams to meet simultaneously and ensure the sites' ability to connect in real time with network access, plus establish audio and video capabilities. The organizations must also establish meeting times that share the burden for those working off-hours across multiple time zones. In other words, even the headquarter locations must devote some of their time to working off-hours during the PI planning events.

Another important element of PI planning is risk management. SAFe recommends the **ROAM** approach to categorize risks. Under the guidance of the RTE, ART and Agile team members participate in risk identification and mitigation discussions during PI planning and later throughout the PIs. The ROAM acronym stands for *Resolved, Owned, Accepted, Mitigated*. The elements of ROAM are defined as follows:

- **Resolved**: The team judges whether the risk is not or is no longer a problem.

- **Owned**: Someone from within the ART, or an affected Agile team member, accepts responsibility to resolve the risk or issue.

- **Accepted**: The ART, or affected Agile team members, agree that the risk is acceptable and take no action to resolve the risk or develop mitigation strategies.

- **Mitigated**: The ART, or affected Agile team members, develop a mitigation strategy for execution should the risk be realized as an issue.

The members of an Agile team or ART identify risks during PI planning events and collaborate on how best to handle each of the identified risks. The ARTs and Agile teams make the risks visible, typically presented as a grid that separates each of the four ROAM categories. The ROAM chart helps the ART and Agile team members, as well as other stakeholders to view, discuss, and build a shared understanding of the risks the teams may face in the upcoming PI.

Maintaining continuous delivery pipelines

A SAFe **continuous delivery pipeline** includes the value stream activities, workflows, and automation necessary to bring a product or solution ideation to delivery. The continuous delivery pipeline includes four aspects of the value stream involving continuous exploration, continuous integration, continuous deployment, and release on demand.

Customer Exploration (CE) includes the set of activities to define the features and capabilities that can deliver a minimum viable product. **Continuous integration (CI)** includes the product backlog refinement of prioritized features through design thinking, plus build, integration, testing, and staging activities. **Continuous Deployment (CD)** includes the activities to move products from the staging environments into the production environments and to verify that the products are working correctly in the production environments. **Release on Demand (RoD)** is a SAFe concept that organizations may need to build out multiple product features across several iterations before it makes sense to release a product as a functionally usable solution. Depending on the type of products, some releases can be rolled out to customers incrementally, while other products or capabilities can be rolled out all at once.

For more information on SAFe's CD pipeline, please visit `https://www.scaledagileframework.com/continuous-delivery-pipeline/`.

For more information on SAFe's CE, please visit `https://www.scaledagileframework.com/continuous-exploration/`.

For more information on SAFe's CI, please visit `https://www.scaledagileframework.com/continuous-integration/`.

For more information on SAFe's CD, please visit `https://www.scaledagileframework.com/continuous-deployment/`.

For more information on SAFe's RoD, please visit `https://www.scaledagileframework.com/release-on-demand/`.

> **Note**
>
> While the features and capabilities under development flow sequentially through a value stream, the work spanning the four aspects of the CD pipeline runs in parallel and are overlapping.

Riding on the ART

The ART brings all the resources together that are necessary to support operational and development value stream activities. ARTs are typically limited to a size of 50 to 125 people to maximize human abilities to maintain interpersonal relationships. ARTs stay together to support the entire life cycle of a deliverable product or product line. A typical ART – in support of a large and complex product – might include the following cross-functional elements, as depicted in *Figure 12.8*, often oriented around development and operation-oriented value streams:

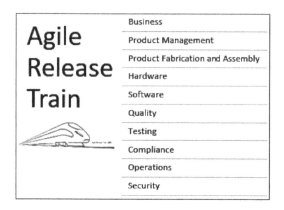

Figure 12.8 – ART cross-functional elements

ARTs have all the cross-functional resources necessary to define, build, test, deploy, release, and potentially operate the solutions they support. SAFe assumes the organization starts by building their SAFe implementations upon an existing hierarchical organizational structure. Rather than turn the organization upside down, ARTs start as virtual teams to flesh out the cross-functional needs of a product's operational and development value streams. Over time, when the organization is comfortable with the changes, the ARTs become permanent across the life span of the product and its value streams.

The metaphor of the ART should be clear. The organization has a common goal to release one or more quality products or solutions at various points along the line. Everyone needs to work together toward the common objective. In SAFe, conceptually, everyone jumps on the virtual train to reach that destination together. You can extend the metaphor further by thinking of the PIs as train stations en route, each representing a step in progress along the way.

Of course, under Lean-Agile practices, the ARTs represent the resources applied to value streams (the tracks of the ARTs), and the PIs represent the increments of new value (features, enablers, and capabilities) along the way.

You will recall from the chapters on Lean that value streams are a consistent set of activities dedicated to creating new value in a single type of product or related product line. The goal of a value stream is to eliminate variances that are wasteful.

Here again, the train metaphor works as the tracks guide the train most safely and directly to its destination. The tracks are improved over time to make the trip safer and more efficient, as it's never a good thing to have a train derail.

The same principle is valid for the Lean-Agile organization; value stream improvements eliminate waste and help implement new capabilities that add value, but you should never derail an ART traveling along its value stream. They are following the most direct path to create value and release their products.

For more information on SAFe's ARTs, visit `https://www.scaledagileframework.com/agile-release-train/`.

Scaling with ARTs

An ART is similar conceptually to having multiple Scrum teams working in collaboration on a large product or solution requirement. However, SAFe implements more structure and discipline on how these teams have to plan, integrate, and synchronize their collective efforts.

Depending on the scope of a product or solution, an ART has *50 to 125 people* working collaboratively in support of one or more value streams. Each ART is a persistent and self-organizing team of multiple smaller Agile teams. Agile teams within the ARTs follow the same small size pattern found in most Scrum teams. The combined size constraints limit each ART to 5 to 12 Agile teams.

The implementation of both small Agile teams and ARTs is not an accident. There is research that supports why an organization needs two forms of structure. It's part of the reason why SAFe promotes the concept of a *dual operating system* for business—one operating system focused on innovations, and the other to support large, complex initiatives. As it turns out, smaller teams are better at creating innovations, while larger teams provide the economies of scale necessary to build and deliver big and complicated things.

In an article published in the **Harvard Business Review** entitled *Research: When Small Teams Are Better Than Big Ones* (by Dashun Wang; James A. Evans. Feb 21, 2019, hbr.org), the authors note that after researching *65 million papers, patents, and software products that came out between 1954 and 2014,* they concluded that *Large Teams Develop, Small Teams Disrupt.* They go on to make two important observations:

1. *"In general, large teams remain important on multiple levels, including for large-scale work related to patents, software development, and other areas. But supporting large teams alone could stunt the growth of innovative ideas by impeding the flourishing ecology of science and technology."*

2. *"This means that both types of teams are essential for the long-term vitality of innovation: while small teams can drive disruption and innovation, larger teams can pick up the ball and engage in greater development of a given area, as part of a virtuous cycle."*

We know from our chapters on Scrum that the optimal small team size is *7 ± 2* (*5 to 9* people). Small teams are more innovative and don't tend to get bogged down from having too many nodes of communications and interactions between individuals that would otherwise prevent any real work from getting done.

But if we need larger organizations to build large, complex things, how do we organize the numerous teams, and how do they work with the other teams? Fortunately, some research helps us answer those questions.

For further details on scaling with ARTs, please refer to the related article at `https://www.scaledagileframework.com/agile-release-train/`.

Leveraging Dunbar's Number

In previous chapters, you've learned that most scaled-Scrum disciplines use a network model to manage network density issues associated with coordinating the work of multiple Scrum teams. Network-based communications structures limit the number of communications links across teams to a handful of people operating in a hub and spoke model. Ideally, the communication links within each hub conform to the model of 7 ± 2 people allowed to participate in the interactions.

This subsection introduces research that suggests humans can manage more personal relationships than the Scrum guide's prescriptive limits of 7 ± 2 team members. This research, referred to as Dunbar's Number, is the foundation behind SAFe's approach.

Specifically, Robin Dunbar, a British anthropologist and evolutionary psychologist who researches primate behavior, found that there are limitations on the number of stable social relationships that primates, humans included, can maintain with others. Dunbar suggests that the number is around 50 to 150 for humans (a.k.a. *Dunbar's Number*) and that each individual's neocortical processing capacity bounds the limitations.

Humans form the strongest personal relationships with between 5 and 15 people. However, Dunbar found that humans can still form close relationships with 50 or more people, up to an average cognitive limit of around 150 people. Dunbar's Number is a mean average that he based on the average capacity of our brains, both memory and processing capabilities, which, in turn, limits the number of long term social relationships we can manage at any given time (Dunbar, 2010).

Going beyond Dunbar's Number

Of course, large businesses can have many times more than 150 people. Rules, regulations, laws, societal norms, common goals, and culture help us obtain cohesiveness and purpose in large groups. It's no different with SAFe, or any other scaled Agile discipline. We need to establish a set of rules, common purpose, and cultural norms for the large organization to succeed in their collective efforts.

SAFe implements its rules, in effect, through its principles, values, core competencies, events, and artifacts. Moreover, starting with the Essential SAFe configuration, SAFe establishes large Lean-Agile teams in the form of Agile Release Teams, scaled in conformance with Dunbar's Number. Yes, the recommended ART sizes fall below Dunbar's Number, but we need some mental cycles to support our network of family and friends.

Also, each ART has a shared purpose in the form of providing support for one or more value streams. Each ART plan commits and executes their work together iteratively across timeboxed *PIs* to deliver new increments of value. An ART can support a single value stream, or the ART can support multiple value streams by having their underlying Agile teams sustain individual value streams. Those decisions are left to the organization to decide, informed by the size and complexity of the products and solutions they must deliver.

The ARTs remain in place and support the continuous delivery of new increments of value for as long as the efforts are economically viable. Their budgets are likewise ongoing, but based on delivering increments of new value via the prioritized items within a product or solution backlog. This approach is quite different from the cost accounting forms of budgeting that sustain functional departments over time, or project-based funding that allocates funding based on completing a predefined amount of work over a set period of time. You'll learn more about Lean budgeting within the Portfolio SAFe configuration section.

Now that you understand the basics of Essential SAFe, let's get into more of the details of how it all works.

Establishing a solution context

Anyone who has worked in sales understands that customers inherently do not value features and functions. In many cases, the customers may not know why they should value a particular feature or functionality. Instead, what makes those features and functions valuable is the capabilities they provide. In other words, features and functions are collectively part of a solution to some set of needs your customers have.

This book fundamentally is about leveraging Agile and Lean practices to build large and complex products, so I won't bore you with too many details on sales and marketing. But, before we move on, you must understand that customers inherently value things for only a handful of fundamental reasons:

- The capabilities provided make them more efficient.
- The capabilities provided support their economic objectives.
- The capabilities provided make them feel good.
- The capabilities provided make them look good in front of others.

Think about it carefully, and you can probably fit every purchase decision you have made into one or more of these four fundamental categories. Companies and other entities exist, and ultimately survive, based on their ability to uncover customers' needs, and then deliver high value in the form of solutions to those customers' needs.

For more information on the solution context, please refer to the article at `https://www.scaledagileframework.com/solution-context/`.

Understanding the solution context

A primary issue when building large and complex solutions is that no single person within the organization has a complete understanding of the solution requirements, nor do they have control over all of the value streams required to build, deliver, and sustain the products. Moreover, market conditions and opportunities and customer demands can and will change over time, and the organization as a whole must respond to build the right solutions, for the right customers, at the right time.

Everyone within the organization, working across all value chains, must have a solid understanding of what value means and how they contribute to the delivery of value. In other words, the organization must place a premium on communications, collaboration, integration, and synchronization of their efforts around adding value in the form of integrated solutions.

The *solution context* in SAFe is an assessment of needs beyond product requirements, to also include usage, installation, operation, support, packaging, and delivery considerations. These considerations collectively drive the *solution intent*, which further drives the scoping of features, capabilities, stories, non-functional requirements, software and system architectures, system and component designs, and testing.

For more information on solution intent, please refer to the article at `https://www.scaledagileframework.com/solution-intent/`.

It should be apparent that the development of solution context and solution intent requires a customer-centric mindset, not only across the organization, but also across its suppliers and partners. More precisely, the enterprise forms value streams, supporting both value-adding business operations and solution development activities, with all participants working in collaboration to deliver a complete solution context.

Later, in the Portfolio SAFe configuration section, you will learn how investment priorities and decisions support both operational and development value streams across multiple planning horizons. Portfolio-level analysis helps ensure that the organization looks across products, components, and value streams to ensure refinement and fulfillment of the solution context over time.

Developing solution intent and solution context

SAFe practitioners document requirements in pretty much the same way Scrum and XP practitioners define requirements. For example, SAFe practitioners develop stories to define features, capabilities, and enablers. Later, in the Portfolio SAFe section, you'll also learn how SAFe leverages the concepts of **Epics** at the portfolio level.

A **feature** is a deliverable item that fulfills a stakeholder need. Each feature includes a benefit hypothesis and acceptance criteria. A benefit hypothesis is simply a measurable benefit to customers and end users. Acceptance criteria define what good looks like when the feature passes testing. A typically written format for acceptance criteria is the **Given-When-Then** (**GWT**) format. For example, *Given (a situation), When (something happens), Then (some result or behavior is expected).*

For more information on SAFe's implementation of Epics, please refer to the article at `https://www.scaledagileframework.com/epic/`.

For more information on features and capabilities, please refer to the article at `https://www.scaledagileframework.com/features-and-capabilities/`.

The size of any single feature is limited to the amount of work that can be delivered by a single ART within a single PI. If not, the teams break apart the features into smaller elements that fit within a single ART and a single PI.

SAFe defines a **capability** as a higher-level solution that involves the development of multiple features and components, usually split across several ARTs. The features developed as part of a more substantial capability are produced concurrently and delivered together. The work is sized and split into multiple features, so that entire functionality is deliverable within a single PI.

For more information on features and capabilities, please refer to the article at `https://www.scaledagileframework.com/features-and-capabilities/`.

Enablers within SAFe are a particular type of capability that supports the future needs of the business or future products or product enhancement needs. SAFe divides enablers into four types: exploration, architecture, infrastructure, and compliance. *Exploration enablers* support research and prototyping activities. *Architectural enablers* build the architectural runway that makes future development more straightforward. *Infrastructure enablers* help build, extend, or automate the organization's development, testing, and deployment environments. *Compliance enablers* have a focus on helping the organization achieve regulatory, industry, or customer compliance requirements. For more information on enablers, please refer to the article at `https://www.scaledagileframework.com/enablers/`.

Breaking down silos with DevOps

DevOps started as a relatively simple strategy to link the efforts of development and operational support organizations through improved communication and collaboration. The early proponents of DevOps advocated a cultural change to break down the silos that separated these organizations. This cultural change helped development teams build and deliver products that were more easily supported and sustained. Also, the collaborations helped ensure that development teams received input from customers on usability and functionality issues that came in through the help desks.

The initial concept of DevOps has evolved in large part due to technology and tool enhancements that not only supported communication and collaboration requirements, but also enabled improvements in IT process integration and automation across the entire product life cycle. As a former business process re-engineering consultant, I liken modern DevOps implementations to the re-engineering of the entire software development and support functions.

The linked activities of DevOps include requirement gathering and analysis, product architectures and designs, coding/fabrication, testing, delivery, deployment, maintenance, and support functions. The modern goals of DevOps are to improve communications and collaborations, shorten development life cycles, and enable continuous delivery of high-quality software products.

For more information on SAFe's DevOps implementation concepts, please visit `https://www.scaledagileframework.com/devops/`.

Building in quality

Quality has to be built in. By the time you inspect something for quality, it's too late. Whatever quality was built into the product is the quality it will have. If that level of quality is unsatisfactory, the organization has no choice but to scrap the work or repair or rework the defective deliverables. Defects cost money and time and are a prime example of non-value-added waste. No customer wants to pay for those activities.

SAFe further breaks quality down into five dimensions: flow, architecture and design, code, system, and release. SAFe also employs the testing concepts you learned in previous chapters, such as TDD, the use of acceptance criteria, and BDD. For more information on SAFe's concepts to incorporate quality, please visit `https://www.scaledagileframework.com/built-In-quality/`.

Remaining Essential SAFe artifacts

On the right sidebar, SAFe associates three additional artifacts with the Essential SAFe configuration. These are as follows:

- **Vision**: This describes a future state for the solutions under development. The vision describes the requirements in terms of customer value, and the features and capabilities proposed to deliver that value: `https://www.scaledagileframework.com/vision/`

- **Roadmap**: This provides a schedule of events and milestones mapped to the deliverables of the solution over the current planning horizon: `https://www.scaledagileframework.com/roadmap/`

- **System Teams**: These are specialized Agile teams that build and maintain the infrastructure that supports Agile development. The systems team can include the development and maintenance of the toolchains that supports DevOps and the continuous delivery pipeline: `https://www.scaledagileframework.com/system-team/`

Evaluating best fits

The Essential SAFe configuration provides the information you need to get started with a SAFe implementation, although some organizations may never grow beyond the Essential SAFe configuration. Essential SAFe coordinates and integrates the activities of multiple yet small Agile teams across both value creation and value delivery activities. Specifically, the Essential SAFe configuration provides the organizational structures, roles, events, and artifacts that help direct customer-centric and value-adding activities across the Agile teams.

The ART structure of Essential SAFe facilitates the guidance of multiple Agile teams spanning 50 to 125 people. The ART structure supports product development or value stream activities, depending on the size and complexity of the products under development. Large products may require multiple ARTs to coordinate and integrate all the work. In such cases, the ARTs typically align with development and operational value streams. The development value streams produce the component items that make up the broader solution. In contrast, the operational value streams support the delivery of end user value by promoting, selling, taking orders, deploying, and supporting the solutions created by the development value streams.

In short, the ARTs within Essential SAFe best support large entities that need to synchronize and integrate multiple Agile teams to deliver one or more products on a large scale. The entities can be commercial enterprises, government agencies, or non-profits. The main point is that the Essential SAFe approach to Lean-Agile helps the organization efficiently deliver products and services on a large scale.

The term *large scale* can imply the development of a single product, such as constructing a ship, airplane, or building. But the term *large scale* can also apply to the mass production of cyber-physical systems and enterprise-class software solutions.

In most cases, Essential SAFe best supports an existing enterprise that needs to remain competitive in a rapidly evolving or highly competitive market. Such entities can leverage their economies of scale to deliver products and services at scale. The executives of the organization must be willing to take charge and direct the training, coaching, and mentoring activities to drive the organization forward through the transformations. But, again, that statement is also true for all scaled Scrum and scaled Lean-Agile practices.

Summary

In this chapter, you have learned what it means to become safe in the context of the Scaled Agile Framework. Specifically, you've learned that SAFe integrates Lean and Agile practices to enable business agility on a large scale. This approach represents a massive shift away from traditional hierarchical and functional organizational structures that tend to be bureaucratic. The benefit is improved operational efficiencies and customer focus that may help the entity stay in business.

In this chapter, you have learned how SAFe integrated Lean and Agile concepts within a framework that supports the development of large cyber-physical systems. The objective of SAFe's essential configuration is to leverage a large organization's economies of scale while also achieving enterprise scale business agility.

You've learned that the critical organizational structure of Essential SAFe is the ART, which provides the necessary structure, roles and responsibilities, events, and artifacts to manage multiple Agile teams involving 50 to 125 people. You've learned how *PIs* keep the activities synched and integrated across both the ARTs and their associated Agile teams. PI planning activities allow the ARTs and Agile teams to assess current priorities and align their work over the next PI.

Finally, you've learned something about the numerous elements that make up Essential SAFe. Collectively, these Lean-Agile practices enable Team and Technical Agility and Agile Product Delivery in a continuous and integrated fashion, building-in quality from the start, and constantly working to improve from a value-added perspective.

This section completes the chapter on Essential SAFe. In the next chapter, we'll continue our exploration of SAFe to understand how to coordinate multiple ARTs to develop comprehensive solutions and multiple products and solutions. We'll also learn how to implement SAFe's **Lean Portfolio Management (LPM)** concepts to align business strategy with execution.

Questions

1. What is the target market/audience for SAFe?

2. Companies that embrace SAFe tend to have what characteristics?

3. What is a primary competitive advantage that large enterprises can take advantage of within their industries?

4. How has competition changed for existing, large enterprises?

5. What is the primary purpose of Essential SAFe?

6. What is the smaller organizational structure within Essential SAFe?

7. What are the primary roles of Essential SAFe?

8. What is the integrating function for Agile teams within Essential SAFe?

9. What two core competencies does Essential SAFe incorporate?

10. What is the purpose of PIs in the context of Essential SAFe?

13
Full Scaled Agile Framework® (SAFe®)

In this chapter, we continue our studies of Scaled Agile Framework (SAFe)™. In the previous chapter, you learned the Essential configuration of SAFe, which allows multiple Agile Teams to work in collaboration to produce large-scale products. The organizing structure at that level of scale is the **Agile Release Train (ART)**, and the function of the ART is to coordinate and integrate the work of the underlying Agile Teams.

The guiding principle behind the formation of ARTs is to keep the size of each ART to between 50 and 120 people, following Dunbar's law. However, many large enterprises have many more people than this number. Therefore, we need to understand how to organize, coordinate, and integrate the work of multiple ARTs to support both a large-scale solution's development requirements and to align those efforts with corporate strategies and investment priorities.

Lastly, of course, we have to do all these things while keeping our focus on the needs of our target market customers. Without them, we don't have a business.

In this chapter, we're going to cover the following main topics:

- Scaling with Large Solution SAFe
- Core competencies supporting Large Solution SAFe
- Elements of the Large Solution SAFe configuration
- Riding on the Solution Train
- Remaining Large Solution artifacts
- Managing investment risks with Portfolio SAFe
- Defining Portfolio SAFe's roles and responsibilities
- Elements of Portfolio SAFe
- Creating Portfolio Backlogs
- Establishing Lean Budgets
- Supporting value streams
- Achieving Full SAFe
- Following the SAFe Implementation Roadmap
- Evaluating best fits

In this chapter, you will learn how SAFe scales beyond 150 team members to facilitate the development of large solutions, while building on the foundations of **Essential SAFe**. You will also learn how SAFe implements **Lean Portfolio Management** concepts as a means to align investment in products and services with business strategies over multiple planning Horizons while staying focused on adding customer-centric value. Finally, given the size and scope of the SAFe configurations, you will learn how the SAFe Implementation Roadmap helps guide organizational implementations incrementally, building buy-in and adoption through early successes, and ultimately scaling SAFe across the enterprise.

Scaling with Large Solution SAFe®

Now that you understand the most fundamental elements of SAFe, as outlined in the *Essential SAFe configuration* section in the previous chapter, we can now move on to discuss how SAFe scales to support the development of very large solutions spanning software applications, networked systems, and cyber-physical systems. The Large Solution SAFe configuration does not stand alone. It builds on the foundations of the Essential SAFe configuration, but installs additional roles, responsibilities, and elements that enable the implementation of multiple ARTs, all operating in a coordinated fashion to develop much larger and more complex solutions.

Figure 13.1 shows how Large Solution SAFe builds upon the Essential SAFe configuration. In other words, the Large Solution SAFe configuration applies all the same concepts as Essential SAFe, such as solution intent, built-in quality, Agile teams and ARTs, Scrum, Kanban, and other Agile practices:

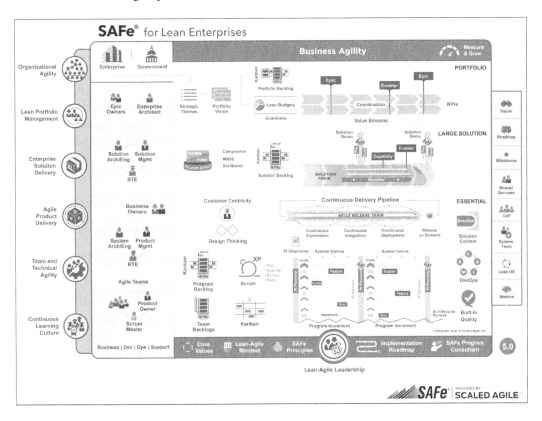

Figure 13.1 – Large Solution SAFe configuration: https://www.scaledAgileframework.com/

Some of the Essential SAFe concepts are modified to enable scaling in support of large solution development and delivery applications. One such example is the integration, coordination, and synchronization of multiple ARTs working in collaboration as larger **Solution Trains**, which is the topic of the next subsection.

Scaling with Solution Trains

By now, you should be pretty comfortable with understanding how SAFe implements small Agile teams and ARTs to build and deliver large products and services. Smaller Agile teams fit the Scrum model by supporting iterative and incremental development practices without the complexities and inefficiencies associated with large team dynamics. The ARTs follow the guidance of Dunbar's number, which bounds team ART sizes to a limit of 150 people, as that is the maximum number of relationships most human beings can maintain.

Unfortunately, there is not another principal or research finding that suggests how to form larger teams without causing *unsupportable complexities* and *network density* issues that result from the enormous number of potential communication interconnections. For example, the traditional hierarchical management structures organize skills and resources into departments by function; but that creates layers of bureaucracy that work against product-oriented flows and value stream efficiencies. As you know, in the case of Lean Development, those management structures brought along with them a host of quality and inefficiency issues, resulting from batch and unsynchronized production processes. Moreover, functional departments do not naturally align with supporting product flows oriented around adding customer-centric value.

The SAFe approach resolves these issues through the implementation of Solution Trains. A Solution Train loosely binds multiple ARTs and external suppliers together in support of a single product or product line. They share a joint mission, solution Vision, Backlog, and Roadmap. They also align their activities to a standard length **Program Increment (PI)**.

Since each of the ARTs are limited in size by Dunbar's number, the SAFe organization needs a way to align and coordinate the activities of the supporting ARTs and suppliers. SAFe accomplishes this by implementing a new level of leadership to aid in the coordination of cross-team activities. Beyond that, the same structure of **Program Increments (PI)**, **Program Increment (PI) Planning events**, **Program Increment (PI) Objectives**, and **Innovation and Planning (IP) Iterations** help keep the disparate teams working in lock-step toward the same solution vision and goals. For more information on Solution Trains, please refer to the article at `https://www.scaledagileframework.com/solution-train/`.

Core competencies supporting Large Solution SAFe®

As with the Essential SAFe configuration, the implementation of the Large Solution SAFe configuration requires the development of the *Agile Product Delivery* and *Team and Technical Agility* core competencies. But achieving scale in large solutions development also requires the additional core competency of **Enterprise Solution Delivery**.

- For more information on Agile Product Delivery, please refer to the article at `https://www.scaledagileframework.com/agile-product-delivery/`.

- For more information on Team and Technical Agility, please refer to the article at `https://www.scaledagileframework.com/team-and-technical-agility/`.

- For more information on Enterprise Solution Delivery, please refer to the article at `https://www.scaledagileframework.com/enterprise-solution-delivery/`.

Distinguishing Large Solution SAFe® roles and responsibilities

The Large Solution configuration also establishes three sets of roles and responsibilities, to include the **Solution Train Engineer (STE)**, plus the **Solution Architect/ Engineering** and **Solution Management** functions. As noted in the introductory section of this chapter, SAFe installs three sets of roles and responsibilities across the various SAFe configurations. As in the other SAFe configurations, each role has a specific set of responsibilities, shown here:

- **Solution Management**: What gets built: `https://www.scaledagileframework.com/product-and-solution-management/`

- **Solution Architect/Engineering**: How it gets built: `https://www.scaledagileframework.com/system-and-solution-architect-engineering/`

- **Solution Train Engineer**: Servant leadership, coaching, and mentoring: `https://www.scaledagileframework.com/release-train-engineer-and-solution-train-engineer/`

In this section, you will learn the roles and responsibilities of the people supporting Large Solution configurations of SAFe.

Elements of the Large Solution SAFe® configuration

Since the Large Solution SAFe configuration builds upon the foundations of the Essential SAFe configuration, much of the operational and development value stream capabilities are in place. The Large Solution SAFe configuration adds the activities, events, and artifacts necessary to coordinate multiple ARTs toward the vision and goals of the larger solution.

The primary activities of the Large Solution SAFe configuration include developing the *Solution Intent*, defining and refining the *Solution Backlog*, and integrating, coordinating, and synchronizing the activities of the underlying ARTs. Let's start with the Solution Intent.

Building the Solution Intent

SAFe introduces the **Solution Intent** concept as *a repository for storing, managing, and communicating the knowledge of current and intended Solution behavior*. Solutions have capabilities that support the needs of their customers. Solution behaviors represent the features that implement a solution's capabilities. The scope of work involved in developing large solutions drives an organizational need to install multiple Agile release teams to develop all the features that are necessary to deliver the capabilities of the solution. Putting this all together, the Solution Intent represents the combined set of features, developed across multiple ARTs, that deliver the capabilities of the solution.

Large solutions have both a current and a future Solution Intent. Developers of large-scale solutions must always bear this fact in mind as they develop their knowledge base of capabilities and features. The collective knowledge of the Solution Intent includes **specifications**, **designs**, and **tests**, and together this collection of knowledge assets provides traceability from requirements through design to development and testing. To ensure that the deployed solution meets the definition of done.

The Solution Intent is dynamic in the sense that it must evolve along with the solution. The evolving Solution Intent drives the evolution of the solution. Market conditions and customer demands drive that evolution.

The Solution Intent includes both, the **Fixed Intent** and **Variable Intent**:

- The Fixed Intent includes the list of known capabilities and features. They may be non-negotiable items mandated by contracts or derived throughout the development.

- The Variable Intent includes the design elements that are not fully defined. In such cases, the members of the Solution Train, and especially the Solution Architect/ Engineering team members, must explore design alternatives and evaluate economic trade-offs.

> **Note**
> Fixed Intent assessments may involve data analysis, simulations, and other forms of modeling. Decisions made on which approach to use fix the intent, and the Variable Intent elements become Fixed Intent elements.

For more information on the Solution Intent, please review the article at `https://www.scaledagileframework.com/solution-intent/`.

Establishing and refining the Solution Backlog

As you learned in the *Essential SAFe* sections, SAFe implements Program Backlogs and Team Backlogs at the product level. But another level of the backlog is needed to maintain large solution requirements, which is the **Solution Backlog**. The Solution Backlog is the knowledge base of upcoming solution capabilities and enablers of the architectural runway. Each item within the Solution Backlog can drive work across multiple ARTs. Solution Management is responsible for maintaining the Solution Backlog.

While Solution Management is responsible for maintaining the Solution Backlog, they receive input from many stakeholders, including customers, business owners, product management, product owners, system and solution architects/engineering, and other stakeholders whose opinions matter. That's not to say that everyone's opinions shouldn't matter, but some people have more influence, both good and bad, than others. Solution Backlog development and refinement is part of the continuous exploration process.

The Solution Backlog items flow through a Solution Kanban system, which is usually a Kanban board in one form or another, as depicted in Figure 13.2. As in other Kanban systems, Solution Kanbans provides a method to view and manage the flow of features and capabilities from concept to their release through the Continuous Delivery pipeline:

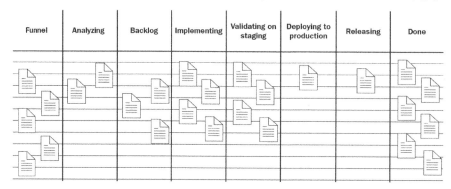

Figure 13.2 – Solution Kanban board

Organizations are free to define the states that most work for them. However, the typical Solution Kanban board includes the states of **Funnel**, **Analyzing**, **Backlog**, **Implementing**, **Validating on staging**, **Deploying to production**, **Releasing, and Done**.

The ARTs within the Solution Train use the Kanban board to limit demand flow to capacity based on **Work in Process (WIP)** limits. The queuing of backlog items within the segments of the Kanban board helps the team see the bottlenecks forming in each process state. This information helps the Agile teams and ARTs identify areas that would benefit from **relentless improvements**. The Kanban system also specifies policies governing the entry and exit of work items in each state.

- For more information on Solution Backlogs, please refer to the article at `https:// www.scaledagileframework.com/program-and-solution- backlogs/`.

- For more information on Solution Kanbans, please refer to the article at `https:// www.scaledagileframework.com/program-and-solution-kanbans/`.

Weighted Shortest Jobs First

SAFe uses a **Weighted Shortest Job First** (**WSJF**) strategy for prioritizing the sequence of work (that is, features, enablers, capabilities, and epics) through a Kanban, and the Solution Kanban is no different. Calculate the WSJF by dividing the Cost of Delay by Job Duration:

$$WSJF = Cost\ of\ Delay\ /\ Job\ Duration\ (Job\ Size)$$

The Cost of Delay includes **user-business value**, **time criticality**, **risk-reduction**, and **opportunity enablement**. These may sound like subjective factors, and they are. The Scaled Agile Framework implements the same estimating techniques described in previous chapters as a team-based activity to define each of the four contributors to the cost of delay. SAFe refers to its version of *planning poker* as **estimating poker** and uses modified Fibonacci numbers as the basis for the estimates:

$$Cost\ of\ Delay = User\ Business\ Value + Time\ Criticality$$
$$+ Risk\ Reduction\ and/or\ Opportunity\ Enablement$$

Recall that the key to backlog refinement is to prioritize those items that have the highest value for the lost cost of development and delivery. WSJF provides the means to make these types of value-oriented estimates and priorities.

Now that you understand how to form priorities within the Solution Backlog, we can now move on to learning how the Solution Trains execute against those priorities. Solution Train execution is the subject of the next subsection. For more information on WSJF, please refer to the article at `https://www.scaledagileframework.com/wsjf/`.

Riding on the Solution Train

The Solution Train is an organizational structure that SAFe implements to support the development and delivery of large and complex solutions. A Solution Train consists of multiple Agile Release Trains operating in a coordinated fashion toward a standard set of business and product objectives. Also, the Solution Training coordinates the activities of external suppliers and partners who contribute to the solution objectives.

The Solution Train aligns the activities of the ARTs to support a shared business and technology mission. The Solution Train implements a shared solution Vision, Backlog, and Roadmap, and aligns the arts to work within the same PI cadence.

Large and complex solutions within SAFe are often described as a **system of systems**. For example, whether we are building autonomous automobiles, ships, aircraft, or the systems that support a commercial insurance company or healthcare provider, the more extensive solutions integrate any number of lower-level systems, components, and subsystems.

These large solutions may require hundreds or even thousands of people to develop. Since we learned from Dunbar's number that humans have a limit on how many viable social relationships they can maintain, the ARTs have a limitation on size. The only way around the limits on scaling the size of the ARTs is to divide and conquer the work by distributing it across multiple ARTs. The Solution Train provides the organizational structures, events, and artifacts to coordinate and manage this collective work.

Some large solutions are so critical that failure can have intolerable social or economic consequences. For example, the loss of an aircraft or cruise ship can cost the lives of hundreds or even thousands of passengers. Some banks are so large and vital to our economy that we refer to them as *too big to fail*. In these cases, the industry requires additional safety considerations and attention to development details. Many of these solutions are subject to industry standards and federal, state, and international regulations and subject to audits and compliance. The leadership teams must pay attention to all of these factors and across all affected ARTs and their value stream activities.

Solution Trains follow similar principles, as outlined in the Essential SAFe configuration. The Solution Train develops on a fixed cadence and delivers a new increment of value over each program increment. Each program increment ends with a new **Solution Demo** to ensure the **PI Objectives** were met and conform to the acceptance criteria and **definitions of Done**.

- For more information on Solution Demos, please refer to the article at `https:// www.scaledagileframework.com/solution-demo/`.

- For more information on PI objectives, please refer to the article at `https:// www.scaledagileframework.com/pi-objectives/`.

The individuals assigned to Large Solution roles and responsibilities define the Solution Context and refine the requirements into an actionable and prioritized set of capabilities, features, and non-functional requirements, maintained within the Solution Backlog. The ARTs pull work from the Solution Backlog based on the highest priorities and their capacities to perform the work. The Solution Kanban helps the Solution Train members visualize and manage the work.

The individuals assigned to Large Solution roles and responsibilities coordinate, integrate, and synchronize the activities of the underlying ARTs and the third-party suppliers to accomplish the Solution Vision. The next section provides more elaboration on the Solution Train coordination activities.

Coordinating trains and teams

One final note: Solution Trains are responsible for the development and delivery activities of each PI, but they don't do the work. The underlying ARTs and third-party suppliers assigned or subcontracted to the Solution Train perform the work. The Solution Train also sets the cadence and synchronizes the development and delivery activities of the ARTs and suppliers and facilitates the PI Planning events and the Solution Demos.

Figure 13.3 shows the Solution Train events and how they relate to the Program and Agile Team events. As noted previously, the developers of large solutions often require suppliers to develop components, subsystems, or capabilities for the value stream. These suppliers also participate in the Solution Train events. In effect, suppliers are another form of ART:

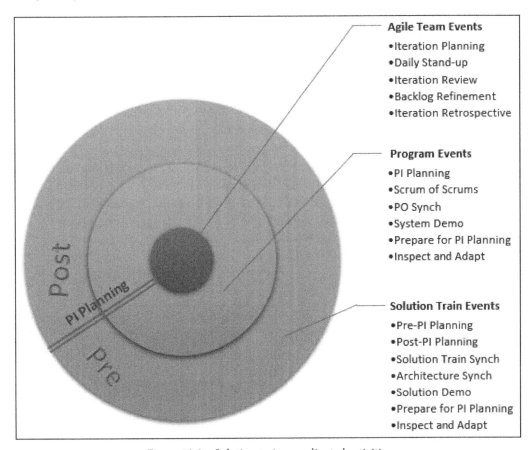

Figure 13.3 – Solution train coordinated activities

You now have a basic understanding of the role of Solution Trains, and how they build upon the foundations laid down in the Essential SAFe configuration. You will have noticed that the bar to the right of the Solution Train configuration graphic adds four new artifacts to this configuration – you will learn what these artifacts are for in the next subsection.

Remaining Large Scale SAFe® artifacts

In the previous section, we learned that the Large Solution SAFe configuration includes five additional artifacts. Let's take a closer look at the purpose of each of these artifacts.

- **Milestones**: Help Solution Trains track progress toward the achievement of specific goals and events—SAFe implements three types of milestones: PI Milestones, Fixed-Date Milestones, and Learning Milestones.

- **Shared Services**: Provide individuals with specialized skills to augment the resources of the ARTs or Solution Trains. However, the shared services personnel do not get assigned as dedicated or full-time resources. They augment resources, and the trains need to plan to coordinate the use of shared services personnel on an as-needed basis.

- **Communities of Practices** (CoPs): Organized groups of people who have a common interest in a specific technical or business domain. They get together frequently to share information, improve or develop new skills, and work collaboratively to advance the general knowledge of the domain across the organization. CoPs share in common a domain of knowledge, a community of practitioners, and a set of practices. CoPs have a life cycle that starts with a shared interest or need and ends when there is no longer a need to continue the collaboration.

- **Lean UX**: *User experience design (UXD)* is an approach to enhance a product's usability by studying the users' behaviors and needs when interacting with a product. SAFe extends the UXD concepts further, through **Lean User Experience (Lean UX)** design concepts, by encompassing Lean-Agile practices to build and deliver minimum viable or marketable products (MVP/MMP).

- **Metrics**: Those who have participated in a process improvement or process reengineering activity understand the importance of **Metrics**. Metrics are equally useful in defining the desired outcomes of our product development efforts. In that sense, metrics are expressions of *what good looks like* after we implement the desired change. Without metrics, we can't know if we have achieved our goals. Metrics can be quantitative and qualitative, depending on the objectives they support. In SAFe, metrics help us evaluate the organization's progress toward meeting portfolio, large solution, program, and each team's business and technical objectives.

This concludes the section on Large Solution configuration. In the next section, you will learn how SAFe integrates portfolio management processes to align product investment with business strategy in a manner that supports Lean-Agile development practices:

- For more information on SAFe Milestones, please review the article at `https://www.scaledagileframework.com/milestones/`.

- For more information on SAFe Shared Services, please review the article at `https://www.scaledagileframework.com/shared-services/`.

- For more information on SAFe Communities of Practices (CoPs), please review the article at `https://www.scaledagileframework.com/communities-of-practice/`.

- For more information on SAFe Lean UX, please review the article at `https://www.scaledagileframework.com/lean-ux/`.

- For more information on SAFe Metrics. please review the article at `https://www.scaledagileframework.com/metrics/`.

Managing investment risks with Portfolio SAFe®

In this section, you will learn how SAFe applies Lean and systems thinking approaches to strategy and investment funding, Agile portfolio operations, and governance. The goal of Lean Portfolio Management is to align corporate strategy with execution. In other words, we need to make sure the efforts of the organization, spanning the Solution Trains, ARTs, and Agile Teams, support the goals and objectives outlined by the chief executives within the corporate strategy:

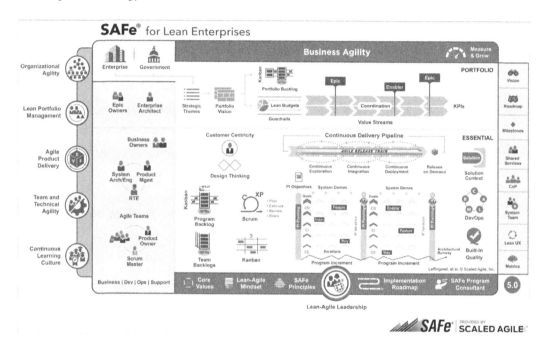

Figure 13.4 provides a graphic illustrating the scope of Portfolio SAFe:

Portfolio SAFe configuration: https://www.scaledAgileframework.com/

Lean portfolio management is an important and foundational element to SAFe's Portfolio configuration, so let's take a moment to understand what this is all about.

Applying Lean principles to Portfolio Management

Value stream assessments are the responsibility of LPM teams, along with strategy and business alignment, portfolio investment analysis, and governance. The LPM teams do not work in a silo to perform their value stream assessments. Instead, they must collaborate with all levels of the organization. Within LPM, there are three primary collaborations:

- The *Strategy and Investment Funding* collaboration works to align portfolio investment decisions with corporate strategy, and to ensure the right solutions are created and maintained that support the goals and objectives of the organization.

- *Agile Portfolio Operations* enable decentralized program execution and operational excellence by defining the objectives of each portfolio investment and then communicating, coordinating, and guiding the activities across the associated value streams that ultimately deliver the value.

- *Lean Governance* provides oversight and decision-making responsibility across all portfolio investments, including audit and compliance, forecasting expenses, and determining and reviewing measurements to gauge the success of each portfolio.

SAFe provides detailed guidance on all these topics in the LPM article at `https://www.scaledagileframework.com/lean-portfolio-management/`.

Defining Portfolio SAFe® roles and responsibilities

Portfolio SAFe breaks the defined three-role pattern found in the Essential SAFe and Large Solution SAFe configurations. As part of the **LMP Team**, the Portfolio SAFe configuration implements two additional roles and responsibilities, **Epic Owners** and the **Enterprise Architect**. In addition, the LPM team includes the Business Owners of the products. We've already discussed the role of Business Owners, as their primary duties support the products at the level of the Essential SAFe configuration. But, let's take a quick look at the roles and responsibilities of the LPM team as a whole, and the Epic Owners and Enterprise Architect. Information on Portfolio SAFe® roles and responsibilities is provided in the article at `https://www.scaledagileframework.com/portfolio-safe/`.

The LPM team

As noted in the previous section, there is a team of individuals who support SAFe's portfolio management configuration, and that is the Lean Portfolio Management team. The LPM team consists of Enterprise Executives, Business Owners, and the Enterprise Architect. Collectively, they have decision making and financial authority within and across SAFe portfolios. Their purpose is to organize the Lean-Agile Enterprise around the flow of value through one or more value streams. Further details about LPM Team member roles are identified in the LPM article at `https://www.scaledagileframework.com/lean-portfolio-management/`.

Epic owners

The Scaled Agile Framework implements the concept of **Epics** at the portfolio level (a.k.a. **Portfolio Epics**). In Large Solution development, the epics can be quite large, requiring dedicated Solution Trains, multiple ARTs, numerous Agile teams, and perhaps hundreds or even thousands of employees and contractors to support. An epic may require months or possibly years to complete all the work under its definition of Done.

There are two types of epics in SAFe, business and enabler epics. Business epics involve the delivery of business value to customers, while enabler epics support future operational and development needs. SAFe refers to enablers as *advancing the Architectural Runway* in support of future business and technical needs.

Epic owners are responsible for defining the epic. Analyzing the capabilities required to form a **Minimum Viable Product** (**MVP**), they develop a Lean Business Case to justify the portfolio investments and then facilitate its implementation. The business case is reviewed and approved by the LPM. Additional details on the role of EPIC owners in general and with a defining MVP are provided in the SAFe article at `https://www.scaledagileframework.com/epic-owner/`.

The Enterprise Architect

In Portfolio SAFe, the Enterprise Architect is responsible for establishing the technology strategy and a roadmap to implement current and future business capabilities within the Portfolio Epic. Their architectures drive the designs and engineering tasks necessary to build the organization's solutions.

As part of their responsibilities, Enterprise Architects must keep in mind the enabler epics required to support future operations and development needs. Enabler epics are not components of the organization's products and solutions. Rather, enabler epics install organizational capabilities that are necessary to build operational and development value streams. For example, an Enabler EPIC might involve the development of IT systems, facilities, or production equipment necessary to support development and delivery activities.

When possible, the Enterprise Architect should encourage the reuse of architecture patterns for software application architectures to reduce future development time and costs. They should also encourage the use of *evolutionary architecture* concepts to build just enough architecture to support the current and upcoming instantiations of the product. The role of the Enterprise Architect is further defined in the SAFe article at `https://www.scaledagileframework.com/enterprise-architect/`.

Elements of Portfolio SAFe®

The concept of **Portfolio Management** has its origins in **modern portfolio theory (MPT)**, introduced by economist Harry Markowitz in an essay he wrote in 1952, entitled *Portfolio Selection*. MPT provides a mathematical framework to analyze a portfolio of assets to maximize the expected returns across identified levels of risk. Markowitz applied his MPT concepts as a risk management strategy to diversify financial assets within a broader investment portfolio. He won a Nobel Prize in Economics for his work in this area.

In a modern context, the word *portfolio* describes a combination of financial, intellectual, and physical assets held by investors, financial institutions, and business enterprises. Portfolio management is the discipline organizations implement to both select and oversee their investments, in whatever form those investments might take, that is, securities, facilities, property, equipment, technologies, IT systems, supply chain and delivery partnerships, and products and service offerings. The primary objective of portfolio management is to weigh the strengths, weaknesses, opportunities, and threats across a broad variety of investments.

Traditional portfolio management concepts align organizational investments in support of achieving corporate strategies. SAFe preserves this objective but with one clear distinction. Rather than leveraging the project management paradigm for portfolio management, SAFe takes a Lean-Agile approach to managing portfolios.

Connecting portfolios to strategy

Corporate strategies define the goals and objectives the chief executives want the organization to achieve over a specific period of time. The strategies must usefully differentiate the organization from other competitive offerings in a way that adds customer-centric value.

SAFe installs **Strategic Themes** as a means to align business or government strategies with one or more SAFe portfolios. In turn, SAFe portfolios provide the necessary funding and guidance to ensure the organization builds the right products and services in the most efficient manner possible. In other words, Portfolio SAFe uses *Strategic Themes* as the means to connect the portfolio to the strategy of the business.

However, strategic objectives are of no value if no one else in the organization knows they exist or how they impact their work and the products and services they deliver. The business executives work with the Lean Portfolio Management team, the Enterprise Architect, and other portfolio stakeholders to define, communicate, and coordinate the work associated with executing the strategy of the business. To ensure the responsible teams understand the strategic directions and related impacts of their work, the executives and portfolio stakeholders must define and communicate a vision for their respective portfolios. Further details on Strategic Themes are provided in the LPM article at `https://www.scaledagileframework.com/strategic-themes/`.

Implementing a Portfolio Vision

The *Portfolio Vision* is a future state description of what good looks like in terms of portfolio investment decisions, solutions, and value streams. In other words, the portfolio vision identifies the boundaries of organizational investments and priorities that are consistent with achieving the strategic goals and objectives of the enterprise.

From the chapters on *Lean*, you already know that efficient value streams give us that type of competitive edge. In this context, portfolio investment decisions must go beyond the definition of solutions to also encompass the delivered capabilities and features, and the efficiencies of our value stream processes.

SAFe incorporates the concepts from the core competency of **Lean Portfolio Management (LPM)** to map a portfolio's vision to the enterprise's mission, strategy, goals, and objectives. LPM also provides the governance that guides the subsequent direction of the Agile teams, Agile release trains, and Solution trains in their day-to-day decision-making.

Further details on Portfolio Vision are provided in the LPM article at `https://www.scaledagileframework.com/portfolio-vision/`.

Lean Portfolio Management (LPM)

The core competency of **Lean Portfolio Management** (**LPM**) guides the configuration of Portfolio SAFe, to align business strategy with execution at an organizational level. LPM applies Lean and Systems Thinking approaches to strategy and investment funding, Agile portfolio operations, and governance. In short, LPM supports portfolio management practices within the Lean-Agile organization.

Since we touched on LPM in the previous section on core competencies, we'll not spend much more time on the topic here. The main point to take away is that LPM helps the organization look ahead from the current "as is" state to a target "to be" state and to ensure adequate planning and financial resources are available to guide the efforts. Further details on Portfolio Vision are provided in the LPM article at `https://www.scaledagileframework.com/lean-portfolio-management/`.

Governing Lean Portfolios

SAFe implements Lean governance concepts to manage expenditures, implement auditing and compliance capabilities, forecast expenses, and implement useful metrics to observe business performance against desired strategic and portfolio objectives. Lean governance is a joint responsibility of the Agile PMO/LACE, business owners, and Enterprise Architects.

Further details on governance are provided in the Portfolio SAFe article at `https://www.scaledagileframework.com/portfolio-safe/`.

Additional guidance is provided in the Lean Portfolio Management article at `https://www.scaledagileframework.com/lean-portfolio-management/`.

Decentralizing Portfolio Operations

SAFe, following Lean-Agile principles, decentralizes authority to the ART and Solution Train levels. They manage risks by collaboratively making decisions involving the **Agile Program Management Office/Lean-Agile Center of Excellence** (**APMO/LACE**) and **Communities of Practice** (**CoPs**) for the **Release Train Engineers** (**RTEs**) and Scrum Masters. In other words, decision making is a collaborative act, at an operational level, by those who are most informed and involved.

Leveraging portfolio-level Kanbans

A **Portfolio Kanban** visually depicts the portfolio backlog items, typically in the form of epics. There is always more work that an organization might like to accomplish than they have the budget, time, and resources to complete. Rather than pushing all the portfolio investment objectives out into the organization at once, hoping for the best, the organizational resources should pull the new work from the portfolio Kanban board when they can do so. The portfolio Kanban provides a visualization of portfolio items in the form of *epics*. Further guidance on Portfolio Kanban is provided in the Portfolio SAFe article at `https://www.scaledagileframework.com/portfolio-kanban/`.

Defining epic portfolio objectives

The Scaled Agile Framework implements the concept of *epics* to document and describe portfolio-level investment objectives and criteria. The epics define the high-level requirements, while the Kanban board visually displays the priorities and progress of value stream assessments at a strategic level. When epics are ready for release, the Agile teams, Agile release trains, and solution trains refine the requirements – in the form of user stories – and ultimately schedule, define, and execute the necessary work tasks across their program increments.

LPM implements two forms of epics, Business Epics and Enabler Epics. Business Epics are investments that directly deliver value to customers. Enabler Epics are investments that help the organization support upcoming needs in exploration, architecture, infrastructure, and compliance. SAFe describes Enablers, through analogy, as an *Architectural Runway*, which supports the efficient development and delivery of future business requirements.

In keeping with the tenets of Lean philosophies, we never want to build more than our customers want. To do so is to create waste in the form of non-value-added work. Instead, for both the business and enabler epics, the organization must always focus on defining and delivering the **Minimum Viable Product** (**MVP**). It is the responsibility of the LPM to review, approve, and then monitor the delivery of epics to the MVP specifications.

- Guidance on Business Epics is provided in the SAFe article at `https://www.scaledagileframework.com/implementation-strategies-for-business-epics/`.

- Guidance on Enabler Epics is provided in the SAFe article at `https://www.scaledagileframework.com/enablers/`.

- Guidance on Architectural Runways is provided in the SAFe article at `https://www.scaledagileframework.com/architectural-runway/`.

Creating Portfolio Backlogs

The portfolio level is the highest-level backlog in SAFe. The portfolio backlog contains the prioritized list of portfolio investment items in the form of *Business and enabler EPICs*. Portfolio epics are analyzed in sufficient detail to establish the feasibility of the work, demonstrate business viability, develop a Lean business case, and describe the MVP. Guidance on Portfolio Backlogs is provided in the SAFe article at `https://www.scaledagileframework.com/portfolio-backlog/`.

Marshaling investments across planning horizons

SAFE's LPM competency implements Portfolio Kanban boards to visualize and monitor the progress of investment option assessments across four planning Horizons. One of the primary responsibilities of the portfolio teams is to honestly assess identified investment priorities in terms of value, determine what's possible in the short run, and to move out lower-priority investments into future planning Horizons.

SAFe implements a version of the McKinsey horizon model (Baghai, Mehrdad, *et al.* 2000) to define a conceptual investment horizon model. These investment Horizons include the following:

- **Horizon 3** – *Evaluating* potential investment options
- **Horizon 2** – *Emerging* investment options that appear to have value
- **Horizon 1** – *Investing* in the highest value options
- **Horizon 1** – *Extracting* value from investments
- **Horizon 0** – *Retiring* value streams that no longer have value

Space limitations preclude a lengthy discussion on this particular topic. The main takeaway is that the portfolio team must always assess potential and existing investments in terms of their value, assign priorities accordingly, and quickly move to decommission value stream options and investments that do not enhance the organization's value.

Delivering the highest value across program increments

When making portfolio investment decisions about investment priorities, we must consider life cycle costs and return on investments (ROI). In other words, customers may value two product upgrades equally. Still, if one upgrade is half the cost to develop and deliver, it's only sensible to make the lower-cost upgrade the priority. We should not look at the costs of products or projects as a whole. Instead, we need to be much more concise and analyze the cost benefit of delivering each increment of value across each program increment. This type of cost-benefit analysis is Lean thinking applied to financial forecasting.

Conceptually, lean budgeting is quite different from traditional budgeting via cost accounting and project-based funding models. *Cost accounting* evaluates the variable and fixed costs of each step in a production process and thereby supports the traditional batch production processes mentioned in the chapters on *Lean*. *Project-based funding* supports the traditional Waterfall model, where the development organization attempts to pre-plan and define all activities and tasks as a set of linear-sequential processes across a project. In the project-based funding model, task and activity costs roll up to the project's deliverables. Neither cost accounting nor project-based funding evaluates costs in terms of adding value.

In contrast, the focus of Lean-Agile processes is always on maximizing customer value and eliminating all non-value-added activities. Value stream activities are made efficient by eliminating queues – and therefore WIP, eliminating batch processes, reducing cycle times across value stream activities, and pulling work in at the rate of customer demand – but never faster than the slowest activity within the value stream.

Establishing Lean Budgets

Portfolio SAFe establishes *Lean Budgets* as the mechanism to provide financial governance over the organization's portfolio, solution, and team investments. In this manner, the organization as a whole remains always focused on maximizing value.

Instead of funding departments or projects, SAFe funds value streams. In other words, the organizations make funds available to the streams of activities that collectively add value to each of the portfolio investments. Moreover, the Lean-Agile discipline of program increments allows product and solutions managers, in collaboration with the ART and solution train members, to reassess priorities, and therefore the allocation of funds and other resources to each value stream, on a frequent and iterative basis.

The mechanics of lean budgeting starts with the Portfolios' Epic Owners, who assess value and cost estimates at a strategic level, assign budgets to portfolio items, and provide governance downstream to the solution and Agile release teams. Yet, SAFe implements a participatory budgeting process that allows the solution and release teams to access value priorities, typically on a bi-annual basis. We'll talk about that in the next subsection. Guidance on Portfolio Backlogs is provided in the SAFe article at `https://www.scaledagileframework.com/lean-budgets/`.

Harnessing participatory budgeting practices

Organizations need to balance how often they can manage changes to their value streams. If they adjust too frequently, it's difficult to achieve anything of consequence. Yes, they may know what their customers want, but they will too often fail to deliver. Adjust budgeting priorities too infrequently, and the organization limits its ability to address evolving requirements and opportunities. So, SAFe proposes biannual budget adjustments as a more optimal strategy.

Participatory budgeting is an iterative process that typically requires multiple rounds of meetings to come to an accommodation among the participants. It's important to note that the organization cannot allow the participants to look at self-interests from a narrow perspective. They must instead look at the bigger picture and understand that they are part of a more significant team effort, and therefore must apply the resources of their teams to the highest value opportunities. Participatory budgeting practices are another example of applying systems thinking, where the whole as an integrated collective of ideas is greater than the sum of its parts.

The inputs to participatory budgeting analysis include business strategy assessments, portfolio epics, and value stream estimates for operational costs and architecture runway investments. The outputs from the participatory budgeting analysis include new value stream budgets and agreements on which epics to pull from the Portfolio Kanban.

The outcome of participatory budgeting is the assignment of budgets to value streams across multiple planning Horizons, and with guardrails at the value stream levels to control spending. Guidance on Portfolio Backlogs is provided in the SAFe LPM article and in the Lean Budgets article at `https://www.scaledagileframework.com/lean-budgets/`.

Implementing guardrails

SAFe budget guardrails give each portfolio and their associated value streams the flexibility to be responsive to customer or market demands while providing the structure to ensure proper oversight and accountability in the management of the organization's financial resources. Specifically, **Lean Budget Guardrails** include the policies and practices for budgeting, expenditures, and governance policies and controls for identified portfolio items.

Having budget guides across investment Horizons ensures the organization is continually looking across time to ensure the organization has the strategies and funding available to both run and grow the business. Each portfolio item that reaches an investment horizon has an approved budget for the development and deployment of the associated epic. As noted previously, each epic contains guidance for a business solution or architectural runway enabler.

In SAFe, Business Owners have the responsibility to guide the priorities of the ARTs and Solution Trains to ensure they stay in alignment with the LPM objectives, customer requirements, and the directions of the Product and Solution Managers. Such alignment is the purpose of the continuous Business Owner engagement guardrail:

- Guidance on Lean Budget Guardrails is provided in the SAFe article at `https://www.scaledagileframework.com/guardrails/`.

- Guidance on Business Owners is provided in the SAFe article at `https://www.scaledagileframework.com/business-owners/`.

Supporting value streams

Each SAFe portfolio contains one or more value streams, and each value stream supports business operations or the development of one or more products or solutions. As you learned in the chapters on *Lean*, the whole point of having value streams is to eliminate functional or organizational silos that hinder the focus on the delivery of value. Instead, value streams have a singular focus on improving value across a single product or product line.

Operational value streams include the activities and people who support the business of the organization. For example, commercial manufacturing organizations may have teams within the ARTs, or Solution Trains, focused on order entry, finance, legal, human resources, accounting, marketing, sales, product or solution delivery, and support.

In contrast, the *development value streams* include the activities and people who define, build, test, and release products. Note that the term **release** in this context does not mean to imply release directly to end-user customers. Products and solutions released to the operational value streams are responsible for product delivery and support. Also, some products may support the function of the operational value streams – such as software constructed to support the order entry activities. Guidance on operational and development value streams is provided in the SAFe article at `https://www.scaledagileframework.com/value-streams/`.

Coordinating across large value streams

Many organizations deliver large and complex solutions that involve the integration of multiple products, offerings, and components. For example, imagine the number of disparate value streams required to deliver the components that make up an automobile, or a ship, or a passenger jet aircraft. As another example, large software systems, such as **Enterprise resource planning (ERP)** and **electronic health record (EHR)** systems, can have numerous integrated modules and software applications. In all those cases, the activities of any number of solution and component value streams need to be integrated and coordinated to deliver the final solution.

Anyone who has conducted a do-it-yourself project at home or put together their children's toys for birthday and Christmas presents knows that there is a specific sequence of work that you must follow. For example, if you get to the end of the project and you have parts left over, it's likely something went wrong, and the outcome will be less than optimal.

The same issue occurs when building large and complex products, services, and solutions. Leave something out, or attempt to perform work out of sequence, and something along the line will fail or come to a grinding halt. In this case, the "line" is the organization's value streams. To prevent these types of failures, the organization must implement a *cadence* and *synchronize* work across development iterations. Each synchronization gives the organization time to set priorities, resolve issues, and integrate their efforts. The ability to integrate work and delivery is the primary purpose of the program increments.

In a previous subsection, you learned about Portfolio Kanbans as a tool to visualize and control the flow of portfolio epics through their life cycles – spanning ideation through analysis, implementation, and completion. Another useful visualization is the **Portfolio Roadmap**, which shows a high-level plan of events and milestones to communicate planned Solution deliverables over the planning Horizons. Roadmaps are higher-level abstractions that link portfolio vision and strategy to the execution of specific tactics to deliver value:

- Guidance on cadence, synchronization, and integration is provided in SAFe at `https://www.scaledagileframework.com/apply-cadence-synchronize-with-cross-domain-planning/`.

- Guidance on the Portfolio Roadmap is provided in SAFe at `https://www.scaledagileframework.com/value-stream-coordination/`.

Monitoring value stream Key Performance Indicators (KPIs)

The concept of **Key Performance Indicators** (**KPIs**) has been around for quite a while and in use across industries and departmental and government applications. KPIs define *what good looks like* when an organization achieves its goals and objectives. KPIs can take the form of both quantitative (that is, data-driven) and qualitative (that is, subjective) measures and metrics.

Portfolio SAFe implements KPIs as the means to assess how each value stream is performing against the forecasted business outcomes that justified the organizational investments. The development of KPIs begins in concert with the development of strategic themes and on through the Portfolio Kanban and Lean budgeting processes that determine the business case and justifications for the investments. The KPIs then become the guiding measures and metrics that allow the decentralization of decision making to the ARTs and Solution Trains.

Put another way, the MVP specifications and KPIs help keep the value streams focused on adding value and achieving the mission and strategic goals of the organization.

A web service attracting and retaining users	AARRR (also known as 'pirate metrics'): acquisition rate, activation rate, revenue, retention rate, referrals
Product or service support value stream	First response time, mean time to resolution, net promoter score (NPS), customer experience score, cost per ticket
Product value stream	Units sold, revenue, gross margin, market share, quality metrics, customer satisfaction, trends on all
Software or hardware development value stream	Cost versus budget, predictability, internal NPS, feature cycle time, quality, release frequency, horizon investments, capacity allocation (growth versus sustaining), leading indicators
On-line membership value stream	Total members, revenue per member, active members, feature usage, churn, NPS, trends
Professional services delivery value stream	Revenue, margin, customer retention, NPS, referrals, personnel utilization

Figure 13.5 – Example of KPIs for value streams © Scaled Agile, Inc.

KPIs are particularly valuable in defining objectives in value streams, as shown in *Figure 13.5*. Guidance on value stream KPIs are provided by SAFe at `https://www.scaledagileframework.com/value-stream-kpis-2/`.

Achieving Full SAFe®

Full SAFe is not a SAFe configuration, per se. Instead, it is the acknowledgment that large organizations often have multiple SAFe configurations and multiple instances of SAFe configurations operating in parallel. In this regard, Full SAFe is the most comprehensive configuration that blends all other SAFe configurations into an integrated whole:

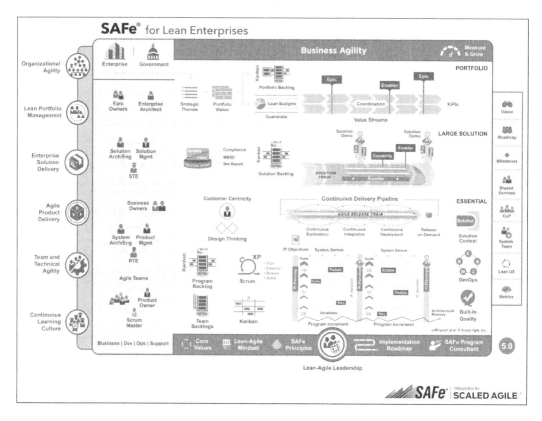

Figure 13.6 – Full SAFe configuration: https://www.scaledAgileframework.com/

Full SAFe supports the development and delivery of large integrated solutions that involve hundreds or even thousands of people to develop and maintain. Figure 13.6 illustrates the Full SAFe configuration.

Let's now have a look at the SAFe Implementation Roadmap.

Following the SAFe® Implementation Roadmap

The lower bar on the various SAFe configuration graphics provides links to the topics on the SAFe Core Values, Lean-Agile Mindset, Principles, and Implementation Roadmap (`https://www.scaledAgileframework.com/#`). Except for the **Implementation Roadmap**, we discussed all these topics in *Chapter 10, Large-Scale Scrum (LeSS)* as part of *Essential SAFe*. It did not make sense to introduce you to the Implementation Roadmap before you understood the total scope of the Scaled Agile Framework. Now that you do understand the comprehensive nature of SAFe, the value of the Implementation Roadmap becomes apparent.

The SAFe Implementation Roadmap (shown in Figure 13.7) provides detailed guidance on how to incrementally move an organization to implement SAFe across an enterprise successfully. This degree of change doesn't happen overnight. Full implementation across a large enterprise can take 2 to 3 years. As with scaling Scrum practices, it takes time to educate the people within the organization, implement prototype engagements, build upon early successes, and ultimately let the culture evolve to adopt this new way of working fully. But the good news is that the benefits from early implementations can start accruing immediately:

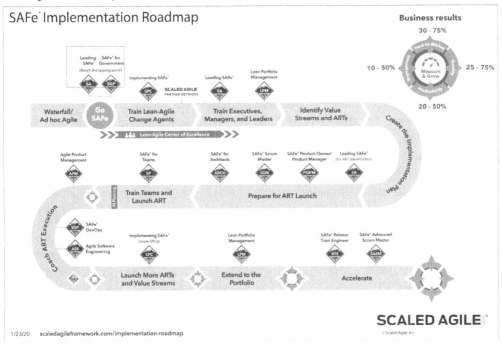

Figure 13.7 – SAFe Implementation Roadmap

The SAFe Implementation Roadmap provides an ordered set of activities that were developed over time and proved to be successful in implementing SAFe on a large scale. SAFe guides 12 articles that describe the process in detail.

It would be a mistake to think other Scrum-based scaling approaches are more straightforward to install across an enterprise. People need to buy into any change initiative. They will resist. Instead, it's better to start small with a group of highly motivated individuals on a scope of work that justifies the installment of multiple Agile teams coordinating their work in a single ART. You don't have to start with a full ART. You can build to the optimal size for a single ART over time.

Make sure those small Agile Teams have the training, resources, and tools to be effective. And give those Agile Teams enough time to demonstrate success, and then build on that success. Allow people within the organization to see the benefits of SAFe, and they will buy into the changes. Ultimately, the culture will evolve to support the new organizational structures and disciplines. That necessary evolutionary process is no different to any large-scale change initiative, or the implementation of any of the large-scale Scrum and Lean-Agile practices presented in this book.

SAFe is not a straightforward framework to implement. On the other hand, it should be apparent that SAFe encompasses virtually all of the methods, practices, and tools described in the chapters within module one. In that regard, SAFe provides a framework for implementing Lean-Agile practices that would not be easy to evolve should the organization choose to go it alone. Though there are investments the organization must make, they can have more confidence in the outcome given the educational and training resources provided by Scaled Agile, Inc., and its affiliates.

Also, your SAFe implementation will benefit from the early establishment of a dedicated **Lean-Agile Center of Excellence (LACE)** to aid the Agile teams and ARTs during the transition. A LACE is a small team with the knowledge and skills to help the organization implement Lean-Agile practices, configurations, teams, trains, events, and artifacts of SAFe. Scaled Agile has found that organizations that implement a LACE tend to have more successful and lasting implementations of SAFe's Lean-Agile practices.

One final note. No two adoptions of SAFe are identical. Every business situation is unique, and adoption within and across a large enterprise is not always uniform. But the benefits of using the SAFe Implementation Roadmap are that the bases are covered, and there is a lot of information available from the hundreds of SAFe implementations that preceded yours. Guidance on LACE is provided in SAFe at `https://www.scaledagileframework.com/lace/`.

Evaluating best fits

In this chapter, you have learned about Large Solutions SAFe configuration and Lean Portfolio Management. Large Solution SAFe offers guidance on organizational structures, roles and responsibilities, events, and artifacts necessary to grow beyond the size of a single ART. Large Solution SAFe only applies to organizations that have multiple Agile Teams containing a total of more than 120 people.

The Large Solution SAFe configuration helps organizations leverage their economies of scale to develop cyber-physical systems with the efficiencies of Agile at the small team level and large-scale efficiencies from Lean Development practices across operational and development value streams. The Large Solution SAFe configuration applies to organizations that build small numbers of very large products (that is, ships, aircraft, or buildings). It also applies to organizations that mass-produce smaller cyber-physical products (that is, self-driving cars, electronic equipment, manufacturing control systems, robotics, or IoT-based products). Finally, large software development companies can likewise benefit from the Large Solution SAFe configuration.

The SAFe Portfolio Management configuration applies to companies of all sizes that wish to organize solution development around the flow of value through one or more value streams, even at the lowest SAFe configuration level of Essential SAFe. The discipline of Lean Development requires a different way to evaluate investment decisions, budgets, and financial transactions.

For example, organizations with traditional development structures and practices allocate funds to programs and projects based on planned activities and resources. However, people report to their functional departments. Those individuals assign their costs to the product, program, or project teams, as assigned. Therefore, the traditional budgeting processes are *after the fact* cost allocations and offer limited ability to highlight or affect operational and development efficiencies. After all, the whole point of having a project is to limit variances in planned scope, schedules, budgets, and quality.

In contrast, Lean practices directly allocate funds to value streams, with both fixed and variable cost components. Improvements to those value streams have an immediate and demonstrable impact on the cost of development and delivery activities, lowering the cost of the products.

Summary

In this chapter, you have learned that *the Scaled Agile Framework (SAFe)* implements virtually all of the practices introduced in the chapters within Section 1 of this book. These include Lean Development, the values and principles of the Agile Manifesto, systems thinking, Scrum, versus, iterative and incremental development practices, and DevOps.

In this chapter, you now have an understanding of how SAFe extends the Essential SAFe configuration with Large Solution, Portfolio, and Full SAFe configurations. The *Large Solution* configuration adds in the *Solution Train* structures and roles and responsibilities necessary to manage multiple ARTs in a coordinated, integrated, and synchronized manner to build large and complex solutions. This knowledge can help you and your organizations scale the Lean-Agile concepts of SAFe to the domains of very large product-oriented applications.

The *Portfolio SAFe* configuration provides the executive-level management structures to align corporate portfolio investment with corporate strategies, goals, and objectives. Moreover, SAFe's *Lean Portfolio Management (LPM)* activities apply Lean and systems thinking to strategic planning and investment funding. Portfolios consist of Portfolio Epics that define the *Solution Context* around value. The long-lived Solution Trains, ARTs, and Agile Teams form to support the value operational and development streams that deliver the value. With this knowledge, you and your organization can implement financial controls that work within a Lean-Agile environment and ensure that your corporate investments in new and maintained products and services align with corporate strategies.

Finally, in this chapter, you learned that the SAFe *Implementation Roadmap* provides detailed guidance on how to go about installing SAFe's Lean-Agile practices and organizational structures on an enterprise scale. The Implementation Roadmap helps ensure you and your organization do not need to go it alone in figuring out how to deploy Lean-Agile practices on a large product or enterprise scale.

This concludes your introduction to the current leaders in scaled Scrum and Lean-Agile practices. There is only one remaining chapter in this book, and that chapter will review the strengths, weaknesses, and best fits for each of the scaled Scrum and Lean-Agile disciplines introduced previously in this book.

Questions

1. SAFe is an amalgamation of Lean-Agile practices for what specific purpose?

2. At the Agile team level, SAFe supports the use of which three Agile disciplines?

3. What configuration of SAFe integrates, coordinates, and synchronizes multiple Agile Release Trains (ARTs) to develop much larger and more complex solutions?

4. What configuration of SAFe provides the foundation to integrate, synchronize, and coordinate the efforts of multiple Lean-Agile teams to create incremental value?

5.   What configuration of SAFe aligns investment decisions with corporate strategies?

6. What is the purpose of Product and Solution Management within SAFe?

7. Which roles have the responsibilities to determine what gets built?

8. Which roles have the responsibilities to determine how a product or solution gets built?

9. Which roles have the responsibilities to provide servant leadership, coaching, and mentoring to the Agile teams, ARTs, and Solution Trains?

10. What are some of the issues organizations face when implementing Lean-Agile practices on an enterprise scale?

Further reading

*   SAFe® for Lean Enterprises 5.0. `https://www.scaledAgileframework.com/` Scaled-Agile, Inc. Boulder, CO Accessed April 19, 2020.

*   Beck, K. *et al.* (2001). *Manifesto for Agile Software Development. Principles behind the Agile Manifesto.* `https://Agilemanifesto.org/principles.html.` Accessed April 14, 2020.

*   Tapscott, D. (1997). *The Digital Economy: Promise and Peril In The Age of Networked Intelligence.* McGraw-Hill. New York, NY

*   Corporate (2019). Gartner Says 5.8 Billion Enterprise and Automotive IoT Endpoints Will Be in Use in 2020. https://www.gartner.com/en/newsroom/press-releases/2019-08-29-gartner-says-5-8-billion-enterprise-and-automotive-io. Newsroom, Press Release. Gartner, Inc.

*   Dashun W., James A. E. (2019). Research: "*When Small Teams Are Better Than Big Ones*", February 21, 2019, hbr.org.

- Dunbar, Robin I. M. (2010). *How many friends does one person need? Dunbar's number and other evolutionary quirks*. London: Faber and Faber. ISBN 978-0-571-25342-5.

- Carlota, P. (2002). *Technological Revolutions and Financial Capital. The Dynamics of Bubbles and Golden Ages*. Edward Elgar Publishing Limited. Cheltenham, UK, and Northampton, MA

- Wenger, Etienne. (1999). *Communities of Practice: Learning, Meaning, and Identity*. Cambridge University Press, Cambridgeshire, England.

- Markowitz, H. M. (March 1952). *Portfolio Selection*. The Journal of Finance. 7 (1): 77–91. doi:10.2307/2975974. JSTOR 2975974.

- Lanning, M. J. (1998). *Delivering Profitable Value: A Revolutionary Framework to Accelerate Growth, Generate Wealth, and Rediscover the Heart of Business*. Perseus Publishing. New York, NY.

- Baghai, Mehrdad, and Coley, Steve. *The Alchemy of Growth: Practical Insights for Building the Enduring Enterprise*. Basic Books, 2000.

- Ford, N., Parsons, R., Kua, P. (2017). *Building Evolutionary Architectures. Support Constant Change*. O'Reilly Media, Inc. Sebastopol, CA

Section 3: Implementation Strategies

The decision to implement Scrum at scale requires executive-level support. More than that, it requires executive-level commitment directly from the CEO or business owner. No one else can make this type of decision as it affects every level of the organization, including governance policies, organizational structures, hiring decisions, compensation plans, corporate training and coaching programs, hiring external implementation consultants, the role and support of partners, performance metrics, and a host of other details. In short, scaled Scrum is an enterprise change initiative and ultimately needs to be treated that way. In this section, you will learn about various considerations and approaches to making a "best fit" decision for your scaled approach.

The section comprises the following chapter:

- *Chapter 14, Contrasting Scrum/Lean-Agile Scaling Approaches*

14
Contrasting Scrum/Lean-Agile Scaling Approaches

This chapter offers a comparative review of the scaled Scrum and Lean-Agile approaches introduced in this book, spanning typical organizational and regulatory environments and development scenarios. You will learn how modern DevOps practices support the Lean-Agile enterprise. We'll also look at how scaled Scrum and Lean-Agile practices impact financial planning and portfolio management capabilities.

In this chapter, we're going to cover the following main topics:

- Assimilating capabilities
- Maximizing value
- Building unanimity through options
- Revisiting module one
- Revisiting module two
- Revisiting Scrum and Lean-Agile strategies

- Selecting based on context

- Side-by-side comparison of all assessment criteria

Let's get started!

Assimilating capabilities

Congratulations! You have made it to the final module of this book. In this third module, you will have a chance to see a side-by-side comparison of the Scrum and Lean-Agile practices presented in this book. But before we start, let me make this one statement to put everything you've read in this book into the proper context for this chapter:

"One size does not fit all!"

In other words, as you read through this final chapter, you should not assume that a methodology that checks off more boxes is better than another. Situation and context are far more important than how many attributes a particular Scrum or Lean-Agile approach includes. Moreover, in your unique situation, you may find it makes more sense to draw ideas from multiple Scrum and Lean-Agile methodologies.

The bottom line is that if a capability is not needed, don't implement it. However, if a capability proves to be useful, not only implement it but improve upon it. And don't be afraid to experiment to find other useful approaches to maximizing your organization's value. The only caveat is to ensure that all practices maximize the primary objective of adding value.

Maximizing value

This strategy, which is to discover useful techniques that add value and improve upon them, is a fundamental concept in both Scrum and Lean-Agile development. Competitive factors and good stewardship on the use of resources drive our organizations to improve continuously. As we improve, we must always bear in mind that our primary objective is to add customer value, and do no more – except where legal, regulatory compliance, and liability issues are involved.

Yes, I realize your customers may not want to pay for those legal, regulatory, and compliance activities – and ultimately, they do. Still, if you are adding real value, they don't need your company to go out of business, either.

I know many of you are probably thinking – "those types of activities add costs without providing customer-centric value." If this is what you are thinking, I ask that you look at things differently. When all companies compete fairly, taking shortcuts does not confer a competitive advantage – not in the long run. It just puts more risk on the company, its employees, the environment, and the safety of others, including its consumers. Taking shortcuts inevitably leads to costly, if not terminal, failures.

The purpose of commercial enterprise, and other entities – such as government agencies and non-profits – is to provide value at the lowest possible cost with the most desirable options, as seen from the eyes of the customer. This sentence encapsulates, in its entirety, what this book is about – how to economically develop and deliver value-centric software and cyber-physical products.

Recall the words of my early mentor, Jim O'Malley: *"People do business with people."* Most people want to do business with people they can trust to deliver value honestly, morally, and ethically. And people will often pay a premium price based on a product's higher value. Having read this book, it should be clear to you that the adoption of Lean-Agile practices offers a clear competitive advantage by putting the focus on improving customer-centric value. There is no need to cheat to compete if we just do the work.

With this understanding, let's take a look at how these methods stand up in a side-by-side comparison. But more importantly, as you read through this chapter, evaluate each approach at a more granular level to extract the concepts and techniques that are useful in your particular organizational and business context.

Building unanimity through options

Years ago, I had the opportunity to lead a corporate professional services development organization that had the responsibility of developing a standard set of IT-based professional consulting services offerings. The professional services supported business process improvements relevant to our retail and banking clients, plus we had to design the services so that they supported delivery on an international scale. The products of our corporate business consulting services development team were information artifacts related to methods and tools. These enabled the company's 4,000 consultants to deliver IT-based professional services with consistently and at a high level.

Operating across nearly 100 countries, each Country Manager, in effect, ran their consulting practices independently. The loosely coupled organizational structure made it very challenging to build consensus in anything. But I also quickly learned that preferences in methods and tools are very emotional subjects and that it was best to provide options.

As a result of these experiences, there is no attempt in this book to imply that one Scrum or Lean-Agile methodology is better than another. You and your teams must make such decisions based on your situational needs, experiences, resources, and preferences. With this in mind, let's quickly revisit what you've learned in modules one and two of this book.

Revisiting module one

In module one, you learned how lightweight software development methodologies, mainly created by software engineers, evolved to eliminate many of the problems associated with the traditional linear-sequential practices related to the so-called **Waterfall** approach. The Agile Manifesto formalized the fundamental values and principles behind the movement to develop less prescriptive and inefficient development methodologies.

Out of all the lightweight development methodologies, the widescale adoption of Scrum made it the *de facto* Agile standard in the software industry. Nevertheless, many of the software engineering practices that were developed as part of other lightweight development strategies persist in use today. For example, Kent Beck's test-driven development and extreme programming techniques are still widely used.

The Scrum Guide makes it clear that Scrum, as a framework, helps teams and organizations develop, deliver, and sustain complex products. However, Scrum doesn't address the development of software exclusively; instead, it is a framework that's used to apply empirical process control and complex adaptive theories, in an iterative development environment, to deliver incremental and ever-improving customer-centric value.

Beyond that, those who implement Scrum's process framework can use whatever methods and tools they prefer to develop whatever it is they need to develop. And, as you discovered later in *Chapter 11, Disciplined Agile*, there are hundreds of potentially useful methods, depending on your needs, situations, and context.

Scrum's generalized approach to improving organizational agility made it highly adaptable to all sorts of business needs. Its success quickly drove Scrum employments across increasingly larger and more complex products and business situations. The Scrum Guide notes that the Scrum Framework can support multiple teams collaborating on the development of a single product. However, the Scrum Guide does not explain how to manage a group of Scrum Teams that must work in a coordinated and integrated fashion. As you learned in module two, later generations of Scrum and Lean-Agile-based disciplines evolved to address the issues of scaling Scrum and Agile practices across multiple teams, and across the enterprise.

Revisiting module two

In module two, you learned that multiple variants of Scrum evolved to address the needs to scale agile structures and practices across both large products and enterprise deployment needs. This module presented four relatively *pure* but scaled extensions to the original Scrum Framework, and two Lean-Agile based extensions to Scrum.

Staying true to Scrum

As a group, **Scrum-of-Scrums (SoS)**, *Scrum@Scale*, the *Nexus Framework*, and **Large-Scale Scrum (LeSS)** all address Scrum scaling issues but do not stray too far from the original concepts employed in Scrum. They all retain Scrum's roots in empiricism and Scrum's minimalist rules, roles, responsibilities, artifacts, and events.

The SoS approach is Schwaber's and Sutherland's original concept of how to scale Scrum across multiple teams working in collaboration to develop a single product. Except for having Scrum Team members serve as Ambassadors in order to help coordinate cross-team activities, SoS does not vary from the concepts presented in the original Scrum Guide.

Scrum@Scale is Sutherland's latest variant of Scrum and retains the generalized Scrum-of-Scrums approach to scaling Scrum in any type of development situation, but at an enterprise scale. In other words, Scrum@Scale is not devoted to pure software development activities but instead offers an approach to implementing Scrum that promotes enterprise-wide business agility. Scrum@Scale employs the concepts of scale-free architectures as repetitive small team structures operating in networks to resolve network density issues with **minimum viable bureaucracy**. To coordinate the activities of these small teams, Scrum@Scale implements additional roles and leadership teams at scale.

In contrast, *The Nexus Framework* and *LeSS* are much more focused on scaling Scrum on larger single software or cyber-physical product development efforts. Let's take another quick look at these two Scrum-based scaled development strategies.

With guidance from Ken Schwaber, a software developer, the Nexus Framework not only stays true to its Scrum roots, but also as a framework that primarily supports software development activities. The alignment with software development is clearly evident in both **The Nexus Guide** and the detailed description of Nexus in the book titled *The Nexus™ Framework for Scaling Scrum* (Bittner, Kong, West, 2018).

Given the complexities of integrating and coordinating the efforts of multiple software development teams, the Nexus Framework implements a new role of **Network Integration Teams (NITs)**. NITs have the responsibility of delivering the maximum increments of integrated product value across every development iteration. NIT team members are the integration coaches and internal consultants for all things related to coordinating multiple teams and building integrated products. They may help develop tools and methods to support the integration needs of the Nexus. In short, the NIT provides useful guidance on how to manage synchronization, coordination, and integration issues associated with multiple Scrum Teams collaborating on the development of a single product.

LeSS implements two Scrum frameworks, *LeSS* – up to seven ScrumTeams – and *LeSS Huge* – to coordinate the activities of eight or more Scrum Teams. LeSS implements Feature, Functional Areas, and Area Feature teams to keep the focus on adding customer value while simultaneously minimizing cross-team integration and coordination concerns. LeSS employs the concept of Systems Thinking to avoid local optimizations that lead to poor system-level performance. The term "system" refers to both the products we build and the organizations that develop the products. LeSS installs sets of rules and guides for each framework to help teams assess practical solutions to problems they might face.

The LeSS Framework orients developers into Feature Teams, to keep each team's focus on adding customer-centric value. At the scale of LeSS Huge, Scrum teams organize into functionally related Requirements Areas that retain the focus on adding customer-centric value to large multifaceted products. Breaking out teams into Requirements Areas minimizes the scope of the product and the domain knowledge each team would otherwise have to master.

Leveraging Lean-Agile practices

The original Scrum Guide offers no guidance on applying Systems Thinking and Lean Development practices in an Agile environment, nor does it offer guidance on implementing portfolio or financial management guidance in an agile environment. Scrum@Scale, Nexus, and LeSS all make some minimal adjustments when applying systems-oriented thinking and Lean development concepts but provide very little, if any, guidance on implementing financial controls and portfolio management under Agile. These shortcomings opened the door to the development of more comprehensive Lean-Agile development methodologies, such as **Disciplined Agile (DA)** and the **Scaled-Agile Framework (SAFe)**.

The focus of DA is all about providing options. For example, DA implements six life cycle approaches and identifies hundreds of useful methods used to address issues across life cycle phases in terms of desired process goals and outcomes. DA also implements four levels of business-oriented agility, from foundational Lean-Agile practices to DevOps, value streams, and enterprise-scale applications. PMI's acquisition of DA will raise its visibility and adoption significantly.

SAFe is perhaps the most comprehensive approach to implementing Scrum and Lean-Agile practices on an enterprise scale, and has additional guidance for government implementations. The focus of SAFe is on improving business agility while leveraging the economies of scale of the large enterprise.

SAFe builds on Scrum and XP practices at the Agile Team level but builds from there to coordinate multiple Agile Teams in **Agile Release Trains** (**ART**), encompassing anywhere from 50 to 120 people. An ART can have a single product focus, or a value stream focus for more extensive solutions.

For larger solutions and organizations with multiple products, SAFe coordinates and integrates the work of multiple ARTs into Solution Trains. Agile Teams, ARTs, and Solution Trains each have three prominent roles that mirror the original Scrum roles, but at scale. SAFe implements comprehensive guidance on DevOps, architecture, product management, and on product, program, and portfolio management activities, roles, and responsibilities.

Now that we've reviewed what you learned in modules one and two of this book, let's take a quick look at how each of the Scrum and Lean-Agile approaches address scalability issues.

Revisiting Scrum and Lean-Agile strategies

The previous section provided as contrast to the Scrum and Lean-Agile approaches discussed in this book. This section presents a quick review of the capabilities and value provided by each of the Scrum and Lean-Agile approaches described in this book. We'll also quickly recap what you learned about Systems Thinking and Lean development practices:

- **Scrum** implements the foundations of empiricism, frequent iterations, customer-centricity, and incremental delivery of new value across each iteration, but does not provide direction on how to scale Scrum across multiple teams.

- **Systems Thinking** provides methods and tools used to evaluate systems that are too complex through the analysis of its parts; that is, *the whole is greater than the sum of its parts.*

- **Lean development** is a strategy that's continuously improved to eliminate all forms of waste, as viewed from the eyes of our customers. Equally important is the understanding that organizations must respect their people to get their buy-in to seek ways to improve their way of working continuously. The objectives of Lean development are to streamline value creation and value delivery activities by improving flows, minimizing if not eliminating queues, avoiding batch processing, and reducing work in the process through pull-oriented order entry. In other words, the goal is to create development and delivery processes that produce what customers want when they want it, without delays or inventories.

- **Scrum@Scale** implements a scalable linear approach based on scalable architectures to organically grown Scrum teams interoperating in loosely coupled network configurations. The scalable architecture strategy minimizes network density issues by limiting the number of people communicating across teams and their types of communications. Specifically, the small Scrum Teams have similar structures and rules when it comes to connecting the Product Owner, Scrum-of-Scrum, and leadership teams, which serve as nodes or hubs to direct and minimize cross-team communications.

- **The Nexus Framework** stays true to its focus on software development by encouraging the adoption of **Continuous Integration** (**CI**) and test automation environments. Nexus also implements the **Network Integration Team** (**NIT**) to coordinate cross-team dependency, coordination, and integration issues. Also, Nexus identifies many useful techniques for planning and improving transparency in multi-team Scrum environments.

- **LeSS** builds on Scrum and Nexus but also implements robust system thinking and organizational design concepts to assist with scaling Scrum across a large multi-team product or enterprise implementation requirement. LeSS focuses on building Scrum Teams around features and requirements areas, plus its many rules and guides help teams gain proficiency in their LeSS adoptions.

- **Disciplined Agile (DA)** implements Lean-Agile practices across four types of product life cycles and four layers of processes supported within the DA toolkit. The key differentiator of DA is its encouragement and knowledge assets to support your team's preferred **way of working** (**WOW**). As part of this strategy, DA identifies hundreds of techniques in the context of process goals and decision points.

- The **Scaled-Agile Framework** (**SAFe**) implements Lean-Agile practices across four configurations – Essential, Large Solution, Portfolio, and Full SAFe. SAFe implements a dual business operating system model to improve business agility while minimizing upheaval and resistance to enterprise change during the transition. SAFe also builds on modern research, such as Dunbar's Number, to define an approach to organizing small teams into larger Agile and solution release trains. SAFE installs robust practices and organizational structures to support product alignment with corporate strategies, portfolio management, and product management. Finally, SAFe provides a comprehensive implementation roadmap to help organizations successfully adopt SAFe and overcome organizational barriers.

Selecting based on context

Revisiting the initial section on *Assimilating capabilities*, it's not fair to state one method or another is more robust or better than another. All of the practices described in this book are comprehensive in terms of their scope and capabilities but evolved to address different needs and purposes. No one should be calling someone else's baby ugly. Please read this section from this perspective – *context is everything*.

This section provides a series of tabular information that evaluates the application of each of the Scrum and Lean-Agile approaches in a particular situation or context. The contextual situations presented include the following:

- Implementation of the Scrum Framework
- Implementation of Systems Thinking
- Implementation of Lean development
- Guidance on business drivers
- Overcoming cultural influences
- Software development practices rules, guides, and techniques
- Implementation of portfolio management
- Implementation of product management
- Implementation of DevOps
- Generalized development-oriented practices
- Team integration and coordination
- Roadmaps to scaling

Each table starts with an explanation of what is meant by the stated contextual situation. The columns separate each of the described approaches. The cells have brief statements that explain the level of support or guidance offered by each approach for each contextual situation.

Implementation of the Scrum framework

This section deals with how closely each of the approaches follows the original concepts of the Scrum Guide in terms of empiricism, as well as the rules, roles, responsibilities, events, and artifacts of Scrum:

Approach	Capabilities
SoS	SoS is the original scaling extension to Scrum. The only real extension is the concept of having a subset of team members having the role of Ambassadors to meet with other Team Ambassadors to discuss integration and coordination issues in daily or less frequently Scrum of Scrums.
Scrum@Scale	S@S scales the original Scrum Framework by interconnecting small Scrum Teams through Scrum of Scrums that serving as nodes in a scale-free architecture. The SoS pattern is replicated as the organization continues to grow. S@S extends the Scrum Framework with additional roles, events, and the Executive Action Team (EAT) and Executive MetaScrum Team (EMT) leadership teams at scale.
Nexus	Adheres firmly to Scrum Guide but extends the Scrum Framework with the Network Integration Team (NIT) to support cross-team dependency, integration, and coordination requirements, plus adds Scrum Planning and Retrospective events.
LeSS	Adheres tightly to Scrum Guide but extends Scrum with two scaled frameworks to support coordination and synchronization of multiple teams, LeSS (from 3 to 7 Scrum Teams) and LeSS Huge (8 or more Scrum Teams.)
DA	DA builds its Agile life cycles based on Scrum and XP but implements new roles, names, events, and artifacts. As the Agile Teams mature, DA implements CD/ DevOps capabilities on top of the basic Scrum/ XP life cycle.
SAFe	SAFe builds its small Agile teams on Scrum and XP practices. Conceptually, Scum-based Agile Teams support non-software related value streams, while XP practices support Software Development-oriented value streams. SAFe's Agile Release Trains (ARTs) coordinate and integrate the work of multiple Agile Teams.

Figure 14.1 – Implementation of the Scrum Framework

This concludes this section on comparing the implementation of the Scrum Framework. Now, we'll look at the degree to which each of the Scrum and Lean-Agile practices implement Systems Thinking.

Implementation of Systems Thinking

This section identified the level of guidance provided in the use of Systems Thinking concepts to address the complexities associated with multiple components interoperating in a large and complex environment. Specifically, we want to know how well each of the approaches evaluates the elements that affect the development and delivery activities of an organization and its products:

Approach	Capabilities
SoS	SoS does not incorporate Systems Thinking in any traditional sense.
Scrum@Scale	S@S does not employ Systems Thinking methods or tools. Instead, it retains Scrum's empiricism to deal with issues of system complexities. S@S also employs the concept of scale-free architectures and networked teams to deal with issues of network density and complexity at scale.
Nexus	Nexus does not employ the methods and tools of Systems Thinking. As with SoS and S@S, Nexus relies on Scrum's traditional empirical process control theories to help organizations address issues of complexity.
LeSS	Though this is another "pure" implementation of Scrum, LeSS training employs Systems Thinking extensively to prevent local optimizations that would otherwise lead to bottlenecks, queues, and inefficient flows.
DA	DA implements Systems Thinking as part of its FLEX (FLow for Enterprise Transformation) and DevOps implementation strategies. The objective is to determine the most value-added approach to prioritize transition activities keeping in mind the influences of people and culture.
SAFe	Systems Thinking is the second of twelve SAFe Principles, and one of its four foundational bodies of knowledge. SAFe leverages System Thinking to evaluate and address complexities across large solutions, organizational structures, and processes, and value streams.

Figure 14.2 – Implementation of Systems Thinking

This concludes this section on comparing the various implementations of Systems Thinking. Now, we'll look at the degree to which each of the Scrum and Lean-Agile practices implement Lean development concepts and practices.

Implementation of Lean development

This section reviews the implementation of Lean development concepts. Where Scrum relies on empiricism to address complex adaptive problems, Lean development practices aim to eliminate waste in the form of non-value-added activities.

Waste comes in many forms, including mixed-matched and inefficient process flows, push-oriented order entry, queuing of materials and work, batch processing, excessive work in progress, lengthy setup and cycle times, defects, bugs, and poor quality. In short, Lean development is all about streamlining workflows, pulling new product orders or work items on demand, and building quality into a product:

Approach	Capabilities
SoS	SoS does not incorporate the concepts or practices of Lean Development.
Scrum@Scale	S@S does not incorporate the concepts or practices of Lean Development.
Nexus	The Nexus Framework does not incorporate the concepts or practices of Lean Development.
LeSS	Lean Thinking is one of the 10 Principles of which LeSS sits, and LeSS draws heavily from Lean Thinking practices. LeSS builds on two pillars of Lean Development: Respect for People, and Continuous Improvement. Additionally, LeSS identifies 14 Principles of Lean Development consistent with the practices defined as the Toyota Way system of Lean Thinking.
DA	PMI acquired both DA and Flex to build their Agile practice offerings, and the two offerings are in the process of being integrated (a.k.a. DA FLEX). Relevant to this context, FLEX is a Lean Thinking Agile approach designed to improve workflows as opposed to processes. DA FLEX has the objective of improving business agility across the organization and all its value streams by removing delays in workflow, feedback, and the time it takes to act on the information. The DA FLEX approach to Lean provides visibility of work, workflow, blockages, workload, and value stream capacities. DA FLEX also supports the principle of building in quality through the use of Acceptance Test-Driven Development, Sustainable Test-Driven Development, and automated testing.
SAFe	SAFe implements ten Lean-Agile principles as fundamental components of its approach to building enterprise-class software and cyber-physical system and achieving business agility on an enterprise scale. Besides using Lean Development concepts to drive value stream efficiencies, SAFe outlines Lean concepts for leadership, budgeting, and portfolio management. SAFe practitioners teach the need to install a Lean-Agile Mindset across the organization. The goal of establishing a Lean-Agile Mindset is to build a culture around the values and principles outlined in the Agile Manifesto combined with the values, principles, and practices of Lean Development.

Figure 14.3 – Implementation of Lean development

This concludes this section on comparing the implementations of Lean development capabilities. Now, we'll look at the degree to which each of the Scrum and Lean-Agile practices provide guidance on evaluating the impact of external business drivers.

Guidance on business drivers

Most Scrum advocates would agree that they have a focus on building what customers want and when they want it. Or, at least they should have that kind of focus. However, the reality is that many approaches do not provide comprehensive guidance on how to go about identifying customer needs. This section identifies which approaches place more emphasis on this area of product and portfolio management:

Approach	Capabilities
SoS Scrum@Scale Nexus	Neither the Scrum Guide, SoS, S@S, nor the Nexus Framework explicitly address the impact of business drivers on an organization, beyond the most rudimentary concepts of needing to be agile to remain competitive. Yes, all of these Scrum-based frameworks address the need to build the products that customers want with the features and capabilities they value. One can also argue that the empiricism of Scrum helps the organization resolve structural issues brought on by the external factors driving the business. Nevertheless, none of these Scrum-based Frameworks discuss the issues that might drive organization-wide change initiatives to achieve business agility nor the potential impacts of the drivers affecting the business. However, some of Schwaber's and Sutherland's books delve into these issues with customer examples.
LeSS	LeSS provides a bit more guidance on how to deal with organizational changes driven by business needs, primarily through its adoption of Systems Thinking and Lean Development concepts. Its employment of Causal Loop Diagrams (CLDs) to evaluate complex system dynamics - as described in this book in Chapter 3, The Scrum Approach on Systems Thinking, provides the methods and tools to assess the impacts of external business drivers.
DA	The Disciplined Agile Enterprise (DAE) provides four layers of tools that help the organization respond rapidly to changes in its marketplace that is to external factors or business drivers). DAE helps the organization create both a structure and culture that is responsive to the situations that drive the need for change. DA takes the view that three fundamental forces are driving the marketplace today: 1) all businesses are software businesses; 2) every industry is undergoing constant disruptions; 3) Agile organizations are most prepared to dominate in their markets. The DA Toolkit deals with external factors through DA tools that support portfolio management, product management, business operations, marketing, sales, finance, legal, procurement, and controls.

Figure 14.4 – Guidance on business drivers

This concludes this section on comparing the approach each practice takes to evaluating and responding to the impacts from external business drivers. Now, we'll look at the degree to which each of the Scrum and Lean-Agile practices help the organization overcome cultural influences and resistance to change.

Overcoming cultural influences

Organizational change is difficult and scary, and subject to high resistance if not handled correctly. Here, again, some approaches spend more time dealing with these issues than others. This section discusses the approach taken by each of the identified Scrum and Lean-Agile practices:

Approach	Capabilities
SoS	SoS does not deal with the issues of overcoming cultural resistance to change. Some of Jeff Sutherland's books do.
Scrum@Scale	The Scrum@Scale Guide does not deal with the issues of overcoming cultural resistance to change.
Nexus	The Nexus Guide does not deal with the issues of overcoming cultural resistance to change. Some of Ken Schwaber's books do.
LeSS	LeSS deals with the subject of changing culture and overcoming resistance through its guidance on '*Adoptions*.' The instructions on LeSS Adoptions include three guiding principles, how to get started, coaching, continuous improvements, Feature Team Adoption Maps, how to stay sane through the adoption period, and seven organizational design principles.
DA	DA is all about allowing teams and organizations to choose their **Way of Working (WOW)**. The entire DA Toolkit provides options in life cycle approaches and hundreds of useful techniques presented in context with desired process goals and decision points. This approach, to enable choice and options, helps reduce potential resistance from those who might have other ideas about the practices they prefer. However, each team must still come to a consensus on the life cycles they prefer. Moreover, teams are encouraged to evolve their WOW with time and maturity in their DA implementations.
SAFe	SAFe is the most comprehensive Lean-Agile development and delivery approach introduced in this book, and it takes training, mentoring, coaching, and time for the organization to become fluent and accepting of its practices. As a result, SAFe provides a comprehensive *Implementation Roadmap* to help guide the initial and follow-on implementations, and to help overcome organizational resistance.

Figure 14.5 – Overcoming cultural influences

> **Note**
>
> Ultimately – and this statement is true for all scaled Scrum and Lean-Agile practices – changes in culture cannot be forced. Cultural change comes naturally over time, driven by human nature to be part of something successful. The executives must drive the early adoptions, provide the time and resources for success, and then promote those successes.

This concludes this section on comparing how each Scrum and Lean-Agile approach facilitates the process of change in terms of overcoming cultural influences and organizational resistance. Now, we'll look at the degree to which each of the Scrum and Lean-Agile practices provides specific guidance on techniques related to software development and software engineering.

Software development support

Scrum evolved initially to support the implementation of Agile practices in the software industry. However, its ability to help organizations address complex adaptive problems at any time quickly led to its implementation in all types of applications and domains. Since this is a book mainly for individuals, teams, and organizations building software and cyber-physical products, we want to make sure we identify those practices that provide specific guidance useful for software development teams:

Approach	Capabilities
SoS Scrum@Scale	The original Scrum Guide, SoS, and S@S all have historical ties to software development. However, none of these Scrum Frameworks offer specific guidance on methods, tools, or techniques that support software engineering practices. They are generalized Agile frameworks, useful and applied across all types of business problems.
Nexus	Ken Schwaber founded Scrum.org and developed the Nexus Framework precisely to scale Scrum across multiple teams working in collaboration to develop a single product or software – with an emphasis on software. Ken Schwaber is a software development veteran, and the Nexus Framework shows his systems engineering influence through its employment of the Nexus Integration Team. Also, the Nexus Framework for Scaling Scrum book (Bittner, Kong, West 2018) offers guidance on the employment of continuous integration and continuous delivery practices, open code base, API management, code reviews, and other useful software engineering practices. Still, the Nexus Guide remains true to the Scrum Guide's original product development concepts.
LeSS	Craig Larman and Bas Vode are both software engineers and, likewise, slant their training in LeSS toward supporting software development and software engineering practices. LeSS provides comprehensive guidance related to *Technical Excellence* in software development including CI/CD, clean code, architecture and design, unit testing, test-driven development, thinking about testing, test automation, acceptance testing, and specification by example.
DA	The DA Toolkit has an entire layer devoted to IT. The process guides, decision points, and techniques within DA IT span Enterprise Architecture, Continuous Improvement, IT Governance, People Management, Reuse Engineering, Portfolio Management, and Product Management. Also, the DA Toolkit has another layer devoted to DevOps, spaning IT Operations, Support, Security, Data Management, and Release Management. DA also identifies numerous IT and software engineering roles supporting DA IT and Disciplined DevOps.
SAFe	At its heart, SAFe is all about implementing Lean-Agile practices in support of large products and large solutions and evolving to implementations on an enterprise scale. SAFe also takes the view that disruptions from the emergent digital economy make software and cyber-physical systems development capabilities mainstream for all entities seeking relevance in this digital world. SAFe implements XP practices at the Agile Team level to support software development teams and also implements continuous integration, continuous deployment, and DevOps practices.

Figure 14.6 – Software development support

This concludes this section on comparing the specific guidance each practice provides related to software development and software engineering. Now, we'll look at the degree to which each of the Scrum and Lean-Agile practices support or extend the Portfolio Management function.

Implementation of Portfolio Management

Many Scrum advocates disparage the concept of Portfolio Management. This issue comes from Scrum's initial focus on eliminating wasteful practices associated with the traditional Waterfall development model. I get it! However, it's also a problem when organizations, particularly large organizations, fail to align their product development and delivery investments with corporate strategies.

Moreover, there are always more things we can do and products we can build than our organizations have the resources to manage. While we can assume Portfolio Management is someone else's problem at the small team level, that is no longer tolerable when an organization wants to implement Scrum and Lean-Agile practices at an enterprise scale. This section explores each of the Scrum and Lean-Agile practices in terms of their guidance on Portfolio Management:

Approach	Capabilities
SoS Scrum@Scale Nexus LeSS	As relatively pure scaled Scrum implementations, SoS, S@S, Nexus, and LeSS do not offer guidance on Portfolio Management practices. Their focus lies strictly on implementing rules, roles, responsibilities, and artifacts to scale Scrum across multiple teams working in collaboration on the development of a single product. Each approach can support the development of multiple products; however, it's up to the organizations to figure out the organizational structures to do so.
DA	DA provides a process group with related process guides and decision points and techniques for Product Management.
SAFe	The Scaled-Agile Framework implements an entire configuration to support Portfolio Management. The Portfolio Management configuration implements the Organizational Agility Competency. The Portfolio Management configuration provides guidance on developing strategic themes, establishing Portfolio Vision, developing a Portfolio Kanban, developing business opportunities as Epics and Enablers, and establishing Value Stream Key Performance Indicators (KPIs) to assess value stream performances against quantifiable objectives.

Figure 14.7 – Implementation of Portfolio Management

This concludes this section on comparing the implementation of Portfolio Management capabilities. Now, we'll look at the degree to which each of the Scrum and Lean-Agile practices support or extend the Product Management function.

Implementation of Product Management

Product Management is another area that Scrum Advocates often disparage or ignore. For example, it's one thing to say that the Product Owner must work with customers and stakeholders to determine what adds value and priorities based on customer needs and costs to deliver. How those activities occur is actually quite complicated and challenging.

The duties of a Product Owner are a small part of a Product Manager's job, assuming the organization combines these roles. As with Portfolio Management, this issue becomes increasingly essential with scale, and some practices provide more guidance than others. In this section, you will learn the extent that each of the assessed practices provides aid in the area of product management:

Approach	Capabilities
SoS Scrum@Scale Nexus LeSS	The SoS, S@S, Nexus, and LeSS Frameworks all inherently apply the concepts of product management due to their Scrum lineage. The whole point of Agile was to move away from short-term project-oriented development practices and instead support the development and delivery of products as a continuous activity. Having said this, they tend to trivialize or ignore the more significant Product Management function. The role of the Product Owner is a small subset of the broader responsibilities of Product Management.
DA	DA devotes a Process Group to the Product Management function within its DAIT toolkit, including process goals, decision points, and techniques.
SAFe	Product and Solution Management have defined roles within SAFe and provides detailed guidance on their responsibilities. SAFe offers guidance on how the product management function differs across internal versus external customers. For large product offerings, SAFe explains how multiple product managers collaborate to define the larger solution. The product management functions coordinate the activities of both development and delivery value streams, which can include coordinating the efforts of marketing, sales, and channel, service, and supply chain partners. They must assess customer and stakeholder needs in the context of the product's life cycle adoption curve. They participate in pre and post PI planning activities and solution demos to ensure the value streams remain aligned.

Figure 14.8 – Implementation of Product Management

This concludes this section on comparing the implementation of Portfolio Management capabilities. Now, let's look at the degree to which each of the Scrum and Lean-Agile practices support or extend the implementation of DevOps capabilities.

Implementation of DevOps

Scrum came about in the early to mid-1990s, well before **Development-Operations (DevOps)** became a thing. In contrast, DevOps started as a communication and collaboration strategy to break down the silos that often exist between software development teams and operational support groups. This two-way communication is vital to continuous improvements in both products and processes.

However, modern improvements in software development, integration, and testing environments, plus automation capabilities, led to the subsumption of continuous integration, automated testing, automated provisioning, and continuous delivery and deployment capabilities within DevOps. As a result, the modern view of DevOps is much broader in scope than its original communications and collaborations foundations.

Some scaled Scrum practices, such as Nexus and LeSS, incorporate modern systems engineering and automation practices in a general context. However, DA and SAFe address these software engineering capabilities within the modern context of both enabling software engineering capabilities and DevOps. This section discusses the approach each of the identified practices takes concerning these advanced software development concepts:

Approach	Capabilities
SoS Scrum@Scale Nexus LeSS	As the relatively pure Scrum practices, SoS, S@S, Nexus, and LeSS do not address DevOps. DevOps came out much later, first described in a conference titled Devopsdays, held in Ghent, Belgium, in 2019. Still, while these Scrum-based practices do not provide instructions on DevOps, there is no reason not to employ DevOps practices with Scrum, with one caveat. When DevOps implements automation capabilities that reduce development life cycles times less than the Sprint duration times, those two activities become decoupled. In other words, use Scrum Sprints for planning purposes if you believe there is merit to synch and coordinate the teams' activities, but understand day-to-day direction is probably better implemented through a Kanban-oriented system.
DA	The DA Toolkit devotes an entire layer to DevOps. The Disciplined DevOps toolkit provides process groups and related decision points and techniques spanning IT Operations, Support, Security, Data Management, and Release Management.
SAFe	DevOps is an established practice within the Essential SAFe configuration. SAFe implements its CALMR approach to DevOps, which stands for: • Culture of Shared Responsibility • Automation and Continuous Delivery Pipeline • Lean Flow Accelerates Delivery • Measurement of everything • Recovery enables low-risk releases

Figure 14.9 – Implementation of DevOps

This concludes this section on comparing the implementation of DevOps capabilities. Now, let's look at the degree to which each of the Scrum and Lean-Agile practices support the development and delivery of physical products and services where software development is not the primary focus.

Generalized development-oriented practices

All of the Scrum and Lean-Agile practices we've identified in this book support the development of software and cyber-physical systems to one degree or another. However, some have applicability to broader use in industry, non-profit, and government entities. This section breaks down the degree to which each Scrum and Lean-Agile practice guides non-software development-related entities or entities where software development is peripheral to their mainline business activities:

Approach	Capabilities
SoS Scrum@Scale	Both SoS and S@S maintain Scrum's generalized approach to use empiricism and the Scrum Framework to support product development activities of virtually any type and to address complex adaptive problems in general.
Nexus LeSS	The Nexus Framework and LeSS can both support general product development needs as a Scrum-based Agile approach. However, both of their target markets are pretty organizations and teams that develop software and cyber-physical products. Non-developers may not fully understand some of their terms and concepts related to integration, test automation, and continuous delivery capabilities.
DA	DA was initially developed to support the software engineering community, and it still retains a heavy focus on information technology. With PMI's acquisition of DA and FLEX, I suspect the use of DA will expand beyond its traditional software development community.
SAFe	SAFe is all about installing Lean-Agile practices to build and deliver really big things. In our modern digital world, most of those things will have software-driven enhancements that provide a competitive advantage, even when the physical parts of the product may require much more time and resources to build. For example, think of building large ships, airplanes, utilities, and self-driven cars. Computers and software significantly advance the capabilities of all of these products, though few people would think about the underlying computing systems that control these products.

Figure 14.10 – Generalized development-oriented practices

This concludes this section on comparing each Scrum and Lean-Agile's ability to support non-software oriented development requirements. Now, let's look at the contrast between each of the Scrum and Lean-Agile practices in terms of how they support team integration, synchronization, and coordination activities.

Team integration, synchronization, and coordination

Scaling Scrum and Lean-Agile practices requires the integration, synchronization, and coordination of small teams working in collaboration on a single product or more extensive and integrated solution. However, some practices provide more guidance than others and often take different approaches. This section contrasts the different approaches taken to coordinate the activities of multiple Scrum and Lean-Agile Teams:

Approach	Capabilities
SoS	SoS coordinates the efforts of multiple teams through the employment of Team Ambassadors who represent the teams in daily SoS meetings.
Scrum@Scale	S@S integrates, synchronizes, and coordinates networks of teams through its network-oriented scale-free architecture concepts.
Nexus	The Nexus Framework incorporates Nexus Integration Teams (NITs) to address coordination, synchronization, and dependency issues. These teams may be permanent or temporary, and NIT members may be dedicated resources or drawn from the Scrum Teams as an additional assignment. Nexus splits Sprint Retrospectives into three parts: 1) Cross-team event with representative to discuss integration and coordination issues; 2) Scrum Team level meetings to address the team and cross-team issues and to come up with potential changes for the next Sprint; 3) another Cross-team event with selected team representatives to agree on how to visualize and track the identified actions.
LeSS	Less implements Feature teams at the level of LeSS Frameworks (3 to 7 Scrum Teams) and Requirements Areas and Area Feature Teams at the level of LeSS Huge (8 or more Scrum Teams). The primary objective of LeSS is to reduce integration and dependency concerns by building fully self-contained Feature and Area Feature teams supporting the slice of the product they have the responsibility to build. LeSS splits Sprint Planning out into two events, one for the Requirement Area level of planning, and the second event for team level planning.
DA	DA implements six life cycle development approaches that teams choose as their preferred WOW. Cross-team integration and coordination issues differ cross each approach. But as a general strategy, DA implements daily coordination meetings to address dependency, integration, and synchronization issues.
SAFe	SAFe implements cross-team integration and coordination controls at two levels of cadence. The small Scrum/ XP Agile teams operate on a higher frequency, consistent with Agile practices. In other words, their Sprints may operate on a frequency of one to four weeks, and the teams will employ Scrum-of-Scrum type meetings to coordinate their activities during this time frame. However, there is a Program Level Increment that operates on a frequency of typically 8 to 12 weeks to realign and coordinate the Solution Train, ARTs, and Agile Teams around the current priorities of the large product or solution. The Program Increment (PI) Planning sessions are all-hands affairs that provide an opportunity for all participants to build relationships and plan and integrate their efforts for the upcoming PI cycle. Program level demos and reviews occur at the beginning of each PI Planning event.

Figure 14.11 – Team integration, synchronization, and coordination

This concludes this section on providing a comparison of how each practice supports team integration, synchronization, and coordination activities. Now, we'll look at the degree to which each of the Scrum and Lean-Agile practices provide guidance on implementation and adoption at an enterprise scale.

Roadmaps to scaling

Once an organization's executives decide to implement Scrum and Lean-Agile practices enterprise-wide, they cannot merely send out a mandate and expect everyone to make it happen. There are too many difficult challenges and blocks that will make the proclamation fail. The executives must provide leadership and resources and guide the effort.

Here, again, some of the Scrum and Lean-Agile practices provide more assistance than others on the topic of enterprise-scale adoptions. This section identifies how much and the form of implementation guidance provided by each identified Scrum and Lean-Agile practice:

Approach	Capabilities
SoS	SoS does not provide any guidance on overcoming resistance to scaled Scrum implementations.
Scrum@Scale	S@S recommends each organization build a reference model depicting types of small sets of Scrum Teams. Scrum teams are installed incrementally, building on the success of the previous teams. The Executive Action Team (EAT) is accountable for the development and execution of the S@S transformation strategy. The EAT members must be empowered, politically, and financially, to implement the Reference Model across the organization.
Nexus	The Nexus Guide does not offer guidance on the approach to implement Nexus on a large scale nor how to overcome organizational resistance. The premise in Nexus is that a Scrum-based product development activity has grown to include multiple teams, and they have come to a logical conclusion that they need better techniques to manage their cross-team coordination, dependency, and integration issue.
LeSS	LeSS has a similar premise as Nexus. But, LeSS provides more guidance on how to resolve issues that arise with the increased number of teams or an organizational mandate to employ Scrum on an enterprise scale.
DA	DA discusses *Agility at Scale* as the concept that defines how organizations go about implementing Lean-Agile practices at scale. There are two levels of scale within DA, Tactical (team-level scaling factors) and Strategic (enterprise-level scaling factors). DA does not provide a roadmap to implement tactical or strategic Agility but instead points to its process groups and toolkits to implementation issues.
SAFe	SAFe provides twelve articles Implementation Roadmap to guide organizations through the journey of launching relatively small-scale Safe trials to ultimately scaling SAFe across an enterprise. SAFe starts wit the premise that organizations must come to a *tipping point* where change becomes necessary or mandated. The next steps are to train Lean-Agile Change Agents, executives, managers, and other leaders., and then to develop a center of excellence (COE) to provide the foundations for growth. The next course of action is to define the necessary value streams and ARTs, develop an implementation plan, and prepare for the first launch. At that point, the members of the Agile Teams and ART must be trained in SAFe, and then launched. SAFe coaches and mentors must be available to help guide the efforts of the Agile Teams and ARTs. Building on the success of the initial AR launches, the organizations similarly prepares new Arts and Solution trains while expanding their portfolios to encompass the new efforts. Each new success allows the organization to overcome resistance and accelerate the process.

Figure 14.12 – Roadmaps to scaling

This concludes this section on comparing the types and extent of guidance provided by the Scrum and Lean-Agile approaches with regard to the implementation and adoption of their practices at an enterprise scale. Now, we'll look at the degree to which each of the Scrum and Lean-Agile practices provide guidance on unique considerations related to the public sector and highly regulated environments.

Guidance on government and highly regulated industries

Highly regulated industries have unique compliance issues created by legislative mandates. There are severe legal and even criminal consequences for failing to abide by these compliance requirements. Some of the Scrum and Lean-Agile practices deal with this topic head-on and in great detail, while others merely mention the issues. This section identifies the degree to which each practice provides instructions on dealing with compliance issues:

Approach	Capabilities
SoS Scrum@Scale Nexus LeSS	SoS, S@S, Nexus, and LeSS all build off Scrum's foundations as a general approach to install empiricism and Agility supporting problem-solving and organizational development needs. Since they are generic, they offer no specific guidance related to issues of regulatory compliance, or supporting government services and legislated mandates. However, there is no reason that these practices cannot support such requirements.
DA	DA is similarly a general approach but with a broader focus that encompasses Scrum as part of a larger offering of Lean-Agile life cycles and practices. Again, there is no reason that DA cannot support the development of government services, or handle issues associated with compliance and legislated mandates.
SAFe	SAFe is unique in its efforts to support the implementation of Lean-Agile practices in public sector organizations. Because government organizations tend to be large, complex, and often bureaucratic, there are tremendous opportunities to improve development and operation efficiencies. SAFe not only offers guidance and case studies on its application in the public sector, but it also offers a certification to designate qualified government specialists in SAFe. that is Certified SAFe® Government Practitioner (SGP)

Figure 14.13 – Guidance on government and highly regulated industries

This concludes this section on comparing the types and extent of guidance provided by the Scrum and Lean-Agile approaches with regard to providing guidance on applications within government or highly regulated industries. Now, we'll finish this chapter by going back through everything we've learned and provide a side-by-side comparison of each Scrum, scaled Scrum, and Lean approach across all the previous assessment criteria.

Side-by-side comparison of all assessment criteria

This section provides a quick overview of what we have covered in this chapter, and is especially useful as an executive summary or for those who have skipped ahead and didn't want to run through all the nitty-gritty details. Admit it! Even if you didn't skip ahead to this section, you were probably tempted:

Application	Scrum	SoS	S@S	Nexus	LeSS	DA	SAFe
Based exclusively on Scrum Framework	☑	☑	☑	☑	☑	◪	◪
Incorporates Systems Thinking	☐	☐	☐	☐	☑	☑	☑
Incorporates Lean Development	☐	☐	◪	☐	☑	☑	☑
Supports concepts of enabling Business Agility	▣	☐	☑	☐	☐	☑	☑
Specific guidance on how to overcome cultural resistance	▣	☐	◪	☐	☑	☑	☑
Specific Techniques to support software development	☐	☐	☐	☑	☑	☑	◪
Implements technique for Portfolio Management	▣	▣	▣	▣	▣	☑	☑
Implements technique for Product Management	☐	☐	☐	☐	☐	☑	☑
Implements Guidance for DevOps	☐	☐	☐	☐	☐	☑	☑
General Use Scrum/ Agile Frameworks	☑	☑	☑	◪	◪	☑	☑
Team Integration, Coordination, Cross-team Synchronization	▣	☑	☑	☑	☑	☑	☑
Implementation Roadmaps/ Scaling Guidance	▣	◪	◪	◪	☑	☑	☑
Guidance on compliance and regulated industries	☐	☐	☐	☐	☐	◪	☑

Figure 14.14 – Side-by-side comparison of the previous assessment criteria

The preceding diagram provides a side-by-side comparison of each of the identified Scrum, Scaled Scrum, and Lean-Agile practices across the assessment areas covered in this chapter. The assessment ratings are identified by their respective icons, as identified here:

☑ Core capability

▨ Some guidance/capability

☐ Limited guidance, but extendable

▨ Not applicable

These assessments are admittedly subjective. The highest ratings for each set of assessments (☑)went to those originating bodies that provide specific guidance in their guides and assessable website content. In other words, those organizations that specifically speck to an assessment area got the highest ratings. The ratings go down from there as to whether they provide some limited guidance or capability (▨) or no specific guidance on the assessment criteria, but the approach is extendable (☐). The lowest ratings went to those assessment criteria that are not applicable to an approach (▨)We have now completed our comparative assessments of Scrum and Lean-Agile practices across a broad range of capabilities, and this section concludes the instruction portion of this chapter and this book. As with previous chapters, we'll conclude with *Summary* and *Questions* sections.

I hope you have enjoyed reading this book and learned some things in the process. If you are new to Scrum and Lean-Agile, you now have a solid foundation of understanding to continue your professional growth. On the other hand, you may have already been using Scrum and Lean-Agile practices in your career and wondered, perhaps, what you have been missing from the other disciplines. Well, now you know, and I hope you will use this new knowledge to likewise continue your professional growth.

Summary

In this chapter, you learned that all the scaled Scrum and Lean-Agile approaches have something to offer and that the assimilation of situationally useful techniques across disciplines will make you a better Agilist. You learned that the discovering useful techniques that add value and then improving upon them is a fundamental concept in both Scrum and Lean-Agile development.

You also learned that having multiple methods and tools as options is not a bad thing. Not every practice is optimal or even practical in every situation. Knowing how to find the available scaled Scrum and Lean-Agile practices, as well as how to use them situationally, is the primary skill you have gained from reading this book.

This chapter provided a comparative analysis for you to assess the scaled Scrum and Lean-Agile disciplines in situational contexts, both in narrative and tabular formats. You now have the knowledge and skills to apply these practices to your sometimes unique, and other times not, situations.

Questions

1. In the context of this chapter, what is meant by the statement, "One size does not fit all?"

2. Do customers typically value legal, regulatory, and compliance-related activities?

3. In a large organization, why is unanimity a consideration in terms of providing access to optional practices, methods, and tools?

4. What was the primary driver behind the development of scaled Scrum frameworks?

5. What value does Systems Thinking bring to Agile-based development practices?

6. What is the approach taken by Scrum@Scale to scale Scrum?

7. What role does the Nexus Framework implement to address issues of cross-team dependencies, integration, and coordination?

    The **Nexus Integration Team** (**NIT**) and its NIT members

8. What is the primary differentiator of the Disciplined Agile approach?

9. What are the two frameworks of LeSS?

10. Can organizational change be forced through directives?

Further reading

- Bittner, K., Kong, P., West, D. (2018) *The Nexus Framework for Scaling Scrum. Continuously Delivering an Integrated Product with Multiple Scrum Teams.* Boston, MA. Prentice Hall.

- Jacobson, I., Stimson, R. (2017, JUN) *Escaping Method Prison*. Retrieved from https://www.infoq.com/articles/escape-method-prson/.

Assessments

This section is for answers to questions from all chapters.

Chapter 1 – Origins of Agile and Lightweight Methodologies

1. What makes software development unique from the development of other large, complex products, such as ships, utilities, bridges, roads, or buildings?

   - Software addresses functional business and user needs that are always changing, and modern software development practice supports the evolution of software to address those changing needs.

2. Why do plan-driven and linear-sequential development practices often fail when developing software?

   - Often referred to as the Waterfall development model, plan-driven and linear-sequential development practices assume customer and end user needs don't change, and that architectures and designs cannot adapt to support the evolving needs.

3. What are some of the development practices often associated with lightweight and agile-based software development practices?

   - **Adaptive Software Development (ASD)**, Crystal Clear, **Extreme Programming (XP)**, **Feature Driven Development (FDD)**, ICONIX, **Rapid Application Development (RAD)**, and Scrum.

4. Why did the software engineers who defined the Agile Manifesto focus on defining values and principles for Agile, as opposed to defining specific agile development practices?

   - The original Agile practices didn't always agree on specific approaches. However, they could agree that "Agile Methodologies" is about the mushy stuff of values and culture'.

5. Why is **Extreme Programming (XP)** considered a methodology and not a framework?

- Software development methodologies, such as XP, tend to include highly prescriptive practices that developers explicitly follow with minimal variations.

6. Why is Scrum considered a framework instead of a methodology?

- Software development frameworks, such as Scrum, serve as a structure to implement minimal guidance to install iterative workflows, Incremental deliveries of enhanced value, roles, events, artifacts, and rules. However, within the framework's structure, development teams can use whatever practices, techniques, methods, and tools support their unique needs.

7. Agilists prefer individuals and interactions over what?

- Processes and tools

8. Agilists prefer working software over what?

- Comprehensive documentation

9. Agilists prefer customer collaboration over what?

- Contract negotiation

10. Agilists prefer responding to change over what?

- Following a plan

Chapter 2 – Scrum Beyond Basics

1. Who are the originators of the Scrum framework?

- Ken Schwaber and Jeff Sutherland

2. The foundations of the Scrum framework are based upon which theory?

- Empirical process control theory

3. How many roles are there in Scrum, and what are they?

- Three roles; Product Owner, Scrum Master, and Developers

4. What are the three pillars of empirical process control?

-   Transparency, inspection, and adaptation.

5. Is it OK to add the role of Project Manager in Scrum? (Yes or No)

-   No

6. What are the Scrum Events?

-   The Sprint – a timeboxed development iteration that delivers Incremental value.
-   Sprint Planning – builds the Sprint Goal and defines the Sprint Backlog.
-   Daily Scrum – short daily team meeting to discuss what was accomplished, what impediments exist, and what is planned to be accomplished over the next 24 hours.
-   Sprint Review – a demo to customers, users, and other stakeholders to obtain feedback on new features and to obtain guidance for future items.
-   Sprint Retrospective – a discussion on what actions can be taken in the next Sprint to improve the team's performance.

7. What are the Scrum artifacts?

-   Product Backlog – the prioritized items that the Product Owner maintains, prioritizes, and approves for development with input from stakeholders, customers, and the Scrum Teams
-   Sprint Backlog – items pulled from the Product Backlog that achieve the Sprint Goal
-   Increment – the additional customer-centric value each Scrum Team delivers over the course of a Sprint

8. Why is transparency so important in Scrum?

-   Improves the ability to make decisions on the optimization of value and the controlling of risks by bringing visibility to the current state of all artifacts.

9. What is the definition of "Done" in Scrum?

-   Varies by team, but all members must have a shared understanding of what it means for work to be complete, to ensure transparency.

10. What is an Increment?

- The sum of all the Product Backlog items completed during a Sprint and the value of the Increments of all previous Sprints. Each Increment must meet the definition of Done at the end of each Sprint. Each new Increment must be fully integrated and tested with previous Increments. Each Increment represents progress toward a vision or goal. The Increment must be useable and potentially shippable irrespective of whether the Product Owner chooses to release it.

Chapter 3 – The Scrum Approach

1. Why is Scrum described as a framework?

- The implication is Scrum is a container that provides only minimal guidance on baseline practices, rules, artifacts, and events to implement the values and principles of Agile and use empiricism to solve complex adaptive problems.

- Within the Scrum, Scrum Teams are free to use any other methods, tools, and practices that support their specific product delivery requirements.

2. How does the traditional development model most differ from the Scrum model?

- The traditional (waterfall) model is plan-driven and implements a linear-sequential life cycle development process. In contrast, Scrum implements an iterative development life cycle to deliver Increments of customer-centric value frequently.

3. Who has the final say on the scope for work that a Scrum Team can complete within a Sprint?

- Only the Scrum Team

4. Why does the Product Owner have the final say on the items and priorities established within the Product Backlog?

- Because they have the P&L responsibility and must look at the organization's ability to deliver an item in context with the value it has and the cost to deliver the items.

5. What is the purpose of the Daily Scrums?

- To synch up as a team to identify work completed, upcoming work, and impediments to progress against the Sprint Goal.

6. What is the purpose of the Sprint Reviews?

-   To synch up with customers, end users, and other interested stakeholders, to provide them with a demo of the product, and update on future enhancements, and to get their feedback on the Increment and current priorities.

7. What is the purpose of the Sprint Retrospectives?

-   To schedule a time to review the team's performance in the preceding Sprint and discuss and agree on actions for improvements over the next Sprint.

8. What are some of the issues that can cause a Scrum Team to fail?

-   Lacking executive sponsorship; failure to obtain executive, customer, and stakeholder buy-in; lacking an Agile mindset; failing to invest; lacking effective communication; and failing to encourage continuous learning

9. What is the potential problem with hiring a Scrum Master based solely on their technical skills, domain knowledge, or their project management experience?

-   As experts in their field, they may be inclined to direct the activities of the Scrum Team, as opposed to providing coaching, training, mentoring, and team facilitation services. Scrum Masters are servant leaders, not managers.

10. What is the primary issue with continuing to develop a product beyond its economic value?

-   The corresponding feature glut can make the product less attractive to customers and end users due to its increased size and complexities.

Chapter 4 – Systems Thinking

1. Provide examples of complex things that act as a system related to information technology.

-   Software applications, integrated systems, IT organizations and teams, business processes, components in an application, hypertext linkages, or connected computers and applications across the internet.

2. Explain why complexity increases with the number of participating elements and relationships within a system.

-   System complexity increases exponentially with the number of elements involved in the system. The mathematical expression for such growth is $n(n-1)/2$.

3. Use the mathematical model of *N(N-1)/2* to demonstrate how systems, complexity increases.

- If we have two elements involved in our system, they have only that one relationship between them.

- If we have 10 elements within our team, the number of potential relationships grows to 45.

- Increase the number of elements to 100, and the number of potential interfaces between them exponentially increases to 4,950

4. What is an element or node within a system?

- Virtually anything that has a potential relationship and related cause and effect impacts in a larger collection of things.

5. Explain the difference between negative and positive causal links.

- Positive Causal Link: This means that the cause and effect impact of two linked nodes is changing the observed attributes in the same direction.

- Negative Causal Link: This means that the cause and effect impact of two linked nodes is changing the observed attributes in the opposite direction.

6. What are the primary differences between open and closed systems?

- Open systems: These are characterized by having inflows and outflows external to the system. That is, things can enter or leave the system.

- Closed systems: These are characterized by having no flows in or out of the system. That is, the system is fully self-contained.

7. What are stocks within a system?

- These are tangible, quantifiable, and measurable variables within a system that is subject to dynamic changes over time through the actions of a flow. Where the term element implies a type of thing at any given time, the term stock implies attributes of the elements that have observable values at specific points in time.

8. Explain the concept of flows within a system, including inflows and outflows.

- Flows are actions that dynamically change the directions of stocks within a system as inflows and outflows.

- Inflows: These indicate a direction of flow that serves to increase the measurable amount of stock. Inflows are shown in Casual loop diagrams as arrows that point to the elements accumulating stock.

- Outflows: These indicate a direction of flow that serves to decrease the measurable amount of stock. Shown in diagrams as arrows that point to the elements accumulating stock. Outflows are shown in Casual loop diagrams as arrows that point away from the elements losing stock.

9. What types of feedback loops exist within a system, and what are their differences?

- Feedback loops are mechanisms that adjust flows to either stabilize a system or to reinforce a certain trend within the system.

- Balancing Feedback Loops: They provide information or resources that bring a system or elements within a system into equilibrium and maintained within a desired range.

- Reinforcing Feedback Loops: They provide information or resources that support a trend within a system or elements within a system, and the trend can be either positive or negative.

10. What is the purpose of causal modeling?

- Causal modeling is a technique that helps organizations, teams, and individuals evaluate the cause and effect of behaviors between elements that participate in a system.

Chapter 5 – Lean Thinking

1. Why is the concept of value important in Lean thinking?

-   Value is defined by the customer, and essentially includes anything and everything your customer is willing to pay for, and not one item more. Adding more than a customer wants is waste. Anything less leaves the customer dissatisfied and potentially open to looking at alternative products and solutions.

2. What are the five foundational principles of Lean thinking (Womack and Jones, 2003)?

-   Value, Value Stream, Flow, Pull, and Perfection.

3. What are the eight common forms of waste?

-   Waiting, overproduction, extra-processing, transportation, motion, inventory, defects, and unused human talent and intellect.

4. What are the three primary types of value streams?

-   The process of product conceptualization and design
-   Demand creation and order handling
-   Product development and delivery

5. What is the purpose of TAKT time, and how is it calculated?

-   It is a mathematical approach to limit the intake of new orders to align with production capacities.
-   Calculated as the total time available for production divided by customer demand in terms of individual products or services.

6. Explain why large-scale batch processes are not efficient?

-   They add cycle time, delayed deliveries, and hide bugs and defects.

7. What is the purpose of changing production scheduling from a push-oriented system to a pull-oriented system?

-   Helps match production intake with production capacities. Pushing orders into a production/development system only introduces bottlenecks that reduce operational efficiencies, and hides problems and defects.

8. True or False: The principle of **Just in Time (JIT)** is to procure and store raw materials so that they are available when customers send in their orders.

•   False. JIT is a concept where material is ordered and delivered, just in time for the development process when the capacity exists to produce the order.

9. How does the concept of transparency support the goal of perfection?

•   Transparency gives the organization access to the information they require to accurately assess customer value and value stream efficiencies and production issues.

10. What are the three states of value and can you define them?

•   Unambiguous value – the activity clearly and provenly provides capabilities that a customer is willing to pay for.

•   Unavoidable waste – the organization does not have a viable approach to address the issue in the short-term.

•   No value – this type of waste must be eliminated as soon as possible as it typically provides the quickest opportunity to improve the value of a product or service.

Chapter 6 – Lean Practices in Software Development

1. What two aspects of Lean thinking are applicable across industries, government agencies, and non-profit organizations?

•   **Value Creation** – activities to create a product, service, or result.

•   **Value Delivery** – activities that support the needs of the customers, such as marketing, sales, order taking, order processing, inventory management, product delivery or fulfillment, and customer support.

2. Identify common value streams that apply to the software industry.

•   Add value, kaizen, implement visual controls, build in quality, improve knowledge, delay decision making, implement testing automation (jidoka), eliminate mistakes (poka-yoke), eliminate waste, eliminate multi-tasking/task switching, implement gemba (management by walking around), single-piece flows, leveling workloads (heijunka), optimize the whole/eliminate local optimizations, produce just in time, reject unfinished work, and respect people.

3. Is designing a product a value creation or value delivery value stream?

    - Design is a value delivery activity, or value stream (that is, set of activities), as the function supports the needs of the customers by figuring out what it is they want.

4. Is developing a software product a value creation or value delivery value stream?

    - As the name implies, software development is a value development value stream

5. Is order taking a value creation or value delivery value stream?

    - Order taking is a value delivery value stream, as it directly supports the needs of our customers.

6. Identify Lean practices that support building in quality.

    - Test-driven development (TDD), continuous integration/Incremental testing, test automation, and code refactoring.

7. Explain how traditional waterfall-based practices differ from Lean-Agile practices in terms of handling feature development flows.

    - The traditional waterfall-based software development model forced development teams to identify and build all features within a single product development and test cycle. Unidentified requirements required extensive reviews and approvals and changes to budgets and schedules.

    - Agile practices anticipate requirements will change and therefore teams never plan project development tasks too far out into the future, and Continuously reevaluate needs and priorities with every development iteration.

8. How does a Kanban Board support Agile-based software development?

    - Visual controls for workflows and blockages to level production

    - Control/minimize WIP

    - Support pull-based intake strategies to match customer orders to production capacities

9. Explain the differences between overproducing and extra or non-value-added processing.

- Overproduction occurs when a development team continues to build software products and features simply because they have capacity or the skills to do so and not because the items have the highest priorities in the Product Backlog.

- Extra processing occurs when features, enhancements, or higher levels of quality are added to a product that are not valued by the customer – usually because they were not validated in the first place.

10. Explain the type of waste associated with multitasking and context switching.

- Humans beings are sequential thinkers, and it takes time and effort for them to reorient their minds and pick up where they left off before starting new tasks.

Chapter 7 – Scrum of Scrums

1. What is the purpose of Scrum of Scrums (SOS)?

- To minimally extend the underlying Scrum Framework in order to manage large product dependency, coordination, and integration issues, across multiple teams, with negligible overhead and complexity.

2. What are the two typical approaches taken to scaling Scrum in the original Scrum model?

- Bottom up-led by engineering/developers
- Top down-led by executive management

3. In the context of an innovation's adoption curve applied to Scrum, what stage is Agile adoption within the software industry?

- Early to late majority stage

4. Why did software engineers and consultants largely lead the movement to promote agile practices?

- They too often received most of the blame for failures caused by strict adherence to the traditional waterfall-based development model

5. What does it mean to prioritize Product Backlog items in terms of highest value?

    • Development priority goes to those items with the highest customer value with the lowest cost of delivery.

6. Instead of hierarchical organizations, which business structures better fit the scaled Scrum model?

    • A network of independent and largely autonomous teams guided by enterprise-level Scrum teams.

7. What are the two elements necessary to build a foundation of excellence?

    • Individual mastery of Scrum practices
    • Team development

8. What are the five stages of team development?

    • Forming–storming–norming–performing-adjourning

9. Since Scrum does not advocate the use of the traditional hierarchical management structures, where is it most logical to place executive-level functions, roles, and responsibilities? And what is their primary function?

    • Within a Center of Excellence.
    • Primary function to remove impediments to enterprise scaling.

10. Scrum has two seemingly conflicting objectives in IT governance. What are they?

    • A need to implement standards to reduce acquisition and sustainment costs and minimize productivity loss during adoptions of new methods and tools.
    • A need to ensure the Scrum teams have enough flexibility to experiment, innovate, and be responsive to change.

Chapter 8 – Scrum@Scale

1. True or False: The purpose of Scrum@Scale is to extend the original Scrum framework to support the development of large and complex products, processes, services, and systems.

    • True

2. How many Scrum Teams did the original Scrum Guide anticipate as working in its framework at optimal capacity while maintaining a sustainable pace?

*   One single Scrum Team

3. What are the two goals of the Scrum@Scale framework?

*   Linear scalability
*   Business agility

4. The Scrum@Scale framework is described as a network of teams, and operating consistently with the Scrum Guide can address complex adaptive problems, while creatively delivering products of the highest possible value. What type of architecture is this an example of?

*   A scale-free architecture.

5. What is a business operating system?

*   A standard collection of business processes employed by an entity, be it a government agency, commercial company, or a non-profit.

6. What are the two cycles within Scrum@Scale?

*   Scrum Master Cycle
*   Product Owner Cycle

7. What is meant by the term "Team Process"?

*   Original Scrum practiced at the team level.

8. A Scrum of Scrums (SoS) in an idealized structure looks like what?

*   A pentagram of five teams consisting of five people each with an assigned SOSM and Chief Product Owner providing leadership and guidance.

9. A Scrum of Scrum of Scrums (SoSoS) in an idealized structure looks like what?

*   A pentagram of five Scrum of Scrum (SoS) teams, for a total of 25 teams consisting of five people each, and each SoS having an assigned SOSM and Chief Product Owner providing leadership and guidance. The roles of Scrum of Scrums Master and Chief Product Owner scale into the leadership groups.

10. What are the roles of the Executive Action Team (EAT) and the Executive MetaScrum (EMS)?

- The Executive Action Team (EAT) fulfills the Scrum Master role for an entire agile organization.

- The Executive MetaScrum (EMS) fulfill the Product Owner role for the entire agile organization.

Chapter 9 – The Nexus Framework

1. What is the definition of a Nexus?

- A connection or series of connections linking two or more people or things.

2. What is the primary objective of Nexus Sprint Planning?

- To eliminate cross-team dependencies and sequence work to coordinate the integration and testing of individual team deliverables.

3. What are the six Nexus Events?

- Refinement, Nexus Sprint Planning, Nexus Sprint Goal, Nexus Daily Scrum, Nexus Sprint Review, and the Nexus Sprint Retrospective.

4. What are two common Scrum Team work partitioning strategies?

- Persona outcome-oriented Scrum teams and value area-oriented Scrum teams

5. What are the five strategies listed for large-scale development efforts?

- Trunk-based development, **continuous integration (CI)**, automated API-based testing, versioned API management, and code reviews.

6. What are the Nexus planning visual aids mentioned in this book?

- Impact maps; cross-team Product Backlog refinement boards; Story mapping; Cross-team visual dependency refinement board; Relative Sizing Board; Outcome and measures planning board; and Nexus Sprint Backlog board.

7. Why are Nexus Daily Scrum meetings held in advance of the Daily Scrum team meetings?

- Nexus Daily Scrums focus on identifying dependency and integration issues in advance of the Scrum Daily Scrums so that the Scrum Teams have the information to discuss and resolve the identified issues.

8. What are the three methods and tools identified for measuring and judging Sprint velocities?

- Velocity chart, burndown chart, and burnup chart.

9. What is the primary reason Nexus implements a single Nexus Sprint Review in lieu of holding multiple Scrum team Product Reviews?

- There is only so much time customers, users, and other stakeholders will devote to the reviews, especially given the iterative updates across each Sprint.

10. What are the steps in the Nexus Sprint Retrospective process?

- Initial Nexus Sprint Retrospective – to identify dependency and integration issues that need to be improved
- Scrum Team Retrospectives – to discuss opportunities to improve both Scrum Team and Nexus Integration performance
- Final Nexus Sprint Retrospective – to discuss how to provide transparency to visualize and track the identified actions

Chapter 10 – Large-Scale Scrum (LeSS)

1. True or False: LeSS is a nearly sufficient framework that is deliberately incomplete and allows for situational learning through observation and experimentation, as opposed to enforcing prescriptive rules and formulas.

- True

2. Why does an organization use LeSS to scale Scrum?

- To eliminate complexity, bureaucracy, and overhead, with the goal of achieving agility on a larger scale.

3. Production of non-value-added Increments, excessive work in progress, and non-value-added processes are all examples of what?

- Waste

4. What is Shu-Ha-Ri?

- A Japanese Martial Arts view on how mastery is obtained:
- Shu – Follow the rules to learn the basics
- Ha – Break the rules to understand context
- Ri – Mastering and finding your own way

5. What are the three common elements in LeSS and LeSS Huge?

- One Product Owner and one Product Backlog
- One common Sprint across all teams
- One shippable product Increment

6. What is the dual role of the Product Owner in the LeSS framework?

- Product Owner role and responsibilities
- Product management or product marketing functions

7. What is the outcome of a Sprint in LeSS?

- One common potentially shippable product Increment.

8. What is the unique artifact associated with LeSS Huge, and what is its purpose?

- Requirements Area.
- To simplify the organization and management of teams in scaled Scrum Product Groups by organizing work around major areas of customer concerns.

9. What is the major difference in rules between LeSS and LeSS Huge adoptions?

- LeSS adoptions occur all at once, while LeSS Huge adoptions are achieved through an evolutionary Incremental approach.

10. Why do the initial LeSS Huge teams operate in parallel but in distinctly different reporting structures during LeSS adoptions?

- To prevent non-productive rivalries – since their short-term goals are different and to keep the new feature teams focused on learning how to create potentially shippable Increments of customer-centric value at the lowest possible cost.

Chapter 11 – Disciplined Agile (DA)

1. What does WOW mean in DA, and why is it important?

- WOW is an acronym for "Way of Working."
- Because DA teams choose their WOW to improve their outcomes

2. What are the components of establishing a Lean and Agile mindset in DA?

- Principles, promises, and guidelines

3. What are the essential DA Team-level roles?

- Product Owner, Architecture Owner, Team Lead, Team Members, and Stakeholders

4. Within a DA Team-of-Teams, cross-team integration, dependency, and coordination activities mimic what type of organizational structure?

- Scrum of Scrums (SOS)

5. What types of leadership teams support large team and program-level DA implementations?

- Product Coordination Team (includes Team Leaders), Product Management Leadership Team (includes Product Owners), Architecture Owner Leadership Team (Includes Architecture Owners), Test and Integration Team, CoPs, CoEs, and Work Teams.

6. What are the six types of product life cycles promoted by DA?

- Agile, Lean, Continuous Delivery: Agile, Continuous Delivery: Lean, Exploratory, and Program.

7. How do Continuous Delivery Agile and Lean product life cycles differ from their Lean and Agile counterparts?

*   They include the implementation of test-driven development, continuous integration, test automation, and automated provisioning capabilities.

8. What are the components of a process goal diagram?

*   Desired process goal or process outcome

*   Decision Points

*   Optional Techniques

9. What are the four layers of the Disciplined Agile tool kit?

*   Foundation Layer

*   Disciplined Agile Layer

*   Value Stream Layer

*   Disciplined Agile Enterprise Layer

10. How are the process blades, goals, decision points, and techniques of the Disciplined Agile tool kit organized?

*   By DA's product life cycles, Phases of Inception, Construction, and Transition, plus ongoing processes.

Chapter 12 – Essential Scaled-Agile Framework (SAFe®)

1. What is the target market/audience for the Scaled Agile Framework (SAFe)?

*   The world's largest and most sophisticated software applications, networks, and cyber-physical systems

2. Companies that embrace SAFe tend to have what characteristics?

*   Produce the world's largest and most sophisticated software applications, networks, and cyber-physical systems.

3. What is a primary competitive advantage that large enterprises can take advantage of within their industries?

- Economies of sale

4. How has competition changed for existing, large enterprises?

- Many existing companies face disruption within their industries from smaller, more Agile entities that have leveraged advanced digital technologies to gain competitive advantage.

5. What is the primary purpose of Essential SAFe?

- Provides the enabling infrastructure to establish Lean-Agile practices in development activities involving 50 to 120 people, and the foundations for continued growth to implement Lean-Agile practices on an enterprise scale via the other SAFe configurations.

6. What is the smaller organizational structure within Essential SAFe?

- Agile teams that install Scrum, XP, Kanban, and design thinking practices.

7. What are the primary roles of Essential SAFe?

- Agile team – Team members, Product Owner, and Scrum Master
- ART – Systems Architect/Engineer, Product Management, and Release Train Engineer (RTE)
- Business Owners

8. What is the integrating function for Agile teams within Essential SAFe?

- Agile Release Trains

9. What two core competencies does Essential SAFe incorporate?

- Agile Product Delivery
- Team and Technical Agility

10. What is the purpose of Program Increments (PIs) in the context of Essential SAFe?

- They are timeboxed (typically 8–12 weeks) intervals during which an Agile Release Train plans and delivers Incremental value in the form of working, tested software and systems.

- Conceptually similar to the iterations at the Agile team level but focused on PI planning, limiting work in process, gathering, and distributing feedback, and facilitating ART-wide retrospectives.

Chapter 13 – Full Scaled-Agile Framework (SAFe®)

1. What is the purpose of the Large Solution SAFe configuration?

- Building large and complex products in organizations that do not require the additional constructs of Portfolio Management

2. What are the core competencies necessary to support the Large Solution SAFe configuration?

- Enterprise Solution Delivery
- Agile Product Delivery
- Team and Technical Agility

3. What is the purpose of the Portfolio SAFe configuration?

- Strategic alignment of portfolio investments with corporate strategies, Lean Portfolio Management and budgeting, management of large scale Epics across multiple planning horizons, and Lean governance.

4. What are the core competencies necessary to support the Portfolio SAFe configuration?

- Organizational Agility
- Lean Portfolio Management
- Agile Product Delivery
- Team and Technical Agility
- Continuous Learning Culture

5. What is the purpose of the Full SAFe configuration?

- To coordinate the efforts of hundreds of team members, or more, to develop, deliver, support, and sustain large and integrated solutions.

6. What is the purpose of product and solution management within SAFe?

- Defining and supporting the development of desirable, feasible, viable, and sustainable products and large scale business solutions

7. Which roles have the responsibilities to determine what gets built?

- Product Owners, Product Management, Solution Management

8. Which roles have the responsibilities to determine how a product or solution gets built?

- Agile teams, System Architect/Engineering, Solution Architect/Engineering

9. Which roles have the responsibilities to provide servant leadership, coaching, and mentoring to the Agile teams, ARTs, and solution trains?

- Scrum Master, Release Train Engineer (RTE), Solution Train Engineer (STE)

10. What are some of the issues organizations face when implementing Lean-Agile practices on an enterprise scale?

- Executive support, education and training, organizational buy-in, need for early successes, and cultural change.

Chapter 14 – Contrasting Scrum/Lean-Agile Scaling Approaches

1. In the context of this chapter, what is meant by the statement "One size does not fit all?"

- You cannot assume that a methodology that checks off more boxes is better than another. Situation and context are far more important.

2. Do customers typically value legal, regulatory, and compliance-related activities?

- No, but if you are adding customer-centric value, they don't need your company to go out of business.

3. In a large organization, why is unanimity a consideration in terms of providing access to optional practices, methods, and tools?

•   Because these are emotional issues for many, especially when folks have spent time and energy building skills with their preferred methods and tools. The issues, for instances, are that customers may not want to pay for certain things, such as staying compliant with regulatory and legal mandates, employee training, or making equipment upgrades. However, those kinds of things are necessary for the long term survival of the company.

4. What was the primary driver behind the development of the scaled Scrum frameworks?

•   Scrum lacked techniques to manage a group of Scrum teams that needed to work in a coordinated and integrated fashion on the development of a single product.

5. What value does systems thinking bring to Agile-based development practices?

•   Provides methods and tools to evaluate systems that are too complex through analysis of its independent parts. Systems thinking helps agile teams look at their development and delivery processes as a complex mix of elements and activities, as opposed to optimizing single elements within a system. The latter strategy is called local optimization, which may not help improve the system as a whole. In fact, local optimization of certain activity cycle times, equipment setup time reductions, or batch processing may cause more harm and create queues and bottlenecks elsewhere. Or improvements to a component of the development and delivery value streams may have no impact at all because they are not the slowest operation in the chain of activities.

•   Helps prevent local optimizations that hinder system-level performance

6. What is the approach taken by Scrum@Scale to scale Scrum?

•   S@S implements a scalable linear approach based on scalable architectures to organically grown Scrum teams interoperating in loosely coupled network configurations.

7. What role does the Nexus framework implement to address issues of cross-team dependencies, integration, and coordination?

- The Nexus Integration Team (NIT) and its NIT members

8. What is the primary differentiator of the Disciplined Agile approach?

- Flexibility to choose your Way of Working (WOW) by providing options in product development life cycles and useful techniques.

- What are the two frameworks of LeSS?

- LeSS Framework (coordinating and integrating the work of 3 to 7 Scrum Teams)

- LeSS Huge Framework (coordinating and integrating the work of 8 or more Scrum Teams)

9. Can organizational change be forced through directive?

- Typically, not People will resist, particularly if they feel threatened by the change.

- The better approach is to communicate the drivers for change, train staff and provide mentors and coaches, launch some early adopter projects, have some early successes, and promote the successes of the new approach. As people see the successes, more and more will want to join in. Over time, the new practices drive the culture of how work is done.

Other Books You May Enjoy

If you enjoyed this book, you may be interested in these other books by Packt:

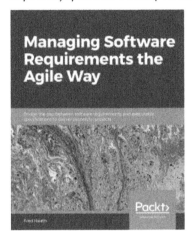

Managing Software Requirements the Agile Way
Fred Heath

ISBN: 978-1-80020-646-5

- Kick-start the requirements-gathering and analysis process in your first meeting with the client
- Accurately define system behavior as features
- Model and describe requirement entities using Impact Mapping and BDD
- Create a feature-based product backlog and use it to drive software development
- Write verification code to turn features into executable specifications
- Deliver the right software and respond to change using either Scrum or Kanban
- Choose appropriate software tools to provide transparency and traceability to your clients

Solutions Architect's Handbook

Saurabh Shrivastava, Neelanjali Srivastav

ISBN: 978-1-83864-564-9

- Explore the various roles of a solutions architect and their involvement in the enterprise landscape

- Approach big data processing, machine learning, and IoT from an architect's perspective and understand how they fit into modern architecture

- Discover different solution architecture patterns such as event-driven and microservice patterns

- Find ways to keep yourself updated with new technologies and enhance your skills

- Modernize legacy applications with the help of cloud integration

- Get to grips with choosing an appropriate strategy to reduce cost

Leave a review - let other readers know what you think

Please share your thoughts on this book with others by leaving a review on the site that you bought it from. If you purchased the book from Amazon, please leave us an honest review on this book's Amazon page. This is vital so that other potential readers can see and use your unbiased opinion to make purchasing decisions, we can understand what our customers think about our products, and our authors can see your feedback on the title that they have worked with Packt to create. It will only take a few minutes of your time, but is valuable to other potential customers, our authors, and Packt. Thank you!

Index

Made in the USA
Coppell, TX
26 February 2021